INTRODUCTORY
QUANTUM MECHANICS

PRENTICE-HALL PHYSICS SERIES

INTRODUCTORY
QUANTUM MECHANICS

BY

VLADIMIR ROJANSKY

PROFESSOR OF PHYSICS
UNION COLLEGE

Englewood Cliffs, N. J.
PRENTICE-HALL, INC.

First printing.......... October, 1938
Second printing......... April , 1942
Third printing......... January , 1946
Fourth printing..... September , 1946
Fifth printing....... November , 1947
Sixth printing.......... August , 1950
Seventh printing....... January , 1956
Eighth printing........... July , 1957
Ninth printing............ July , 1959
Tenth printing ...... September , 1960

Eleventh printing...... January, 1964

PRINTED IN THE UNITED STATES OF AMERICA
50164-C

PREFACE

This book is addressed to the reader who wishes to become familiar with some of the simpler physical ideas and mathematical methods of quantum mechanics, either because of their own intrinsic interest, or in preparation for a comprehensive and critical survey of the theory, or for a study of its applications. Although written primarily for graduate and advanced undergraduate students beginning a study of quantum mechanics, the text should also be of service to persons who are already acquainted with some of the concepts and results of the theory, and who wish to inquire into its formulation.

The prerequisites are the elements of calculus and of ordinary differential equations, and a recognition of the failure of classical mechanics in the domain of atomic physics. The reader's acquaintance with partial differential equations and with matrices is assumed to be slight at best.

Quantum mechanics is a large subject, and even introductory courses in it differ greatly in content and emphasis. Certain rudimentary topics, however, come up in almost every quantum mechanics course; and it is to some of these topics that this book is confined. I hope that its plan will be found convenient for the interpolation and addition of further material in the classroom.

The discussion proceeds from the outset toward a coherent view of the main mathematical forms of the theory; but the exposition makes little pretense to rigor and often aims to make plausible rather than to prove. The arrangement of the book is essentially as follows:

CHAPTERS

Mathematical topics		I and IX
Problems in one-dimensional motion	the classical method	II
	the Schroedinger (wave) method	III–VII
	the momentum method	VIII
	the Heisenberg (matrix) method	X
	the Dirac (symbolic) method	XI
Problems in three-dimensional motion; the Schroedinger method.		XII
Electron spin	the Pauli theory	XIII
	the Dirac theory	XIV

The reader interested primarily in the Schroedinger method may take up Chapter XII directly after Chapter VII; §§53 to 58 of Chapter IX and §69 of Chapter X will then prepare him for the two chapters on electron spin.

v

The exercises provide drill in the material already covered, tie up some of the loose ends in the discussion of the text, and clear the ground for the topics to come. Most of the exercises are short, and a good understanding of the text should enable the reader to do many of them mentally.

The main results and proofs presented here are of course well known to theoretical physicists, while most of the supplementary arguments can perhaps also be found elsewhere, between the lines if not in print. The courses of Professor J. H. Van Vleck, Professor E. U. Condon, Professor P. A. M. Dirac, and Professor H. P. Robertson, various lectures by others, a few letters, and many conversations have all put their imprint on these pages. Through their reactions to different ways of presenting various topics, the persons who attended my own classes have also played a large part in shaping this book. The entire manuscript was thoroughly improved by my colleague Professor A. H. Fox, and further important refinements were made by Dr. Condon, Editor of the Prentice-Hall Physics Series. In the handling of the manuscript and the preparation of the diagrams I had student asistance sponsored by the N. Y. A. To the editorial department of Prentice-Hall, Inc. I am indebted for sympathetic cooperation.

V. ROJANSKY

CONTENTS

NOTE: The numbering of equations, exercises, tables, and figures is described on page 27 (footnote), page 29 (footnote), and page 74.

Latin and Greek symbols are listed in the index, the latter in the alphabetical order of their English names.

Mathematical symbols not admitting of alphabetical listing are grouped in the index under the heading 'symbols.'

INTRODUCTORY
QUANTUM MECHANICS

Chapter I

MATHEMATICAL PRELIMINARIES

1. Introduction

In 1900 Max Planck introduced the idea of a quantum of action. In 1905 Albert Einstein suggested the wave-particle duality of radiation. In 1913 Niels Bohr formulated the first substantially successful theory of atomic phenomena. In 1923 Louis de Broglie injected the wave-particle duality into the theory of matter. And a quarter of a century after Planck's discovery came *quantum mechanics*.

Quantum mechanics was invented twice: first by Werner Heisenberg, and a few months later by Erwin Schroedinger. But Heisenberg's *matrix mechanics* and Schroedinger's *wave mechanics* were so different that for a time their mathematical equivalence remained unrecognized.[1]

Then began the widespread and remarkably successful activity in developing the new mechanics for application to a growing range of problems in physics and chemistry. As the theory became better understood, generalized and clarifying formulations of it were put forward, notably by Paul Adrien Maurice Dirac and by Pascual Jordan. A relativistic quantum mechanics of the electron was constructed by Dirac. A mathematically rigorous formulation of the theory was given by Johann von Neumann. And, as a result of all these developments, quantum mechanics is today not only much wider in scope than it was at its inception, but also more compact, more orderly, and easier to learn.

The mathematics required for the quantum-mechanical treatment of the motion of a particle is more elaborate than that necessary for the classical treatment of particle motion, so that a person beginning the study of the quantum-mechanical behavior of a particle may find his mathematical preparation quite inadequate, even though he is well versed in the corresponding classical

---

[1] For a vivid account of the early history of quantum mechanics see J. H. Van Vleck's reports in *Jour. Optical Soc. Am. and Rev. Sci. Instr.*, **14**, 108 (1927), and **16**, 301 (1928).

problem. For this reason, whenever such background cannot be
expected to have been acquired in connection with a study of
classical particle motion, we shall make it a part of our aim to
develop the mathematical background necessary for the work.
But the purely mathematical discussion will be restricted to the
necessary minimum, and will often forego mathematical rigor.

In order that the reader may not be confronted concurrently
with two quite distinct tasks—that of becoming acquainted with
certain standard mathematical methods, and that of learning the
use and the physical significance of these methods in quantum
mechanics—we devote this chapter to an elementary account of
the mathematical methods involved in the physical considerations
of Chapter III, where quantum-mechanical ideas will first be
introduced.

2. Differential Operators

A central part in the mathematical structure of quantum mechanics is played by *operators* of several types; of these we shall
now consider the so-called differential operators, which are used
in the theory of ordinary differential equations.

Among the various mathematical operations that can be performed on a function $u(x)$ of the variable x [such as $u(x) = x^3$
and $u(x) = \sin x$] are differentiation of $u(x)$ with respect to x,
multiplication of $u(x)$ by x, and multiplication of $u(x)$ by a constant, say c. In studying the properties of these and other operations it is convenient to introduce the concepts of an *operator*
and an *operand*. It is convenient, for example, to regard the
expression $\dfrac{d}{dx} u(x)$ as consisting of two constituents: the operator
$\left[\dfrac{d}{dx}\right]$ and the operand $u(x)$; to regard the expression $xu(x)$ as
consisting of the operator $[x]$ and the operand $u(x)$; and to regard
the expression $cu(x)$ as consisting of the operator $[c]$ and the
operand $u(x)$. The operator $\left[\dfrac{d}{dx}\right]$ is, in fact, defined by the
requirement that the relation

$$\left[\frac{d}{dx}\right] u(x) = u'(x) \tag{1}$$

hold for an arbitrary differentiable function $u(x)$, $u'(x)$ being the first derivative of $u(x)$ obtained by the rules of differential calculus; the operator $[x]$ is defined by the requirement that

$$[x]u(x) = xu(x) \tag{2}$$

for an arbitrary $u(x)$, the right side of (2) being the algebraic product of x and $u(x)$; and the operator $[c]$ is defined by the requirement that

$$[c]u(x) = cu(x) \tag{3}$$

for an arbitrary $u(x)$, the right side of (3) being the algebraic product of $u(x)$ and the constant c.

We shall usually denote the operators $\left[\dfrac{d}{dx}\right]$, $[x]$, and $[c]$ by $\dfrac{d}{dx}$ (or d/dx), x, and c, respectively; brackets were used above in order that Equations (1) to (3) might not appear trivial. The operator symbols d/dx, x, and c must not be confused with symbols representing ordinary functions and numbers. This is perhaps clear at once in the case of the operator d/dx; that this is also so in the case of the operators x and c will become clear later. The reader should acquire the habit of inquiring whether a mathematical expression that he encounters in a quantum-mechanical calculation has to do with operators, or with ordinary functions and numbers, or with operators *and* ordinary functions and numbers.

The processes of operating with the operators d/dx, x, and c, are called, respectively, differentiation with respect to x, multiplication by x, and multiplication by the constant c. Among the operators of type c are the operator 1 (the *unit operator*, *idemfactor*, or simply *unity*), which leaves every operand unaltered, and the operator 0 (the *zero operator* or simply *zero*), which annihilates every operand. Operators of type c are often called *constants*. When discussing operators in general, we usually denote them by Greek letters.

If the respective results of operating on the operand u with the operators α and β are added together, then the final result

$$\alpha u + \beta u \tag{4}$$

is usually denoted by

$$(\alpha + \beta)u, \tag{5}$$

this convention being suggested by the notation of algebra; thus the expression $(d/dx)u(x) + xu(x)$, that is, the sum of the respective results of operating on $u(x)$ with d/dx and with x, is written as $(d/dx + x)u(x)$. This notation is readily extended to sums of the respective results of operating on the same operand with more than two operators.

Another convention concerns consecutive operations. If we first operate on u with the operator α, getting the result αu, and next operate on this result with the operator β, then the final result

$$\beta(\alpha u) \tag{6}$$

of the two successive operations is usually denoted by

$$\beta \alpha u, \tag{7}$$

it being understood that to evaluate an expression of type (7) we must *first* operate on u with α, and *next* operate on the result so obtained with β. For example, if we first operate on $u(x)$ with the operator x, getting $xu(x)$, and next operate on this result with d/dx, then the final result $d/dx[xu(x)]$ must be written in the conventional notation as $(d/dx)xu(x)$; on the other hand, if we first operate on $u(x)$ with d/dx, getting $(d/dx)u(x)$, and next operate on this result with x, then the final result $x[(d/dx)u(x)]$ must be written as $x(d/dx)u(x)$. Incidentally, by the rule for differentiating a product, $(d/dx)[xu(x)] = x(d/dx)u(x) + u(x)$, that is,

$$\frac{d}{dx} xu(x) = x \frac{d}{dx} u(x) + u(x), \tag{8}$$

so that

$$\frac{d}{dx} xu(x) \neq x \frac{d}{dx} u(x) \tag{9}$$

unless $u(x) = 0$. The inequality (9) illustrates the importance of remembering the order in which the individual operations must be carried out when the conventional notation is used for successive operations. Extending this notation to cases involving more than two consecutive operations, we write $\gamma \beta \alpha u$ for $\gamma[\beta(\alpha u)]$, $\beta \alpha \gamma u$ for $\beta[\alpha(\gamma u)]$, $\delta \gamma \beta \alpha u$ for $\delta\{\gamma[\beta(\alpha u)]\}$, and so forth; if a certain operation is repeated without the intervention of other operations, we use the exponent notation and write, for example, $\alpha\beta^2\alpha^3\beta\alpha u$ for $\alpha\beta\beta\alpha\alpha\alpha\beta\alpha u$.

Operator algebra. In investigating the properties of a given class of operators, we may proceed along two lines. One is to consider the results of operating with the operators on various operands, and to obtain the desired information through a study of the *relations among the results of the operations*. The other is to introduce the concept of certain *relations among the operators themselves*, to define (using operands) the criteria for the existence of such relations, to establish (using operands) the existence of certain fundamental relations among some of the operators of the class, and then, by deducing additional relations among the operators from the fundamental ones, to continue the study without further reference to operands. The latter method, that of *operator algebra*, rests on the following definitions of equality, sum, and product of operators.

If the operators α and β are of such a nature that

$$\alpha u = \beta u \tag{10}$$

for *every* operand u on which both can operate, then α and β are defined to be *equal* to each other, and we write

$$\alpha = \beta, \tag{11}$$

adopting the notation of ordinary algebra. We need not consider here the possibility of existence of operands on which one of the operators can operate and the other cannot. Relations of type (11) between operators are called *operator equations*, and in stating such symbolic equations in words we use the language of ordinary algebra. Two operators, α and β, are said to be unequal if there exists an operand u on which both can operate and for which (10) does not hold.

If the operators α, β, and γ are of such a nature that

$$\gamma u = \alpha u + \beta u \tag{12}$$

for every operand u for which the operations involved in (12) can be carried out, then γ is defined to be the *sum of α and β*, and we write

$$\gamma = \alpha + \beta. \tag{13}$$

In particular, we may regard the symbol $\alpha + \beta$ in $(\alpha + \beta)u$ as a distinct operator, the sum of α and β. For example, $d/dx + x$ in $(d/dx + x)u(x)$ may be regarded as a *distinct operator*, defined as the sum of d/dx and x, and *having properties of its own*.

If the operators α, β, and γ are of such a nature that

$$\gamma u = \alpha(\beta u) \tag{14}$$

for every operand u for which the operations in (14) can be carried out, then γ is defined to be the *product $\alpha\beta$ of α and β*, and we write

$$\gamma = \alpha\beta. \tag{15}$$

In particular, we may regard $\alpha\beta$ in $\alpha\beta u$ as a distinct operator, the product $\alpha\beta$ of α and β. For example, $(d/dx)x$ in $(d/dx)xu(x)$ may be regarded as a distinct operator. Incidentally, the operator $(d/dx)x$ may serve to illustrate the importance of not confusing the operator x with the ordinary function x: the operator symbol $(d/dx)x$ must be understood to symbolize the double operation of first multiplying an operand by x and then differentiating the result so obtained with respect to x; no numerical value must be ascribed to this symbol, even though the symbol, when no operand is written after it, may be mistaken for the derivative of the function x with respect to x.

Note that γ in (14) was defined as the product $\alpha\beta$ of α and β, rather than simply the product of α and β. The reason for this is that the product $\beta\alpha$ may be different from the product $\alpha\beta$; for example, it follows from (9) that

$$\frac{d}{dx} x \neq x \frac{d}{dx}. \tag{16}$$

The definitions of equality, sum, and product of operators given above enable us to construct any number of distinct operators from our three fundamental operators d/dx, x, and c, such as $d/dx + x$, $d/dx + x + 3$, x^2, $3d/dx$, $-d/dx$, $(d/dx)^2$, $(d/dx)^2 + x^2$, $(d/dx + x)^2$, and so forth; for lack of a more descriptive short term, we shall call these operators *differential operators*. The operator-algebraic rules for handling differential operators are quite similar to those of ordinary algebra, the conspicuous exception being, however, that the order of the factors in a product is, in general, important. An algebra in which the order of the factors may affect the significance of a product is said to be *noncommutative.* The algebra of the differential operators is non-commutative, as illustrated by (16). If the products $\alpha\beta$ and $\beta\alpha$ of two operators α and β are equal, we say that α and β *commute;* otherwise we say that they do not commute. We may add equal operators to both sides of an operator equation without destroying the equality; but if the algebra is noncommutative we must be careful in multiplying an equation through by'an operator; for example, if $\alpha = \beta$, then $\gamma\alpha = \gamma\beta$, and $\alpha\gamma = \beta\gamma$, but $\alpha\gamma$ does not necessarily equal $\gamma\beta$, nor does $\gamma\alpha$ necessarily equal $\beta\gamma$. The process of getting $\gamma\alpha = \gamma\beta$ from $\alpha = \beta$ is called *multiplication by γ from the left;* that of getting $\alpha\gamma = \beta\gamma$ from $\alpha = \beta$ is called *multiplication by γ from the right.*

Commutators. The operator $\alpha\beta - \beta\alpha$ is called the *commutator* of the operators α and β. The commutator of two operators may sometimes be identified with an operator having a simpler form than the defining expression $\alpha\beta - \beta\alpha$. For example, the commutator

$$\frac{d}{dx}\, x - x\, \frac{d}{dx} \tag{17}$$

of the operators d/dx and x can be put into a simpler form as follows: we write (8) as

$$\frac{d}{dx}\, xu(x) = \left(x\, \frac{d}{dx} + 1 \right) u(x); \tag{18}$$

since (18) holds for an arbitrary differentiable operand $u(x)$, we have

$$\frac{d}{dx}\, x = x\, \frac{d}{dx} + 1, \tag{19}$$

that is,

$$\frac{d}{dx}\, x - x\, \frac{d}{dx} = 1. \tag{20}$$

The commutator of d/dx and x is thus the unit operator. Similarly, the commutator of x and d/dx is -1.

The commutator of d/dx and x^2 can be simplified in appearance as follows: By the rules of the calculus,

$$\left(\frac{d}{dx}\, x^2 - x^2\, \frac{d}{dx} \right) u(x) = \frac{d}{dx}\, x^2 u(x) - x^2\, \frac{d}{dx}\, u(x)$$

$$= 2xu(x) + x^2\, \frac{d}{dx}\, u(x) - x^2\, \frac{d}{dx}\, u(x) = 2xu(x); \tag{21}$$

hence the equation

$$\left(\frac{d}{dx}x^2 - x^2\frac{d}{dx}\right)u(x) = 2xu(x) \tag{22}$$

holds for an arbitrary differentiable $u(x)$, and we have

$$\frac{d}{dx}x^2 - x^2\frac{d}{dx} = 2x. \tag{23}$$

The commutators of pairs of more complicated operators can often be simplified in appearance in a similar manner. The commutator of two commuting operators is, of course, the operator zero.

Let us now illustrate the symbolic methods of *operator algebra* by deriving (23) from* (20) *without further reference to operands*. Multiplication of (20) by x from the left yields

$$x\frac{d}{dx}x - x^2\frac{d}{dx} = x, \tag{24}$$

while multiplication of (20) by x from the right gives

$$\frac{d}{dx}x^2 - x\frac{d}{dx}x = x; \tag{25}$$

adding (24) and (25), we now get

$$\frac{d}{dx}x^2 - x^2\frac{d}{dx} = 2x, \tag{26}$$

in agreement with (23).

Linear operators. An operator α is said to be *linear* if for arbitrary operands u and v

$$\alpha(u + v) = \alpha u + \alpha v, \tag{27}$$

and for an arbitrary constant c

$$\alpha c = c\alpha. \tag{28}$$

The simple differential operators discussed above are examples of linear operators. In quantum mechanics we are concerned almost exclusively with linear operators, and throughout our work the term *operator* will be used to mean *linear operator*, unless the contrary is explicitly stated.

Exercises

1. Verify that the result of operating on the operand sin x with the operator $[(d/dx)x]^2$ is sin $x + 3x$ cos $x - x^2$ sin x, and that the result of operating on the same operand with the operator $[x(d/dx)]^2$ is x cos $x - x^2$ sin x.

2. Verify that $(d/dx + 1)^2 = (d/dx)^2 + 2d/dx + 1$, and that $(d/dx + x)^2 = (d/dx)^2 + (d/dx)x + x(d/dx) + x^2$. Note that $(d/dx + x)^2$ is *not* equal to $(d/dx)^2 + 2(d/dx)x + x^2$.

3. In ordinary algebra we have: $(\alpha + \beta)(\alpha - \beta) = \alpha^2 - \beta^2$. Under what condition can this formula be used when α and β are operators? What formula should be used instead when this condition is not fulfilled?

4. Consider the products $\alpha\beta\gamma$, $\alpha\gamma\beta$, $\beta\gamma\alpha$, $\beta\alpha\gamma$, $\gamma\alpha\beta$, and $\gamma\beta\alpha$ of operators α, β, and γ. How many of these products are different operators if no two of the three operators α, β, and γ commute? If α and β commute with each other, but neither α nor β commutes with γ? If α commutes with β and with γ, but β and γ do not commute? If every two of the three operators commute? Illustrate each of these possibilities, using operators of the types discussed in the text.

5. Show that the commutator of the operator x and the operator $(\cos^2 a)x(d/dx) + (\sin^2 a)(d/dx)x$, where a is a constant, is independent of a. Show that the commutator of d/dx and $(\cos^2 a)x(d/dx) + (\sin^2 a)(d/dx)x$ is also independent of a.

6. Show, using calculus, that for all positive integral values of n we have: $(d/dx)x^n - x^n(d/dx) = nx^{n-1}$.

7. Show by operator algebra that, if $\alpha\beta - \beta\alpha = 1$, then $\alpha\beta^2 - \beta^2\alpha = 2\beta$, $\alpha\beta^3 - \beta^3\alpha = 3\beta^2$, and, in general, $\alpha\beta^n - \beta^n\alpha = n\beta^{n-1}$.

8. Derive the result of Exercise 6, taking for granted (20) and the result of Exercise 7.

9. Reduce the commutator of $(d/dx)^n$ and x to a form not involving the operator x.

10. Verify the following identities, in which the Greek letters denote arbitrary linear operators, c denotes a constant, and $\{\alpha, \beta\}$ denotes $\alpha\beta - \beta\alpha$:

$$\{\xi, \eta\} = -\{\eta, \xi\}$$

$$\{\xi, c\} = 0$$

$$\{\xi_1 + \xi_2, \eta\} = \{\xi_1, \eta\} + \{\xi_2, \eta\}$$

$$\{\xi, \eta_1 + \eta_2\} = \{\xi, \eta_1\} + \{\xi, \eta_2\} \qquad \text{(29 a-g)}$$

$$\{\xi_1\xi_2, \eta\} = \{\xi_1, \eta\}\xi_2 + \xi_1\{\xi_2, \eta\}$$

$$\{\xi, \eta_1\eta_2\} = \{\xi, \eta_1\}\eta_2 + \eta_1\{\xi, \eta_2\}$$

$$\{\xi, \{\eta, \zeta\}\} + \{\eta, \{\zeta, \xi\}\} + \{\zeta, \{\xi, \eta\}\} = 0.$$

11. Show that the operator $\partial/\partial x$, which stands for partial differentiation of any operand (now explicitly allowed to be a function of several variables) with respect to x, satisfies the equation

$$\frac{\partial}{\partial x} x - x \frac{\partial}{\partial x} = 1. \qquad (30)$$

12. By a generalization of the arguments given below, prove the following theorem for the case when the operand u can be expanded into a power series in the variable x: if the operator α commutes with x and with $\partial/\partial x$, that is, if

$$\alpha x - x\alpha = 0 \tag{31}$$

and

$$\alpha \frac{\partial}{\partial x} - \frac{\partial}{\partial x} \alpha = 0, \tag{32}$$

then, for an arbitrary u,

$$\alpha u = cu, \tag{33}$$

where c is independent of x and $\partial/\partial x$, so that, insofar as dependence on x and $\partial/\partial x$ is concerned, α is a constant.[2]

[Let $u = u_1 = 1$; then, in view of (32), $(\partial/\partial x)\alpha u_1 = \alpha(\partial/\partial x)u_1 = 0$, and

$$\frac{\partial}{\partial x}(\alpha u_1) = 0, \tag{34}$$

so that $\alpha u_1 = c$, where c is independent of x, or

$$\alpha u_1 = cu_1. \tag{35}$$

Next let $u = u_2 = x$, so that $\alpha u_2 = \alpha x$, or $\alpha u_2 = \alpha x u_1$, $\alpha x u_1$ being the result of operating with α on the product of the variable x and the number 1. Now, we may regard x in $\alpha x u_1$ as being the operator x instead of the variable x, and write $\alpha x u_1 = (\alpha x)u_1$ without affecting the result; but, in view of (31), $(\alpha x)u_1 = x\alpha u_1$, so that, because of (35), we have $\alpha u_2 = xc$, and hence

$$\alpha u_2 = cu_2. \tag{36}$$

Thus (33) follows from (31) and (32) in the two special cases $u = 1$ and $u = x$.]

13. Show that, if α satisfies the two operator equations

$$x\alpha - \alpha x = 0, \qquad \frac{\partial}{\partial x}\alpha - \alpha \frac{\partial}{\partial x} = 2x, \tag{37}$$

then the operator $(\alpha - x^2)$ commutes with x and with $\partial/\partial x$; then, using the result of Exercise 12, show that the general solution of Equations (37) is

$$\alpha = x^2 + c, \tag{38}$$

where c is a constant insofar as dependence on x and $\partial/\partial x$ is concerned. Show in a similar way that the general solution of the simultaneous operator equations $x\alpha - \alpha x = 0$ and $(\partial/\partial x)\alpha - \alpha(\partial/\partial x) = Ax^n$, where A is a constant, is $\alpha = A(n+1)^{-1}x^{n+1} + c$.

---

[2] The operator $\dfrac{d}{dx} x - x \dfrac{d}{dx}$ is an example of a constant in disguise.

3. The Operator $-\dfrac{d^2}{dx^2}$

We shall be concerned for the present with real and complex functions $u(x)$ of the real variable x, and shall usually write u, u', u'', and so forth, for $u(x)$, $du(x)/dx$, $d^2u(x)/dx^2$, and so forth. The moduli (or absolute values, see §8) of x and $u(x)$ will be denoted, respectively, by $|x|$ and $|u|$; since our x is real, $|x|$ equals x when x is positive, and $-x$ when x is negative. The statement that a function of x remains finite when $x \to \infty$ will mean that when x increases without limit this function does not tend to ∞ (as does, say, e^x) or to $-\infty$ (as does, say, $-e^x$), and does not oscillate with amplitude approaching ∞ (as do, say, $x \sin x$ and $-x \cos^2 x$); the meaning of the statement that a function of x remains finite when $x \to -\infty$ is similar. The words "when $|x| \to \infty$" will mean "when $x \to \infty$ *and also* when $x \to -\infty$."

If $u(x)$ and $du(x)/dx$ are both continuous for all real values of x, we say that $u(x)$ satisfies our *standard continuity conditions*.

If $u(x)$ [or $|u|$, if u is complex or pure imaginary] remains finite when $|x| \to \infty$, we say that $u(x)$ satisfies our *standard boundary conditions*.[3] If $u(x)$

    (a), satisfies our standard continuity conditions,

    (b), satisfies our standard boundary conditions, and

    (c), is not identically zero,

we call $u(x)$ a *well-behaved* function. For example, the four functions shown in the top row of Fig. 1 are well-behaved, while the

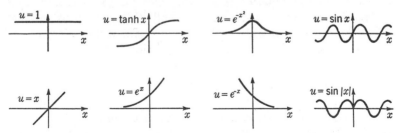

Fig. 1. Top row: examples of well-behaved functions; bottom row: examples of ill-behaved functions.

---

[3] It should perhaps be emphasized that to satisfy our boundary conditions a function must remain finite when $x \to \infty$ *and also* when $x \to -\infty$.

four functions in the bottom row are *ill-behaved*, that is, not well-behaved.

The problem of immediate interest to us is to consider the conditions under which certain second-order differential equations possess well-behaved solutions. Some differential equations have a well-behaved general solution; for example, the general solution of

$$u'' = -u \tag{1}$$

is

$$u = A \sin x + B \cos x, \tag{2}$$

and satisfies our standard boundary and continuity conditions for any choice of the arbitrary constants[4] A and B, so that (2) is well behaved for any choice of A and B except $A = B = 0$. Some differential equations do not have any well-behaved solutions at all; for example, the general solution of

$$u'' = u \tag{3}$$

is

$$u = Ae^x + Be^{-x}; \tag{4}$$

the first term in (4) increases without limit when $x \rightarrow \infty$, and the second does so when $x \rightarrow -\infty$; hence no adjustment of A and B (except $A = B = 0$) yields a solution satisfying our boundary conditions.

Finally, a differential equation may not possess well-behaved solutions in general, but does possess them if a numerical constant appearing in the equation is suitably chosen. This case will be of special interest to us, and we shall illustrate it by several examples, the first of which will be to determine the values of the numerical constant λ for which the equation

$$-\frac{d^2}{dx^2} u = \lambda u, \tag{5}$$

---

[4] In anticipation of working with several independent variables, note that the statement that a quantity involved in a mathematical expression is a *constant* means only that this quantity does not depend on the independent variable or variables explicitly appearing in the expression; for example, the statement that A in (2) is a constant means that A does not depend on x, but does not exclude the possibility that A depends on independent variables other than x.

of which (1) and (3) are special cases, possesses well-behaved solutions, and to find these solutions.

Now, if $\lambda \neq 0$, the general solution of (5) is

$$u = A_1 \cos \lambda^{\frac{1}{2}} x + A_2 \sin \lambda^{\frac{1}{2}} x, \tag{6}$$

where the A's are arbitrary constants, and where $\lambda^{\frac{1}{2}}$ denotes $+\sqrt{\lambda}$. The solution (6) satisfies the continuity conditions regardless of the values of the A's, and it remains to be seen if the boundary conditions are also fulfilled; in doing this we shall consider several cases separately.

First, let

$$\lambda > 0, \tag{7}$$

so that $\lambda^{\frac{1}{2}}$ is a nonvanishing positive number; (6) then remains finite everywhere, and hence the boundary conditions are satisfied.

Next, let

$$\lambda < 0, \tag{8}$$

so that $\lambda^{\frac{1}{2}}$ is a nonvanishing pure imaginary number, say ia, where a is positive. It is convenient in this case to write the general solution of (5) as

$$u = B_1 e^{ax} + B_2 e^{-ax} \tag{9}$$

rather than as (6), and it is seen that if $\lambda < 0$, then neither the general solution of (5) nor any of its particular solutions are well behaved.

We shall leave it to the reader to show that if λ is a complex or a pure imaginary number, then (5) does not possess any well-behaved solutions, and we shall proceed to the remaining case,

$$\lambda = 0. \tag{10}$$

The general solution of (5) is now

$$u = Bx + C, \tag{11}$$

where B and C are arbitrary constants. The term Bx does not satisfy our boundary conditions, while the term C does; hence the special solution

$$u = C, \tag{12}$$

obtained by setting $B = 0$ in (11), satisfies all our conditions, and consequently (5) does possess well-behaved solutions when $\lambda = 0$. Note that the results in the two cases $\lambda > 0$ and $\lambda = 0$

differ in an important respect. In the case $\lambda > 0$ the general solution itself is well-behaved; while in the case $\lambda = 0$ the general solution is not, but the particular solution (12), containing a single arbitrary constant, is. Note also that, although (6) is not the general solution of (5) when $\lambda = 0$, the substitution $\lambda = 0$ into (6) yields, nevertheless, the solution (12), that is, the solution satisfying the boundary conditions when $\lambda = 0$.

To summarize: Equation (5) possesses well-behaved solutions if, and only if,

$$\lambda \geq 0; \tag{13}$$

and the well-behaved solutions have the form (6), or the equivalent form

$$u = A e^{i\lambda^{\frac{1}{2}}x} + B e^{-i\lambda^{\frac{1}{2}}x}, \tag{14}$$

which for most of our purposes is more convenient than (6); it is to be understood that the trivial case $A = B = 0$ in (14) is to be excluded.

Eigenvalues and eigenfunctions. To simplify further discussion, we introduce the following terminology. If, for the specific value λ_i of the numerical constant λ, a well-behaved operand u_i satisfies the equation

$$\alpha u = \lambda u, \tag{15}$$

where α is a given operator (that is, if

$$\alpha u_i = \lambda_i u_i, \tag{16}$$

and u_i is well behaved), we say that the number λ_i is an *eigenvalue*[5] of the operator α, that the operand u_i is an *eigenfunction*[6] of α, and that the eigenvalue λ_i and the eigenfunction u_i of the operator α belong to each other.

For example, since the operand $\sin 3x$ is well-behaved, and since

$$-\frac{d^2}{dx^2} \sin 3x = 9 \sin 3x, \tag{17}$$

we say that the number 9 is an eigenvalue of the operator $-d^2/dx^2$, that the operand $\sin 3x$ is an eigenfunction of the operator $-d^2/dx^2$, and that

---

[5] This term is half-translated (to use Professor Kemble's expression) from the German *Eigenwert*; alternative terms are *proper value* (or *number*) and *characteristic value* (or *number*).

[6] Alternative terms are *proper function* and *characteristic function*.

the eigenvalue 9 and the eigenfunction $\sin 3x$ of the operator $-d^2/dx^2$ belong to each other.

Our definitions can be restated as follows: an eigenfunction of the operator α is a well-behaved operand such that operating on it with α is equivalent to multiplying it by a numerical constant, this constant then being the corresponding eigenvalue of α. If

$$\alpha = -\frac{d^2}{dx^2}, \tag{18}$$

Equation (15) goes over into (5), and consequently the problem concerning (5) treated above (our first example of the *eigenvalue problem*) can be stated as follows: to find the eigenvalues and the eigenfunctions of the operator $-d^2/dx^2$. And our conclusions can be stated thus: any positive number, zero included, is an eigenvalue of the operator $-d^2/dx^2$, and the eigenfunction of $-d^2/dx^2$ belonging to the eigenvalue λ is (14).

We call the totality of the eigenvalues of an operator its *eigenvalue spectrum*, or simply its *spectrum*; thus we say that the spectrum of the operator $-d^2/dx^2$ consists of all positive numbers, zero included.

The eigenvalue problem, which plays a fundamental part in the quantum mechanics of particle motion, arises also quite frequently in classical theoretical physics, particularly in the theory of continuous media; but the definition of good behavior of a function is then usually somewhat different from that adopted above, and the problem usually goes over into what is called the *Sturm-Liouville* problem.

Exercises

1. Show that the function $\cos 4x$ is an eigenfunction of the operator d^2/dx^2 belonging to the eigenvalue -16. Show that the function $xe^{-\frac{1}{2}x^2}$ is an eigenfunction of the operator $-d^2/dx^2 + x^2$ belonging to the eigenvalue 3. Show that the function $\sinh 2x$ is not an eigenfunction of the operator d^2/dx^2 in spite of the equation $(d^2/dx^2) \sinh 2x = 4 \sinh 2x$.

2. Show that the operator $-d^2/dx^2$ has no complex or pure imaginary eigenvalues.

3. Show that, if u_i is an eigenfunction of a linear operator α belonging to the eigenvalue λ_i, then Cu_i, where C is an arbitrary nonvanishing constant, is also an eigenfunction of α belonging to the eigenvalue λ_i.

4. The operator $-\partial^2/\partial x^2$ is of interest when the operands are explicitly permitted to be functions not only of x but also of other independent variables. Show that, if the operands are required to be well behaved so far as their dependence on x is concerned, then the spectrum of $-\partial^2/\partial x^2$

is the same as that of $-d^2/dx^2$ found in the text, and that the eigenfunctions of $-\partial^2/\partial x^2$ have the form (14) and can depend on independent variables other than x only through the coefficients A and B.

4. The Operator $-\dfrac{d^2}{dx^2} + x^2$

Our next problem is to determine the eigenvalues and the eigenfunctions of the operator

$$-\frac{d^2}{dx^2} + x^2,$$ (1)

that is, to find the values of the numerical constant λ for which the equation $\alpha u = \lambda u$ possesses well-behaved solutions when α is the operator (1), and to find these solutions. The operator (1) will come into play in connection with the first dynamical system that we shall study from the quantum-mechanical standpoint, namely, the linear harmonic oscillator.

Remarks on curvature. If a curve $u = u(x)$ is concave downward wherever it lies above the x-axis, and concave upward wherever it lies below the x-axis, we say that it is *concave toward the x-axis* in the region in question; for example, the function $\sin x$ is concave toward the x-axis throughout the infinite region. Now, according to a theorem in elementary calculus, u is concave downward if u'' is negative, and concave upward if u'' is positive. Hence u is concave toward the x-axis if u and u'' have opposite algebraic signs; in other words,

u is concave toward the x-axis if $u''/u < 0$. (2a)

If a curve is concave upward wherever it lies above the x-axis, and concave downward wherever it lies below the x-axis, we say that it is *convex toward the x-axis* in the region in question; for example, the function x^3 is convex toward the x-axis throughout the infinite region. An argument similar to that used above shows that

u is convex toward the x-axis if $u''/u > 0$. (2b)

The results (2a) and (2b) will find immediate application in our study of the operator (1).

When α is the particular operator (1), the eigenvalue equation $\alpha u = \lambda u$ becomes the differential equation

$$\left(-\frac{d^2}{dx^2} + x^2\right) u = \lambda u.$$ (3)

The general solution of (3) cannot be expressed in any simple way in terms of the elementary functions; consequently, we shall have to proceed in a manner less direct than that of §3, and a few preliminary remarks are perhaps in order.

Since, as the reader will verify,

$$\left(-\frac{d^2}{dx^2} + x^2\right) e^{-\frac{1}{2}x^2} = 1 \cdot e^{-\frac{1}{2}x^2}, \tag{4}$$

and the function $e^{-\frac{1}{2}x^2}$ (Fig. 3) is well-behaved, the operator (1) has the eigenvalue 1. Similarly, since

$$\left(-\frac{d^2}{dx^2} + x^2\right) xe^{-\frac{1}{2}x^2} = 3xe^{-\frac{1}{2}x^2}, \tag{5}$$

and the function $xe^{-\frac{1}{2}x^2}$ (Fig. 4) is well-behaved,[7] the operator (1) has also the eigenvalue 3. The question may now be asked: Does the operator (1) have the eigenvalue 2? To answer it we must find whether the equation

$$\left(-\frac{d^2}{dx^2} + x^2\right) u = 2u \tag{6}$$

has well-behaved solutions.

To get an idea of the behavior of the solutions of (6), we calculate by numerical integration[8] two particular solutions U_0 and U_1 of (6) satisfying the following conditions at $x = 0$:

$$
\begin{aligned}
U_0(0) &= 1 & U_0'(0) &= 0 \\
U_1(0) &= 0 & U_1'(0) &= 1.
\end{aligned}
\tag{7}
$$

Graphs of U_0 and U_1 are shown in the lower part of Fig. 2; in the upper part are plotted the parabola x^2 and the constant $\lambda = 2$. The graphs

---

[7] (In this footnote, as well as in some other places, we write exp s for e^s.) When $x \to \pm \infty$ the first factor of $x \exp(-\frac{1}{2}x^2)$ approaches $\pm\infty$ while the second approaches zero, so that the product, as it stands, becomes indeterminate. To resolve the indeterminacy, we rewrite $x \exp(-\frac{1}{2}x^2)$ as $x/\exp(\frac{1}{2}x^2)$ and recall (see *indeterminate forms* in a calculus text) that, if the ratio of two functions of x becomes indeterminate for some value of x, then it can be replaced at this value of x by the ratio of the derivatives of the numerator and the denominator; thus, the limit of $x/\exp(\frac{1}{2}x^2)$ when $x \to \infty$ or $x \to -\infty$ may be replaced by the corresponding limit of $[dx/dx]/[d \exp(\frac{1}{2}x^2)/dx]$, that is, of $1/x \exp(\frac{1}{2}x^2)$, and we conclude that $x \exp(-\frac{1}{2}x^2) \to 0$ when $|x| \to \infty$. Similar arguments show that the product of $\exp(-\frac{1}{2}x^2)$ and of any *polynomial* in x (that is, any *terminating* power series in x) approaches zero when $|x| \to \infty$.

[8] Even when the general solution of an ordinary differential equation cannot be obtained analytically, particular solutions satisfying prescribed numerical initial conditions can usually be evaluated by numerical methods; for references, see §33.

suggest that U_0 is even[9] in x, while U_1 is odd in x; that this is indeed so will be shown rigorously later. Also, we observe that in the region $|x| < \sqrt{2}$ (where the parabola in the upper part of Fig. 2 lies below the line $\lambda = 2$) both U's are concave toward the x-axis, while in the regions $|x| > \sqrt{2}$ (where the parabola lies above the line $\lambda = 2$) both U's are convex toward the x-axis. That the curvature of *any* solution of (6) has these properties can be shown, without reference to graphs, as follows: For $u \neq 0$, Equation (6) can be written as $u''/u = x^2 - 2$, and therefore

$$u''/u < 0 \quad \text{for} \quad |x| \lesssim \sqrt{2}, \tag{8}$$

and

$$u''/u > 0 \quad \text{for} \quad |x| > \sqrt{2}, \tag{9}$$

so that, according to (2a), u is concave toward the x-axis when $|x| < \sqrt{2}$, and, according to (2b), u is convex toward the x-axis when $|x| > \sqrt{2}$.

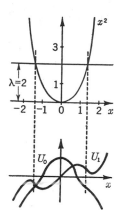

Now, at $x = 2$, say, the value of U_1'' is seen from the graph to be positive; in view of (9), U_1'' will remain positive for all values of x greater than 2 as long as U_1 remains positive, so that, since both U_1 and its slope are positive at $x = 2$, U_1 is certain to increase without limit when $x \to \infty$. We find in a similar way that U_1 decreases without limit when $x \to -\infty$, and that U_0 decreases without limit when $|x| \to \infty$. In brief, both U_0 and U_1 are ill-behaved.

The general solution of (6) is

$$u = AU_0 + BU_1, \tag{10}$$

Fig. 2. Two solutions of (6); curvature exaggerated.

where A and B are arbitrary constants. In view of the behavior of U_0 and U_1 discussed above, we now conclude that, although A and B can perhaps be so chosen that (10) remains finite when $x \to \infty$ *or* when $x \to -\infty$, it is certainly impossible to choose A and B so that (10) remains finite when $x \to \infty$ *and also* when $x \to -\infty$, if the trivial case $A = B = 0$ is excluded. Consequently, (6) does not possess any well-behaved solutions, and hence the operator (1) does not have the eigenvalue 2; it will presently be shown, in fact, that the only eigenvalues of (1) are the odd positive integers.

Let us return for a moment to (4), which shows that $Ae^{-\frac{1}{2}x^2}$ is an eigenfunction of (1) belonging to the eigenvalue 1. Now, the general solution of the equation

$$\left(-\frac{d^2}{dx^2} + x^2\right) u = 1 \cdot u \tag{11}$$

---

[9] The function $u(x)$ is called *even in x*, or simply *even*, if $u(x) = u(-x)$ for all values of x, and is called *odd in x*, or simply *odd*, if $u(x) = -u(-x)$ for all values of x; thus $\cos x$ is even in x, $\sin x$ is odd in x, and $\cos(x + \frac{1}{4}\pi)$ is neither even nor odd in x.

turns out to be

$$u = Ae^{-\frac{1}{2}x^2} + BU_1, \qquad (12)$$

where U_1, calculated numerically under the conditions $U_1(0) = 0$ and $U_1'(0) = 1$, is shown in Fig. 3, and where A and B are arbitrary constants; U_1 is odd in x and is readily shown to be ill-behaved. Since $e^{-\frac{1}{2}x^2}$ is well-behaved and U_1 is not, the only way to get well-behaved solutions of (11) is to set $B = 0$ in (12), thus leaving out the odd part of the general solution.

Again, (5) shows that $Bxe^{-\frac{1}{2}x^2}$ is an eigenfunction of (1) belonging to the eigenvalue 3. The general solution of the equation

$$\left(-\frac{d^2}{dx^2} + x^2\right)u = 3u \qquad (13)$$

Fig. 3. Two solutions of (11); curvature exaggerated. Here $U_0 = e^{-\frac{1}{2}x^2}$.

turns out to be

$$u = AU_0 + Bxe^{-\frac{1}{2}x^2}, \qquad (14)$$

where U_0, calculated numerically under the conditions $U_0(0) = 1$ and $U_0'(0) = 0$, is shown in Fig. 4, and where A and B are arbitrary constants; U_0 is even in x and is ill-behaved. Since $xe^{-\frac{1}{2}x^2}$ is well-behaved and U_0 is not, the only way to get well-behaved solutions of (13) is to set $A = 0$ in (14), thus leaving out the even part of the general solution.

The principal features of the solutions of (3) that will be proved below and that have been illustrated to a certain extent by the examples given above are:

(a) For any value of λ, the particular solutions U_0 and U_1 of (3) satisfying the conditions (7) are, respectively, even in x and odd in x, and the general solution of (3) has the form

$$u = AU_0 + BU_1, \qquad (15)$$

where A and B are arbitrary constants.

(b) Unless λ is an odd positive integer, both U_0 and U_1 are ill-behaved, and u is ill-behaved for every choice of A and B in (15).

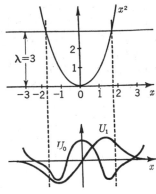

Fig. 4. Two solutions of (13); curvature exaggerated. Here $U_1 = xe^{-\frac{1}{2}x^2}$.

(c) If λ is an odd positive integer, then either U_0 is well-behaved and U_1 is not, or U_1 is well-behaved and U_0 is not; well-behaved solutions of (3) can in this case be obtained by equating to zero the coefficient of the ill-behaved term in (15), and consequently the eigenvalues of (1) are the odd positive integers.

A convenient procedure for a systematic identification of the eigenvalues of the operator (1) is the following: We let[10]

$$u = ve^{-\frac{1}{2}x^2}, \tag{16}$$

where $v = v(x)$, and find by substituting (16) into (3) that, in order that (16) be a solution of (3), v must satisfy the equation

$$v'' - 2xv' + (\lambda - 1)v = 0, \tag{17}$$

where the primes denote differentiation with respect to x. The boundary conditions to be imposed on v are less stringent than our standard conditions imposed on u; v may be allowed to become infinite when $|x| \to \infty$, provided that the product $ve^{-\frac{1}{2}x^2}$ remains finite when $|x| \to \infty$.

We now seek the general solution of (17) expressed as a power series:

$$v = a_\tau x^\tau + a_{\tau+1} x^{\tau+1} + a_{\tau+2} x^{\tau+2} + \cdots, \qquad \text{with } a_\tau \neq 0, \tag{18}$$

that is,

$$v = \sum_i a_i x^i, \qquad i = \tau, \tau + 1, \tau + 2, \cdots, \tag{19}$$

with $a_\tau \neq 0$. To identify this series, we must adjust the a's so that when (18) is substituted into the left side of (17) the coefficient of each power of x in the resulting expression vanishes. We expect two arbitrary constants to appear in the solution, since (17) is a differential equation of the second order. Substituting (18) into (17), we get

$$\sum_i [a_i i(i - 1)x^{i-2} + a_i(\lambda - 1 - 2i)x^i] = 0, \tag{20}$$

and note that terms in x^k in (20) come from two sources: from the first term in the brackets when $i = k + 2$, and from the second when $i = k$. Hence the complete coefficient of x^k in (20) is

$$(k + 2)(k + 1)a_{k+2} + (\lambda - 1 - 2k)a_k. \tag{21}$$

---

[10] The substitution (16) is suggested by the fact that, for an arbitrary m, the function $x^m e^{-\frac{1}{2}x^2}$ is, for any value of λ, an approximate solution of (3) in the regions where $|x|$ is sufficiently large. The method for handling (3) that we use here is called the *Sommerfeld polynomial method*; see A. Sommerfeld, *Wave-Mechanics* (hereafter cited as Sommerfeld), page 14, London, Methuen and Co., (1930).

In order that (20) hold, the coefficient (21) must vanish for every value of k, so that the relation

$$\frac{a_{k+2}}{a_k} = \frac{2k + 1 - \lambda}{(k + 1)(k + 2)} \tag{22}$$

must hold for every value of k.   This relation enables us to calculate the coefficients a_{k+2}, a_{k+4}, a_{k+6}, and so forth, if the coefficient a_k is available.   Note that (22) involves alternate rather than consecutive coefficients of (18).

To determine the powers of x with which the series (18) may start, we observe that the complete coefficient of the lowest power of x, that is, of $x^{\tau-2}$, in (20), is $a_\tau \tau(\tau - 1)$, so that the equation

$$\tau(\tau - 1) = 0 \tag{23}$$

must hold, and we have the two possibilities $\tau = 0$ and $\tau = 1$. The series, which we denote by V_0, obtained from (18) by letting $\tau = 0$, letting $a_0 = 1$, and omitting the odd powers of x, that is,

$$V_0(x) = 1 + a_2 x^2 + a_4 x^4 + \cdots, \tag{24}$$

is a particular solution of (17), provided the a's satisfy (22). Similarly, the series, which we denote by V_1, obtained from (18) by letting $\tau = 1$, letting $a_1 = 1$, and omitting the even powers of x, that is,

$$V_1(x) = x + a_3 x^3 + a_5 x^5 + \cdots, \tag{25}$$

is also a particular solution of (17) if the a's satisfy (22).   The general solution of (17) can thus be written as

$$v = A V_0(x) + B V_1(x), \tag{26}$$

where A and B are arbitrary constants.

If the series (24) happens to terminate, that is, if V_0 is a polynomial, then the product $V_0 e^{-\frac{1}{2}x^2}$ approaches zero[7] when $| x | \rightarrow \infty$, and the first term of (26) contributes a well-behaved term to u when substituted into (16).   But if (24) is an infinite series, then the product $V_0 e^{-\frac{1}{2}x^2}$ is ill-behaved, as the following argument would indicate.   For large values of k, (22) goes over into the approximate equation $a_{k+2}/a_k \cong 2/k$, so that for large values of k the ratio of the coefficients of x^{k+2} and x^k in V_0 approaches the ratio of the coefficients of x^{k+2} and x^k in the power series for the function e^{x^2}; thus V_0 then behaves for large values of x somewhat like e^{x^2}, and $V_0 e^{-\frac{1}{2}x^2}$ behaves for large values of x somewhat like the ill-behaved function $e^{\frac{1}{2}x^2}$. To summarize: V_0 contributes a well-behaved term to the solution (16) of (3) if, and only if, V_0 is a *polynomial*, that is, a terminating series. Similar considerations show that V_1 contributes a well-behaved term to the solution of (3) if, and only if, V_1 is a polynomial.

Now, inspection of (22) shows, first, that the only condition under which one of the two series in (26) will terminate is that, for some k,

$$2k + 1 - \lambda = 0, \tag{27}$$

in which case $a_{k+2} = a_{k+4} = a_{k+6} = \cdots = 0$, and, second, that it is impossible to choose λ so as to make *both* series in (26) terminate. Thus the only way to obtain well-behaved solutions of (3) is

(a) *to let* $\lambda = 2n + 1$ *where n is a positive integer or zero* (thus causing V_0 to terminate if n is even, or V_1 if n is odd) and

(b) *to set the arbitrary multiplier of the nonterminating series in* (26) *equal to zero.*

Consequently, the only eigenvalues of the operator (1) are the odd positive integers 1, 3, 5, $\cdots$; we shall label them λ_1, λ_2, λ_3, $\cdots$, according to the scheme

$$\lambda_n = 2n + 1, \qquad n = 0, 1, 2, 3, \cdots, \tag{28}$$

and shall denote the eigenfunction belonging to λ_n by u_n. This eigenfunction contains an arbitrary nonvanishing numerical factor.

The eigenfunction of (1) belonging to a particular eigenvalue can be obtained by computing the appropriate solution of (17) and substituting the result into (16).

To illustrate, we shall find the eigenfunction u_5 belonging to $\lambda_5 = 11$. Since n is odd, the terminating series in (26) is V_1, and the coefficient A in (26) is to be set equal to zero. Equation (22) gives for $\lambda = 11$

$$\frac{a_3}{a_1} = -\frac{4}{3}, \qquad \frac{a_5}{a_3} = -\frac{1}{5}, \qquad \frac{a_7}{a_5} = 0; \tag{29}$$

consequently,

$$a_3 = -\frac{4}{3}a_1, \qquad a_5 = \frac{4}{15}a_1, \qquad a_7 = a_9 = a_{11} = \cdots = 0, \tag{30}$$

and the required solution of (17) is

$$a_1\left(x - \frac{4}{3}x^3 + \frac{4}{15}x^5\right). \tag{31}$$

This may be written as

$$A_5(32x^5 - 160x^3 + 120x), \tag{32}$$

where A_5 is the arbitrary constant, and where the coefficient of x^5 within the parentheses is made equal to 2^5 in order that u_5 may appear in the form that we shall later adopt as standard. Substitution of (32) into (16) finally yields

$$u_5 = A_5(32x^5 - 160x^3 + 120x)e^{-\frac{1}{2}x^2}. \tag{33}$$

Hermite polynomials.[11] We shall now verify that the polynomial solution of (17) involved in u_n can, apart from an arbitrary multiplicative constant, be written in the form

$$e^{x^2} \frac{d^n}{dx^n} e^{-x^2}; \tag{34}$$

note that (34) *is* a polynomial, since $d^n e^{-x^2}/dx^n$ is e^{-x^2} times a polynomial. When $\lambda = \lambda_n = 2n + 1$, Equation (17) becomes

$$v'' - 2xv' + 2nv = 0, \tag{35}$$

and substitution of (34) into this yields

$$\frac{d^{n+2}}{dx^{n+2}} e^{-x^2} + 2x \frac{d^{n+1}}{dx^{n+1}} e^{-x^2} + 2(n+1) \frac{d^n}{dx^n} e^{-x^2} = 0, \tag{36}$$

so that we shall have verified that (34) is a solution of (35) if we show that (36) holds for $n = 0, 1, 2, 3, \cdots$. Now, if we differentiate (36) with respect to x, we get the same equation as that obtained by writing $n + 1$ for n in (36); therefore, if (36) holds for one value of n, it holds also for the next-higher value of n; but (36) is seen to hold for $n = 0$; hence[12] it holds also for $n = 1$, for $n = 2$, and so forth, that is, for all positive integral values of n, and our proof is completed.

The product of (34) and the constant $(-1)^n$ is called the *Hermite polynomial* of the nth degree and is denoted by $H_n(x)$:

$$H_n(x) = (-1)^n e^{x^2} \frac{d^n}{dx^n} e^{-x^2}; \tag{37}$$

---

[11] C. Hermite, *Comptes Rendus*, **58**, 93 (1864).
[12] A proof of this type is called a proof by *mathematical induction*.

thus

$$H_0(x) = 1 \qquad\qquad H_1(x) = 2x \qquad (38a, \cdots)$$
$$H_2(x) = 4x^2 - 2 \qquad\qquad H_3(x) = 8x^3 - 12x$$
$$H_4(x) = 16x^4 - 48x^2 + 12 \quad H_5(x) = 32x^5 - 160x^3 + 120x,$$

and so forth.

The eigenfunction of the operator (1) belonging to the eigenvalue $\lambda_n = 2n + 1$ can now be written as

$$u_n = A_n H_n(x) e^{-\frac{1}{2}x^2}, \qquad (39)$$

where A_n is an arbitrary constant. The function (39) is called the nth *Hermite function*. Graphs[13] of Hermite functions are shown in Fig. 5; the choice of A_n made in this figure will be discussed in §8.

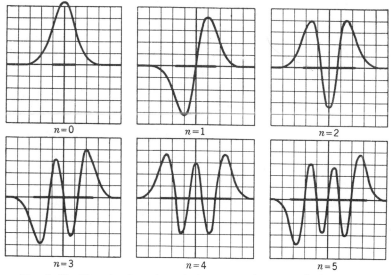

Fig. 5. Six Hermite functions (39), with $A_n = (2^n n! \pi^{\frac{1}{2}})^{-\frac{1}{2}}$. The horizontal and vertical scale units are approximately 1 and .1, respectively. The thick horizontal lines extend along the x-axes from $-\sqrt{2n+1}$ to $\sqrt{2n+1}$.

---

[13] Drawn after those in L. Pauling and E. B. Wilson's *Introduction to Quantum Mechanics* (hereafter cited as Pauling and Wilson); New York, McGraw-Hill Book Co., 1935.

To establish certain properties[14] of the Hermite polynomials, we consider the auxiliary function

$$z(x, s) = e^{-s^2 + 2sx} = e^{x^2} e^{-(s-x)^2} \tag{40}$$

of two independent variables x and s. The nth partial derivative of $e^{-(s-x)^2}$ with respect to s, evaluated at $s = 0$, satisfies the relation

$$\left[\frac{\partial^n}{\partial s^n} e^{-(s-x)^2} \right]_{s=0} = (-1)^n \frac{d^n}{dx^n} e^{-x^2}. \tag{41}$$

[Equation (41) can be proved, for example, by mathematical induction: we verify it for $n = 0$ and $n = 1$ and show, with the help of (36), that, if it holds for $n = n'$ and for $n = n' + 1$, then it holds also for $n = n' + 2$.] Therefore,

$$\left[\frac{\partial^n}{\partial s^n} z(x, s) \right]_{s=0} = (-1)^n e^{x^2} \frac{d^n}{dx^n} e^{-x^2} = H_n(x). \tag{42}$$

Next we expand $z(x, s)$ into a Taylor (Maclaurin) series in s. The coefficient of s^n in the series is the nth partial derivative of $z(x, s)$ taken with respect to s, evaluated at $s = 0$, and divided by $n!$ In view of (42), we then have

$$e^{-s^2 + 2sx} = \sum_n \frac{s^n}{n!} H_n(x), \quad n = 0, 1, 2, \cdots. \tag{43}$$

Thus the function (40), when expanded in powers of s, gives rise, so to speak, to the totality of the Hermite polynomials; for this reason it is called the *generating function* of these polynomials.

Now, our $z(x, s)$ satisfies the equation

$$\frac{\partial}{\partial x} z(x, s) = 2sz(x, s), \tag{44}$$

so that, in view of (43), the relation

$$\sum_n \frac{s^n}{n!} H_n'(x) = \sum_n \frac{2s^{n+1}}{n!} H_n(x), \tag{45}$$

where the prime denotes differentiation with respect to x, holds identically in s. Equating the coefficients of s^n on both sides of (45), we find that[15]

$$H_n'(x) = 2nH_{n-1}(x). \tag{46}$$

The function $z(x, s)$ also satisfies the equation

$$\frac{\partial}{\partial s} z(x, s) = -2sz(x, s) + 2xz(x, s), \tag{47}$$

---

[14] These are (43), (46), (49) and (50); familiarity with their proofs is not essential for the present.

[15] $H_{-1}(x)$ should be interpreted as zero when (46) or (49) is used with $n = 0$.

and consequently

$$\sum_n \frac{s^{n-1}}{(n-1)!} H_n(x) + 2 \sum_n \frac{s^{n+1}}{n!} H_n(x) - 2 \sum_n \frac{s^n}{n!} x H_n(x) = 0. \quad (48)$$

Equating to zero the coefficient of s^n, we get the relation[15]

$$H_{n+1}(x) - 2x H_n(x) + 2n H_{n-1}(x) = 0, \quad (49)$$

called the *recursion formula* for the Hermite polynomials.
The differential equation satisfied by $H_n(x)$ is (35):

$$H_n''(x) - 2x H_n'(x) + 2n H_n(x) = 0. \quad (50)$$

Exercises

1. Calculate $H_6(x)$ in three ways: by the method used in the text for getting the $H_5(x)$ involved in (32); using (37); and using (49) and (38).

2. Show that (50) follows from (46) and (49).

3. Verify that $H_{k+1}(x)e^{-x^2} = -(d/dx)[H_k(x)e^{-x^2}]$; then show, using Rolle's theorem[16] and mathematical induction, that the n *nodes* of $H_n(x)$ [that is, the roots of the equation $H_n(x) = 0$] are all real and distinct.

4. Show that every solution of (3) inflects at each of its nodes, at $x = -\lambda^{\frac{1}{2}}$, and at $x = \lambda^{\frac{1}{2}}$; that every solution of (3) is concave toward the x-axis in the region $-\lambda^{\frac{1}{2}} < x < \lambda^{\frac{1}{2}}$, and is convex toward the x-axis outside this region; that no solution of (3) can have more than one node in the region $x < -\lambda^{\frac{1}{2}}$, or more than one node in the region $x > \lambda^{\frac{1}{2}}$; and that, if a solution of (3) has a node at a finite value of x in the region $x < -\lambda^{\frac{1}{2}}$, or at a finite value of x in the region $x > \lambda^{\frac{1}{2}}$, then this solution is ill-behaved. Show further that (39) has n nodes in the region $-\sqrt{2n+1} < x < \sqrt{2n+1}$, one node at $x = -\infty$, and another at $x = \infty$, that is, $n + 2$ nodes in all.

5. Show that the functions (39) satisfy the identities

$$x u_n = \frac{n A_n}{A_{n-1}} u_{n-1} + \frac{A_n}{2 A_{n+1}} u_{n+1}, \quad (51)$$

and

$$\frac{d}{dx} u_n = \frac{n A_n}{A_{n-1}} u_{n-1} - \frac{A_n}{2 A_{n+1}} u_{n+1}. \quad (52)$$

Then deduce directly from (51) and (52) that

$$x^2 u_n = \frac{n(n-1)A_n}{A_{n-2}} u_{n-2} + \tfrac{1}{2}(2n+1)u_n + \frac{A_n}{4 A_{n+2}} u_{n+2}, \quad (53)$$

$$\frac{d^2}{dx^2} u_n = \frac{n(n-1)A_n}{A_{n-2}} u_{n-2} - \tfrac{1}{2}(2n+1)u_n + \frac{A_n}{4 A_{n+2}} u_{n+2}, \quad (54)$$

---

[16] Rolle's theorem states that, if $u(x)$ satisfies our standard continuity conditions and vanishes at $x = a$ and at $x = b$, then there is at least one point within the interval $a < x < b$ at which $u'(x) = 0$.

and

$$\left(\frac{d}{dx} + x\right)^k u_n = \frac{2^k n! \, A_n}{(n-k)! \, A_{n-k}} \, u_{n-k}, \qquad \text{for } k \leq n. \tag{55}$$

6. By a k-fold application of (53), the function $x^{2k} u_n$ can be expressed as

$$x^{2k} u_n = \cdots + c_{n-4} u_{n-4} + c_{n-2} u_{n-2} + c_n u_n + c_{n+2} u_{n+2}$$
$$+ c_{n+4} u_{n+4} + \cdots. \tag{56}$$

Show, without evaluating the c's, but by comparing the structures of (53) and (54), that

$$(-1)^k \frac{d^{2k}}{dx^{2k}} u_n = \cdots + c_{n-4} u_{n-4} - c_{n-2} u_{n-2} + c_n u_n - c_{n+2} u_{n+2}$$
$$+ c_{n+4} u_{n+4} - \cdots, \tag{57}$$

where the c's are, respectively, the same as those in (56).

7. Show that, if the operands are required to be well-behaved so far as their dependence on x is concerned, then the spectrum of $-\partial^2/\partial x^2 + x^2$ is the same as that of $-d^2/dx^2 + x^2$ found in the text, and that the eigenfunctions of $-\partial^2/\partial x^2 + x^2$ have the form (39) and can depend on independent variables other than x only through the coefficient A_n.

5. The Operators $-i\,\dfrac{\partial}{\partial x}$, x, and c

An operator of fundamental importance in quantum mechanics is

$$-i\,\frac{\partial}{\partial x}, \tag{1}$$

where $i^2 = -1$. In the case of this operator, the eigenvalue equation 15^3 (see footnote[17]), that is,

$$\alpha u = \lambda u, \tag{2}$$

---

[17] In cross references, we specify the section number by a superscript (a notation patterned after that of E. U. Condon and G. H. Shortley). For example, the symbol 15^3 denotes Equation (15) of §3; similarly, 'Exercise 7^{44}' denotes Exercise 7 of §44. Section numbers are printed at the right of page headings, so that the number in the upper right of a reference symbol is the number in the upper right of a page. Note that the section number heading a page on which one section ends and another begins usually refers to the *former* section. References to the Appendix carry the superscript A.

The figures and the tables are numbered consecutively throughout the book; but to help in locating them we sometimes append the section number as a superscript. For example, the superscript in 'Fig. 22^{15}' means that **Fig. 22** appears in §15.

is

$$-i\frac{\partial}{\partial x}u = \lambda u, \tag{3}$$

and its general solution is

$$u = Ae^{i\lambda x}, \tag{4}$$

where A is independent of x, but is otherwise arbitrary. This solution is well-behaved if λ is any real number (positive, negative, or zero), but is ill-behaved if λ is a nonvanishing complex or a pure imaginary number. The spectrum of $-i\partial/\partial x$ thus consists of all real numbers, and the eigenfunctions of $-i\partial/\partial x$ belonging to the eigenvalue λ are (4). This spectrum is quite different from the continuous spectrum of $-\partial^2/\partial x^2$ because it contains *all* real numbers.

To determine the eigenvalues and eigenfunctions of an operator of type c, we set $\alpha = c$ in (2), and obtain

$$cu = \lambda u. \tag{5}$$

In view of the definition of the operator c, this equation is satisfied if, and only if, $\lambda = c$, when the trivial case $u = 0$ is excluded. The operator c thus has only *one* eigenvalue, the number c. When $\lambda = c$, any u—in particular, any well-behaved u—satisfies (5), so that any well-behaved function is an eigenfunction of the operator c.

To find the eigenvalues and eigenfunctions of the operator x, we set $\alpha = x$ in (2) and consider the equation

$$xu = \lambda u. \tag{6}$$

Since u is not permitted to be identically zero, and since x is a variable, while λ is a constant, we conclude that u must vanish for all values of x except the value $x = \lambda$, for which it must not vanish. A function of this kind will be discussed at the end of §12, where, with the help of a nonrigorous argument, we shall conclude that every real number (positive, negative, or zero), and no other number, is an eigenvalue of the operator x. The operators x and $-i\partial/\partial x$ thus have spectra of the same type.

6. Simultaneous Eigenfunctions

The well-behaved function

$$e^{3ix} \tag{1}$$

is an eigenfunction of the operator $-i\partial/\partial x$ belonging to the eigenvalue 3 of $-i\partial/\partial x$, since

$$-i\,\frac{\partial}{\partial x}\,e^{3ix} = 3e^{3ix}; \tag{2}$$

the function (1) is also an eigenfunction of the operator $-\partial^2/\partial x^2$ (belonging to the eigenvalue 9 of $-\partial^2/\partial x^2$), since

$$-\frac{\partial^2}{\partial x^2}\,e^{3ix} = 9e^{3ix}. \tag{3}$$

An operand that is an eigenfunction of two or more operators is said to be a *simultaneous eigenfunction* of these operators; for example, (1) was shown above to be a simultaneous eigenfunction of $-i\partial/\partial x$ and $-\partial^2/\partial x^2$.

An eigenfunction u of an operator α belonging to the eigenvalue λ of α is simultaneously an eigenfunction of the operator α^2 belonging to the eigenvalue λ^2 of α^2; indeed, if

$$\alpha u = \lambda u, \tag{4}$$

then $\alpha^2 u = \alpha(\alpha u) = \alpha\lambda u = \lambda\alpha u = \lambda^2 u$, that is,

$$\alpha^2 u = \lambda^2 u. \tag{5}$$

We can thus conclude, for example, that, since $-\partial^2/\partial x^2 = (-i\partial/\partial x)^2$, an eigenfunction of $-i\partial/\partial x$ belonging to the eigenvalue λ of $-i\partial/\partial x$ is simultaneously an eigenfunction of $-\partial^2/\partial x^2$ belonging to the eigenvalue λ^2 of $-\partial^2/\partial x^2$; Equations (2) and (3) illustrate this result for the case of the function (1).

The converse of this theorem is in general not true: an eigenfunction of α^2 need not be simultaneously an eigenfunction of α. To illustrate: the general eigenfunction of the operator $-\partial^2/\partial x^2$ belonging to the eigenvalue λ, that is,[18]

$$(14^3) \qquad\qquad u = Ae^{i\lambda^{\frac{1}{2}}x} + Be^{-i\lambda^{\frac{1}{2}}x}, \tag{6}$$

is, in general, not an eigenfunction of the operator $-i\partial/\partial x$, since

$$-i\,\frac{\partial}{\partial x}\,u = \lambda^{\frac{1}{2}}(Ae^{i\lambda^{\frac{1}{2}}x} - Be^{-i\lambda^{\frac{1}{2}}x}), \tag{7}$$

---

[18] The marginal number at the left of an equation is its old number, or the number of an equation which, for one reason or another, might advantageously be recalled.

so that

$$-i\frac{\partial}{\partial x}u \neq \text{constant} \times u, \tag{8}$$

unless A, B, or λ is zero.

Certain pairs of operators (for example, the operators $-i\partial/\partial x$ and $-\partial^2/\partial x^2 + x^2$) do not have any eigenfunctions in common.

If an operand u is a simultaneous eigenfunction of two operators α and β, so that

$$\alpha u = \lambda u, \qquad \beta u = \mu u, \tag{9}$$

where λ and μ are numerical constants, then u is also an eigenfunction of the operator $\alpha\beta - \beta\alpha$, and belongs to the eigenvalue 0 of $\alpha\beta - \beta\alpha$. Indeed, in view of (9),

$$\alpha\beta u = \alpha\mu u = \mu\alpha u = \mu\lambda u, \tag{10}$$

and

$$\beta\alpha u = \beta\lambda u = \lambda\beta u = \lambda\mu u, \tag{11}$$

so that

$$(\alpha\beta - \beta\alpha)u = 0; \tag{12}$$

Equation (12) can be written as

$$(\alpha\beta - \beta\alpha)u = 0\cdot u, \tag{13}$$

and the theorem is proved.

Exercises

1. Show that an eigenfunction of $-i\partial/\partial x$ belonging to the eigenvalue λ of $-i\partial/\partial x$ is an eigenfunction of $i\partial^3/\partial x^3$ belonging to the eigenvalue λ^3 of $i\partial^3/\partial x^3$.

2. Show that, if u is an eigenfunction of α belonging to the eigenvalue λ, then u is also an eigenfunction of $c\alpha$ belonging to the eigenvalue $c\lambda$.

3. Show that, if u is an eigenfunction of α belonging to the eigenvalue a, and if $P(\alpha)$ is a polynomial in the operator α, then u is an eigenfunction of $P(\alpha)$ belonging to the eigenvalue $P(a)$.

4. Show by means of an example that a well-behaved operand u may satisfy the equation $(\alpha\beta - \beta\alpha)u = 0$ without being an eigenfunction of either α or β.

5. Inspect the commutator of x and $-i\partial/\partial x$, and show (without reference to their explicit eigenfunctions) that these operators have no eigenfunctions in common.

6. Show that, if α and β commute, and if u is an eigenfunction of α belonging to the eigenvalue λ, then the operand βu, if well-behaved, is also an eigenfunction of α belonging to the eigenvalue λ.

7. Let α, β, and γ be operators satisfying the equations $\alpha\beta - \beta\alpha = -\gamma$, $\beta\gamma - \gamma\beta = -\alpha$, and $\gamma\alpha - \alpha\gamma = -\beta$. Show that, if u is a simultaneous eigenfunction of any two of these operators, then it is also an eigenfunction of the third, and the eigenvalues of α, β, and γ belonging to u are all zero.

8. Show that, if α, β, and γ satisfy the commutation rules of Exercise 7, then each of these operators commutes with $\alpha^2 + \beta^2 + \gamma^2$.

7. Degenerate Eigenvalues

It was shown in Exercise 3[3] that, if u_i is an eigenfunction of a linear operator α belonging to the eigenvalue λ_i of α, then Cu_i, where C is an arbitrary constant, is also an eigenfunction of α belonging to the same eigenvalue, so that to every eigenvalue of a linear operator α there belongs an infinite set of eigenfunctions. In this connection, we must distinguish two cases: (a) when every eigenfunction of α belonging to λ_i can be obtained from any other such eigenfunction by multiplying the latter by a constant (we then call λ_i a *nondegenerate* eigenvalue of α); and (b) when not all eigenfunctions of α belonging to λ_i have the form Cu_i, where u_i is one of these eigenfunctions (we then call λ_i a *degenerate* eigenvalue of α). To illustrate: the eigenvalue 0 of the operator $-d^2/dx^2$ is nondegenerate, because, as shown in §3, all eigenfunctions of $-d^2/dx^2$ belonging to this eigenvalue are constants, so that every one of them can be obtained from any other by multiplying the latter by a constant; on the other hand, every eigenvalue of $-d^2/dx^2$ greater than 0 is degenerate, because, when $\lambda > 0$, this operator has such eigenfunctions as

$$u = Ae^{i\lambda^{\frac{1}{2}}x} \tag{1}$$

and

$$u = Be^{-i\lambda^{\frac{1}{2}}x}, \tag{2}$$

which cannot be converted into each other by a multiplication by a constant.

A set of n functions, f_1, f_2, $\cdots$, f_n, is said to be *linearly independent* if it is impossible to choose n constants c_1, c_2, $\cdots$, c_n, not all of which are zeros, in such a way that the equation

$$c_1 f_1 + c_2 f_2 + \cdots + c_n f_n = 0 \tag{3}$$

holds for all values of the arguments of the f's; otherwise the f's are said to be *linearly dependent*. The *multiplicity*, or the *degree of degeneracy*, of an eigenvalue of an operator is now defined as follows: if the aggregate of the eigenfunctions belonging to λ_i contains n, and not more than n, linearly independent eigenfunctions (that is, if the explicit general expression for the eigenfunctions belonging to λ_i contains just n essentially arbitrary constants), then the degeneracy of λ_i is said to be n-fold (except that λ_i is said to be *nondegenerate* when $n = 1$). For example, the degeneracy of each eigenvalue $\lambda > 0$ of $-d^2/dx^2$ is twofold, since the functions (1) and (2) are linearly independent, and since, when $\lambda > 0$, Equation 5^3 possesses no solutions that are not linear combinations of (1) and (2).

Exercises

1. Show that the three functions 1, $\cos^2 x$, and $\sin^2 x$ are linearly dependent, and that the three functions 1, $\cos x$, and $\sin x$ are linearly independent.

2. Show that none of the three operators $-i\partial/\partial x$, x, and $-\partial^2/\partial x^2 + x^2$ has any degenerate eigenvalues. Show that the single eigenvalue of the operator c is degenerate to an infinite degree.

3. Show that, if α and β commute, if u is an eigenfunction of α belonging to a nondegenerate eigenvalue of α, and if βu is well-behaved, then u is also an eigenfunction of β.

4. Show that if λ is real the function $Ae^{i\lambda x}$ is an eigenfunction of every differential operator that commutes with $-i\partial/\partial x$.

8. Orthogonal Sets of Functions

The eigenfunctions of some of the operators of quantum mechanics form so-called *discrete orthogonal sets*, and we shall now make a few remarks concerning such sets. We shall deal, in general, with complex functions of real variables, and shall employ the following terminology and notation. If f_1 and f_2 are real numbers or real functions of real variables, and

$$f = f_1 + if_2, \tag{1}$$

where $i^2 = -1$, we call f_1 the *real part of f*, call f_2 the *imaginary part of f*, and write

$$f_1 = \operatorname{Re} f, \quad \text{and} \quad f_2 = \operatorname{Im} f; \tag{2}$$

for example, since $e^{ix} = \cos x + i \sin x$, the real part of e^{ix} is $\cos x$, the imaginary part of e^{ix} is $\sin x$, and we write $\operatorname{Re} e^{ix} = \cos x$, and $\operatorname{Im} e^{ix} = \sin x$. The function $f_1 - if_2$, which we denote by $\bar{f}$, is called the *complex conjugate* of f; for example, if $f = e^{ix}$, then $\bar{f} = e^{-ix}$. The complex conjugate of a given function is obtained from the function itself by reversing the algebraic sign of i wherever i appears in the given function; it is unnecessary first to rewrite the function in the form (1). The function $+\sqrt{f_1^2 + f_2^2}$, which we denote by $|f|$, is called the *modulus*, or the *absolute value*, of f; for example, if $f = e^{ix}$, then $|f| = 1$. The principal value of arc tan (f_2/f_1) is called the *phase* of f. The product of f and its complex conjugate, that is, the square of the modulus of f, will be denoted by $\bar{f}f$ or by $|f|^2$. If Im $f = 0$, so that f is real, the complex conjugate of f is f itself, and $\bar{f}f = f^2$. The product of a function g and the complex conjugate $\bar{f}$ of a function f will be written in the form $\bar{f}g$, rather than in the equivalent form $g\bar{f}$; the convenience of this convention will become apparent when we come to quantum mechanics.

If the product of a function $u_1(x)$ and of the complex conjugate $\bar{u}_2(x)$ of a function $u_2(x)$ vanishes when integrated with respect to x over the interval $a \leq x \leq b$, that is, if

$$\int_a^b \bar{u}_2(x)u_1(x)\, dx = 0, \tag{3}$$

then $u_1(x)$ and $u_2(x)$ are said to be *mutually orthogonal*,[19] or, simply, *orthogonal* in the interval (a, b).

If every two functions contained in the set

$$u_1(x),\ u_2(x),\ u_3(x),\ u_4(x),\ \cdots \tag{4}$$

are mutually orthogonal in the interval (a, b) of x, that is, if

$$\int_a^b \bar{u}_m(x)u_n(x)\, dx = 0 \text{ when } n \neq m \text{ and } n,\, m = 1, 2, 3, \cdots, \tag{5}$$

then the *set* (4) is said to be *orthogonal* in the interval (a, b) of x.

For example, the infinite set

$$\left.\begin{aligned} 1,\ \cos x,\ \cos 2x,\ \cos 3x,\ \cdots \\ \sin x,\ \sin 2x,\ \sin 3x,\ \cdots \end{aligned}\right\} \tag{6}$$

is orthogonal in the interval $(-\pi, \pi)$ of x because the integral of the product of any member of (6) and the complex conjugate[20] of any other member of the set vanishes when the limits of inte-

---

[19] Some of the definitions given here differ from those usually employed in discussions restricted to *real* functions of real variables.

[20] Since every member of (6) is real, the words *complex conjugate* may be omitted in the present case.

gration are $-\pi$ and π; the set (6) is in fact orthogonal in any interval of x of length 2π.

The set (6) is of great interest in mathematical physics because a large class of functions[21] of x can be expressed in an interval of length 2π as linear combinations[22] of members of (6), so that a large class of periodic functions having the period 2π can be expressed in this manner in the infinite interval $(-\infty, \infty)$. When a function is expressed as a linear combination of the members of (6), it is said to be expanded into its *Fourier series*. Certain Fourier series are encountered in elementary trigonometry; for example, the right side of the familiar identity

$$\sin^2 x = \tfrac{1}{2} - \tfrac{1}{2} \cos 2x \qquad (7)$$

is the Fourier series of the function $\sin^2 x$.

The Fourier expansion (that is, the Fourier series) of a given function, if it exists, can sometimes be found in several superficially distinct ways; for example, the expansion (7) can be carried out by trigonometric or by equally elementary algebraic methods. But a general method exists for finding the Fourier expansion of a given function by means of integration; this method applies equally well to orthogonal sets other than (6), and we shall now present it for the general case.

If it can be shown that in the interval (a, b) the function $f(x)$ admits of an expansion

$$f = c_1 u_1 + c_2 u_2 + c_3 u_3 + \cdots + c_k u_k + \cdots \qquad (8)$$

in terms of the set

$$u_1, u_2, u_3, \cdots, \qquad (9)$$

which is orthogonal in the interval (a, b) then the *expansion coefficients*,[23] that is, the c's in (8), can be evaluated as follows:

1) write (8) with the c's undetermined;

---

[21] Only highly discontinuous functions (not satisfying the Dirichlet conditions discussed in mathematical books) cannot be expanded into Fourier series in a finite interval.

[22] By a *linear combination* of the functions $u_1, u_2, u_3, \cdots$, we mean an expression of the form $c_1 u_1 + c_2 u_2 + c_3 u_3 + \cdots$, where the c's are constants.

[23] Expansion coefficients are sometimes called *Fourier coefficients*, even when sets other than (6) are concerned.

2) multiply (8) through by $\bar{u}_k$, getting

$$\bar{u}_k f = c_1 \bar{u}_k u_1 + c_2 \bar{u}_k u_2 + c_3 \bar{u}_k u_3 + \cdots + c_k \bar{u}_k u_k + \cdots;\quad (10)$$

3) integrate (10) term by term over the interval (a, b); in view of the orthogonality of the u's, all terms on the right side of (10) except that involving $\bar{u}_k u_k$ will vanish, and hence

$$\int_a^b \bar{u}_k f\, dx = c_k \int_a^b \bar{u}_k u_k\, dx,\quad (11)$$

so that

$$c_k = \frac{\displaystyle\int_a^b \bar{u}_k f\, dx}{\displaystyle\int_a^b \bar{u}_k u_k\, dx},\quad k = 1, 2, 3, \cdots\quad (12)$$

Note that (12) was derived on the assumptions that $f(x)$ does admit of an expansion of type (8), and that a term-by-term integration of the right side of (10) is permissible; hence the fact that the c's given by (12) can be computed for a given $f(x)$ and a given orthogonal set (9) does not guarantee that the expansion (8) exists; and therefore the use of the method of integration for the evaluation of expansion coefficients should be accompanied by an investigation of the question whether the series so obtained converges to the values of $f(x)$ for the value of x under consideration. If a computation presumes the convergence of series or integrals without proving the validity of this presumption for the case on hand, we call it a *formal* computation. Incidentally, the fact that the c's are given by (12) if the expansion (8) exists shows that the expansion of a given function in terms of a given orthogonal set, if it exists, is *unique*.

In the case of some of the more important orthogonal sets, general conditions have been set up that enable us to determine, prior to a formal evaluation of the expansion coefficients, whether or not the expansion is possible; for example, it is known that every continuous[21] periodic function of period 2π can be expanded in terms of the set (6). If every function of a certain type admits of an expansion in terms of a given orthogonal set, the set is said to be *complete* with respect to functions of this type; for example, the set (6) is complete with respect to continuous periodic functions of period 2π.

To illustrate the use of (12), let us obtain the Fourier series of the function $f(x)$, shown in Fig. 6 and defined as follows:

$$f(x) = \begin{cases} -\dfrac{2}{\pi}(x + \pi) & \text{for} \quad -\pi \leq x \leq -\tfrac{1}{2}\pi \\[2mm] \dfrac{2}{\pi}x & \text{for} \quad -\tfrac{1}{2}\pi \leq x \leq \tfrac{1}{2}\pi \\[2mm] -\dfrac{2}{\pi}(x - \pi) & \text{for} \quad \tfrac{1}{2}\pi \leq x \leq \pi, \end{cases} \tag{13a}$$

$$f(x + 2\pi) = f(x) \qquad \text{for} \quad -\infty < x < \infty. \tag{13b}$$

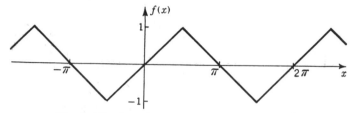

Fig. 6. The function defined by (13a) and (13b)

This function is continuous, and hence we are assured that the series obtained by a formal use of (6) and (12) will represent it. Writing

$$f(x) = a_0 + a_1 \cos x + a_2 \cos 2x + \cdots + a_n \cos nx + \cdots$$
$$+ b_1 \sin x + b_2 \sin 2x + \cdots + b_n \sin nx + \cdots , \tag{14}$$

we have, in view of (12):

$$a_n = \frac{\displaystyle\int_{-\pi}^{\pi} \cos nx f(x)\, dx}{\displaystyle\int_{-\pi}^{\pi} \cos^2 nx\, dx} = 0, \tag{15}$$

$$b_n = \frac{\displaystyle\int_{-\pi}^{\pi} \sin nx f(x)\, dx}{\displaystyle\int_{-\pi}^{\pi} \sin^2 nx\, dx} = \frac{1}{\pi}\left\{ \int_{-\pi}^{-\frac{1}{2}\pi} \left[-\frac{2}{\pi}(x + \pi) \right] \sin nx\, dx \right.$$

$$\left. + \int_{-\frac{1}{2}\pi}^{\frac{1}{2}\pi} \left[\frac{2}{\pi}x \right] \sin nx\, dx + \int_{\frac{1}{2}\pi}^{\pi} \left[-\frac{2}{\pi}(x - \pi) \right] \sin nx\, dx = \frac{8}{\pi^2 n^2} \sin \tfrac{1}{2}n\pi, \tag{16}$$

where the a's vanish because $f(x)$ is odd in x, $\cos nx$ is even in x, and the interval of integration is symmetric about $x = 0$. Consequently, the Fourier series of the function shown in Fig. 6 is

$$f(x) = \frac{8}{\pi^2}\left(\sin x - \frac{1}{3^2} \sin 3x + \frac{1}{5^2} \sin 5x - \frac{1}{7^2} \sin 7x + \cdots \right). \tag{17}$$

We shall now define certain additional terms. If the integral

$$\int_a^b \bar{u}u \, dx \tag{18}$$

is finite, the function u is said to be *of integrable square*, or *quadratically integrable*, in the interval (a, b).

If u and all of its derivatives approach zero when $|x| \to \infty$, and if $\int_{-\infty}^{\infty} \bar{u}u \, dx$ is finite, we call u a *normalizable* function (this use of the term is not standard in the literature); functions, such as $e^{-x^2} \sin(e^{x^2})$, which are quadratically integrable, but whose derivatives do not vanish when $|x| \to \infty$, will not be of interest to us.

If

$$\int_a^b \bar{u}u \, dx = 1, \tag{19}$$

the function u is said to be *normal, unitary, normalized to unity*, or, simply, *normalized*, in the interval (a, b).

If every function in the set

$$u_1, u_2, u_3, \cdots \tag{20}$$

is normalized to unity in (a, b), the *set* (20) is said to be *normal, unitary, normalized to unity*, or, simply, *normalized*, in the interval (a, b).

If a set is both normal and orthogonal in an interval, it is said to be *orthonormal* in this interval. If the set (9) is orthonormal in (a, b), the formula (12) for the expansion coefficients in (8) becomes

$$c_k = \int_a^b \bar{u}_k f \, dx, \quad k = 1, 2, 3, \cdots. \tag{21}$$

In speaking of quadratic integrability, orthogonality, and normalization, we usually omit a specific mention of the interval whenever it can be readily inferred from the context.

If a function f, which is of integrable square in (a, b) and is not identically zero, is multiplied by a constant N such that

$$\bar{N}N = \left(\int_a^b \bar{f}f \, dx \right)^{-1}, \tag{22}$$

then the function Nf is normalized to unity in (a, b). A number N satisfying (22) is called a *normalizing factor* of f; note that (22), regarded as an equation to be solved for N, determines only the modulus of N and leaves N indeterminate to the extent of a *phase factor* $e^{i\gamma}$, where γ is an arbitrary real constant, the *phase* of N. Consequently, the process of normalizing a given function does not lead to an unambiguous result unless the phase factor is specified.

By normalizing every function of a set, we may convert the set into a normalized set. To illustrate: the set (6), as it stands, is not normalized in the interval $(-\pi, \pi)$ because

$$\int_{-\pi}^{\pi} dx = 2\pi, \qquad \int_{-\pi}^{\pi} \cos^2 kx \, dx = \int_{-\pi}^{\pi} \sin^2 kx \, dx = \pi; \quad (23)$$

to normalize it, the function 1 must be multiplied by a constant of modulus $(2\pi)^{-\frac{1}{2}}$, and each of the other members of the set must be multiplied by a constant of modulus $\pi^{-\frac{1}{2}}$, so that the set

$$\left. \begin{array}{llll} \dfrac{e^{i\gamma_0}}{\sqrt{2\pi}}, & \dfrac{e^{i\gamma_1}}{\sqrt{\pi}} \cos x, & \dfrac{e^{i\gamma_2}}{\sqrt{\pi}} \cos 2x, & \dfrac{e^{i\gamma_3}}{\sqrt{\pi}} \cos 3x, \cdots, \\[3mm] & \dfrac{e^{i\delta_1}}{\sqrt{\pi}} \sin x, & \dfrac{e^{i\delta_2}}{\sqrt{\pi}} \sin 2x, & \dfrac{e^{i\delta_3}}{\sqrt{\pi}} \sin 3x, \cdots, \end{array} \right\} \quad (24)$$

is normal and orthogonal in $(-\pi, \pi)$, the γ's and δ's being arbitrary real constants. Any particular choice of these arbitrary phases leads to a distinct orthonormal set, and, in order that a set be completely specified, each phase factor must be fixed by some suitable convention. For example, we may choose each γ and δ in (24) equal to zero, and get the set

$$\left. \begin{array}{llll} \dfrac{1}{\sqrt{2\pi}}, & \dfrac{1}{\sqrt{\pi}} \cos x, & \dfrac{1}{\sqrt{\pi}} \cos 2x, & \dfrac{1}{\sqrt{\pi}} \cos 3x, \cdots \\[3mm] & \dfrac{1}{\sqrt{\pi}} \sin x, & \dfrac{1}{\sqrt{\pi}} \sin 2x, & \dfrac{1}{\sqrt{\pi}} \sin 3x, \cdots \end{array} \right\} \quad (25)$$

which is orthonormal in the interval $(-\pi, \pi)$ and is free from ambiguity.

If an orthogonal set is given, then other orthogonal sets may be constructed from it, the members of a new set being special linear combinations of the members of the original set. To illustrate: the two functions $e^{ix} = \cos x + i \sin x$ and $e^{-ix} = \cos x - i \sin x$ are mutually orthogonal in $(-\pi, \pi)$, and each of them is orthogonal to every member of (6) except $\cos x$ and $\sin x$. Therefore, the set

$$\left. \begin{array}{l} e^{-ix}, \; 1, \; e^{ix}, \; \cos 2x, \; \cos 3x, \; \cos 4x, \; \cdots \\ \sin 2x, \; \sin 3x, \; \sin 4x, \; \cdots \end{array} \right\} \qquad (26)$$

is orthogonal in the interval $(-\pi, \pi)$. In a similar way, we may convert (6) into the set

$$\cdots, \; e^{-3ix}, \; e^{-2ix}, \; e^{-ix}, \; 1, \; e^{ix}, \; e^{2ix}, \; e^{3ix}, \; \cdots . \qquad (27)$$

Normalizing (27) to unity in $(-\pi, \pi)$, and setting the phases of the normalizing factors equal to zero, we get the symmetric orthonormal set

$$\frac{e^{inx}}{\sqrt{2\pi}}, \qquad n = \cdots, -2, -1, 0, 1, 2, \cdots, \qquad (28)$$

which is in many respects more convenient than (25). We shall call an expansion in terms of (28) a *Fourier series*; no confusion need arise regarding the use of this term also in connection with expansions in terms of (6), because either expansion can be immediately converted into the other through the relations $e^{inx} = \cos nx + i \sin nx$, $\sin nx = -\frac{1}{2}ie^{inx} + \frac{1}{2}ie^{-inx}$, and $\cos nx = \frac{1}{2}e^{inx} + \frac{1}{2}e^{-inx}$.

Many of our equations will contain definite integrals, usually involving certain standard limits of integration. In the main one-dimensional equations, these limits will be indicated explicitly; but to simplify the printing of numerous auxiliary equations we shall let the symbol $\int f(s) \, d\!s$ (note the crossed d) stand for the definite integral of $f(s)$ taken over the complete range of the variable s or, if s is an angle, over its principal range. For example, in the case of the variable x, whose range extends from $-\infty$ to ∞, we set

$$\int f(x) \, d\!x = \int_{-\infty}^{\infty} f(x) \, dx. \qquad (29)$$

Exercises

1. Outline the procedure for deriving (7) by means of (12).

2. Show that each of the two sets

$$\left\{ \begin{array}{c} \dfrac{1}{\sqrt{L}}, \quad \sqrt{\dfrac{2}{L}} \cos \dfrac{2\pi x}{L}, \quad \sqrt{\dfrac{2}{L}} \cos \dfrac{4\pi x}{L}, \quad \sqrt{\dfrac{2}{L}} \cos \dfrac{6\pi x}{L}, \cdots \\[3mm] \sqrt{\dfrac{2}{L}} \sin \dfrac{2\pi x}{L}, \quad \sqrt{\dfrac{2}{L}} \sin \dfrac{4\pi x}{L}, \quad \sqrt{\dfrac{2}{L}} \sin \dfrac{6\pi x}{L}, \cdots, \end{array} \right. \tag{30}$$

and

$$\frac{1}{\sqrt{L}} e^{2\pi i n x / L}, \quad n = \cdots, -2, -1, 0, 1, 2, \cdots \tag{31}$$

is orthonormal in any interval of length L. These sets are used for the expansion of periodic functions of period L, and the resulting series are called *Fourier series*, just as in the case of the sets (25) and (28).

3. Show that, if the function $\cos 137x$ is omitted from (6), then the remaining orthogonal set is no longer complete with respect to continuous periodic functions of period 2π.

4. Show formally that if a function f, which is *unitary* in the interval (a, b), admits of the expansion $f = c_1 u_1 + c_2 u_2 + c_3 u_3 + \cdots$ in terms of a set $u_1, u_2, u_3, \cdots$, which is *orthonormal* in the interval (a, b), then

$$\sum_k |c_k|^2 = 1, \qquad k = 1, 2, 3, \cdots. \tag{32}$$

5. Using repeated integration by parts[24] and the formulas 37[4] and 46[4'] show that the Hermite functions 39[4] form an orthogonal set in the infinite interval $(-\infty, \infty)$, and that normalization of this set yields

$$u_n = \frac{e^{i\gamma_n} H_n(x) e^{-\frac{1}{2}x^2}}{\sqrt{2^n\, n!\, \pi^{\frac{1}{2}}}}, \quad n = 0, 1, 2, 3, \cdots, \tag{33}$$

where each γ_n is an arbitrary real constant. Graphs of the first six members of (33), ith the γ's set equal to zero, are given in Fig. 5.

The Hermite functions form an orthogonal set that is complete with respect to normalizable functions satisfying certain mild continuity conditions.[25] An expansion in terms of the Hermite functions is called a *Gram-Charlier series*.

---

[24] Formula for indefinite integration by parts (primes denote differentiation with respect to x): $\displaystyle \int uv'dx = uv - \int u'vdx$; for definite integration by parts: $\displaystyle \int_a^b uv'dx = uv \Big|_a^b - \int_a^b u'vdx$, where $uv \Big|_a^b = u(b)v(b) - u(a)v(a)$.

[25] R. Courant and D. Hilbert, *Methoden der Mathematischen Physik*, Vol. I, Second Edition, page 81. Berlin: Springer, 1931.

6. Recall Exercise 5[4] and show that the expansion of the function xu_n [where u_n is given by (33)] in terms of the set (33) is

$$xu_n = \sqrt{\tfrac{1}{2}n}\, e^{i(\gamma_n - \gamma_{n-1})}\, u_{n-1} + \sqrt{\tfrac{1}{2}(n+1)}\, e^{i(\gamma_n - \gamma_{n+1})}\, u_{n+1}. \qquad (34)$$

In a similar way, obtain the expansion

$$\frac{d}{dx}\, u_n = \sqrt{\tfrac{1}{2}n}\, e^{i(\gamma_n - \gamma_{n-1})}\, u_{n-1} - \sqrt{\tfrac{1}{2}(n+1)}\, e^{i(\gamma_n - \gamma_{n+1})}\, u_{n+1}, \qquad (35)$$

and also the expansions for $x^2 u_n$ and $(d^2/dx^2)u_n$.

7. According to (21), the coefficient c_k in the expansion of the function xu_n in terms of the orthonormal set (33), that is, in

$$xu_n = \sum_k c_k u_k, \qquad k = 0, 1, 2, \cdots \quad (36)$$

is [remember (29)]

$$c_k = \int \bar{u}_k\, xu_n\, dx. \qquad (37)$$

Now, comparison of (36) with (34) shows, for example, that

$$c_{n-1} = \sqrt{\tfrac{1}{2}n}\, e^{i(\gamma_n - \gamma_{n-1})}, \qquad (38)$$

so that in view of (37) we have

$$\int \bar{u}_{n-1}\, xu_n\, dx = \sqrt{\tfrac{1}{2}n}\, e^{i(\gamma_n - \gamma_{n-1})}, \qquad (39)$$

a result which can be written in the form

$$\text{if } m = n + 1, \text{ then } \quad \int \bar{u}_n\, xu_m\, dx = \sqrt{\tfrac{1}{2}(n+1)}\, e^{i(\gamma_{n+1} - \gamma_n)}. \qquad (40)$$

This calculation shows that, in view of the uniqueness of the expansion of a given function in terms of a given orthogonal set, if the expansion coefficients can be found in some way without recourse to integration— as were the coefficients in (34)—then certain definite integrals can be evaluated by comparing the known coefficients with (12).

Working along these lines with the functions (33), verify the following formulas, in which the symbol ' stands for the phase factor $e^{-i(\gamma_n - \gamma_m)}$, so that the entry $\sqrt{\tfrac{1}{2}n}$' in the first line of (41) stands for $\sqrt{\tfrac{1}{2}n} \exp[-i(\gamma_n - \gamma_{n-1})]$, the entry $\sqrt{\tfrac{1}{2}(n+1)}$' in the second line of (41) stands for $\sqrt{\tfrac{1}{2}(n+1)} \exp[-i(\gamma_n - \gamma_{n+1})]$, and so forth:

$$\int \bar{u}_n\, xu_m\, dx = \begin{cases} \sqrt{\tfrac{1}{2}n}\,' & \text{if } m = n - 1 \\ \sqrt{\tfrac{1}{2}(n+1)}\,' & \text{if } m = n + 1 \\ 0 & \text{otherwise.} \end{cases} \qquad (41)$$

$$\int \bar{u}_n\, \frac{d}{dx}\, u_m\, dx = \begin{cases} -\sqrt{\tfrac{1}{2}n}\,' & \text{if } m = n - 1 \\ \sqrt{\tfrac{1}{2}(n+1)}\,' & \text{if } m = n + 1 \\ 0 & \text{otherwise.} \end{cases} \qquad (42)$$

$$\int \bar{u}_n x^2 u_m \, dx = \begin{cases} \frac{1}{2}\sqrt{(n-1)n}\,' & \text{if } m = n - 2 \\ \frac{1}{2}(2n+1) & \text{if } m = n \\ \frac{1}{2}\sqrt{(n+1)(n+2)}\,' & \text{if } m = n + 2 \\ 0 & \text{otherwise.} \end{cases} \tag{43}$$

$$\int \bar{u}_n \frac{d^2}{dx^2} u_m \, dx = \begin{cases} \frac{1}{2}\sqrt{(n-1)n}\,' & \text{if } m = n - 2 \\ -\frac{1}{2}(2n+1) & \text{if } m = n \\ \frac{1}{2}\sqrt{(n+1)(n+2)}\,' & \text{if } m = n + 2 \\ 0 & \text{otherwise.} \end{cases} \tag{44}$$

8. Recall Exercise 6[4], and show that for u_n given by (33)

$$\int \bar{u}_n \frac{d^{2k}}{dx^{2k}} u_n \, dx = (-1)^k \int \bar{u}_n x^{2k} u_n \, dx. \tag{45}$$

CHAPTER II

REMARKS ON CLASSICAL MECHANICS

9. Hamiltonian Functions

According to the classical theory, the one-dimensional motion (which we shall take to be along the x-axis of a Cartesian coordinate frame) of a particle of mass m acted on by a force f is described by the differential equation

$$m\ddot{x} = f, \tag{1}$$

which can be inferred from Newton's laws of motion; the symbol $\ddot{x}$ in (1) stands for d^2x/dt^2: we use dotted symbols for *total* derivatives with respect to the time t. Given a force field, Equation (1) enables us to express the position x of the particle as a definite function of the time, provided the initial conditions of the motion are known, so that the two arbitrary constants in the general solution of (1) can be evaluated.

The force field f is said to be *conservative* if a function $V(x)$, called the *potential function* of the force field, or simply the *potential*, can be found such that[1]

$$f = -\frac{\partial V(x)}{\partial x}. \tag{2}$$

When a conservative force field is given, the corresponding potential, as found by the use of (2), is indeterminate to the extent of an arbitrary additive constant; this constant can be given a specific value by choosing the origin from which the potential is measured. We restrict ourselves to conservative fields.

If the field is conservative, (1) can be written as

$$m\ddot{x} = -\frac{\partial V(x)}{\partial x}, \tag{3}$$

---

[1] In the one-dimensional case, ordinary rather than partial derivatives may be used on the right sides of (2) and (3). Equation (2) means essentially that the force acting on the particle depends only on the position of the particle—a condition which, in the *one-dimensional* case, assures conservation of mechanical energy.

and we get the familiar result that the quantity

$$\tfrac{1}{2}m\dot{x}^2 + V(x) \tag{4}$$

is independent of the time, and is thus a *constant of motion* (or an 'integral' of the motion); (4) is called the *total energy*, or simply the *energy* of the particle, and is the sum of the *kinetic energy* $\tfrac{1}{2}m\dot{x}^2$ of the particle, and the *potential energy* $V(x)$ of the particle. We shall denote the numerical value of the energy by the letter E, although the letter W also is often used for this purpose. The constancy of (4) is referred to as the *conservation of the mechanical energy* of the particle, and accounts for the use of the term *conservative* for one-dimensional force fields of type (2).

The quantity

$$p = m\dot{x} \tag{5}$$

is called the *momentum* (of the particle) associated with the Cartesian coordinate x.

We refer to a particle executing one-dimensional motion as a one-dimensional *dynamical system*, and speak of such quantities as the position x, the velocity $v = \dot{x}$, the momentum p, the energy E, and so forth, as *dynamical variables*, even though some of these, such as E and E^2, may, in fact, be constants. We often substitute the word *system* for the word *particle*, and say 'energy of the system' for 'energy of the particle,' and so on; also, we say 'conservative system' for 'a system consisting of a particle moving in a conservative field.' There are as many different one-dimensional systems involving a single particle of mass m as there are force fields in which a particle can execute one-dimensional motion.

The energy of a one-dimensional system expressed in terms of x and p (*not* in terms of x and v) is called the *Hamiltonian function* of the system, or simply the *Hamiltonian* of the system, and is denoted by H. In the case of a conservative one-dimensional system, we have, in view of (4) and (5),

$$H = \frac{1}{2m}p^2 + V(x). \tag{6}$$

To symbolize that the energy of a system is conserved and is numerically equal to E we write:

$$H = E. \tag{7}$$

Equation (1), a single ordinary differential equation of the second order, is equivalent to the system of two partial differential equations of the first order,

$$\frac{\partial H}{\partial p} = \dot{x}, \qquad \frac{\partial H}{\partial x} = -\dot{p}, \qquad (8)$$

called *Hamilton's canonical equation*; these equations follow directly from (1), (5), and (6): $\partial H/\partial p = p/m = \dot{x}$, and $\partial H/\partial x = \partial V(x)/\partial x = -f = -m\ddot{x} = -\dot{p}$.

If two dynamical variables, say r and s, are of such a nature that the Hamiltonian can be expressed entirely in terms of them, and that when this is done the equations

$$\frac{\partial H}{\partial s} = \dot{r}, \qquad \frac{\partial H}{\partial r} = -\dot{s} \qquad (9)$$

hold, the variables r and s are said to be *canonically conjugate*. Comparison of (8) and (9) shows that the position x and the momentum p of a particle executing one-dimensional motion are canonically conjugate regardless of the specific form that the potential $V(x)$ may have.

A classical dynamical variable to which we shall refer early in our study of quantum mechanics is the so-called *Poisson bracket* of a pair of variables. The Poisson bracket of two dynamical variables, say the variables ξ and η, is denoted by $[\xi, \eta]$ and in the case of one-dimensional motion is defined as

$$[\xi, \eta] = \frac{\partial \xi}{\partial x} \cdot \frac{\partial \eta}{\partial p} - \frac{\partial \xi}{\partial p} \cdot \frac{\partial \eta}{\partial x}. \qquad (10)$$

For example, the Poisson bracket of the variables x and x^2 is

$$[x, x^2] = \frac{\partial x}{\partial x} \cdot \frac{\partial x^2}{\partial p} - \frac{\partial x}{\partial p} \cdot \frac{\partial x^2}{\partial x} = 1 \cdot 0 - 0 \cdot 2x = 0; \qquad (11)$$

the Poisson bracket of x and p is

$$[x, p] = \frac{\partial x}{\partial x} \cdot \frac{\partial p}{\partial p} - \frac{\partial x}{\partial p} \cdot \frac{\partial p}{\partial x} = 1 \cdot 1 - 0 \cdot 0 = 1; \qquad (12)$$

and the Poisson bracket of xp and x is

$$[xp, x] = \frac{\partial xp}{\partial x} \cdot \frac{\partial x}{\partial p} - \frac{\partial xp}{\partial p} \cdot \frac{\partial x}{\partial x} = p \cdot 0 - x \cdot 1 = -x. \qquad (13)$$

Insofar as our discussion is concerned, it is important to remember the definition (10) of the Poisson brackets, but acquaintance with their use in classical mechanics is not essential.

Our attention will be focused on dynamical variables which (like x, x^2, p, and $ax^2 + bp^2$, where a and b are constants) can be expressed entirely in terms of the variables x and p, that is, which (unlike t, xt, and p^2t^2) do not involve the time t explicitly.

Exercises

1. Show that $[x^2, p^2] = 4xp$, $[f(x, p), f(x, p)] = 0$, $[f(x), g(x)] = 0$, and $[f(p), g(p)] = 0$.

2. Show that, if the Greek letters are dynamical variables pertaining to a one-dimensional system, and c is a constant, then

$$[\xi, \eta] = -[\eta, \xi]$$

$$[\xi, c] = 0$$

$$[\xi_1 + \xi_2, \eta] = [\xi_1, \eta] + [\xi_2, \eta]$$

$$[\xi, \eta_1 + \eta_2] = [\xi, \eta_1] + [\xi, \eta_2] \qquad \text{(14a–g)}$$

$$[\xi_1\xi_2, \eta] = [\xi_1, \eta]\xi_2 + \xi_1[\xi_2, \eta]$$

$$[\xi, \eta_1\eta_2] = [\xi, \eta_1]\eta_2 + \eta_1[\xi, \eta_2]$$

$$[\xi, [\eta, \zeta]] + [\eta, [\zeta, \xi]] + [\zeta, [\xi, \eta]] = 0.$$

Note the resemblance of these relations to the relations 29^2 among commutators of linear operators.

3. Show that, if ξ is any dynamical variable pertaining to a one-dimensional system, then $[\xi, p] = \partial\xi/\partial x$, and $[\xi, x] = -\partial\xi/\partial p$, so that, in particular, Hamilton's canonical equation can be written in the symmetric form

$$\dot{x} = [x, H], \qquad \dot{p} = [p, H]. \qquad (15)$$

4. Show that, if ξ is a dynamical variable which does not explicitly depend on the time t, then

$$\dot{\xi} = [\xi, H] \qquad (16)$$

Thus, in particular, $[\xi, H]$ vanishes if, and only if, ξ is a constant of motion.

5. Denote the elevation of a ball thrown vertically upward by x, and show that (2) holds if the motion is frictionless, but does not hold otherwise.

10. Examples of Classical Motion

We shall now consider briefly some aspects of the classical theory of certain one-dimensional systems that we shall presently consider from the quantum-mechanical standpoint, since later it will be instructive to compare the respective conclusion of the two theories.

The free particle. The simplest one-dimensional problem of classical mechanics is that of a free particle, that is, a particle not acted on by any forces. In this case, 1^9 is

$$m\ddot{x} = 0, \tag{1}$$

so that

$$x = At + B, \tag{2}$$

where A and B are arbitrary constants. When the initial conditions of the motion are,

$$\text{at } t = t_0, \quad x = x_0 \text{ and } p = p_0, \tag{3}$$

Equation (2) becomes

$$x = \frac{p_0}{m}(t - t_0) + x_0. \tag{4}$$

According to classical theory, the physical meaning, that is, the experimental implication, of (4) is that, if the position and the momentum of a free particle of mass m are measured experimentally (precisely, simultaneously, and without disturbing the particle) at a time t_0 and are found to be x_0 and p_0, and if another precise experimental measurement of position is to be made at a time t, then the result of the latter measurement is certain to be the number obtained by substituting the numerical values of m, t_0, p_0, x_0, and t into the right side of (4). [Classical equations of the type $x = F(t)$ also permit us to form a mental picture of the manner in which the particle behaves between observations.]

Integrating (1) once, we find that the momentum of the free particle is a constant of motion, so that, under the conditions (3),

$$p(t) = p_0. \tag{5}$$

In view of 2^9, the potential describing the field-free case is a constant, and we may, without loss of generality, set

$$V(x) = 0. \tag{6}$$

The total energy then equals the kinetic energy:

$$E = \frac{1}{2m} p^2 = \frac{1}{2m} p_0^2. \tag{7}$$

The linear harmonic oscillator. Next we consider the one-dimensional system known as a *linear harmonic oscillator*, that is, the system consisting of a particle of mass m moving on the x-axis under the influence of a restoring force that is proportional to the displacement of the particle from some fixed point on the axis, say the point $x = 0$. If the force per unit displacement is $-k$, the equation of motion is

$$m\ddot{x} = -kx. \tag{8}$$

Using the abbreviation

$$\omega = \sqrt{k/m}, \tag{9}$$

we write the general solution of (8) as

$$x = A \cos \omega t + B \sin \omega t, \tag{10}$$

where A and B are arbitrary constants. The particle thus executes a simple harmonic motion of frequency

$$\nu = \frac{\omega}{2\pi} = \frac{1}{2\pi} \sqrt{\frac{k}{m}}. \tag{11}$$

If the initial conditions are (3), Equation (10) becomes

$$x = x_0 \cos \omega(t - t_0) + \frac{p_0}{\omega m} \sin \omega(t - t_0), \tag{12}$$

and the momentum at the time t is

$$p = -x_0 \omega m \sin \omega(t - t_0) + p_0 \cos \omega(t - t_0). \tag{13}$$

Although (12) exhibits x as a function of the time in a most explicit fashion, another expression for x will also be of interest to us. Our system is conservative, and the force $-kx$ is the negative gradient of the potential function

$$V(x) = \tfrac{1}{2}kx^2, \tag{14}$$

the arbitrary constant in $V(x)$ having been set equal to zero, as we shall usually do in studying the oscillator. The Hamiltonian of the system is

$$H = \frac{1}{2m} p^2 + \tfrac{1}{2}kx^2, \tag{15}$$

so that, if the energy of the oscillator has the numerical value E, we have

$$E = \frac{1}{2m} p^2 + \tfrac{1}{2}kx^2. \tag{16}$$

Now, the general solution (10) can be rearranged so that E appears as one of two arbitrary constants. Let a constant τ be defined by $\sin \omega\tau = A/(A^2 + B^2)^{\frac{1}{2}}$; then (10) becomes $x = (A^2 + B^2)^{\frac{1}{2}} \sin \omega(t + \tau)$, and consequently $p = m\omega(A^2 + B^2)^{\frac{1}{2}} \cos \omega(t + \tau)$; substitution of these expressions for x and p into (16) yields $A^2 + B^2 = 2E/k = 2E/m\omega^2$, and we finally get

$$x = \sqrt{\frac{2E}{k}} \sin \omega(t + \tau) \qquad (17)$$

and

$$p = \sqrt{2mE} \cos \omega(t + \tau). \qquad (18)$$

The two arbitrary constants in (17) are E and τ; when the general solution of the equations of motion of a dynamical system is written in such a way that one of the arbitrary constants, say τ, and the time t appear only in the combination $t + \tau$, then τ is called the *phase* of the motion.

Incidentally, Equation (17) shows that according to classical theory a precise experimental measurement of the position of a particle comprising a linear harmonic oscillator of energy E cannot yield a result lying outside the region $-\sqrt{2E/k} \leq x \leq \sqrt{2E/k}$; for this reason the positions $-\sqrt{2E/k}$ and $\sqrt{2E/k}$ are called the *classical limits* of x of the oscillator. The momenta $-\sqrt{2mE}$ and $\sqrt{2mE}$ are, for a similar reason, called the classical limits of p of an oscillator.

We often find it convenient to represent the potential $V(x)$ of a one-dimensional system and the energy E of the system in a single graph, E being represented by a horizontal line. Such an energy diagram for a linear harmonic oscillator is shown in Fig. 7, where the parabola is the potential function $\frac{1}{2}kx^2$, and where x_1 and x_2 are the classical limits of motion. Note that an energy diagram makes no reference to the time t.

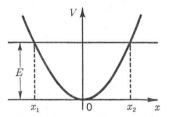

Fig. 7. Energy diagram of a linear harmonic oscillator.

Potential wells. Let three metallic cylinders (the two outer ones infinitely long) and the fine grids across their ends be maintained at the electric potentials indicated in Fig. 8 (a); the potential field, Fig. 8(b), acting on a particle carrying a unit positive charge and moving along the axis of the

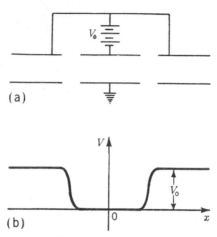

(a)

(b)

Fig. 8. A potential well.

cylinders then has the form of a *well*.   If the members of each
pair of adjacent grids are imagined to approach each other, we
get the idealized potential of Fig. 9, sometimes called a (one-

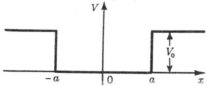

Fig. 9. A rectangular potential well.

dimensional) *rectangular potential well*; the vertical lines at
$x = \pm a$ in Fig. 9 are drawn to help the eye.   If the potential
V_0 in Fig. 9 is increased indefinitely, we get the potential describing what is often called a (one-dimensional) *box with perfectly reflecting walls*; this field is usually represented graphically
as in Fig. 10, where the 'box' extends
from $x = 0$ to $x = l$.

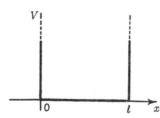

Fig. 10. A potential box.

Exercises

1. What are the experimental implications of the classical results (13) and (16)?
2. Evaluate τ in (17) if at $t = 0$ the particle is at $x = 0$ and is moving toward the
right.

3. Show that the coordinate x, the momentum p, and the variables x^2, p^2, and xp for a linear harmonic oscillator can be expressed as functions of t by means of the following Fourier series, in which γ ($= \omega\tau$) is a real constant:

$$x = \left\{-i\sqrt{\frac{E}{2k}}\,e^{i\gamma}\right\}e^{i\omega t} + \left\{i\sqrt{\frac{E}{2k}}\,e^{-i\gamma}\right\}e^{-i\omega t} \tag{19}$$

$$p = \left\{\sqrt{\frac{mE}{2}}\,e^{i\gamma}\right\}e^{i\omega t} + \left\{\sqrt{\frac{mE}{2}}\,e^{-i\gamma}\right\}e^{-i\omega t} \tag{20}$$

$$x^2 = \left\{-\frac{E}{2k}e^{2i\gamma}\right\}e^{2i\omega t} + \frac{E}{k} + \left\{-\frac{E}{2k}e^{-2i\gamma}\right\}e^{-2i\omega t} \tag{21}$$

$$p^2 = \{\tfrac{1}{2}mEe^{2i\gamma}\}\,e^{2i\omega t} + mE + \{\tfrac{1}{2}mEe^{-2i\gamma}\}\,e^{-2i\omega t} \tag{22}$$

$$xp = \left\{-\frac{E}{2}\sqrt{\frac{m}{k}}\,ie^{2i\gamma}\right\}e^{2i\omega t} + \left\{\frac{E}{2}\sqrt{\frac{m}{k}}\,ie^{-2i\gamma}\right\}e^{-2i\omega t}. \tag{23}$$

4. Show that, if a particle of mass m and energy E moves in the one-dimensional box of Fig. 10, then

$$x = \frac{l}{2} - \frac{2li}{\pi^2}\sum_k \frac{(-1)^k}{(2k+1)^2}\,e^{i(2k+1)\gamma}\,e^{i(2k+1)\Omega t},$$

$$k = \cdots, -2, -1, 0, 1, 2, \cdots, \tag{24}$$

where $\Omega = 2\pi\sqrt{E/2ml^2}$, and where $\gamma = \Omega\tau$, τ being the phase. Evaluate γ if at $t = 0$ the particle is at $x = \frac{1}{2}l$ and is moving toward the right.

11. Distribution Functions

The type of experiment that is in some respects most informative consists in determining experimentally the condition of a system at an instant t_0 and then measuring the value of some dynamical variable at a later instant t. In order that a theoretical calculation may be carried out to the point at which it becomes directly useful in interpreting the results of such an experiment, the person performing the theoretical computations must be informed, first of all, as to what *kind* of a system is under consideration, so that he may properly choose the force field f in the fundamental equation $m\ddot{x} = f$; secondly, he must be given information regarding the condition of the system at the instant t_0, or, as we shall say, the *state* of the system must be specified for him. In classical mechanics, the standard method of specifying the state of a system consists in quoting the initial conditions of the motion, as was done in 3^{10}, or by providing information from which x_0 and p_0 can be unambiguously determined. A self-consistent set of data is called a *maximal* set if it describes the condition of the system at some instant in all theoretically attainable detail; according to classical theory, the initial conditions 3^{10} are an example of a maximal set of conditions for a particle executing one-dimensional motion.

If the information concerning the condition of the system at the instant t_0 available to the experimentalist does not constitute a maximal set of conditions, he will know that the results of at least some of the experiments which might be performed at the instant t are not certainties, and will not expect the theoretical computer to provide unambiguous answers to all questions; again, the computer will not be able to carry out his work entirely on the basis of the laws of motion, but will have to be guided also by considerations of probabilities.

To illustrate: We are requested to provide theoretical data concerning the outcome of a precise measurement, to be made at the instant t, of the momentum p of a particle of mass m moving in the potential box of Fig. 10, and we are told that

$$\left. \begin{array}{l} \text{(a) the energy of the particle is certainly } E \\ \text{(b) no other information is available.} \end{array} \right\} \tag{1}$$

Under these circumstances, we are obviously not able to compute the result of the contemplated measurement with certainty; yet we can tell what the possible results and what their respective probabilities are. In fact, we can draw from the available information the conclusions concerning the outcome of a precise measurement of the momentum at the time t summarized in Table 1.

TABLE 1

Possible results of a precise measurement of p	$\sqrt{2mE}$	$-\sqrt{2mE}$
Respective probabilities	$\frac{1}{2}$	$\frac{1}{2}$

Discrete distributions. Let the different possible results of an experiment, yet to be performed and designed to measure precisely the value of a dynamical variable, say s, be s_1, s_2, s_3, and so forth, and let the respective probabilities of getting these results be $P(s_1)$, $P(s_2)$, $P(s_3)$, and so forth. Then the list of the s's and the P's shown in Table 2 is called the *expected absolute distribution function* of s, or the *distribution function* of s, or

TABLE 2

Possible results of a precise measurement of s	s_1	s_2	s_3	$\cdots$
Respective probabilities	$P(s_1)$	$P(s_2)$	$P(s_3)$	$\cdots$

simply the *distribution-in-s*. Table 1, for example, is the expected absolute distribution function of the momentum of our boxed particle, or the distribution function of the momentum of the particle, or simply the distribution-in-p of the particle. The word *expected* appears in the full title of the term to suggest that the measurement is yet to be performed, a circumstance that must be kept in mind when the abbreviated terminology is employed.[2] The word *absolute* is used to distinguish the present case from *relative* distribution functions to be discussed later. If the possible results of a precise measurement of s, or, as we shall often say for short, 'the possible values of s,' are separated from each other by finite amounts, then the distribution-in-s is said to be *discrete*. The concept of a distribution-in-s implies, of course, that s can be measured with absolute precision. The probabilities $P(s_i)$ occurring in an absolute distribution satisfy the relation

$$\sum_i P(s_i) = 1, \qquad\qquad i = 1, 2, 3, \cdots . \quad (2)$$

A quantity of considerable interest to us is

$$\sum_i s_i P(s_i), \qquad\qquad i = 1, 2, 3, \cdots , \quad (3)$$

called the *mathematical expectation* of s, or simply the *expectation* of s. The expectation of s is the arithmetic mean of the results that our contemplated precise measurement of s might yield, each result being weighted by its estimated probability. Thus the expectation of the momentum of our particle in the box is, according to Table 1,

$$(\sqrt{2mE})(\tfrac{1}{2}) + (-\sqrt{2mE})(\tfrac{1}{2}) = 0; \quad (4)$$

this example shows that the expectation of a quantity need not itself be a possible result of a precise measurement of the quantity.

---

[2] The term *distribution function* is used also to denote a list of experimental values and of the frequencies of occurrence of the individual values (or values in specified ranges) found by a series of experiments on a single system or on an assemblage of similar systems; we shall have no occasion to use the term in these senses, although in a rigorous formulation of quantum mechanics the consideration of assemblages is quite important.

Although the terms *mathematical expectation* of s or *expectation* of s seem to be the only ones that can be legitimately used for the quantity (3), it has become a custom in quantum-mechanical literature to speak of (3) as the *average* of s, even though the unqualified term *average* usually refers to the arithmetic mean of already available experimental data, rather than to the probability-weighted mean of the possible results of a single experiment yet to be performed on a single particle; accordingly, we shall, as a rule, speak of (3), with mental reservations, as the *average* of s, and shall abbreviate it by the symbols av s or s_a :

$$\text{av } s = s_a = \sum_i s_i P(s_i), \qquad i = 1, 2, 3, \cdots . \quad (5)$$

As a measure of the inexactitude of the information concerning s contained in a distribution-in-s, we shall adopt the quantity

$$\Delta s = \sqrt{\sum_i (s_i - \text{av } s)^2 P(s_i)}, \qquad i = 1, 2, 3, \cdots , \quad (6)$$

that is, the probability-weighted root-mean-square of the deviations of the possible values of s from av s, shall call Δs the *expected inexactitude*[3] of s, or simply the *inexactitude* of s, and shall use the symbol Δ_s interchangeably with Δs. The inexactitude of the momentum of our boxed particle, for example, is

$$\Delta p = \sqrt{\left(+\sqrt{2mE} - 0\right)^2 \left(\tfrac{1}{2}\right) + \left(-\sqrt{2mE} - 0\right)^2 \left(\tfrac{1}{2}\right)}$$
$$= \sqrt{2mE}. \quad (7)$$

Since Δs as defined by (6) cannot vanish unless every possible value of s equals av s, the vanishing of Δs implies that only one value of s is possible, and that hence the result of a precise measurement of s is a certainty. Whether the value of s is a certainty is shown of course by the distribution-in-s; but sometimes it is possible to determine Δs without the knowledge of $P(s)$.

If the distribution-in-s is available, then the possible results of a precise measurement of a variable $f(s)$ and their respective probabilities, that is, the distribution-in-$f(s)$, can be calculated from

---

[3] The quantity Δs has a variety of names; in statistics it is called the *standard deviation* of s, the *dispersion* of s, and so on; in quantum mechanics it is called the *uncertainty* of s, the *indeterminacy* of s, the *indefiniteness* of s, and so on. In quantum mechanics the symbol Δs is sometimes used for the product of our Δs and $\sqrt{2}$, in which case certain formulas differ from those to be derived here.

the distribution-in-s.   The expectation of $f(s)$ can be computed directly in terms of the distribution-in-s:

$$\text{av} f(s) = \sum_i f(s_i) P(s_i), \qquad i = 1, 2, 3, \cdots . \quad (8)$$

Thus the expected average of the square of the momentum of our particle in the box is

$$\text{av} \, p^2 = (+\sqrt{2mE})^2(\tfrac{1}{2}) + (-\sqrt{2mE})^2(\tfrac{1}{2}) = 2mE; \quad (9)$$

this example shows that in using (8) we must sum over all possible values of s even when the inverse of $f(s)$ is not single-valued, that is, even when $f(s_i)$ and $f(s_j)$ are not necessarily different if i and j are different.

Continuous distributions. To introduce the so-called *continuous* distributions, let us consider, on the basis of the information (1), the result of an experiment designed to measure at the time t the precise value of the coordinate x of the particle moving in the box of Fig. 10, redrawn in Fig. 11(a).   A relation of the type $x = x(t)$ cannot be set up, but several signifi-

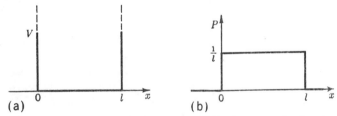

(a)

(b)

Fig. 11. A potential box.   (a) The potential.   (b) The distribution-in-x under the conditions (1).

cant conclusions regarding the outcome of the experiment can nevertheless be drawn.   In the first place, since the particle never leaves the box, the probability of finding it in any region which lies wholly outside the box, that is, outside the interval $0 \leq x \leq l$, is zero.   Further, although the experiment will certainly locate the particle at some one point within the box, the probability of locating the particle at any one *preassigned* point is zero, since the number of points at which the particle might be located is infinitely great.   But the probability of locating the particle between any two preassigned noncoincident points within the box is finite, and we may compute the probability of locating it between x and $x + dx$, or, as we shall say for short, of locating it in dx at x.   Since the particle moves with a constant speed inside the box, and hence spends equal intervals of time in regions of equal length, the probability of finding it in dx at x inside the box is proportional to dx and is independent of x.   The probability of finding the particle in dx at x— which we denote by $P(x)dx$—is consequently of the form

$$P(x)dx = \begin{cases} 0 & \text{for} \quad x < 0 \\ Cdx & \text{for } 0 \leq x \leq l \\ 0 & \text{for} \quad l < x, \end{cases} \quad (10)$$

where C is a constant. To evaluate C we note that according to (10) the probability of locating the particle *somewhere* is

$$\int_{-\infty}^{\infty} P(x)\,dx = \int_0^l C\,dx = Cl, \quad (11)$$

and that, since the particle will certainly be found somewhere, we must have $Cl = 1$; hence

$$P(x) = \begin{cases} 0 & \text{for} \quad x < 0 \\ l^{-1} & \text{for } 0 \leq x \leq l \\ 0 & \text{for} \quad l < x, \end{cases} \quad (12)$$

and $P(x)$ has the form shown in Fig. 11(b).

When the probability that the result of a precise measurement of s will yield a result lying in ds at s is written in the form $P(s)ds$, the function $P(s)$ is called the *expected absolute distribution function of s*, or simply the *distribution-in-s*. This terminology is an extension of that given before; but note that in the case of a discrete distribution $P(s)$ is itself a probability and hence a pure number, while if the distribution is continuous $P(s)$ must be multiplied by ds before a probability is obtained, so that, in the continuous case, $P(s)$ has the physical dimensions of s^{-1}.

If the distribution-in-s is continuous, the following formulas take the places of (2), (5), (6), and (8) [recall the convention stated above Equation 29[8]]:

$$\int P(s)\,ds = 1, \quad (13)$$

$$\text{av } s = \int sP(s)\,ds, \quad (14)$$

$$\Delta s = \sqrt{\int (s - \text{av } s)^2 P(s)\,ds}, \quad (15)$$

$$\text{av } f(s) = \int f(s)P(s)\,ds. \quad (16)$$

In the case of our boxed particle, we have, for example,

$$\text{av } x = \int_{-\infty}^{\infty} x P(x)\, dx = \int_{0}^{l} l^{-1} x\, dx = \tfrac{1}{2}l, \tag{17}$$

and

$$\Delta_x^2 = \int_{-\infty}^{\infty} (x - \text{av } x)^2 P(x)\, dx = \int_{0}^{l} (x - \tfrac{1}{2}l)^2 l^{-1}\, dx = \tfrac{1}{12}l^2, \tag{18}$$

so that

$$\Delta x = \frac{1}{\sqrt{12}} l. \tag{19}$$

Relative distributions. The possible values of a variable may comprise a set that is in part discrete and in part continuous, a case which we shall not discuss here. But we shall illustrate the so-called *relative* distribution functions, which are to be distinguished from the *absolute* distribution functions discussed so far.

We may be informed, for example, that a particle of mass m and total energy E, $E > V_0$, moves classically in the potential field of Fig. 9, redrawn in Fig. 12(a), and may wish to investigate, on the basis of this information alone, the result of an experiment designed to measure precisely the coordinate x of the particle at the time t. The probability that x will be found to have any one preassigned value is then zero, just as in the case of a particle in a box; but, in addition, the probability that x will be found to have a value in any preassigned finite interval is also zero, since an infinite region is accessible to the particle. Hence the absolute distribution function $P(x)$ defined above vanishes everywhere.

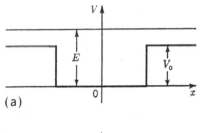

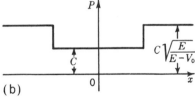

Fig. 12. A potential well. (a) The energy diagram for the case $E > V_0$. (b) The corresponding relative distribution-in-x when only E is known.

Now, the distribution function $P(x) = 0$ contains significant information regarding our particle; yet it fails to display an important fact: when the particle is in the middle region, where $V(x) = 0$, its speed is $\sqrt{2E/m}$, but when it is in an outer region its speed is $\sqrt{2(E - V_0)/m}$, so that the time spent by the particle in any interval in the middle region is shorter, in the ratio $\sqrt{(E - V_0)/E}$, than the time spent in an interval of equal length but lying in an exterior region.

In cases of this kind, it is advantageous to abandon the absolute distribution function $P(s)$ and employ instead a function (denoted by $P(s)$ also) such that $P(s)ds$ is *proportional* to, rather than *equal* to, the probability that s have a value in ds at s. In our specific example we may choose the relative probability $P(x)$ to be some nonvanishing constant C in the middle region, and then its value everywhere else will be $C\sqrt{E/(E - V_0)}$; this relative distribution-in-x is shown in Fig. 12(b).

If the only information available regarding a *free* particle moving classically along the x-axis is that its kinetic energy is E, then the relative distribution-in-x can be taken as $P(x) = C$, C being an arbitrary nonvanishing constant, preferably a positive one; if the momentum (rather than the kinetic energy) of a free particle, and nothing else, is specified, the relative distribution-in-x is again $P(x) = C$; this distribution is shown in Fig. 13. When an absolute distribution function is multiplied by a nonvanishing constant other than 1, the result is a relative distribution function of the same variable.

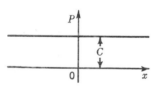

Fig. 13. The relative distribution-in-x for a free particle when only E (or only p) is known.

Stationary distributions. In discussing, under the conditions (1), the outcome of an experiment designed to measure the position of a particle in a box, we specified that the measurement is to be performed at the time t; yet the distribution function (12) is independent of t. Whenever a distribution-in-s is independent of the time at which the contemplated measurement of s is to be made, the distribution is said to be *stationary*. The distribution-in-x given by (12) and the distribution-in-p given by Table 1 are examples of stationary distributions.

A uniqueness theorem. When a distribution-in-s is given, then the averages of all integral powers of s (that is, av s^k, $k = 1$,

2, $\cdots$) are uniquely determined; in the case of the simpler distributions, the converse is also true, namely, *the aggregate of the averages of all positive integral powers of s determines (at least in principle) the distribution-in-s uniquely.*[4] In what follows, we shall sometimes be given the values of av s^k for $k = 1, 2, 3, \cdots$, and shall be able to identify *one* distribution $P(s)$ yielding just the correct averages; the uniqueness theorem quoted above will then enable us to conclude that this $P(s)$ is *the* correct distribution.

The state of a system. We remarked earlier that both the *kind* and the *state* of a dynamical system must be specified in order that certain theoretical calculations may be carried out, and we noted that the standard method of specifying the state in classical mechanics consists in quoting the initial conditions of the motion. To make the term *state*, as we shall use it, more precise, we shall now agree on the following definition: *the state of a dynamical system at an instant t is specified by whatever information is available concerning the system at the instant t, apart from the information that the system is of a certain kind.* In practice, then, the state of the system at some instant t_0 is usually specified by experimental data; and the state at a later instant t is specified by whatever information concerning the system at this instant that can be inferred, with the help of the laws of motion, from that relating to the instant t_0.

The state of an isolated system at any instant t can always be inferred from that at an earlier instant t_0, and consequently the specification of the state for an instant t_0 is equivalent to specifying the state for all time;[5] hence we may, for brevity, suppress the mention of a particular instant of time when speaking of a state of a system, it being understood that such a mention would be made in a more careful statement.

An essential feature of our definition of the term *state* is that it does not require that the information concerning the system constitute a maximal set of conditions. For example, we can say

---

[4] The problem of inferring the distribution function from the averages of the integral powers of the variable is discussed, for example, in J. V. Uspensky's *Introduction to Mathematical Probability* (hereafter cited as Uspensky), Appendix II; New York: McGraw-Hill Book Co., (1937).

[5] We disregard the possibility that the computations may be upset by the arrival of delayed information.

that the state of the boxed particle discussed in this section is specified by the statements (1), and can refer to (12) as 'the distribution-in-x for a boxed particle in the state (1),' even though the conditions (1) are obviously not maximal. Although the reader will probably not deny the convenience of this terminology, yet our use of the term *state* may seem to him unattractive; he may prefer, for example, to say that the state of a system is specified if, and only if, a maximal set of conditions is available, when, according to classical mechanics, the result of every precise measurement can be computed with certainty. We shall see later, however, that conditions which are maximal according to quantum mechanics are not maximal classically, and leave the results of some precise measurements uncertain.

Exercises

1. Show that for either a discrete or a continuous distribution

$$\Delta^2 s = \text{av } s^2 - \text{av}^2 s, \tag{20}$$

where $\Delta^2 s$ is the square of the inexactitude of s, av s^2 is the average of the square of s, and av$^2 s$ is the square of the average of s. In computing Δs it is often expedient to use (20) rather than (6) or (15).

2. Show that, if the distribution-in-s is discrete and $c \neq$ av s, then $\sum_i (s_i - c)^2 P(s_i) > \Delta^2 s$; prove the corresponding inequality for continuous distributions.

3. One of the most important distributions, the *Gaussian* or *normal* distribution, is

$$P(s) = \frac{1}{\sigma\sqrt{2\pi}} e^{-\frac{(s-m)^2}{2\sigma^2}}, \tag{21}$$

where the variable s ranges from $-\infty$ to ∞, m is a real constant, and σ is a positive constant. Show that for this distribution av $s = m$ and $\Delta s = \sigma$, so that we may write (21) as (see Fig. 14)

$$P(s) = \frac{1}{\Delta_s\sqrt{2\pi}} e^{-\frac{(s-s_a)^2}{2\Delta_s^2}}. \tag{22}$$

Note that (22) inflects at $s = s_a - \Delta_s$ and at $s = s_a + \Delta_s$.

4. Show that the distribution function[6]

$$P(s) = \frac{b}{\pi [b^2 + (s - m)^2]} \tag{23}$$

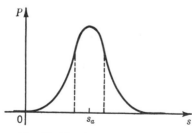

Fig. 14. The Gaussian distribution. The dotted lines mark the inflections at $s_a \pm \Delta_s$.

[6] Uspensky, page 242.

(where the variable s ranges from $-\infty$ to ∞, m is a real constant, and b is a positive constant) satisfies (13), and that its graph resembles that of (21). Then use (15) to show that, when the distribution-in-s is (23), the inexactitude of s is infinite and that hence the average value of s is not significantly representative of the distribution.

5. Show that, if the distribution-in-x is (12), then the average of x^k is $l^k/(k+1)$, and [here (20) is helpful] the inexactitude of x^k is $k(k+1)^{-1}(2k+1)^{-\frac{1}{2}}l^k$.

6. Let $P(s)$ be a continuous distribution-in-s, and let $P[f(s)]$ be the corresponding distribution-in-$f(s)$, so that $P[f(s)]\,df(s)$ is the probability that $f(s)$ will have a value between $f(s)$ and $f(s)+df(s)$; show that then

$$P[f(s)] = P(s)/\,|\,f'(s)\,|. \tag{24}$$

Indicate how $P[f(s)]$ can be expressed as a function of $f(s)$—rather than a function of s—when the inverse of $f(s)$ is single-valued, and also when the inverse of $f(s)$ is not single-valued.

7. Show that, if the distribution-in-x is (12), then the distribution-in-u, where $u = x^k$ and k is a positive integer, vanishes outside the region $0 \le u \le l^k$, and is $P(u) = k^{-1}l^{-1}u^{(1-k)/k}$ within. Use this distribution to verify the results of Exercise 5.

8. Let the only information available concerning a classical oscillator ($V = \frac{1}{2}kx^2$) be that its energy is certainly E. Show that then the absolute distribution-in-x at the time t is (see Fig. 15)

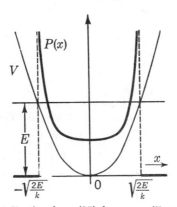

Fig. 15. The distribution-in-x (25) for an oscillator (heavy lines)

$$P(x) = \begin{cases} 0 & \text{for} \quad x < -\sqrt{2E/k} \\[2mm] \dfrac{1}{\pi\sqrt{2E/k - x^2}} & \text{for} \quad -\sqrt{2E/k} \le x \le \sqrt{2E/k} \\[2mm] 0 & \text{for} \quad \sqrt{2E/k} < x, \end{cases} \tag{25}$$

and that av $x = 0$, av $x^2 = E/k$, $\Delta x = \sqrt{E/k}$, and av $x^4 = 3E^2/2k^2$.

9. Show that for the oscillator of Exercise 8 the absolute distribution-in-p at the time t is (see Fig. 16)

$$P(p) = \begin{cases} 0 & \text{for} \quad p < -\sqrt{2mE} \\[2mm] \dfrac{1}{\pi\sqrt{2mE - p^2}} & \text{for} \quad -\sqrt{2mE} \leq p \leq \sqrt{2mE} \quad (26) \\[2mm] 0 & \text{for} \quad \sqrt{2mE} < p, \end{cases}$$

and that av $p = 0$, av $p^2 = mE$, and $\Delta p = \sqrt{mE}$; note also that $\Delta x\,\Delta p = E\sqrt{m/k}$.

10. Explain why the following argument is fallacious: "The speed of a particle executing simple harmonic motion is small when the displacement is large, and is large when the displacement is small; according to Fig. 15, large displacements are more probable than small ones; hence small speeds are more probable than large ones, and $P(p)$ should have a *maximum* at $p = 0$, rather than a *minimum* as indicated in Fig. 16."

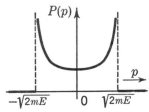

Fig. 16. The distribution-in-p (26) for an oscillator (heavy lines).

11. Show that the expected averages of the potential and the kinetic energies of the oscillator of Exercise 8 are $\frac{1}{2}E$ each.

12. Let s be a dynamical variable pertaining to a one-dimensional system, and let only the energy E of the system be known. Show that then the expected average of s at the time t can be obtained by expressing s in terms of E and the phase τ, and then averaging the resulting expression over τ. To illustrate, use the results of Exercise 3[10] to verify the averages computed in Exercises 8 and 9. What condition must the dynamical variable s satisfy in order that its distribution be stationary when E and nothing else is known?

13. We instruct a person to toss a well-balanced coin and to adjust the energy of a classical oscillator ($V = \frac{1}{2}kx^2$) to be certainly E_I if heads come up, and to be certainly E_{II}, $E_{II} \neq E_I$, if tails do; in our absence he does as instructed, and then returns the oscillator to us without comment. Show that on the basis of this information: (a) the result of a contemplated precise measurement of the energy of the oscillator at the time t is not a certainty, and av $E = \frac{1}{2}(E_I + E_{II})$; (b) the result of a contemplated precise measurement of the jth power of the energy at the time t is not a certainty, and av $E^j = \frac{1}{2}(E_I^j + E_{II}^j)$; (c) the distribution-in-x of the oscillator at the time t is $P(x) = \frac{1}{2}[P_I(x) + P_{II}(x)]$, where $P_I(x)$ and $P_{II}(x)$ are obtained from (25) by using E_I and E_{II}, respectively, for E.

14. A particle moves in a one-dimensional potential box with a slanting bottom, shown in Fig. 17; its energy is certainly E, but the phase of its motion is unknown. Show that if E is sufficiently large the particle is more likely to be found in the shallow, rather than in the deep half of the box, while for sufficiently small values of E the situation is reversed.

For what value of E is the particle as likely to be found in the deep as in the shallow half?

15. Show that, if $P(s)$ is a continuous relative distribution and $\int P(s)\,ds$ is finite, then

$$\text{av } f(s) = \frac{\int f(s)P(s)\,ds}{\int P(s)\,ds}; \qquad (27)$$

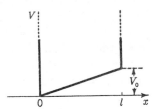

Fig. 17. A potential box with a slanting bottom.

discuss the case when $\int P(s)\,ds$ is infinite. Consider the corresponding cases for discrete relative distributions.

16. Explain how the distribution-in-$f(s)$ can be deduced from the distribution-in-s when the latter is discrete.

17. Show that, if the distribution-in-s is such that one of the possible values of s, say s_l, is less than every other possible value,[7] then av $s \geq s_l$.

12. Probability Packets

Classical mechanics imposes no limitation on the accuracy with which any set of dynamical variables pertaining to a given system can be simultaneously measured. Any particular apparatus used for the measurement of x, say, will of course have its own limit of precision; but, if greater precision is required, another, more delicate, apparatus can in principle be constructed. Classical mechanics implies that the improvement of the apparatus for measuring x can be carried on indefinitely, so that the precision will exceed any preassigned standard, however fine. Similarly, the precision of apparatus for the measurement of p, or of apparatus for the simultaneous measurement of x and p, can, according to the classical view, be improved without limit.

In practice, however, the experimental information regarding the values of physical quantities is never absolutely precise; the statement, for example, that the coordinate of a particle at the time t_0 is x_0 usually means that at a time near the instant t_0 the coordinate has a value near x_0, and that a value much different from x_0 is unlikely to be the true value; such a statement is usually accompanied by quoting some estimates of the reliability of t_0 and x_0, commonly, their probable errors, which depend on the technique used in the measurement. Having measured x with a

---

[7] This condition is not satisfied, for example, when the possible values of s form the infinite set $1, \frac{1}{2}, \frac{1}{3}, \frac{1}{4}, \cdots$.

certain apparatus, we obtain in fact a distribution function giving the probability that an absolutely precise measurement of x would have resulted in a value lying in dx at x.

In the text and in some of the exercises of §11 we investigated the results of experiments to be performed at a time t and designed to measure accurately the value of a dynamical variable pertaining to a system whose state is specified by its energy alone. We shall now continue to consider classical systems whose states are specified by information that is not equivalent to a precise knowledge of the initial conditions; but, instead of assuming that the energy and nothing else is known, we shall turn to cases in which the information refers to the values of x and p at the time t_0, but does not provide the initial conditions of the motion with absolute precision.

An example. Let us consider the result of a precise measurement, to be made at the time t, of the position of a free particle, the available information being as follows: The momentum of the particle at the instant $t = 0$ was precisely p_0; the position at $t = 0$ is not known with absolute precision, but the probability that the particle was in dx at x at the instant $t = 0$ is $P^0(x)\,dx$, where

$$P^0(x) = \frac{1}{\Delta_x \sqrt{2\pi}}\, e^{-\frac{(x-x_0)^2}{2\Delta_x^2}} ; \qquad (1)$$

this information concerning x may be regarded as having been obtained by means of an instrument having a resolving power of the order of Δx; the assumption that $P^0(x)$, is a *normal* distribution, made principally for mathematical convenience, is perhaps not unreasonable.

We are not able to compute the result of a precise measurement of x at an instant t with certainty, and the best we can do is to calculate the probability that the measurement will yield a result lying in dx at x; we shall denote the distribution-in-x at the time t by $P(x)$. Now, our particle is moving with a uniform velocity $v_0 = p_0/m$, so that it will be exactly at $x = X$ when $t = T$ if it was exactly at $x = X - v_0T$ when $t = 0$, and it will be exactly at $X + dX$ when $t = T$ if it was exactly at $X + dX - v_0T$ when $t = 0$; the probability that it will be between X and $X + dX$ at the instant T thus equals the probability that it was between $(X - v_0T)$ and $(X - v_0T) + dX$ when $t = 0$. According to (1), the latter probability is $(\Delta_x \sqrt{2\pi})^{-1} \exp \{ - [(X - v_0T) - x_0]^2 / 2\Delta_x^2 \} dX$, so that, writing x for X and t for T, we get

$$P(x) = \frac{1}{\Delta_x \sqrt{2\pi}} e^{-\frac{[x-(x_0+v_0t)]^2}{2\Delta_x^2}} \qquad (2)$$

Graphs of (2) for several equally spaced values of t, beginning with $t = 0$, are indicated in Fig. 18, where p_0 is taken as positive.

It is often convenient to speak of the distribution function of a dynamical variable as the *probability packet* describing this variable, particularly if the distribution function vanishes or nearly vanishes everywhere except in a limited region. The expected average of the variable

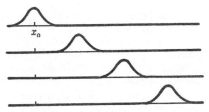

Fig. 18. Successive graphs of the packet (2).

is then called the *center* of the packet. If this average varies with the time, the packet is said to be moving. In our case, for example, the position of the particle is described by the probability packet (2), whose center lies at $x = x_0 + v_0t$ at the time t; the center of this packet thus moves in precisely the way in which our particle would move were its position and momentum at $t = 0$ exactly x_0 and p_0.

Since our particle is not being accelerated, the result of a precise measurement of its momentum at any time will be certainly p_0; similarly, the result of a precise measurement of its energy at any time will be certainly $E = p_0^2/2m$.

Second example. Let us consider next the result of a precise position measurement, to be made on a free particle at the time t, if the available information is that the position of the particle at $t = 0$ was precisely x_0, while the momentum at $t = 0$ is not known with absolute precision, but the probability that the momentum was in dp at p when $t = 0$ is dp times

$$P^0(p) = \frac{1}{\Delta_p \sqrt{2\pi}} e^{-\frac{(p-p_0)^2}{2\Delta_p^2}}. \qquad (3)$$

Since our particle is not being accelerated, its momentum at any time is the same as it was at $t = 0$, whatever its value at $t = 0$ may have been. Now, the particle will be exactly at X when $t = T$ if its momentum is exactly $m(X - x_0)/T$, and it will be exactly at $X + dX$ when $t = T$ if its momentum is exactly $m(X + dX - x_0)/T$, that is, $m(X - x_0)/T + mdX/T$; the probability that the particle will be between X and $X + dX$ when $t = T$ thus equals the probability that its momentum is between $m(X - x_0)/T$ and $m(X - x_0)/T + mdX/T$. According to (3), the latter probability is $(\Delta_p\sqrt{2\pi})^{-1} \exp\{-[m(X - x_0)/T - p_0]^2/2\Delta_p^2\}\cdot mdX/T$, so that, writing $v = p/m$, and $\Delta_v = \Delta_p/m$, using x and t for X and T, and rearranging the result, we get

$$P(x) = \frac{1}{t\Delta_v \sqrt{2\pi}} e^{-\frac{[x-(x_0+v_0 t)]^2}{2t^2\Delta_v^2}}. \tag{4}$$

Comparison of (4) with 22^{11} shows that (4) is a normal distribution, av x at the time t being $x_0 + v_0 t$, and Δ_x at the time t being $t\Delta_v$, where Δ_v is the constant inexactitude of the velocity. Thus the packet not only moves with the constant velocity v_0, but also spreads out in the course of time, so that our estimates concerning the outcome of a precise measurement of x become less and less reliable as the instant at which the measurement is to be made is postponed relatively to $t = 0$. Graphs of (4) for several equally spaced values of t are given in Fig. 19, where p_0 is taken

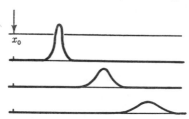

Fig. 19. Successive graphs of the packet (4). The arrow indicates that at $t = 0$ the particle was certainly at x_0.

as positive, and where the arrow indicates that the particle was certainly at x_0 at $t = 0$.

The energy of our particle is, of course, not a certainty, because the value of p is not certain; but the packet describing the energy, that is, the distribution-in-E, is stationary, just as is the distribution-in-p.

Third example. We shall finally consider the case when the available information regarding a free particle is that neither its position nor its momentum at $t = 0$ is known with absolute precision, but that the distribution-in-x and the distribution-in-p at $t = 0$ are, respectively,

$$P_1^0(x) = \frac{1}{\Delta_x\sqrt{2\pi}} e^{-\frac{(x-x_0)^2}{2\Delta_x^2}}, \tag{5}$$

and

$$P_2^0(p) = \frac{1}{\Delta_p\sqrt{2\pi}} e^{-\frac{(p-p_0)^2}{2\Delta_p^2}}. \tag{6}$$

The distributions (5) and (6) are to be regarded as independent, so that the probability that x had a value in dx at x at $t = 0$ and that at the same instant p had a value in dp at p is $P_1^0(x)P_2^0(p)\,dx\,dp$. The simultaneous distribution-in-x-and-p at $t = 0$, given by $P_1^0(x)P_2^0(p)$, may be pictured (see Fig. 20) as a surface lying above the xp-plane. Note that we may legitimately speak of the simultaneous distribution of x and p only if no limitations are put on the precision with which x and p can be measured simultaneously.

Now, our particle will be certainly at X when $t = T$, if its position x and momentum p at $t = 0$ satisfy the relation

$$x + pT/m = X; \tag{7}$$

Equation (7) may be interpreted as specifying a straight line in the xp-plane of Fig. 20. Again, the particle will be certainly at $X + dX$ when $t = T$, if its position and momentum at $t = 0$ satisfy the relation

$$x + pT/m = X + dX, \tag{8}$$

specifying another straight line in the xp-plane. The probability, $P(X)dX$, that the particle be between X and $X + dX$ when $t = T$ is thus equal to the probability that the point in the xp-plane corresponding to the true (but unknown) initial conditions will lie between the two parallel straight lines (7) and (8). This latter probability, in turn, equals the volume bounded at the top by the surface $P_1^0(x)P_2^0(p)$, at the bottom by the xp-plane, and at the sides by the two vertical planes cutting the xp-plane along the lines (7) and (8); that is,

Fig. 20. The simultaneous distribution of x and p for the case given by (5) and (6). The horizontal plane is the xp-plane.

$$P(X)\,dX = \int_{-\infty}^{\infty} \int_{m(X-x)/T}^{m(X-x)/T+mdX/T} P_1^0(x)P_2^0(p)\,dp\,dx. \tag{9}$$

Now, if ϵ is sufficiently small, then

$$\int_a^{a+\epsilon} f(s)\,ds = \epsilon f(a), \tag{10}$$

so that (9) becomes

$$P(X)\,dX = \frac{mdX}{T}\int P_1^0(x)P_2^0\,[m(X-x)/T]\,dx$$

$$= \frac{mdX}{2\pi T\Delta_x\Delta_p}\int \exp\left\{-\frac{(x-x_0)^2}{2\Delta_x^2}\right\}\exp\left\{-\frac{[m(X-x)/T-p_0]^2}{2\Delta_p^2}\right\}dx. \tag{11}$$

If a, b, c, d, f, α, and β are independent of s, we have the standard formula

$$\int_{-\infty}^{\infty} \exp\left\{ -\frac{[s-a]^2}{2\alpha^2} - \frac{[b(f-cs)-d]^2}{2\beta^2} \right\} ds$$

$$= \frac{1}{b} \sqrt{\frac{2\pi\alpha^2\beta^2}{c^2\alpha^2 + \beta^2/b^2}} \exp\left\{ -\frac{(f-ac-d/b)^2}{2(c^2\alpha^2 + \beta^2/b^2)} \right\}. \quad (12)$$

The integral in (11) has the form (12), and, after writing x and t for X and T in the result of the integration, we finally get

$$P(x) = \frac{1}{\sqrt{\Delta_z^2 + t^2\Delta_v^2}\ \sqrt{2\pi}} e^{-\frac{[x-(x_0+v_0 t)]^2}{2(\Delta_x^2 + t^2\Delta_v^2)}}. \quad (13)$$

The x-packet (that is, the packet describing x) is therefore again a normal distribution, av x at the time t being $x_0 + v_0 t$, and the inexactitude of x at the time t being $\sqrt{\Delta_z^2 + t^2\Delta_v^2}$. The x-packet thus moves (see Fig. 21) with a constant velocity and spreads at the same time. The p-packet (that is, the packet describing p) is at all times the stationary packet (6). The E-packet is of course also stationary.

Fig. 21. Successive graphs of the packet (13).

The δ-function. In conclusion, let us return to Fig. 19, where we used an arrow to indicate that at $t = 0$ the particle is certainly at x_0, and consider what function of x might be used for the distribution-in-x when x is certainly equal to x_0. When the particle is certainly at x_0 the probability of finding it in any region not including x_0 is zero, so that the required function, which we shall denote by $\delta(x - x_0)$, should satisfy the relation

$$\delta(x - x_0) = 0 \qquad \text{for } x \neq x_0. \quad (14)$$

Further, if the distribution is to be absolute, we must have

$$\int_{-\infty}^{\infty} \delta(x - x_0)dx = 1. \quad (15)$$

Now, (14) and (15) are not consistent if the integral in (15) is thought of in the usual sense, because, if a function differs from zero at only one point, its integral vanishes when interpreted in the usual way. We shall, nevertheless, employ the function $\delta(x - x_0)$, defined by (14) and (15), with the understanding that the results obtained by using it can be verified by recourse to appropriate limiting processes, and without reference to a function satisfying both (14) and (15). In quantum mechanics the function $\delta(x - x_0)$ (the δ-function) was first used by Dirac.

To visualize $\delta(x - x_0)$ we may return to Equation (4) and allow t to decrease toward zero. The numerator of the exponent in (4) will approach $(x - x_0)^2$ when $t \to 0$, so that, writing ξ for $t\Delta_v\sqrt{2}$, we get

$$\lim_{\xi \to 0} \frac{1}{\xi\sqrt{\pi}} e^{-\frac{(x-x_0)^2}{\xi^2}} \tag{16}$$

for $\delta(x - x_0)$. The definition of $\delta(x - x_0)$ is, however, (14) and (15) rather than[8] (16). At $x = x_0$, $\delta(x - x_0)$ is of course infinite.

Our interest in the δ-function is due chiefly to the fact that in view of (14)

$$x\delta(x - x_0) = x_0\delta(x - x_0), \tag{17}$$

so that $\delta(x - x_0)$ satisfies the eigenvalue equation 6[5] for the operator x. According to (16), $\delta(x - x_0)$ can be interpreted as a limit of a well-behaved function; but $\delta(x - x_0)$ itself is not well-behaved in the sense of §3. We shall nevertheless adopt $\delta(x - x_0)$ as an eigenfunction of the operator x belonging to the eigenvalue x_0 of x, even though this step will undermine the mathematical rigor of a few of our computations. It then follows that any real number (positive, negative, or zero) is an eigenvalue of the operator x, and that x has no complex or pure imaginary eigenvalues.

Exercises

1. Suppose that at $t = 0$ the distribution-in-x and the distribution-in-p of particle comprising a linear harmonic oscillator are (5) and (6), respectively, and show that then the x-packet and the p-packet at the instant t are

$$P(x) = \frac{1}{\sqrt{\Delta_x^2 \cos^2 \omega t + \Delta_p^2 m^{-2}\omega^{-2}\sin^2 \omega t}\,\sqrt{2\pi}}$$

$$\exp\left\{-\frac{[x - (x_0 \cos \omega t + p_0\omega^{-1}m^{-1}\sin \omega t)]^2}{2(\Delta_x^2 \cos^2 \omega t + \Delta_p^2 m^{-2}\omega^{-2}\sin^2 \omega t)}\right\} \tag{18}$$

---

[8] Note, for example, the equation following Equation (543) of J. H. Jeans's *The Mathematical Theory of Electricity and Magnetism* (hereafter cited as Jeans) Fifth Edition, Cambridge, The University Press, 1925.

and

$$P(p) = \frac{1}{\sqrt{\Delta_x^2 m^2 \omega^2 \sin^2 \omega t + \Delta_p^2 \cos^2 \omega t}\, \sqrt{2\pi}}$$
$$\exp\left\{-\frac{[p - (-x_0 \omega m \sin \omega t + p_0 \cos \omega t)]^2}{2(\Delta_x^2 m^2 \omega^2 \sin^2 \omega t + \Delta_p^2 \cos^2 \omega t)}\right\}. \quad (19)$$

Consider the motions of the centers of the two packets in the light of 12^{10} and 13^{10}, and note the periodic changes in the shapes of the packets.

2. Show that, for the oscillator of Exercise 1, av $E = (p_0^2 + \Delta_p^2)/2m + k(x_0^2 + \Delta_x^2)/2$.

3. Note that, if $\Delta_p^2 = mk\Delta_x^2$, then the results of Exercises 1 and 2 reduce to

$$P(x) = \frac{1}{\Delta_x\sqrt{2\pi}} \exp\left\{-\frac{[x - (x_0 \cos \omega t + p_0 \omega^{-1} m^{-1} \sin \omega t)]^2}{2\Delta_x^2}\right\}, \quad (20)$$

$$P(p) = \frac{1}{m\omega\Delta_x\sqrt{2\pi}} \exp\left\{-\frac{[p - (-x_0 \omega m \sin \omega t + p_0 \cos \omega t)]^2}{2m^2 \omega^2 \Delta_x^2}\right\}, \quad (21)$$

and

$$\text{av } E = \frac{1}{2m} p_0^2 + \frac{1}{2} kx_0^2 + k\Delta_x^2, \quad (22)$$

so that in this special case the packets move without change in shape. Illustrate the motions of the packets (20) and (21) by diagrams.

4. Show that if $\Delta_p^2 = mk\Delta_x^2$, and $x_0 = p_0 = 0$, then the distribution-in-E of the oscillator of the preceding exercises is

$$P(E) = \frac{1}{k\Delta_x^2} e^{-\frac{E}{k\Delta_x^2}}, \qquad E \geq 0, \quad (23)$$

av $E = k\Delta_x^2$, and the most probable value of E is zero. Note that in this special case the probability packets for x and p are both stationary, even though the energy is not a certainty.

5. Show that in the case of a linear harmonic oscillator the probability packets for x and p are periodic functions of t of period $2\pi\sqrt{m/k}$, regardless of the form that they may have initially.

6. Discuss the behavior and the physical meaning of the various probability packets of this section for times prior to $t = 0$.

7. With the help of the formulas

$$\int_{-\infty}^{\infty} e^{-\frac{s^2}{\xi^2}}\, ds = \sqrt{\pi}\, \xi \quad (24a)$$

and

$$\int_{-\infty}^{\infty} s^{2n} e^{-\frac{s^2}{\xi^2}}\, ds = \frac{1 \cdot 3 \cdot 5 \cdots (2n-1)\, \sqrt{\pi}}{2^n} \xi^{2n+1}, \quad (24b)$$

where n is a positive integer, show that, if $f(x)$ can be expanded into a power series in x in the vicinity of x_0, then

$$\lim_{\xi \to 0} \int_{-\infty}^{\infty} f(x) \left[\frac{1}{\xi \sqrt{\pi}} e^{-\frac{(x-x_0)^2}{\xi^2}} \right] dx = f(x_0). \tag{25}$$

Equation (25) can be interpreted as meaning that if a normal distribution-in-x is varied in such a way as to confine the particle to a greater and greater extent to the immediate neighborhood of x_0, then the expected average of $f(x)$ approaches $f(x_0)$, as of course it should.

8. Show that in view of (14) and (15)

$$\int_{-\infty}^{\infty} f(x)\delta(x - x_0)\, dx = f(x_0); \tag{26}$$

one interpretation of this equation is that, if the distribution-in-x is $\delta(x - x_0)$, that is, if the value of x is certainly x_0, then the expected average of $f(x)$ is $f(x_0)$. Comparison of (26) with (25) illustrates that a result obtained by means of the δ-function can also be obtained without its use if appropriate limiting processes are employed.

9. Discrete distributions, which we have so far presented in the form of tables, can be expressed in terms of δ-functions, and then treated formally as continuous ones. Consider the 'continuous' distribution-in-p

$$P(p) = \tfrac{1}{2}\delta(p + \sqrt{2mE}) + \tfrac{1}{2}\delta(p - \sqrt{2mE}) \tag{27}$$

and show [by computing av p^k, using (27) and 16^{11}, and comparing the result with av p^k obtained from Table 1 by means of 8^{11}] that (27) is equivalent to the discrete distribution-in-p of Table 1. Note that the physical dimensions of the right side of (27) are just those required for a continuous absolute distribution-in-p.

Chapter III

ELEMENTS OF THE SCHROEDINGER METHOD; ONE DIMENSION

In §13 we shall state two quantum-mechanical assumptions which are quite general in that they do not refer specifically to any one of the several distinct mathematical methods that the theory may use. In §14 we shall turn to the Schroedinger method (as it appears in the light of developments that followed its inception) and, disregarding historical order, shall base this method in part on the assumptions of §13. Incidentally, the Schroedinger method is sometimes called the use of the 'Schroedinger representation.'

13. Two Assumptions

The postulates of any mathematical theory of physical phenomena—for example, Newton's laws of classical mechanics, or the fundamental assumptions of quantum mechanics—are a set of categorical statements that the student is asked to take for granted. Back of such postulates there is a long story of search, trial, and achievement, a story both instructive and inspiring. But, once a set of postulates is formulated, its worth is to be judged solely by its effectiveness in leading to theoretical results that are in agreement with experimental facts, and by the generality of its applicability.

How easily the postulates of a theory can be made to appear intelligible and reasonable to the student depends in a large measure on the readiness with which physical conclusions regarding some familiar phenomena can be derived from the postulates. Now, Newton's laws can be made to appear sensible by a quite elementary discussion of the student's experiences in daily life. But in the case of quantum mechanics the deduction of the properties of large-scale phenomena encountered in daily life involves much calculation, while the results obtained most easily have to do with atomic phenomena, with which none of us is acquainted through intimate personal contact. Consequently we cannot expect that the physical significance of the postulates given below will be clear as soon as they are stated; but we hope that as the reader studies their use in answering specific physical questions about specific dynamical systems, he will gradually perceive their physical content.

A rigorous and complete statement of the fundamental rules and assumptions of quantum mechanics is of necessity quite mathematical and abstract, and is therefore not the best starting point for a beginner. The rules and assumptions which we shall state and which will take the reader a long way toward understanding the quantum-mechanical method are easy to memorize, and, in almost every case, each of them can be put to use before the next is introduced; but not all of them are free from defects. For example, in the second sentence of our first assumption we use the term 'precise experimental measurement' without a word of explanation, although the subject of quantum-mechanical measurement requires pages of advanced discussion;[1] we fail to mention certain relevant matters, such as the radiative effects hinted at in §31; besides, the assumption made in this sentence is eventually shown to be contained in another assumption made later.

Our introductory assumption, which we shall call the *operator assumption*, is as follows:

I. The physical properties of any dynamical variable pertaining to a given dynamical system can be inferred theoretically from the mathematical properties of an operator to be associated with this dynamical variable. In particular, the possible numerical results of a precise experimental measurement of a dynamical variable are the eigenvalues of an operator associated with this dynamical variable, and vice versa.

With every *dynamical variable* we thus associate in quantum mechanics an *operator*. A dynamical variable and•an operator associated with it will be denoted by the same letter, it being left for the reader to determine from the context whether a symbol, say α, stands for the dynamical variable α or for an operator α associated with the dynamical variable α. To minimize the

---

[1] E. C. Kemble, *The Fundamental Principles of Quantum Mechanics* [hereafter cited as Kemble], Chapter IX. New York: McGraw-Hill Book Co., 1937.

possibility of confusion, we shall (until Chapter XIII) usually employ the following convention:[2] if an expression (or equation) contains a symbol that is to be interpreted as an operator associated with a dynamical variable, rather than as the dynamical variable itself, then the marginal number of the expression (or equation) is enclosed in angular brackets rather than in parentheses.

Although the operator assumption does not provide a method for associating operators with dynamical variables, it does require that operators to be associated with real dynamical variables must have only real eigenvalues; it also suggests that the operators to be associated with numerical constants, such as 0, 1, 2, π, m, and so forth, are the corresponding operators of type c, that is, the operators 0, 1, 2, π, m, and so forth. A detailed program for associating operators with dynamical variables not involving t explicitly is provided by the following rule[3] (the symbol $\hbar$, introduced by Dirac, stands for $h/2\pi$, where h is Planck's constant, equal to approximately 6.6×10^{-27} erg · seconds; as usual, $i^2 = -1$):

II. The operators α and β, to be associated, respectively, with the dynamical variables α and β, must be so chosen that

$$\alpha\beta - \beta\alpha = i\hbar[\alpha, \beta], \qquad \langle 1 \rangle$$

where $[\alpha, \beta]$ is the operator to be associated with the classically-computed Poisson bracket of α and β.

Equation $\langle 1 \rangle$, through which Planck's constant is introduced into the theory, is called the *quantum condition*. The appearance of $[\alpha, \beta]$ in $\langle 1 \rangle$ implies that the dynamical system to be studied is described classically in terms of some coordinate system, and, unless the contrary is explicitly stated, we shall take these coordinates to be Cartesian (rectangular) coordinates.

Equation $\langle 1 \rangle$ involves the constant $i\hbar$ and *three* operators: that to be associated with the classical dynamical variable α, that to be

---

[2] Patterned after the convention used by J. H. Van Vleck in his *Theory of Electric and Magnetic Susceptibilities*. Oxford: The Clarendon Press, 1932.

[3] P. A. M. Dirac, *The Principles of Quantum Mechanics*, Second Edition [hereafter cited as Dirac], page 90. Oxford: The Clarendon Press, 1935.

associated with the classical dynamical variable β, and that to be associated with the classical dynamical variable $[\alpha, \beta]$. The structure of $\langle 1 \rangle$ depends, therefore, on the form of $[\alpha, \beta]$, and is particularly simple if the Poisson bracket is a constant, because then the latter can be immediately associated with an operator of type c, and the number of operators involved in $\langle 1 \rangle$ is essentially reduced to two.

To illustrate the implications of $\langle 1 \rangle$, let us consider the operators—which we denote[4] by x and p—to be associated, respectively, with the Cartesian coordinate x and the momentum p of a particle undergoing one-dimensional motion. In this case, $\langle 1 \rangle$ becomes

$$xp - px = i\hbar[x, p]. \qquad \langle 2 \rangle$$

Now, classically,

$$(12^9) \qquad\qquad [x, p] = 1, \qquad\qquad (3)$$

so that we can write the operator 1 for the operator $[x, p]$ on the right side of $\langle 2 \rangle$, getting

$$xp - px = i\hbar 1, \qquad \langle 4 \rangle$$

or simply,

$$xp - px = i\hbar. \qquad \langle 5 \rangle$$

Consequently, the operators to be associated, respectively, with the coordinate x and the conjugate momentum p must be so chosen that their commutator is the constant $i\hbar$. Incidentally, the theory imposes no conditions on the operators to be associated with x and p, apart from $\langle 5 \rangle$ and the requirement that the respective eigenvalues of these operators be real.

In view of $\langle 1 \rangle$, the quantum conditions for the operators α, β,

---

[4] Heretofore we used the symbol x for the independent variable and for the operator x in mathematical computations, and also for the dynamical variable x describing the position of a particle in physical problems. In equations such as $\langle 2 \rangle$ the symbol x is used in a still different sense, namely, for an operator (whatever its specific form may be) to be associated in quantum theory with the dynamical variable x. These distinct uses of the same symbol should not be confused; it is of course possible to decrease the likelihood of a misunderstanding by employing several symbols instead of one, but the disadvantages of such a procedure, in the long run, outweigh its advantages, especially since but little care on the reader's part is required to avoid falling into error.

and γ, to be associated, respectively, with three dynamical variables α, β, and γ, which do not involve t explicitly, are

$$\alpha\beta - \beta\alpha = i\hbar[\alpha, \beta], \quad \gamma - \gamma\beta = i\hbar[\beta, \gamma], \quad \gamma\alpha - \alpha\gamma = i\hbar[\gamma, \alpha], \quad \langle 6 \rangle$$

where $[\alpha, \beta]$, $[\beta, \gamma]$, and $[\gamma, \alpha]$ are the operators to be associated with the respective classically calculated Poisson brackets. The case of more than three variables is similar. The reason for the self-consistency of the large set of commutation rules that comes into play when the number of variables under consideration is great is that commutators of functions of operators satisfy relations much like those satisfied by the Poisson brackets of functions of dynamical variables—recall 29^2 and 14^9.

The quantum-mechanical method of associating operators with dynamical variables determines, through the quantum conditions, the commutation rules that the operators must satisfy, but does not specify in detail the individual operators themselves. This implies that detailed specification of individual operators is not necessary for the calculation of the theoretical data to be compared with experiment, and that quantum-mechanical calculations may be carried out by the purely symbolic methods of operator algebra. But if a set of some specific operators is available whose eigenvalues are real and whose commutation rules are just those required by quantum mechanics, it is usually expedient to associate the various dynamical variables with these specific operators.

The method of associating variables and operators embodied in $\langle 1 \rangle$ applies to dynamical variables that are a part of the structure of classical mechanics. It appears, however, that dynamical variables exist in nature (those having to do with the so-called electron spin are an example) which defy classical description, or, as we shall say, have no classical analogues. For such variables the present method is insufficient.

As implied in the operator assumption, the calculation of the possible values of a dynamical variable[5] consists, in quantum mechanics, in the computation of the eigenvalues of an operator associated with this dynamical variable. Now, as illustrated in

---

[5] From now on we shall, for brevity, say *the possible values of a dynamical variable* instead of *the possible numerical results of a precise experimental measurement of a dynamical variable.*

Chapter I, the question of the eigenvalues of certain operators may not arise unless the operands are restricted by some auxiliary conditions, such as continuity and boundary conditions. But we shall not make here any general assumption to take care of such additional conditions, because they depend on the specific mathematical procedure adopted in the solution of a quantum-mechanical problem.

14. Schroedinger Operators

Quantum-mechanical calculations may be carried out either by purely symbolic methods of operator algebra based on the quantum conditions 1[13], or by associating the various dynamical variables with operators of specific explicit forms. The latter alternative, which we shall consider first, leaves us a certain freedom of choice, and we shall begin with a particularly simple and useful scheme of association, the Schroedinger scheme.

The operators associated in the Schroedinger method with dynamical variables pertaining to one-dimensional systems are specific functions of the operators $\partial/\partial x$ and x, and of operators of type c, studied in Chapter I. The operands employed in the Schroedinger theory of one-dimensional systems are, accordingly, functions of x; they are usually denoted by the symbol ψ, and are called *Schroedinger functions, wave functions, ψ-functions*, or simply ψ's. **All Schroedinger functions are required to be well-behaved.** We shall not attempt here to give a comprehensive definition of good behavior; for our elementary purposes it is sufficient to say that *one-dimensional Schroedinger functions are required to be well-behaved in the sense of §3.*

To begin the process of association, we turn to the fundamental dynamical variables of one-dimensional motion, that is, the Cartesian coordinate x and the momentum p conjugate to it. In consequence of the quantum condition, the operators x and p, associated, respectively, with these dynamical variables, must, in any scheme of association, satisfy the relation

$$\langle 5^{13} \rangle \qquad\qquad xp - px = i\hbar, \qquad\qquad \langle 1 \rangle$$

and it remains to recognize a pair of specific operators, of the kind studied in Chapter I, whose commutator is $i\hbar$ and whose eigenvalues are all real. Now, since $i\hbar$ is a constant, it follows from 30^2 that

$$x\left(-i\hbar\,\frac{\partial}{\partial x}\right) - \left(-i\hbar\,\frac{\partial}{\partial x}\right)x \;=\; i\hbar, \qquad\qquad \langle 2\rangle$$

so that the specific operators x and $-i\hbar\partial/\partial x$ have just the commutator required by $\langle 1\rangle$; further, the eigenvalues of each of these operators are all real. Consequently, *one of the methods—the Schroedinger method—of associating specific operators with the dynamical variables x and p is to associate the operator x with the dynamical variable x, and the operator $-i\hbar\partial/\partial x$ with the dynamical variable p.* In symbols,

$$\begin{cases} \text{dynamical variable } x \rightleftharpoons \text{operator } x \\[2mm] \text{dynamical variable } p \rightleftharpoons \text{operator } -i\hbar\,\dfrac{\partial}{\partial x}. \end{cases} \qquad \langle 3\rangle$$

We shall next indicate the operators associated in the Schroedinger scheme with dynamical variables that are functions of x and p, but do not involve explicitly the time t, and shall begin with the dynamical variable x^2. The Poisson brackets of x^2 with x and with p are

$$[x^2,\, x] = 0, \qquad\qquad [x^2,\, p] = 2x, \qquad\qquad (4)$$

so that, if the operator to be associated with x^2 be temporarily denoted by α, the commutators of α with the operators already introduced for x and p must, according to the quantum conditions, be

$$\alpha x - x\alpha = 0, \qquad \alpha\left(-i\hbar\,\frac{\partial}{\partial x}\right) - \left(-i\hbar\,\frac{\partial}{\partial x}\right)\alpha = i\hbar 2x. \qquad \langle 5\rangle$$

Equations $\langle 5\rangle$ are just the equations 37^2, and their general solution is

$$\alpha = x^2 + c, \qquad\qquad \langle 6\rangle$$

where c is an arbitrary constant. The physical assumptions introduced so far do not enable us to assign a specific value to c, but an additional assumption, to be made in §17, has as one of its consequences the following rule: *the operator to be associated with a dynamical variable $\alpha(\xi)$* [that is, a dynamical variable which is explicitly a function of the dynamical variable ξ only] *is the operator* $\alpha(\xi)$, *where ξ is the operator associated with the dynamical variable ξ itself.* This rule requires that we set $c = 0$ in $\langle 6 \rangle$, getting the association

$$\text{dynamical variable } x^2 \rightleftarrows \text{operator } x^2. \qquad \langle 7 \rangle$$

The statement just made in italics requires that, having adopted the associations $\langle 3 \rangle$, we must also adopt the associations

$$\text{dynamical variable } \alpha(x) \rightleftarrows \text{operator } \alpha(x) \qquad \langle 8 \rangle$$

$$\text{dynamical variable } \alpha(p) \rightleftarrows \text{operator } \alpha\left(-i\hbar\,\frac{\partial}{\partial x}\right), \qquad \langle 9 \rangle$$

and hence the association $\langle 7 \rangle$ can be set up without going through the steps (4) and $\langle 5 \rangle$; we used these steps to illustrate the possibility that the quantum conditions may leave an operator undetermined to the extent of an additive constant.

An important dynamical variable is p^2; according to $\langle 9 \rangle$ the operator associated with it in the Schroedinger scheme is the square of the operator $-i\hbar\partial/\partial x$ associated with p itself:

$$\text{dynamical variable } p^2 \rightleftarrows \text{operator } -\hbar^2\,\frac{\partial^2}{\partial x^2}. \qquad \langle 10 \rangle$$

For a dynamical variable that is the sum of a function of x only and a function of p only, we adopt the association

dynamical variable $\alpha(x) + \beta(p)$

$$\rightleftarrows \text{operator } \alpha(x) + \beta\left(-i\hbar\,\frac{\partial}{\partial x}\right), \qquad \langle 11 \rangle$$

of which all our previous associations are special cases. That $\langle 11 \rangle$ is consistent with the quantum conditions follows from the appropriateness of $\langle 3 \rangle$ and the similarity between 29^2 and 14^9.

The identification of a Schroedinger operator to be associated with a dynamical variable of the form $\alpha(x)\beta(p)$ requires special consideration. In the simple case of the variable xp (which classically can be denoted equally well by px) we may proceed as follows: We note that xp is the Poisson bracket of the variables $\frac{1}{2}x^2$ and $\frac{1}{2}p^2$:

$$xp = [\tfrac{1}{2}x^2, \tfrac{1}{2}p^2]. \qquad (12)$$

The quantum condition 1^{13} then requires that the operator associated with the dynamical variable xp be $-i\hbar^{-1}$ times the commutator of the operators already associated with $\frac{1}{2}x^2$ and $\frac{1}{2}p^2$, that is, $-i\hbar^{-1}$ times the operator

$$(\tfrac{1}{2}x^2)\left(-\tfrac{1}{2}\hbar^2\frac{\partial^2}{\partial x^2}\right) - \left(-\tfrac{1}{2}\hbar^2\frac{\partial^2}{\partial x^2}\right)(\tfrac{1}{2}x^2) = \tfrac{1}{4}\hbar^2\left(\frac{\partial^2}{\partial x^2}x^2 - x^2\frac{\partial^2}{\partial x^2}\right)$$

$$= \tfrac{1}{2}\hbar^2\left(1 + 2x\frac{\partial}{\partial x}\right) = \tfrac{1}{2}\hbar^2\left(x\frac{\partial}{\partial x} + \frac{\partial}{\partial x}x\right), \quad \langle 13\rangle$$

and hence

dynamical variable xp (or px)

$$\rightleftarrows \text{ operator } \tfrac{1}{2}\left[x\left(-i\hbar\frac{\partial}{\partial x}\right) + \left(-i\hbar\frac{\partial}{\partial x}\right)x\right]. \quad \langle 14\rangle$$

This operator is, so to speak, an average of the operators $x(-i\hbar\partial/\partial x)$ and $(-i\hbar\partial/\partial x)x$, suggested, respectively, by the classical expressions xp and px.

Dynamical variables of the form $\alpha(x)\beta(p)$, or sums of such variables, will appear in our work only indirectly, and we shall not consider them any further here. Also, we shall postpone until later the proof that all the operators adopted above have only real eigenvalues, a property which, in view of the operator assumption I, is very vital.

A dynamical variable of particular interest is the Hamiltonian, given in the case of one-dimensional motion by

$$(6^9) \qquad\qquad H = \frac{1}{2m}p^2 + V(x). \qquad\qquad (15)$$

The operator, denoted by H, associated with the Hamiltonian in the Schroedinger method is, in view of $\langle 8\rangle$ and $\langle 10\rangle$,

$$H = \frac{1}{2m}\left(-\hbar^2\frac{\partial^2}{\partial x^2}\right) + V(x), \qquad\qquad \langle 16\rangle$$

where the operator $V(x)$ is the same function of the operator x as the potential $V(x)$ is of the coordinate x. When we introduce the *Schroedinger constant*

$$\kappa = \frac{8\pi^2 m}{h^2} = \frac{2m}{\hbar^2}, \qquad\qquad (17)$$

which we shall use throughout our work, Equation $\langle 16 \rangle$ becomes

$$H = -\frac{1}{\kappa}\frac{\partial^2}{\partial x^2} + V(x). \qquad \langle 18 \rangle$$

In view of the operator assumption, the calculation of the possible values of the energy of a dynamical system consists in determining the eigenvalues of an operator to be associated with the Hamiltonian of this system; these eigenvalues will be denoted by E.   In the Schroedinger scheme, the operator associated with the Hamiltonian is $\langle 18 \rangle$, and the operands are required to be well-behaved; hence *the Schroedinger procedure for calculating the possible results of a precise experimental measurement of the energy of a conservative one-dimensional system described classically by the potential function $V(x)$ is to determine those values of the number E for which the equation*

$$H\psi = E\psi \qquad \langle 19 \rangle$$

possesses well-behaved solutions, the operator H in $\langle 19 \rangle$ being given by $\langle 18 \rangle$.

Equation $\langle 19 \rangle$, with H given by $\langle 18 \rangle$, is the one-dimensional form of a fundamental equation of quantum mechanics, discovered by Schroedinger[6] and called the *first Schroedinger equation,* or simply the *Schroedinger equation.*

The one-dimensional first Schroedinger equation is often written, in a more explicit form, as

$$\frac{\partial^2 \psi}{\partial x^2} + \frac{8\pi^2 m}{h^2}[E - V(x)]\psi = 0. \qquad (20)$$

Exercises

1. Consider the multiplied-out form of the Schroedinger operator associated with the dynamical variable $(Ax + Bp)^2$, where A and B are constants, and note that it suggests the association $\langle 14 \rangle$.

2. Examine the fitness of the following associations as alternatives for $\langle 3 \rangle$: (a) dyn. var. $x \rightleftarrows$ operator ix, and dyn. var. $p \rightleftarrows$ operator $-\hbar\partial/\partial x$; (b) dyn. var. $x \rightleftarrows$ operator $i\hbar\partial/\partial x$, and dyn. var. $p \rightleftarrows$ operator x; (c) dyn. var. $x \rightleftarrows$ operator $-i\hbar\partial/\partial x$, and dyn. var. $p \rightleftarrows$ operator x.

15. Energy Levels of an Oscillator

To illustrate the Schroedinger method of dealing with physical problems, we shall now consider a linear harmonic oscillator of mass m moving in the potential field

---

[6] E. Schroedinger, Ann. der Physik, **79**, 361, (1926).

(14^{10}) $$V(x) = \tfrac{1}{2}kx^2,\tag{1}$$

and shall take up the question: *What are the possible results of a precise experimental measurement of the energy of this oscillator?*

Incidentally, we would hardly ask this question in classical theory, because, when $V(x)$ is given by (1), the energy of a classical oscillator can obviously have any positive value whatever, zero included, depending on the initial conditions of the motion. But in quantum theory we shall draw a conclusion quite different from this.

To answer our question, we must, according to the operator assumption, calculate the eigenvalues of the operator associated with the Hamiltonian of the oscillator; in view of 18^{14} and (1) this operator is

$$H = -\frac{1}{\kappa}\frac{\partial^2}{\partial x^2} + \frac{1}{2}kx^2,\tag{2}$$

so that the Schroedinger equation, $H\psi = E\psi$, is

$$\left(-\frac{1}{\kappa}\frac{\partial^2}{\partial x^2} + \frac{1}{2}kx^2\right)\psi = E\psi.\tag{3}$$

The fact that (3) is a partial differential equation implies that ψ may be a function of other independent variables besides x; but, since x is the only independent variable appearing in (3) explicitly, the dependence of ψ on x is determined by the equation

$$\left(-\frac{1}{\kappa}\frac{d^2}{dx^2} + \frac{1}{2}kx^2\right)\psi = E\psi,\tag{4}$$

and ψ can depend on variables other than x only through the arbitrary constants contained in the solutions of (4). Now, (4) is of the same general form as the equation

(3^4) $$\left(-\frac{d^2}{dx^2} + x^2\right)u = \lambda u,\tag{5}$$

which possesses well-behaved solutions when, and only when,

(28^4) $$\lambda = 2n + 1, \qquad n = 0, 1, 2, 3, \cdots,\tag{6}$$

and we shall transform (4) into (5) by a change of variable. The substitution

$$s = x/a, \qquad (7)$$

where a is an as yet undetermined constant, carries (4) into

$$-\frac{d^2\psi}{ds^2} + \frac{1}{2} k\kappa a^4 s^2 \psi = a^2 \kappa E \psi. \qquad (8)$$

We now choose

$$a = \sqrt[4]{2/k\kappa} = \sqrt[4]{\hbar^2/km} \qquad (9)$$

and set

$$E = \lambda/a^2 \kappa = \tfrac{1}{2}\lambda\hbar\sqrt{k/m} \qquad (10)$$

so that (8) goes over into

$$\left(-\frac{d^2}{ds^2} + s^2\right)\psi = \lambda\psi, \qquad (11)$$

that is, into an equation precisely like (5). The eigenvalues of our H can now be obtained by substituting into (10) the numbers listed in (6):

$$E_n = (n + \tfrac{1}{2})\hbar\sqrt{\frac{k}{m}}, \qquad n = 0, 1, 2, 3, \cdots. \qquad (12)$$

The eigenvalues of the operator $\langle 2 \rangle$ associated with the Hamiltonian of the oscillator are thus the numbers (12), and in accordance with our operator assumption we conclude that *the only possible results of a precise experimental measurement of the energy of a linear harmonic oscillator of mass m and restoring constant k are*

$$E_0 = \tfrac{1}{2}\hbar\sqrt{\frac{k}{m}}, \qquad E_1 = \tfrac{3}{2}\hbar\sqrt{\frac{k}{m}}, \qquad E_2 = \tfrac{5}{2}\hbar\sqrt{\frac{k}{m}}, \cdots. \qquad (13)$$

By means of the abbreviation

$$(11^{10}) \qquad\qquad \nu_c = \frac{1}{2\pi}\sqrt{\frac{k}{m}}, \qquad (14)$$

where the symbol ν_c is used to remind us that the right side of (14) is just the frequency of a classical linear harmonic oscillator of mass m and restoring constant k, we may write (12) as

$$E_n = (n + \tfrac{1}{2})h\nu_c, \qquad n = 0, 1, 2, 3, \cdots. \qquad (15)$$

The answer given by quantum mechanics to the question asked

at the beginning of this section is thus quite different from the classical answer. Which is the more correct must be determined by experiment; but we shall not discuss this point here.

When quantum mechanics implies that not all of the classically permissible values of a dynamical variable can be results of a precise experimental measurement of this variable, we say that this dynamical variable is *quantized*; for example, we say that the energy of a linear harmonic oscillator is quantized, for, instead of all the positive values of the energy expected on the classical theory, only those contained in (15) are the possible results of a precise measurement. The possible values of the energy of a system are called the *energy levels* of the system, and their totality is called the *energy spectrum*, or the *term spectrum*, of the system. The term spectrum of the linear harmonic oscillator is entirely discrete, the successive energy levels being separated by the amount $h\nu_c$; and the lowest possible value of the energy is not zero, but

$$E_0 = \tfrac{1}{2}h\nu_c , \qquad (16)$$

the so-called *zero-point energy* of the oscillator. The five lowest energy levels of a linear harmonic oscillator are shown diagram-

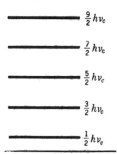

$\tfrac{9}{2}h\nu_c$

$\tfrac{7}{2}h\nu_c$

$\tfrac{5}{2}h\nu_c$

$\tfrac{3}{2}h\nu_c$

$\tfrac{1}{2}h\nu_e$

Fig. 22. Energy-level diagram for a linear harmonic oscillator. The thick lines show the five lowest levels given by (15).

matically in Fig. 22. Pure numbers, such as n in (15), contained in quantum-mechanical formulas for the possible values of a dynamical variable are called *quantum numbers*. The Bohr theory of the atom—the forerunner of quantum mechanics—gives $E_n = nh\nu_c$, rather than (15), as the formula for the energy levels of a linear harmonic oscillator.

Incidentally, quantum mechanics does not imply that the energy of *every* dynamical system is quantized; in this connection, the reader might at this point read the first two paragraphs of §28.

Exercises

1. The pendulum of an ordinary clock executes approximately simple harmonic motion. Discuss the feasibility of discriminating, by experimenting with such a pendulum, between the classical and the quantum-mechanical conclusions regarding the possible values of the energy of a linear harmonic oscillator.

2. Show that a normalized eigenfunction of $\langle 2 \rangle$ belonging to the eigenvalue E_n given by (15) has the form $e^{i\gamma_n} N_n H_n(x/a) \exp\left[-\frac{1}{2}(x/a)^2\right]$, where γ_n is independent of x but otherwise arbitrary, H_n is the nth Hermite polynomial 37[4], a is given by (9), and $N_n = 1/\sqrt{a2^n n! \pi^{\frac{1}{2}}}$.

3. Let A be an arbitrary real constant, let H be the operator $\langle 2 \rangle$, and let f be any function for which the integrals in $\langle 17 \rangle$ are finite. Show that then

$$\int \bar{f}(H - A)^2 f \, dx = \int |(H - A)f|^2 \, dx. \qquad \langle 17 \rangle$$

16. Schroedinger Functions

The portion of quantum mechanics discussed so far and yielding the one-dimensional first Schroedinger equation enables us to calculate the energy levels, that is, the possible results of a precise measurement of the energy, for any conservative one-dimensional system; the procedure is quite direct: when confronted with a system described by a specific potential $V(x)$, we seek mathematically the eigenvalues of the operator $H = -\kappa^{-1}\partial^2/\partial x^2 + V(x)$. The details of the computation may be very involved on account of mathematical complications; but in principle the procedure is straightforward. Consequently, were we interested exclusively in the energy levels of conservative one-dimensional systems, we would not need to introduce any quantum-mechanical assumptions beyond those stated already. We shall not, however, proceed at once to systems other than the oscillator, but, in order to get a more detailed idea of the quantum-mechanical behavior of an oscillator, we shall first consider the information that the theory provides regarding results of experiments other than measurements of energy. To do this, we must examine more closely the operands of the Schroedinger scheme (that is, the Schroedinger functions that are involved only indirectly in the calculation of energy levels) and must augment our list of assumptions. This will be done in this section and the next; and illustrations of the physical implications of our formal results in specific problems will be begun in §18.

The only condition imposed so far on the Schroedinger operands is the requirement of good behavior. We now add another, which we denote by III[S], rather than by III, to indicate that it refers specifically to the Schroedinger method.

III$^\text{S}$. Every Schroedinger operand ψ pertaining to a given dynamical system depends on the time t in such a way that

$$H\psi = i\hbar \frac{\partial}{\partial t} \psi, \tag{1}$$

where H is the Schroedinger operator associated with the Hamiltonian of this system.

The partial differential equation $\langle 1 \rangle$ is called the *second Schroedinger equation*. It is to be understood from now on that (with a minor exception to be mentioned in a moment) *all* Schroedinger functions depend on t, and that the symbol ψ, by which we shall continue to denote them, is, in the case of one-dimensional systems, an abbreviation for $\psi(x, t)$.

To illustrate: In the case of a linear harmonic oscillator, H is given by 2^{15}, and $\langle 1 \rangle$ becomes

$$\left(-\frac{1}{\kappa} \frac{\partial^2}{\partial x^2} + \frac{1}{2} kx^2 \right) \psi = i\hbar \frac{\partial}{\partial t} \psi, \tag{2}$$

so that, when the Schroedinger method is used for the study of a linear harmonic oscillator, then every operand, besides being a well-behaved function of x, must depend on t so as to satisfy the partial differential equation (2).

We shall now outline a procedure for computing the Schroedinger function $\psi = \psi(x, t)$, belonging to a one-dimensional system with a Hamiltonian H, for times other than $t = 0$, if it is known to be $\psi^0 = \psi(x, 0)$ at $t = 0$. The desired function must satisfy $\langle 1 \rangle$ and must reduce to ψ^0 at $t = 0$; since $\langle 1 \rangle$ is a differential equation of the first order in $\partial/\partial t$, the problem has a unique solution.

We consider first the case when ψ^0 is an eigenfunction of the operator H, so that, denoting it by ψ_E^0, we have

$$H\psi_E^0 = E\psi_E^0, \tag{3}$$

where E is a constant. Now, the function

$$\psi_E = \psi_E^0 e^{-iEt/\hbar} \tag{4}$$

satisfies $\langle 1 \rangle$, since

$$H\psi_E = e^{-iEt/\hbar} H\psi_E^0 = e^{-iEt/\hbar} E\psi_E^0 = E\psi_E \tag{5}$$

and

$$i\hbar \frac{\partial}{\partial t} \psi_E = i\hbar\psi_E^0 \frac{\partial}{\partial t} e^{-iEt/\hbar} = i\hbar\psi_E^0 (-iE/\hbar) e^{-iEt/\hbar} = E\psi_E; \tag{6}$$

further, (4) reduces to ψ_E^0 at $t = 0$. Consequently, our first problem has been solved: an eigenfunction of H belonging to the eigenvalue E depends on the time through the factor $e^{-iEt/\hbar}$, a factor whose formal appearance is the same for all dynamical systems. As shown by $\langle 5 \rangle$, in the case of a conservative system, a Schroedinger function which, at $t = 0$, is an eigenfunction of H belonging to the eigenvalue E will always remain an eigenfunction of H belonging to the same eigenvalue. Again, we have $\bar{\psi}_E \psi_E = \bar{\psi}_E^0 \psi_E^0$, so that an eigenfunction of H, if normalized at $t = 0$, will always remain normalized. Note that, if E in (4) should equal zero, we get an exception to our statement that *all* Schroedinger functions depend on t; but this exception is too unimportant to emphasize.

We can now write down the explicit expressions for those of the normalized Schroedinger functions, pertaining to the oscillator, which are eigenfunctions of the operator H of the oscillator. In view of the results of this section and of Exercise 2^{15} we have:

$$\psi_n = e^{i\gamma_n} N_n H_n\left(\frac{x}{a}\right) e^{-\frac{1}{2}\left(\frac{x}{a}\right)^2} e^{-iE_nt/\hbar}, \qquad n = 0, 1, 2, \cdots, \quad (7)$$

where

$$E_n = (n + \tfrac{1}{2})h\nu_c, \qquad N_n = 1/\sqrt{a 2^n n! \pi^{\frac{1}{2}}}, \qquad (8)$$

$$a = \sqrt[4]{\frac{\hbar^2}{km}}, \qquad \nu_o = \frac{1}{2\pi}\sqrt{\frac{k}{m}}, \qquad (9)$$

H_n is the Hermite polynomial 37^4, and the γ's are real and independent of both x and t, but otherwise arbitrary. The results of Exercise 5^8 show that the functions (7) form, at any instant t, an orthonormal set, complete with respect to functions that are of integrable square in the infinite interval and satisfy certain mild continuity conditions.

In describing a method for deducing $\psi = \psi(x, t)$ from $\psi^0 = \psi(x, 0)$ when ψ^0 is not an eigenfunction of H, we shall restrict ourselves to the case of the oscillator; that is, we shall look for that function ψ which satisfies (2) and reduces to ψ^0 for $t = 0$. The method employs the ψ-functions (7), which have the form

$$\psi_n = f_n(x)e^{-iE_nt/\hbar}, \qquad n = 0, 1, 2, \cdots \quad (10)$$

and satisfy the equations

$$H\psi_n = E_n\psi_n, \qquad\qquad \langle 11 \rangle$$

where H is the operator associated with the Hamiltonian of the oscillator. We assume that the arbitrary phases of the functions (7) have been fixed by some suitable convention. Letting the superscript ^{0} denote that $t = 0$, we write

$$\psi_n^0 = f_n(x), \qquad\qquad n = 0, 1, 2, \cdots . \quad (12)$$

We next expand the given function ψ^0 in terms of the orthonormal set (12), getting

$$\psi^0 = \sum_n c_n \psi_n^0, \qquad\qquad n = 0, 1, 2, \cdots , \quad (13)$$

the expansion coefficients being given by 21^8, so that $c_n = \int \bar{\psi}_n^0 \psi^0 \, dx$. Consider now the function

$$\psi = \sum_n c_n \psi_n, \qquad\qquad n = 0, 1, 2, \cdots , \quad (14)$$

where the c's are the same as in (13), and where the ψ's are the time-dependent functions (10). We have

$$H\psi = H \sum_n c_n \psi_n = \sum_n c_n H \psi_n = \sum_n c_n E_n \psi_n, \quad \langle 15 \rangle$$

and

$$i\hbar \frac{\partial}{\partial t} \psi = i\hbar \frac{\partial}{\partial t} \sum_n c_n \psi_n = \sum_n c_n i\hbar \frac{\partial}{\partial t} \psi_n = \sum_n c_n E_n \psi_n, \quad (16)$$

so that (14) satisfies (2). Further, (14) reduces to ψ^0 for $t = 0$, and hence it constitutes the solution of our problem. The case when ψ^0 does not admit of the expansion (13) is of no physical interest.

Exercises

1. How does the choice of the phases of the functions (7) affect the c's in (14)? How does this choice affect the ψ-function (14)?

2. Outline the computation of $\psi(x, t)$ for an oscillator when $\psi(x, t_0)$ is known, and $t_0 \neq 0$.

3. Use 45^8 to show that if j is a positive integer and ψ_n is (7) then

$$\int \bar{\psi}_n \left(-i\hbar \frac{\partial}{\partial x} \right)^{2j} \psi_n \, dx = k^j m^j \int \bar{\psi}_n x^{2j} \psi_n \, dx. \quad (17)$$

4. Show that if ψ is a normalizable solution of $\langle 1 \rangle$ then

$$\frac{d}{dt} \int \bar{\psi}\psi \, dx = 0, \quad (18)$$

even if ψ is not an eigenfunction of H. *Hint*: first differentiate with respect to t under the integral sign.

17. Specification of States

Calculations of the results of certain experiments on a dynamical system must be based on information specifying both the *kind* and the *state* of the system under consideration. The state of a classical harmonic oscillator, for example, may be specified by designating the precise initial conditions of the motion, as in §10; by stating that its energy is E and that nothing else is known, as in Exercise 8[11]; by designating the distributions in x and in p at some instant t_0, as in Exercise 1[12]; or in some other manner. Such descriptions of the state are readily translated into mathematical terms and enable us to proceed to calculations concerning outcomes of experiments.

In quantum theory it is of course also necessary to have information regarding the kind of dynamical system, and we already know how this information is translated into mathematical terms: the *kind* of system is taken care of by the operator V in the operator H associated with the Hamiltonian. Again, in certain quantum-mechanical problems it is also necessary to have physical information concerning the *state* of the system, and to summarize this information mathematically before calculations of the physical properties of the system in this state can be begun. It is our next task to consider how a verbal specification of the state of a system is to be translated into the mathematical terms of the Schroedinger method, and how, this translation having been made, calculations of results of experiments are to be carried out. In this connection we introduce the following general assumption, which we shall call the *operand rule*:

IV. States of dynamical systems are to be associated with the operands of the quantum-mechanical operators, and vice versa.

This assertion, taken by itself, is not very informing, since it does not provide a method for associating operands with states; it does suggest, however, that, in the Schroedinger scheme, states are associated with and specified by well-behaved functions satisfying 1[16], and that, when verbal information concerning the state of a system is provided, the computer's first task is to determine just which ψ-function summarizes this information mathematically.

The operand rule is elaborated in the Schroedinger method by the following assumption, about which most computations center; in stating it, we use the symbol $av_\psi\ \alpha$ (read, for short, 'the average of α for the state ψ') to denote the expected average of the dynamical variable α for the state specified by the Schroedinger function ψ :

V^S. **When a dynamical system is in the state specified by the Schroedinger function ψ, then the expected average, $av_\psi\alpha$, of any dynamical variable α is given by the formula**

$$av_\psi\ \alpha = \frac{\int^{e.c.s.} \bar{\psi}\alpha\psi d\tau}{\int_{e.c.s.} \bar{\psi}\psi d\tau}, \qquad \langle 1 \rangle$$

where α in the integrand is the Schroedinger operator associated with the dynamical variable α, and where the integrals extend over the entire configuration space.

We shall call $\langle 1 \rangle$ the *Schroedinger expectation formula*. Until Chapter XII we shall be concerned with one-dimensional motion, and consequently there is for the present no need to define the term *configuration space* in detail. Suffice it to say that in the case of a single particle confined to the x-axis the term 'entire configuration space' means the totality of points comprising the x-axis. In the one-dimensional case our latest assumption reduces, in fact, to the following form:

V_1^S. *When a one-dimensional system is in the state specified by the Schroedinger function ψ, then the expected average, $av_\psi\alpha$, of any dynamical variable α is given by the formula*

$$av_\psi\ \alpha = \frac{\int_{-\infty}^{\infty} \bar{\psi}\alpha\psi\, dx}{\int_{-\infty}^{\infty} \bar{\psi}\psi\, dx}, \qquad \langle 2 \rangle$$

where α in the integrand is the Schroedinger operator associated with the dynamical variable α.

The expectation formula $\langle 2 \rangle$ implies, for example, that, if we are told that the state of a one-dimensional system is specified by a given Schroedinger function ψ, then we can compute the average value of the momentum p of the particle for this state by evaluating the right side of the equation

$$\text{av}_\psi\, p = \frac{\int \bar{\psi}\left(-i\hbar\, \frac{\partial}{\partial x}\right) \psi\, dx}{\int \bar{\psi}\psi\, dx}. \tag{3}$$

Note that, since ψ in $\langle 2 \rangle$ is a function of t, $\text{av}_\psi\, \alpha$ is in general also a function of t, even though the dynamical variable α may have the form $\alpha = \alpha(x, p)$ and not depend on t explicitly.

The implications of the expectation formula $\langle 2 \rangle$ are far-reaching. Thus, having been given the Schroedinger function specifying the state of a one-dimensional system, we can compute the expected average of any dynamical variable for this state for any time; again, by calculating the respective expected averages of all integral powers of α, we are, in view of the uniqueness theorem of §11, enabled, at least in principle, to infer the distribution-in-α for this state; in particular we can compute the inexactitude, to be denoted by $\Delta_\psi\alpha$, of α for this state by means of the formula

$$(20^{11}) \qquad\qquad \Delta_\psi^2\, \alpha = \text{av}_\psi\, \alpha^2 - \text{av}_\psi^2\, \alpha, \tag{4}$$

and test the possibility that the result of a precise measurement of α be a certainty.

Conversely, having been given a verbal specification of a state, we can determine the Schroedinger function that will specify the state mathematically, by looking for that ψ which, when used in $\langle 2 \rangle$, yields data in agreement with those given us; this done, we are ready to make computations concerning further properties of the system in this state, computations in which, as we shall see, Equation $\langle 2 \rangle$ again plays a central part.

The following three general implications of $\langle 2 \rangle$ are very important:

1. Since operators associated with dynamical variables are linear, a substitution of $c\psi$ for ψ in $\langle 2 \rangle$ does not affect the right side of $\langle 2 \rangle$ if c is a numerical constant. The results of quantum-mechanical calculations for a state specified by a Schroedinger function ψ are thus exactly the same as those for a state specified by the Schroedinger function $c\psi$, and we conclude that, *if c is a constant, then the Schroedinger functions ψ and $c\psi$ specify the same state.* In particular, the ψ-function obtained by normalizing a

given ψ-function specifies the same state as does the original ψ-function; hence, in dealing with a normalizable ψ-function, we may, without loss of generality and usually with a gain in simplicity, replace it by the corresponding normalized ψ-function.

2. If the dynamical variable α is a function only of the coordinate x, that is, if $\alpha = f(x)$, then it follows from $\langle 2 \rangle$ and 8^{14} that

$$\mathrm{av}_\psi f(x) = \frac{\int \bar{\psi} f(x) \psi \, dx}{\int \bar{\psi} \psi \, dx}. \tag{5}$$

If the operator α involves differentiation, it is of course not permissible to rearrange the factors in the integrand in the numerator of $\langle 2 \rangle$; but (5) can obviously be rewritten as

$$\mathrm{av}_\psi f(x) = \frac{\int f(x) \bar{\psi} \psi \, dx}{\int \bar{\psi} \psi \, dx}. \tag{6}$$

Equation (6), valid for any $f(x)$, holds in particular when $f(x) = x^k$, $k = 1, 2, 3, \cdots$. Therefore, a comparison of (6) with 27^{11} in the light of the uniqueness theorem of §11 yields the result: *when a one-dimensional system is in the state specified by the Schroedinger function ψ, then the distribution-in-x of the particle is $\bar{\psi}\psi$.* For this reason, one-dimensional Schroedinger functions are called *amplitudes* of distributions-in-x, or simply *probability amplitudes*. If ψ is normalized to unity, then $\bar{\psi}\psi$ is the absolute distribution-in-x for the state specified by the Schroedinger function ψ. In the sequel we shall, for brevity, usually say 'the state ψ' instead of 'the state specified by the Schroedinger function ψ.'

3. If the state is specified by a ψ-function that is an eigenfunction of the operator α associated with the dynamical variable α, then

$$\alpha\psi = a\psi, \tag{7}$$

where a is a numerical constant, so that $\langle 2 \rangle$ yields the result

$$\mathrm{av}_\psi \alpha = \frac{\int \bar{\psi} \alpha \psi \, dx}{\int \bar{\psi} \psi \, dx} = \frac{\int \bar{\psi} a \psi \, dx}{\int \bar{\psi} \psi \, dx} = \frac{a \int \bar{\psi} \psi \, dx}{\int \bar{\psi} \psi \, dx} = a, \tag{8}$$

and also the result

$$\mathrm{av}_\psi \alpha^2 = \frac{\int \bar{\psi} \alpha^2 \psi \, dx}{\int \bar{\psi} \psi \, dx} = \frac{\int \bar{\psi} a^2 \psi \, dx}{\int \bar{\psi} \psi \, dx} = a^2, \tag{9}$$

so that according to (4)

$$\Delta_\psi \alpha = 0. \tag{10}$$

Now, as pointed out in §11, the inexactitude of a quantity cannot vanish unless only one value of this quantity is possible, and we conclude: *if ψ is an eigenfunction of the operator α belonging to its eigenvalue* a, *then the result of a precise measurement of the dynamical variable α when the system is in the state ψ is certainly* a.

Equation ⟨2⟩ enables us to compute the average of any dynamical variable α for any state for which the Schroedinger function, that is, the amplitude of the distribution-in-x, is known A calculation of $\mathrm{av}_\psi \alpha$ by means of ⟨2⟩ involves no preliminary inquiries concerning the distribution-in-α for the state in question, even if α is a function of both x and p, or of p alone; all we need to do is to use the appropriate operator in the integrand of ⟨2⟩. This procedure has no analogue in classical mechanics or statistics where distribution functions, rather than their amplitudes, are of primary significance.

18. Energy States of an Oscillator

In Exercises 8[11] and 9[11] we investigated on the classical basis some of the properties of an oscillator on the assumption that the energy of the oscillator is known to be certainly E and that no other information is available. We are now prepared to consider the corresponding problems from the quantum-mechanical standpoint. The ψ-functions with which we shall have to deal are of integrable square (Exercise 14); therefore, in view of theorem 1 of §17, they may without loss of generality be assumed to be normalized. If ψ is normalized, that is, if

$$\int_{-\infty}^{\infty} \bar{\psi}\psi \, dx = 1, \tag{1}$$

the Schroedinger expectation formula 2[17] becomes

$$\mathrm{av}_\psi \alpha = \int_{-\infty}^{\infty} \bar{\psi}\alpha\psi \, dx. \tag{2}$$

Thus, for example, the expected average of the energy of the oscillator for a state specified by a normalized Schroedinger function ψ is

$$\mathrm{av}_\psi E = \int \bar{\psi}H\psi \, dx, \tag{3}$$

where

$$H = -\frac{1}{\kappa} \frac{\partial^2}{\partial x^2} + \tfrac{1}{2}kx^2. \tag{4}$$

Similarly, the expected average of the square of the energy for this state is

$$\mathrm{av}_\psi E^2 = \int \bar\psi H^2 \psi \, dx. \tag{5}$$

The basis on which we regard equations such as $\langle 3 \rangle$ and $\langle 5 \rangle$ as correct is, of course, the assumption V_1^S of §17.

The Schroedinger function for the normal state. The statement that the energy of the oscillator is certainly E means that the result of a precise experimental measurement of the energy is certain to be E. According to quantum mechanics, the only possible results of a precise measurement of the energy of an oscillator are

$$(15^{15}) \qquad E_n = (n + \tfrac{1}{2})h\nu_c, \qquad n = 0, 1, 2, \cdots. \tag{6}$$

Hence, saying that the energy of the oscillator is certainly E implies, in quantum theory, that E is one of the numbers listed in (6).

For the present, we shall restrict ourselves to an oscillator whose energy is certainly

$$E_0 = \tfrac{1}{2}h\nu_c = \tfrac{1}{2}\hbar\sqrt{k/m}, \tag{7}$$

the lowest value listed in (6); an oscillator whose energy is certainly E_0 is said to be in its *normal* state. Our first concern is to identify the Schroedinger function describing the normal state; that is, we must deduce the Schroedinger function from the information that the energy of the oscillator is certainly E_0.

Now, the energy for a state is certainly E_0 if, and only if, the average of the energy for this state is E_0 and the inexactitude of the energy is zero; further, in view of 20^{11}, the inexactitude of the energy vanishes if, and only if, the square of the average of the energy equals the average of the square of the energy. Consequently, if ψ is the normalized Schroedinger function that we are seeking, then the statement that the energy of the oscillator for the state ψ is certainly E_0 can be summarized by the two equations

$$\int \bar{\psi} H \psi \, dx = E_0, \qquad \int \bar{\psi} H^2 \psi \, dx = E_0^2, \qquad \langle 8 \rangle$$

where H is the operator $\langle 4 \rangle$.

Consider now the quantity $\int \bar{\psi}(H - E_0)^2 \psi \, dx$. If ψ satisfies Equations $\langle 8 \rangle$ and (1) we have

$$\int \bar{\psi}(H - E_0)^2 \psi \, dx$$

$$= \int \bar{\psi} H^2 \psi \, dx - 2E_0 \int \bar{\psi} H \psi \, dx + E_0^2 \int \bar{\psi} \psi \, dx = 0; \quad \langle 9 \rangle$$

again, the finiteness of the integrals (1) and $\langle 8 \rangle$ implies that our ψ satisfies the conditions of Exercise 3^{15}, and that hence $\int \bar{\psi}(H - E_0)^2 \psi \, dx = \int |(H - E_0)\psi|^2 \, dx$. We thus get the equation

$$\int |(H - E_0)\psi|^2 \, dx = 0. \qquad \langle 10 \rangle$$

The integrand in $\langle 10 \rangle$ is nowhere negative, and hence it must vanish everywhere in order that $\langle 10 \rangle$ may hold. Consequently, $(H - E_0)\psi = 0$; that is, the ψ-function that we have been seeking is a well-behaved solution of the equation

$$H\psi = E_0\psi. \qquad \langle 11 \rangle$$

Equation $\langle 11 \rangle$ is just the Schroedinger equation 3^{15} for the oscillator, with E set equal to E_0, and its normalized solution, denoted by ψ_0, is given in Exercise 2^{15}; this solution, adjusted to be properly time-dependent, is given in 7^{16}:

$$\psi_0 = \frac{1}{\sqrt{a\pi^{\frac{1}{2}}}} e^{i\gamma} e^{-\frac{1}{2}\left(\frac{x}{a}\right)^2} e^{-i\pi\nu_c t}, \qquad (12)$$

where

$$a = \sqrt[4]{\hbar^2/km}, \qquad 2\pi\nu_c = \sqrt{k/m}, \qquad (13)$$

and where γ is an arbitrary real constant independent of both x and t.

Our first task has been accomplished: we now know that the normalized Schroedinger function, specifying the state of the oscillator for which the energy is certainly E_0, is (12).

By the theorem 3 of §17, the condition that ψ be an eigenfunction of H belonging to the eigenvalue E is *sufficient* in order that the result of a precise energy measurement for the state ψ be certainly E; the present argument illustrates that this condition is also *necessary*.

The distribution-in-x for the normal state. In §17 we concluded that when a one-dimensional system is in the state specified by the Schroedinger function ψ, then the distribution-in-x of the particle is $\bar{\psi}\psi$. The distribution-in-x for an oscillator whose energy is certainly E_0 [we denote this distribution by $P_0(x)$] is consequently

$$P_0(x) = \bar{\psi}_0\psi_0 = \frac{1}{a\sqrt{\pi}}\, e^{-\left(\frac{x}{a}\right)^2}. \tag{14}$$

This absolute distribution, unlike its amplitude (12), is independent of the time and is free from any arbitrariness. A graph of (14) is shown in Fig. 23, where V is the potential $\frac{1}{2}kx^2$, and the horizontal line, labeled E_0 and drawn to the same scale as V, represents the total energy of the oscillator. Fig. 23 also shows by a dotted line the distribution-in-x of a classical oscillator having the same mass, restoring constant, and total energy as those of the quantum-mechanical oscillator whose distribution function is (14); the classical distribution is obtained from 25^{11} and is drawn to the same scale as $\bar{\psi}_0\psi_0$. The two distributions are seen to be very different from each other.

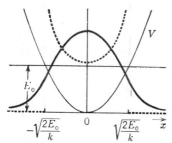

Fig. 23. The distribution-in-x of a linear harmonic oscillator in the normal state (thick solid curve).

Perhaps the most striking property of the quantum-mechanical distribution in Fig. 23 is that the distribution-in-x does not vanish outside the classical limits of x for oscillator of energy E_0, that is, outside the limits $-\sqrt{2E_0/k}$ and $\sqrt{2E_0/k}$: *according to the quantum theory, a particle may be found in regions that are not accessible to it on the classical basis.* This feature of the theory provides an interpretation of certain physical phenomena that cannot be accounted for classically.

Since a direct experimental measurement of p will obviously never yield an imaginary value for p, the quantum-mechanical possibility of finding the particle outside the classical limits implies that the classical relation connecting the numerical values of x, p, and E of the oscillator at any instant, that is,

$$E = \frac{1}{2m} p^2 + \tfrac{1}{2}kx^2, \tag{15}$$

does not hold in quantum mechanics. The situation is somewhat as follows: According to the classical view, we can determine the energy of an oscillator either by some direct measurement or by measuring the precise simultaneous values of x and p at some instant and substituting the results into the right side of (15). But, according to quantum mechanics, although a precise measurement of x *or* of p at any instant is possible, these measurements cannot be carried out simultaneously (§§23 and 24); hence, no equations relating simultaneous values of x and p, or simultaneous values of x, p, and E, appear in the theory. The fact that (15) is not to be found among quantum-mechanical equations signifies, in essence, that, if the energy of an oscillator is to be determined, it must be measured *directly*, and that it cannot be deduced indirectly from the results of measurements of x and p.

If a precise experiment, designed to determine the position of the particle, be performed at the instant t_0 on an oscillator in the normal state, a definite value of x will be obtained, lying, according to (14), somewhere in the infinite region from $-\infty$ to ∞; but such a measurement will violently perturb the oscillator, so that, for example, were a precise measurement of p to follow immediately the measurement of x, the result of the second measurement could not be expected to be the same as it would have been had the measurement of x not been made.

The absolute distribution-in-x being available, we can calculate by the standard statistical method the average of any function of x for the normal state. Using the symbol av_0 to denote an expected average for the state ψ_0, we have, for example,

$$\mathrm{av}_0 x^s = \int \frac{x^s}{a\pi^{\frac{1}{2}}} e^{-\left(\frac{x}{a}\right)^2} dx. \tag{16}$$

If s is an odd integer, (16) vanishes, since the integrand is odd in x and the interval of integration is symmetric about $x = 0$. If $s = 2j$, where j is a positive integer, we get, using 24b[12],

$$\mathrm{av}_0 x^{2j} = 1 \cdot 3 \cdot 5 \cdots (2j - 1) 2^{-j} a^{2j}. \qquad (17)$$

In particular, $\mathrm{av}_0 x^2 = \frac{1}{2} a^2 = \frac{1}{2} \hbar / \sqrt{km}$, that is,

$$\mathrm{av}_0 x^2 = E_0 / k. \qquad (18)$$

Comparison of (18) with the corresponding result of Exercise 8[11] shows that, in spite of the dissimilarity between the classical and the quantum-mechanical distributions-in-x of Fig. 23, the expected average of x^2 is the same for both. The inexactitude of x for the normal state is

$$\Delta_0 x = \sqrt{\mathrm{av}_0 x^2 - \mathrm{av}_0^2 x} = \sqrt{E_0 / k}. \qquad (19)$$

The distribution function of any dynamical variable that depends explicitly only on x can be calculated, for the normal state of the oscillator, by means of (14) and 24[11].

The distribution-in-p for the normal state. Let us consider next the momentum of a linear harmonic oscillator in the normal state. According to $\langle 2 \rangle$ we have, for example,

$$\mathrm{av}_0 p^s = \int \bar{\psi}_0 \left(-i\hbar \frac{\partial}{\partial x} \right)^s \psi_0 \, dx, \qquad (20)$$

that is,

$$\mathrm{av}_0 p^s = \frac{1}{a\pi^{\frac{1}{2}}} \int e^{-\frac{1}{2}\left(\frac{x}{a}\right)^2} \left(-i\hbar \frac{\partial}{\partial x} \right)^s e^{-\frac{1}{2}\left(\frac{x}{a}\right)^2} \, dx. \qquad (21)$$

Since ψ_0 is even in x, $\mathrm{av}_0 p^s$ vanishes whenever s is an odd positive integer, because the integrand is then odd in x. When $s = 2j$, where j is a positive integer, we have, in view of (20) and 17[16],

$$\mathrm{av}_0 p^{2j} = \int \bar{\psi}_0 \left(-i\hbar \frac{\partial}{\partial x} \right)^{2j} \psi_0 \, dx = k^j m^j \int \bar{\psi}_0 x^{2j} \psi_0 \, dx, \qquad (22)$$

that is,

$$\mathrm{av}_0 p^{2j} = k^j m^j \, \mathrm{av}_0 x^{2j}, \qquad (23)$$

so that, according to (17),

$$\mathrm{av}_0 p^{2j} = 1 \cdot 3 \cdot 5 \cdots (2j - 1) 2^{-j} b^{2j}, \qquad (24)$$

where

$$b = a\sqrt{km} = \sqrt[4]{km\hbar^2}. \tag{25}$$

In particular, $\mathrm{av}_0\, p^2 = \tfrac{1}{2}b^2 = \tfrac{1}{2}\hbar\sqrt{km}$, that is,

$$\mathrm{av}_0\, p^2 = mE_0, \tag{26}$$

a result in agreement with the corresponding classical result of Exercise 9^{11}. The inexactitude of p for the normal state is

$$\Delta_0 p = \sqrt{\mathrm{av}_0 p^2 - \mathrm{av}_0^2 p} = \sqrt{mE_0}. \tag{27}$$

The product of the respective inexactitudes of x and p for the normal state is of interest. From (19) and (27) we get

$$\Delta_0 x\, \Delta_0 p = E_0\, \sqrt{m/k}, \tag{28}$$

in agreement with the corresponding classical result of Exercise 9^{11}; but, eliminating E_0 by means of (7), we find that

$$\Delta_0 x\, \Delta_0 p = \frac{h}{4\pi}, \tag{29}$$

so that $\Delta_0 x\, \Delta_0 p$ of a linear harmonic oscillator is a universal constant independent of m and k.

We now proceed to find the distribution-in-p, $P_0(p)$, for the normal state of the oscillator. Were $P_0(p)$ available, we could calculate $\mathrm{av}_0 p^s$ by the standard statistical method:

$$\mathrm{av}_0 p^s = \int_{-\infty}^{\infty} p^s P_0(p)\, dp. \tag{30}$$

Now, we do not know what $P_0(p)$ is, but we do know from (21) the values of (30) for all positive integral values of s:

$$\int_{-\infty}^{\infty} p^s P_0(p)\, dp = \begin{cases} 1 \cdot 3 \cdot 5 \,\cdots\, (2j-1)2^{-j}b^{2j} & \text{if } s = 2j, \\ 0 & \text{if } s = 2j+1. \end{cases} \tag{31}$$

In view of the resemblance of these formulas to those which we proved a moment ago for the coordinate x, that is

$$\int_{-\infty}^{\infty} x^s P_0(x)\, dx = \begin{cases} 1 \cdot 3 \cdot 5 \,\cdots\, (2j-1)2^{-j}a^{2j} & \text{if } s = 2j \\ 0 & \text{if } s = 2j+1, \end{cases} \tag{32}$$

$P_0(p)$ is found rather simply. Indeed, we note that, if we use for $P_0(p)$ in (31) the function obtained from $P_0(x)$ by writing p for x and b for a, then (31) will follow from (32); and [since, in view of the uniqueness theorem of §11, $P_0(p)$ is presumably determined by Equations (31) uniquely][7] we conclude that the distribution-in-p for an oscillator in the normal state is

$$P_0(p) = \frac{1}{b\pi^{\frac{1}{2}}} e^{-\left(\frac{p}{b}\right)^2}. \tag{33}$$

The distribution (33), superimposed on the classical distribution-in-p of an oscillator of energy E_0 obtained from 26^{11}, is shown in Fig. 24. The two distributions are quite different from each other; in particular, quantum mechanically, a precise measurement of the momentum of an oscillator of energy E_0 may yield any value between $-\infty$ and ∞, while classically only values between $-\sqrt{2mE_0}$ and $\sqrt{2mE_0}$ are possible.

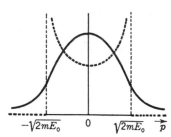

$-\sqrt{2mE_0}$ 0 $\sqrt{2mE_0}$ $\vec{p}$

Fig. 24. The distribution-in-p of a linear harmonic oscillator in the normal state (thick solid curve).

The method used above for computing $P_0(p)$ is effective only because of the symmetry of the Hamiltonian of the oscillator in x and p; for other systems a comparison of the averages of powers of p with those of powers of x is not very helpful, and in §27 we shall develop a general method by which the distribution-in-p can be calculated directly from the Schroedinger function for any one-dimensional system.

Before (33) was established, we had only one way to calculate the expected average of a function of p for the normal state, that is, by using $\langle 2 \rangle$:

$$\text{av}_0 f(p) = \int_{-\infty}^{\infty} \bar{\psi}_0 f\left(-i\hbar \frac{\partial}{\partial x}\right) \psi_0 \, dx; \tag{34}$$

but now we have an alternative method that will yield the same result:

$$\text{av}_0 f(p) = \frac{1}{b\pi^{\frac{1}{2}}} \int_{-\infty}^{\infty} f(p) e^{-\left(\frac{p}{b}\right)^2} \, dp. \tag{35}$$

[7] For a proof of the validity of the uniqueness theorem in the present case, see Uspensky, page 383.

The distribution function of any dynamical variable that depends explicitly only on p can be computed, for the normal state of the oscillator, by means of (33) and 24^{11}.

If a dynamical variable depends on both x and p, then its average and the averages of all of its powers can be computed for the normal state of the oscillator by means of $\langle 2 \rangle$ and (12); consequently, the distribution function of every dynamical variable that depends only on x and p can be found, at least in principle. The phase factors of ψ_0 and $\bar{\psi}_0$ cancel in $\langle 2 \rangle$, and therefore the average of any dynamical variable is free from any ambiguity. The time factors of ψ_0 and $\bar{\psi}_0$ also cancel in $\langle 2 \rangle$, so that the expected average of any dynamical variable not involving t explicitly is independent of t, and hence the respective distribution functions of all such variables are independent of t; for this reason, the state ψ_0 is called a *stationary state*.

Summary. We began the study of the normal state of an oscillator by translating into mathematical terms suitable for further calculations by the Schroedinger method the statement that the energy of the oscillator is certainly E_0 ; that is, assuming the energy to be certainly E_0 , we identified the particular Schroedinger function ψ_0 that would properly summarize this information. The amplitude of the distribution-in-x being then known, we discussed the distribution-in-x and computed the averages of the powers of x. We turned next to the momentum, calculated the averages of the powers of p by means of our fundamental equation $\langle 2 \rangle$, and, finding these averages to be very similar to the averages of the powers of x, were able to infer the distribution-in-p for the normal state. Our illustrations of the manipulation of the Schroedinger function in the course of computations of the physical properties of a state were chosen partly on account of their mathematical simplicity, but our examples are perhaps sufficient to show how the answering of any question relative to the outcome of any experiment, to be performed on an oscillator in the normal state and designed to measure the value of any dynamical variable not depending explicitly on t, can be reduced to a definite mathematical problem by the straightforward application of $\langle 2 \rangle$.

The questions that we treated are analogous to those considered from the classical standpoint in Exercises 8^{11} and 9^{11}. The mathematical methods that we employed in the classical theory and in the quantum theory of these analogous problems cannot very well be compared; they are different, and little more can be said. But the respective physical conclusions drawn on the basis of the two theories can be compared in detail; we made some comparisons and found illustrations of fundamental incompatibility, such as quantization of the energy, the possibility that a precise measurement of x will yield a value lying outside the classical limits, and so forth, as well as illustrations of agreement, such as the fact that both the classical and the quantum-mechanical distributions-in-x are stationary, that Δx is the same for both distributions, and so on. We shall now contrast the physical background used in the classical treatment of these problems with that employed in the quantum-mechanical calculations.

In Exercises 8^{11} and 9^{11}, the classical treatment of an oscillator was based on the premise that the *only* information available about the condition of the oscillator is that the energy is certainly E; that is, we assumed that

(a) the energy is certainly E,

(b) no further information is available.

It was quite essential to make the assumption (b) explicitly, because information relevant to the problem and consistent with (a) could be given in addition to (a) in such a way as to lead to results quite different from those that we derived from (a) *and* (b); for example, if, in addition to (a), we were given the values of x and p at some instant t_0 , our conclusions would be expressed in terms of certainties rather than probabilities. In other words, (a) does not alone constitute a maximal set of conditions from the classical viewpoint.

The classical distribution-in-x, 25^{11}, was derived from (a) and (b) along lines such as these: it follows from (a) and from the classical laws of motion that the particle moves on a perfectly definite schedule between the points $-\sqrt{2E/k}$ and $\sqrt{2E/k}$, and has a calculable speed at every point of its path; it follows from (b) that we are not able to set up any connection between the schedule of the particle and the time as recorded by our laboratory clock; consequently, the probability that the particle will be found in dx at x at the time t is proportional to the time spent by the particle in dx at x in the course of its motion and is independent of the instant t at which the measurement is to be made; this probability is therefore inversely proportional to the known speed with which the particle passes the point x. This reasoning yields the distribution-in-x, and similar reasoning can be used in finding the distribution functions of other dynamical variables.

The quantum-mechanical treatment of the problem proceeded along quite different lines. We assumed that

(a′) the energy is certainly E_0,

and showed how any physical question regarding the oscillator could be answered by straightforward mathematical means and without ambiguity on the basis of this information alone. No references to details of the motion were made; it was not implied that the particle moves on any particular schedule, or that its speed varies in any definite way; in short, no relation of the classical type $x = F(t)$ was presumed to exist between the position of the particle and the time. [Except in the case of heavier particles, when many of its results merge into those of classical theory, quantum mechanics does not yield results of the type $x = F(t)$, and hence does not permit us to form mental pictures of the manner in which a particle behaves between observations.]

The fact that no assumption similar to (b) was necessary before we could proceed with the calculations and carry them out to the end implies that no assumption relevant to the problem, compatible with (a′), and not included in (a′) can be made in the quantum theory of the oscillator. This result holds also when E_0 is replaced by E_n, and means that, according to quantum mechanics, it is not possible experimentally to establish the fact that the energy of the oscillator is a certainty, and (still being sure of the energy) to get further information regarding the particle, information that cannot be deduced from the knowledge of the energy alone. For example, according to quantum mechanics, it is impossible to make sure experimentally that at $t = t_0$ the energy of the oscillator is certainly E_0 and that the particle is at that instant in a definite position. Thus, from the quantum-mechanical standpoint, the condition (a′) is alone a maximal set of conditions for the oscillator.

Excited states. States of the oscillator for which its energy is respectively certainly $E_1 = \frac{3}{2}h\nu_c$, $E_2 = \frac{5}{2}h\nu_c$, and so forth, are called its *first excited state*, its *second excited state*, and so on. Any state for which the energy is a certainty is called an *energy* *state.* The state of the oscillator for which the energy is certainly $E_n = (n + \frac{1}{2})h\nu_c$ is called the nth energy state or the nth *quantum state*. A state for which the value of a dynamical variable α is a certainty is often called an *eigenstate* of α; energy states are thus eigenstates of the Hamiltonian.

The argument used at the beginning of this section to identify the ψ-function describing the normal state leads to the conclusion that the normalized ψ-function describing the state for which the energy of the oscillator is certainly E_n is the function ψ_n given by 7^{16}. Graphs[8] of the right-hand halves of the distributions-in-x $\bar{\psi}_n\psi_n$ for $n = 0, 1, 2, 3$, and 4 are shown in Fig. 25; the first diagram

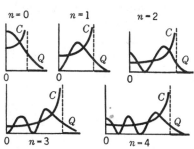

in this figure is a part of Fig. 23. The corresponding classical distributions are also shown, and it is seen that, for the higher values of the quantum number n, the quantum-mechanical distribution is more like the corresponding classical one, and that, in particular, the probability of finding the particle outside the classical limits is smaller for higher energies. An interesting characteristic of the excited states is the *nodes* of

Fig. 25. Distributions-in-x for energy states of a linear harmonic oscillator. The quantum-mechanical distributions are marked Q; the classical distributions for the same m, k, and E are marked C.

the distribution-in-x, that is, values of x at which the distribution-in-x is zero. They signify impossible values of x, that is, places at which the particle can never be found by a precise position measurement, although it may be found on either side of a node. These nodes may serve to emphasize the fact that quantum mechanics concerns itself with results of observations, and not with mental pictures of the behavior of a particle between observations.

In the exercises below, we let $P_n(\alpha)$, $\mathrm{av}_n \, \alpha$, and $\Delta_n\alpha$ denote,

---

[8] Taken from E. U. Condon and P. M. Morse's *Quantum Mechanics*, page 51. New York: McGraw-Hill Book Co., 1929.

[9] 'Imposible value' is a stronger restriction than 'value having zero probability,' since, in the case of a continuous distribution, any preassigned value has zero probability.

respectively, the distribution-in-α, the average of α, and the inexactitude of α for the nth energy state of the oscillator.

Exercises

1. Show that, if a linear harmonic oscillator is in its normal state, then the probability of finding the particle outside the classical limits is approximately 16 per cent.

2. Show that, if a linear harmonic oscillator is in its normal state, then the expected average of the dynamical variable xp is zero.

3. Show that the condition that the state of an oscillator be specified by the Schroedinger function ψ_n in 7^{16} is, apart from normalization, both necessary and sufficient in order that the energy of the oscillator be certainly E_n .

4. Show that

$$P_n(x) = \frac{1}{a2^n n! \, \pi^{\frac{1}{2}}} \left[H_n \left(\frac{x}{a} \right) \right]^2 e^{-\left(\frac{x}{a} \right)^2}, \qquad (36)$$

and that the n nodes of $P_n(x)$ lying at finite values of x lie within the classical limits of x.

5. Show that $\mathrm{av}_n x^4 = 3(n^2 + n + \frac{1}{2})E_n^2/2(n + \frac{1}{2})^2 k^2$, and note that, when $n \to \infty$, this result approaches the corresponding classical result of Exercise 8^{11}. *Hint:* use 53^4 twice over and remember the orthogonality of the ψ's.

6. Show that if j is a positive integer or zero, then $\mathrm{av}_n p^{2j+1} = \mathrm{av}_n x^{2j+1} = 0$, and $\mathrm{av}_n p^{2j} = m^j k^j \mathrm{av}_n x^{2j}$. *Hint:* note 17^{16}.

7. The function ψ_n in 7^{16} satisfies the Schroedinger equation $-\kappa^{-1}\psi_n'' + \frac{1}{2}kx^2 \psi_n = E_n\psi_n$. Multiply every term of this equation on the left by $\bar{\psi}_n$, integrate with respect to x from $-\infty$ to ∞, and show that

$$\frac{1}{2m} \, \mathrm{av}_n p^2 + \frac{1}{2}k \, \mathrm{av}_n x^2 = E_n'. \qquad (37)$$

Equation (37) is, in a sense, the nearest approach possible in quantum mechanics to the classical equation (15).

8. Using (37) and the results of Exercise 6, show that $\mathrm{av}_n x^2 = E_n/k$, $\mathrm{av}_n p^2 = mE_n$, and $\Delta_n x \, \Delta_n p = (2n + 1)h/4\pi$; compare with the corresponding classical results of Exercises 8^{11} and 9^{11}.

9. Show that the respective expected averages of the kinetic and the potential energies of an oscillator in the nth energy state are $\frac{1}{2}E_n$ each; compare Exercise 11^{11}.

10. Let ξ be the dynamical variable $p/\sqrt{mk}$. Recall Exercise 6 and show that $\mathrm{av}_n \xi^s = \mathrm{av}_n x^s$ for every positive integral value of s. Infer $P_n(\xi)$, and show that

$$P_n(p) = \frac{1}{b2^n n! \, \pi^{\frac{1}{2}}} \left[H_n \left(\frac{p}{b} \right) \right]^2 e^{-\left(\frac{p}{b} \right)^2}, \qquad (38)$$

where b is (25), and that the n nodes of $P_n(p)$ lying at finite values of p lie within the classical limits of p.

11. Show that if both (36) and (38) be expressed in terms of m, k, and

E_n , rather than in terms of a and b, then (36) can be transformed into (38) by exactly the same substitutions that carry 25^{11} into 26^{11}.

12. Equation (15) implies that p can have a value outside the limits $-\sqrt{2mE}$ and $\sqrt{2mE}$ only if x is imaginary. An apparatus designed to measure the position of a particle, for example, a microscope, will obviously never yield an imaginary result. How do these comments bear upon the feasibility of the quantum-mechanical claim (illustrated, for example, by Fig. 24) that the momentum of a linear harmonic oscillator may, upon a precise measurement, be found to lie outside the classical limits of p?

13. Use (33) to recompute the value of $\Delta_0 p$ given in (27).

14. Consider 2^{17} under the assumption that α is $\langle 4 \rangle$ and ψ is not quadratically integrable, and show that in the study of the oscillator we may restrict ourselves to quadratically integrable ψ's.

19. Composition of States

The discussion of §18 was concerned with a linear harmonic oscillator whose energy is a certainty. We shall next consider cases in which the energy is not a certainty, and, in preparation for a more general treatment, shall take up from the quantum-mechanical viewpoint the problem studied classically in Exercise 13^{11}. The problem is to make calculations regarding the outcomes of various experiments to be performed on an oscillator prepared as follows: we instruct a person to toss a well-balanced coin and then to adjust the energy of an oscillator to be certainly E_I if heads come up, and to be certainly E_{II} , $E_{II} \neq E_I$, if tails do; he, in our absence, does as instructed and then returns the oscillator to us without comment. We shall assume that, whatever the energy is once adjusted to be, the oscillator will retain it indefinitely (§31). Both E_I and E_{II} must, of course, now be quantum-mechanically permissible energy values of the oscillator.

The energy of our oscillator is either E_I or E_{II} , but, on the basis of only the information given above, we cannot decide which. A suitable experiment would reveal what the energy actually is; we wish, however, to investigate the properties of the oscillator before getting any information besides that given above, and consequently we must allow for both alternatives.

Our first concern is to describe the state of the oscillator by an appropriate Schroedinger function; therefore, we enumerate the conditions which this function, to be denoted by ψ, must satisfy. In the first place, ψ, being a Schroedinger function describing a state of an oscillator, must satisfy the second Schroedinger equation

$$H\psi = i\hbar \frac{\partial}{\partial t}\psi, \qquad\qquad \langle 1 \rangle$$

where $H = -\kappa^{-1}\partial^2/\partial x^2 + \frac{1}{2}kx^2$. Secondly, ψ must not be an eigenfunction of H, that is, the inequality

$$H\psi \neq \text{constant} \times \psi \qquad\qquad \langle 2 \rangle$$

must hold, because otherwise ψ would specify a state for which the result of an energy measurement is a certainty, while the energy of our oscillator is definitely uncertain. Further, in view of theorem 1 of §17 and the result of Exercise 14[18], we may take ψ to be normalized:

$$\int \bar{\psi}\psi \, dx = 1. \qquad\qquad (3)$$

We next recall that in the classical treatment of the problem we concluded that, for the state of the oscillator in question,

$$\text{av } E^j = \frac{1}{2}(E_{\mathrm{I}}^j + E_{\mathrm{II}}^j), \qquad j = 0, 1, 2, 3, \cdots . \quad (4)$$

The infinite set of equations (4) was obtained essentially from probability considerations and without reference to mechanics, so that we may expect it to hold in quantum mechanics as well as in classical theory. Now, when ψ is normalized, the Schroedinger expectation formula gives $\int \bar{\psi}H^j\psi \, dx$ for $\text{av}_\psi E^j$; therefore, if Equations (4) are to hold in the quantum-mechanical case, our ψ must satisfy the infinite set of equations

$$\int \bar{\psi}H^j\psi \, dx = \frac{1}{2}(E_{\mathrm{I}}^j + E_{\mathrm{II}}^j), \qquad j = 0, 1, 2, 3, \cdots . \quad \langle 5 \rangle$$

The problem of specifying the state of our oscillator by a Schroedinger function has now been stated in mathematical terms: the ψ that we need is a solution of $\langle 1 \rangle$, $\langle 2 \rangle$, (3), and $\langle 5 \rangle$. We shall not attempt at this point to deduce ψ from these conditions, but shall merely verify that a certain function, to be written down presently, satisfies them all.

Let ψ_{I} be a properly time-dependent and normalized eigenfunction of H belonging to the eigenvalue E_{I}, so that

$$H\psi_{\mathrm{I}} = E_{\mathrm{I}}\psi_{\mathrm{I}}, \qquad H\psi_{\mathrm{I}} = i\hbar \frac{\partial}{\partial t}\psi_{\mathrm{I}}, \qquad \int \bar{\psi}_{\mathrm{I}}\psi_{\mathrm{I}} \, dx = 1. \quad \langle 6 \rangle$$

The function ψ_{I} is thus one of the functions listed in 7^{16}; the phases of the members of 7^{16} will be assumed to be fixed by some suitable convention. Similarly, let ψ_{II} be a properly time-dependent and normalized eigenfunction of H belonging to the eigenvalue E_{II}, so that

$$H\psi_{II} = E_{II}\psi_{II}, \qquad H\psi_{II} = i\hbar\frac{\partial}{\partial t}\psi_{II}, \qquad \int \bar{\psi}_{II}\psi_{II}\,dx = 1; \quad \langle 7\rangle$$

ψ_{II} is another member of 7^{16}, and in view of the orthogonality of the set 7^{16} we have

$$\int \bar{\psi}_I\psi_{II}\,dx = \int \bar{\psi}_{II}\psi_I\,dx = 0. \tag{8}$$

We now claim that the following Schroedinger function, a linear combination of ψ_I and ψ_{II}, satisfies $\langle 1\rangle$, $\langle 2\rangle$, (3), and $\langle 5\rangle$:

$$\psi = \frac{1}{\sqrt{2}}e^{i\delta_I}\psi_I + \frac{1}{\sqrt{2}}e^{i\delta_{II}}\psi_{II}, \tag{9}$$

where δ_I and δ_{II} are any two real numbers independent of x and t; the verification of this claim will be based on Equations $\langle 6\rangle$, $\langle 7\rangle$, and (8). First,

$$\begin{aligned}
H\psi &= \frac{1}{\sqrt{2}}e^{i\delta_I}H\psi_I + \frac{1}{\sqrt{2}}e^{i\delta_{II}}H\psi_{II} \\
&= \frac{1}{\sqrt{2}}e^{i\delta_I}i\hbar\frac{\partial}{\partial t}\psi_I + \frac{1}{\sqrt{2}}e^{i\delta_{II}}i\hbar\frac{\partial}{\partial t}\psi_{II} \\
&= i\hbar\frac{\partial}{\partial t}\left(\frac{1}{\sqrt{2}}e^{i\delta_I}\psi_I + \frac{1}{\sqrt{2}}e^{i\delta_{II}}\psi_{II}\right) = i\hbar\frac{\partial}{\partial t}\psi, \quad \langle 10\rangle
\end{aligned}$$

so that $\langle 1\rangle$ holds. Secondly,

$$\begin{aligned}
H\psi &= \frac{1}{\sqrt{2}}e^{i\delta_I}H\psi_I + \frac{1}{\sqrt{2}}e^{i\delta_{II}}H\psi_{II} \\
&= \frac{1}{\sqrt{2}}e^{i\delta_I}E_I\psi_I + \frac{1}{\sqrt{2}}e^{i\delta_{II}}E_{II}\psi_{II}, \quad \langle 11\rangle
\end{aligned}$$

so that the inequality $\langle 2\rangle$ holds, since $E_I \neq E_{II}$. Finally,

$$\begin{aligned}
\int \bar{\psi}H^j\psi\,dx &= \tfrac{1}{2}\int (e^{-i\delta_I}\bar{\psi}_I + e^{-i\delta_{II}}\bar{\psi}_{II})\,H^j(e^{i\delta_I}\psi_I + e^{i\delta_{II}}\psi_{II})\,dx \\
&= \tfrac{1}{2}\int (e^{-i\delta_I}\bar{\psi}_I + e^{-i\delta_{II}}\bar{\psi}_{II})(e^{i\delta_I}H^j\psi_I + e^{i\delta_{II}}H^j\psi_{II})\,dx \\
&= \tfrac{1}{2}\int (e^{-i\delta_I}\bar{\psi}_I + e^{-i\delta_{II}}\bar{\psi}_{II})(e^{i\delta_I}E_I^j\psi_I + e^{i\delta_{II}}E_{II}^j\psi_{II})\,dx \\
&= \tfrac{1}{2}E_I^j\int \bar{\psi}_I\psi_I\,dx + \tfrac{1}{2}e^{-i\delta_I+i\delta_{II}}E_{II}^j\int \bar{\psi}_I\psi_{II}\,dx \\
&\qquad + \tfrac{1}{2}e^{-i\delta_{II}+i\delta_I}E_I^j\int \bar{\psi}_{II}\psi_I\,dx + \tfrac{1}{2}E_{II}^j\int \bar{\psi}_{II}\psi_{II}\,dx \\
&= \tfrac{1}{2}(E_I^j + E_{II}^j), \qquad\qquad\qquad\qquad\qquad \langle 12\rangle
\end{aligned}$$

and hence our ψ satisfies the infinite set of equations $\langle 5 \rangle$; Equation (3) is a special case of $\langle 12 \rangle$, obtained by letting $j = 0$.

It will be shown presently that no function other than (9) satisfies $\langle 1 \rangle$, $\langle 2 \rangle$, (3), and $\langle 5 \rangle$, and consequently we adopt (9) as the Schroedinger function describing the state of our oscillator. The Schroedinger function being available, calculations concerning the outcomes of various experiments on the oscillator can be carried out by the routine methods based on the Schroedinger expectation formula 2^{17}.

The special problem which we have been discussing, and to which we shall return in §22, was taken up by way of introduction, and is not of any particular interest in itself; it does show, however, that physical situations can arise in which the Schroedinger function is not an eigenfunction of the operator H, but a *linear combination* (or a *superposition*) of such eigenfunctions. If the Schroedinger function for a certain state of a system is a linear combination of Schroedinger functions for some other states of the system, we say that the former *state* is a *superposition* of the latter *states*; for example, the state of the oscillator discussed above is a superposition of two energy states, one of energy E_I and the other of energy E_{II}.

20. Resolution of States

The problem considered above was that of finding the Schroedinger function for a state which is known not to be an energy state, but for which the distribution-in-energy is known. We shall now turn to the converse problem: to find the distribution-in-energy for a state for which the Schroedinger function is known, but is not an eigenfunction of the operator associated with the Hamiltonian of the system. The solution will incidentally explain why the function ψ of §19 must have the form 9^{19}.

Let us assume then that the state of a linear harmonic oscillator is specified at the instant $t = 0$ by a Schroedinger function ψ^0 that is normalized,

$$\int \bar{\psi}^0 \psi^0 \, dx = 1, \qquad (1)$$

and that is not an eigenfunction of H; and let us calculate the probability, to be denoted by P_n, that a precise energy measurement to be made at the time t will yield the result $E_n =$

$(n + \frac{1}{2})h\nu_c$—according to quantum theory, results not of this form are impossible.

Since we are interested in the results of an experiment to be performed at the time t, we must first calculate the Schroedinger function for the time t; ψ^0 being given, this can be done by the method of §16. We have, in fact,

$$\psi = \sum_n c_n \psi_n, \qquad n = 0, 1, 2, \cdots, \quad (2)$$

where ψ_n is a properly time-dependent and normalized eigenfunction of H belonging to the eigenvalue E_n, listed in 7^{16}, and where $c_n = \int \bar{\psi}_n^0 \psi^0 \, dx$, ψ_n^0 being obtained from ψ_n by letting $t = 0$.

Now, if the respective absolute probabilities of the results E_0, E_1, E_2, and so forth, of an energy measurement to be made on our oscillator at the instant t are P_0, P_1, P_2, and so forth, then, according to the standard statistical formula 8^{11}, the average of the kth power of the energy at the instant t is

$$\sum_n E_n^k P_n, \quad n = 0, 1, 2, 3, \cdots. \quad (3)$$

On the other hand, the Schroedinger function being available, the average of E^k of our oscillator can be calculated by quantum-mechanical means; it is, in fact (since ψ^0 is normalized, so is ψ; see 18^{16}),

$$\int \bar{\psi} H^k \psi \, dx, \qquad \langle 4 \rangle$$

where ψ is given by (2) and where $H = -\kappa^{-1}\partial^2/\partial x^2 + \frac{1}{2}kx^2$. Both (3) and $\langle 4 \rangle$ represent the same number, and consequently the P's that we are seeking must satisfy the infinite set of equations

$$\sum_n E_n^k P_n = \int \bar{\psi} H^k \psi \, dx \qquad \text{for } k = 0, 1, 2, \cdots. \quad \langle 5 \rangle$$

Inserting the expansion (2) for ψ into $\langle 4 \rangle$, we get[10]

$$\int \bar{\psi} H^k \psi \, dx = \int \left(\sum_j \bar{c}_j \bar{\psi}_j \right) H^k \left(\sum_n c_n \psi_n \right) dx$$

$$= \int \left(\sum_j \bar{c}_j \bar{\psi}_j \right) \left(\sum_n c_n E_n^k \psi_n \right) dx = \sum_j \sum_n \bar{c}_j c_n E_n^k \int \bar{\psi}_j \psi_n \, dx; \quad \langle 6 \rangle$$

the integral of $\bar{\psi}_j \psi_n$ vanishes for $j \neq n$ and equals unity for $j = n$

---

[10] In the equations that follow, the summation indices all run through the values $0, 1, 2, 3, \cdots$.

because of the orthonormality of the ψ's, so that we are left with

$$\int \bar{\psi} H^k \psi \, dx = \sum_n E_n^k \mid c_n \mid^2, \tag{7}$$

and $\langle 5 \rangle$ becomes

$$\sum_n E_n^k P_n = \sum_n E_n^k \mid c_n \mid^2 \qquad \text{for } k = 0, 1, 2, \cdots. \tag{8}$$

The obvious solution of these equations is

$$P_n = \mid c_n \mid^2, \qquad\qquad n = 0, 1, 2, \cdots, \tag{9}$$

and, in view of the uniqueness theorem of §11, this is the only solution.

Thus the problem of calculating the distribution-in-energy for a state of the oscillator for which the Schroedinger function is known has been solved: *the probability that a precise energy measurement will yield the result E_n when the state is specified by a normalized Schroedinger function ψ equals the square of the modulus of the coefficient of ψ_n in the expansion of ψ in terms of the normalized eigenfunctions of H.* The process of expanding a given ψ in terms of the eigenfunctions of H is usually called *resolution* of the given state into energy states.

Summary. The physical information regarding the state of an oscillator may imply that its energy is a certainty; in this case, as was shown in §18, the state is to be specified by an eigenfunction of H; on the other hand, the physical information may imply that the energy is not a certainty—an illustration is the oscillator of §19—and in that case a superposition of eigenfunctions of H is necessary to specify the state. Conversely, if the state is specified by an eigenfunction of H, then, in view of the results of §17, the energy is a certainty; but if the state is specified by a ψ-function that is not an eigenfunction of H, then the result of measuring the energy is not a certainty, and the probability of getting any particular result can be computed by means of the theorem given in italics above.

Exercises

1. The function 9^{19} was written down without inquiry as to how it could be obtained. Show that the form 9^{19} follows from the theorem in italics above.

2. We instruct a person to toss a well-balanced die and to adjust the energy of an oscillator to be certainly E_{I} if the score is 1, to be certainly E_{II} if the score is 2 or 3, and to be certainly E_{III} if the score is 4, 5, or 6; he, in our absence, does as instructed and then returns the oscillator to us without comment. Set up the normalized Schroedinger function representing the state of the oscillator as defined by the information available to us, and enumerate the arbitrary features of this function.

3. Show that the condition 5^{19} includes the condition 2^{19}.

4. How does the choice of the phases of the ψ_n's used in (2) affect the P's in (9)? Compare Exercise 1^{16}.

5. How does the distribution-in-E given by (9) depend on t? Is the answer one that is to be expected from intuitive physical considerations?

6. Show that the P's given by (9) satisfy 2^{11}.

7. Show that the result of Exercise 3^{18} follows at once from (9).

21. Probability Packets

We shall now consider from the quantum-mechanical viewpoint a special case of the problem treated classically in Exercise 1^{12}, where we investigated the oscillator on the assumption that the precise values of x and p at $t = 0$ are unknown, but that the respective distributions in x and in p at $t = 0$ are Gaussian.

Were we to consider precisely the same problem from the quantum-mechanical standpoint, we would have to investigate first of all how the available information is to be summarized by means of a Schroedinger function; this we are not prepared to do, and we shall therefore confine ourselves to a rather special case, chosen principally on account of its mathematical simplicity. We shall, in fact, assume outright that the state of the oscillator is specified at $t = 0$ by the Schroedinger function

$$\psi^0 = \frac{1}{\sqrt{a\pi^{\frac{1}{2}}}} e^{-\frac{(x-x_0)^2}{2a^2}}, \tag{1}$$

where $x_0 \neq 0$, and where a is the constant $\sqrt[4]{\hbar^2/km}$ given in 9^{16}. The distribution-in-x of our oscillator at $t = 0$ is then

$$P^0(x) = \bar{\psi}^0 \psi^0 = \frac{1}{a\sqrt{\pi}} e^{-\frac{(x-x_0)^2}{a^2}} \tag{2}$$

Now, the average of p^s at $t = 0$ is

$$\int \bar{\psi}^0 \left(-i\hbar \frac{\partial}{\partial x}\right)^s \psi^0 dx$$

$$= \frac{1}{a\sqrt{\pi}} \int e^{-\frac{(x-x_0)^2}{2a^2}} \left(-i\hbar \frac{\partial}{\partial x}\right)^s e^{-\frac{(x-x_0)^2}{2a^2}} dx. \tag{3}$$

The change of variable from x to $y = x - x_0$ transforms the right side of (3) into

$$\frac{1}{a\sqrt{\pi}} \int e^{-\frac{1}{2}\left(\frac{y}{a}\right)^2} \left(-i\hbar\frac{\partial}{\partial y}\right)^s e^{-\frac{1}{2}\left(\frac{y}{a}\right)^2} dy. \qquad (4)$$

This integral is precisely the same as 21^{18}, so that the average of p^s at $t = 0$ is, for any s, the same as that for the normal state of the oscillator; consequently the distribution-in-p of our oscillator is, at $t = 0$, the same as that for an oscillator in the normal state, and in view of 33^{18} we have:

$$P^0(p) = \frac{1}{b\sqrt{\pi}} e^{-\left(\frac{p}{b}\right)^2}, \qquad (5)$$

where $b = \sqrt[4]{km\hbar^2}$.

Comparison of (2) and (5) with 5^{12} and 6^{12} shows that, having started with the ψ-function (1), we are treating essentially the problem of Exercise 1^{12}, except that instead of all four quantities x_0, Δ_x, p_0, and Δ_p, only one, namely, x_0, is left arbitrary, while the others are assigned the following values:

$$p_0 = 0, \qquad \Delta_x = a/\sqrt{2}, \qquad \Delta_p = b/\sqrt{2}. \qquad (6)$$

We note further that $\Delta_p^2 = \frac{1}{2}b^2 = \frac{1}{2}\hbar\sqrt{km} = \frac{1}{2}kma^2 = km\,\Delta_x^2$, so that the restriction of Exercise 3^{12} holds. Consequently, were we to treat classically the problem of an oscillator whose distributions in x and in p at $t = 0$ are (2) and (5), we would find them to be the packets

$$(20^{12}) \qquad P(x) = \frac{1}{a\sqrt{\pi}} e^{-\frac{(x - x_0\cos\omega t)^2}{a^2}}, \qquad (7)$$

and

$$(21^{12}) \qquad P(p) = \frac{1}{m\omega a\sqrt{\pi}} e^{-\frac{(p + x_0\omega m\sin\omega t)^2}{m^2\omega^2 a^2}}, \qquad (8)$$

where $\omega = \sqrt{k/m}$.

In order to find the corresponding quantum-mechanical distributions, we proceed to calculate the Schroedinger function for the time t, that is, to find that solution of the equation

$$H\psi = i\hbar\frac{\partial}{\partial t}\psi, \qquad (9)$$

where $H = -\kappa^{-1}\partial^2/\partial x^2 + \frac{1}{2}kx^2$, which equals our ψ^0 at $t = 0$.

To compute the required solution of $\langle 9 \rangle$ by the systematic method of §16, we set all the γ's in 7^{16} equal to zero,[11] in which case the normalized eigenfunctions of H at $t = 0$ are

$$\psi_n^0 = N_n H_n \left(\frac{x}{a}\right) e^{-\frac{1}{2}\left(\frac{x}{a}\right)^2}, \qquad n = 0, 1, 2, \cdots, \quad (10)$$

where $N_n = (a2^n n! \pi^{\frac{1}{2}})^{-\frac{1}{2}}$, and expand our ψ^0 in terms of the set (10):

$$\psi^0 = \sum_n c_n \psi_n^0 = \sum_n c_n N_n H_n \left(\frac{x}{a}\right) e^{-\frac{1}{2}\left(\frac{x}{a}\right)^2}, \quad n = 0, 1, 2, \cdots. \quad (11)$$

The step corresponding to that from 13^{16} to 14^{16} then yields the desired solution:

$$\psi = \sum_n c_n \psi_n = \sum_n c_n N_n H_n \left(\frac{x}{a}\right) e^{-\frac{1}{2}\left(\frac{x}{a}\right)^2} e^{-iE_n t/\hbar},$$

$$n = 0, 1, 2, \cdots, \quad (12)$$

where $E_n = (n + \frac{1}{2})h\nu_c$.

To get ψ explicitly, we must evaluate the c's in (11). According to 21^8, we have $c_n = \int \bar{\psi}_n^0 \psi^0 \, dx$; but, in view of the special form of our ψ^0 and the relation 43^4, actual integration in evaluating the c's can be avoided as follows. We write 43^4 as

$$\exp\left[-s^2 + \frac{2sx}{a} - \frac{x^2}{2a^2}\right] = \sum_n \frac{s^n}{n!} H_n \left(\frac{x}{a}\right) e^{-\frac{1}{2}\left(\frac{x}{a}\right)^2}, \quad (13)$$

and (1) as

$$\psi^0 = \frac{1}{\sqrt{a\pi^{\frac{1}{2}}}} \exp\left[-\frac{x_0^2}{4a^2}\right] \exp\left[-\frac{x_0^2}{4a^2} + \frac{x_0 x}{a^2} - \frac{x^2}{2a^2}\right]; \quad (14)$$

we then set $s = x_0/2a$ in (13), making its left side identical with the second exponential in (14), and substitute for this exponential the right side of (13); the result, when rearranged, is

$$\psi^0 = \sum_n \left[\frac{(x_0/a)^n}{\sqrt{2^n n!}} e^{-\left(\frac{x_0}{2a}\right)^2}\right]\left[N_n H_n \left(\frac{x}{a}\right) e^{-\frac{1}{2}\left(\frac{x}{a}\right)^2}\right], \quad (15)$$

and comparison with (11) shows that

$$c_n = \frac{(x_0/a)^n}{\sqrt{2^n n!}} e^{-\left(\frac{x_0}{2a}\right)^2}. \quad (16)$$

---

[11] This leads to a superficial simplification in the work and does not affect the results; see Exercises 1^{16} and 4^{20}.

The explicit form of (12) is consequently

$$\psi = \sum_n c_n \psi_n$$
$$= \sum_n \left[\frac{(x_0/a)^n}{\sqrt{2^n n!}} e^{-\left(\frac{x_0}{2a}\right)^2} \right] \left[N_n H_n \left(\frac{x}{a}\right) e^{-\frac{1}{2}\left(\frac{x}{a}\right)^2} e^{-iE_n t/\hbar} \right]. \quad (17)$$

The problem of finding that solution of $\langle 9 \rangle$ which reduces to our ψ^0 at $t = 0$ has now been solved explicitly: the desired solution is (17). The infinite series in (17) can, however, be readily summed. Since $E_n = (n + \frac{1}{2})\hbar\omega$, where $\omega = \sqrt{k/m}$, (17) can be written as

$$\psi = \frac{1}{\sqrt{a\pi^{\frac{1}{2}}}} \exp\left(-\frac{x_0^2}{4a^2} - \frac{i\omega t}{2}\right)$$
$$\sum_n \frac{1}{n!} \left(\frac{x_0}{2a} e^{-i\omega t}\right)^n H_n\left(\frac{x}{a}\right) e^{-\frac{1}{2}\left(\frac{x}{a}\right)^2}; \quad (18)$$

the summation in (18) is of the same form as that in (13) and can be eliminated by means of (13) with $s = (x_0/2a) \exp(-i\omega t)$; the result, when rearranged, is

$$\psi = \frac{1}{\sqrt{a\pi^{\frac{1}{2}}}} \exp\left(-\frac{x_0^2}{4a^2} - \frac{i\omega t}{2} - \frac{x_0^2}{4a^2} e^{-2i\omega t} + \frac{x_0 x}{a^2} e^{-i\omega t} - \frac{x^2}{2a^2}\right). \quad (19)$$

Lest the mathematical steps that resulted in (19) confuse the reader as to what the main object of our calculation has been, we shall repeat that, being given that at $t = 0$ the Schroedinger function describing the state of our oscillator is (1), we computed the Schroedinger function ψ describing the state at the time t. To do this, we had to find that solution of $\langle 9 \rangle$ which reduces to our ψ^0 at $t = 0$, and this solution, when simplified in appearance, turned out to be (19). The procedure used in finding ψ is really immaterial; were we able to guess that the solution of $\langle 9 \rangle$ which reduces to ψ^0 at $t = 0$ is (18), our aim would have been accomplished. In fact, we used the systematic procedure of §16, and, besides, the special form of our ψ^0 and the relation 43[4] enabled us to carry out the calculations with relatively little labor and to obtain the solution in a closed form rather than in the form of an infinite series.

The Schroedinger function for the time t now being known, we are ready to make calculations concerning the behavior of our oscillator at any time. We can, for example, compute the distribution-in-x of the particle at the instant t: multiplying (19) by its complex conjugate, we get

$$P(x) = \bar{\psi}\psi = \frac{1}{a\sqrt{\pi}} e^{-\frac{(x - x_0 \cos\omega t)^2}{a^2}}. \quad (20)$$

This result is identical with (7), so that, for the special case under consideration, classical mechanics and quantum theory agree insofar as the probability packet describing the position of the oscillator at any time is concerned, a conclusion that appears remarkable in view of the wide differences between the classical and quantum-mechanical concepts and methods employed in the study of this problem. Note that in investigating the behavior of the x-packet classically we used the simultaneous distribution-in-x-and-in-p of the oscillator, while in the quantum-mechanical treatment no recourse to such a simultaneous distribution was made.

The quantum-mechanical distribution-in-p for the state (19) also agrees with the corresponding classical distribution, namely, (8); the proof will be postponed until we develop in §27 a direct method for computing distributions-in-p from Schroedinger functions.

Although (19) presents ψ in a simpler form than does (17), the expression (17) is of greater interest in calculations concerning the energy of our oscillator, since (17) displays explicitly the expansion coefficients c_n. If $x_0 \neq 0$, the Schroedinger function (1) is not an eigenfunction of H, and consequently the energy of our oscillator is not a certainty; and, according to the theorem of §20, the probability that a precise energy measurement made at any time will yield the result $E_n = (n + \frac{1}{2})h\nu_c$ is

$$| c_n |^2 = \frac{(x_0/a)^{2n}}{2^n n!} e^{-\frac{1}{2}\left(\frac{x_0}{a}\right)^2} \qquad (21)$$

Exercises

1. Verify by direct substitution that (19) satisfies ⟨9⟩ and that it reduces to (1) at $t = 0$.

2. Verify by a straighforward summation that (as is to be expected from the general result of Exercise 6²⁰) the probabilities (21) add up to unity.

3. Assume that x_0/a in (1) is large compared to unity and show that then the most probable result of an energy measurement is that value of $E_n = (n + \frac{1}{2})h\nu_c$ which lies nearest to $\frac{1}{2}kx_0^2$. Show also, using the first term of Stirling's formula for factorials of large integers $[n! = \sqrt{2\pi n}\, n^n e^{-n}(1 + n^{-1}/12 + n^{-2}/288 - \cdots)]$, that the probability of the most probable result is approximately $\pi^{-\frac{1}{2}}a/x_0$. Can two or more possible values of the energy of our oscillator be equally probable?

4. Show that the average of the energy of an oscillator in the state (19) is $\frac{1}{2}h\nu_c + \frac{1}{2}kx_0^2$; note that this result is greater than $E_0 = \frac{1}{2}h\nu_c$, in agreement with the conclusion of Exercise 17¹¹.

5. Explain why the following argument is fallacious: "At $t = t' = (4\nu_c)^{-1}$, the distribution-in-x (20) is identical with the distribution-in-x 14^{18} for the normal state of the oscillator; hence the oscillator whose state is specified at $t = 0$ by (1) is in the normal state at $t = t'$, and a precise energy measurement made at the instant t' is certain to yield the result $E_0 = \frac{1}{2}h\nu_c$."

6. Consider the state obtained by letting $x_0 = 0$ in (1); in particular, contrast the conclusions concerning the energy with the classical results of Exercise 4^{12}.

7. Let the state of an oscillator be specified at $t = 0$ by the Schroedinger function $(d\pi^{\frac{1}{2}})^{-\frac{1}{2}} \exp(-x^2/2d^2)$, where $d \neq \sqrt[4]{h^2/km}$, that is, $d \neq a$. Show that then the values $E_n = (n + \frac{1}{2})h\nu_c$ with n an *odd* integer cannot be results of a precise energy measurement.

8. Show that the classical theorem of Exercise 5^{12} holds in quantum theory.

22. Coherent and Incoherent Superpositions of States

Let us return for a moment to the state

$$(9^{19}) \qquad \psi = \frac{1}{\sqrt{2}} e^{i\delta_{\mathrm{I}}} \psi_{\mathrm{I}} + \frac{1}{\sqrt{2}} e^{i\delta_{\mathrm{II}}} \psi_{\mathrm{II}}. \qquad (1)$$

Here ψ_{I} and ψ_{II} are free from any arbitrariness, but the real constants δ_{I} and δ_{II} are both arbitrary; in particular, the constant $\delta_{\mathrm{I}} - \delta_{\mathrm{II}}$, the *relative phase* of the energy states ψ_{I} and ψ_{II}, is arbitrary. A superposition involving arbitrary relative phases is called an *incoherent* superposition. Incoherent superposition arises in connection with states specified by sets of conditions less stringent than maximal sets.

In dealing with incoherent superpositions, it is sometimes necessary to average over the arbitrary relative phases when computing theoretical data for comparison with experiment; to illustrate, we shall consider the distribution-in-x for the state (1). Recalling that $\psi_{\mathrm{I}} = f_{\mathrm{I}}(x)e^{-iE_{\mathrm{I}}t/\hbar}$ and $\psi_{\mathrm{II}} = f_{\mathrm{II}}(x)e^{-iE_{\mathrm{II}}t/\hbar}$, where f_{I} and f_{II} are free from any arbitrariness, we get

$$\bar{\psi}\psi = \frac{1}{2}(\bar{\psi}_{\mathrm{I}}\psi_{\mathrm{I}} + \bar{\psi}_{\mathrm{II}}\psi_{\mathrm{II}}) + \frac{1}{2}\left[\bar{f}_{\mathrm{I}}(x)f_{\mathrm{II}}(x) \exp i\left(\frac{E_{\mathrm{I}} - E_{\mathrm{II}}}{\hbar}t\right.\right.$$

$$\left.\left. + \delta_{\mathrm{II}} - \delta_{\mathrm{I}}\right) + \bar{f}_{\mathrm{II}}(x)f_{\mathrm{I}}(x) \exp i\left(\frac{E_{\mathrm{II}} - E_{\mathrm{I}}}{\hbar}t + \delta_{\mathrm{I}} - \delta_{\mathrm{II}}\right)\right]. \qquad (2)$$

The first term in (2) is independent of t, but the terms in brackets involve t explicitly; yet the question What is the distribution-in-x when our laboratory clock reads t? cannot be answered with certainty because the relative phase $\delta_I - \delta_{II}$ is involved in the bracketed terms in essentially the same way as t, and because the physical information that led us to adopt (1) as the proper Schroedinger function provides no clue as to what the value of $\delta_I - \delta_{II}$ should be. The dependence of (2) on t is therefore only formal. The best we can do in estimating the distribution-in-x at the time t is to average the bracketed terms over all possible values of $\delta_I - \delta_{II}$, regarded as equally likely. Now, the average of $\exp i(\delta_I - \delta_{II})$ calculated in this manner is just the average of all complex numbers of modulus unity (that is, zero), so that, upon averaging, the bracketed terms in (2) vanish. The estimate of the distribution-in-x at the time t is consequently

$$\tfrac{1}{2}(\bar{\psi}_I \psi_I + \bar{\psi}_{II} \psi_{II}) \tag{3}$$

and is independent of t. Note that (3) is just what we would get by using the quantum-mechanical $P_I(x)$ and $P_{II}(x)$ in the classical formula for $P(x)$ given in Exercise 13[11].

Superpositions, such as 17[21], in which the relative phases of the component states are fixed are called *coherent*; for a state that is a coherent superposition of energy states of different energies the distribution-in-x is necessarily nonstationary. Further remarks on coherent superposition will be made in §27.

Exercise

1. Discuss the distribution-in-x of the oscillator of Exercise 2[20].

23. Heisenberg Inequalities

In the preceding sections we illustrated how the physical properties of an oscillator can be investigated from the standpoint of quantum mechanics when it is known that the energy of the oscillator is a certainty, or when the information regarding its state refers to the values of x and p at a certain instant of time but does not provide the initial conditions of the motion with precision; and we compared the quantum-mechanical results with those given under analogous circumstances by the classical theory. We shall finally consider the quantum-mechanical status of the problem of the motion of the oscillator when the information regarding its state provides the precise values x_0 and p_0 of the coordinate x and the momentum p at the instant t_0; and we shall find that, in quantum mechanics, this fundamental problem of the classical theory of the oscillator is divested of physical content. Our arguments will not be restricted to the oscillator and will apply to any one-dimensional system.

We shall begin by assuming that the following converse of theorem 3 of §17 is true: *If the result of a precise measurement of the dynamical variable* α *is certain to be the number* a, *then the* ψ-*function describing the state of the system is an eigenfunction of the operator* α *belonging to the eigenvalue* a. Now, the information that the values of x and p at the instant t_0 are precisely x_0 and p_0 means that a precise simultaneous measurement of x and p at this instant is certain to yield the results x_0 and p_0. In the light of the theorem stated above, the ψ-function describing the state of the system at $t = t_0$ must therefore be a simultaneous eigenfunction of the operators associated with the dynamical variables x and p; but according to Exercise 5^6 these operators do not have eigenfunctions in common because their commutator is a non-vanishing constant. Consequently, the statement that the position and momentum of a particle are known simultaneously with unlimited precision cannot be translated into the mathematical terms of quantum mechanics, and, if we are to regard quantum mechanics as a good physical theory, no physical content can be ascribed to this statement.

The general argument just given relies on the theorem stated above in italics, a theorem, which we have not proved.[12] We shall therefore present an alternative detailed argument, which the reader can verify step by step, and which, incidentally, shows how near we can come, so to speak, to a precise simultaneous specification of x and p in quantum theory.

Let a state of an arbitrary one-dimensional system at an arbitrary instant of time be specified by a normalized Schroedinger function ψ, so that at this instant

$$\text{av } x = \int \bar{\psi} x \psi \, dx \qquad \text{av } x^2 = \int \bar{\psi} x^2 \psi \, dx \qquad (1)$$

$$\text{av } p = -i\hbar \int \bar{\psi} \psi' \, dx \qquad \text{av } p^2 = -\hbar^2 \int \bar{\psi} \psi'' \, dx. \qquad (2)$$

We assume that all the integrals above exist for the ψ in question, so that each quantity enumerated above has a definite finite

---

[12] We have, however, proved special cases in §18.

numerical value; integration by parts then yields the following relations:

$$\int \bar{\psi}'\psi' \, dx = -\int \bar{\psi}\psi'' \, dx \tag{3}$$

$$\int \psi\bar{\psi}' \, dx = -\int \bar{\psi}\psi' \, dx \tag{4}$$

$$\int x(\psi\bar{\psi}' + \bar{\psi}\psi') \, dx = \int x\frac{d}{dx}(\bar{\psi}\psi) \, dx = -\int \bar{\psi}\psi \, dx. \tag{5}$$

Our proof will consist in writing down the obvious inequality (6) and deducing from it the inequality (13) that has an immediate physical significance;[13] more direct proofs of (13) are less elementary. We begin with the inequality

$$|\,\psi' + (\alpha x + \beta + i\delta)\psi \,|^2 \ge 0, \tag{6}$$

where ψ is the Schroedinger function in question, and where α, β, and δ are real constants that for the present we leave arbitrary. We then rewrite (6) as

$$\bar{\psi}'\psi' + \alpha x(\psi\bar{\psi}' + \bar{\psi}\psi') + \beta(\psi\bar{\psi}' + \bar{\psi}\psi') + i\delta(\psi\bar{\psi}' - \bar{\psi}\psi')$$
$$+ \alpha^2 x^2 \bar{\psi}\psi + 2\alpha\beta x\bar{\psi}\psi + (\beta^2 + \delta^2)\bar{\psi}\psi \ge 0, \tag{7}$$

integrate (7), and, using (3), (4), and (5), write the result as

$$-\int \bar{\psi}\psi'' \, dx - \alpha \int \bar{\psi}\psi \, dx - 2i\delta \int \bar{\psi}\psi' \, dx + \alpha^2 \int \bar{\psi}x^2\psi \, dx$$
$$+ 2\alpha\beta \int \bar{\psi}x\psi \, dx + (\beta^2 + \delta^2) \int \bar{\psi}\psi \, dx \ge 0. \tag{8}$$

Next we use (1) and (2) to reduce (8) to

$$\hbar^{-2}\operatorname{av} p^2 - \alpha + 2\delta\hbar^{-1}\operatorname{av} p + \alpha^2 \operatorname{av} x^2 + 2\alpha\beta \operatorname{av} x + \beta^2 + \delta^2 \ge 0, \tag{9}$$

and finally assign the following specific numerical values to α, β, and δ:

$$\alpha = \frac{1}{2\Delta^2 x}, \qquad \beta = -\frac{\operatorname{av} x}{2\Delta^2 x}, \qquad \delta = -\frac{\operatorname{av} p}{\hbar}. \tag{10}$$

Equation (9) then becomes

$$\frac{1}{\hbar^2}(\operatorname{av} p^2 - \operatorname{av}^2 p) - \frac{1}{2\Delta^2 x} + \frac{1}{4\Delta^4 x}(\operatorname{av} x^2 - \operatorname{av}^2 x) \ge 0, \tag{11}$$

---

[13] This proof is a modification of that given by W. Heisenberg in his *Physical Principles of the Quantum Theory*, page 18. The University of Chicago Press, 1930.

that is,

$$\frac{\Delta^2 p}{\hbar^2} - \frac{1}{4\Delta^2 x} \geq 0, \tag{12}$$

and we conclude that

$$\Delta x \, \Delta p \geq \frac{h}{4\pi}. \tag{13}$$

Thus *the quantity* $\Delta x \, \Delta p$ *(the product of the respective inexactitudes of the coordinate x and the momentum p) for any state of an arbitrary one-dimensional system cannot be smaller than the universal constant* $h/4\pi$. Therefore, a verbal description of a state cannot be summarized by means of a Schroedinger function whenever this description implies that x and p are known simultaneously with a precision exceeding that allowed by (13), and, according to quantum mechanics, a state so described cannot be realized physically.

The proof of (13) given above is readily extended from normalized ψ's to quadratically integrable ψ's, provided the integrals in (1) and (2) exist. Schroedinger functions which are not quadratically integrable, and ones for which some of the integrals in (1) and (2) do not exist, are of course of no interest in the present connection.

Applying our results to the case of an oscillator, we conclude that the problem of the motion of an oscillator whose position and momentum at $t = t_0$ are precisely x_0 and p_0 cannot be properly stated in quantum theory, and consequently, from the standpoint of this theory, has no physical significance.

The inequality (13)—a *Heisenberg inequality*—is an example of the limitations that are imposed by the quantum theory on the precision with which the values of canonically conjugate pairs of dynamical variables can be known simultaneously. Among the Heisenberg inequalities referring to three-dimensional motion of a particle are

$$\Delta x \, \Delta p_x \geq \frac{h}{4\pi}, \qquad \Delta y \, \Delta p_y \geq \frac{h}{4\pi}, \qquad \Delta z \, \Delta p_z \geq \frac{h}{4\pi}. \tag{14}$$

Exercises

1. Verify that if $\Delta x = 0$ the inequality (9) can be converted into

$$\hbar^{-2}\Delta^2 p + (\alpha \text{ av } x + \beta)^2 - \alpha \geq 0, \tag{15}$$

and that hence Δp would have to be greater than any preassigned number. Thus the vanishing of Δx is inconsistent with the finiteness of all integrals in (1) and (2), so that the substitutions (10) are permissible whenever these integrals are finite.

2. Deduce from (9) that Δp cannot vanish if all integrals in (1) and (2) are finite.

3. Verify that the quantum-mechanical values of $\Delta x \Delta p$ for the various specific states of an oscillator studied in this chapter satisfy (13).

4. Consider the energy states of an oscillator and show that the statement, "The more accurately one knows the position of a particle, the less accurately one knows its momentum," is not always true, and consequently should not be made unless properly qualified.

24. The Heisenberg Principle

The fact that the Heisenberg inequalities follow directly from the assumptions of quantum mechanics shows that the quantum theory satisfies the requirements of a fundamental physical principle enunciated by Heisenberg, requirements that, in the light of the present-day knowledge, must be fulfilled by any theory in order that it may hold promise of being capable of correlating physical phenomena without the introduction of irrelevancies. The Heisenberg principle has to do with the simultaneous experimental measurement of any two canonically conjugate dynamical variables; if, for definiteness, these variables are taken to be the coordinate x and its conjugate momentum p, this principle can be stated as follows: *it is impossible to devise an experimental procedure for the measurement of x and p that would yield simultaneously absolutely precise values of x and p: the information provided by any experiment regarding the simultaneous values of x and p is always inaccurate to such an extent that* $\Delta x \Delta p \geq h/4\pi$.

To quote from §12: "Any particular apparatus used for the measurement of x, say, will of course have its own limits of precision, but, if greater precision is required, another, more delicate, apparatus can in principle be constructed. Classical mechanics implies that the improvement of the apparatus for measuring x can be carried on indefinitely so that the precision will exceed any preassigned standard, however fine. Similarly, the precision of apparatus for the measurement of p, or of apparatus for the simultaneous measurement of x and p, can, according to the classical view, be improved without limit." The words 'according to the classical view' now acquire special significance because, in contradistinction to the classical ideas, the Heisenberg principle implies a fundamental limitation on the precision with which a simultaneous measurement of x and p can be made.

Our belief in the correctness of the Heisenberg principle rests at present on the following foundations:

(a) When any one of the experiments proposed so far for the simultaneous measurement of two canonically conjugate dynamical variables is studied in the light of the present-day knowledge of the properties of the physical agencies employed in the measurement, it is found that no precise simultaneous values of these variables can be inferred from the results of the experiment, and that the reliability of whatever inferences can be drawn is in accord with the Heisenberg principle.

(b) The only theory known at present that has a claim to a general applicability to atomic phenomena—the quantum theory—is in accord with the principle.

To illustrate the basis of contention (a) by means of an example, we shall now show that the measurement of the position of a particle by means of a microscope is accompanied by an alteration of the momentum of the particle, and that a precise correction for this alteration cannot be made; and we shall also estimate the orders of magnitude of the attendant inexactitudes. In doing this we shall confine ourselves to the x-components of position and momentum, the x-direction being that from left to right in the plane of Fig. 26, which shows the direction of the light of wave length λ used to illuminate a particle in the vicinity of the point 0; I and II are the extreme paths that the light scattered by the particle may take and still get through the microscope.

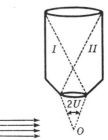

Fig. 26. A microscope.

The precision with which a microscope can yield information regarding the position of a particle depends on the resolving power determined by the lenses and their arrangement, by the angle U, and by the wave length λ_1 of the light scattered by the particle into the microscope; in particular, if perfect lenses are arranged in the most satisfactory way, then the smallest interval d that can be optically resolved is

$$d = \frac{\lambda_1}{2 \sin U}. \tag{1}$$

The inexactitude of the information provided by an actual micro-scope concerning the x-coordinate of the particle is therefore *at best* of the order of magnitude of d:

$$\Delta x \sim \frac{\lambda_1}{2 \sin U}.$$ (2)

Let us now suppose that at an instant t_0 the particle was actually observed near the point O, so that its position at that instant is known with a precision Δx. This means that at least one photon coming from the light source was deflected by the particle into the microscope. The path taken by this photon after it struck the particle cannot be determined, because the microscope is con-structed so as to focus the light coming from O regardless of the direction in which this light may have entered the microscope; hence, if the photon remained in the plane of Fig. 26, it may have taken any path between the extremes I and II. Now, as known from the studies of the *Compton effect*, the deflection of a photon by a material particle is accompanied by a change in momentum of both the photon and the particle; in particular, the change in the x-component of the momentum of the particle is $h(\lambda_1 - \lambda \sin U)/\lambda\lambda_1$, or approximately

$$h(1 - \sin U)/\lambda$$ (3)

if the photon took path I, and approximately

$$h(1 + \sin U)/\lambda$$ (4)

if it took path II; here λ is the wave length of the light used for illumination. Consequently, the fact that an observation of the position of the particle was made implies that an alteration of its momentum lying between $h(1 - \sin U)/\lambda$ and $h(1 + \sin U)/\lambda$ was also made. The very construction of the microscope makes it impossible to determine the exact amount of the alteration, so that, whatever the information regarding the x-component of the momentum of the particle may have been prior to the instant t_0, the act of locating the particle made the knowledge of its momentum inexact, the inexactitude being of the order of mag-nitude of $h(1 + \sin U)/\lambda - h(1 - \sin U)/\lambda$; that is,

$$\Delta p_x \sim 2h\lambda^{-1} \sin U.$$ (5)

Now, because of the Compton effect, λ_1 is greater than λ, and hence it follows from (2) and (5) that *at best*

$$\Delta x \, \Delta p_x \sim h.$$ (6)

The argument resulting in (6) is in a sense a hybrid, since it uses the wave theory of light in (1) and the photon theory in (3) and (4); yet there is abundant evidence for the fact that (1) does give the maximum resolving power of a microscope, and that the Compton effect does take place when light is scattered by a particle.

A microscope, of course, is not the only instrument that can be used for the measurement of position, but consideration of other types of apparatus shows again that a measurement of x with a precision Δx causes the information available regarding p_x to become inexact in such a way that, after the position has been observed, $\Delta x \, \Delta p_x \geq h/4\pi$; similarly, devices intended primarily for the measurement of p_x render the knowledge of x inexact. These matters are discussed very lucidly by Heisenberg in his book cited in footnote 13.

With regard to contention (b) given above in support of the Heisenberg principle, we can but reiterate that the Heisenberg inequalities are, as we have seen, deducible from the fundamental assumptions of the quantum theory, and that hence the theory does not permit the translation into its mathematical terms of just the kind of information that, in the light of the Heisenberg principle, is to be regarded as not physically obtainable. All deductions from the quantum theory are thus bound to be in accord with the demands of this principle.

Exercise

1. Why cannot a correction for the alteration in p_x of the particle observed by means of a microscope be made, without affecting the accuracy of the knowledge of x, by measuring the wave length of the light coming out of the microscope at the instant t_0, and then computing the angle through which the photon was deflected?

25. Kennard Packets

We shall next determine the form that the Schroedinger function ψ must have at a given instant of time in order that $\Delta_x \Delta_p$ have at that instant its smallest possible value $h/4\pi$. The replacement of $\geq$ by $=$ in 13^{23} is permissible if and only if it is permissible in 6^{23}, that is, if and only if ψ satisfies the equation

$$\psi' + (\alpha x + \beta + i\delta)\psi = 0, \tag{1}$$

whose general solution is

$$\psi = Ae^{-\frac{1}{2}\alpha x^2 - (\beta + i\delta)x}. \tag{2}$$

If we choose A so as to normalize (2), the resulting ψ may be written as

$$\psi = e^{i\gamma} \sqrt[4]{\frac{\alpha}{\pi}} \exp\left[-\frac{1}{2}\left(\sqrt{\alpha}x + \frac{\beta}{\sqrt{\alpha}}\right)^2 - i\delta x\right], \tag{3}$$

where γ is real and independent of x, but otherwise arbitrary.

A computation of av$x$ ($= x_a$), av$p$ ($= p_a$), and Δ_x for the state (3) shows that these quantities are related to α, β, and δ through Equations 10^{23}, so that (3) can be written as

$$\psi = \frac{e^{i\gamma}}{\sqrt[4]{2\pi\Delta_x^2}} e^{-\frac{(x-x_a)^2}{4\Delta_x^2} + \frac{i p_a x}{\hbar}}. \tag{4}$$

The distribution-in-x corresponding to the amplitude (4) is the Gauss distribution

$$\bar{\psi}\psi = \frac{1}{\Delta_x\sqrt{2\pi}} e^{-\frac{(x-x_a)^2}{2\Delta_x^2}} \tag{5}$$

and has a maximum at $x = x_a$; hence x_a is not only the average of x but also its most probable value. The distribution-in-p for the state (4) is (§27)

$$\frac{1}{\Delta_p\sqrt{2\pi}} e^{-\frac{(p-p_a)^2}{2\Delta_p^2}}, \tag{6}$$

where

$$\Delta_p = \frac{h}{4\pi\Delta_x}; \tag{7}$$

the distribution (6) is also Gaussian, so that p_a is the average and also the most probable value of p.

The Schroedinger function (4) thus represents a state for which the most probable value of x is x_a, the most probable value of p is p_a, and for which $\Delta_x\Delta_p$ has its least possible value $h/4\pi$. In specifying the state of a one-dimensional system by the function (4) we consequently come, so to speak, as near to the specification of precise initial conditions of the motion (to which we are accustomed in the classical theory) as is possible to do in quantum mechanics. For this reason, states that at some instant of time have the form (4) are of special interest; we shall call such states one-dimensional *Kennard packets*.[14] The packet 1^{21}, for example, is a Kennard packet having x_0 for the most probable value of x, zero for the most probable value of p, and $a/\sqrt{2}$ for Δ_x .

The manner in which a Kennard packet varies with the time depends of course on the dynamical system under consideration, because the time dependence of a Schroedinger function is determined by the equation $H\psi = i\hbar \partial\psi/\partial t$, whose solutions depend on the explicit form of the Hamiltonian. In a linear restoring field, the Kennard packet 1^{21} was found to vary with the time as shown by 19^{21}; in another field, the behavior of the packet would be different. The fact that the Hamiltonian must be known in order that the behavior of a Kennard packet (for that matter, of any Schroedinger function) may be determined corresponds to the fact that in classical theory the force field must be known before the motion of a particle can be calculated.

Quantum theory does not provide for us an opportunity for employing in a strict sense the mental picture of a moving particle cultivated by daily experience and also by classical mechanics, the picture that associates with the particle a definite position and momentum at every instant of time and allows us to follow mentally the motion of the particle between observations. The best we can do in seeking a mental image of the motion of a particle that is justified by both the quantum and the classical theory is to turn to probability packets; but, while in the classical theory the probability packets describing x and p of a particle may be made more and more narrow without limit (so that in the end we get a precise specification of the simultaneous values of x and p), in quantum theory we must stop with $\Delta x \, \Delta p = h/4\pi$, that is, with a Kennard packet.

Exercises

1. Show that 19^{21} can be written as

$$\psi = \frac{1}{\sqrt{a\pi^{\frac{1}{2}}}} \exp i \left(\frac{x_0^2}{4a^2} \sin 2\omega t - \tfrac{1}{2}\omega t \right) \cdot \exp \left[- \frac{(x - x_0 \cos \omega t)^2}{2a^2} - i \, \frac{xx_0 \sin \omega t}{a^2} \right], \quad (8)$$

and find by inspection av x and av p for this state for any time.

---

[14] E. H. Kennard, *Zeits. f. Physik*, **44**, 326 (1927). Note that for brevity we use the term *packet* for both a distribution function and its amplitude.

2. The quantum-mechanical problem that in a sense corresponds most nearly to the classical problem of determining the motion of a linear harmonic oscillator if the position and momentum of the particle at $t = 0$ are x_0 and p_0 is that of determining the motion, in a linear restoring field, of a Kennard packet that at $t = 0$ represents a state for which the most probable value of x is x_0 and the most probable value of p is p_0. In §21 we discussed the special case $p_0 = 0$ and $\Delta_p^2 = mk\Delta_x^2$.

Consider now the somewhat more general case when $\Delta_p^2 = mk\Delta_x^2$, but $p_0 \neq 0$. Set up the appropriate Kennard packet for $t = 0$ to take place of the packet 1^{21}, expand the new ψ^0 in terms of the eigenfunctions of the Hamiltonian of the oscillator, compute approximately the most probable value of the energy, obtain the time-dependent Schroedinger function and check it by means of 1^{16}, find the most probable values of x and p at the time t, and calculate the average of the energy. Point out whatever similarities exist between the quantum-mechanical results and the corresponding classical results of Exercise 3^{12}.

3. Recompute the time-dependent Schroedinger function of Exercise 2 by writing $t' - \tau$ for t and x' for x_0 in (8) and adjusting x' and τ in the result in such a way that for $t' = 0$ the x-dependent exponential in it equals the corresponding exponential in the Kennard packet set up for $t = 0$ in Exercise 2. Explain why we may expect this transformation to yield the proper result, and compare the values of x' and τ obtained by this process with those suggested by classical analogy.

26. Summary

We began this chapter by stating in §13 the *operator assumption* I, and then introduced rule II, which requires that quantum-mechanical operators be associated with dynamical variables according to the *quantum condition* 1^{13}. This assumption and this rule do not commit us to any specific mathematical form for the quantum-mechanical operators.

In §14 we described the *Schroedinger method* of associating *specific* operators with dynamical variables pertaining to one-dimensional systems and not involving explicitly the time t, and stated that the Schroedinger operands (the significance of which was as yet unclarified) are subject to a *condition of good behavior*. We also constructed the *first Schroedinger equation* 19^{14} for the case of one-dimensional motion.

The Schroedinger machinery for computing energy levels of conservative one-dimensional systems was then complete, and we illustrated it in §15 for the case of a linear harmonic oscillator.

To develop the technique for handling problems other than those concerning energy levels, we then introduced rule III^8, which requires that the time dependence of the Schroedinger operands be controlled by the *second Schroedinger equation* 1^{16}; and we showed how the Schroedinger function pertaining to the instant t can be computed from that pertaining to the instant t_0. Next we introduced the *operand rule* IV of §17, which implies, in particular, that a Schroedinger function is associated with a *state* of a dynamical system, and conversely. Finally, we introduced assumption V^S (and its one-dimensional form V_1^S), which provides the *Schroedinger expectation formula* 1^{17} (and its one-dimensional form 2^{17}).

The Schroedinger expectation formula supplies a method for inferring detailed physical information concerning a dynamical system in a certain state from the Schroedinger function which specifies this state; it also supplies (at least in principle) a method for handling the converse problem, namely, the problem of identifying the Schroedinger function to be associated with a verbally described state. Three particular implications of the expectation formula, pointed out in §17, are: (a) if c is a numerical constant, then the Schroedinger functions ψ and $c\psi$ specify the same state; (b) in the one-dimensional case, the distribution-in-x for a state specified by the Schroedinger function ψ is $\bar{\psi}\psi$; and (c) if the Schroedinger function ψ satisfies the equation $\alpha\psi = a\psi$ (where α is the Schroedinger operator associated with the dynamical variable α, and a is a numerical constant), then the value of the dynamical variable α for the state specified by this Schroedinger function is certainly a.

In §18 we began the work of applying the Schroedinger method to a number of one-dimensional problems, the work that will be continued in the next four chapters. In particular, we derived the *Heisenberg inequality* 13^{23}, and, in §24, we discussed the *Heisenberg principle*.

Exercise

1. Show that, having adopted the expectation formula 2^{17}, we may, insofar as the one-dimensional Schroedinger method is concerned, omit from among our fundamental assumptions the second sentence of the operator assumption I.

CHAPTER IV

FURTHER PROBLEMS IN THE SCHROEDINGER METHOD

27. Linear Momentum

The operator associated in the Schroedinger scheme with the x-component of momentum is

$$\langle 3^{14} \rangle \qquad\qquad -i\hbar\frac{\partial}{\partial x}, \qquad\qquad (1)$$

an operator closely related to 1^5. For brevity, we shall speak of (1) as the 'momentum operator' or simply as the 'momentum,' rather than as the 'operator associated in the Schroedinger scheme with the momentum'; the same term will thus be used for the dynamical variable and for the operator associated with it. Furthermore, whenever we shall not need to rewrite the operator (1) in full, we shall denote it by the letter p:

$$p = -i\hbar\frac{\partial}{\partial x}, \qquad\qquad \langle 2 \rangle$$

thus using the same symbol for the dynamical variable and for the operator associated with it.

In Chapter III we considered the momentum of a linear harmonic oscillator for various states of this particular dynamical system. The form of the operator (1), however, is independent of the force field in which the particle may be moving; hence certain general properties of the momentum can be investigated without specifying any particular dynamical system. Incidentally, so long as we do not specify the force field, we cannot determine explicitly the time dependence of the Schroedinger functions, because doing this involves using the second Schroedinger equation, that is, the equation $H\psi = i\hbar\partial\psi/\partial t$; hence our ψ-functions pertaining to an unspecified dynamical system will be *instantaneous* ψ's, that is, will refer to some particular instant of time.

Let us consider first the possible results of a precise measurement

of the momentum.   According to the operator assumption of §13·
these are the eigenvalues of (1), so that to calculate them we must
determine those values of the number λ for which the equation
$-i\hbar\partial\psi/\partial x = \lambda\psi$ has well-behaved solutions.   To suggest that
the eigenvalues which we are seeking are the possible values of the
momentum rather than of some other dynamical variable, we
shall use the symbol p' instead of λ and shall write the eigenvalue
equation for the momentum as

$$-i\hbar\frac{\partial}{\partial x}\psi = p'\psi \tag{3}$$

rather than as $-i\hbar\partial\psi/\partial x = \lambda\psi$, with the understanding that the
symbol p' stands for an ordinary number.[1]   Equation (3) can be
contracted to $p\psi = p'\psi$, it being understood that p is the operator
(1) and p' is a number.   The general solution of (3),

$$\psi = Ae^{ip'x/\hbar}, \tag{4}$$

where A is independent of x but otherwise arbitrary, is well-
behaved if and only if p' is a real number, zero included.   Consequently, every real number is an eigenvalue of our operator p,
and we conclude that, so long as no restriction to any special
dynamical system in a particular state is made, every real value of
linear momentum is a possible one, just as in classical mechanics.
This result is to be expected in the light of some of our previous
results, such as, for example, the distribution-in-p for the normal
state of an oscillator.

The eigenfunction of momentum belonging to the eigenvalue
p' is (4), so that, in view of the theorem 3 of §17, if the state of a
system at a given instant is specified by the Schroedinger function
(4), then a precise momentum measurement made at that instant
is certain to yield the numerical result p'.   Unless $p' = 0$, (4)
is a complex function of x, and it is impossible to plot it against x
as abscissa by means of a single line in a plane; an eigenfunction of
momentum is thus somewhat difficult to visualize.   We speak
of a state described by a Schroedinger function of type (4) as a
momentum state.

It follows from (4) that

$$\bar{\psi}\psi = |A|^{2}, \tag{5}$$

---

[1] The symbols α', α'', and so on, are often used for the possible values of a
dynamical variable α.

so that for a momentum state the distribution-in-x is a constant independent of x; that is, precise knowledge of p implies complete ignorance of x. The graph of (5) is exactly like that of Fig. 13[11]; but, while in obtaining Fig. 13[11] in the classical theory we deliberately disclaimed all knowledge of position, in quantum mechanics we are compelled to disclaim all knowledge of position as soon as we claim a precise knowledge of the conjugate momentum.

The choice of the constant A in (4) is of course arbitrary, especially since (4) cannot be normalized to unity. Our discussion will, however, be made more concise if we agree to refer to the function[2]

$$\psi_{p'} = e^{ip'x/\hbar}, \tag{6}$$

obtained from (4) by letting $A = 1$, as *the* Schroedinger function specifying the state for which the momentum of the particle is certainly p', or as *the* eigenfunction of p belonging to the eigenvalue p'.

By letting p' in (6) take on every (real) value between $-\infty$ and ∞, we obtain the infinite set of momentum eigenfunctions. This set is a *continuous* one, and is to be contrasted with, say, the *discrete* set of the eigenfunctions of H of the oscillator listed in 7[16].

We shall now proceed to show that a large class of functions ψ can be 'expanded' in terms of the momentum eigenfunctions in the form

$$\psi = \int_{-\infty}^{\infty} c_{p'} \psi_{p'} \, dp', \tag{7}$$

and that the distribution-in-p for the state ψ can be inferred from the expansion coefficients, that is, the c's in (7).

Fourier integrals. To pave the way for expansions of the form (7), we return to the set

$$(31^8) \qquad L^{-\frac{1}{2}} e^{2\pi inx/L}, \qquad n = \cdots, -2, -1, 0, 1, 2, \cdots, \tag{8}$$

which is orthonormal in any interval of length L. If $f(x)$ can be expanded in terms of this set in the interval $(-\frac{1}{2}L, \frac{1}{2}L)$, so that, in this interval,

$$f(x) = \sum_n c_n L^{-\frac{1}{2}} e^{2\pi inx/L}, \tag{9}$$

---

[2] Since (6) is an amplitude of a *relative* distribution, its physical dimensions are not of importance.

then, in view of 21^8, the expansion coefficients are

$$c_n = \int_{-\frac{1}{2}L}^{\frac{1}{2}L} L^{-\frac{1}{2}} e^{-2\pi i n x / L} f(x)\, dx. \tag{10}$$

Using s instead of x for the variable of integration in (10), we put (9) into the form

$$f(x) = L^{-1} \sum_n \left[\int_{-\frac{1}{2}L}^{\frac{1}{2}L} f(s)\, e^{-2\pi i n s / L}\, ds \right] e^{2\pi i n x / L}. \tag{11}$$

Since the right side of (11) is periodic in x with period L, the equality (11) holds outside the interval $(-\frac{1}{2}L, \frac{1}{2}L)$ only if $f(x)$ is also periodic in x with period L: a nonperiodic function cannot be represented by a Fourier series in the infinite interval.

We shall now indicate, by allowing L in (11) to grow large without limit, how a nonperiodic function can be expressed in the infinite interval in a form resembling (11). Let $u = n/L$; then, as n runs through its successive integral values, u increases at each step by the amount $\Delta u = L^{-1}$, so that (11) can be written as

$$f(x) = \sum_u \left[\int_{-\frac{1}{2}L}^{\frac{1}{2}L} f(s)\, e^{-2\pi i u s}\, ds \right] e^{2\pi i u x} \Delta u,$$

$$u = \cdots, -\frac{2}{L}, -\frac{1}{L}, 0, \frac{1}{L}, \cdots. \tag{12}$$

If L in (12) is allowed to increase without limit, we obtain the improper integral with the limits $-\infty$ and ∞; further, an integration with respect to u can be substituted for the summation, and we get

$$f(x) = \int_{-\infty}^{\infty} \left[\int_{-\infty}^{\infty} f(s)\, e^{-2\pi i u s}\, ds \right] e^{2\pi i u x}\, du, \tag{13}$$

that is,

$$f(x) = \int_{-\infty}^{\infty} c_u\, e^{2\pi i u x}\, du, \tag{14}$$

where x ranges over the entire infinite interval $(-\infty, \infty)$, and where

$$c_u = \int_{-\infty}^{\infty} f(x)\, e^{-2\pi i u x}\, dx. \tag{15}$$

In view of (6), Equation (14) is of the same form as (7), so that we are getting nearer to the solution of the problem of resolving a state in terms of momentum states. Equation (13) is one form of the *Fourier integral theorem*.[3]

The quantity c_u given by (15) is a function of u; its value for $u = u_1$ is the weight, so to speak, with which the function $e^{2\pi i u_1 x}$ enters into the expansion of $f(x)$ in terms of functions of the form $e^{2\pi i u x}$ The rôle of c_u in the expansion (14) is analogous to that of the whole list of the coefficients $\cdots , c_{-2} , c_{-1} , c_0 , c_1 , c_2 , \cdots$ in the expansion (9).

Let $f = f(x)$ and $g = g(x)$ be any two functions that can be expanded into Fourier series in the interval $(-\tfrac{1}{2}L, \tfrac{1}{2}L)$:

$$f = \sum_n a_n L^{-\frac{1}{2}} e^{2\pi i n x/L}, \qquad n = \cdots , -2, -1, 0, 1, \cdots \quad (16)$$

$$g = \sum_m b_m L^{-\frac{1}{2}} e^{2\pi i m x/L}, \qquad m = \cdots , -2, -1, 0, 1, \cdots \quad (17)$$

and let the Fourier series for the function $f(x)g(x)$ be

$$fg = \sum_k c_k L^{-\frac{1}{2}} e^{2\pi i k x/L}, \qquad k = \cdots , -2, -1, 0, 1, \cdots . \quad (18)$$

The a's, b's and c's can all be obtained by means of 21^8; in particular,

$$c_0 = L^{-\frac{1}{2}} \int_{-\frac{1}{2}L}^{\frac{1}{2}L} fg \, dx, \qquad (19)$$

so that the term in (18) that does not depend on x is

$$L^{-1} \int_{-\frac{1}{2}L}^{\frac{1}{2}L} fg \, dx. \qquad (20)$$

By direct multiplication of (16) and (17) we get

$$fg = L^{-1} \sum_n \sum_m a_n b_m e^{2\pi i (n+m)x/L}, \qquad (21)$$

so that the constant term in (18) can also be found by summing the right side of (21) under the condition $n + m = 0$, the result being

$$L^{-1} \sum_m a_{-m} b_m . \qquad (22)$$

Equating (20) to (22), and using 21^8 to eliminate a_{-m} and b_m, we get

$$\int_{-\frac{1}{2}L}^{\frac{1}{2}L} fg \, dx = \sum_m L^{-1} \left[\int_{-\frac{1}{2}L}^{\frac{1}{2}L} f e^{2\pi i m x/L} \, dx \right] \cdot \left[\int_{-\frac{1}{2}L}^{\frac{1}{2}L} g e^{-2\pi i m x/L} \, dx \right]. \quad (23)$$

If we now write $s = m/L$ and allow L to become infinite, (23) goes over into

$$\int_{-\infty}^{\infty} f(x)g(x)dx = \int_{-\infty}^{\infty} \left[\int_{-\infty}^{\infty} f(x) e^{2\pi i s x} \, dx \right] \cdot \left[\int_{-\infty}^{\infty} g(x) e^{-2\pi i s x} \, dx \right] ds. \quad (24)$$

---

[3] For the conditions that must be satisfied by $f(x)$ in order that (13) may hold rigorously, see a mathematical discussion of Fourier integrals.

Now, let g in (24) be the kth derivative of some function (which we shall denote by g in order that our final result have a convenient form), and let the new g and its first $k - 1$ derivatives vanish when $|x| \to \infty$. Equation (24) then becomes

$$\int_{-\infty}^{\infty} f \frac{d^k}{dx^k} g\, dx = \int_{-\infty}^{\infty} \left[\int_{-\infty}^{\infty} f e^{2\pi i s x}\, dx \right] \cdot \left[\int_{-\infty}^{\infty} e^{-2\pi i s x} \frac{d^k}{dx^k} g\, dx \right] ds, \quad (25)$$

and the second bracketed factor in (25), when integrated by parts k times, becomes $(2\pi i s)^k \int e^{-2\pi i s x} g\, dx$. The final result, namely,

$$\int_{-\infty}^{\infty} f(x) \frac{d^k}{dx^k} g(x)\, dx$$
$$= (2\pi i)^k \int_{-\infty}^{\infty} \left[\int_{\infty}^{\infty} f(x) e^{2\pi i s x}\, dx \right] s^k \left[\int_{-\infty}^{\infty} g(x) e^{-2\pi i s x}\, dx \right] ds, \quad (26)$$

will find immediate application in our work.

Amplitudes of distributions-in-p. If a normalized Schroedinger function ψ describing the state of an oscillator is expanded in terms of the normalized eigenfunctions ψ_n of H in the form

$$\psi = \sum_n c_n \psi_n, \quad (27)$$

then, as shown in §20, the probability that the energy for the state ψ be E_n is $|c_n|^2$, so that c_n is an amplitude of the probability that the energy for the state ψ be E_n. We may, by analogy, expect that if a Schroedinger function ψ is expanded in terms of the eigenfunctions of p in the form

$$(7) \qquad \psi = \int_{-\infty}^{\infty} c_p \psi_p\, dp = \int_{-\infty}^{\infty} c_p e^{ipx/h}\, dp, \quad (28)$$

where for simplicity p is written for p', then c_p, a function of p, should be proportional to the amplitude of the probability that for the state ψ the momentum lie in dp at p. This surmise is a correct one, as we shall now show. Since p ranges from $-\infty$ to ∞, the symbol d in integrals with respect to p will imply that the limits of integration are $-\infty$ and ∞.

Let the state of a one-dimensional system be specified by a Schroedinger function ψ which, together with all of its derivatives, vanishes when $|x| \to \infty$ and which can be expressed as a Fourier integral:

$$\psi = \int_{-\infty}^{\infty} c_u e^{2\pi i u x}\, du, \quad (29)$$

where, according to (15), $c_u = \int \psi e^{-2\pi i u x}\, dx$. Letting $u = p/h = p/2\pi\hbar$ in (29), we get

$$\psi = \int h^{-1} c_p e^{ipx/h}\, dp, \tag{30}$$

where

$$c_p = \int \psi e^{-ipx/h}\, dx, \tag{31}$$

so that ψ has been expanded in terms of the momentum states. We expect then that the amplitude [which we denote by $A_\psi(p)$] of the distribution-in-p for the state ψ is proportional to (31) and, choosing the constant of proportionality to be $h^{-\frac{1}{2}}$, we write tentatively

$$A_\psi(p) = h^{-\frac{1}{2}} \int_{-\infty}^{\infty} \psi e^{-ipx/h}\, dx. \tag{32}$$

Having arrived at a plausible expression for $A_\psi(p)$, we proceed to prove that it is consistent with our fundamental assumptions. According to the expectation formula 2^{17}, the average of p^k for the state specified by the Schroedinger function ψ is

$$\int \bar{\psi}\left(-i\hbar \frac{\partial}{\partial x}\right)^k \psi\, dx \Big/ \int \bar{\psi}\psi\, dx. \tag{33}$$

Now, if the amplitude of the distribution-in-p is $A_\psi(p)$, then the distribution-in-p is $\bar{A}_\psi(p)A_\psi(p)$, so that, if $A_\psi(p)$ is available, then the average of p^k for the state ψ, calculated by means of 27^{11}, is

$$\int \bar{A}_\psi(p) p^k A_\psi(p)\, dp \Big/ \int \bar{A}_\psi(p) A_\psi(p)\, dp; \tag{34}$$

the factors in the integrands of (34) are arranged in our customary order, although in the present case the order does not matter. To verify (32) we need only to show that for $A_\psi(p)$ given by (32) the numerical value of (34) is, for every positive integral value of k, the same as the numerical value of (33).

We write $g = h^{-\frac{1}{2}}\psi, f = \bar{g} = h^{-\frac{1}{2}}\bar{\psi}$, and $s = p/h$ in (26), and get[4]

$$\int \bar{\psi}\left(-i\hbar \frac{\partial}{\partial x}\right)^k \psi\, dx$$

$$= \int \left[h^{-\frac{1}{2}}\int \bar{\psi}e^{ipx/h}\, dx\right] p^k \left[h^{-\frac{1}{2}}\int \psi e^{-ipx/h}\, dx\right] dp, \tag{35}$$

---

[4] It is of course permissible to write $\partial/\partial x$ for d/dx in (26).

so that for $A_\psi(p)$ given by (32) the numerators of (33) and (34) are equal; the case $k = 0$ in (35) shows that the denominators of (33) and (34) are also equal. Consequently (32) yields the correct values of $\mathrm{av}_\psi\, p^k$, and its validity is established: *the amplitude of the distribution-in-p for a state of a one-dimensional system described by a Schroedinger function ψ is given by (32)*.

The formula (32) enables us to transform, so to speak, the amplitude of the distribution-in-x for a given state into the amplitude of the distribution-in-p for the same state; we therefore call it a *transformation formula*.

Note that multiplication of the right side of (32) by a factor of the form $Ce^{i\gamma}$, where C is a constant and γ is a real function of p and t, does not affect that value of (34), so that we have not shown that (32) is the only suitable expression for $A_\psi(p)$. But a closer study, which we shall not undertake here, shows that the multiplication of the right side of (32) by a function of p or t is not permissible, and that consequently our result is indeterminate to the extent of only a trivial constant factor. The factor $h^{-\frac{1}{2}}$ in (32) is convenient because, as was shown above, it makes the numerators of (33) and (34) precisely equal to each other, so that, in particular, if $\bar\psi\psi$ is an absolute distribution-in-x, then $\bar A_\psi(p)A_\psi(p)$ is an absolute distribution-in-p.

Examples. To illustrate the applications of the transformation formula (32), we shall now calculate the distribution-in-p for the normal state of an oscillator. This distribution was found in §18 by a method that involved a comparison of the averages of the powers of p with those of x, a method successful only because of the symmetry of the Hamiltonian of the oscillator in x and p; the present method, on the other hand, will not involve the computation of any averages.

According to (32), the amplitude, which we denote by $A_0(p)$, of the distribution-in-p for the normal state of the oscillator is

$$A_0(p) = h^{-\frac{1}{2}} \int \psi_0 e^{-ipx/h}\, dx, \tag{36}$$

where ψ_0 is the Schroedinger function for the normal state, given in the normalized form by 12^{18}; that is,

$$A_0(p) = \frac{e^{i\gamma_0} e^{-\pi i \nu_c t}}{\sqrt{ah\pi^{\frac{1}{2}}}} \int e^{-\frac{1}{2}\left(\frac{x}{a}\right)^2} e^{-ipx/h}\, dx. \tag{37}$$

Integrating with the help of the formula 23^{28}, we get

$$A_0(p) = \frac{e^{i\gamma_0}}{\sqrt{b\pi^{\frac{1}{2}}}} e^{-\frac{1}{2}\left(\frac{p}{b}\right)^2} e^{-\pi i\nu_c t}, \qquad (38)$$

where b is the constant $\sqrt[4]{km\hbar^2} = \hbar/a$, first introduced in 25^{18}. The distribution-in-p for the normal state is thus the product of (38) and its complex conjugate, and we have

$$P_0(p) = \bar{A}_0(p)A_0(p) = \frac{1}{b\sqrt{\pi}} e^{-\left(\frac{p}{b}\right)^2}, \qquad (39)$$

in agreement with 33^{18}. The present calculation is of course much more straightforward than that of §18.

The amplitude of the absolute distribution-in-p for the nth energy state of the oscillator is, according to (32),

$$A_n(p) = h^{-\frac{1}{2}} \int \psi_n e^{-ipx/\hbar} dx, \qquad (40)$$

where ψ_n is 7^{16}; integration yields[5]

$$A_n(p) = \frac{e^{i(\gamma_n + \frac{1}{2}n\pi)}}{\sqrt{b 2^n n! \pi^{\frac{1}{2}}}} H_n\left(\frac{p}{b}\right) e^{-\frac{1}{2}\left(\frac{p}{b}\right)^2} e^{-iE_n t/\hbar}. \qquad (41)$$

The absolute distribution-in-p corresponding to (41) is just 38^{18}.

Further examples. The validity of (32) was proved above only for severely restricted ψ-functions, and the question as to whether or not this transformation formula holds when some of the restrictions on ψ are removed has been left open. We shall, however, use (32) even if ψ is not of integrable square, although we shall then have occasionally to use mathematical methods formally rather than rigorously.

To illustrate, let us see what kind of a result is given by (32) for the state specified by the Schroedinger function (6), that is, for a state for which the momentum is certainly p'. We have

$$A(p) = h^{-\frac{1}{2}} \int e^{ip'x/\hbar} e^{-ipx/\hbar} dx = h^{-\frac{1}{2}} \int e^{i(p'-p)x/\hbar} dx. \qquad (42)$$

The integral is indeterminate for $p \neq p'$ and is infinite for $p = p'$; but it will be shown in Exercise 4 that setting $\int e^{i(p'-p)x/\hbar} dx$ equal to $h\delta(p' - p)$ is consistent with the definition of the δ-function.

---

[5] See, for example, G. A. Campbell and R. M. Foster, *Fourier Integrals for Practical Applications*, page 14. New York: Bell Telephone System, 1931.

Since $\delta(p' - p) = \delta(p - p')$, we then get from (42)

$$A(p) = h^{\frac{1}{2}}\delta(p - p').$$
(43)

The distribution-in-p for our momentum state is thus $h\delta(p - p')$ $\delta(p - p')$, which we denote by $h\delta^2(p - p')$; it vanishes for every value of p except p', for which it is infinite. This type of result is of course to be expected, since we are trying to represent a discrete distribution by a continuous distribution function. At the end of §12 we concluded that, if the value of a quantity is a certainty, then the absolute distribution in this quantity can be taken to be a δ-function; in the present calculation, the amplitude, rather than the distribution itself, is a δ-function, so that the resulting distribution must be interpreted as a relative one.

As a further illustration of the use of (32) when ψ is not quadratically integrable, let us consider the case when the state of a system is specified at a given instant by the Schroedinger function

$$\psi = c_1 e^{ip'x/h} + c_2 e^{ip''x/h},$$
(44)

where the numbers p' and p'' are not equal to each other and where the c's are known constants, and let us calculate the distribution-in-p for that instant. Since $p' \neq p''$, our ψ is not an eigenfunction of the momentum operator, and the structure of (44) suggests that the possible values of p are p' and p'', that their respective relative probabilities are $|c_1|^2$ and $|c_2|^2$, and that hence their respective absolute probabilities are $|c_1|^2/(|c_1|^2 + |c_2|^2)$ and $|c_2|^2/(|c_1|^2 + |c_2|^2)$.

Substituting (44) into (32) and treating the resulting integrals in the same way as we did (42), we get

$$
\begin{aligned}
A_\psi(p) &= h^{-\frac{1}{2}} \int (c_1 e^{ip'x/h} + c_2 e^{ip''x/h}) e^{-ipx/h}\, dx \\
&= c_1 h^{\frac{1}{2}}\delta(p - p') + c_2 h^{\frac{1}{2}}\delta(p - p'').
\end{aligned}
$$
(45)

The distribution-in-p is the product of (45) and its complex conjugate, and since $\delta(p - p')\delta(p - p'') = 0$ when $p' \neq p''$, we have

$$P_\psi(p) = |c_1|^2 h\delta^2(p - p') + |c_2|^2 h\delta^2(p - p'').$$
(46)

This result implies just what we expected in the first place: at the instant at which the Schroedinger function is (44), the possible values of p are p' and p'', and their relative probabilities are $|c_1|^2$ and $|c_2|^2$.

Letting $c_1 = |c_1| e^{i\phi_1}$ and $c_2 = |c_2| e^{i\phi_2}$, we get the following result for the distribution-in-x at the instant at which the Schroedinger function is (44):

$$\bar{\psi}\psi = |c_1|^2 + |c_2|^2 + 2|c_1| \cdot |c_2| \cos\left(\frac{p' - p''}{\hbar} x + \phi_1 - \phi_2\right); \quad (47)$$

its form is shown in Fig. 27. The distribution-in-x is periodic in x, period $h/|p' - p''|$, and not all values of x are equally likely.

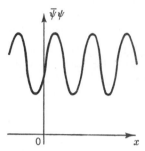

Fig. 27. Distribution-in-x for a state of the form (44).

A Schroedinger function of type (44) is $\psi_c = \cos kx$. We have

$$\psi_c = \cos kx = \tfrac{1}{2}e^{i(k\hbar)x/\hbar} + \tfrac{1}{2}e^{i(-k\hbar)x/\hbar}, \quad (48)$$

so that the possible values of p are $k\hbar$ and $-k\hbar$, and these values are equally probable; the expected average of the momentum is therefore zero. Another function of the same type is

$$\psi_s = \sin kx = \frac{1}{2i}e^{i(k\hbar)x/\hbar} - \frac{1}{2i}e^{i(-k\hbar)x/\hbar}; \quad (49)$$

the distribution-in-p is the same as for (48), but the two distributions-in-x are different.

The Schroedinger functions (48) and (49) may serve to illustrate a curious feature of coherent quantum-mechanical superposition. The ψ-function (48) implies that the momentum is not certain; the ψ-function (49) also implies that the momentum is not certain; yet the ψ-function

$$\psi = \psi_c + i\psi_s = e^{i(k\hbar)x/\hbar}, \quad (50)$$

that is, a special coherent superposition of (48) and (49), implies that the momentum is a certainty! Examples of this kind show that, although the discussion of systems whose preparation involves ·the tossing of a coin (for example, a discussion along the lines of §19) may be helpful in giving a beginner a start toward understanding quantum-mechanical superposition, such discussion loses its effectiveness when the superposition is *coherent*, because neither the classical theory of probability nor the classical theory of particle motion can serve as a starting point for a discussion of the physical meaning of the *phases* of probability amplitudes. To be sure, an analogy to the quantum-mechanical superposition of states can, as we shall presently see, be found in the classical theory of wave motion; but this analogy is one of mathematical method rather than of physical content.

Notation. In dealing with one-dimensional systems, we have used the symbol ψ for a Schroedinger function, with the understanding that ψ is a function of x and t, interpreted as the amplitude of a distribution-in-x; but when we consider concurrently amplitudes of the distributions of more than one variable, say of x and of p, as we have been doing in this section, the following notation, due to Dirac, is usually more convenient.

Instead of denoting a Schroedinger function by ψ, we denote it by $(x \mid)$, the symbol $(x \mid)$ being read "x, line." Instead of denoting the complex conjugate of the Schroedinger function by $\bar{\psi}$, we denote it by $(\mid x)$, so that $(\mid x) = \overline{(x \mid)}$; the symbol $(\mid x)$ is read "line, x." The corresponding distribution-in-x is then denoted by $(\mid x)(x \mid)$ instead of $\bar{\psi}\psi$.

The spaces to the right and to the left, respectively, of the vertical lines in $(x \mid)$ and $(\mid x)$ are reserved for whatever symbols may be required to particularize a state. For example, we write $(x \mid k)$ for ψ_k, the symbol $(x \mid k)$ being read "x, line, k"; $\bar{\psi}_k$ is then denoted by $(k \mid x)$, so that $(k \mid x) = \overline{(x \mid k)}$, and $\bar{\psi}_k\psi_k$ is written as $(k \mid x)(x \mid k)$.

To illustrate, we rewrite in the new notation some expressions taken from the preceding pages. The Schroedinger equation for the linear harmonic oscillator:

$$(3^{15}) \qquad \left(-\frac{1}{\kappa}\frac{\partial^2}{\partial x^2} + \frac{1}{2}kx^2 \right)(x \mid) = E(x \mid). \qquad (51)$$

The normalized Schroedinger eigenfunctions of the Hamiltonian of the oscillator:

$$(7^{16}) \qquad (x \mid n) = e^{i\gamma \dot{n}} N_n H_n\left(\frac{x}{a}\right) e^{-\frac{1}{2}\left(\frac{x}{a}\right)^2} e^{-iE_n t/\hbar}. \qquad (52)$$

The eigenfunction of the momentum belonging to the eigenvalue p' of p:

$$(6) \qquad (x \mid p') = e^{ip'x/\hbar}. \qquad (53)$$

The complex conjugate of (53):

$$(p' \mid x) = e^{-ip'x/\hbar}. \tag{54}$$

The distribution-in-x for the normal state of the oscillator:

$$(14^{18}) \qquad\qquad (0 \mid x)(x \mid 0) = \frac{1}{a\sqrt{\pi}} e^{-\left(\frac{x}{a}\right)^2}. \tag{55}$$

The symbols for the amplitudes of distributions in dynamical variables other than x are constructed in an analogous manner. For example, when the amplitude of the distribution-in-x for a state is denoted by $(x \mid)$, the amplitude of the distribution-in-p for the same state is denoted by $(p \mid)$, $(\mid p)$ is used for $\overline{(p \mid)}$, and the distribution-in-p is denoted by $(\mid p)(p \mid)$. Again, if the amplitude of the distribution-in-x for a specific state is $(x \mid k)$, then the amplitude of the distribution-in-p, the complex conjugate of this amplitude, and the distribution-in-p for this state are denoted, respectively, by $(p \mid k)$, $(k \mid p)$, and $(k \mid p)(p \mid k)$. Thus we denote the amplitude of the distribution-in-p for the normal state of the oscillator by $(p \mid 0)$:

$$(38) \qquad\qquad (p \mid 0) = \frac{e^{i\gamma_0}}{\sqrt{b\pi^{\frac{1}{2}}}} e^{-\frac{1}{2}\left(\frac{p}{b}\right)^2} e^{-\pi i \nu_c t}, \tag{56}$$

the complex conjugate of the right side of (56) is denoted by $(0 \mid p)$, and the distribution-in-p for the normal state by $(0 \mid p)$ $(p \mid 0)$:

$$(39) \qquad\qquad (0 \mid p)(p \mid 0) = \frac{1}{b\sqrt{\pi}} e^{-\left(\frac{p}{b}\right)^2}. \tag{57}$$

The transformation formula (32), the most important single result of this section, now takes on the form

$$(32) \qquad\qquad (p \mid) = h^{-\frac{1}{2}} \int_{-\infty}^{\infty} (x \mid)e^{-ipx/\hbar} \, dx. \tag{58}$$

Exercises

1. The state of a one-dimensional system is specified at a certain instant by a Schroedinger function of the form $\psi = CR(x)$, where C is independent of x, and $R(x)$ is a normalizable real function of x; show that at this instant av $p = 0$.

2. Show that, if

$$g(u) = \int_{-\infty}^{\infty} f(s)e^{-2\pi i u s}\, ds, \tag{59}$$

then

$$f(s) = \int_{-\infty}^{\infty} g(u)e^{2\pi i u s}\, du, \tag{60}$$

and conversely.   The process of deducing one of the relations (59) and (60) from the other is called *inversion* of a Fourier integral.   Two functions, $f(s)$ and $g(u)$, related to each other through (59) and (60) are called *Fourier transforms* of one another.

3. Derive the following theorems from (59) and (60): (a) if one of the two functions f and g is identically zero, then the other is also identically zero; (b) if one of the two functions f and g is even,[6] then the other is also even, while if one of them is odd, then the other is also odd; and (c) if both f and g are real, then both are even.

4. Recall 26^{12} and verify that $e^{2\pi i s u_0} = \int_{-\infty}^{\infty} c_u\, e^{2\pi i s u}\, du$, with $c_u = \delta(u - u_0)$;

this formula means that, when $e^{2\pi i s u_0}$ is expanded in terms of the continuous set of functions $e^{2\pi i s u}$, then the coefficients of the functions for which $u \neq u_0$ are all zero, while the coefficient of the function $e^{2\pi i s u_0}$ is so great that the integral is finite even though the integrand vanishes everywhere except at the single point $u = u_0$.   Then show by inversion that

$$\int_{-\infty}^{\infty} e^{2\pi i (u - u_0)s}\, ds = \delta(u - u_0). \tag{61}$$

Try to evaluate the integral in (61) directly, and discuss the rigor of (61).

5. If we try to compute av p^k for the state (44) by means of the expectation formula 2^{17}, we get meaningless integrals.   But show that, if the integrals in 2^{17} are evaluated between the limits $-l$ and l (rather than $-\infty$ and ∞), and av p^k is taken to be the limit of the quotient of the two integrals as $l \to \infty$, then the result is in agreement with that implied in (46).

6. Determine the absolute distributions-in-p, and plot rough graphs of the distributions-in-x implied by the following Schroedinger functions: $\psi = 3e^{ik_1 x} + 4e^{-ik_2 x}$; $\psi = 3e^{-ik_1 x} + 4e^{ik_2 x}$; $\psi = 3e^{-ik_1 x} - 4e^{ik_2 x}$; $\psi = (12 + 9i)e^{-ik_1 x} + (16 - 12i)e^{ik_2 x}$; $\psi = \sin^2 kx$; $\psi = \cos^3 kx$.

7. The only information available concerning a particle is that at a certain instant its momentum is either p' or p'', the probability of the first alternative being 0.36 and that of the second being 0.64.   Write down the Schroedinger function for this instant and show that in view of the incoherency of the superposition all values of x are at that instant equally likely.

---

[6] To say that f is even means that $f(-s) = f(s)$; to say that g is odd means that $g(-u) = -g(u)$; and so forth.

8. Show that if the Schroedinger function at a certain instant is the Kennard packet 4^{25}, then the amplitude of the distribution-in-p at that instant is $(2\pi\Delta_p^2)^{-\frac{1}{2}}e^{i\gamma_1}\exp\left[-(p-p_a)^2/4\Delta_p^2 - ipx_a/\hbar\right]$, where $\gamma_1 = \gamma + x_a p_a/\hbar$ and $\Delta_p = \hbar/2\Delta_x$. Verify that 6^{25} is the distribution-in-p corresponding to the ψ-function 4^{25}.

9. Show that the distribution-in-p for the state 19^{21} is 8^{21}.

10. Show that the condition that the Schroedinger function at a given instant be (4) is not only sufficient but necessary in order that the momentum of the particle at that instant be certainly p'.

11. Derive the transformation formula $(x \mid \ ) = h^{-\frac{1}{2}} \displaystyle\int_{-\infty}^{\infty} (p \mid \ )e^{ipx/\hbar}\,dp.$

28. The Free Particle in One Dimension

The only specific dynamical system that we have considered so far is the linear harmonic oscillator; the next one will be the free particle in one dimension. If a particle of mass m moves along the x-axis without being subjected to any forces, the Hamiltonian function is $H = \dfrac{1}{2m}p^2 + V_0$, where V_0 is an arbitrary constant that can without loss of generality be set equal to zero. The operator associated in the Schroedinger scheme with the resulting H is

$$H = -\frac{1}{\kappa}\frac{\partial^2}{\partial x^2}, \tag{1}$$

where, as before, $\kappa = 2m/\hbar^2$. We shall, for brevity, often call the operator associated with the Hamiltonian of a given system the *Hamiltonian operator* of the system, or simply the *Hamiltonian*.

To compute the possible values of the energy of a free particle, we must find the eigenvalues of $\langle 1 \rangle$, that is, the values of the number E for which the equation

$$-\frac{1}{\kappa}\frac{\partial^2}{\partial x^2}\psi = E\psi, \tag{2}$$

the first Schroedinger equation for the free particle, has well-behaved solutions. Equation (2) is of the form 5^3 and has well-behaved solutions if and only if

$$E \geq 0, \tag{3}$$

so that the eigenvalue spectrum of our Hamiltonian consists of all positive numbers, zero included. We conclude that (when $V_0 = 0$)

any positive value of the energy, zero included, is a possible value of the energy of a free particle, and that no other values are possible. This result is in agreement with the corresponding result of the classical theory of a free particle: *the energy of a free particle is not quantized.*

The eigenfunctions of H belonging to the eigenvalue E have the form $a \exp (i\sqrt{\kappa E}\, x) + b \exp (-i\sqrt{\kappa E}\, x)$, that is,

$$ae^{i\sqrt{2mE}\, x/\hbar} + be^{-i\sqrt{2mE}\, x/\hbar}, \tag{4}$$

where a and b are independent of x, but are otherwise arbitrary; (4) is the general solution of (2), except when $E = 0$.

To compute the properly time-dependent Schroedinger function for a free particle of energy E, we substitute (4) into the second Schroedinger equation 1[16] (which in the case of an energy state reduces to $E\psi = i\hbar\partial\psi/\partial t$), and find that this function, to be denoted by ψ_E, is

$$\psi_E = Ae^{i\sqrt{2mE}\, x/\hbar}e^{-iEt/\hbar} + Be^{-i\sqrt{2mE}\, x/\hbar}e^{-iEt/\hbar}, \tag{5}$$

where A and B are independent of both x and t, but are otherwise arbitrary. Every nonvanishing positive value of E is a doubly degenerate eigenvalue of H, since the two special eigenfunctions

$$Ae^{i\sqrt{2mE}\, x/\hbar}e^{-iEt/\hbar} \tag{6}$$

and

$$Be^{-i\sqrt{2mE}\, x/\hbar}e^{-iEt/\hbar}, \tag{7}$$

of which (5) is a linear combination, are linearly independent when $E \neq 0$. The energy spectrum of a free particle is continuous and degenerate, and the eigenfunctions of H are not quadratically integrable; for these reasons, the theory of a free particle is in some respects more involved than the theory of a linear harmonic oscillator.

Comparison of (6) and (7) with 4[27] shows that each of these functions, besides being an eigenfunction of our H, is simultaneously an eigenfunction of p, and that (6) belongs to the eigenvalue $\sqrt{2mE}$ of p, while (7) belongs to the eigenvalue $-\sqrt{2mE}$ of p; the values $\pm \sqrt{2mE}$ of p (corresponding, respectively, to *rightward* and *leftward* motion) are just the possible values of p of a classical free particle of energy E. The general energy state (5) of a free particle is thus a superposition of two momentum states; in fact, the possible results of a precise measurement of the momentum of a free particle whose state is specified by the Schroedinger function (5) are $\sqrt{2mE}$ and $-\sqrt{2mE}$, the respective relative probabilities of these results at any time being $|Ae^{-iEt/\hbar}|^2$ and $|Be^{-iEt/\hbar}|^2$, that is, $|A|^2$ and $|B|^2$. The distribution-in-x, $\bar{\psi}_E\psi_E$, for the state (5) is stationary and has the general form shown in Fig. 27[27].

We saw in §18 that the knowledge of the energy of a linear harmonic oscillator with certainty leaves the Schroedinger function specifying the state of the oscillator undetermined only to the extent of an arbitrary multiplicative constant, and that consequently the condition that the energy of the oscillator is a certainty constitutes a maximal set of conditions on the oscillator: if the statement that the energy of the oscillator is a certainty is made, no relevant information, not already implied in this statement, can be added to it. In the case of a free particle, the situation is different on account of the degeneracy of the energy spectrum: the knowledge that the energy of a free particle is a certainty does imply that the Schroedinger function is (5), yet it leaves both A and B in (5) arbitrary. This means that the condition that the energy of a free particle is certainly E does not constitute a maximal set of conditions when $E > 0$, and can be supplemented by further information concerning the particle. For example, the statement that the energy of a free particle is certainly E, $E > 0$, may be accompanied by the statement that the momentum is also a certainty and equals $+\sqrt{2mE}$; in this case the Schroedinger function has the form (6) and is undetermined only to the extent of an arbitrary multiplicative constant: these conditions that both E and p be certainties constitute a maximal set of conditions on a free particle. In fact, the condition that the momentum of a free particle be a certainty constitutes a maximal set, since if the momentum is certainly p the energy is necessarily certainly $\frac{1}{2m}p^2$. The ψ-function (5) can be written as

$$\psi_E = \left(C \sin \frac{\sqrt{2mE}}{\hbar}x + D \cos \frac{\sqrt{2mE}}{\hbar}x\right)e^{-iEt/\hbar}; \text{ but this expression}$$

does not display ψ_E as an explicit superposition of momentum states, and the form (5) is usually preferable.

Nonstationary states.[7] We consider next how the Schroedinger

---

[7] C. G. Darwin, *Proc. Roy. Soc.*, 117A, 258 (1927).

function ψ describing the state of a free particle at the instant t can be found if it is known to be ψ^0 at $t = 0$; in the field-free case, the second Schroedinger equation 1^{16} has the form

$$\frac{i\hbar}{2m} \frac{\partial^2}{\partial x^2}\psi = \frac{\partial}{\partial t}\psi, \tag{8}$$

so that, stated in mathematical terms, our problem is to find that solution of (8) which at $t = 0$ reduces to the given ψ^0. If ψ^0 is an eigenfunction of H belonging to the eigenvalue E, then, as has been shown, ψ is simply $\psi^0 e^{-iEt/\hbar}$; but, if the energy of the particle is not a certainty, ψ is more complicated.

In §16 we found that the solution of the corresponding problem for the case of an oscillator can be obtained by first resolving ψ^0 in terms of the eigenfunctions of H referring to $t = 0$, and then attaching the appropriate time factor to each term in the summation. Essentially the same procedure can be used in the present case, except that: (a) since to all but one eigenvalue of H there belong two linearly independent eigenfunctions, the simultaneous eigenfunctions of H and p, rather than the eigenfunctions of H alone, are to be used in the expansions; and (b) integrals must be employed instead of sums. The functions that will play a fundamental part in our calculation are thus the functions (6) and (7), which all have, apart from a multiplicative constant, the form

$$\psi_p = e^{ipx/\hbar} e^{-ip^2 t/2m\hbar}, \tag{9}$$

where p is the numerical value of the momentum (positive, negative, or zero) and where ψ_p is used for brevity instead of the more explicit symbol $\psi_{E,p}$. For $t = 0$, the functions (9) become

$$\psi_p^0 = e^{ipx/\hbar}. \tag{10}$$

We now proceed formally in a manner parallel to that of §16. First, we expand the given ψ^0 in terms of the (continuous) set (10):

$$\psi^0 = \int c_p \psi_p^0 \, dp; \tag{11}$$

Equation (11) is analogous to 13^{16}. Secondly, we substitute ψ_p, given by (9), for ψ_p^0 in (11), and denote the resulting function of x and t by ψ:

$$\psi = \int c_p \psi_p \, dp; \tag{12}$$

Equation (12) is analogous to 14^{16}. More explicitly, according to

(10), 30^{27}, and 31^{27}, Equation (11) is

$$\psi^0 = h^{-1} \int \left[\int \psi^0 e^{-ipx/\hbar} \, dx \right] e^{ipx/\hbar} \, dp, \qquad (13)$$

while (12) is

$$\psi = h^{-1} \int_{-\infty}^{\infty} \left[\int_{-\infty}^{\infty} \psi^0 e^{-ipx/\hbar} \, dx \right] e^{ipx/\hbar} e^{-ip^2 t/2m\hbar} \, dp. \qquad (14)$$

At $t = 0$, the right sides of (14) and (13) are the same, and consequently it remains only to show that (14) satisfies (8). Now, differentiation of (14) once with respect to t under the integral sign introduces the factor $-ip^2/2m\hbar$ in the integrand of the integral with respect to p; differentiation[8] of (14) twice with respect to x under the integral sign introduces the factor $(ip/\hbar)^2$ in the integrand of the integral with respect to p; and, since $(i\hbar/2m)\,(ip/\hbar)^2 = -ip^2/2m\hbar$, (14) is a solution of (8). Our problem has been solved: if the Schroedinger function describing the state of a free particle is ψ^0 at $t = 0$, then it is (14) at the instant t.

The case when ψ^0 is a discrete superposition of momentum states, that is, has the form

$$\psi^0 = c_1 e^{ip'x/\hbar} + c_2 e^{ip''x/\hbar} + c_3 e^{ip'''x/\hbar} + \cdots, \qquad (15)$$

is a special case of the continuous superpositions considered above; but it can be treated without reference to (14), since we can readily verify that the function

$$\psi = c_1 e^{ip'x/\hbar} e^{-iE_1 t/\hbar} + c_2 e^{ip''x/\hbar} e^{-iE_2 t/\hbar} + c_3 e^{ip'''x/\hbar} e^{-iE_3 t/\hbar} + \cdots, \qquad (16)$$

where $E_1 = (p')^2/2m$, $E_2 = (p'')^2/2m$, and so forth, satisfies (8) and reduces to (15) at $t = 0$.

Constancy of p. According to classical mechanics, the momentum of a free particle is a constant of motion, so that if it is certainly p (that is, if it certainly has the numerical value p) at the instant $t = 0$, then it will continue to be certainly p for all time; or, if the momentum of a classical free particle at $t = 0$ is not a certainty, then the distribution-in-p at any subsequent time is the same as it is at $t = 0$. The situation is similar in quantum mechanics.

In the first place, if the momentum of a free particle at $t = 0$

---

[8] Note that the bracketed part of (14) is independent of x.

is certainly p, then the Schroedinger function at $t = 0$ is a constant multiple of (10), and the time-dependent Schroedinger function is a constant multiple of (9); and, since (9) is at any time an eigenfunction of momentum belonging to the eigenvalue p, it follows that, if the momentum of a free particle is certainly p at $t = 0$, it will continue to be certainly p for all time.

'Secondly, if the momentum of a free particle at $t = 0$ is not a certainty, so that the Schroedinger function for the instant t has the general form (14), then by inversion (Exercise 2^{27}) we get

$$\left[\int \psi^0 e^{-ipx/\hbar} \, dx \right] e^{-ip^2 t/2m\hbar} = \int \psi e^{-ipx/\hbar} \, dx. \qquad (17)$$

Now, according to the transformation formula 58^{27}, the right side of (17) is $h^{\frac{1}{2}}$ times the amplitude, $(p \mid)$, of the distribution-in-p at the time t, while the bracket on the left side of (17) is $h^{\frac{1}{2}}$ times the amplitude, $(p \mid)^0$, of the distribution-in-p at the instant $t = 0$; consequently

$$(p \mid) = (p \mid)^0 e^{-ip^2 t/2m\hbar}, \qquad (18)$$

so that the amplitude of the distribution-in-p for any state of a free particle depends on t in a rather simple way. The distribution-in-p at the time t is

$$(\mid p)(p \mid) = (\mid p)^0 (p \mid)^0, \qquad (19)$$

and is always the same as at $t = 0$. The stationary character of the distribution-in-p for an arbitrary state of a free particle, expected in the light of classical analogy, has thus been proved.

Exercises

1. Show that the distribution-in-E for any state of a free particle is stationary.

2. In the text we let the potential V_0, describing the force-free case, be zero.[9] Consider the case $V_0 = $ constant $\neq 0$.

3. Set up the Schroedinger function which implies that the energy of a free particle is certainly zero. Consider its time dependence, and the information it contains concerning the momentum.

4. Show that if the state of a free particle is specified at $t = 0$ by the Schroedinger function $\psi^0 = A \sin^2 kx$, then the time-dependent ψ-function is

$$\psi = -\tfrac{1}{4} A (e^{-2ikx} + e^{2ikx}) e^{-iE_k t/\hbar} + \tfrac{1}{2} A, \qquad (20)$$

where $E_k = 2k^2 \hbar^2/m$.

---

[9] The condition $V_0 = 0$ is implied also in the exercises below.

5. Find by inspection the distribution-in-p for the state (20); then show that the possible values of the energy of a free particle in the state (20) are E_k and 0, and that the respective probabilities of these values are $\frac{1}{3}$ and $\frac{2}{3}$.

6. Let the state of a free particle by specified at $t = 0$ by the ψ-function

$$\psi^0 = \frac{1}{\sqrt[4]{2\pi\Delta_x^2}} e^{-\frac{(x-x_0)^2}{4\Delta_x^2} + i\frac{p_0 x}{\hbar}}, \tag{21}$$

that is, by a Kennard packet. Show that the time-dependent ψ is then

$$\psi = \frac{\exp\left(-i p_0^2 t/2\hbar m\right)}{2^{\frac{1}{4}}\pi^{\frac{1}{4}}\sqrt{\Delta_x + i\Delta_v t}} \exp\left\{-\frac{[x-(x_0+v_0 t)]^2}{4(\Delta_x^2 + i\Delta_x\Delta_v t)} + i\frac{p_0 x}{\hbar}\right\}, \tag{22}$$

where $v = p/m$. Note the formula[10]

$$\int_{-\infty}^{\infty} e^{-(\alpha s^2 + \beta s + \gamma)} e^{i(\delta s^2 + \epsilon s + \zeta)} ds$$

$$= \sqrt{\frac{\pi}{\alpha - i\delta}} \exp\left[-\gamma + \frac{\alpha(\beta^2 - \epsilon^2) + 2\beta\delta\epsilon}{4(\alpha^2 + \delta^2)}\right] \exp\left[i\zeta + i\frac{(\beta^2 - \epsilon^2)\delta - 2\alpha\beta\epsilon}{4(\alpha^2 + \delta^2)}\right]. \tag{23}$$

Show that the distribution-in-x for the state (22) is 13^{12}. Compare the present problem with that which was considered classically in §12 and which led to 13^{12}; point out a condition under which the above-mentioned problem of §12 cannot be translated into the mathematical terms of quantum mechanics and is consequently meaningless from the quantum-mechanical standpoint.

7. Show that for the state (22) $\mathrm{av}_\psi E = \frac{1}{2m}p_0^2 + \frac{1}{2m}\Delta_p^2$.

8. The theorem that the distribution-in-p for any state of a free particle is stationary was proved in the text with the help of the transformation formula 58^{27}. Prove this theorem for the case of states specified by normalizable ψ's by computing the time derivative of $\mathrm{av}_\psi p^k$, and without reference to 58^{27}. Note that in the field-free case, according to (8), $\partial\psi/\partial t = i\hbar\psi''/2m$, and $\partial\bar\psi/\partial t = -i\hbar\bar\psi''/2m$.

29. One-Dimensional Rectangular Potential Wells

The energy spectrum of a linear harmonic oscillator is discrete, while that of a free particle is continuous. To give an example of an energy spectrum that contains a discrete part and also a

---

[10] See integrals 6 and 7, Table 269, D. Bierens de Haan, *Nouvelles Tables d'Intégrales Définies*; Leyden, 1867.

continuous part we shall now consider the motion of a particle in the field of the rectangular potential well of Fig. 9[10]. The energy diagram

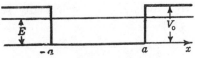

Fig. 28. A potential well. Energy diagram for the case $0 < E < V_0$.

of this system is shown in Fig. 28 for the case when the total energy E of the particle is less than the depth V_0 of the well, and in Fig. 33 for the case when $E > V_0$.

The Schroedinger equation is now

$$-\frac{1}{\kappa}\frac{\partial^2}{\partial x^2}\psi + V(x)\psi = E\psi, \tag{1}$$

where

$$V(x) = \begin{cases} V_0 > 0 & \text{for} \quad x \leq -a \\ 0 & \text{for} -a \leq x \leq a \\ V_0 & \text{for} \quad a \leq x. \end{cases} \tag{2}$$

To find the possible energies of our particle, we must compute the values of E for which (1), with $V(x)$ given by (2), has well-behaved solutions; and in view of the discontinuities in $V(x)$ we proceed as follows. We subdivide the infinite interval into the *left* region $(x \leq -a)$, the *central* region $(-a \leq x \leq a)$, and the *right* region $(a \leq x)$; writing ψ in the form

$$\psi = \begin{cases} \psi_l & \text{for} \quad x \leq -a \\ \psi_c & \text{for} -a \leq x \leq a \\ \psi_r & \text{for} \quad a \leq x, \end{cases} \tag{3}$$

we now find that, if (3) is to be a solution of (1), then the three pieces into which we have divided ψ must satisfy, respectively, the simple equations

$$\psi_l'' + \kappa(E - V_0)\psi_l = 0, \qquad \psi_c'' + \kappa E\psi_c = 0,$$
$$\psi_r'' + \kappa(E - V_0)\psi_r = 0; \tag{4}$$

next we find the respective general solutions of Equations (4); and finally we determine the circumstances under which ψ_l, ψ_c, and ψ_r, when pieced together, will yield a well-behaved ψ.

We shall carry out this procedure in detail for the case

$$0 < E < V_0, \tag{5}$$

to which Fig. 28 specifically refers. In terms of the abbreviations

$$\alpha = \sqrt{\kappa E}, \qquad\qquad \beta = \sqrt{\kappa(V_0 - E)}, \qquad (6)$$

the respective general solutions of Equations (4) are

$$\psi_l = B_1 e^{\beta x} + B_2 e^{-\beta x}, \qquad \psi_c = A_1 e^{i\alpha x} + A_2 e^{-i\alpha x},$$
$$\psi_r = C_1 e^{\beta x} + C_2 e^{-\beta x}, \qquad (7)$$

where the A's, B's, and C's are arbitrary constants. In view of (5), β is positive; hence the term $B_2 e^{-\beta x}$ in ψ_l misbehaves when $x \rightarrow -\infty$, and we must set $B_2 = 0$ in order that (3) may behave properly at $-\infty$; the term $B_1 e^{\beta x}$ in ψ_l misbehaves when $x \rightarrow \infty$, but, since our ψ is equal to ψ_l only in the left region, this does not imply a violation of the boundary conditions by ψ. Similarly, the boundary condition at $+\infty$ requires that $C_1 = 0$. The solution

$$\psi = \begin{cases} \psi_l = B_1 e^{\beta x} \\ \psi_c = A_1 e^{i\alpha x} + A_2 e^{-i\alpha x} \\ \psi_r = C_2 e^{-\beta x} \end{cases} \qquad (8)$$

of (1) thus satisfies the boundary conditions for an arbitrary choice of B_1, A_1, A_2, and C_2. The general character of (8) is indicated in Fig. 29, which is drawn on the assumption that ψ is real and that B_1 and C_2 are positive.

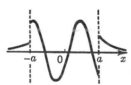

We turn next to our standard continuity conditions, which require that ψ and ψ' be continuous throughout the infinite region. Each of the three pieces of ψ in (8), when taken by itself, is continuous and has a continuous derivative, and hence we need to consider only the points $-a$ and a at which

Fig. 29. A function of the form (8). This function is ill-behaved; well-behaved functions of the form (8) are shown in Fig. 32.

the pieces join. Now, ψ will be continuous at $-a$ if and only if $\psi_l(-a) = \psi_c(-a)$; similarly, ψ' will be continuous at $-a$ if and only if $\psi_l'(-a) = \psi_c'(-a)$. Analogous conditions must hold at a, so that our ψ will satisfy the continuity conditions if and only if

$$\psi_l(-a) = \psi_c(-a), \qquad\qquad \psi_l'(-a) = \psi_c'(-a), \qquad (9)$$
$$\psi_r(a) = \psi_c(a), \qquad\qquad \psi_r'(a) = \psi_c'(a). \qquad (10)$$

In trying to subject (8) to the conditions (9) and (10), we might proceed as follows: Taking ψ_l in (8) as it stands, we adjust ψ_c so as to satisfy the continuity conditions at $-a$; this can be done without difficulty because ψ_c contains two adjustable constants, and there are just two conditions to satisfy. After this, no arbitrariness will remain in ψ_c, and the values of ψ_c and ψ_c' at a will become fixed. Next we try to satisfy the continuity conditions at a by adjusting ψ_r ; but here we encounter a complication, because ψ_r must be made to satisfy the *two* conditions (10), although it contains only *one* adjustable constant, namely, C_2. We may therefore expect that in general it is impossible to adjust the coefficients in (8) so as to satisfy Equations (9) and (10), and that exceptional cases in which this can be done can arise only if α, β, and a are related in some special way.

To carry out the calculations explicitly, we substitute ψ_l and ψ_c, given in (8), into (9), getting

$$B_1 e^{-\beta a} = A_1 e^{-i\alpha a} + A_2 e^{i\alpha a} \tag{11}$$

$$B_1 \beta e^{-\beta a} = A_1 i\alpha e^{-i\alpha a} - A_2 i\alpha e^{i\alpha a}. \tag{12}$$

Elimination of B_1 yields the relation between A_1 and A_2 that is required for the proper joining of ψ_l and ψ_c :

$$A_2 = -\frac{\beta - i\alpha}{\beta + i\alpha} e^{-2i\alpha a} A_1. \tag{13}$$

Similarly, substitution of ψ_c and ψ_r into (10) yields

$$C_2 e^{-\beta a} = A_1 e^{i\alpha a} + A_2 e^{-i\alpha a} \tag{14}$$

$$-C_2 \beta e^{-\beta a} = A_1 i\alpha e^{i\alpha a} - A_2 i\alpha e^{-i\alpha a}, \tag{15}$$

and eliminating C_2 we get the relation between A_1 and A_2 that is required for the proper joining of ψ_c and ψ_r :

$$A_2 = -\frac{\beta + i\alpha}{\beta - i\alpha} e^{2i\alpha a} A_1. \tag{16}$$

Now, Equations (13) and (16) are in general inconsistent, and hence it is impossible in general to piece the three parts of (8) together so that the resulting ψ satisfies the continuity conditions. In other words, the Schroedinger equation for our particle does not possess well-behaved solutions for an arbitrary value of E lying between 0 and V_0 ; and we draw the physical conclusion that not every energy value lying between 0 and V_0 is a possible value of the energy of a particle moving in the field of Fig. 28.

It remains to investigate the circumstances under which (13) and (16) are consistent, that is, under which

$$\frac{\beta + i\alpha}{\beta - i\alpha} e^{2i\alpha a} = \frac{\beta - i\alpha}{\beta + i\alpha} e^{-2i\alpha a} \tag{17}$$

Equation (17) is a condition on the quantities α, β, and a, and not on the arbitrary constants in (7); if a, V_0, and κ are fixed, as they are in our problem, (17) is a condition on E. Elimination of the complex exponentials in (17) yields

$$(\beta^2 - \alpha^2) \sin 2\alpha a = -2\alpha\beta \cos 2\alpha a, \tag{18}$$

so that, in view of (6), Equations (13) and (16) are consistent if and only if

$$\tan 2a \sqrt{\kappa E} = \frac{2\sqrt{E(V_0 - E)}}{2E - V_0} \tag{19}$$

Thus the values of E, lying between 0 and V_0, for which our Schroedinger equation possesses well-behaved solutions, are the roots of the transcendental equation (19) lying between 0 and V_0. These roots, which turn out to be real, discrete, and finite in number, are the energy levels of our dynamical system lying between 0 and V_0; they will be labeled E_1, E_2, E_3, and so on, in such a way that $E_1 < E_2 < E_3 < \cdots$ and so on.

To complete the discussion of the case $0 < E < V_0$, we shall now find the explicit form of the Schroedinger function ψ_n belonging to energy value E_n lying between 0 and V_0, the calculation to be based on the assumption that E_n satisfies (19), so that (17) holds, and (13) and (16) are both true. The product of the left sides of (13) and (16) is A_2^2, and that of the right sides is A_1^2; hence $A_2 = \pm A_1$, and (16) goes over into

$$\frac{\beta + i\alpha}{\beta - i\alpha} e^{2i\alpha a} = \mp 1. \tag{20}$$

When B_1 and C_2 are evaluated in terms of A_1 [note that (11) and (12) are consistent when (17) holds, and so are (14) and (15)], the solution (8) takes the form

$$\psi_n = \begin{cases} A(e^{-i\alpha_n a} \pm e^{i\alpha_n a})e^{\beta_n(a+x)} & x \leq -a \\ A(e^{i\alpha_n x} \pm e^{-i\alpha_n x}) & -a \leq x \leq a \\ A(e^{i\alpha_n a} \pm e^{-i\alpha_n a})e^{\beta_n(a-x)} & a \leq x, \end{cases} \tag{21}$$

where

$$\alpha_n = \sqrt{\kappa E_n}, \qquad \beta_n = \sqrt{\kappa(V_0 - E_n)}, \qquad (22)$$

and where A is the factor, independent of x but otherwise arbitrary, previously denoted by A_1. To determine whether the upper or the lower signs in (21) are to be used in ψ_n, we may substitute E_n into (20) and thus determine whether the upper or the lower sign is appropriate in (20).

To make ψ_n properly time dependent, we let A depend on t through the factor $e^{-iE_n t/\hbar}$, for then $i\hbar \partial \psi_n/\partial t = E_n \psi_n$ and ψ_n satisfies the second Schroedinger equation 1^{16}.

Besides the discrete energy spectrum lying between 0 and V_0, our system has a continuous spectrum consisting of all energies greater than V_0 (Exercise 6); if $E = V_0$ is a solution of (19), there is also an energy level at $E = V_0$ (Exercise 7). Each level belonging to the continuous spectrum is doubly degenerate, while, as we have already seen, each level of the discrete spectrum is nondegenerate. The system has no energy levels besides those enumerated above.

Exercises

1. Show that every ψ-function (21) is either even or odd in x, and can be made real by a proper choice of A.

2. Show that the choice $A = N_n = \frac{1}{2}(a + \beta_n^{-1})^{-\frac{1}{2}} e^{i\gamma}$, where γ is an arbitrary real constant, normalizes (21) to unity.

3. The substitution $s = 2a\sqrt{\kappa E}$ sends (19) into $\tan s = s(4V_0 a^2 \kappa - s^2)^{\frac{1}{2}} \times (s^2 - 2V_0 a^2 \kappa)^{-1}$; graphs of the two sides of this equation for the case $V_0 a^2 \kappa = 36$ are given in Fig. 30. Use Fig. 30 to show that, in the special case $V_0 a^2 \kappa = 36$, the system[11] has four energy levels lying between 0 and V_0, and that these are, approximately, $E_1 = .05V_0$, $E_2 = .20V_0$, $E_3 = .44V_0$, and $E_4 = .74V_0$. These discrete levels are shown in the lower part of Fig. 31; the corresponding normalized ψ-functions are shown in Fig. 32.

4. Verify that, in terms of $\xi = a\sqrt{\kappa E}$, Equation (20), taken with the upper sign, can be written as

$$\tan \xi = (V_0 a^2 \kappa - \xi^2)^{\frac{1}{2}} \xi^{-1}, \qquad (23)$$

and, taken with the lower sign, as

$$\tan \xi = -\xi (V_0 a^2 \kappa - \xi^2)^{-\frac{1}{2}}. \qquad (24)$$

Draw *rough* graphs of $\tan \xi$ and of the right sides of (23) and (24), regarded as functions of ξ, and show that the energy levels of the system[11] lying between 0 and V_0 are spaced as follows:

$$0 < a\sqrt{\kappa E_1} < \tfrac{1}{2}\pi < a\sqrt{\kappa E_2} < \tfrac{3}{2}\pi < a\sqrt{\kappa E_3} < \tfrac{3}{2}\pi < \cdots < a\sqrt{\kappa V_0}, \qquad (25)$$

---

[11] That is, a particle of mass m in the field of the one-dimensional rectangular potential well of Fig. 9^{10}.

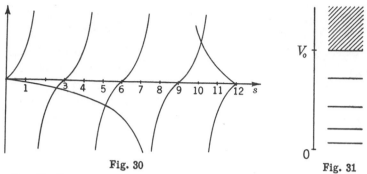

Fig. 30

Fig. 31

Fig. 30. Graph for Exercise 3.

Fig. 31. The energy spectrum of the well of Exercise 3. In this case, the value $E = V_0$ is not included in the spectrum.

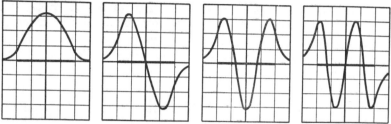

Fig. 32. Instantaneous ψ-functions for the discrete energy states of the well of Exercise 3. The heavy horizontal lines extend on the x-axes from $x = -a$ to $x = a$.

and that the system has at least one level between 0 and V_0. Under what condition are there just ten levels between 0 and V_0?

5. Show that (21) is even in x if n is odd, and odd in x if n is even; show also that (21) has altogether $n + 1$ nodes: one at $-\infty$, one at ∞, and $n - 1$ between $-a$ and a.

6. Consider the case $E > V_0$, shown in Fig. 33. Note that β in (6) is now a pure imaginary, so that the terms $B_2 e^{-\beta x}$ and $C_1 e^{\beta x}$ in (7) are no longer ill-behaved in their respective regions; show that consequently (as indicated in Fig. 31) any energy greater than V_0 is a possible energy of the system,[11] and verify that the ψ-functions belonging to the energy value E, $E > V_0$, can be written in

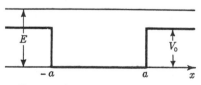

Fig. 33. A potential well. Energy diagram for the case $E > V_0$.

the form

$$\psi = \begin{cases} \psi_l = (A + Bs_4)e^{-i\alpha_1 x} + Bs_3 e^{i\alpha_1 x} \\ \psi_o = (As_2 + Bs_1)e^{-i\alpha x} + (As_1 + Bs_2)e^{i\alpha x} \\ \psi_r = As_3 e^{-i\alpha_1 x} + (As_4 + B)e^{i\alpha_1 x}, \end{cases} \quad (26)$$

where A and B are arbitrary constants, and where $\alpha = \sqrt{\kappa E}$, $\alpha_1 = \sqrt{\kappa(E - V_0)}$, $s_1 = (\alpha - \alpha_1)(2\alpha)^{-1} e^{i(\alpha_1 + \alpha)a}$, $s_2 = (\alpha + \alpha_1)(2\alpha)^{-1} e^{i(\alpha_1 - \alpha)a}$, $s_3 = (2\alpha\alpha_1)[2\alpha\alpha_1 \cos 2\alpha a - i(\alpha^2 + \alpha_1^2) \sin 2\alpha a] e^{2i\alpha_1 a}$, and $s_4 = i(2\alpha\alpha_1)^{-1} (\alpha^2 - \alpha_1^2) \sin 2\alpha a$.

7. Show that $E = V_0$ is a possible energy of the system[11] if and only if $E = V_0$ is a root of (19); and that the corresponding ψ-function contains only one arbitrary constant, and can be obtained by letting $E = V_0$ in (21); is this ψ-function normalizable?

8. Show that energies less than or equal to zero are not possible energies of the system.[11]

9. Consider a particle moving in one dimension in the field of the *rectangular potential barrier*

$$V(x) = \begin{cases} 0 & x \leq -\tfrac{1}{2}l \\ V_0 > 0 & -\tfrac{1}{2}l \leq x \leq \tfrac{1}{2}l \\ 0 & \tfrac{1}{2}l \leq x \end{cases} \quad (27)$$

drawn in Fig. 34. Show that any energy greater than 0 is a possible energy of the system. Verify that the Schroedinger functions describing a state of energy E have the following forms: For $0 < E < V_0$,

$$\psi = \begin{cases} \psi_l = Ae^{i\alpha x} + (Ac_2 + Bc_1)e^{-i\alpha x} \\ \psi_c = (Ac_4 + Bc_3)e^{\beta x} + (Ac_3 + Bc_4)e^{-\beta x} \\ \psi_r = (Ac_1 + Bc_2)e^{i\alpha x} + Be^{-i\alpha x}, \end{cases} \quad (28)$$

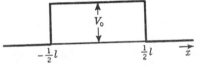

Fig. 34. The potential barrier (27).

where A and B are arbitrary constants, where α and β are given by (6), and where $c_1 = 2\alpha\beta[2\alpha\beta \cosh \beta l + i(\beta^2 - \alpha^2) \sinh \beta l]^{-1} e^{-i\alpha l}$, $c_2 = -ic_1(2\alpha\beta)^{-1}(\beta^2 + \alpha^2) \sinh \beta l$, $c_3 = c_1(2\beta)^{-1}(\beta - i\alpha)e^{\frac{1}{2}(\beta + i\alpha)l}$, and $c_4 = c_1(2\beta)^{-1}(\beta + i\alpha)e^{\frac{1}{2}(-\beta + i\alpha)l}$. For $E = V_0$,

$$\psi = \begin{cases} Ae^{-i\alpha_0 x} + B[(1 - \tfrac{1}{2}i\alpha_0 l)e^{i\alpha_0(l+x)}) - \tfrac{1}{2}i\alpha_0 l e^{-i\alpha_0 x}] \\ Ae^{\frac{1}{2}i\alpha_0 l}[1 - i\alpha_0(\tfrac{1}{2}l + x)] + Be^{\frac{1}{2}i\alpha_0 l}[1 - i\alpha_0(\tfrac{1}{2}l - x)] \\ A[-\tfrac{1}{2}i\alpha_0 l e^{i\alpha_0 x} + (1 - \tfrac{1}{2}i\alpha_0 l)e^{i\alpha_0(l-x)}] + Be^{i\alpha x}, \end{cases} \quad (29)$$

where A and B are arbitrary constants, and $\alpha_0 = \sqrt{\kappa V_0}$. For $E > V_0$, the ψ-functions have the form (28), where $\beta = \sqrt{\kappa(V_0 - E)} = i\sqrt{\kappa(E - V_0)}$.

30. The One-Dimensional Box

A dynamical system of some interest is that consisting of a particle in a one-dimensional box; the potential describing it is shown in Fig. 36, a reproduction of Fig. 10[10]. We shall begin with a box located as in Fig. 35.

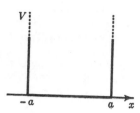

Fig. 35. A potential box extending from $x = -a$ to $x = a$.

On account of the highly singular character of our new $V(x)$, we shall treat it as a limiting case of the well of §29, to be obtained by letting V_0 increase without limit, and shall compute the energy levels for the box by letting $V_0 \to \infty$ in the expression for the energy levels for the well. In doing this, we may restrict ourselves to the discrete levels of the well, because the continuous spectrum lies above V_0 and is of no interest when $V_0 \to \infty$.

When $V_0 \to \infty$ the energy level equation 19^{29} for the well goes over into $\tan 2a\sqrt{\kappa E} = 0$, that is, into $2a\sqrt{\kappa E} = n\pi$, and hence the energy levels of the boxed particle are

$$E_n = n^2\pi^2/4a^2\kappa = n^2h^2/32ma^2, \qquad n = 1, 2, 3, \cdots. \quad (1)$$

The reason for omitting $n = 0$ will appear presently.

To obtain the Schroedinger function ψ_n describing the nth energy state of the particle in the box of Fig. 35, we allow $V_0 \to \infty$ in 21^{29}. When $V_0 \to \infty$, Equations 22^{29} become, in the limit,

$$\alpha_n = n\pi/2a, \qquad\qquad \beta_n = +\infty, \qquad (2)$$

while 20^{29} becomes $e^{n\pi i} = \mp 1$, so that the upper sign is to be used in 21^{29} when n is odd, and the lower when n is even. Consequently, $e^{-i\alpha a} \pm e^{i\alpha a}$ vanishes for every integral n, $e^{\beta_n(a+x)}$ vanishes for $x < -a$, $e^{\beta_n(a-x)}$ vanishes for $x > a$, and 21^{29} becomes

$$\psi_n = \begin{cases} 0 & x \le -a \\ A[e^{n\pi ix/2a} - (-1)^n e^{-n\pi ix/2a}] & -a \le x \le a \quad (3) \\ 0 & a \le x. \end{cases}$$

Fig. 36. A potential box extending from $x = 0$ to $x = l$.

In view of (2) and the result of Exercise 2^{29}, the ψ-function (3) is normalized when $A = \frac{1}{2}a^{-\frac{1}{2}}e^{i\gamma}$; the normalizing factor of (3) can of course be readily evaluated directly. The vanishing of (3) for $n = 0$ is the reason for excluding $n = 0$ from (1).

The ψ-function for the nth energy state of a particle in the box of Fig. 36, extending from $x = 0$ to $x = l$, can be obtained from (3) by writing $\frac{1}{2}l$ for a and $x + \frac{1}{2}l$ for x; when normalized and made properly time-dependent, this function is

$$\psi_n = \begin{cases} 0 & x \le 0 \\ e^{i\gamma_n} \sqrt{\frac{2}{l}} \sin \frac{n\pi x}{l} e^{-iE_n t/\hbar} & 0 \le x \le l \\ 0 & l \le x, \end{cases} \qquad (4)$$

where γ_n is real and independent of x and t, but otherwise arbitrary, and where

(1)
$$E_n = \frac{n^2 h^2}{8ml^2}, \qquad n = 1, 2, 3, \cdots. \quad (5)$$

The energy spectrum of a particle in a box is thus entirely discrete and nondegenerate.

Graphs of (4) for $n = 1, 2, 3,$ and 4 for times at which $\exp i(\gamma_n - E_n t/\hbar) = 1$ are shown in Fig. 37; since ψ_n is in general complex, it can be represented by a single line in a plane only for exceptional values of t.

The function (4) is continuous everywhere in the infinite region; but its first derivative is discontinuous at the ends of the box, so that our standard continuity conditions are violated. We adopt (4) nevertheless, because it is a limit of the function 21^{29} that does satisfy all the requirements, and because from the physical standpoint it is certainly permissible to regard the box problem as a limit of the well problem. This situation shows that our elementary criteria of good behavior are not adequate for the treatment of all one-dimensional problems; but the exceptional cases are rather rare.

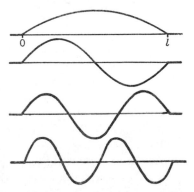

Fig. 37. Instantaneous ψ-functions for energy states of a particle in a one-dimensional box.

The distribution-in-x for the nth quantum state is

$$\bar{\psi}_n \psi_n = \begin{cases} 0 & x \le 0 \\ \frac{2}{l} \sin^2 \frac{n\pi x}{l} & 0 \le x \le l \\ 0 & l \le x \end{cases} \qquad (6)$$

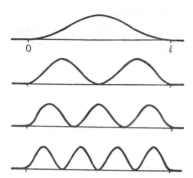

Fig. 38. Distributions-in-x for energy states of a particle in a one-dimensional box.

and is of course stationary. Equation (6) implies that the probability of finding the particle outside the box is zero, just as in the classical theory. Graphs of (6) for $n = 1, 2, 3,$ and 4 are shown in Fig. 38.

Distributions-in-p. Since the ψ_n given by (4) vanishes outside the box, an integral of the form $\int \bar{\psi}_n f(x)\psi_n \, dx$ can be replaced by $\int_0^l \bar{\psi}_n f(x)\psi_n \, dx$, and hence the computation of averages of functions of x is straightforward. The situation is more involved in the case of averages of functions of p. For example, since ψ_n is normalized, we have, according to the expectation formula 2[17],

$$\text{av}_n \, p^k = (i\hbar)^k \int_{-\infty}^{\infty} \bar{\psi}_n \frac{\partial^k}{\partial x^k} \psi_n \, dx. \tag{7}$$

Now, the derivatives of ψ_n are discontinuous and very irregular at 0 and at l, and consequently limiting processes must be used in evaluating (7). For example, we may choose some function, $F(x, c)$, of x and of a parameter c, which has k continuous derivatives when $c \neq 0$ and approaches ψ_n when $c \to 0$, evaluate (7) with $F(x, c)$ taking the place of ψ_n, and let $c \to 0$ in the result. In particular, we should be prepared to find that this process will yield a result different from that obtained by writing 0 and l for $-\infty$ and ∞ in (7), and then carrying out the integration directly.

The limiting processes can, however, be circumvented as follows: The unsatisfactory feature of (7) is that it involves differentiation of ψ_n; now, neither the formula for the amplitude, $(p \mid n)$, of the distribution-in-p for the nth quantum state,

$$(32^{27}) \qquad (p \mid n) = h^{-\frac{1}{2}} \int \psi_n e^{-ipx/\hbar} \, dx, \tag{8}$$

nor the formula expressing $\text{av}_n \, p^k$ in terms of $(p \mid n)$,

$$\text{av}_n \, p^k = \int (n \mid p) p^k (p \mid n) \, dp, \tag{9}$$

involves differentiation of ψ_n. The evaluation of $\text{av}_n \, p^k$ can thus be effected without complications by means of (8) and (9).

To be sure, in deriving (8), we used 35^{27}, whose validity depends on that of 26^{27}, while in proving the latter we assumed that differentiation of $g(x)$ causes no irregularities; but it is perhaps tolerably clear that, were we to use in (8) the function $F(x, c)$ mentioned above, then calculate (9), and finally let $c \to 0$, the result would be the same as that obtained by a direct use of ψ_n in (8), followed by the evaluation of (9).

Omitting the phase factor and the time factor in (4), since these can be appended to the result later, and remembering that ψ_n vanishes outside the box, we find by means of (8) that

$$(p \mid n) = h^{-\frac{1}{2}} \int_{-\infty}^{\infty} \psi_n e^{-ipx/\hbar} dx = h^{-\frac{1}{2}} \int_0^l \sqrt{\frac{2}{l}} \sin \frac{n\pi x}{l} e^{-ipx/\hbar} dx$$

$$= \sqrt{\frac{l}{2h}} \left[\frac{1 - \exp(in\pi - ipl/\hbar)}{n\pi - pl/\hbar} + \frac{1 - \exp(-in\pi - ipl/\hbar)}{n\pi + pl/\hbar} \right]. \quad (10)$$

Multiplication of (10) by its complex conjugate yields the absolute distribution-in-p for the nth quantum state:[12]

$$(n \mid p)(p \mid n) = \frac{2n^2 \pi l}{\hbar} \cdot \frac{1 - \cos n\pi \cdot \cos(pl/\hbar)}{(n^2 \pi^2 - p^2 l^2/\hbar^2)^2}. \quad (11)$$

The value of (11) at $p = \pm n\pi\hbar/l$, that is, at $p = \pm\sqrt{2mE_n}$, where both the numerator and denominator of (11) vanish, is $\frac{1}{2}lh^{-1}$ and is independent of n. Graphs of (11) for $n = 1, 2, 3$, and 4 are shown in Fig. 39. The distribution (11) is very different

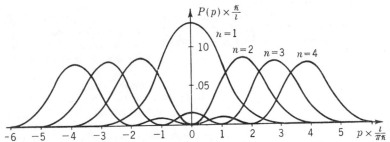

Fig. 39. Distributions-in-p for energy states of a particle in a one-dimensional box.

---

[12] Note that the short-cut argument, "The energy of a boxed particle is all kinetic, and hence, whenever the result of a precise energy measurement is certainly E_n, the result of a precise momentum measurement is certainly either $\sqrt{2mE_n}$ or $-\sqrt{2mE_n}$," which, were it correct, would contradict (11), fails to inquire into the experimental technique to be used in the measurements.

from the corresponding classical distribution-in-p given in Table 1^{11} and again in Equation 27^{12}.

The use of (11) in (9) yields the following values for the averages of the integral powers of p:

$$\text{av}_n\, p^k = \begin{cases} 0 & \text{if } k \text{ is odd} & (12) \\ 2mE_n & \text{if } k = 2 & (13) \\ \infty & \text{otherwise.} & (14) \end{cases}$$

The results (12) and (13) agree with those to be expected by classical analogy in spite of the dissimilarity between the quantum-mechanical and the classical distributions-in-p.

Exercises

1. Show that, for a particle in the box of Fig. 36, $\text{av}_n\, x = \frac{1}{2}l$, $\text{av}_n\, x^2 = \frac{1}{3}l^2\left(1 - \dfrac{3}{2n^2\pi^2}\right)$, and $\text{av}_n\, x^k = \dfrac{l^k}{k+1} - \dfrac{k(k-1)l^2}{4n^2\pi^2}\,\text{av}_n\, x^{k-2}$. Verify that for large values of n the two last results approach the corresponding classical results.

2. Obtain (4) and (5) without a limiting process, but by assuming outright that ψ should vanish outside and at the ends of the box, and that ψ and ψ' should be continuous inside the box.

3. Study (11) for large values of n.

4. To verify that the discontinuities in the derivatives of ψ_n at 0 and at l play an important part in determining the distribution-in-p, show that, if the limits of integration in (7) are changed from $-\infty$ and ∞ to 0 and l, then, in spite of the vanishing of ψ_n outside the box, we get results in disagreement with (14); incidentally, the results we then get are those expected by classical analogy.

5. To elaborate on Exercise 4, draw a curve like the top curve in Fig. 37, except that the corners at 0 and at l are smoothed out; also draw rough graphs of several derivatives of this curve. Then allow the bends at 0 and at l to become sharper and sharper, and study graphically the behavior of the derivatives.

6. A boxed particle is in the nth quantum state. Assume that, if the length of the box is varied slowly, the system will remain in the nth quantum state, so that, in particular, its energy at any instant can be computed from (5) by letting l be the length of the box at that instant; then show that the force exerted by the particle on a wall of the box is $2E_n/l$. Note that this force equals the classical average force.

31. Radiative Transitions

From our discussion of the stationary states, it would appear that if an isolated system is once in an energy state it will remain in that state forever. Experimental evidence regarding the behavior of atoms and molecules indicates, however, that a dynamical system in an excited state may spontaneously go over to a state of lower energy, the transition being accompanied by emission of energy in the form of radiation. The reason for the failure of our elementary calculations to provide for spontaneous transitions is not far to seek: in using the expression $H =$ $p^2/2m + V(x)$ for the total energy of the system, we have at the outset excluded the possibility of conversion of mechanical energy into electromagnetic energy. In the general quantum-mechanical theory,[13] the interaction of matter and radiation is allowed for from the beginning; there we start with the dynamical system[14]

$$\text{atom + radiation,} \tag{1}$$

and the Hamiltonian then consists of terms describing the mechanical energy of the atom, terms describing the energy of the radiation, and terms describing the interaction energy of the atom and the radiation. It then comes about that every energy value of the system (1) given by the theory can be interpreted as a possible energy of the atom alone, plus a possible energy of the radiation alone, plus a small interaction energy, so that it is still permissible to speak of the energy levels of the atom itself. Now, the feature of the general theory that is of particular interest to us at present is this: if we start with the system (1) at $t = 0$ in a state that can be described roughly as

$$\text{atom in an excited state II + no radiation,} \tag{2}$$

we find that by a subsequent instant t the system may have passed over into a state

$$\text{atom in a state I + radiation,} \tag{3}$$

which has the same total energy as the initial state (2), although the energy of the atom itself is now smaller. Whether or not the transition (2) → (3) will actually occur, or the precise instant at which it takes place if it does take place, cannot, according to the theory, be inferred from the information that at $t = 0$ the system is certainly in the state (2); in other words, an excited

---

[13] Dirac, Chapter XI; E. Fermi, *Rev. Mod. Phys.*, **4**, 87 (1932); W. Heitler, *The Quantum Theory of Radiation*, Oxford, The Clarendon Press, 1936.

[14] We use the word *atom* for *material dynamical system*.

atom may 'jump' *spontaneously* into a state of lower energy and in doing so emit radiation.

In our elementary discussion, the subject of radiative transitions is introduced as an afterthought, the formulas for the calculation of transition probabilities and of the frequency of the emitted light are taken for granted, and the relation of these formulas to the fundamental postulates of the general theory is left unclarified. The calculations we shall perform concern systems consisting of a particle moving along the x-axis and are therefore only of academic interest; but the mathematical technique to be employed is a fair prototype of that involved in actual physical problems. Having as yet made no provisions for dealing with physical phenomena taking place in three-dimensional space, we are of course entirely unprepared to discuss the polarization of the light emitted by actual systems, or the dependence of its intensity on the direction from which it may be viewed.

Our first assumption is the celebrated *Bohr frequency condition*:[15]

A. *A spontaneous transition of a dynamical system from an energy state* II *of energy* E_{II} *to an energy state* I *of lower energy* E_I *is accompanied by the emission of radiation of spectroscopic frequency* $\nu_{II \to I}$, *given by the formula*

$$\nu_{II \to I} = \frac{1}{h}(E_{II} - E_I), \tag{4}$$

where h is Planck's constant.

The measure of the likelihood of a spontaneous transition from a state II to a state I is taken to be the constant, denoted by $A_{II \to I}$, such that $A_{II \to I}\, dt$ is the probability that the transition II → I will occur during the infinitesimal interval dt if the system is certainly in the state II at the beginning of the interval dt; $A_{II \to I}$ is called the *transition probability* of the quantum jump II → I, although $A_{II \to I}\, dt$, rather than $A_{II \to I}$ itself, is a probability. In connection with transition probabilities, we introduce the following assumption, essentially equivalent to that first made by Heisenberg in his paper[16] inaugurating quantum mechanics:

B. *The transition probability* $A_{II \to I}$ *for a spontaneous quantum jump of a one-dimensional dynamical system from an energy state*

[15] N. Bohr, *Phil. Mag.*, **26**, 476, 857 (1913).
[16] W. Heisenberg, *Zeits. f. Physik*, **33**, 879 (1925).

II *to an energy state* I *of lower energy is, to a high degree of approximation,*[17] *given by the formula*

$$A_{\text{II}\to\text{I}} = \frac{64\pi^4\epsilon^2(\nu_{\text{II}\to\text{I}})^3}{3hc^3} \left| \frac{\displaystyle\int_{-\infty}^{\infty} \bar{\psi}_{\text{II}}\, x\psi_{\text{I}}\, dx}{\displaystyle\int_{-\infty}^{\infty} \bar{\psi}_{\text{II}}\psi_{\text{II}}\, dx \int_{-\infty}^{\infty} \bar{\psi}_{\text{I}}\psi_{\text{I}}\, dx} \right|^2, \tag{5}$$

where ϵ *is the electric charge of the particle,* c *is the velocity of light,* h *is Planck's constant,* ψ_{I} *and* ψ_{II} *are Schroedinger functions specifying, respectively, the states* I *and* II *of the system, and where* $\nu_{\text{II}\to\text{I}}$ *is given by* (4).

If ψ_{I} and ψ_{II} are both normalized to unity, (5) becomes

$$A_{\text{II}\to\text{I}} = \frac{64\pi^4\epsilon^2(\nu_{\text{II}\to\text{I}})^3}{3hc^3} \left| \int_{-\infty}^{\infty} \bar{\psi}_{\text{II}}\, x\psi_{\text{I}}\, dx \right|^2. \tag{6}$$

The line spectrum of an oscillator. To illustrate the application of the assumptions A and B, we shall now compute the transition probabilities for a linear harmonic oscillator consisting of a particle acted on by a restoring force $-kx$, and having mass m and charge ϵ; in view of the factor ϵ^2 in (5), a system cannot radiate unless it carries an electric charge. The normalized Schroedinger functions for the energy states of the system are

$$(7^{16}) \quad \psi_n = e^{i\gamma_n} N_n H_n\left(\frac{x}{a}\right) e^{-\frac{1}{2}\left(\frac{x}{a}\right)^2} e^{-iE_nt/h}, \qquad n = 0, 1, 2, \cdots, \tag{7}$$

where $a = (\hbar^2/km)^{\frac{1}{4}}$ and $N_n = (a2^n n!\, \pi^{\frac{1}{2}})^{-\frac{1}{2}}$.

The transition probability, $A_{n\to n'}$, for a spontaneous quantum jump of the oscillator from the nth to the n'th energy state depends, according to (6), on the integral

$$\int \bar{\psi}_n\, x\psi_{n'}\, dx, \tag{8}$$

---

[17] We shall treat (5) as exact; in the general theory, besides terms having the form (5) and describing the so-called *dipole* radiation, there appear terms describing *multipole* radiation. See E. U. Condon and G. H. Shortley, *The Theory of Atomic Spectra* [hereafter cited as Condon and Shortley], Chapter IV; Cambridge: The University Press, 1935.

where the ψ's are given by (7). According to 41[8] the values of this integral are

$$\int \bar{\psi}_n x \psi_{n'} \, dx = \begin{cases} e^{-i(\gamma_n - \gamma_{n-1})} a\sqrt{\tfrac{1}{2}n} \, e^{i(E_n - E_{n-1})t/h} & \text{if } n' = n - 1 \\ e^{-i(\gamma_n - \gamma_{n+1})} a\sqrt{\tfrac{1}{2}(n+1)} \, e^{i(E_n - E_{n+1})t/h} & \\ & \text{if } n' = n + 1 \\ 0 & \text{otherwise.} \end{cases} \quad (9)$$

The first line of (9), when used in (6), yields

$$A_{n \to n-1} = \frac{32\pi^4 \epsilon^2 a^2 (\nu_{n \to n-1})^3}{3hc^3} \, n. \quad (10)$$

For an oscillator, $E_n = (n + \tfrac{1}{2})h\nu_c$, so that, according to (4),

$$\nu_{n \to n-1} = \frac{1}{h}[(n + \tfrac{1}{2})h\nu_c - (n - 1 + \tfrac{1}{2})h\nu_c] = \nu_c, \quad (11)$$

and consequently

$$A_{n \to n-1} = \frac{32\pi^4 \epsilon^2 a^2 \nu_c^3}{3hc^3} \, n = \frac{2\epsilon^2 k}{3c^3 m^2} \, n. \quad (12)$$

As we should expect, $A_{n \to n-1}$ vanishes for $n = 0$.

We next consider transitions from the nth state to a state other than the $(n - 1)$th. The second line in (9) does not concern spontaneous transitions, because there $n' > n$; the third line shows that $A_{n \to n'}$ vanishes whenever $n' < n - 1$. Consequently the only possible direct spontaneous transition that an oscillator in the nth quantum state can make is into the $(n - 1)$th level. The spontaneous transitions of an oscillator are represented diagramatically in Fig. 40, which refers to the five lowest quantum states; the horizontal lines indicate the relative positions of the energy levels, and the arrows represent possible spontaneous transitions. Such a diagram summarizes what we call the *selection rules* for the transitions; but it does not display the respective probabilities of the possible transitions.

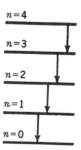

Fig. 40. Transition diagram for a linear harmonic oscillator.

In an experimental study of the light emitted in the spontaneous transitions of an atom, an assemblage of similar atoms is confined in a chamber and is subjected to the action of a suitable exciting agent; and the light emitted by those atoms that become excited and then make spontaneous 'downward' transitions is analyzed spectroscopically. The positions of the resulting spectral lines can be calculated theoretically from the knowledge of the energy levels and selection rules; but the intensities, both absolute and relative, of the possible lines depend also on the method of excitation, and so forth.

Note that the spectroscopic frequency of the light emitted in *any* spontaneous transition of an oscillator is equal to the classical vibration frequency of the oscillator; hence the line spectrum of a linear harmonic oscillator consists of a single line of frequency ν_c. According to our elementary calculations, this line is sharp; the so-called *natural width* of a spectral line (to be distinguished from the width due to the Doppler effect and collision effects) is accounted for by the general theory.

Exercises

1. Let the energy states of a dynamical system having energies smaller than that of a state II be denoted by I', I'', I''', and so on, and let $P_{II}(t)$ denote the probability that the system will still be in the state II at the instant t if it is certainly in this state at $t = 0$; show that $P_{II}(t) = \exp[-(A_{II\to I'} + A_{II\to I''} + A_{II\to I'''} + \cdots)t]$. The time interval during which $P_{II}(t)$ decreases by the factor e^{-1} is called the *mean life* of the state II.

2. A linear harmonic oscillator is certainly in the state $n = 2$ at $t = 0$; show that the probability that it will be in the normal state at the time t is $(1 - e^{-\alpha t})^2$, where $\alpha = 2\epsilon^2 k/3c^3 m^2$. *Hint:* show first that the probability that the oscillator will be in the normal state at the time t, *having jumped from the state $n = 2$ to the state $n = 1$ between the instants t_1 and $t_1 + dt_1$*, is $2\alpha e^{-2\alpha t_1}[1 - e^{-\alpha(t-t_1)}] dt_1$.

3. A linear harmonic oscillator is certainly in the nth quantum state at $t = 0$; show that the probability that it will be in the normal state at the time t is $(1 - e^{-\alpha t})^n$, where $\alpha = 2\epsilon^2 k/3c^3 m^2$.

4. Show that if ψ_n and ψ_k are any two of the functions 4^{30}, then

$$\int \bar{\psi}_n x \psi_k \, dx = \begin{cases} -e^{-i(\gamma_n - \gamma_k)} \dfrac{8lnk}{\pi^2(n^2 - k^2)^2} e^{i(E_n - E_k)t/\hbar} & \text{if } n + k \text{ is odd,} \\ \frac{1}{2}l & \text{if } n = k, \\ 0 & \text{otherwise.} \end{cases} \tag{13}$$

5. Use (13) to show that the transition probabilities of a particle of mass m and charge ϵ in a one-dimensional box of length l are

$$A_{n\to k} = \begin{cases} \dfrac{8\epsilon^2 h^2}{3c^3 m^3 l^4} \cdot \dfrac{n^2 k^2}{n^2 - k^2} & \text{if } n + k \text{ is odd} \\ 0 & \text{if } n + k \text{ is even,} \end{cases} \tag{14}$$

and verify the transition diagram for the six lowest levels given in Fig. 41.

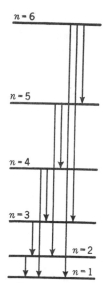

Fig. 41. Transition diagram for a particle in a one-dimensional box.

6. Show that for a charged particle in a one-dimensional box there are sixteen transitions involving only the eight lowest levels, and that these produce fifteen spectral lines. How are these lines spaced on a frequency scale?

7. Show that the respective mean lives of the states $n = 1, 2, 3$, and 4 of a particle in a one-dimensional box are ∞, $3\beta/4$, $5\beta/36$, and $105\beta/2272$, where $\beta = 3c^3ml^4/8e^2h^2$. What is the mean life of the nth quantum state of a charged linear harmonic oscillator?

8. Convince yourself that a free particle cannot make spontaneous radiative transitions even if it carries an electric charge. *Hints*: consider a free particle as a limiting case of a particle in a box, or use (5) and some appropriate limiting procedure, say that of Exercise 5[27].

32. Properties of the One-Dimensional First Schroedinger Equation

In the case of a linear harmonic oscillator, a free particle, a particle in a rectangular potential well, or a particle in a box, the Schroedinger eigenfunctions of H can, as we have seen, be computed readily. There are a few other special cases for which the eigenfunctions of H have been computed explicitly; but in general the solutions of the Schroedinger equation cannot be expressed in terms of the elementary functions. Fortunately, important properties of the solutions can be inferred without solving the equation explicitly; and it is the purpose of this section to enumerate several of these and to provide hints concerning the more involved proofs.[18]

We assume that the first Schroedinger equation for one-dimensional motion, namely, $\psi'' + \kappa[E - V(x)]\psi = 0$, has been transformed into[19]

$$u'' + [\lambda - g(x)]u = 0, \tag{1}$$

where the new independent variable x, the function $g(x)$, and the parameter λ are all free from physical dimensions; $V(x)$, and con-

---

[18] Much of the discussion of this section is based on the work of W. E. Milne, *Trans. Amer. Math. Soc.*, **30**, 797 (1928), and *Phys. Rev.*, **35**, 863 (1930).

[19] See, for example, the transformation from 1[33] to 4[33].

sequently $g(x)$, and all their derivatives will be assumed to be continuous. The symbol u will denote (a) particular solutions of (1) that are not identically zero, but that are not necessarily well-behaved; (b) particular *real* solutions of (1) that are not identically zero, but that are not necessarily well-behaved; and (c) the general solution of (1). It should be clear from the context which use of the symbol u is implied. By *eigenfunctions and eigenvalues of equation* (1) we shall mean the eigenfunctions and eigenvalues of the operator $-d^2/dx^2 + g(x)$, that is, well-behaved solutions of (1) and values of λ for which such solutions exist. Several of the theorems that we proved in Exercise 4^4 and elsewhere are special cases of those taken up here.

1. If a solution of (1) and its first derivative both vanish at a finite value of x, then this solution is identically zero; both u and u' may, however, approach zero when $x \rightarrow \pm \infty$, if u is not identically zero.

2. If $u(x_0) \neq 0$ and $\lambda > g(x_0)$, then $u''(x_0)/u(x_0)$ is negative, and hence u is concave toward the x-axis at $x = x_0$; similarly, if $u(x_0) \neq 0$ and $\lambda < g(x_0)$, then $u''(x_0)/u(x_0)$ is positive, and hence u is convex toward the x-axis at $x = x_0$.

3. If $u(x_0) = 0$ and $\lambda \neq g(x_0)$, then $u''(x_0) = 0$ and $u'''(x_0) \neq 0$, so that u inflects at $x = x_0$.

4. If $u(x_0) \neq 0$, $\lambda = g(x_0)$, and $g'(x_0) \neq 0$, then $u''(x_0) = 0$ and $u'''(x_0) \neq 0$, so that u inflects at $x = x_0$.

5. If u' vanishes at x_1 and at x_2 , and if $\lambda > g(x)$ everywhere between x_1 and x_2 , then u vanishes at least once between x_1 and x_2 .

{Integration of (1) between x_1 and x_2 gives $u'(x_2) - u'(x_1) + \int_{x_1}^{x_2} [\lambda - g]u\,dx$
$= 0$, that is, $\int_{x_1}^{x_2} [\lambda - g]u\,dx = 0$, so that, if $[\lambda - g]$ does not change sign between x_1 and x_2 , then u must do so.}

6. The function uu' can, at most, vanish once in a region throughout which $\lambda < g(x)$; for example, u cannot have two nodes, or a maximum and a node in such a region.

{If uu' vanishes at x_1 and x_2, then, by Rolle's theorem, $d(uu')/dx$ must vanish at least once between x_1 and x_2; now, $d(uu')/dx = u'u' + uu'' = (u')^2 + [g - \lambda]u^2$, and hence $d(uu')/dx > 0$ wherever $\lambda < g$.}

7. If u_1 and u_2 are two particular solutions of (1) then

$$u_1 u_2' - u_2 u_1' = c, \tag{2}$$

where c is a constant.

{Differentiate (2) and eliminate u_1'' and u_2'' by means of (1).}

8. The condition $c = 0$ in (2) is necessary and sufficient in order that u_1 and u_2 be linearly dependent.

{Necessity: if u_1 and u_2 are linearly dependent (so that $u_2 = \text{const.} \times u_1$), then the left side of (2) vanishes. Sufficiency: set $c = 0$ in (2), getting $u_1'/u_1 = u_2'/u_2$, and integrate, getting $\log u_1 = \log u_2 + \text{constant}$, that is, $u_2 = \text{constant} \times u_1$.}

9. Two linearly independent solutions of (1) cannot vanish at the same value of x.

10. If u_1 is a particular solution of (1), then $u_2 = u_1 \displaystyle\int_{x_0}^{x} u_1^{-2}\, dx$, where x_0 is an arbitrarily fixed value of x, is another particular solution of (1); further, u_1 and u_2 are linearly independent, so that

$$u = A u_1 + B u_1 \int_{x_0}^{x} u_1^{-2}\, dx, \tag{3}$$

where A and B are arbitrary constants, is the general solution of (1).

{$u_2' = u_1' \displaystyle\int_{x_0}^{x} u_1^{-2}\, dx + u_1 u_1^{-2} = u_1' \displaystyle\int_{x_0}^{x} u_1^{-2}\, dx + u_1^{-1}$; $u_2'' = u_1'' \displaystyle\int_{x_0}^{x} u_1^{-2}\, dx + u_1' u_1^{-2} - u_1^{-2} u_1' = u_1'' \displaystyle\int_{x_0}^{x} u_1^{-2}\, dx = [g - \lambda] u_1 \displaystyle\int_{x_0}^{x} u_1^{-2}\, dx = [g - \lambda] u_2$; hence u_2 satisfies (1). Substitution of u_1 and u_2 into (2) yields $c = 1$, and hence (theorem 8) u_1 and u_2 are linearly independent.}

11. If u_1 and u_2 are the two particular solutions of (1) that satisfy the conditions[20]

$$u_1(0) = 1, \qquad u_1'(0) = 0, \qquad u_2(0) = 0, \qquad u_2'(0) = 1, \tag{4}$$

---

[20] It is quite immaterial for our purposes whether the explicit analytic expressions for u_1 and u_2 are available or not.

and v is the function

$$v(x) = \sqrt{u_1^2 + u_2^2},\tag{5}$$

then

$$v(0) = 1, \qquad\qquad v'(0) = 0 \tag{6}$$

and

$$v(x) > 0,\tag{7}$$

so that v is a nodeless function of x.

{The equation

$$u_1 u_2' - u_2 u_1' = 1 \tag{8}$$

holds for $x = 0$ and hence (theorem 7) it holds for all values of x; consequently u_1 and u_2 are linearly independent (theorem 8), and (7) follows from theorem 9. Fig. 42, computed numerically, shows v for $\lambda = 1$, 2, and 3 when $g(x) = x^2$.}

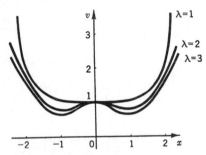

Fig. 42. Graphs of $v(x)$ for the case $g(x) = x^2$.

12. If u_1 and u_2 are the particular solutions (4), and ϕ is the function

$$\phi(x) = \tan^{-1} u_2/u_1,\tag{9}$$

then

$$\phi(0) = 0 \tag{10}$$

and

$$\phi'(x) = v^{-2},\tag{11}$$

so that ϕ is an increasing function of x.

{$\phi' = d(\tan^{-1} u_2/u_1)/dx = (u_1 u_2' - u_2 u_1')(u_1^2 + u_2^2)^{-1}$; (11) then follows from (8) and (5). Graphs of ϕ for $\lambda = 1$, 2, and 3 when $g(x) = x^2$ are shown in Fig. 43, computed numerically.}

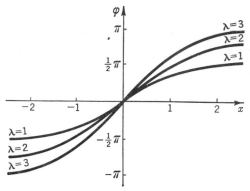

Fig. 43. Graphs of $\phi(x)$ for the case $g(x) = x^2$.

13. The general solution of (1) can be written in the form

$$u = Cv(x) \sin [\phi(x) - \theta], \qquad (12)$$

where C and θ are arbitrary constants;[21] it is then the factor $\sin [\phi(x) - \theta]$ that is responsible for the nodes of u.

{Since u_1 and u_2 satisfying (4) are linearly independent (theorem 8), the general solution of (1) is $u = Au_1 + Bu_2$. Using (5) and (9), we get $Au_1 + Bu_2 = (u_1^2 + u_2^2)^{\frac{1}{2}}[Au_1/(u_1^2 + u_2^2)^{\frac{1}{2}} + Bu_2/(u_1^2 + u_2^2)^{\frac{1}{2}}] = v[A \cos \phi + B \sin \phi] = (A^2 + B^2)^{\frac{1}{2}} v[A \cos \phi/(A^2 + B^2)^{\frac{1}{2}} + B \sin \phi/(A^2 + B^2)^{\frac{1}{2}}]$, and, introducing the constants $C^2 = A^2 + B^2$ and $\theta = - \tan^{-1} A/B$, we get (12).}

14. The function $v(x)$ is the particular solution of the equation

$$v'' + [\lambda - g(x)]v = v^{-3} \qquad (13)$$

that satisfies the conditions

$$(6) \qquad v(0) = 1, \qquad\qquad v'(0) = 0. \qquad (14)$$

{To verify (13), substitute (12) into (1), noting that, in view of (11), $u'' = C(v'' - v^{-3}) \sin [\phi - \theta] = (v'' - v^{-3})v^{-1}u$.}

15. If

$$u'' + [\lambda - g(x)]u = 0, \qquad (15)$$

and

$$U'' + [\lambda + \epsilon - g(x)]U = 0, \qquad (16)$$

---

[21] It should perhaps be emphasized that, when g and λ in (1) are given, then both v and ϕ are definite functions of x even though their analytical forms may not be available.

where ϵ is a positive constant, then U has a node between every two nodes of u; that is, the nodes of u are separated by nodes of U. This theorem is a special case of *Sturm's first comparison theorem*.[22]

{Multiply (15) by U and (16) by u; subtract, getting $Uu'' - uU'' = \epsilon uU$, that is, $d(u'U - uU')/dx = \epsilon uU$; integrate this between two successive nodes x_1 and x_2 of u, getting $u'(x_2)U(x_2) - u(x_2)U'(x_2) - u'(x_1)U(x_1) + u(x_1)U'(x_1) = \epsilon \int_{x_1}^{x_2} uU dx$, that is,

$$u'(x_2)U(x_2) - u'(x_1)U(x_1) = \epsilon \int_{x_1}^{x_2} uU \, dx. \qquad (17)$$

Suppose now that u is positive between x_1 and x_2 and that U is positive at and between x_1 and x_2 ; then (Fig. 44) the left side of (17) is *negative*, while the right side of (17) is *positive*, and we have an inconsistency. We may change the sign of u, of U, or of both, and may allow U to have a node at x_1 , or a node at x_2 , or nodes at both x_1 and x_2 ; but the inconsistency persists until we allow U to have a node *between* x_1 and x_2 .}

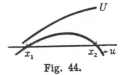

Fig. 44.

The bound case. If $V(x) \to \infty$ when $|x| \to \infty$, then the classical motion of a particle of given total energy does not extend outside certain values of x, and we call the motion *bound*. If x_1 and x_2 are, respectively, the smallest and the greatest roots of the equation $g(x) = \lambda$ in a bound case (Fig. 45), then we use the terms *left outer*, *inner*, and *right outer region* to denote, respectively, the region at the left of x_1 , that between x_1 and x_2 , and that at the right of x_2 .

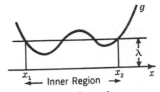

Fig. 45. A bound case.

16. In the bound case, u has at most a finite number of nodes.

{It is perhaps obvious that u has a finite number of nodes (if any) in the finite inner region; and it has at most one node in each of the two outer regions (theorem 6).}

---

[22] E. L. Ince, *Ordinary Differential Equations* [hereafter cited as Ince], page 228.

17. In the bound case, ϕ satisfies the conditions

$$\lim_{x \to -\infty} \phi(x) = \phi_1, \qquad\qquad \lim_{\to \infty} \phi(x) = \phi_2, \qquad (18)$$

where the numbers ϕ_1 and ϕ_2 are finite.

{Were ϕ to decrease without limit when $x \to -\infty$, or to increase without limit when $x \to \infty$, the sine factor in (12) would cause u to have infinitely many nodes, in contradiction to theorem 16. Fig. 43 provides an illustration of the conditions (18).}

18. In the bound case, $\phi' \to 0$ when $|x| \to \infty$.

{Otherwise Equations (18) cannot hold, ϕ' never being negative.}

19. In the bound case, $v \to \infty$ and $v' \to \infty$ when $|x| \to \infty$.

{That $v \to \infty$ when $|x| \to \infty$ follows from (11) and theorem 18; it then follows from (13) that $v'' \to \infty$ when $|x| \to \infty$, and that hence $v' \to \infty$ when $|x| \to \infty$.}

20. In the bound case, Equation (1) possesses (a) solutions that approach zero when $x \to -\infty$; (b) solutions that approach $\pm\infty$ when $x \to -\infty$; (c) solutions that approach zero when $x \to \infty$; and (d) solutions that approach $\pm\infty$ when $x \to \infty$.

{Solutions of type (a) are

$$Av(x) \sin [\phi(x) - \phi_1], \qquad (19)$$

where A is an arbitrary constant. When $x \to -\infty$, (19) becomes $\infty \cdot 0$; to resolve the indeterminacy, we rewrite (19) as $A \sin [\phi - \phi_1]/v^{-1}$, and replace this by the quotient of the derivatives of the numerator and denominator, that is, by $A \cos [\phi - \phi_1]\phi'/(-v^{-2}v') = -A \cos [\phi - \phi_1]/v'$; the last fraction tends to zero when $x \to -\infty$ (theorem 19), and hence (19) does also.

Solutions of Equation (1) pertaining to the case $g = x^2$ and having the form (19) are shown in Fig. 46. All of the solutions shown have the same A. The point at which a curve emerges from the inner into the right outer region is marked by a crossline. In the left portion of the figure, some curves lie too close together to be drawn separately. Note that as λ increases the nodes (except that at $-\infty$) move leftward (as is to be expected from theorem 15 when all u's under consideration have a node at $-\infty$) and that after the rightmost node has moved into the inner region a new node forms at $+\infty$. Note also the good behavior of the curves for $\lambda = 1$ and $\lambda = 3$, that is, for λ's that, according to 28⁴, are eigenvalues of Equation (1) when $g = x^2$.

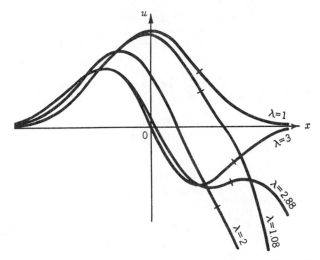

Fig. 46. Solutions of the form (19) for the case $g(x) = x^2$.

Solutions of type (c) are

$$Cv(x) \sin [\phi(x) - \phi_2].\tag{20}$$

Solutions of type (b) are linear combinations of $Bv(x) \cos [\phi(x) - \phi_1]$ and (19); those of type (d) are linear combinations of $Dv(x) \cos [\phi(x) - \phi_2]$ and (20).}

21. If u remains finite in an outer region, then it approaches zero when x recedes outward in this region.

{The solutions $v \sin [\phi - \phi_2]$ and $v \cos [\phi - \phi_2]$ are linearly independent (theorem 8), so that the general solution of (1) can be written as

$$u = Cv(x) \sin [\phi(x) - \phi_2] + Dv(x) \cos [\phi(x) - \phi_2],\tag{21}$$

where C and D are arbitrary constants. When $x \to \infty$, the first term in (21) approaches zero and the second term increases without limit (theorem 20); hence u remains finite when $x \to \infty$ only if $D = 0$; but in this case u approaches zero when $x \to \infty$. Substituting ϕ_1 for ϕ_2 in (21), we get the general solution in the form suitable for proving the theorem for the left outer region.

A graphical argument runs as follows: Let $u(x_0) > 0$ (Fig. 47), where x_0 lies in the right outer region, so that u is convex toward the x-axis everywhere at the right of x_0 (theorem 2). Now (a) if $u'(x_0) \geq 0$, then $u \to \infty$ when $x \to \infty$. If $u'(x_0) < 0$, there are three possibilities: (b) when $x \to \infty$, u remains positive, has a minimum at the right of x_0, and then goes to ∞;

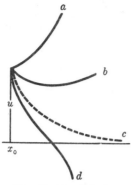

Fig. 47. Possible forms of u in the right outer region.

(c) u approaches the x-axis when $x \to \infty$; (d) u crosses the x-axis at the right of x_0, inflects at the crossing (theorem 3), and then goes to $-\infty$. Thus u remains finite only in the case (c). Similar arguments apply when x_0 is in the right outer region and $u(x_0) \leq 0$, and when x_0 is in the left outer region.}

22. In the bound case, an eigenfunction of Equation (1) vanishes when $|x| \to \infty$.

23. The quantity $\phi_2 - \phi_1$ is an increasing function of λ and tends to ∞ when $\lambda \to \infty$.

{Differentiate (1) partially with respect to λ, multiply the result by u, and substitute $-u''$ for $[\lambda - g]u$, getting $u'' \partial u/\partial \lambda - u \partial u''/\partial \lambda = u^2$, that is, $d(u' \partial u/\partial \lambda - u \partial u'/\partial \lambda)/dx = u^2$; substitute (12) into this, getting

$$\frac{d}{dx}\left\{\left(v'\frac{\partial v}{\partial \lambda} - v\frac{\partial v'}{\partial \lambda}\right)\sin^2[\phi - \theta] + \frac{\partial \phi}{\partial \lambda} + v^{-1}\frac{\partial v}{\partial \lambda}\sin 2[\phi - \theta]\right\} = v^2\sin^2[\phi - \theta].$$

(22)

Choose some value of x, say x_0, and set $\theta = \phi(x_0)$; the expression in { } which vanishes at $x = 0$ in view of (6) and (10), then becomes $\partial \phi(x_0)/\partial \lambda$ at $x = x_0$, so that, integrating (22) from 0 to x_0, we get

$$\frac{\partial \phi(x_0)}{\partial \lambda} = \int_0^{x_0} v^2 \sin^2[\phi(x) - \phi(x_0)]\, dx.$$

(23)

The integrand in (23) is never negative, so that the algebraic sign of the integral is the same as that of x_0; hence, when λ increases, ϕ increases for positive and decreases for negative values of x, as illustrated in Fig. 43.}

24. In order that λ be an eigenvalue of Equation (1) in the bound case, it is necessary and sufficient that

$$\phi_2 - \phi_1 = n\pi, \qquad n = 1, 2, 3, \cdots . \quad (24)$$

{Sufficiency: if (24) holds, then $v \sin[\phi - \phi_1] = v \sin[\phi + n\pi - \phi_2] = \pm v \sin[\phi - \phi_2]$, so that a solution of type (19) is also of type (20), and hence remains finite when $|x| \to \infty$. Necessity: if u is an eigenfunction, then $u \to 0$ when $|x| \to \infty$ (theorem 22), so that both $\phi_1 - \theta$ and $\phi_2 - \theta$ in (12) must be integral multiples of π. The condition (24) is illustrated by the graphs of ϕ for $\lambda = 1$ and $\lambda = 3$ in Fig. 43.}

25. In the bound case, Equation (1) possesses a discrete and nondegenerate eigenvalue spectrum of the form

$$\lambda_1, \lambda_2, \cdots, \lambda_n, \cdots \tag{25}$$

where $\lambda_1 < \lambda_2 < \cdots$, and where λ_1 is greater than the smallest value of $g(x)$.

{An eigenfunction of (1) vanishes when $x \to -\infty$ (theorem 22) and hence has the form (19). If λ is smaller than the smallest value of g, then (19) has no nodes besides that at $-\infty$ (theorem 6); hence $\phi_2 - \phi_1 < \pi$, so that (24) does not hold, and λ is not an eigenvalue. As λ increases, the quantity $\phi_2 - \phi_1$ increases also (theorem 23), and we have an eigenvalue whenever (24) holds. Were an eigenvalue degenerate, the corresponding *general* solution of (1) would be well-behaved; but this is impossible in view of the existence of solutions of types (b) and (d) of theorem 20.}

26. In the bound case, an eigenfunction u_n of Equation (1) belonging to the eigenvalue[23] λ_n has $n + 1$ nodes: one at $-\infty$, one at ∞, and $n - 1$ in the inner region.

27. In the bound case, every eigenfunction of Equation (1) is quadratically integrable in the infinite region.[18]

28. In the bound case, eigenfunctions of Equation (1) belonging to distinct eigenvalues are orthogonal.

{Let u_n and u_m be eigenfunctions of (1) belonging to eigenvalues λ_n and λ_m, so that $u_n'' + [\lambda_n - g]u_n = 0$ and $u_m'' + [\lambda_m - g]u_m = 0$. Multiply the first equation by u_m, the second by u_n, and subtract, getting $u_m u_n'' - u_n u_m'' = (\lambda_m - \lambda_n)u_n u_m$, that is, $d(u_n' u_m - u_n u_m')/dx = (\lambda_m - \lambda_n)u_n u_m$. Integration from $-\infty$ to ∞ yields $0 = (\lambda_m - \lambda_n) \int u_n u_m \, dx$, so that $\int u_n u_m \, dx = 0$ whenever $\lambda_n \neq \lambda_m$. The case of complex u's is taken up in Exercise 3.}

29. If $g(x)$ is even in x in the bound case, then every eigenfunction of Equation (1) belonging to the eigenvalue[23] λ_n is even in x if n is odd, and odd in x if n is even.

{Write $-x$ for x in (1), getting $d^2u(-x)/d(-x)^2 + [\lambda - g(-x)]u(-x) = 0$; since $d^2/d(-x)^2 = d^2/dx^2$ and since in the case under consideration $g(-x) = g(x)$, this equation becomes $d^2u(-x)/dx^2 + [\lambda - g(x)]u(-x) = 0$, so that $u(-x)$ satisfies (1) when $u(x)$ does so. If $u(x)$ is well-behaved, then $u(-x)$ is also well-behaved, so that if $u_n(x)$ is an eigenfunction of (1) belonging to the eigenvalue λ_n, then $u_n(-x)$ is also an eigenfunction of

---

[23] The labeling is that of (25).

(1) belonging to the same eigenvalue; since the spectrum is nondegenerate (theorem 25), it then follows that $u_n(-x) = cu_n(x)$, where c is some constant. Writing $-x$ for x in the last equation, we get $u_n(x) = cu_n(-x)$, and hence $u_n(x) = c^2 u_n(x)$; thus $c^2 = 1$, and $u_n(-x) = \pm u_n(x)$, so that, when $g(x)$ is even in x, then every eigenfunction of (1) is either even or odd in x. The correlation between n and the oddness or evenness of u_n follows from theorem (26) and the fact that an odd function has an odd number of nodes, while an even function has an even number of nodes, zero being counted as an even number.}

30. In order that λ be an eigenvalue of Equation (1) in the bound case, it is necessary and sufficient that

$$\int_{-\infty}^{\infty} v^{-2}\,dx = n\pi, \qquad\qquad n = 1, 2, 3, \cdots . \quad (26)$$

{According to (11) and (10), $\phi = \displaystyle\int_0^x v^{-2}\,dx$; hence $\phi_1 = \displaystyle\int_0^{-\infty} v^{-2}\,dx$, $\phi_2 = \displaystyle\int_0^{\infty} v^{-2}\,dx$, and (24) is equivalent to (26).}

Conditionally bound cases. Certain general characteristics of the eigenvalue spectrum of the Schroedinger equation can be inferred also for cases other than the bound one. For example, if, as shown in Fig. 48 (a), $V(x)$ has a minimum, increases without

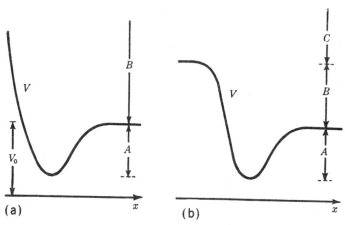

Fig. 48. Conditionally bound cases. A, discrete spectrum; B, continuous nondegenerate spectrum; C, continuous degenerate spectrum.

limit when $x \rightarrow -\infty$, and approaches a constant when $x \rightarrow \infty$, then the spectrum is discrete and nondegenerate in the region A, and continuous and nondegenerate in region B. Again, if, as shown in Fig. 48 (b), $V(x)$ has a minimum, and approaches one constant when $x \rightarrow -\infty$ and another when $x \rightarrow \infty$, then the spectrum is discrete and nondegenerate in region A, continuous and nondegenerate in region B, and continuous and doubly degenerate in region C.

Exercises

1. Taking $g(x)$ and λ from Fig. 45, draw the graph of a function that violates each of the theorems 1, 2, 3, 4, 5, 6, and 21.

2. Show that in the bound one-dimensional case every instantaneous eigenfunction ψ of the Schroedinger equation has the form $\psi = CR(x)$, where $R(x)$ is a real function of x, and C is a constant, real, imaginary, or complex.

3. Prove theorem 28 when the eigenfunctions are allowed to be complex.

4. Show that when $V(x)$ is as in Fig. 48 (a) then (1) possesses, for every real value of λ, solutions of types (a) and (b) of theorem 20.

5. Show that if $V(x)$ is as in Fig. 48 (a) or in Fig. 48 (b) and if λ is less than V_0, then (1) possesses solutions of types (a), (b), (c), and (d) of theorem 20.

6. Justify the classifications of spectra given in Fig. 48.

7. Let u_1 and u_2 be solutions of (1) such that $u_1(x_0) = 1$, $u_1'(x_0) = 0$, $u_2(x_0) = 0$, $u_2'(x_0) = a > 0$, and let $w(x) = (u_1^2 + u_2^2)^{\frac{1}{2}}$; then show that w is the particular solution of the equation $w'' + [\lambda - g(x)]w = a^2 w^{-3}$ that satisfies the conditions $w(x_0) = 1$ and $w'(x_0) = 0$; that the general solution of (1) is $u = Cw \sin\left[a \int_{x_0}^{x} w^{-2}\, dx - \theta\right]$, where C and θ are arbitrary constants; and that in the bound case the condition $a \int w^{-2}\, dx = n\pi$, where $n = 1, 2, 3, \cdots$, is necessary and sufficient in order that λ be an eigenvalue of (1).

8. Examine (3) for the case when a node of u_1 lies between x_0 and x.

9. Set $g(x) = 0$ in (1) and compute analytically the function v defined by (5) and the function ϕ defined by (9). Contrast the results with those shown in Fig. 42 and Fig. 43, referring to a bound case.

10. Set $g(x) = 0$ in (1) and compute analytically the function w defined in Exercise 7. Note the simplification that results when a is taken to be $\lambda^{\frac{1}{2}}$.

Chapter V

APPROXIMATE METHODS FOR TREATING THE ONE-DIMENSIONAL SCHROEDINGER EQUATION

33. Numerical Approximations

The Schroedinger equation can be solved explicitly in terms of known functions for only a few special forms of $V(x)$, so that in many problems approximate methods must be employed. A number of such methods, adapted to various types of situations, have been developed, and in this chapter we shall illustrate a few of them. We shall be concerned with instantaneous ψ-functions, so that in dealing with bound motion we may, according to the result of Exercise 2^{32}, restrict ourselves without loss of generality to *real* solutions of the Schroedinger equation.

We begin with two numerical methods, which we shall use to compute the lowest eigenvalue and the corresponding ψ-function for the Schroedinger equation

$$\psi'' + \kappa(E - Kx^4)\psi = 0, \tag{1}$$

which concerns the motion of a particle in one dimension under the action of a restoring force proportional to the cube of the displacement from $x = 0$. Introducing the parameter

$$\lambda = \kappa^{\frac{3}{5}} K^{-\frac{1}{5}} E \tag{2}$$

and the new independent variable

$$\kappa^{\frac{1}{5}} K^{\frac{1}{5}} x, \tag{3}$$

which we denote (risking an ambiguity) by x, and writing u for ψ, we transform (1) into

$$u'' + (\lambda - x^4)u = 0, \tag{4}$$

an equation of type 1^{32} with $g(x) = x^4$. In view of theorems 22, 25, and 29 of §32, the spectrum of (4) is discrete and nondegenerate, the eigenfunctions vanish when $|x| \to \infty$, and u_1 (the eigenfunction belonging to the lowest eigenvalue λ_1) is even in x, so that we may restrict ourselves to the positive half of the x-axis.

The methods of this section employ numerical integration oᵢ differential equations. Given an ordinary differential equatioɪ involving no literal symbols besides the independent and de- pendent variables and the derivatives of the latter, and given thε numerical initial conditions that a particular solution must satisfɣ at some point $x = x_0$, it is in general possible to calculate nu- merically the values of this particular solution step by step foɪ points other than x_0 and to extend the solution through anɣ desired finite interval of x. Several ways of doing this are avail- able,[1] but it would take us too far afield to describe any of them here. The choice of a particular process of numerical integration depends on the type of equation to be handled, on the mechanical computing devices available, and on the computer's judgment.

The method of two-way integration. Let us assume that $\lambda = \lambda_1$ in (4), λ_1 being precisely the lowest eigenvalue of (4). Further, let $x = x_1$ be some positive value of x, let u_α be the solution of (4) such that $u_\alpha(0) = 1$ and $u'_\alpha(0) = 0$, and let u_β be the solution of (4) such that $u_\beta(x_1) = u_\alpha(x_1)$ and $u_\beta(x) \to 0$ when $x \to \infty$. It is perhaps obvious that then u_α and u_β match properly at x_1, that is, that in addition to the equation $u_\beta(x_1) = u_\alpha(x_1)$ we have $u'_\beta(x_1) = u'_\alpha(x_1)$. The method of two-way integra- tion, about to be illustrated, enables us to approximate λ_1 by studying the departure from proper matching of solutions u_α and u_β computed for trial values of λ_1.

First trial value of λ_1. It is necessary first to make at least a rough estimate of λ_1. In practice, such estimates can be made by reference to experimental data, by comparing the equation in question with similar equations whose properties are known, or by other methods; in treating (4), we shall rely on an approximate analytical formula to be discussed in §34, which estimates the two lowest eigenvalues of (1) as $.87\ \kappa^{-\frac{3}{2}}K^{\frac{1}{2}}$ and $3.77\ \kappa^{-\frac{3}{2}}K^{\frac{1}{2}}$, and shall accordingly adopt

$$\lambda'_1 = .87 \tag{5}$$

as our first approximation to the correct value of λ_1 in (4).

---

[1] See, for example, A. A. Bennett, W. E. Milne, and H. Bateman, *Nu- merical Integration of Differential Equations*, Bulletin No. 92 of the National Research Council, Washington, D. C., 1933; or J. B. Scarborough, *Nu- merical Mathematical Analysis*, Baltimore, The Johns Hopkins Press, 1930.

First rightward integration. We put (5) into (4), getting

$$u'' + (.87 - x^4)u = 0, \tag{6}$$

and calculate numerically that particular solution u_A of (6) which equals 1 at $x = 0$ and has a horizontal tangent there, the computation extending to $x_1 = 1.2$, say. The resulting u_A is shown in Fig. 49; the terminal values of u_A and u_A' are given in Table 3, where the initial conditions are printed in boldface.

TABLE 3: $\lambda_1' = .87$

x	u_A	u_A'
0.0	**1.000**	**.000**
1.2	.504	−.541

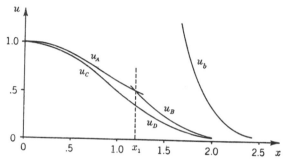

Fig. 49. Solutions of (4) for trial values of λ.

First leftward integration. Our next task is to compute that solution of (6) which equals .504 at $x_1 = 1.2$ and vanishes when $x \to \infty$. It is impossible to do this without using some analytic approximation,[2] and hence we compute instead the solution that equals .504 at $x = 1.2$ and has a horizontal tangent at a sufficiently large value of x, say at $x_2 = 3.0$. To begin with, we compute, working from right to left, the solution u_b that equals .001 at $x_2 = 3.0$ and has a horizontal tangent there; this solution will turn out to have a wrong value at $x_1 = 1.2$, but a correction for this can be made

TABLE 4: $\lambda_1' = .87$

x	u_b	u_b'
1.2	4.010	−7.536
3.0	**.001**	**.000**

later by multiplying u_b by a constant. A portion of the graph of u_b, computed by numerical integration, is shown in Fig. 49; the terminal values of u_b and u_b' are given in Table 4, the initial conditions being again printed in boldface. .

---

[2] It is usually expedient to combine the purely numerical work with an analytical study of the behavior of the solutions for large values of $|x|$.

Matching u_A and u_b at x_1. According to Tables 3 and 4, the ratio of u_A to u_b at $x_1 = 1.2$ is $.504/4.010 = .126$. Consequently we can get the solution of (6) that equals .504 at x_1 and has a horizontal tangent at x_2—the solution

TABLE 5: $\lambda_1' = .87$

x	u_B	u_B'
1.2	.504	$-.947$
3.0	.0001	.0000

denoted by u_B—simply by multiplying u_b by .126; see Fig. 49 and Table 5.

An estimate of $u_1'(x_1)$. Although u_A and u_B are equal at x_1, their derivatives at x_1, equal respectively to $-.541$ and $-.947$, are different; hence .87 is not the correct value of λ_1, and we proceed to improve it. Let u_1 be the as yet unknown eigenfunction of (4) belonging to the lowest eigenvalue and equal to 1 at $x = 0$. The slope of u_1 at $x_1 = 1.2$ is not available, but an estimate of it can be made by taking the average of $u_A'(x_1)$ and $u_B'(x_1)$:

$$u_1'(1.2) \sim \tfrac{1}{2}(-.541 -.947) = -.744. \tag{7}$$

Second trial value of λ_1. Let $\lambda_1'' = \lambda_1' + \Delta\lambda'$ be the second trial value of λ_1, presumably better than λ'_1, and let u_C be the solution of

$$u'' + (\lambda_1'' - x^4)u = 0 \tag{8}$$

that equals 1 at $x = 0$ and has a horizontal tangent there. Then

$$u_C'' = (x^4 - \lambda_1')u_C - \Delta\lambda' u_C, \tag{9}$$

and integrating this between 0 and x_1, we get

$$u_C'(x_1) = \int_0^{x_1} (x^4 - \lambda_1')u_C \, dx - \Delta\lambda'\int_0^{x_1} u_C \, dx. \tag{10}$$

Let us now assume that in the region from 0 to x_1 the function u_C does not differ much from u_A, so that it is permissible to replace u_C by u_A on the right of (10):

$$u_C'(x_1) \sim \int_0^{x_1} (x^4 - \lambda_1')u_A \, dx - \Delta\lambda'\int_0^{x_1} u_A \, dx. \tag{11}$$

Since $u_A'' = (x^4 - \lambda_1')u_A$, the first integral on the right of (11) is just $u_A'(x_1)$, namely $-.541$. The second integral can be obtained either from the numerical values of u_A not given here, or graphically from Fig. 49; it equals approximately .90. Equation (11) thus yields

$$u_C'(1.2) \sim -.541 -.90\Delta\lambda'. \tag{12}$$

Using (7), our estimate of the correct value of the derivative at 1.2, to eliminate $u'_c(1.2)$ from (12), we find that $\Delta\lambda' \sim (.744 - .541)/.90 = .23$, so that

$$\lambda''_1 = .87 + .23 = 1.10. \tag{13}$$

Second rightward and leftward integrations. Equation (8) now becomes

$$u'' + (1.10 - x^4)u = 0; \tag{14}$$

we compute in the region from 0 to 1.2 its solution u_c such that $u_c(0) = 1$ and $u'_c(0) = 0$ (Fig. 49 and Table 6), compute in the region from 3.0 to 1.2 its solution u_d such that $u_d(3.0) = .001$ and $u'_d(3.0) = 0$ (Table 7), and then multiply u_d by $.366/3.798 = .0964$ to get the solution u_D that equals u_c at $x_1 = 1.2$ and has a horizontal tangent at $x_2 = 3.0$ (Fig. 49 and Table 8). The derivatives

TABLE 6: $\lambda''_1 = 1.10$			TABLE 7: $\lambda''_1 = 1.10$			TABLE 8: $\lambda''_1 = 1.10$		
x	u_c	u'_c	x	u_d	u'_d	x	u_D	u'_D
0.0	1.000	.000	1.2	3.798	-6.952	1.2	.366	$-.670$
1.2	.366	$-.752$	3.0	.001	.000	3.0	.0001	.0000

of u_c and u_D do not match at 1.2 (Tables 6 and 8), so that 1.10 is not the correct value of λ_1; but as seen from Fig. 49 the curves u_c and u_D join at $x_1 = 1.2$ much more smoothly than do the curves u_A and u_B, and hence 1.10 is a decided improvement over the first trial value .87.

Third trial value of λ_1. The respective ratios of the slopes at $x_1 = 1.2$ of the solutions obtained above by the rightward and the leftward integrations are

$$\lambda = .87: \quad u'_A(x_1)/u'_B(x_1) = (-.541)/(-.947) = .571 \tag{15}$$

$$\lambda = 1.10: \quad u'_c(x_1)/u'_D(x_1) = (-.752)/(-.670) = 1.122. \tag{16}$$

For the correct value of λ_1, the ratio would be 1; so we interpolate between (15) and (16) for the value of λ corresponding to the ratio 1, and get

$$\lambda'''_1 = [.87(1.122 - 1.000) + 1.10(1.000 - .571)]/$$

$$[1.122 - .571] = 1.049 \tag{17}$$

as our third approximation to λ_1.

Concluding remarks.   It appears that the lowest eigenvalue of (4) lies between .87 and 1.10, and that the value 1.049 is likely to be a good approximation; further approximations can be made by further two-way integration.   If high accuracy is desired, the numerical integration must at an appropriate stage be made correspondingly accurate and the point at which the final[3] leftward integration is begun must be chosen with particular care. As we shall see below, the value of λ_1, correct to at least four significant figures, is 1.0605, so that the result 1.049 obtained above is in error by about 1 per cent.

Approximate numerical eigenvalues and eigenfunctions of (1) can of course be obtained from those of (4) by means of (2) and (3).

Milne's method.[4]   This method is particularly expedient when several eigenvalues and eigenfunctions of a given Schroedinger equation are to be computed.   Adapting the results of Exercise 7[32] to our special equation (4) and setting[5] $x_0 = 0$ and $a = \lambda^{\frac{1}{4}}$, we find that, if w is the solution of the equation

$$w'' + (\lambda - x^4)w = \lambda w^{-3} \qquad (18)$$

such that $$w(0) = 1, \qquad w'(0) = 0, \qquad (19)$$

then the condition

$$\pi^{-1}\lambda^{\frac{1}{4}} \int w^{-2}\,dx = n, \quad n = 1, 2, 3, \cdots \quad (20)$$

is necessary and sufficient in order that λ be an eigenvalue of (4). Rough estimates show that λ_1 and λ_2 are likely to lie between .5 and 4.5; so we set λ, in turn, equal to 1, 2, 3, and 4, and for each of these values of λ compute numerically the solution (19) of (18), starting at $x = 0$ and ending at a point beyond which w^{-2} is sufficiently small.[6]   We then compute the left side of (20) [which we denote by J]

TABLE 9

λ	J
1	.9699
2	1.3995
3	1.7487
4	2.0602

[3] To shorten the preliminary work, the earlier approximations may be obtained without using too large a value of x_2.

[4] W. E. Milne, *Phys. Rev.*, **35**, 863 (1930).

[5] The choice $x_0 = 0$ causes w to be even in x, so that the computations may be restricted to positive values of x; the choice $a = \lambda^{\frac{1}{4}}$ then makes w particularly flat at $x = 0$ (Exercise 6), thus simplifying the numerical work still further.

[6] A sample computation is given in detail in reference 4.

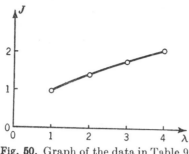

Fig. 50. Graph of the data in Table 9.

for each of the four λ's, getting Table 9 and Fig. 50. Inspection of these results in the light of (20) shows that the first eigenvalue is a little greater than 1, while the second is a little smaller than 4, and interpolation by means of Table 9 yields $\lambda_1 = 1.0605$ and $\lambda_2 = 3.7998$. Substituting these results into (2), we get the following rather accurate estimates of the two lowest eigenvalues of (1):

$$E_1 = 1.0605\,\kappa^{-\frac{2}{3}}K^{\frac{1}{3}}, \qquad E_2 = 3.7998\,\kappa^{-\frac{2}{3}}K^{\frac{1}{3}}. \tag{21}$$

Milne's method for computing eigenfunctions is outlined in reference 4.

Exercises

1. Explain why we may expect, on the basis of Tables 3 and 5, that $u_1'(1.2)$ lies within rather than outside the limits $-.541$ and $-.947$.

2. Suppose the solutions u_A and u_B of (6) and u_C and u_D of (14) to be extended rightward in Fig. 49; then describe the behavior of each for large values of x. Note that $.87 < \lambda_1 < 1.10 < \lambda_2$.

3. When dealing with (4) we should choose x_2 greater than the fourth root of the trial value of λ. Why?

4. Outline the steps for the calculation of the second eigenvalue of (4) by two-way integration.

5. Propose a procedure for using two-way integration to compute eigenvalues and eigenfunctions when $V(x)$ is not even in x.

6. Show that the first five derivatives of the solution (19) of Equation (18) vanish at $x = 0$.

34. Expansions in Powers of $\hbar$

The next method[7] of approximation to be outlined consists in expressing the solutions of the Schroedinger equation

$$\psi'' + \frac{2m}{\hbar^2}[E - V(x)]\psi = 0 \tag{1}$$

----

[7] Developed by L. Brillouin (1926), H. Jeffreys (1923), H. A. Kramers (1926), and G. Wentzel (1926), and in quantum-mechanical discussions variously called the J. W. B. K. method, the B. W. K. method, the W. B. K. method, and so on. For a rigorous discussion, extensive references, and

in a form involving power series in h and then neglecting the higher powers of h.

We look for solutions of (1) of the form

$$\psi = Ce^{i\phi(x)/h}, \tag{2}$$

where C is a constant and ϕ is an as yet undetermined function of x which, as seen by substituting (2) into (1), must satisfy the equation

$$i\hbar\phi'' - (\phi')^2 + 2m[E - V(x)] = 0. \tag{3}$$

To get an approximate solution of (3), we express ϕ in the form

$$\phi(x) = \phi_0(x) + \hbar\phi_1(x) + \hbar^2\phi_2(x) + \cdots, \tag{4}$$

where the subscripted ϕ's are independent of $\hbar$, and assume that on account of the smallness of $\hbar$ the first two terms in (4) give a sufficiently good approximation to ϕ; a close scrutiny of (3) is of course required to tell just how good this approximation may actually be for various values of x. Substituting (4) into (3) and neglecting powers of $\hbar$ higher than the first, we then get the equation

$$\{2m[E - V] - (\phi_0')^2\} + \hbar\{i\phi_0'' - 2\phi_0'\phi_1'\} = 0. \tag{5}$$

In order that (5) may hold identically in $\hbar$, each $\{\ \}$ must vanish separately, so that

$$\phi_0' = \pm \sqrt{2m[E - V]} \tag{6}$$

and

$$\phi_1' = \tfrac{1}{2}i\phi_0''/\phi_0' = \tfrac{1}{2}i\frac{d}{dx}\log\phi_0'. \tag{7}$$

Integrating (6), we get $\phi_0 = \pm\int\sqrt{2m[E - V]}\,dx$, that is,

$$\phi_0 = \pm\int_{x_0}^{x} \sqrt{2m[E - V(x)]}\,dx + c_1, \tag{8}$$

where x_0 is an arbitrarily fixed value of x and c_1 is an arbitrary constant. Integrating (7), we get $\phi_1 = \tfrac{1}{2}i\log\phi_0' + c_2$; this result is inconvenient if ϕ_0' is negative, and therefore we replace it by

---

cautions concerning this important method, see Kemble, Section 21. For an application of this method to the classical problem of the vibrations of a string of nonuniform density, see J. C. Slater and N. H. Frank, *Introduction to Theoretical Physics* [hereafter cited as Slater and Frank], Chapter XIV; New York and London: McGraw-Hill Book Co., 1933.

$\phi_1 = \frac{1}{2}i \log |\phi_0'| + c_2$, recalling that the logarithm of a negative function differs only by an imaginary constant from the logarithm of the absolute value of the function, and that c_2 is an arbitrary constant in any case. Thus we get the approximate equation

$$\phi(x) \cong \phi_0(x) + \tfrac{1}{2}i\hbar \log |\phi_0'|, \qquad (9)$$

where ϕ_0 is given by (8) and c_2 is absorbed in c_1. Substituting (9) into (2) and rearranging the result, we finally get our approximate solution in the form

$$\psi_{\text{app.}} = C\{2m \,|\, E - V(x)\,|\}^{-\frac{1}{4}}$$

$$\exp\left(\pm\frac{i}{\hbar}\int_{x_0}^{x} \sqrt{2m[E - V(x)]}\,dx\right), \quad (10)$$

where C remains arbitrary. The two solutions contained in (10) and differing in the sign of the exponent are linearly independent, and hence the approximate general solution of (1) is

$$\psi_{\text{app.}} = \{2m \,|\, E - V\,|\}^{-\frac{1}{4}}\left\{A \exp\left(\frac{i}{\hbar}\int_{x_0}^{x} \sqrt{2m[E - V]}\,dx\right)\right.$$

$$\left. + B \exp\left(-\frac{i}{\hbar}\int_{x_0}^{x} \sqrt{2m[E - V]}\,dx\right)\right\}, \quad (11)$$

where A and B are arbitrary constants; an alternative form of (11) is

$$\psi_{\text{app.}} = C\{2m \,|\, E - V\,|\}^{-\frac{1}{4}} \cos\left\{\frac{1}{\hbar}\int_{x_0}^{x} \sqrt{2m[E - V]}\,dx + \theta\right\}, \quad (12)$$

where C and θ are arbitrary constants.

The approximate solutions (11) and (12) of the Schroedinger equation are usually called W. B. K. ψ-functions, or B. W. K. ψ-functions.[7]

Connection formulas. Consider now the case (Fig. 51), when V is greater than E everywhere in region I lying at the left of x_1. Then set $x_0 = x_1$ in (11), and recall that the precise solutions of (1) that are of interest to us are required to be well-behaved. Writing $[E - V]^{\frac{1}{2}} = i [V - E]^{\frac{1}{2}}$ and remembering that $x \leq x_1$ in region

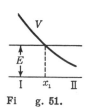

Fig. 51.

I, we then find that as $x \to -\infty$ the A-term in (11) increases without limit while the B-term approaches zero. Hence, in order that (11) may approximate a solution of (1) which remains finite when $x \to -\infty$, we must set $A = 0$ and adopt the function

$$\psi_{\text{app.}}^{\text{I}} = B\{2m[V - E]\}^{-\frac{1}{4}} e^{\frac{1}{\hbar} \int_{x_1}^{x} \sqrt{2m[V-E]}\, dx} \qquad (13)$$

as the appropriate approximation for region I. Incidentally, at $x = x_1$ the function (13) becomes infinite on account of the factor $\{\ \}^{-\frac{1}{4}}$, and hence, although (13) may be a good approximation to a precise solution of (1) for values of x lying sufficiently far to the left of x_1, it certainly departs violently from this solution when $x \to x_1$; this departure is illustrated in Fig. 54, which presents the correct ψ-function for the fifth energy state of an oscillator together with a W. B. K. approximation to this function.

In region II of Fig. 51 no limitations are put on the arbitrary constants, and we may take the approximate general solution to have the form (12).

Now, how should the adjustable constants in (12) be chosen in order that (12) may connect properly with (13), that is, in order that (12) may approximate in region II the same exact solution of (1) which (13) approximates in region I? A complicated computation, which we omit, gives the following answer: the approximate solution for region II that connects properly with (13) is

$$\psi_{\text{app.}}^{\text{II}} = 2B\{2m[E - V]\}^{-\frac{1}{4}} \cos\left\{\frac{1}{\hbar} \int_{x_1}^{x} \sqrt{2m[E - V]}\, dx - \tfrac{1}{4}\pi\right\}, \qquad (14)$$

which is obtained from (12) by letting $C = 2B$, $x_0 = x_1$, and $\theta = -\tfrac{1}{4}\pi$. Incidentally, from the elementary standpoint, (13) and (14) do not join at all smoothly at x_1, where both are infinite; but both are, of course, poor approximations near x_1.

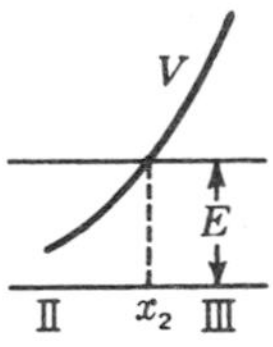

For the case (Fig. 52) when V is greater than E everywhere at the right of x_2, it is found that the appropriate approximation for the region III is

Fig. 52.

$$\psi_{\text{app.}}^{\text{III}} = A\{2m[V - E]\}^{-\frac{1}{4}} e^{\frac{1}{\hbar} \int_{x}^{x_2} \sqrt{2m[V-E]}\, dx} \qquad (15)$$

and that the function approximating in region II of Fig. 52 the same exact solution of (1) that (15) approximates in region III is

$$\psi_{\text{app.}}^{\text{II}} = 2A \{2m[E - V]\}^{-\frac{1}{4}} \cos\left\{\frac{1}{\hbar} \int_{x_2}^{x} \sqrt{2m[E - V]}\, dx + \tfrac{1}{4}\pi\right\}. \quad (16)$$

The bound case. We turn next to the bound case, restricting ourselves to a potential V such that V' vanishes only once, as in Fig. 53. According to theorem 25 of §32, the energy in this case is

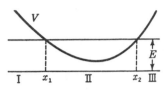

Fig. 53. A bound case.

quantized, a fact that shows up in our present approximate work as follows: On the one hand, $\psi_{\text{app.}}$ must have the form (13) in region I, so that in region II it must have the form (14); on the other hand, $\psi_{\text{app.}}$ must have the form (15) in region III, so that in region II it must have the form (16). Consequently, the proper connections can be made only if the functions (14) and (16) are equal to each other, that is, only if throughout region II we have

$$B \cos\left\{\frac{1}{\hbar}\int_{x_1}^{x} - \frac{1}{4}\pi\right\} = A \cos\left\{\frac{1}{\hbar}\int_{x_2}^{x} + \frac{1}{4}\pi\right\}, \quad (17)$$

where $\int$ stands for $\int \sqrt{2m[E - V]}\, dx$. Now, differentiating (17) with respect to x and canceling the factor common to both sides of the result, we get an equation precisely like (17), except that the cosines are replaced by sines; and combining this equation with (17), we get

$$\tan\left\{\frac{1}{\hbar}\int_{x_1}^{x} - \frac{1}{4}\pi\right\} = \tan\left\{\frac{1}{\hbar}\int_{x_2}^{x} + \frac{1}{4}\pi\right\}. \quad (18)$$

Since the period of the tangent is π, the arguments of the two tangents in (18) must differ by $n\pi$, where n is an integer or zero, and we finally get

$$2\int_{x_1}^{x_2} \sqrt{2m[E - V(x)]}\, dx = (n + \tfrac{1}{2})h, \quad n = 0, 1, 2, \cdots, \quad (19)$$

where negative n's are suppressed, since the left side of (19) is positive. For a preassigned V, Equation (19) is a condition on E, and consequently only for particular E's is it possible properly to connect our approximate ψ's. The condition (19) is thus an *approximate quantization rule* for the energy when the potential has the form shown in Fig. 53.

Examples. To illustrate the use of (19), we shall employ it to estimate the energy levels for the case of the particular potential $V(x) = Kx^4$. The integrand in (19) is now even in x, and the classical limits of motion for a particle of energy E are $x_1 = -(E/K)^{\frac{1}{4}}$ and $x_2 = (E/K)^{\frac{1}{4}}$, so that (19) becomes

$$4 \int_0^{(E/K)^{\frac{1}{4}}} \sqrt{2m[E - Kx^4]}\, dx = (n + \tfrac{1}{2})h, \quad n = 0, 1, 2, \cdots. \quad (20)$$

The substitution $y = Kx^4/E$ sends (20) into

$$\sqrt{2m}\, K^{-\frac{1}{4}} E^{\frac{3}{4}} \int_0^1 (1 - y)^{\frac{1}{2}} y^{-\frac{3}{4}}\, dy = (n + \tfrac{1}{2})h. \quad (21)$$

The integral in (21) is approximately[8] 3.50, so that, writing E_n for E, we finally get

$$E_n = .87(2n + 1)^{\frac{4}{3}} \kappa^{-\frac{2}{3}} K^{\frac{1}{3}}, \quad n = 0, 1, 2, \cdots \quad (22)$$

as the approximate formula for the energy levels. The two lowest levels are given by (22) as

$$E_0 = .87\kappa^{-\frac{2}{3}} K^{\frac{1}{3}}, \qquad E_1 = 3.77\kappa^{-\frac{2}{3}} K^{\frac{1}{3}}. \quad (23)$$

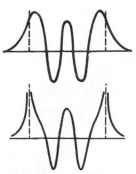

Comparison with 21[33] shows that, when $V = Kx^4$, the formula (19) underestimates the lowest level by about 18 per cent, and the second level by about 1 per cent; this formula usually gives better results for the higher levels.

The B.W.K. ψ-function for the fifth energy state of a linear harmonic oscillator is shown in Fig. 54, together with a correct Schroedinger function for this state. The corresponding distribution-in-x, $\bar{\psi}_{\text{app.}}\psi_{\text{app.}}$, is shown in Fig. 55; note that in the inner region this distribution is a compromise between the

Fig. 54. *Top:* a Schroedinger function. *Bottom:* the W.B.K. approximation to this function.

[8] See, for example, H. B. Dwight, *Tables of Integrals and Other Mathematical Data*, formula 855.2 and table 1018; New York: The Macmillan Co., 1934. Or B. O. Peirce, *A Short Table of Integrals*, formula 482 and the table of logarithms of the gamma function; Boston: Ginn and Co.

Fig. 55. *Top:* a Schroedinger distribution-in-x and the corresponding classical distribution-in-x. *Bottom:* the W.B.K. distribution-in-x for the same state.

classical and the correct quantum-mechanical distributions, both of which are shown at the top of the figure.

A comparison with the Bohr theory. In the Bohr theory, the energy of a particle moving in the field shown in Fig. 53 is quantized by the Wilson-Sommerfeld rule, which states that $2 \int_{x_1}^{x_2} p\, dx = nh$, where p is the momentum of the particle at the point x, and $n = 1, 2, 3, \cdots$; this rule can be rewritten as $2 \int_{x_1}^{x_2} \sqrt{2m\,[E - V(x)]}\ dx = nh$. The Wilson-Sommerfeld rule and the in general more accurate approximate rule (19) may be contrasted by saying that the former uses *integer quantization* and the latter *odd half-integer quantization*. Note that the Wilson-Sommerfeld rule bears some resemblance to the exact formula 26[32].

Exercises

1. Show that (19) yields (fortuitously) the correct energy levels for the linear harmonic oscillator. Remember Fig. 54, however.

2. Show that if $V(x) = c \mid x \mid$, where c is a positive constant, then the approximate energy levels given by (19) are $E_n = [3c(n + \tfrac{1}{2})h/8\sqrt{2m}]^{\frac{2}{3}}$.

3. Apply, in turn, the rule (19) and the Wilson-Sommerfeld rule to a particle in a box and compare the results with 5[30].

4. Consider a region in which $E > V$ and show that the factor $\{\ \}^{-\frac{1}{2}}$ in (11) contributes to the approximate distribution-in-x, $\bar{\psi}_{app.}\psi_{app.}$, a factor that is just the classical distribution-in-x. What is the nature of the remaining factor in $\bar{\psi}_{app.}\psi_{app.}$?

5. Consider a particle in a potential box with a slanting bottom, Fig. 17[11], and show (essentially by inspection) that for the higher energies the W. B. K. method gives a result in qualitative agreement with the corresponding classical result of Exercise 14[11]. We do not stress the agreement for the lower energies, because for lower energies this method might be unreliable; but see Exercise 8[36].

6. Show that our disregard for the physical dimensions of ϕ_0' in (7) does not invalidate (10).

35. A Variation Method[9]

In preparation for the next method of approximation, we shall say a word about ordinary curve fitting. If a given curve (say a trace made by a recording instrument), whose correct equation $y = F(x)$ is either unknown or inconveniently too complicated, happens to be approximately straight, it is often expedient to write $y = ax + b$, to adjust the numerical values of the constants a and b so as to obtain a 'best fit' to the given curve, and then to use the linear equation as an approximation to the correct one. Similarly, if the given curve resembles a parabola, the function $y = ax^2 + bx + c$ may be profitably fitted to it; in general, if a given curve has a shape resembling that of some simple function, it is sometimes expedient to adjust the numerical constants in this function so as to fit the given curve best, and then to use the resulting function as an approximation to the given curve. The process of curve fitting consists essentially of three steps:

I, to choose a function $f(x)$ that has the appropriate general shape and contains adjustable constants $a, b, \cdots$,

II, to decide on a criterion of 'best fit,' and

III, to adjust the constants $a, b, \cdots$, in $f(x)$ so as to obtain the best fit.

In its most elementary aspect, which alone we shall consider, the variation method for approximate solution of a one-dimensional first Schroedinger equation can be viewed as essentially a process of curve fitting, consisting of the steps I, II, and III enumerated above. To be sure, in ordinary curve fitting we fit a chosen function to a *given* curve, while in the variation method we fit a chosen function to an *unknown* solution of a given differential equation; the underlying ideas of the two types of computations have, nevertheless, much in common. In describing the method, we shall restrict ourselves to approximating the lowest eigenvalue E_0 and the corresponding normalized eigenfunction ψ_0 of the Schroedinger equation pertaining to bound motion.

I. **The choice of the approximating ψ.** Our first step is to write down a function ψ that has the same general shape as the

---

[9] For important ramifications and extensions of this method (which, from the mathematical standpoint, is best approached through the calculus of variation) and for references see, for example, Pauling and Wilson, and Kemble.

unknown ψ_0 and contains some adjustable constants a, b, $\cdots$. This step is feasible because the theorems of §32 enable us at once to enumerate several important features of the unknown ψ_0 . Thus ψ_0 , being the lowest eigenfunction for a bound motion, can be taken as real, vanishes when $|x| \to \infty$, has no nodes at finite values of x so that it can be taken as everywhere positive, and has one maximum and no minima; if $V(x)$ happens to be even in x, then ψ_0 is also even in x. A person familiar with the shapes of ψ-functions in a variety of special cases could perhaps infer additional information about ψ_0 by inspecting the given $V(x)$ more closely. We shall take it for granted in the sequel that ψ is normalized.

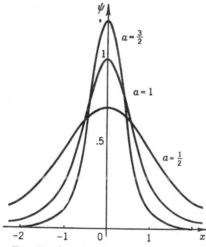

Fig. 56. Graphs of the function (1).

To illustrate: If $V = Kx^4$, say, then ψ_0 vanishes when $|x| \to \infty$, has no nodes at finite values of x, is even in x, and, if taken as positive, has a maximum at $x = 0$. Several simple functions of this general shape come to mind, among them the function $\psi = N(1 + a^2 x^2)^{-2}$, where N is the normalizing factor and a is a single adjustable constant that we shall take to be positive; written out in detail, this function is

$$\psi = 4\sqrt{\frac{a}{5\pi}} \frac{1}{(1 + a^2 x^2)^2}; \quad (1)$$

graphs of (1) for three values of a are shown in Fig. 56. Thus, for example, in dealing with the case $V = Kx^4$, we may adopt (1) as the function to be fitted[10] (by an adjustment of a) to the unknown ψ_0 .

Extraordinary coincidences excepted, the approximating ψ chosen in this manner is of course not precisely equal to the unknown ψ_0 even for special values of the adjustable constants;

---

[10] Incidentally, the function (1) would be a rather bad approximating ψ when $V = Kx^4$, because it does not decrease sufficiently fast when $|x|$ grows large. Indeed, for large values of $|x|$, Equation 1[33] becomes $\psi'' \cong \kappa Kx^4 \psi$; for large values of $|x|$, approximate solutions of the latter equation are $x^p e^{\pm q x^3}$, where p is arbitrary and $9q^2 = \kappa K$; the function (1), on the other hand, behaves for large values of $|x|$ as x^{-4}.

instead, ψ is a superposition of the various unknown instantaneous Schroedinger eigenfunctions of H. But, since ψ has substantially the same shape as ψ_0, ψ_0 appears in this superposition particularly prominently; in other words, *the approximating ψ represents instantaneously a state for which the energy of the system is not a certainty, but is particularly likely to be E_0*.

II. **The criterion of best fit** used in approximating the lowest eigenfunction by the variation method can be set up as follows: Let E_0 be the lowest energy level of the system (that is, the lowest possible result of a precise measurement of the energy of the system). Let av E be the expected average of the energy (that is, the probability-weighted arithmetic average of the possible results of a precise energy measurement) of this system for some state that is either the normal state, or a higher energy state, or, in general, a superposition of the various energy states. It is then perhaps obvious (if not, recall Exercise 17[11]) that av $E \geq E_0$. If the state in question is specified by a Schroedinger function ψ, so that we may replace the symbol av E by av$_\psi$ E, this result takes the form

$$\text{av}_\psi\, E \geq E_0. \tag{2}$$

The $=$ sign in (2) applies if and only if ψ is the Schroedinger function ψ_0 specifying the normal state of the system.

Now, if ψ is normalized, then, according to the Schroedinger expectation formula 2[18],

$$\text{av}_\psi\, E = \int \bar{\psi} H \psi \, dx, \tag{3}$$

where H is the Hamiltonian operator of the system; and, combining ⟨3⟩ with (2), we conclude that

$$\int \bar{\psi} H \psi \, dx \geq E_0, \tag{4}$$

whenever ψ is normalized. The relation ⟨4⟩ holds, of course, whether ψ is an instantaneous or a time-dependent ψ-function.

The relation ⟨4⟩, taken together with its special case

$$\int \bar{\psi}_0 H \psi_0 \, dx = E_0, \tag{5}$$

suggests the following criterion of good fit, adopted in the variation method: *of two normalized ψ's, the one for which the integral $\int \bar{\psi} H \psi \, dx$ has the lesser numerical value is the better approximation to ψ_0*.

III. **Adjustment of the constants in** ψ. Substitution of the approximating ψ into $\int \bar{\psi} H \psi \, dx$ yields a number involving the adjustable constants $a, b, \cdots$, appearing in ψ. According to the criterion quoted above, to make ψ fit the unknown ψ_0 best, we must choose these constants so as to make $\int \bar{\psi} H \psi \, dx$ as small as possible. Thus our problem reduces to that of minimizing a function of $a, b, \cdots$, so that, to determine the best values of $a, b, \cdots$, we need only to solve simultaneously the equations

$$\frac{\partial}{\partial a} \int \bar{\psi} H \psi \, dx = 0, \qquad \frac{\partial}{\partial b} \int \bar{\psi} H \psi \, dx = 0, \cdots . \qquad \langle 6 \rangle$$

To illustrate, we return to the potential $V = K x^4$ and to the approximating function (1). We have

$$\int \bar{\psi} H \psi \, dx$$

$$= \int \left[4 \sqrt{\frac{a}{5\pi}} \, (1 + a^2 x^2)^{-2} \right] \left[-\frac{1}{\kappa} \frac{d^2}{dx^2} + K x^4 \right] \left[4 \sqrt{\frac{a}{5\pi}} \, (1 + a^2 x^2)^{-2} \right] dx$$

$$= \frac{16a}{5\pi} \int \left[\frac{4a^2}{\kappa} \, (1 + a^2 x^2)^{-5} - \frac{24a^4}{\kappa} \, x^2 (1 + a^2 x^2)^{-6} + K x^4 (1 + a^2 x^2)^{-4} \right] dx, \langle 7 \rangle$$

and evaluation of the integral yields

$$\int \bar{\psi} H \psi \, dx = \frac{7a^2}{5\kappa} + \frac{K}{5a^4} . \qquad \langle 8 \rangle$$

Thus

$$\frac{d}{da} \int \bar{\psi} H \psi \, dx = \frac{14a}{5\kappa} - \frac{4K}{5a^5}, \qquad \langle 9 \rangle$$

so that the value of a that minimizes $\int \bar{\psi} H \psi \, dx$ satisfies the equation $14a/5\kappa - 11K/10a^5 = 0$, whose positive solution is

$$a = (2\kappa K/7)^{\frac{1}{6}} \cong .81\kappa^{\frac{1}{6}} K^{\frac{1}{6}}. \qquad (10)$$

Substitution of (10) into (1) now yields that function which, among all functions of the form (1) with a positive a, is (according to the criterion adopted above) the best approximation to ψ_0 for the case $V = K x^4$; when just two significant figures are kept in the numerical coefficients, this function is

$$\psi = \frac{.91\kappa^{1/12} K^{1/12}}{(1 + .66\kappa^{\frac{1}{6}} K^{\frac{1}{6}} x^2)^2} . \qquad (11)$$

The approximate value of E_0. Since the relation

$$\langle 4 \rangle \qquad\qquad E_0 \le \int \bar{\psi} H \psi \, dx \qquad\qquad \langle 12 \rangle$$

holds for any normalized ψ representing instantaneously a state of the system, we can get an upper limit to E_0 by substituting any normalized ψ into the right side of $\langle 12 \rangle$. In particular, having chosen a ψ of a certain form and having minimized the right side of $\langle 12 \rangle$ according to our criterion of best fit, we get as low an upper limit to E_0 as it is possible to obtain with this form of ψ.

For example, in the case $V = Kx^4$, it follows from $\langle 12 \rangle$ and $\langle 8 \rangle$ that

$$E_0 \leq \frac{7a^2}{5\kappa} + \frac{K}{5a^4} \tag{13}$$

for any real a, and, reducing the right side of (13) to a minimum by using a from (10), we get

$$E_0 \leq \left[\frac{7}{5} \left(\frac{2}{7} \right)^{\frac{1}{3}} + \frac{1}{5} \left(\frac{7}{2} \right)^{\frac{2}{3}} \right] \kappa^{-\frac{2}{3}} K^{\frac{1}{3}} \cong 1.38\kappa^{-\frac{2}{3}} K^{\frac{1}{3}}. \tag{14}$$

Thus we now know for certain that in the case $V = Kx^4$ the value of E_0 (which in view of theorem 25 of §32 is positive) is not greater than $1.38\kappa^{-\frac{2}{3}} K^{\frac{1}{3}}$, and that the upper limit $1.38\kappa^{-\frac{2}{3}} K^{\frac{1}{3}}$ is as low an upper limit as can be obtained by means of an approximating ψ of the form (1). Since functions of the form (1) are not suited particularly well[10] for approximating ψ_0 when $V = Kx^4$, we may expect that the upper limit to E_0 set by (14) is rather high; comparison of (14) with our previous result (note the difference in labeling)

(21^{33}) $$E_0 = 1.0605\kappa^{-\frac{2}{3}} K^{\frac{1}{3}} \tag{15}$$

substantiates this surmise.

If the approximating ψ is chosen with particular care (which was not the case in our illustrative computations for the case $V = Kx^4$), we may sometimes be confident that the upper limit to E_0 given by the variation method lies very close to E_0 ; *under these circumstances, the upper limit itself, that is, the minimum of $\int \bar{\psi} H \psi \, dx$, can be taken as a good approximation to E_0* .

The formal proof of $\langle 4 \rangle$, in which we do not make use of physical considerations, runs as follows: We imagine the normalized function ψ to be expanded in terms of the normalized instantaneous eigenfunctions of H:

$$\psi = \sum_i c_i \psi_i, \qquad i = 0, 1, 2, \cdots . \tag{16}$$

Operating on (16) with H, multiplying through by $\bar{\psi}$, and integrating, we get, in succession, the following equations: $H\psi = \Sigma_i c_i H \psi_i = \Sigma_i c_i E_i \psi_i$, $\bar{\psi} H \psi = \Sigma_i c_i E_i \bar{\psi} \psi_i = \Sigma_i c_i E_i (\Sigma_j \bar{c}_j \bar{\psi}_j) \psi_i = \Sigma_i \Sigma_j E_i c_i \bar{c}_j \bar{\psi}_j \psi_i$, and $\int \bar{\psi} H \psi \, dx =$

$\Sigma_i \Sigma_j E_i c_i \bar{c}_j \int \bar{\psi}_j \psi_i \, dx$. In view of the orthonormality of the ψ_i's, it follows that $\int \bar{\psi} H \psi \, dx = \Sigma_i E_i \mid c_i \mid^2$, so that, since E_0 is smaller than any other E_i, we get $\int \bar{\psi} H \psi \, dx \geqq E_0 \Sigma_i \mid c_i \mid^2$, where the = sign is retained to allow for the possibility that all the c's except c_0 vanish in (16). The relation ⟨4⟩ now follows in view of 32³.

Exercises

1. Make a graph comparing (11) with the smoother curve in Fig. 49³³, which, as we know, is a good approximation to ψ_0 when $V = Kx^4$. Remember the matter of normalization, and the fact that x in Fig. 49 stands for the variable 3³³.

2. Explain why, in dealing with ψ_0 when $V = Kx^4$, we may expect the function $Ne^{-c^2 x^2}$, where c is an adjustable constant, to be a better approximating ψ than (1)

3. Show that the function $Ne^{-c^2 x^2}$ best fits ψ_0 for the case $V = Kx^4$ when $c = (3\kappa K/8)^{\frac{1}{6}}$ and that $E_0 < 1.09\kappa^{-\frac{1}{3}} K^{\frac{1}{3}}$. Is the surmise of Exercise 2 correct?

4. Show that, when $V = Kx^4$, then the inexactitude of the energy for the state described by the ψ-function $Ne^{-c^2 x^2}$, with $c = (3\kappa K/8)^{\frac{1}{6}}$, is approximately $.57\kappa^{-\frac{1}{3}} K^{\frac{1}{3}}$. What is the inexactitude of the energy for a state described by a ψ-function of the form (1) when $V = Kx^4$?

5. If the function $\psi = Ne^{-c^2 x^2}$ should be used to fit, by the variation method, the lowest eigenfunction for a linear harmonic oscillator, what would the best value of c and the minimal value of $\int \bar{\psi} H \psi \, dx$ turn out to be? Verify by an explicit computation.

6. Show that, if the motion is bound, if V is even in x, and if the normalized approximating ψ is odd in x, then $\int \bar{\psi} H \psi \, dx \geq E_1$, where E_1 is the next to the lowest energy level.

7. Show that, when it is inconvenient to normalize the approximating ψ before evaluating the adjustable constants[11], then the equations $\partial (\int \bar{\psi} H \psi \, dx / \int \bar{\psi} \psi \, dx) / \partial a = 0$, $\partial (\int \bar{\psi} H \psi \, dx / \int \bar{\psi} \psi \, dx) / \partial b = 0$, and so forth, may be substituted for Equations ⟨6⟩.

36. A Perturbation Method for Nondegenerate States

If the potential V differs only a little from a potential V^0, so that the term V^P in the equation

$$V = V^0 + V^P \tag{1}$$

is small,[12] then we may call V, V^0, and V^P the *perturbed*, the *unperturbed*, and the *perturbing* potentials, respectively; the energy levels and the corresponding ψ-functions (to be denoted by E_0, E_1, E_2, $\cdots$ and ψ_0, ψ_1, ψ_2, $\cdots$) for the potential V may be called

---

[11] For example, when the approximating ψ is so complicated as to necessitate numerical evaluation of the various integrals.

[12] For the present, the terms *a little* and *small* will be used vaguely.

the *perturbed* levels and ψ-functions, and we may refer to the levels and the corresponding ψ-functions (to be denoted by E_0^0, E_1^0, E_2^0, $\cdots$ and ψ_0^0, ψ_1^0, ψ_2^0, $\cdots$) for the potential V^0 as the *unperturbed* levels and ψ-functions. Further, we may then expect that each of the perturbed E's and ψ's differs but little from the corresponding unperturbed quantity; in particular, if the perturbed potential has the form

$$V = V^0 + \epsilon v^{\mathrm{I}} + \epsilon^2 v^{\mathrm{II}} + \epsilon^3 v^{\mathrm{III}} + \cdots, \tag{2}$$

where ϵ is a small parameter and the v's are functions not involving ϵ, then we may expect that

$$E_n = E_n^0 + \epsilon e_n^{\mathrm{I}} + \epsilon^2 e_n^{\mathrm{II}} + \epsilon^3 e_n^{\mathrm{III}} + \cdots, \tag{3}$$

where the e's are constants independent of ϵ, and that

$$\psi_n = \psi_n^0 + \epsilon f_n^{\mathrm{I}} + \epsilon^2 f_n^{\mathrm{II}} + \epsilon^3 f_n^{\mathrm{III}} + \cdots, \tag{4}$$

where the f's are functions independent of ϵ.

To illustrate Equations (2), (3), and (4), we consider the normal state of a linear harmonic oscillator (restoring constant k) perturbed by the potential $\frac{1}{2}\epsilon k x^2$, so that

$$V^0 = \tfrac{1}{2}k x^2, \qquad V^P = \tfrac{1}{2}\epsilon k x^2, \qquad V = \tfrac{1}{2}k x^2 + \tfrac{1}{2}\epsilon k x^2, \tag{5}$$

and assume that $-1 < \epsilon < 1$. In terms of our standard symbols ν_c and a, and the temporary abbreviation $c^2 = \hbar/m^{\frac{1}{2}}$, the lowest level of the unperturbed system is

$$(7^{18}) \qquad\qquad E_0^0 = \tfrac{1}{2}h\nu_c = \tfrac{1}{2}c^2 k^{\frac{1}{2}}, \tag{6}$$

and the corresponding normalized ψ-function is[13]

$$(12^{18}) \qquad \psi_0^0 = \frac{1}{\pi^{\frac{1}{4}}a^{\frac{1}{2}}} e^{-\frac{1}{2}\left(\frac{x}{a}\right)^2} = \frac{k^{\frac{1}{8}}}{\pi^{\frac{1}{4}}c^{\frac{1}{2}}} \exp\left[-\frac{k^{\frac{1}{2}}}{2c^2}x^2\right]. \tag{7}$$

Now, the perturbed potential being $V = \frac{1}{2}(k + \epsilon k)x^2$, the perturbed system is simply a linear harmonic oscillator with restoring constant $k(1 + \epsilon)$, so that E_0 and ψ_0 can be obtained from (6) and (7) by merely substituting $k(1 + \epsilon)$ for k:

$$E_0 = \tfrac{1}{2}c^2 k^{\frac{1}{2}}(1 + \epsilon)^{\frac{1}{2}} = \tfrac{1}{2}h\nu_c(1 + \epsilon)^{\frac{1}{2}}, \tag{8}$$

and

$$\psi_0 = \frac{k^{\frac{1}{8}}(1 + \epsilon)^{\frac{1}{8}}}{\pi^{\frac{1}{4}}c^{\frac{1}{2}}} \exp\left[-\frac{k^{\frac{1}{2}}(1 + \epsilon)^{\frac{1}{2}}}{2c^2}x^2\right] = \frac{(1 + \epsilon)^{\frac{1}{8}}}{\pi^{\frac{1}{4}}a^{\frac{1}{2}}} \exp\left[-\frac{(1 + \epsilon)^{\frac{1}{2}}}{2a^2}x^2\right]. \tag{9}$$

---

[13] In treating the case (5), we restrict ourselves, for simplicity, to instantaneous ψ's, and set the various arbitrary phases equal to zero, that is, set the phase factors equal to unity.

To complete our illustration, we must show that (8) and (9) can be put in the respective forms (3) and (4). To do this, we write $(1 + \epsilon)^{\frac{1}{2}} = 1 + \frac{1}{2}\epsilon - \frac{1}{8}\epsilon^2 + \cdots$ in (8) and get

$$E_0 = E_0^0 + \epsilon\{\tfrac{1}{4}h\nu_c\} + \epsilon^2\{-\tfrac{1}{16}h\nu_c\} + \epsilon^3\{\} + \cdots . \tag{10}$$

In a similar way,[14] we get from (9) the series

$$\psi_0 = \psi_0^0 + \epsilon\left\{\frac{1}{4\pi^{\frac{1}{4}}a^{\frac{3}{2}}}\left(\frac{1}{2} - \frac{x^2}{a^2}\right)e^{-\frac{x^2}{2a^2}}\right\} + \epsilon^2\cdot\{\} + \cdots . \tag{11}$$

In the example just given, the perturbed system is so simple that its precise E's and ψ's can be readily computed even without reference to the unperturbed system. It sometimes comes about, however, that, while the unperturbed system admits of precise treatment, the perturbed system does not; in such cases we turn to the so-called *perturbation theory*, designed for the approximate computation of the perturbed E's and ψ's in terms of the perturbing potential and the unperturbed E's and ψ's. This theory is rather extensive. We shall confine ourselves to one of its simplest and most useful forms, the *Rayleigh-Schroedinger method*, and shall restrict ourselves still further to cases when the motion is bound and the nth energy level of the unperturbed system is nondegenerate. (For bound *one-dimensional* motion, the entire energy spectrum is nondegenerate; see theorem 25 of §32.)

It is advantageous to elaborate our notation by writing $\epsilon v^{\mathrm{I}} = V^{\mathrm{I}}$, $\epsilon^2 v^{\mathrm{II}} = V^{\mathrm{II}}$, and so on, $\epsilon e_n^{\mathrm{I}} = E_n^{\mathrm{I}}$, $\epsilon^2 e_n^{\mathrm{II}} = E_n^{\mathrm{II}}$, and so on, and $\epsilon f_n^{\mathrm{I}} = \psi_n^{\mathrm{I}}$, $\epsilon^2 f_n^{\mathrm{II}} = \psi_n^{\mathrm{II}}$, and so on,[15] that is, by using the following equivalent pairs of series for V, E_n, and ψ_n :

$$\begin{aligned} V &= V^0 + \epsilon v^{\mathrm{I}} + \epsilon^2 v^{\mathrm{II}} + \epsilon^3 v^{\mathrm{III}} + \cdots \\ &= V^0 + V^{\mathrm{I}} + V^{\mathrm{II}} + V^{\mathrm{III}} + \cdots \end{aligned} \tag{12}$$

$$\begin{aligned} E_n &= E_n^0 + \epsilon e_n^{\mathrm{I}} + \epsilon^2 e_n^{\mathrm{II}} + \epsilon^3 e_n^{\mathrm{III}} + \cdots \\ &= E_n^0 + E_n^{\mathrm{I}} + E_n^{\mathrm{II}} + E_n^{\mathrm{III}} + \cdots \end{aligned} \tag{13}$$

$$\begin{aligned} \psi_n &= \psi_n^0 + \epsilon f_n^{\mathrm{I}} + \epsilon^2 f_n^{\mathrm{II}} + \epsilon^3 f_n^{\mathrm{III}} + \cdots \\ &= \psi_n^0 + \psi_n^{\mathrm{I}} + \psi_n^{\mathrm{II}} + \psi_n^{\mathrm{III}} + \cdots . \end{aligned} \tag{14}$$

---

[14] Taylor-Maclaurin theorem: $f(\epsilon) = f(0) + \epsilon[df(\epsilon)/d\epsilon]_{\epsilon=0} + \cdots$.

[15] For example, in (5) we have $v^{\mathrm{I}} = \frac{1}{2}kx^2$, $v^{\mathrm{II}} = v^{\mathrm{III}} = \cdots = 0$ and $V^{\mathrm{I}} = \frac{1}{2}\epsilon kx^2$, $V^{\mathrm{II}} = V^{\mathrm{III}} = \cdots = 0$; in (10) we have $e_0^{\mathrm{I}} = \frac{1}{4}h\nu_c$, $e_0^{\mathrm{II}} = -\frac{1}{16}h\nu_c$, and so on, and $E_0^{\mathrm{I}} = \frac{1}{4}\epsilon h\nu_c$, $E_0^{\mathrm{II}} = -\frac{1}{16}\epsilon^2 h\nu_c$, and so on.

The term V^I is called the *linear* (or *first-order*) perturbing term, E_n^I the linear (or first-order) correction to the nth energy level, ψ_n^I the linear (or first-order) correction to the nth ψ-function, V^{II} the *quadratic* (or *second-order*) perturbing term, and so on.

Our problem, then, is to compute the various corrections in terms of the available quantities (that is, in terms of the unperturbed E's and ψ's, the parameter ϵ, and the v's), it being known that the unperturbed and the perturbed ψ's, *which we shall take to be normalized*, satisfy respectively the Schroedinger equations

$$\left[\frac{d^2}{dx^2} + \kappa(E_n^0 - V^0)\right]\psi_n^0 = 0,$$

$$\left[\frac{d^2}{dx^2} + \kappa(E_n - V)\right]\psi_n = 0. \tag{15a, b}$$

The linear energy correction. Substitution of (12), (13), and (14) into (15b) yields

$$\left[\frac{d^2}{dx^2} + \kappa(E_n^0 + \epsilon e_n^I + \epsilon^2 e_n^{II} + \cdots - V^0 - \epsilon v^I\right.$$
$$\left. - \epsilon^2 v^{II} - \cdots)\right](\psi_n^0 + \epsilon f_n^I + \epsilon^2 f_n^{II} + \cdots) = 0; \tag{16}$$

multiplying this out and collecting like powers of ϵ, we write (16) as

$$\{\ \} + \epsilon\{\ \} + \epsilon^2\{\ \} + \cdots = 0; \tag{17}$$

the first $\{\ \}$ in (17) is given in full on the left of (18), and the second on the left of (19). Since (17) should hold identically in ϵ, each $\{\ \}$ must vanish separately, and we get the series of equations

$$\left[\frac{d^2}{dx^2} + \kappa(E_n^0 - V^0)\right]\psi_n^0 = 0, \tag{18}$$

$$\left[\frac{d^2}{dx^2} + \kappa(E_n^0 - V^0)\right]f_n^I + \kappa(e_n^I - v^I)\psi_n^0 = 0, \tag{19}$$

and so on. Equation (18) is just (15a), and yields nothing new. Equation (19) contains two unknowns, f_n^I and e_n^I, of which f_n^I can be eliminated as follows: We imagine f_n^I to be expanded in terms of the unperturbed ψ's, so that

$$f_n^I = \sum_i c_i \psi_i^0, \quad i = 0, 1, 2, \cdots, \tag{20}$$

and, substituting (20) into (19), we get the equation $\sum_i c_i [d^2/dx^2 + \kappa(E_n^0 - V^0)]\psi_i^0 = \kappa(v^I - e_n^I)\psi_n^0$; according to (15a) $[d^2/dx^2 - \kappa V^0]\psi_i^0 = -\kappa E_i^0 \psi_i^0$, and hence the last equation becomes

$$\sum_i c_i(E_n^0 - E_i^0)\psi_i^0 + (e_n^I - v^I)\psi_n^0 = 0. \tag{21}$$

We now multiply (21) by $\bar{\psi}_n^0$ and integrate from $x = -\infty$ to $x = \infty$. Because of the orthogonality of the unperturbed ψ's, the terms in the summation in (21) for which $i \neq n$ then vanish, while, on account of the factor $(E_n^0 - E_n^0)$, the term $i = n$ is zero even before the integration. Thus (21) reduces to $\int \bar{\psi}_n^0 (e_n^I - v^I)\psi_n^0 \, dx = 0$, that is, to $e_n^I = \int \bar{\psi}_n^0 v^I \psi_n^0 \, dx$, f_n^I having been eliminated. Multiplying the last equation through by ϵ, we get

$$E_n^I = \int_{-\infty}^{\infty} \bar{\psi}_n^0 V^I \psi_n^0 \, dx = \mathrm{av}_{\psi_n^0} V^I. \tag{22}$$

Thus *the linear energy correction for a nondegenerate state is equal to the linear perturbing term averaged over the unperturbed state.* Incidentally, the result (22) is the quantum-mechanical analogue of the classical perturbation theorem which states that the linear energy correction for a nondegenerate orbit is equal to the linear perturbing term averaged, with respect to the time, over the unperturbed orbit.

To illustrate (22), we return to the case (5). Here $V^I = \frac{1}{2}\epsilon k x^2$, so that (22) yields

$$E_0^I = \frac{1}{2}\epsilon k \int \bar{\psi}_0^0 x^2 \psi_0^0 \, dx, \tag{23}$$

where ψ_0^0 is (7). The integral in (23) is listed in 18^{18} as E_0^0/k, and consequently

$$E_0^I = \frac{1}{2}\epsilon k E_0^0/k = \frac{1}{4}\epsilon h \nu_c. \tag{24}$$

Thus the result given by (22) is just that required by (10).

The linear ψ-correction. To determine f_n^I, it is sufficient to compute the c's in (20); so we multiply (21) by $\bar{\psi}_j^0$ with $j \neq n$, integrate from $x = -\infty$ to $x = \infty$, and, remembering the orthonormality of the unperturbed ψ's, get the equation $c_j(E_n^0 - E_j^0) - \int \bar{\psi}_j^0 v^I \psi_n^0 \, dx = 0$, which, with i written for j, yields the formula

$$c_i = -\int \bar{\psi}_i^0 v^I \psi_n^0 \, dx / (E_i^0 - E_n^0), \qquad i \neq n, \tag{25}$$

so that every c except c_n has been evaluated. The computation of c_n can be based on the normalization of ψ_n and ψ_0, and will be taken up in Exercise 9; the result is

$$c_n = 0. \tag{26}$$

We now multiply (20) through by ϵ and, using (25) and (26), get the formula

$$\psi_n^{\mathrm{I}} = -\sum_i' \frac{\int_{-\infty}^{\infty} \bar{\psi}_i^0 V^{\mathrm{I}} \psi_n^0 \, dx}{E_i^0 - E_n^0} \, \psi_i^0, \qquad i = 0, 1, 2, \cdots, \tag{27}$$

where $\sum$ is primed to indicate that the term with $i = n$ is to be omitted in the summation. Thus the linear ψ-correction has been expressed in terms of the available quantities.

To illustrate, we shall use (27) to compute ψ_0^{I} for the case (5). Here $V^{\mathrm{I}} = \frac{1}{2}\epsilon k x^2$, so that

$$\psi_0^{\mathrm{I}} = -\sum_i' \frac{\int \bar{\psi}_i^0 V^{\mathrm{I}} \psi_0^0 \, dx}{E_i^0 - E_0^0} \, \psi_i^0 = -\tfrac{1}{2}\epsilon k \sum_i' \frac{\int \bar{\psi}_i^0 x^2 \psi_0^0 \, dx}{E_i^0 - E_0^0} \psi_i^0. \tag{28}$$

According to 43[8], the integrals in (28) all vanish except those with $i = 0$ and $i = 2$; the integral with $i = 2$ is[13] $a^2/\sqrt{2}$, and the integral with $i = 0$ is not needed in (28), as indicated by the primed Σ. Hence (28) reduces to

$$\psi_0^{\mathrm{I}} = -\tfrac{1}{2}\epsilon k \frac{a^2/\sqrt{2}}{E_2^0 - E_0^0} \, \psi_2^0. \tag{29}$$

Since $E_2^0 - E_0^0 = \tfrac{5}{2}h\nu_a - \tfrac{1}{2}h\nu_c$, we finally get, taking ψ_2^0 from 7[16],

$$\psi_0^{\mathrm{I}} = \frac{\epsilon}{4\pi^{\frac{1}{4}} a^{\frac{1}{2}}} \left(\frac{1}{2} - \frac{x^2}{a^2} \right) e^{-\frac{x^2}{2a^2}}, \tag{30}$$

in agreement with (11).

The quadratic energy correction. The equations obtained by setting each $\{\}$ in (17) equal to zero form an infinite set which is sufficient for the computation, one by one, of the higher-order corrections in (13) and (14) in much the same way that E_n^{I} and ψ_n^{I} were computed above, although the procedure becomes increasingly more tedious. In practice it is seldom of interest to go beyond the linear ψ-correction given by (27) and the quadratic energy correction, which turns out to be

$$E_n^{\mathrm{II}} = \int_{-\infty}^{\infty} \bar{\psi}_n^0 V^{\mathrm{II}} \psi_n^0 \, dx + \sum_i' \frac{\left| \int_{-\infty}^{\infty} \bar{\psi}_n^0 V^{\mathrm{I}} \psi_i^0 \, dx \right|^2}{E_n^0 - E_i^0}, \tag{31}$$

$$i = 0, 1, 2, \cdots,$$

where the $\sum$ is primed to indicate as before that the term with $i = n$ is to be omitted.

To illustrate, we shall use (31) to compute E_0^{II} for the case (5). Here $V^{\mathrm{I}} = \frac{1}{2}\epsilon k x^2$ and $V^{\mathrm{II}} = 0$, so that

$$E_0^{\mathrm{II}} = (\tfrac{1}{2}\epsilon k)^2 \sum_i{}' \frac{\left| \int \bar{\psi}_0^0 x^2 \psi_i^0 \, dx \right|^2}{E_0^0 - E_i^0}. \tag{32}$$

The integrals in (32) all vanish except those for $i = 0$ and $i = 2$. The term with $i = 0$ is to be omitted, and (32) reduces to

$$E_0^{\mathrm{II}} = (\tfrac{1}{2}\epsilon k)^2 \frac{a^4/2}{E_0^0 - E_2^0} = -\tfrac{1}{16}\epsilon^2 h\nu_c, \tag{33}$$

in agreement with (10).

Convergence. The Rayleigh-Schroedinger method outlined above is purely formal, and thus does not guarantee that the series it yields are convergent.[16] Consequently it must be used with caution, and the results that it gives should, strictly, be examined for convergence; rigorous convergence tests, however, are in most cases too laborious to be feasible. Fortunately, the following rather simple though somewhat rough rule can be relied upon in many cases: the method yields the correct approximations to E_n if the quantity $| E_n - E_n^0 |$ (the shift that the perturbation causes in the level in question) is small compared to the quantities $E_{n+1}^0 - E_n^0$ and $E_n^0 - E_{n-1}^0$ (the separations from its immediate neighbors of the unperturbed level in question). This rule is convenient because in practice it can be applied through an examination of the experimental data, that is, prior to any elaborate computations.

The shift caused in a given level by a perturbation is said to be small if it is small compared to the separations of this level from its neighbors. The perturbing potential is said to be small, insofar as a given level is concerned, if the shift that it causes in this level is small; for a given unperturbed system, a given perturbing

---

[16] To illustrate that the process may give incorrect results, we consider once again E_0 for the case (5). The value of E_0, correct whenever $\epsilon > -1$, is (8). Now, as we have seen, our process yields for E_0 the series (10), whatever the value of ϵ may be. But (10) converges to (8) only if $| \epsilon | < 1$, since only then is the relation $(1 + \epsilon)^{\frac{1}{2}} = 1 + \tfrac{1}{2}\epsilon - \tfrac{1}{8}\epsilon^2 + \cdots$ true. Thus in the case (5) the process is certain to yield divergent series whenever $\epsilon > 1$.

potential can thus be small in the case of one level and large in the case of another.

The Rayleigh-Schroedinger method is readily extended to three-dimensional motion, yielding formulas quite similar in structure to those obtained above.   But, in other than one-dimensional motion, energy levels may be degenerate even in the bound case; if so, they must be handled by special methods, because in case of degeneracy the simple formulas derived above acquire zero denominators, so that the simple results are meaningless unless the corresponding numerators vanish also, in which case these results are indeterminate.   Incidentally, it turns out that the levels which coincide in the unperturbed system may be shifted by the perturbation by different amounts, and thus may coincide no longer in the perturbed system; in such a case the perturbation is said to *remove the degeneracy*.   Examples of this effect are found in atomic spectra: the unperturbed levels of an atom are usually degenerate, but perturbations (external electric or magnetic fields) remove this degeneracy at least in part, with the result that the levels and the spectral lines become split (Stark or Zeeman effects).

Exercises

1. Compute the precise value of E_n for the case (5), expand the result in powers of ϵ, assuming that $|\epsilon| < 1$, and verify (22) and (31).

2. Consider a linear harmonic oscillator perturbed by a uniform field $V^P = \epsilon kx$, so that $V = \frac{1}{2}kx^2 + \epsilon kx$.   In the Schroedinger equation for the perturbed system, change to the new independent variable $x + \epsilon$, solve the resulting equation precisely, and show that $E_n = E_n^0 - \frac{1}{2}k\epsilon^2$.   Then verify (22) and (31).

3. Expand ψ_n of Exercise 2 in powers of ϵ and, with the help of 35[8], express ψ_n^I in terms of the unperturbed ψ's, disregarding ϵ^2, ϵ^3, $\cdots$.   Then verify (27).

4. Oscillators perturbed by potentials involving powers of x higher than the second are said to be *anharmonic*; their precise energy levels cannot be computed in a closed form, so that perturbation methods must be relied upon.   Consider the case $V = \frac{1}{2}kx^2 + \epsilon x^3$, and show that $E_n = (n + \frac{1}{2})h\nu_c - (15\epsilon^2 h^2/4mk^2)(n^2 + n + \frac{11}{30}) + \cdots$.   Formulas of Exercise 5[4] are helpful in this work.

5. Consider the behavior of the V of Exercise 4 for large values of $|x|$, and indicate the conditions under which the expression for E_n obtained in Exercise 4 is certain to be faulty.

6. Show that if the unperturbed motion is bound, if V^0 is even in x, and if V^P is odd in x, then $E_n^I = 0$ for any n.

7. Show that if the unperturbed motion is bound, if V^0 is even in x,

if V^P is odd in x, and if the energy levels are labeled E_1, E_2, $\cdots$, then ψ_n^I is odd in x if n is odd, and even in x if n is even.

8. Consider the normal state of a particle in the potential box of Fig. 17^{11}, assume that the bottom of the box slants only slightly, and show by perturbation methods that the particle is slightly more likely to be found in the deeper than in the shallower half of the box. [Hints: place the origin of potential energy at the center of the bottom of the box, and consider only the algebraic signs rather than the precise values of the nonvanishing integrals in (27).] Note that this result is not unexpected in view of a classical result of Exercise 14^{11}. What feature of (27) will allow the result to be just the opposite (recall Exercise 5^{34}) in the case of a highly excited state?

9. Let R be a normalized real function of x involving a parameter ϵ and admitting, in a certain range of ϵ, the expansion $R = R^v + \epsilon R^I + \epsilon^2 R^{II} + \cdots$, where the superscripted R's are independent of ϵ; show that then R^I is orthogonal to R. Then recall Exercise 2^{32} and justify (26).

10. Determine the effect of the phase and time factors of the unperturbed ψ's on the linear ψ-correction (27).

11. Expand (8) into a convergent series in ϵ when $\epsilon > 1$.

CHAPTER VI

ONE-DIMENSIONAL PROBABILITY CURRENTS AND DE BROGLIE WAVES

37. Probability Current

Let the state of a one-dimensional system be specified by a normalized Schroedinger function $\psi(x, t)$, which, in the general case, need not be an eigenfunction of the Hamiltonian of the system; the distribution-in-x, $\bar{\psi}\psi$, is then in general time-dependent. A time-dependent $\bar{\psi}\psi$ is illustrated in Fig. 57, where the full line represents $\bar{\psi}\psi$ for one instant of time and the dotted line for another.

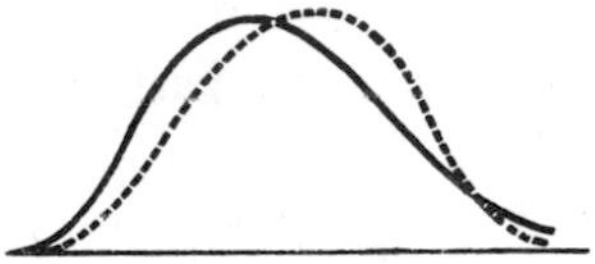

Now, the probability of finding the particle *somewhere* at the left of a point x at the instant t is

$$\int_{-\infty}^{x} \bar{\psi}\psi \, dx, \qquad (1)$$

Fig. 57. A time-dependent $\bar{\psi}\psi$ at two instants of time.

and the time rate of change of this probability at the instant t is

$$\frac{\partial}{\partial t} \int_{-\infty}^{x} \bar{\psi}\psi \, dx. \qquad (2)$$

In view of 18^{16}, our ψ-function remains normalized for all time, so that a decrease in the quantity (1) is accompanied by an equal increase in the probability of finding the particle somewhere at the right of the point x; similarly, an increase in (1) is accompanied by an equal decrease in the probability of finding the particle at the right of the point x. Consequently we may say that the probability *flows from left to right* past the point x whenever (1) decreases with t, and may define the term *probability current at x at the instant t* to mean the time rate at which the probability flows from left to right across the point x at the instant t. This rate, which we denote by $S = S(x, t)$, should

207

equal the rate at which the probability of finding the particle at the left of x decreases at the instant t, so that

$$S = -\frac{\partial}{\partial t} \int_{-\infty}^{x} \bar{\psi}\psi \, dx. \tag{3}$$

If the value of S computed by means of (3) is negative, the implication is that at the point x the probability current flows leftward at the instant t.

To rewrite (3) in a more readily usable form, we differentiate in its right side under the integral sign; we then recall the second Schroedinger equation 1^{16} (which in the present case means that $i\hbar \, \partial\psi/\partial t = -\kappa^{-1}\psi'' + V\psi$ and $-i\hbar \, \partial\bar\psi/\partial t = -\kappa^{-1}\bar{\psi}'' + V\bar\psi$, where $\kappa = 2m/\hbar^2$), and get

$$S = -\frac{\hbar}{2im} \int_{-\infty}^{x} (\bar{\psi}''\psi - \bar\psi\psi'') \, dx; \tag{4}$$

integration by parts now yields

$$S = -\frac{\hbar}{2im} \left\{ \bar{\psi}'\psi \Big|_{-\infty}^{x} - \int_{-\infty}^{x} \bar{\psi}'\psi' \, dx - \bar\psi\psi' \Big|_{-\infty}^{x} + \int_{-\infty}^{x} \bar{\psi}'\psi' \, dx \right\}; \tag{5}$$

the integrals in (5) cancel, the remaining terms vanish at the lower limit, since ψ is normalizable, and we finally get

$$S = \frac{\hbar}{2im} (\bar\psi\psi' - \bar{\psi}'\psi). \tag{6}$$

To illustrate the use of (6), we consider a *free* particle whose state is specified by a Kennard packet 22^{28}; for simplicity, we take the averages of x and of p to be zeros at $t = 0$, and leave arbitrary only Δ_x , the inexactitude of x at $t = 0$; our time-dependent ψ is then

$$\psi = \frac{1}{2^{\frac14} \pi^{\frac14} \sqrt{\Delta_x + i\Delta_v t}} \exp\left\{ -\frac{x^2}{4(\Delta_x^2 + i\Delta_x \Delta_v t)} \right\}, \tag{7}$$

where $\Delta_v \, (= \Delta_p/m = \hbar/2m\Delta_x)$ is the inexactitude of the velocity at $t = 0$.

To compute the probability current for the state (7), we substitute (7) into (6). The result is

$$S = \frac{\Delta_v^2 xt}{\sqrt{2\pi(\Delta_x^2 + \Delta_v^2 t^2)^3}} \exp\left\{ -\frac{x^2}{2(\Delta_x^2 + \Delta_v^2 t^2)} \right\}, \tag{8}$$

that is,

$$S = \frac{\Delta_v^2 xt}{\Delta_x^2 + \Delta_v^2 t^2} \bar\psi\psi. \tag{9}$$

We note in particular that for $t > 0$ the current has the same algebraic sign as x and hence is everywhere directed away from $x = 0$, and that the absolute value of S starts everywhere with the value zero at $t = 0$, grows to a maximum, and eventually vanishes; these qualitative features of the current can of course be inferred directly by inspecting the distribution-in-x for the state (7), namely,

$$\bar{\psi}\psi = \frac{1}{\sqrt{2\pi(\Delta_x^2 + \Delta_v^2 t^2)}} \exp\left\{-\frac{x^2}{2(\Delta_x^2 + \Delta_v^2 t^2)}\right\} \tag{10}$$

An alternative method for obtaining (6) is as follows: Having defined the probability current S as the time rate at which probability flows from left to right past the point x at the instant t, we proceed to consider the time rate of change of the probability of finding the particle between the points x and $x + dx$ (Fig. 58). On the one hand [since the probability of finding the particle at x in dx is $\bar{\psi}\psi\, dx$], this rate is $\dfrac{\partial}{\partial t}\,\bar{\psi}\psi\, dx$; on the other hand

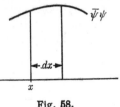

Fig. 58.

$\Bigg[$ since the current at x is $S(x, t)$ and the current at $x + dx$ is $S(x + dx, t) = S(x, t) + \dfrac{\partial S(x, t)}{\partial x}\, dx + \cdots \Bigg]$ this rate, correctly to the first order in dx, is $-\dfrac{\partial S(x, t)}{\partial x}\, dx$; hence $\dfrac{\partial}{\partial t}\,\bar{\psi}\psi\, dx = -\dfrac{\partial S(x, t)}{\partial x}\, dx$, that is,

$$\frac{\partial S}{\partial x} + \frac{\partial}{\partial t}\,\bar{\psi}\psi = 0. \tag{11}$$

Equation (11) is called the *conservation equation* (or *continuity equation*) for probability. The steps that carry (3) into (4) carry (11) into $\partial S/\partial x = -\hbar(\bar{\psi}''\psi - \bar{\psi}\psi'')/2im$, so that

$$\frac{\partial S}{\partial x} = \frac{\partial}{\partial x}\left[\frac{\hbar}{2im}\,(\bar{\psi}\psi' - \bar{\psi}'\psi)\right]. \tag{12}$$

Integrating (12) with respect to x and setting the arbitrary additive 'constant' of integration equal to zero, we once again get (6).

This method avoids the use of the expression (2)—which may be meaningless if ψ is not normalizable—and enables us in fact to show (merely by substituting the terms 'relative probability' and 'current of relative probability' for 'probability' and 'probability current' in the paragraph just above) that whenever ψ is not normalized (or even not normalizable) the right side of (6) represents the *current of relative probability* flowing past the point x at the instant t.

To illustrate the use of (6) when ψ is not normalizable, we consider a free particle whose momentum has certainly the numerical value p, so that the Schroedinger function is

$$\psi = A e^{ipx/\hbar} e^{-iEt/\hbar}, \tag{13}$$

where $E = p^2/2m$. Substituting (13) into (6), we get

$$S = |A|^2 p/m = v |A|^2; \tag{14}$$

thus, as we would expect by classical analogy, the current of relative probability in this case equals the velocity of the particle multiplied by the relative probability of finding the particle in an interval of unit length.

As another example, we consider a free particle in the state specified by the Schroedinger function

$$(5^{28}) \qquad \psi = A e^{ipx/\hbar} e^{-iEt/\hbar} + B e^{-ipx/\hbar} e^{-iEt/\hbar}, \tag{15}$$

that is, in a state for which the energy of the particle is certainly $E = p^2/2m$ while the numerical value of the momentum is either p or $-p$, the relative probabilities of these two possibilities being $|A|^2$ and $|B|^2$, respectively; in other words, if, for definiteness, the number p is taken positive, (15) represents a state in which the *speed* of the particle is certainly $v = p/m$, the relative probability that the particle moves from left to right is $|A|^2$, and the relative probability that the particle moves from right to left is $|B|^2$. The result of substituting (15) into (6) reduces to

$$S = v |A|^2 - v |B|^2. \tag{16}$$

The current thus turns out to consist of two readily distinguishable parts, and we recognize that the first term in (16) takes care of the possibility that the particle moves to the right, and the second of the possibility that the particle moves to the left.

Exercises

1. Extend the example given just below (6) to the case when neither x_a nor p_a in 22^{28} is zero.

2. Use (6) to show that, if a linear harmonic oscillator is in the state that at $t = 0$ is described by 1^{21}, then $S = -\omega x_0 \bar{\psi} \psi \sin \omega t$, where $\bar{\psi} \psi$ is 20^{21}.

3. Let ψ be such that $\bar{\psi} \psi$ is a packet moving with velocity $V(t)$ without change of shape; deduce from (3) with the help of 10^{12} that then $S = V(t) \bar{\psi} \psi$. Use this result to check that of Exercise 2.

4. Show that the probability current for any energy state of a one-dimensional system is independent of x and t.

5. Show that the probability current for any energy state of a bound one-dimensional system is zero.

6. Show that the results of Exercises 4 and 5 are just those suggested by classical analogy.

7. Show that, if ψ is normalized, then $\int S \, dx = \mathrm{av}_\psi \, v$.

8. To exhibit a curious effect of coherent quantum-mechanical superposition of states, compute the probability current for a free particle when $\psi = A e^{ip_1 x/\hbar} e^{-iE_1 t/\hbar} + B e^{ip_2 x/\hbar} e^{-iE_2 t/\hbar}$, with $E_1 \neq E_2$ and with fixed A and B, and note that the result is *not* that suggested by classical analogy; but note that the classical result can be obtained from the quantum-mechanical one by averaging the latter with respect to t. Show also that, if a state of a free particle is an incoherent superposition of two energy states of different energies, then the current is that suggested by classical analogy.

9. Explain why neglecting the additive 'constant' in the result of integrating (12) is permissible in evaluating the probability current.

38. One-Dimensional Potential Barriers

A rectangular barrier. If the force field acting on a particle is zero or nearly zero everywhere except in a limited region (as for example in Fig. 64), it is said to comprise a *potential barrier*. We shall consider first the rather idealized barrier of Fig. 59, restricting ourselves to the case when

$$0 < E < V_0, \qquad (1)$$

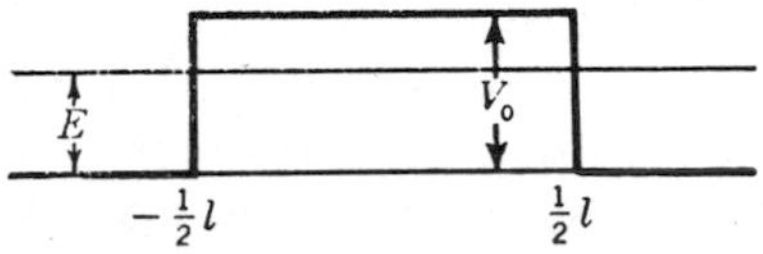

Fig. 59. A rectangular potential barrier.

E being the total energy of the particle and V_0 the 'height' of the barrier.

Incidentally, according to *classical* mechanics, the barrier of Fig. 59 is *impenetrable* for a particle satisfying (1), that is, the condition (1) precludes the possibility that a classical particle should be found in the central region ($-\frac{1}{2}l < x < \frac{1}{2}l$) or should pass from one of the outer regions into the other. For example, if a classical particle satisfying (1) is once certainly in the left region ($x < -\frac{1}{2}l$), then it will remain in the left region forever; in particular, if this particle is at some time moving toward the barrier, it will be reflected back upon reaching the point $x = -\frac{1}{2}l$ and will from then on move away from the barrier. Again, if it is uncertain whether a classical particle satisfying (1) is at some instant t_1 in the left or in the right region, then the probability that the particle is in the left region at any later instant t_2 is the same as that at the instant t_1; in other words, from the classical standpoint, no probability current can flow across the barrier of Fig. 59 under the condition (1). These classical results hold of course whether the energy of the particle is a certainty or not, provided it is certainly smaller than V_0.

Any energy greater than zero is a quantum-mechanically possible energy value of our system (Exercise 9^{29}), and the Schroedinger eigenfunction of the Hamiltonian of the system belonging to the energy value E such that $0 < E < V_0$ is, apart from the time factor $e^{-iEt/\hbar}$,

$$(28^{29}) \qquad \psi = \begin{cases} \psi_l = Ae^{i\alpha x} + (Ac_2 + Bc_1)e^{-i\alpha x} \\ \psi_c = (Ac_4 + Bc_3)e^{\beta x} + (Ac_3 + Bc_4)e^{-\beta x} \\ \psi_r = (Ac_1 + Bc_2)e^{i\alpha x} + Be^{-i\alpha x}, \end{cases} \qquad (2)$$

where the c's are the constants listed in Exercise 9^{29}, A and B are arbitrary constants,

$$\alpha = \sqrt{\kappa E}, \qquad\qquad \beta = \sqrt{\kappa(V_0 - E)}, \qquad (3)$$

and the subscripts l, c, and r stand for *left*, *central*, and *right*.

Reflection and transmission of a probability packet. To study the quantum-mechanical behavior of a particle impinging on our barrier from, say, the left side, we must consider a state for which the particle is at some initial instant moving in the left region toward the barrier, and must set up a ψ-function describing such a state; since no eigenfunction of our H vanishes everywhere except in the left region, the desired ψ-function will have to be a superposition of the eigenfunctions of H. Further, if we wish to consider cases when the energy of the particle is certainly less than V_0, we must restrict ourselves to ψ-functions that are superpositions of only those eigenfunctions of H which belong to E's lying below V_0. The latter limitation turns out to make it impossible to construct a ψ-function that vanishes everywhere except in the left region; in other words, the claim that the energy of the particle is certainly less than V_0 is quantum-mechanically incompatible with the claim that the particle is certainly in the left region. But it is possible to construct states for which the energy of the particle is certainly less than V_0 and for which, at $t = 0$, the particle is as likely to be in the left region as we please; a state of this type was studied by MacColl.[1]

---

[1] L. A. MacColl, *Phys. Rev.*, **40**, 621 (1932). The author is indebted to Dr. MacColl for advice concerning Fig. 60 and the accompanying text.

At $t = 0$, the distribution-in-x, $\bar\psi\psi$, for MacColl's state is a packet whose bulk is located in the left region and whose center is moving toward the barrier. The subsequent behavior of this packet, indicated in Fig. 60 without regard for the finer details, turns out to be as follows: At first the packet moves toward the barrier with uniform velocity and spreads at the same time in much the same way as does a packet in the field-free case; as the bulk of this *incident* packet approaches the barrier, a *transmitted*

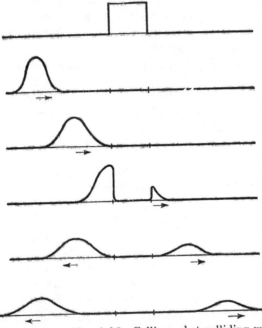

Fig. 60. Successive graphs of MacColl's packet colliding with the rectangular barrier shown at the top. The vertical scale in the diagram of the barrier is of course unrelated to that in the five graphs of packets.

packet emerges from the far side of the barrier, while a *reflected* packet forms at the near side and recedes leftward; and eventually the incident packet becomes replaced by two packets: the transmitted one, moving uniformly rightward (and spreading) in the right-hand region, and the reflected one, moving uniformly leftward (and spreading) in the left-hand region. The formation of the transmitted packet implies, of course, that the probability of finding the particle in the right-hand region has grown from a negligible value to a sizable one.

MacColl's ψ-function is a superposition of only those eigen-functions of H which belong to E's smaller than V_0, so that the possibility that the energy of the particle is greater than V_0 is excluded. Hence the results described above lead to the physical conclusion that *a particle impinging on our barrier with energy certainly smaller than V_0 will not necessarily be reflected by the barrier, but may pass across the barrier and continue its forward motion.*

If a particle whose energy is certainly smaller than the height of a barrier should pass across the barrier, it is said to have gone *through* rather than *over* the barrier. This possibility of going through potential barriers—called the *tunnel effect*—makes it possible to understand in terms of quantum mechanics a number of atomic phenomena that are inexplicable classically.

The probability that a particle in a given state should go through or over a given barrier is called the *transmission coefficient* for this state and is denoted by T; the number

$$R = 1 - T, \tag{4}$$

that is, the probability that the particle should be reflected by the barrier, is called the *reflection coefficient*. For a particle in a state of the type discussed by MacColl, T is the ratio of the final area of the transmitted packet to that of the incident packet, and R is the ratio of the final area of the reflected packet to that of the incident packet.

Reflection and transmission of probability currents. The discussion above was concerned with a particle whose position at some instant is reasonably well known, but whose energy is accordingly uncertain; the effect of a barrier on a particle whose energy is a certainty can be investigated, by means of probability currents, as follows:

If a particle whose energy is certainly E, where $0 < E < V_0$, moves in the potential of Fig. 59, we have, according to 6^{37} and (2),

$$S = \frac{\hbar}{2im} (\bar{\psi}\psi' - \bar{\psi}'\psi) = \begin{cases} S_l = \hbar(\bar{\psi}_l\psi_l' - \bar{\psi}_l'\psi_l)/2im \\ S_c = \hbar(\bar{\psi}_c\psi_c' - \bar{\psi}_c'\psi_c)/2im \\ S_r = \hbar(\bar{\psi}_r\psi_r' - \bar{\psi}_r'\psi_r)/2im, \end{cases} \tag{5}$$

or, more explicitly,

$$S = \begin{cases} S_l = v \mid A \mid^2 - v \mid Ac_2 + Bc_1 \mid^2 \\ S_c \\ S_r = v \mid Ac_1 + Bc_2 \mid^2 - v \mid B \mid^2, \end{cases} \tag{6}$$

where $v = \sqrt{2E/m}$ is the speed that the particle would certainly have were it not for the barrier, and where $S_c = \beta[(\bar{A}\bar{c}_3 + \bar{B}\bar{c}_4)(Ac_4 + Bc_3) - (\bar{A}\bar{c}_4 + \bar{B}\bar{c}_3)(Ac_3 + Bc_4)]/im$. We note that, in general, $S_c \neq 0$, so that, as we already know from the results of MacColl, our barrier transmits probability current even when $E < V_0$.

Now, according to the result of Exercise 4^{37}, S_l, S_c, and S_r are numerically equal to each other; yet useful information is revealed by the details of the structure of (6). Thus we recognize, for example, that the net current S_l flowing in the left region consists of a rightward component $v \mid A \mid^2$ and a leftward component $-v \mid Ac_2 + Bc_1 \mid^2$, while in the right region the net current consists of the rightward component $v \mid Ac_1 + Bc_2 \mid^2$ and the leftward component $-v \mid B \mid^2$. The component currents flowing toward the barrier, that is, $v \mid A \mid^2$ in S_l and $-v \mid B \mid^2$ in S_r, are both quite arbitrary and independent of the barrier, so that they can be interpreted as *incident* currents, originating respectively at $-\infty$ and at ∞. To simplify the problem of interpreting the component currents flowing *away* from the barrier, we consider states for which current is incident from only one side, say the left, and accordingly let $B = 0$, so that (6) becomes

$$S^{\mathrm{I}} = \begin{cases} S_l^{\mathrm{I}} = v \mid A \mid^2 - v \mid Ac_2 \mid^2 \\ S_c^{\mathrm{I}} \\ S_r^{\mathrm{I}} = v \mid Ac_1 \mid^2. \end{cases} \tag{7}$$

Having already noted that probability *can* flow across our barrier even when $E < V_0$, we now interpret S_r^{I} in (7) as the transmitted part of the incident current $v \mid A \mid^2$, and the term $-v \mid Ac_2 \mid^2$ in S_l^{I} as the reflected part. It then follows that the ratios of the reflected and transmitted currents to the incident current, that is, the reflection and transmission coefficients of the barrier for the current, are

$$R_E = \frac{v \mid Ac_2 \mid^2}{v \mid A \mid^2} = \mid c_2 \mid^2 \tag{8}$$

and

$$T_E = \frac{v \mid Ac_1 \mid^2}{v \mid A \mid^2} = \mid c_1 \mid^2, \tag{9}$$

where the subscript E emphasizes the fact that the energy of our particle is certainly E. Using the value of c_1 given in Exercise

9^{29}, we get the following explicit formula for T_E for the case $0 < E < V_0$:

$$T_E = \left[1 + \frac{V_0^2 \sinh^2 l \sqrt{\kappa(V_0 - E)}}{4E(V_0 - E)} \right]^{-1} \tag{10}$$

Graphs of (10) for three particular values of the quantity ml^2V_0 are shown in Fig. 61. Note that, in contradistinction to classical mechanics, our barrier transmits a part of the incident probability current for every E lying between 0 and V_0, that the constants describing the shape of the barrier appear in T_E in the combination l^2V_0, and that, for a barrier of a given shape, T_E is quite sensitive to the value of m.

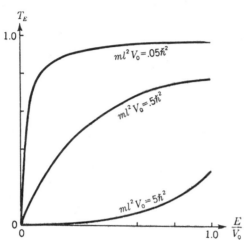

Fig. 61. Graphs of the transmission coefficient (10).

The current (7) is independent of x (Exercise 4^{37}), so that $v \mid A \mid^2 - v \mid Ac_2 \mid^2 = v \mid Ac_1 \mid^2$; thus $1 - \mid c_2 \mid^2 = \mid c_1 \mid^2$, and hence (8) and (9) satisfy the equation $R_E + T_E = 1$, that is, Equation (4). The explicit formulas for R_E and T_E can therefore be checked by means of (4).

The probability current is the measure of the probability that the particle should pass across a given point per unit time, and hence R_E and T_E of a barrier for a current associated with a state of energy E can be said to be the reflection and transmission coefficients of the barrier for a particle whose energy is certainly E.

The current S_c flowing in the barrier region does not admit of a simple resolution into rightward and leftward components, and indicates, so to speak, that, if the particle *is* reflected by the barrier, then the reflection may have taken place at any point of the barrier. But, as we have seen, no detailed consideration of S_c is necessary for the computation of R and T.

The rectangular barrier will be considered further in the Exercises.

A single-step barrier. If the energy E of a particle impinging on a barrier is greater than the height V_0 of the barrier, then, classically, the particle is certain to go over the barrier and to continue its forward motion; but, according to quantum mechanics, the particle may be reflected even if $E > V_0$. To illustrate this point, we shall consider a particle of energy E moving in the potential field of Fig. 62 and subject to the condition

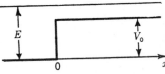

Fig. 62. A single-step barrier.

$$E > V_0. \tag{11}$$

The ψ-function belonging to the energy value E satisfying (11) is, in this case, apart from the time factor,

$$\psi = \begin{cases} \psi_l = A\left(e^{i\alpha_l x} + \dfrac{\alpha_l - \alpha_r}{\alpha_l + \alpha_r}e^{-i\alpha_l x}\right) + B\,\dfrac{2\alpha_r}{\alpha_l + \alpha_r}e^{-i\alpha_l x}, & x \le 0 \\[2mm] \psi_r = A\,\dfrac{2\alpha_l}{\alpha_l + \alpha_r}e^{i\alpha_r x} + B\left(-\dfrac{\alpha_l - \alpha_r}{\alpha_l + \alpha_r}e^{i\alpha_r x} + e^{-i\alpha_r x}\right), & x \ge 0, \end{cases} \tag{12}$$

where

$$\alpha_l = \sqrt{\kappa E}, \qquad \alpha_r = \sqrt{\kappa(E - V_0)}, \tag{13}$$

and where the subscripts l and r mean *left* and *right*. The reader should verify that ψ_l and ψ_r satisfy the respective Schroedinger equations for the left and for the right regions, and that the various coefficients in (12) have been adjusted so that ψ_l and ψ_r join properly at $x = 0$.

The probability current for the state (12) is

$$S = \begin{cases} S_l = v_l\,|A|^2 - v_l\left|\dfrac{(\alpha_l - \alpha_r)A + 2\alpha_r B}{\alpha_l + \alpha_r}\right|^2 \\[3mm] S_r = v_r\left|\dfrac{2\alpha_l A + (\alpha_r - \alpha_l)B}{\alpha_l + \alpha_r}\right|^2 - v_r\,|B|^2, \end{cases} \tag{14}$$

where $v_l = \sqrt{2E/m}$ and $v_r = \sqrt{2(E - V_0)/m}$ are the respective speeds that our particle would certainly have classically in the two regions. Inspection of (14) shows that the general state (12) involves two incident currents: the current $v_l \,|\, A \,|^2$ coming rightward from $-\infty$, and the current $-v_r \,|\, B \,|^2$ coming leftward from ∞. To get the special case in which current is incident only from the left, we set $B = 0$ and reduce (14) to

$$S^{\mathrm{I}} = \begin{cases} S_l^{\mathrm{I}} = v_l \,|\, A \,|^2 - v_l \left(\dfrac{\alpha_l - \alpha_r}{\alpha_l + \alpha_r}\right)^2 |\, A \,|^2 \\[2em] S_r^{\mathrm{I}} = v_r \left(\dfrac{2\alpha_l}{\alpha_l + \alpha_r}\right)^2 |\, A \,|^2. \end{cases} \tag{15}$$

Identifying the first term in S_l^{I} with the incident current, the second term in S_l^{I} with the reflected current, and the single term in S_r^{I} with the transmitted current, we now get

$$R_E = \left[v_l \left(\frac{\alpha_l - \alpha_r}{\alpha_l + \alpha_r}\right)^2 |\, A \,|^2 \right] \Big/ [v_l |\, A \,|^2]$$

$$= \left(\frac{\alpha_l - \alpha_r}{\alpha_l + \alpha_r}\right)^2 = \left(\frac{1 - \sqrt{1 - V_0/E}}{1 + \sqrt{1 - V_0/E}}\right)^2 \tag{16}$$

$$T_E = \left[v_r \left(\frac{2\alpha_l}{\alpha_l + \alpha_r}\right)^2 |\, A \,|^2 \right] \Big/ [v_l |\, A \,|^2]$$

$$= \frac{v_r}{v_l} \left(\frac{2\alpha_l}{\alpha_l + \alpha_r}\right)^2 = \frac{4\sqrt{1 - V_0/E}}{(1 + \sqrt{1 - V_0/E})^2}. \tag{17}$$

T_E is plotted against V_0/E in Fig. 63; the transmission is thus imperfect unless E is much greater than V_0.

The expression (16) is the reflection coefficient of the single-step barrier of Fig. 62 for a probability current coming from the left. Now, what is the reflection coefficient of this barrier for a current coming from the right? We might think offhand that in the latter case the transmission should be perfect,

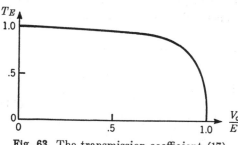

Fig. 63. The transmission coefficient (17).

since the force at $x = 0$ would help the particle to move from right to left, rather than hinder it; a barrier, however, is always equally reflecting on both sides, so to speak (Exercise 8). To verify this for the present case, we set $A = 0$, reduce (14) to

$$S^{II} = \begin{cases} S_l^{II} = -v_l \left(\dfrac{2\alpha_r}{\alpha_l + \alpha_r} \right)^2 |B|^2 \\[2ex] S_r^{II} = v_r \left(\dfrac{\alpha_r - \alpha_l}{\alpha_r + \alpha_l} \right)^2 |B|^2 - v_r |B|^2, \end{cases} \tag{18}$$

and (identifying the second term in S_r^{II} with the incident current coming from ∞, the first term in S_r^{II} with the reflected current, and the single term in S_l^{II} with the transmitted current) get

$$R_E = \left[v_r \left(\frac{\alpha_r - \alpha_l}{\alpha_r + \alpha_l} \right)^2 |B|^2 \right] \Big/ [v_r |B|^2] = \left(\frac{\alpha_l - \alpha_r}{\alpha_l + \alpha_r} \right)^2, \tag{19}$$

as before.

The single-step barrier will be considered further in the Exercises.

One-dimensional barriers in general. The barriers of Figs. 59 and 62, made up of 'step-potentials,' admit of precise mathematical treatment in terms of the elementary functions; but their shapes are quite artificial from the physical standpoint. Barriers of greater physical interest are more difficult to study theoretically because of the mathematical complexities of solving the appropriate Schroedinger equation, and approximate methods must usually be employed. On the assumption that the requisite Schroedinger ψ's are available, we shall now outline the general procedure for the computation of R_E and T_E ; it is essentially the same as that used above, and consequently we need discuss it but briefly.

We consider a barrier of the type shown in Fig. 64, for which $V(x)$ approaches a constant V_l when $x \to -\infty$ and a constant V_r when $x \to \infty$; and we restrict ourselves to the case when $E > V_l$ and $E > V_r$. For definiteness, we assume that the peak of the barrier lies near $x =$ 0, and then specify the (infinite) region in which V is

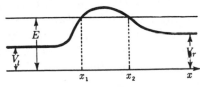

Fig. 64. A potential barrier.

essentially equal to V_l by writing $x \ll -1$, and the (infinite) region in which V is essentially equal to V_r by writing $x \gg 1$.

For $x \ll -1$, the general solution of the Schroedinger equation then has the form

$$Ae^{i\alpha_l x} + Be^{-i\alpha_l x}, \qquad \alpha_l = \sqrt{\kappa(E - V_l)}; \quad (20)$$

for $x \gg 1$ the general solution has the form

$$Ce^{i\alpha_r x} + De^{-i\alpha_r x}, \qquad \alpha_r = \sqrt{\kappa(E - V_r)}; \quad (21)$$

for values of x for which $V(x)$ is markedly dependent on x, that is, in the barrier region, the explicit form of ψ depends of course on the details of the shape of the barrier. The general solution of the Schroedinger equation for the entire region $(-\infty, \infty)$ involves two arbitrary constants; we may take these to be C and D in (21), in which case A and B in (20) are no longer arbitrary. We now set $D = 0$ and get a ψ of the form

$$\psi^{\mathrm{I}} = \begin{cases} A'e^{i\alpha_l x} + B'e^{-i\alpha_l x}, & x \ll -1 \\ \psi^{\mathrm{I}} \\ Ce^{i\alpha_r x}, & x \gg 1, \end{cases} \quad (22)$$

where A and B are primed to indicate that they are not arbitrary. The current for the state (22) has the form

$$S^{\mathrm{I}} = \begin{cases} v_l \, | \, A' \, |^2 - v_l \, | \, B' \, |^2, & x \ll -1 \\ S^{\mathrm{I}} \\ v_r \, | \, C \, |^2, & x \gg 1, \end{cases} \quad (23)$$

which is essentially the form (15). The incident current, coming from $-\infty$, is given by the term $v_l \, | \, A' \, |^2$, and the reflected and the transmitted currents are given by the terms $-v_l \, | \, B' \, |^2$ and $v_r \, | \, C \, |^2$, respectively; hence

$$R_E = \frac{v_l \, | \, B' \, |^2}{v_l \, | \, A' \, |^2} = \frac{| \, B' \, |^2}{| \, A' \, |^2}, \qquad T_E = \frac{v_r \, | \, C \, |^2}{v_l \, | \, A' \, |^2}. \quad (24)$$

The principal mathematical problem in evaluating R_E and T_E is thus the computation of a ψ-function of the form (22), that is, of a solution of the Schroedinger equation which for large values of x behaves like $e^{i\alpha_r x}$. A systematic method for computing approximate ψ's of this form was devised by Born.[2]

---

[2] For further discussion of potential barriers, references, and examples see E. U. Condon, *Rev. Mod. Phys.*, **3**, 43 (1931), and N. H. Frank and L. A. Young, *Phys. Rev.*, **38**, 80 (1931).

The application of the W. B. K. ψ-functions of §34 to the barrier of Fig. 64, under the condition that E is less than the height of the barrier, yields the approximate formula

$$T_E = f(E) \exp\left[-\frac{2}{\hbar} \int_{x_1}^{x_2} \sqrt{2m(V - E)}\, dx \right];$$ (25)

here x_1 and x_2 are the points so marked in Fig. 64, and $f(E)$ is a function of E depending on the shape of the barrier but in general varying with E slower than the exponential in (25); in rough work, $f(E)$ may be set equal to unity.

Some potential barriers of interest in the theory of electron emission from metals are followed by a constant force field (a linearly varying potential), rather than by a field-free space (constant potential) as in Fig. 64. In this case, special methods must be used to recognize the terms representing, respectively, the rightward and the leftward component currents in the expression for the net current flowing in the constant field far from the barrier.[2]

Exercises

1. A 1-volt electron impinges head on on a rectangular barrier 1×10^{-8} cm wide and 3 volts high; use Fig. 61 to show that the probability of transmission is approximately .5.

2. Take c_1 and c_2 from Exercise 9[29] and verify in detail that the sum of (8) and (9) is unity.

3. Show that, if $E > V_0$, then the transmission coefficient of the rectangular barrier of Fig. 59 is

$$T_E = \left[1 + \frac{V_0^2 \sin^2 l\sqrt{\kappa(E - V_0)}}{4E(E - V_0)} \right]^{-1}$$ (26)

The fluctuations of T_E with E are described by saying that for $E > V_0$ the barrier is a *selective* transmitter.

4. Show that, if $E < V_0$, then R_E of the single-step barrier of Fig. 62 is unity, that is, reflection is certain, although the particle may temporarily penetrate into the barrier region.

5. Set $B = A(\alpha_r - \alpha_l)/2\alpha_r$ in (14), and point out a curious effect of coherent superposition of states that then takes place.

6. Show that R_E and T_E in (24) satisfy (4).

7. Show that, if ψ^I and ψ^{II} are solutions of a Schroedinger equation belonging to the same value of E, then the quantities $\psi^I \dfrac{d\psi^{II}}{dx} - \dfrac{d\psi^I}{dx} \psi^{II}$

and $\bar{\psi}^I \dfrac{d\psi^{II}}{dx} - \dfrac{d\bar{\psi}^I}{dx} \psi^{II}$ are both independent of x.

8. Consider the state

$$\psi^{II} = \begin{cases} Be^{-i\alpha_l x}, & x \ll -1 \\ \psi^{II} \\ C'e^{i\alpha_r x} + D'e^{-i\alpha_r x}, & x \gg 1, \end{cases} \quad (27)$$

rather than the state (22), and show that when a current is incident on the barrier of Fig. 64 from the right we have $R_E = |C'|^2/|D'|^2$ and $T_E = \alpha_l |B|^2/\alpha_r |D'|^2$; then use the results of Exercise 7 to show that these coefficients are identical with those in (24).

9. Show that, for large values of the quantity $l\sqrt{\kappa(V_0 - E)}$, Equation (10) reduces to the form (25).

10. Consider the state (22), and compute the average value of $\bar{\psi}\psi$ for $x \ll -1$, and the value of $\bar{\psi}\psi$ for $x \gg 1$; then, using (24), show that the results can be interpreted as follows: the particle may be in the region $x \ll -1$ because it is on its way toward the barrier or because it has been reflected; and it may be in the region $x \gg 1$ because it has been transmitted.

11. Use the transformation formula 58[27] to compute the distribution-in-p for the state (12) with $B = 0$. What possible values of p turn out to be the only ones of interest, and what are their probabilities?

12. S_l in (15) can be written as

$$S_l = v_l [|A|^2 + k] - v_l \left[\left(\frac{\alpha_l - \alpha_r}{\alpha_l + \alpha_r} \right)^2 |A|^2 + k \right], \quad (28)$$

where k is an arbitrary constant. Use the results of Exercise 11 to show that, if $k \neq 0$ it would be improper to interpret the first term in (28) as the incident and the second term as the reflected current for the state (12) with $B = 0$.

13. Show in a qualitative way that the transmitted packet in Fig. 60 should move somewhat faster than the incident MacColl packet, while the reflected packet should move somewhat slower than the incident packet.

39. Virtual Binding

Let us consider next a potential consisting of two symmetrical potential barriers of height V_0 and approaching the value V_a for large values of $|x|$, as in Fig. 65. The classical motion may in this case fall under one of three categories: if $0 < E < V_a$, the particle can move only in a part of the potential valley between the barriers; if $V_a < E < V_0$, the particle can be either in the infinite region at the left of the left barrier, in a

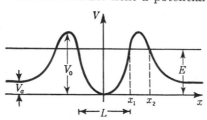

Fig. 65. A two-barrier potential.

part of the valley, or in the infinite region at the right of the right barrier—but it cannot move from one of these three regions into another; if $E > V_0$ the complete infinite region is accessible to the particle. In particular, if a classical particle whose energy is less than V_0 should once be in the valley, it will remain bound in the valley forever.

Even a rough consideration of the Schroedinger ψ's belonging to the potential of Fig. 65 is sufficient to show that in quantum mechanics the classification of the possible motions is quite different. The energy spectrum of the system consists of a discrete part lying between 0 and V_a, and a continuous part lying above V_a. The ψ-functions belonging to the discrete spectrum vanish when $|x| \to \infty$ and differ markedly from zero only between the barriers, so that, if the particle is in an energy state such that $E < V_a$, then it is forever most likely to be found within the valley, and we may say that it is bound there. On the other hand, the ψ-functions belonging to the continuous spectrum are oscillatory outside the barriers, so that a particle whose energy is greater than V_a may be found practically anywhere in the complete infinite region. Thus the quantum-mechanical condition for the confinement of the motion to a portion of the valley is $E < V_a$, rather than the less strict classical condition $E < V_0$, and the confinement is not quite perfect even if $E < V_a$.

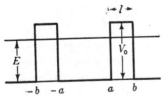

Fig. 66. An idealized two-barrier potential.

Now, for certain E's lying between V_a and V_0, there arises in quantum mechanics a phenomenon which is akin to the binding of the particle in the valley and which we call *virtual binding*. To illustrate: we consider the idealized two-barrier potential of Fig. 66, let E lie between 0 and V_0, and note that the Schroedinger equation then has a particular solution which is even in x and which for positive values of x has the form

$$\psi = \begin{cases} \cos \alpha x, & 0 \leq x \leq a \\ A e^{\beta x} + B e^{-\beta x}, & a \leq x \leq b \\ C \cos \alpha (x + D), & b \leq x, \end{cases} \qquad (1)$$

where $\alpha = \sqrt{\kappa E}$ and $\beta = \sqrt{\kappa(V_0 - E)}$. The conditions on the constants A, B, C, and D for the matching of the ψ's and the ψ''s at $x = a$ and at $x = b$ are

$$A = \tfrac{1}{2}\left(\cos \alpha a - \frac{\alpha}{\beta}\sin \alpha a\right)e^{-\beta a} \tag{2}$$

$$B = \tfrac{1}{2}\left(\cos \alpha a + \frac{\alpha}{\beta}\sin \alpha a\right)e^{\beta a} \tag{3}$$

$$C \cos \alpha(b + D) = Ae^{\beta b} + Be^{-\beta b} \tag{4}$$

$$C \sin \alpha(b + D) = -\frac{\beta}{\alpha}Ae^{\beta b} + \frac{\beta}{\alpha}Be^{-\beta b}. \tag{5}$$

Without working out the details of the general case, we now take the width l ($= b - a$) of each barrier sufficiently large to make $e^{-\beta l}$ negligible compared to $e^{\beta l}$, so that $e^{-\beta b}$ is negligible compared to $e^{\beta b}$. Disregarding for the moment the exceptional case when the factor in parentheses in (2) is zero or very small, we then reduce (4) and (5) to

$$C \cos \alpha(b + D) = Ae^{\beta b} \tag{6}$$

$$C \sin \alpha(b + D) = -\frac{\beta}{\alpha}Ae^{\beta b}. \tag{7}$$

Squaring and adding (6) and (7), we then find, with the help of (2), that

$$C^2 = \frac{1}{4}\left(1 + \frac{\beta^2}{\alpha^2}\right)\left(\cos \alpha a - \frac{\alpha}{\beta}\sin \alpha a\right)^2 e^{2\beta l}. \tag{8}$$

Thus, if l is sufficiently large, then C^2 is in general large compared to unity, so that the amplitude of (1) in the outer regions is large

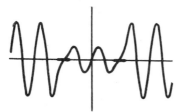

compared to that in the valley, and the particle is less likely to be in the valley than in any other region of length $2a$. A Schroedinger function having a relatively large amplitude outside the barriers is shown in Fig. 67, where the barriers are indicated by the thick parts of the x-axis.

Fig. 67. A Schroedinger function for the system of Fig. 66.

The exceptional cases arise when the factor in parentheses in (2) is zero or very small, that is, when E satisfies or nearly satisfies the equation

$$\tan \alpha a = \beta/\alpha. \tag{9}$$

Equations (2) to (5) then reduce to

$$A = 0, \qquad\qquad B = e^{\beta a} \cos \alpha a \qquad\qquad (10)$$

$$C \cos \alpha(b + D) = e^{-\beta l} \cos \alpha a \qquad\qquad (11)$$

$$C \sin \alpha(b + D) = e^{-\beta l} \sin \alpha a, \qquad\qquad (12)$$

and we get

$$C^2 = e^{-2\beta l}. \qquad\qquad (13)$$

Hence, in the exceptional cases, C^2 is smaller than unity, (1) has the form indicated in Fig. 68, and the particle is more likely to be in the valley than in any other region of length $2a$. The values of E for which the Schroedinger equation for an unbound system possesses solutions having relatively large amplitudes in a limited region are called *virtual energy levels* of the system. It will be shown in Exercise 2 that the virtual levels of our present system are grouped about the discrete true levels of a rectangular well of width $2a$ and depth V_0.

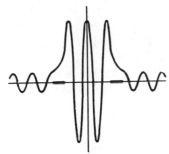

Fig. 68. A Schroedinger function for the system of Fig. 66, illustrating virtual binding.

We shall next estimate roughly the mean time, t_m, which our particle may be expected to spend within the valley if its state is specified by the ψ-function (1). Using $\bar{\psi}\psi$ for the relative distribution-in-x, we obtain for the relative probability of finding the particle within the valley the value $\int_{-a}^{a} \cos^2 \alpha x\, dx$, that is, approximately a. The corresponding relative probability of finding it in an interval of length $2a$ lying outside the barrier is $\int_{x}^{x+2a} C^2 \cos^2 \alpha(x + D)\, dx$, that is, approximately aC^2. Further, when the particle is far outside the barriers, it may be imagined to behave as though it were a free particle of energy E and speed $\sqrt{2E/m}$, and hence the time that it may be expected to spend in an interval of length $2a$ lying outside the barriers is $2a\sqrt{m/2E}$. The proportion

$$\frac{t_m}{2a\sqrt{m/2E}} = \frac{a}{aC^2} \qquad\qquad (14)$$

now yields the approximate result

$$t_m = \frac{2a}{C^2} \sqrt{\frac{m}{2E}}.$$ (15)

According to (8), t_m is, in general, of the order of magnitude of

$$2a \sqrt{\frac{m}{2E}} e^{-2\beta l},$$ (16)

while for a virtual energy level we get, using (13), the much greater mean time

$$t'_m = 2a \sqrt{\frac{m}{2E}} e^{2\beta l}.$$ (17)

In the case of the barrier of Fig. 65, the situation is similar. Thus, if the W. B. K. ψ-functions of §34 are used in an approximate treatment of the problem, we find that, when $V_a < E < V_0$, the square of the amplitude of a ψ-function outside the barrier is, in general, larger than that in the valley by a factor of the order of magnitude of

$$\exp\left[\frac{2}{\hbar} \int_{x_1}^{x_2} \sqrt{2m(V - E)} \, dx\right],$$ (18)

where x_1 and x_2 are the points so marked in Fig. 65; this result corresponds to (8). But, for special values of E, there exist ψ-functions for which the ratio of the square of the amplitude outside to that inside is approximately

$$\exp\left[-\frac{2}{\hbar} \int_{x_1}^{x_2} \sqrt{2m(V - E)} \, dx\right];$$ (19)

this result corresponds to (13). These special values of E, that is, the virtual energy levels, turn out to lie near the discrete levels of the potential well that we get if, in Fig. 65, we replace the two parts of the curve, lying outside the maxima, by horizontal lines through these maxima. For the case of a virtual level, the mean stay inside the valley comes out to be approximately

$$t'_m = L \sqrt{\frac{m}{2E}} \exp\left[\frac{2}{\hbar} \int_{x_1}^{x_2} \sqrt{2m(V - E)} \, dx\right],$$ (20)

where L is the width of the valley at the height E.

To summarize: When $V_a < E < V_0$, the ψ-functions for two-barrier potentials of the form shown in Fig. 65 have, as a rule, large amplitudes outside the barriers, and the mean stay of the particle in the valley is usually very short. But, for special values of E, there exist ψ's having small amplitudes outside the barriers, compared to the amplitudes inside; for the corresponding states, the mean stay of the particle in the valley is long, and the possibility that the particle *is* in the valley and will remain virtually bound there for an appreciable time may be sufficiently probable to be of physical interest.

Radioactive emission of α-particles. When extended to three dimensions, the considerations outlined above permit a theoretical interpretation of the emission of α-particles by radioactive atomic nuclei. To summarize the essentials of the problem, we quote, with a few minor changes, a passage from Rasetti:[3]

We shall first discuss the serious difficulties that are encountered when we try to explain the phenomenon of α-disintegration from the standpoint of the classical theory. These difficulties appear in striking form if we compare the spontaneous emission of α-particles by a nucleus with the scattering of α-particles by the same nucleus. Let us consider, for example, the uranium nucleus.

Rutherford's scattering experiments show that even the fastest α-particles available (those of Th C', whose energy is $14 \cdot 10^{-6}$ ergs) are unable, even in a head-on collision, to penetrate close enough to the nucleus to show departures from the Coulomb law. This observation means that, at least up to a distance of $3 \cdot 10^{-12}$ cm. from, the center of the nucleus, where the potential energy $V(r)$ of the α-particle is $14 \cdot 10^{-6}$ ergs, this potential energy is still expressed by the Coulomb formula:

$$V(r) = 2Ze^2/r,$$

where Ze is the charge of the nucleus, and $2e$ and r are the charge of the α-particle and its distance from the center of the nucleus. At smaller distances, where the α-particle cannot penetrate, we shall certainly find deviations from the Coulomb potential, since the nearly stable binding of α-particles in the nucleus requires the existence of a potential hole in the center of the nucleus.

The general shape of the function $V(r)$ must therefore be the one indicated in Fig. 69, where the dotted line represents the Coulomb potential, and the solid line the actual potential. The inner part of the curve has been traced arbitrarily; but for $r > 3 \cdot 10^{-12}$ cm., the scattering experiments show that there is no appreciable departure from the Coulomb potential.

The uranium nucleus spontaneously emits particles whose energy is $6.6 \cdot 10^{-6}$ ergs. (This energy is indicated in the diagram in Fig. 69.) It is consequently difficult to understand how the particles contained in the inside of the nucleus can go over a potential barrier which is at least twice

---

[3] F. Rasetti, *Elements of Nuclear Physics*, page 100. New York: Prentice-Hall, Inc., 1936.

as high as their total energy. According to the classical theory, particles of this energy could originate only from a point at a distance of $6 \cdot 10^{-12}$ cm. from the center of the nucleus, where the Coulomb potential energy has the value of $6.6 \cdot 10^{-6}$ ergs. However, in this region there is no possibility for the stable binding of an α-particle. In other words, we can say that, in the classical model, an α-particle emitted by a nucleus should have a kinetic energy corresponding at least to the top of the potential barrier. For example, in uranium the energy should be higher than $14 \cdot 10^{-6}$ ergs.

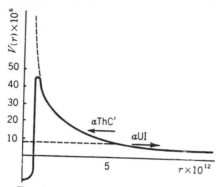

Fig. 69. Potential for the alpha particle in the nucleus.

This difficulty disappears when we treat the problem from the standpoint of quantum mechanics, as has been done independently by Gurney and Condon[4] and by Gamow.[5]

Indeed, according to Fig. 69, the potential on any line passing through the center of the nucleus has essentially the two-barrier form of Fig. 65, so that quantum-mechanically we may suspect, in view of the experimental results, that the situation is as follows: there is a virtual level of $6.6 \cdot 10^{-6}$ ergs; the not-yet-emitted α-particle occupies this level, being virtually bound inside the nucleus; the ψ-function describing this level does not, however, vanish outside the nucleus, and consequently the particle may eventually get out; and when this happens a spontaneous emission of the α-particle is said to have taken place.

When put to the test, this hypothesis fits in well with the experimental data concerning α-activity, for it leads to the exponential law of decay and the Geiger-Nuttall relation between mean life and range, yields the virtual levels at approximately the right places, and, through the exponential factor in (20), accounts for the fact that the mean lives of certain distinct nuclei differ from each other tremendously in spite of the evidence for the essential similarity of the respective potential barriers. An α-particle, however, is acted on by several moving nuclear constituents, the

[4] R. W. Gurney and E. U. Condon, *Nature*, **122,** 439 (1928); *Phys. Rev.*, 33, 127 (1929).

[5] G. Gamow, *Zeits. f. Physik*, **51,** 204 (1928)

valley portion of Fig. 69 can at best be but a time average, and hence even elementary considerations indicate a limit to the precision that we may expect of this simple theory.

The general form of the law of decay can be indicated by the following rough argument based on an interplay of classical and quantum-mechanical ideas. We return to Fig. 65, denote the energy of one of the virtual levels by E, denote by R and T the reflection and transmission coefficients of either *one* of the two barriers for a particle of energy E, and assume that T is so small that the higher-order terms in the expansion $\log (1 - T) = -T - \frac{1}{2}T^2 - \cdots$ can be disregarded and that hence

$$\log R = \log (1 - T) = -T. \tag{21}$$

Next we imagine that a particle (of energy E) which is in the valley at the instant $t = 0$, oscillates classically back and forth between the barriers, but at each collision with a barrier it has a chance T of being transmitted out. The probability $P(t)$ that it is still within the valley at the instant t is then R after one collision, R^2 after two collisions, and so on, that is,

$$P(t) = R^n, \tag{22}$$

where n is the expected number of collisions between the instants 0 and t; in view of (21) we then have

$$P(t) = R^n = e^{n \log R} = e^{-Tn}. \tag{23}$$

To estimate n, we turn again to the classical theory, take the average speed v of the particle to be approximately $\sqrt{2E/m}$, and find that

$$n = vt/L = \sqrt{2E/m}\, t/L, \tag{24}$$

where L is the width of the valley for a particle of energy E. Eliminating n from (23) by means of (24), and T by means of 25^{38}, with $f(E) = 1$, we finally get

$$P(t) = e^{-t/\tau}, \tag{25}$$

where

$$\tau = L \sqrt{\frac{m}{2E}} \exp \left[\frac{2}{\hbar} \int_{x_1}^{x_2} \sqrt{2m(V - E)}\, dx \right], \tag{26}$$

x_1 and x_2 being the points so marked in Fig. 65. Thus $P(t)$

decays exponentially with time, in agreement with experiment. Note that τ turns out to be identical with the t_m' given by (20).

Exercises

1. Show that the Schroedinger equation for the potential of Fig. 66 has a solution that is odd in x and that for positive values of x has the form

$$\psi = \begin{cases} \sin \alpha x, & 0 \leq x \leq a \\ A'e^{\beta x} + B'e^{-\beta x}, & a \leq x \leq b \\ C' \sin \alpha(x + D'), & b \leq x \end{cases} \qquad (27)$$

and that the system possesses virtual levels lying at and near the E's satisfying the equation

$$\tan \alpha a = -\alpha/\beta. \qquad (28)$$

2. Show that (9) and (28) can be combined into the single formula 19[29].

3. Consider the curvature of the ψ's and show graphically why virtual levels may be expected to exist when $V(x)$ is as in Fig. 65.

40. Waves

The assumptions with which we began our discussion of quantum mechanics were formulated sometime after Schroedinger proposed his theory, and our approach to, say, the Schroedinger equation is quite different from that used originally by Schroedinger himself. The stimulus for Schroedinger's researches that resulted in his celebrated equation came from the work of de Broglie,[6] who proposed the remarkable idea that a kind of vibration is associated with a moving particle, just as—so interference experiments suggest—a light wave is associated with a moving photon. Schroedinger's theory in its original form (his *wave mechanics*) made constructive uses of the notion of a wave motion associated with a particle motion, even though no entirely satisfactory physical interpretation of the 'associated waves' was available at the time.[7] In fact, the extraordinary rapidity with which Schroedinger's researches progressed was at least in part due to the similarity that some of the mathematical problems involved bore to certain problems in classical wave motion.

We should then expect that, whatever the manner in which we may introduce the Schroedinger method of studying the motion

---

[6] L. de Broglie, *Ann. de Physique*, **3**, 22 (1925); *Thèses*, Paris, 1924.

[7] The interpretation of ψ's as probability amplitudes was proposed by M. Born: *Zeits. f. Physik*, **37**, 863 (1926).

of a particle, the mathematical apparatus employed in the applications of the method should resemble that used in the classical theory of vibrations of continuous media, and that some of the terms used in the classical theory of wave motion should find a place in the quantum theory of particle motion. The remainder of this chapter is intended to indicate the extent to which this is so; we begin by reviewing certain terms.

Terminology. If the quantity $u = u(x, t)$ depends on the coordinate x and the time t, for all values of x and t, through the relation

$$u = A \cos 2\pi(kx - \nu t + \delta), \tag{1}$$

where A, k, and δ are real constants and ν is a positive[8] constant, we call u a *real cosinusoidal* (or *sinusoidal*) *wave* of infinite extent in x and in t, or simply a *real monochromatic wave*; the term *monochromatic* implies both the sinusoidal shape of the wave and its infinite extent in x and t. The usual names and symbols for the various quantities involved in (1) are listed in Table 10.

TABLE 10

$\|A\|$	*amplitude* of u
A^2	*intensity* of u
k	*propagation constant* of u
$\|k\|$	*wave number* of u
$\|1/k\| = \lambda$	*wave length* of u
ν	*frequency* of u
$\nu^{-1} = T$	*period* of u
$2\pi(kx - \nu t + \delta)$	*phase* of u
$2\pi\delta$	*initial phase* of u

Waves of type (1) arise, for example, in connection with small plane transverse vibrations of a uniform elastic string of infinite length whose equilibrium position coincides with the x-axis; and u may then represent, for every value of x and t, the transverse displacement of the string from its equilibrium position. In our discussion we shall not, however, restrict ourselves to any particular physical interpretation of u.

For a given type of a physical wave, the frequency ν and the wave number $|k|$ are usually dependent on each other in a definite way; for example, if (1) represents the transverse displacement of a uniform elastic string, we have

$$\nu = \left| \sqrt{\frac{\tau}{\rho}}\, k \right|, \qquad k = \pm\sqrt{\frac{\rho}{\tau}}\, \nu, \tag{2}$$

where ρ is the linear density and τ is the tension of the string.

---

[8] This restriction, imposed here for simplicity, is sometimes inadvisable.

Once A in (1) is fixed, the numerical value of u at a given point x at a given instant t is determined by the phase

$$\phi = 2\pi(kx - \nu t + \delta); \tag{3}$$

hence, as t increases, any preassigned value of u drifts, so to speak, along the x-axis with the velocity ν/k, which, in view of the dependence of ν on k, can be regarded as a function of k alone. We denote this velocity by $w_\phi(k)$ or by w_ϕ, so that

$$w_\phi = w_\phi(k) = \nu/k, \tag{4}$$

and call it the *phase velocity* of u (rather than simply the *velocity* of u) to emphasize that it is the velocity with which the values of the phase of u are, in the course of time, transferred along the x-axis. The direction of the phase velocity is determined by the algebraic sign of the propagation constant k.

If

$$u = \sum_s A_s \cos 2\pi(k_s x - \nu_s t + \delta_s), \qquad s = 1, 2, 3, \cdots, \tag{5}$$

we call u a *composite* wave,[9] and say that it is a *discrete superposition* of the monochromatic *component* waves $A_1 \cos 2\pi(k_1 x - \nu_1 t + \delta_1)$, $A_2 \cos 2\pi(k_2 x - \nu_2 t + \delta_2)$, and so forth.

A more general type of a composite wave is a *continuous superposition* of monochromatic waves, that is,

$$u = \int_{k_1}^{k_2} A(k) \cos 2\pi[kx - \nu(k)t + \delta(k)]\, dk. \tag{6}$$

The integral in (6) stands in more or less the same relation to the sum in (5) as does a Fourier integral to a Fourier series.

A monochromatic wave preserves its sinusoidal shape as time goes on, and consequently the concept of the velocity of such a wave is a simple one. This is in general not so in the case of a composite wave, because the respective speeds of the component waves may be different (when we call the propagation *dispersive*), or, even if these speeds are the same, the directions of the motions of the component waves may be different, so that the composite wave as a whole may not preserve its shape; in fact, it is not usually instructive to interpret any single number associated with

---

[9] Note that we regard a wave such as $\cos 2\pi(kx - \nu t) + \cos 2\pi(-kx - \nu t)$ as composite, even though it involves only a single frequency.

a composite wave as its velocity, especially when the propagation is dispersive. An important exception arises, however, when the composite wave is a superposition of monochromatic waves of nearly equal amplitudes and propagation constants. To illustrate, we let u be the superposition of the two monochromatic waves

$$u_1 = A \cos 2\pi(kx - \nu t) \tag{7}$$

and $$u_2 = A \cos 2\pi[(k + \Delta k)x - (\nu + \Delta \nu)t] \tag{8}$$

whose amplitudes are the same, whose propagation constants differ by an amount Δk small compared to k, whose frequencies differ by an amount $\Delta \nu$ small compared to ν, and whose initial phases are both zero. Then

$$u = u_1 + u_2 = 2A \cos \pi[(2k + \Delta k)x - (2\nu + \Delta \nu)t] \cdot$$
$$\cos \pi(\Delta k \cdot x - \Delta \nu \cdot t), \quad (9)$$

or, approximately,

$$u = 2A \cos 2\pi(kx - \nu t) \cdot \cos \pi(\Delta k \cdot x - \Delta \nu \cdot t). \tag{10}$$

Our composite wave is thus approximately a monochromatic wave *modulated* by the factor $\cos \pi(\Delta k \cdot x - \Delta \nu \cdot t)$. The component waves (7) and (8) and their superposition (10) are shown for a fixed instant of time in Fig. 70. The composite wave

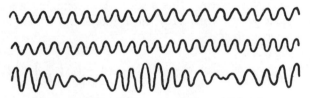

Fig. 70. Superposition of two sinusoidal waves.

consists at any instant of groups of ripples, the arrangement of these groups (or *space beats*) being controlled by the modulating factor. Now, as time goes on, the shape of u changes in detail; but the arrangment into groups persists for all time, and the velocity with which the *groups* move is determined by the velocity with which the phase of the modulating factor drifts along the x-axis. Inspection of (10) shows that this velocity, called the *group velocity* of our composite wave and denoted by $w_g(k)$ or

by w_g , is $\Delta\nu/\Delta k$, so that, if Δk and $\Delta\nu$ are allowed to approach
zero, we have

$$w_g \;=\; w_g(k) \;=\; \frac{d\nu}{dk}. \tag{11}$$

Although (11) was derived above for a special case of no particular interest, it represents in fact the velocity of wave groups
whenever these groups are formed by a superposition of monochromatic waves whose amplitudes are nearly equal and whose
propagation constants all lie near a single value k. To give
another example, we consider a composite wave u whose component waves interfere with each other in such a way as nearly to
cancel everywhere except in a limited region, so that u consists
essentially of a single wave group, that is, as we often say, a single
wave packet. A wave of this type is

$$u \;=\; \int_{k_0-\Delta k}^{k_0+\Delta k} A(k)\cos 2\pi[kx - \nu(k)t]\,dk, \tag{12}$$

provided that within the region of integration $\nu(k)$ can be expressed
sufficiently accurately by the first two terms of its Taylor series
in k, so that

$$\nu(k) \;=\; \nu(k_0) \,+\, (k - k_0)\left(\frac{d\nu}{dk}\right)_0, \tag{13}$$

and provided that within this region $A(k)$ remains essentially
constant. To verify that (12) then represents a single wave
packet, we write it as

$$u \;=\; A(k_0)\int_{k_0-\Delta k}^{k_0+\Delta k} \cos 2\pi\left[kx - \nu(k_0)t - (k - k_0)\left(\frac{d\nu}{dk}\right)_0 t\right]dk, \tag{14}$$

and, integrating and omitting the zero subscripts in the result, get

$$u \;=\; 2A(k)\Delta k\cdot\cos 2\pi[kx - \nu(k)t]\cdot\frac{\sin 2\pi\Delta k\left[x - \left(\dfrac{d\nu}{dk}\right)t\right]}{2\pi\Delta k\left[x - \left(\dfrac{d\nu}{dk}\right)t\right]}. \tag{15}$$

Our u is thus a modulated monochromatic wave whose modulating
factor at the instant t is small everywhere except near the point
$x = (d\nu/dk)t$, and consequently (12) does represent a single
wave packet. The shape of (15) for a single instant is indicated

in Fig. 71. The group velocity of our wave is the velocity with which the maximum of the modulating factor drifts along the x-axis, and inspection of (15) shows that this velocity is given by (11).

Fig. 71. An instantaneous graph of the packet (15).

Sometimes, for short, we speak of $w_g(k)$ as 'the group velocity of a monochromatic wave having the propagation constant k,' this term being an abbreviation for 'the velocity of wave groups formed by a superposition of monochromatic waves whose propagation constants all lie near the value k.'

In some calculations involving real waves, it is convenient to use complex exponentials rather than trigonometric functions and, using the symbolism of 2^8, to write (1) as

$$u = \text{Re } A e^{2\pi i(kx - \nu t + \delta)}. \tag{16}$$

Complex exponentials can be used in a similar way in dealing with real composite waves.

Exercises

1. Use (2) to show that the propagation of the transverse displacements of a uniform elastic string is nondispersive.

2. Show that, in order for a wave propagation to be nondispersive, it is necessary and sufficient that the group speed equal the phase speed.

3. Show in a qualitative way that the wave packet (12) spreads out as it moves unless the right side of (13) expresses $\nu(k)$ *exactly*.

41. De Broglie Waves

The Schroedinger function specifying the state of a free particle moving in one dimension with a definite momentum is

$$\psi = A e^{ipx/\hbar} e^{-iEt/\hbar}, \tag{1}$$

where A is an arbitrary nonvanishing constant (in general complex) whose value does not affect the physical properties of the state in question, and where p and E are the respective definite numerical values of the momentum and the energy of the particle. Now, if we write (1) as

$$\psi = Ae^{2\pi i\left(\frac{p}{h}x - \frac{E}{h}t\right)},$$ (2)

we note that ψ resembles the expression

(16^{40}) $u = \mathrm{Re}\ Ae^{2\pi i(kx - \nu t)}$ (3)

for a real monochromatic wave to such an extent as to suggest that we introduce the notion of a *complex*[10] *monochromatic wave*, intepret our ψ as such a wave, and ascribe to ψ an amplitude A, an intensity $|A|^2$, a propagation constant k, a wave length λ, a frequency ν, and so forth, by correlating the various constants in (2) with those in (3). The correlation yields, in particular,

$$k = p/h,$$ (4)

$$\nu = E/h.$$ (5)

When the Schroedinger function (1) is regarded as a complex wave, it is called a *monochromatic de Broglie wave*, and the quantities $|h/p|$, $|E/h|$, and so on, are then called the *de Broglie wave length of the particle*, the *de Broglie frequency of the particle*, and so on.

Since any Schroedinger function can be expanded at any instant in terms of the eigenfunctions of momentum, we may regard any Schroedinger function as a superposition of monochromatic de Broglie waves and may speak of it as a *wave function* or simply a *wave*. A Kennard packet, for example, may be referred to as a Kennard *wave packet*.

Although complex waves cannot be readily visualized, we may define their velocities by adopting 4^{40} and 11^{40}:

$$w_\phi = \nu/k, \qquad w_g = d\nu/dk.$$ (6)

In view of (4) and (5) we then get

$$w_\phi = E/p, \qquad w_g = dE/dp$$ (7)

for the phase and the group velocity of a de Broglie wave associated with a free particle whose momentum is certainly p. Re-

---

[10] Our terms *complex* and *composite* should not be confused.

calling that, for a free particle, $E = p^2/2m$ and $p = mv$, we get, more explicitly,

$$w_\phi = \tfrac{1}{2}v, \qquad w_g = v \tag{8}$$

from (7), and[11]

$$k = \frac{mv}{h}, \qquad \lambda = \frac{h}{mv} \tag{9a, b}$$

from (4). Thus, in particular, the group velocity of a de Broglie wave associated with a free particle of definite momentum equals the velocity of the particle.[12]

By introducing such terms as de Broglie wave length, frequency, and so on, we have provided new *names* for certain quantities occurring in quantum-mechanical formulas, but have not in any way modified or augmented our fundamental postulates: whether we do or do not refer to Schroedinger functions as waves, we must go through exactly the same mathematical procedure when we wish to determine the physical implications of the assertion that the state of a system is specified by a certain ψ-function. The principal reason for regarding Schroedinger functions as waves and for speaking of the wave length and the frequency of a particle is that the mathematical properties of complex waves are in many respects similar to those of real waves, and that consequently the wave terminology may be helpful, in a subjective way, to one familiar with the properties of the real waves encountered in the classical theory of continuous media.

The classical notion of the entity called a *particle* is inextricably bound up with the possibility of ascribing to this entity at any instant a definite position and, simultaneously, a definite momentum; in view of the Heisenberg inequalities, then, the quantum-mechanical notion of a particle is not precisely the same as the corresponding classical notion. The fact that we now succeed in associating, in a reasonably straightforward way, such terms as wave length and frequency with certain quantities involved in the quantum theory of the entity that we have been calling (and, for lack of a more suitable and generally accepted term, shall continue to call) a *particle*, suggests that under suitable circum-

---

[11] To conform to the notation of §40 we should, strictly, write (9b) as $\lambda = h/m \mid v \mid$ and (5) as $\nu = \mid E \mid/h$.

[12] In the relativistic de Broglie theory, $w_g = v$ and $w_\phi = c^2/v$, so that w_ϕ is not equal to $\tfrac{1}{2}v$, but is greater than the speed of light c.

stances this entity may display properties which are usually ascribed to waves. This is indeed true; and it is for the very reason that quantum mechanics allows for the coexistence of particulate and undulatory properties in a single entity that it is successful in correlating experiments (for example, Compton's) which bring to the fore the corpuscular nature of the electron with experiments (for example, Davisson and Germer's) which reveal its wave properties.

In conclusion, we must emphasize the fact that the de Broglie relation $\lambda = h/mv$ was inferred above from the state (1), which is a momentum state of a free particle and which consequently implies that the position of the particle is entirely indeterminate. Therefore, to use a rather crude illustration, it is quite wrong to point at a billiard ball of mass m moving on a table with velocity v and to say, "With this ball is associated a monochromatic de Broglie wave of wave length h/mv." The very fact that we are pointing at the ball means that we have a considerable amount of information regarding its position, and consequently the state of the ball is not a momentum state and is not described by a ψ-function of the type (1). The true situation is somewhat as follows: we know roughly both the velocity and the position of the ball, so that the distribution-in-x and the distribution-in-p both have the form of packets; the ψ-function representing the state of the ball is consequently a wave packet consisting of a superposition of an infinite number of de Broglie waves of different wave lengths, the component wave of wave length h/mv being particularly prominent; each of the component waves is of infinite extent, but these components interfere with each other so as practically to cancel everywhere except in the immediate vicinity of the most likely position of the ball; and, as time goes on, the x-packet moves with the group velocity $w_g = v$ of the composite wave, that is, with the velocity of the ball.

Exercises

1. Show that the de Broglie wave length of an electron having the kinetic energy of P electron volts is approximately $12.2\,P^{-\frac{1}{2}}$ angstroms.

2. Set $B = 0$ in 2^{38}, interpret the two terms in the resulting ψ_l as an incident and a reflected wave and the resulting ψ_r as a transmitted wave, compare the intensities of the incident and the reflected waves, and show that, when $0 < E < V_0$, the reflection coefficient of the rectangular barrier of Fig. 59^{38} for the incident wave is 8^{38}; then compare the intensities of the incident and the transmitted waves, and derive 9^{38}.

3. Use the procedure of Exercise 2 to derive 16^{38} and 17^{38}; note that in deriving 17^{38} independently of 16^{38} it is necessary to take into account the fact that the potentials on the two sides of $x = 0$ in Fig. 62^{38} are different.

4. Show that 26^{38} vanishes whenever $l = \frac{1}{2}n\lambda$, where $n = 1, 2, \cdots$, and where λ is the de Broglie wave length of the particle in the central region of Fig. 59^{38} when $E > V_0$. What phenomenon in the transmission of a wave incident normally on a refracting plate does this effect resemble?

5. Evaluate the de Broglie wave length and the de Broglie frequency of a free particle when $V(x) = V_0 \neq 0$.

6. Draw a rough graph of the Kennard wave packet 21^{28} for the case $p_0 = 0$ and contrast it with the wave packet of Fig. 71^{40}.

42. A Vibrating String and a Particle in a Box

The mathematical similarity between the methods of the Schroedinger theory of a particle and of the classical theory of wave motion makes it possible to correlate problems in the quantum theory of particle motion with certain problems in classical wave motion in such a way that acquaintance with a problem in one theory is helpful in dealing with a particular problem in the other theory. Thus there is a certain similarity between the methods of handling the classical problem of the small vibrations of an elastic string of infinite length and the Schroedinger method of studying a particle moving freely in one dimension; the Schroedinger treatment of the motion of a particle in a one-dimensional box is analogous in several mathematical details to the classical problem of the small vibrations of a finite string fixed at both ends; the Schroedinger technique for treating the linear harmonic oscillator resembles that used in the classical theory of the diffraction of waves by a parabolic cylinder—these are but a few of the examples that can be quoted. But in pointing out such similarities we must emphasize the fact that the dissimilarities which may accompany them are often so important that it is in general quite unsafe, without a careful scrutiny, to carry the conclusions drawn in the one problem over to the other. For example, the analogy of an infinite string would suggest that the propagation of the de Broglie waves of a free particle should be nondispersive; we know, however, that this is not so, because the values of w_ϕ and w_g given by 8^{41} are not equal to each other.

To illustrate these matters we shall now discuss briefly a classical string and a quantum-mechanical particle in a box.

The small transverse vibrations of an elastic string fixed at both ends. We consider a string fastened at $x = 0$ and at $x = l$, whose equilibrium position coincides with the x-axis, whose linear density is a constant ρ, and whose tension is a constant τ; and we assume that the string is perfectly elastic and can support only tangential stress, that friction can be neglected, that the angle between the x-axis and the tangent to the string at any point is small,[13] that the displacement $u = u(x, t)$ of every point of the string from its position of equilibrium is at every instant transverse to the x-axis, and that the displaced string lies in a plane.

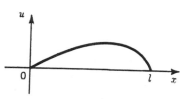

Fig. 72. A string displaced from the equilibrium position.

When the string is displaced (Fig. 72), its length is given by the standard calculus formula as $\int_0^l [1 + (\partial u/\partial x)^2]^{\frac{1}{2}} \, dx$; since $\partial u/\partial x$ is in our case small, we may take this length to be $\int_0^l [1 + \frac{1}{2}(\partial u/\partial x)^2] \, dx$, so that the string is longer than l by the amount $\frac{1}{2} \int_0^l (\partial u/\partial x)^2 \, dx$. Taking the potential energy of the undisturbed string to be zero, we find that the potential energy of the displaced string (elongation times tension) at the instant t is

$$\text{P. E.} = \frac{1}{2}\tau \int_0^l \left(\frac{\partial u}{\partial x}\right)^2 dx. \tag{1}$$

The kinetic energy of a portion dx of the string at the instant t is $\frac{1}{2}(\rho dx)v^2 = \frac{1}{2}\rho dx(\partial u/\partial t)^2$, and hence the kinetic energy of the whole string at the instant t is

$$\text{K. E.} = \frac{1}{2}\rho \int_0^l \left(\frac{\partial u}{\partial t}\right)^2 dx. \tag{2}$$

The total energy of the string is consequently

$$W = \frac{1}{2}\tau \int_0^l \left(\frac{\partial u}{\partial x}\right)^2 dx + \frac{1}{2}\rho \int_0^l \left(\frac{\partial u}{\partial t}\right)^2 dx. \tag{3}$$

To derive the differential equation satisfied by u, we set up the equation

$$\text{force} = \text{mass} \times \text{acceleration} \tag{4}$$

---

[13] For details, see a book on theoretical physics.

for the short portion AB of
the string in Fig. 73. The
external forces T_1 and T_2 are
both of magnitude τ, so that
the resultant upward force
is $\tau(-\sin\alpha_1 + \sin\alpha_2)$; that
is, if we replace the sines of
the small angles by their tangents, it is

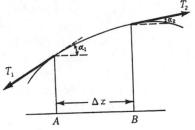

Fig. 73. Force diagram for a portion of a string.

$$\tau(-\tan\alpha_1 + \tan\alpha_2); \quad (5)$$

the resultant horizontal force is $\tau(-\cos\alpha_1 + \cos\alpha_2)$ and, to the
first approximation, is zero. Equation (4) thus becomes

$$\tau(-\tan\alpha_1 + \tan\alpha_2) = \rho\Delta x\, \frac{\partial^2 u}{\partial t^2}. \qquad (6)$$

Now, the slope of u at A is $\tan\alpha_1 = \partial u(x, t)/\partial x$, while the slope of
u at B is $\tan\alpha_2 = \partial u(x + \Delta x, t)/\partial x$, so that, to the first order in
Δx, $\tan\alpha_2 = \partial u(x, t)/\partial x + \Delta x\cdot\partial^2 u(x, t)/\partial x^2$ and $-\tan\alpha_1 +$
$\tan\alpha_2 = \Delta x\cdot\partial^2 u/\partial x^2$. Substituting this result into (6), canceling
Δx, and dividing through by τ, we finally get

$$\frac{\partial^2 u}{\partial x^2} = \frac{\rho}{\tau}\frac{\partial^2 u}{\partial t^2}. \qquad (7)$$

In addition to satisfying (7), the displacement of a string fixed at
$x = 0$ and at $x = l$ satisfies the boundary conditions

$$u(0, t) = 0, \qquad u(l, t) = 0. \qquad (8)$$

The standard method of computing the general solution of (7)
satisfying the conditions (8) runs as follows. To begin with, we
look for solutions of (7) having the rather special form

$$u(x, t) = X(x)T(t), \qquad (9)$$

where $X(x) = X$ is a function only of x, and $T(t) = T$ is a function
only of t. To determine the conditions that must be satisfied by
X and T in order that (9) may be a solution of (7), we substitute (9)
into (7) and, writing X'' for $\partial^2 X(x)/\partial x^2$ and T'' for $\partial^2 T(t)/\partial t^2$, get
$X''T = \rho X T''/\tau$, that is,

$$\frac{X''}{X} = \frac{\rho}{\tau}\frac{T''}{T}. \qquad (10)$$

Since X is a function only of x, the quantity X''/X depends only on x and is independent of t; similarly, the quantity $\rho T''/\tau T$ depends only on t and is independent of x. Now, Equation (10) asserts that the quantity X''/X (which, as we have seen, can depend only on x) is equal to a quantity that is independent of x; hence X''/X does not depend even on x, and we may write $X''/X = -K$, that is,

$$X'' + KX = 0, \tag{11}$$

where K is some constant regarding which we have as yet no information. It now follows from (10) and (11) that $T''/T = -\tau K/\rho$, that is,

$$T'' + \frac{\tau}{\rho} KT = 0. \tag{12}$$

Thus the problem of finding the solutions of (7) having the special form (9) reduces to that of finding the respective solutions of the two equations (11) and (12), each of which involves only one independent variable. The process of converting a differential equation containing several independent variables into several differential equations each of which contains fewer independent variables than does the original equation is called *separation of variables*.

The respective general solutions of Equations (11) and (12) are

$$X = A \sin K^{\frac{1}{2}}x + B \cos K^{\frac{1}{2}}x \tag{13}$$

and

$$T = C \sin\left(\frac{\tau K}{\rho}\right)^{\frac{1}{2}} t + D \cos\left(\frac{\tau K}{\rho}\right)^{\frac{1}{2}} t, \tag{14}$$

so that (9) becomes

$$u = [A \sin K^{\frac{1}{2}}x + B \cos K^{\frac{1}{2}}x] \cdot \left[C \sin\left(\frac{\tau K}{\rho}\right)^{\frac{1}{2}} t + D \cos\left(\frac{\tau K}{\rho}\right)^{\frac{1}{2}} t \right]. \tag{15}$$

The boundary conditions (8) require that the first [ ] in (15) vanish for $x = 0$ and for $x = l$, and consequently we must have

$$B = 0, \qquad K^{\frac{1}{2}} = n\pi/l, \quad n = 1, 2, 3, \cdots, \tag{16}$$

the case $n = 0$ being trivial. Introducing the quantity

$$\nu_n = \frac{n}{2l} \sqrt{\frac{\tau}{\rho}} \tag{17}$$

and writing u_n for u, we now reduce (15) with the help of (16) to

$$u_n = A_n \sin \frac{n\pi x}{l} \cos 2\pi \,(\nu_n t + \delta_n), \qquad (18)$$

where A_n and δ_n are arbitrary constants. The reader will perhaps recognize (17) as giving the *characteristic frequencies* of our string, and (18) as describing its *characteristic vibrations*. Since the values of u outside the limits 0 and l are of no physical interest, we may take them to be zero and may write the expression for the nth characteristic vibration as

$$u_n = \begin{cases} 0 & x \leq 0 \\ \mathrm{Re}\, A_n \sin \frac{n\pi x}{l}\, e^{-2\pi i(\nu_n t + \delta_n)} & 0 \leq x \leq l \quad (19) \\ 0 & l \leq x. \end{cases}$$

Now, the problem that we undertook to solve is to find the general solution of (7) subject to the conditions (8), and at first sight the identification of the solutions of the rather special form (9) may appear to be a digression from our main object. In fact, however, any solution of (7) which is of physical interest and satisfies (8) can be expressed as a superposition of the characteristic vibrations,[13] that is, as

$$u = \sum_n A_n \sin \frac{n\pi x}{l} \cos 2\pi(\nu_n t + \delta_n), \quad n = 1, 2, 3, \cdots . \quad (20)$$

The function (20)—which contains the infinitely many arbitrary constants A_n and δ_n and which no longer has the restricted form (9)—thus comprises the complete solution of (7) subject to the conditions (8); the large number of arbitrary constants is due to the fact that (7) is a partial rather than an ordinary differential equation.

Using (3), we find that the energy of a string executing the nth characteristic vibration (18) is

$$W_n = \frac{A_n^2 \tau \pi^2 n^2}{4l}, \qquad (21)$$

and that the energy for the general vibration (20) is

$$W = \frac{\tau \pi^2}{4l} \sum_n n^2 A_n^2 = \sum_n W_n, \qquad n = 1, 2, 3, \cdots . \quad (22)$$

Thus the energy of a characteristic vibration is, in particular, proportional to the square of the amplitude of the vibration, and the energy of a more complicated motion is the *sum* of the energies of the characteristic component vibrations into which the motion as a whole can be resolved.

A vibrating string and a particle in a box.   Let us now turn to a quantum-mechanical particle in the potential box of Fig. 36[30]. The second Schroedinger equation 1[16] then has, in the region $0 \leq x \leq l$, the form

$$\frac{\partial^2 \psi}{\partial x^2} = -i\hbar\kappa \frac{\partial \psi}{\partial t};$$ (23)

the eigenvalues of H are

(5[30]) $$E_n = n^2 h^2 / 8ml^2;$$ (24)

the (not normalized) eigenfunction of H belonging to E_n can be written as

(4[30]) $$\psi_n = \begin{cases} 0 & x \leq 0 \\ A_n \sin \dfrac{n\pi x}{l}\, e^{-2\pi i(\nu_n t + \delta_n)} & 0 \leq x \leq l \quad (25) \\ 0 & l \leq x, \end{cases}$$

where A_n and δ_n are arbitrary real constants, and

$$\nu_n = E_n/h = n^2 h/8ml^2;$$ (26)

and the ψ-function specifying an arbitrary state of the system can be expressed as a superposition of the ψ-functions (25).

We note first of all the close resemblance of the ψ_n given by (25) to the u_n given by (19)—the resemblance responsible for the drawing of analogies between the particle in the box and the vibrating string.   But we should also note a number of dissimilarities, some of which are listed below.

The Schroedinger equation (23) involves the *first* time derivative of ψ, while the string equation (7) involves the *second* time derivative of u.   This fact is responsible for many differences between the respective properties of ψ and of u, among which the following is perhaps the most fundamental: the knowledge of ψ as a function of x for any single instant t_0 is *sufficient* to determine ψ for all time; on the other hand, the knowledge of u as a function of x for a single instant t_0 is *not sufficient* to determine u for all time—the behavior of the string depends not only on its displacement at some initial instant t_0 , but also on the velocities of all of its points at that instant.[14]

The function u_n is always and everywhere real, and may be pictured at any instant as a line in the ux-plane. On the other hand, owing to the imaginary coefficient in (23), the function ψ_n is real only for special values of t, so that it can be pictured as a line in a fixed plane only at isolated instants and cannot be visualized as readily as u_n .

In dealing with u_n we may restrict ourselves entirely to the range $0 \leq x \leq l$; the values of u_n outside this range do not enter into the computations concerning the physical properties of the string. But the values of ψ_n outside this range are important; for example, the discontinuities of $\partial \psi_n / \partial x$ at the ends of the box (discontinuities that could be disregarded were we permitted to work entirely within the region $0 \leq x \leq l$) affect the distribution-in-p of the particle, as was shown in Exercise 4^{30}.

The value of A_n in u_n is obviously of physical interest; the value of A_n in ψ_n , on the other hand, does not affect any of the physical conclusions[15] to be drawn from the assertion that the state of the system is specified by the ψ-function (25). For example, if the displacement of the string is specified by (19), its energy is certainly (21), while if the particle is in the state (25) its energy is certainly (24); and we note that A_n plays an important part in (21) but does not appear in (24) at all.

The frequency of u_n , given by (17), is proportional to n; while the frequency of ψ_n , given by (26), is proportional to n^2 .

A very important dissimilarity in physical interpretation arises in connection with superposition. For example, if the displacement of the string is

$$u = u_1 + u_2 , \tag{27}$$

---

[14] If θ is the temperature and σ is the diffusivity (that is, the ratio of thermal conductivity to the specific thermal capacity) of a homogeneous body, then the one-dimensional equation for the conduction of heat is $\dfrac{\partial^2 \theta}{\partial x^2} = \dfrac{1}{\sigma} \dfrac{\partial \theta}{\partial t}$. This equation resembles (23) much more closely than does (7); but to make the resemblance complete the diffusivity has to be taken as a pure imaginary, and for this reason the analogy between (23) and the heat-flow equation is drawn rather seldom in elementary work.

[15] It is for this reason that we may once for all assign to A_n in (25) a value which normalizes ψ_n .

where u_1 and u_2 are given by (19), then the energy of the string is a *certainty*, being given by (22) as

$$W = W_1 + W_2 = \frac{\tau \pi^2}{4l} (A_1^2 + 4A_2^2), \tag{28}$$

where W_1 and W_2 are the energies associated, respectively, with the first and second harmonics in (27). On the other hand, if the state of the particle in the box is specified by the Schroedinger function

$$\psi = \psi_1 + \psi_2, \tag{29}$$

where ψ_1 and ψ_2 are given by (25), then the energy of the system is *not a certainty*; in fact, according to the theorem on p. 111, the possible results of a precise energy measurement are then $E_1 = h^2/8ml^2$ and $E_2 = 4h^2/8ml^2$, and their respective probabilities are

$$\frac{|A_1|^2}{|A_1|^2 + |A_2|^2} \quad \text{and} \quad \frac{|A_2|^2}{|A_1|^2 + |A_2|^2}. \tag{30}$$

Note that the simplicity of the result (30) is due to the fact that the normalizing factor of (25) is independent of n.

Exercises

1. Consider the second Schroedinger equation $H\psi = i\hbar\, \partial\psi/\partial t$ for one dimension, restrict yourself to its solutions of the special form $\psi = X(x)T(t)$, and show that this equation then separates into the two ordinary differential equations

$$HX = EX \quad \text{and} \quad i\hbar \frac{\partial T}{\partial t} = ET, \tag{31a, b}$$

where E is the constant which is introduced in the process of separating the variables and which is arbitrary until the conditions of good behavior are imposed. Note that (31a) is just the one-dimensional first Schroedinger equation. Solve (31b), and correlate these computations with those on page 86.

2. Discuss the effect of the choice of the origin from which potential energy is measured (a) on the frequency of u_n for a string, (b) on the frequency of ψ_n for a boxed particle, and (c) on the distributions-in-x for stationary and for nonstationary states of a boxed particle.

CHAPTER VII

CONSTANTS OF MOTION

43. Time Derivatives of Averages of Dynamical Variables

If the state of a one-dimensional dynamical system is specified by a normalized Schroedinger function ψ, then, according to the expectation formula 2^{17}, the average value of a dynamical variable α for this state is

$$\mathrm{av}_\psi \, \alpha = \int \bar{\psi} \alpha \psi \, dx, \qquad \langle 1 \rangle$$

where α in the integrand is the Schroedinger operator associated with the dynamical variable α. Now, in view of the second Schroedinger equation 1^{16}, both ψ and $\bar{\psi}$ are time-dependent; in fact, in the one-dimensional case, they satisfy the equations

$$\frac{\partial \psi}{\partial t} = \frac{i}{\hbar \kappa} \psi'' - \frac{i}{\hbar} V \psi, \qquad \frac{\partial \bar{\psi}}{\partial t} = -\frac{i}{\hbar \kappa} \bar{\psi}'' + \frac{i}{\hbar} V \bar{\psi}. \quad (2a, b)$$

Consequently $\mathrm{av}_\psi \, \alpha$ is usually a function of t, even when α does not involve t explicitly.

The time derivative of $\mathrm{av}_\psi \, \alpha$ is, according to $\langle 1 \rangle$,

$$\frac{d}{dt} \mathrm{av}_\psi \, \alpha = \frac{d}{dt} \int \bar{\psi} \alpha \psi \, dx. \qquad \langle 3 \rangle$$

If α does not involve t explicitly, we get, differentiating in the right side of $\langle 3 \rangle$ under the integral sign,

$$\frac{d}{dt} \mathrm{av}_\psi \, \alpha = \int \left(\frac{\partial \bar{\psi}}{\partial t} \alpha \psi + \bar{\psi} \alpha \frac{\partial \psi}{\partial t} \right) dx. \qquad \langle 4 \rangle$$

Averages of dynamical variables and time derivatives of averages of dynamical variables satisfy, in quantum mechanics, relations similar to those satisfied by dynamical variables and time derivatives of dynamical variables in the classical theory. For example, according to $\langle 4 \rangle$ and (2),

$$\frac{d}{dt} \mathrm{av}_\psi \, x = \int \left(\frac{\partial \bar{\psi}}{dt} x \psi + \bar{\psi} x \frac{\partial \psi}{dt} \right) dx$$

$$= \frac{i\hbar}{2m} \int (\bar{\psi} x \psi'' - \bar{\psi}'' x \psi) \, dx; \qquad (5)$$

247

integration by parts reduces the last integral to $-(i\hbar/m) \int \bar{\psi}\psi' \, dx$, and hence

$$\frac{d}{dt} \operatorname{av}_\psi x = \frac{1}{m} \int \bar{\psi} \left(-i\hbar \frac{\partial}{\partial x} \right) \psi \, dx. \tag{6}$$

Comparing the right side of (6) with that of $\langle 1 \rangle$, and recalling that $-i\hbar\partial/\partial x$ is the Schroedinger operator associated with the momentum p, we finally rewrite (6) as

$$\frac{d}{dt} \operatorname{av}_\psi x = \frac{1}{m} \operatorname{av}_\psi p. \tag{7}$$

Thus, for an arbitrary normalizable state of an arbitrary dynamical system, the quantities $d \operatorname{av}_\psi x/dt$ and $\operatorname{av}_\psi p$ satisfy an equation similar to the classical $\dot{x} = p/m$.

Similarly,

$$\frac{d}{dt} \operatorname{av}_\psi p = \int \left[\frac{\partial \bar{\psi}}{\partial t} \left(-i\hbar \frac{\partial}{\partial x} \right) \psi + \bar{\psi} \left(-i\hbar \frac{\partial}{\partial x} \right) \frac{\partial \psi}{\partial t} \right] dx; \tag{8}$$

eliminating $\partial\bar{\psi}/\partial t$ by means of (2b) and $\partial\psi'/\partial t$ by means of the equation obtained by differentiating (2a) with respect to x, and integrating by parts, we reduce the integral to $- \int \bar{\psi}(\partial V/\partial x)\psi \, dx$, and get

$$\frac{d}{dt} \operatorname{av}_\psi p = \operatorname{av}_\psi \left(-\frac{\partial V}{\partial x} \right), \tag{9}$$

that is, an equation resembling the classical $\dot{p} = -\partial V/\partial x$.

Again, substitution of $\alpha = H = -\kappa^{-1}\partial^2/\partial x^2 + V$ into $\langle 4 \rangle$, the use of (2), and repeated integration by parts, yield $d \operatorname{av}_\psi H/dt = 0$, that is,

$$\frac{d}{dt} \operatorname{av}_\psi E = 0, \tag{10}$$

another result to be expected by classical analogy. Incidentally, we have already shown in §28 that in the case of a *free particle* (when, classically, p is a constant of motion) we have $d \operatorname{av}_\psi p/dt = 0$, as is to be expected by classical analogy.

In deriving Equations (7), (9), and (10), we did not restrict ourselves to any particular dynamical system, and in this sense these equations are general; but we did use normalized ψ-functions. The question now arises, do these equations hold for states specified by nonnormalizable ψ-functions? In reply we shall assert,

waiving mathematical caution, that the relations between averages
of dynamical variables and time derivatives of averages of dynamical
variables which hold for all normalizable states of arbitrary systems
hold also (if only formally) for nonnormalizable states; accordingly, we assume that (7), (9), (10), and other similar equations
hold even for states specified by nonnormalizable ψ's.

Narrow x-packets. The equation

$$m \frac{d^2}{dt^2} \operatorname{av}_\psi x = - \int \bar{\psi} \frac{\partial V(x)}{\partial x} \psi \, dx, \tag{11}$$

which follows from (7) and (9), enables us to indicate an asymptotic connection between quantum theory and classical mechanics.
Let a particle be almost certainly at $x = x_a$ at a certain instant,
so that, at this instant, the probability packet $\bar{\psi}\psi$ is sufficiently
narrow to justify writing $x_a \int \bar{\psi}\psi \, dx = x_a$ for $\int \bar{\psi}x\psi \, dx$, and
$V'(x_a) \int \bar{\psi}\psi \, dx = V'(x_a)$ for $\int \bar{\psi}V'(x)\psi \, dx$. Equation (11) then
becomes

$$m\ddot{x}_a = - \left[\frac{\partial V(x)}{\partial x} \right]_{x=x_a} \tag{12}$$

and comparison with 3^9 shows that, *at an instant at which the
x-packet is sufficiently narrow, the particle may be said to move
according to classical laws.*[1]

Equation (12) is a satisfactory approximation only as long as the
x-packet remains narrow. Now, in view of the Heisenberg
inequality, the statement that the x-packet is narrow implies
that little is known about the momentum of the particle; consequently, to put the matter somewhat roughly, we may expect
that, if the x-packet is very narrow, then it will soon become
broad. To illustrate, we shall consider a Kennard packet and
restrict ourselves to times near $t = 0$. Let $\Delta_x(t)$ denote the
inexactitude of x at the instant t; then, by Taylor's theorem,

$$\Delta_x^2(t) = \Delta_x^2(0) + t \left[\frac{d\Delta_x^2(t)}{dt} \right]_{t=0} + \frac{1}{2} t^2 \left[\frac{d^2 \Delta_x^2(t)}{dt^2} \right]_{t=0} + \cdots, \tag{13}$$

and, for a packet which at $t = 0$ has the Kennard form 4^{25}, we get
(Exercise 4)

$$\Delta_x^2(t) = \Delta_x^2(0) + \frac{1}{2} \left[\frac{\hbar^2}{2m^2 \Delta_x^2(0)} + \frac{2}{m} \int \bar{\psi}(x_a - x)V'\psi \, dx \right]_{t=0} t^2 + \cdots. \tag{14}$$

---

[1] P. Ehrenfest, *Zeits. f. Physik*, **45**, 455 (1927).

Thus Δ_x^2 varies parabolically with t for times near $t = 0$, and the length of time during which (12) is a good approximation depends on the initial value of Δ_x, on the values of V' in the vicinity of x_a, on the mass of the particle, and on the value of Planck's constant h.

Exercises

1. Verify that (7) holds for the state 19^{21}.

2. Show that, if ψ is normalized, then $m\, d\, \mathrm{av}_\psi\, x^2/dt = \int \bar\psi (xp + px)\psi\, dx$, and $m^2\, d^2\, \mathrm{av}_\psi\, x^2/dt^2 = 2 \int \bar\psi (p^2 - mxV')\psi\, dx$.

3. Let Δ_x, Δ_p, x_a, and p_a denote, respectively, the inexactitudes and the averages of x and p at the instant t, and let ψ be normalized; show that then $m\, d\, \Delta_x^2/dt = \int \bar\psi (xp + px)\psi\, dx - 2x_a p_a$, and $m^2\, d^2 \Delta_x^2/dt^2 = 2\Delta_p^2 + 2m \int \bar\psi\, (x_a - x)V'\psi\, dx$.

4. Use the results of Exercise 3 to show that, if ψ is given at $t = 0$ by 4^{25}, then (13) reduces to (14).

5. Show that (14) is consistent with the fact that for the state 19^{21} of an oscillator the x-packet moves without spreading.

6. Discuss the following curious feature of the reflection coefficient 16^{38} for a single-step barrier: it does not involve h at all, and yet it is different from the corresponding classical reflection coefficient, which, of course, is zero.

44. Time Derivatives of Dynamical Variables

From time derivatives of averages of dynamical variables, we now turn to time derivatives of the dynamical variables themselves. In classical mechanics, the time derivative of a dynamical variable α is identified by a reference to states specified by precise initial conditions; for such states, every dynamical variable has an unambiguous numerical value at every instant of time, so that the standard definition

$$\dot\alpha(t) = \lim_{\tau \to 0} \frac{\alpha(t + \tau) - \alpha(t)}{\tau} \tag{1}$$

has an immediate physical significance. According to quantum mechanics, however, the value of a dynamical variable cannot usually be known precisely for every instant of time even for states specified in all physically obtainable detail, and consequently the right side of (1) does not usually have any clear-cut meaning. It is, of course, very convenient to be able to refer in a suggestive way to one dynamical variable as the time derivative of another, and in order to make this possible in quantum mechanics we introduce the following definition,[2] which makes no reference to the classical formula (1): *If the dynamical variables α and β pertaining to a given dynamical system are so related that for every state of the system the average of β at every instant equals the time derivative of the average of α at the same instant, then β is said to be the time derivative of α*, and we write $\beta = \dot{\alpha}$. Or, expressed in symbols, if for every state of the system

$$\frac{d}{dt} \operatorname{av}_\psi \alpha = \operatorname{av}_\psi \beta \tag{2}$$

at every instant of time, then

$$\dot{\alpha} = \beta. \tag{3}$$

To illustrate: Having shown that for every normalizable state of an arbitrary system

$$(7^{43}) \qquad \frac{d}{dt} \operatorname{av}_\psi x = \frac{1}{m} \operatorname{av}_\psi p, \tag{4}$$

and having later asserted that this equation holds for an arbitrary state, we write *in quantum mechanics*

$$\dot{x} = p/m. \tag{5}$$

Equation (5) is precisely the equation connecting x and p/m in classical mechanics; and, lest this identity in form suggest to the reader too great a similarity in the respective physical contents of the classical and the quantum-mechanical equations, we must emphasize that in quantum mechanics Equation (5) is essentially an abbreviation for (4), and means just this: *for an arbitrary state of an arbitrary system, the time derivative of the expected average of x is, at every instant, equal to the expected average of p/m at that instant.* Similarly, the relations

$$\frac{d}{dt} \operatorname{av}_\psi p = \operatorname{av}_\psi \left(-\frac{\partial V}{\partial x} \right), \qquad \frac{d}{dt} \operatorname{av}_\psi H = 0, \tag{6}$$

obtained in §43, enable us to write

$$\dot{p} = -\frac{\partial V}{\partial x}, \qquad \dot{H} = 0, \tag{7}$$

in the case of conservative quantum-mechanical systems.

---

[2] G. Breit, *Rev. Mod. Phys.*, **4**, 537 (1932).

To identify the time derivative of a given dynamical variable α, we must, according to the definition above, rearrange the expression $d\,\mathrm{av}_\psi\,\alpha/dt$ in such a way that it has the form of an average. The process of rearrangement (illustrated, for example, by the step from 5^{43} to 6^{43}) usually involves integrations by parts, and is tedious when α is complicated; but this process can be simplified by the use of an important property of the Schroedinger operators which we now proceed to discuss.

Hermitian operators. The expected average of a dynamical variable is, by definition, the arithmetic mean of the possible results of a precise measurement of this variable, each possible result being weighted by its probability. The possible results of measurements of actual physical variables (to which variables we restrict our attention) are real numbers, and consequently the average of any physical variable for any state at any time must be a real number. Now, if α is the Schroedinger operator associated with a dynamical variable α, and if ψ is a normalized Schroedinger function specifying the state, then, according to the expectation formula 2^{17},

$$\mathrm{av}_\psi\,\alpha = \int \bar{\psi}\alpha\psi\,dx, \tag{8}$$

so that, if the average of α for the state ψ is to be real, the expression $\int\bar{\psi}\alpha\psi\,dx$ must be real; that is, in terms of the symbolism of 2^8, we must have

$$\mathrm{Im} \int \bar{\psi}\alpha\psi\,dx = 0 \tag{9}$$

for an *arbitrary* normalizable ψ. All Schroedinger operators associated with real variables must satisfy this condition.

The complex conjugate of $\int \bar{\psi}\alpha\psi\,dx$ may be written either as $\overline{\int \bar{\psi}\alpha\psi\,dx}$ or as $\int \psi(\overline{\alpha\psi})\,dx$, and hence we have the identity

$$\overline{\int \bar{\psi}\alpha\psi\,dx} = \int \overline{\alpha\psi}\cdot\psi dx, \tag{10}$$

where $\overline{\alpha\psi}$ denotes the complex conjugate of the function $\alpha\psi$, and $\overline{\alpha\psi}\cdot\psi$ denotes $(\overline{\alpha\psi})\psi$. If α satisfies $\langle 9\rangle$, the bar over the left side of $\langle 10\rangle$ can be removed, so that

$$\int \bar{\psi}\alpha\psi\,dx = \int \overline{\alpha\psi}\cdot\psi\,dx. \tag{11}$$

Now, let u and v be any two normalizable functions of x, and let α satisfy $\langle 9\rangle$, so that $\langle 11\rangle$ holds also. Then

$$\int \overline{(u+v)}\alpha(u+v)\,dx = \int \overline{\alpha(u+v)}\cdot(u+v)\,dx, \tag{12}$$

that is,

$$\int \bar{u}\alpha u \, dx + \int \bar{v}\alpha v \, dx + \int \bar{u}\alpha v \, dx + \int \bar{v}\alpha u \, dx$$

$$= \int \overline{\alpha u} \cdot u \, dx + \int \overline{\alpha v} \cdot v \, dx + \int \overline{\alpha u} \cdot v \, dx + \int \overline{\alpha v} \cdot u \, dx. \quad \langle 13 \rangle$$

Because of $\langle 11 \rangle$ the first two terms on the left of $\langle 13 \rangle$ cancel the corresponding terms on the right, and, rearranging the remaining terms, we get

$$\int \bar{u}\alpha v \, dx - \int \overline{\alpha v} \cdot u \, dx = \int \overline{\alpha u} \cdot v \, dx - \int \bar{v}\alpha u \, dx, \quad \langle 14 \rangle$$

a result which can be written equally well as

$$\int \bar{u}\alpha v \, dx - \overline{\int \bar{u}\alpha v \, dx} = \int \overline{\alpha u} \cdot v \, dx - \overline{\int \overline{\alpha u} \cdot v \, dx}, \quad \langle 15 \rangle$$

that is, as

$$2\mathrm{Im} \int \bar{u}\alpha v \, dx = 2\mathrm{Im} \int \overline{\alpha u} \cdot v \, dx. \quad \langle 16 \rangle$$

If we use the function iv instead of v in $\langle 12 \rangle$, we get, instead of $\langle 15 \rangle$,

$$\int \bar{u}\alpha iv \, dx - \overline{\int \bar{u}\alpha iv \, dx} = \int \overline{\alpha u} \cdot iv \, dx - \overline{\int \overline{\alpha u} \cdot iv \, dx}; \quad \langle 17 \rangle$$

cancellation of the factor i in $\langle 17 \rangle$ yields $\int \bar{u}\alpha v \, dx + \overline{\int \bar{u}\alpha v \, dx} = \int \overline{\alpha u} \cdot v \, dx + \overline{\int \overline{\alpha u} \cdot v \, dx}$, that is,

$$2\mathrm{Re} \int \bar{u}\alpha v \, dx = 2\mathrm{Re} \int \overline{\alpha u} \cdot v \, dx. \quad \langle 18 \rangle$$

It now follows from $\langle 16 \rangle$ and $\langle 18 \rangle$ that[3]

$$\int_{-\infty}^{\infty} \bar{u}\alpha v \, dx = \int_{-\infty}^{\infty} \overline{\alpha u} \cdot v \, dx. \quad \langle 19 \rangle$$

If an operator satisfies $\langle 19 \rangle$ whenever u and v are normalizable, we call it *Hermitian, self-adjoint,* or *real* (although, strictly, these terms are not quite synonymous). We have shown above that $\langle 19 \rangle$ is deducible from $\langle 9 \rangle$; and, since $\langle 9 \rangle$ must hold for all Schroedinger operators associated with real dynamical variables, we conclude that *every Schroedinger operator associated with a real dynamical variable is Hermitian.*

That any one of the simpler Schroedinger operators satisfies $\langle 19 \rangle$ can be verified directly without much labor. For example, in the case of the momentum operator $p = -i\hbar \partial/\partial x$, we have $\int \bar{u}pv \, dx = -i\hbar \int \bar{u}v' \, dx$; integrating by parts, remembering that u and v are normalizable, and

---

[3] This derivation of $\langle 19 \rangle$ from $\langle 9 \rangle$ was given in a lecture by Dr. J. von Neumann.

rearranging the result, we get $-i\hbar \int \bar{u}v' \, dx = i\hbar \int \bar{u}'v \, dx = \int (i\hbar\bar{u}')v \, dx = \int \overline{(-i\hbar u')}v \, dx = \int \overline{pu} \cdot v \, dx$, so that

$$\int \bar{u}pv \, dx = \int \overline{pu} \cdot v \, dx, \qquad \langle 20 \rangle$$

and p satisfies $\langle 19 \rangle$. In view of the deducibility of $\langle 19 \rangle$ from $\langle 9 \rangle$ we may, however, use $\langle 19 \rangle$ with any Schroedinger operator associated with a real dynamical variable without verifying it for every particular case.

So far the work of this section has been rigorous; but now we shall assert that if an operator α is Hermitian, that is, if $\langle 19 \rangle$ holds for every pair of normalizable functions u and v, then it holds, at least formally, for every pair of well-behaved functions u and v. This assertion, although not always justifiable from the strict mathematical viewpoint, will expedite our calculations and will not lead us astray in the elementary work.

Every eigenvalue of a Hermitian operator is real. To prove this, we let u be an eigenfunction of a Hermitian operator α belonging to the eigenvalue λ, and set $v = u$ in $\langle 19 \rangle$; the result is $\int \bar{u}\lambda u \, dx = \int \overline{\lambda u} \cdot u \, dx$, that is, $\lambda \int \bar{u}u \, dx = \bar{\lambda} \int \bar{u}u \, dx$, and hence $\lambda = \bar{\lambda}$.

If β and γ are commuting Hermitian operators, then the operator $\beta\gamma$ is also Hermitian. To prove this, we write $\int \bar{u}\beta\gamma v \, dx = \int \bar{u}\beta(\gamma v) \, dx$ and note that, if β is Hermitian, then $\int \bar{u}\beta(\gamma v) \, dx = \int \overline{\beta u} \cdot \gamma v \, dx$, and if γ is Hermitian, then $\int \overline{\beta u} \cdot \gamma v \, dx = \int \overline{\gamma\beta u} \cdot v \, dx$, so that, if β and γ are both Hermitian, then $\int \bar{u}\beta\gamma v \, dx = \int \overline{\gamma\beta u} \cdot v \, dx$; when β and γ commute, this is equivalent to $\int \bar{u}\beta\gamma v \, dx = \int \overline{\beta\gamma u} \cdot v \, dx$, and comparison with $\langle 19 \rangle$ shows that $\beta\gamma$ is Hermitian. In this computation we assumed that not only u and v, but also βu and γv are well-behaved.

Equations of motion. As we have shown, the Schroedinger operators associated with real dynamical variables are all Hermitian, so that, in particular, the Schroedinger operator H associated with the Hamiltonian of a dynamical system is Hermitian. The latter fact can be used in the following way to identify the time derivative of a dynamical variable α which does not involve t explicitly. If the state is specified by a normalized ψ-function, then

$$\langle 4^{43} \rangle \qquad \frac{d}{dt} \text{av}_\psi \, \alpha = \int \left(\frac{\partial \bar{\psi}}{\partial t} \alpha\psi + \bar{\psi}\alpha \frac{\partial \psi}{\partial t} \right) dx. \qquad \langle 21 \rangle$$

The second Schroedinger equation 1^{16} requires that $i\hbar\partial\psi/\partial t = H\psi$, so that, since H does not involve i, we also have the equation

$-i\hbar\partial\bar{\psi}/\partial t = \overline{H\psi}$. Equation $\langle 21 \rangle$ can therefore be written as

$$\frac{d}{dt}\,\mathrm{av}_\psi\,\alpha = \frac{i}{\hbar}\left(\int \overline{H\psi}\cdot\alpha\psi\,dx - \int \bar{\psi}\alpha H\psi\,dx\right). \qquad \langle 22 \rangle$$

Remembering that H is Hermitian and writing $\alpha\psi$ for v, ψ for u, and H for α in $\langle 19 \rangle$, we get

$$\int \bar{\psi}H\alpha\psi\,dx = \int \overline{H\psi}\cdot\alpha\psi\,dx, \qquad \langle 23 \rangle$$

and $\langle 22 \rangle$ becomes

$$\cdot\,\frac{d}{dt}\,\mathrm{av}_\psi\,\alpha = \frac{i}{\hbar}\left(\int \bar{\psi}H\alpha\psi\,dx - \int \bar{\psi}\alpha H\psi\,dx\right), \qquad \langle 24 \rangle$$

that is,

$$\frac{d}{dt}\,\mathrm{av}_\psi\,\alpha = \int \bar{\psi}\left[\frac{i}{\hbar}(H\alpha - \alpha H)\right]\psi\,dx. \qquad \langle 25 \rangle$$

Now, Equation $\langle 25 \rangle$ can be written as

$$\frac{d}{dt}\,\mathrm{av}_\psi\,\alpha = \mathrm{av}_\psi\,\beta, \qquad (26)$$

where β is the dynamical variable associated with the operator $\frac{i}{\hbar}(H\alpha - \alpha H)$, H and α being the operators associated, respectively, with the Hamiltonian and with the dynamical variable α. Equation (26) has the form (2); therefore, assuming that (26) holds for all states rather than only for all states specified by normalizable ψ-functions, and recalling our definition of the time derivative of a dynamical variable, we conclude: $\dot{\alpha}$ *is that dynamical variable which is associated with the operator* $\frac{i}{\hbar}(H\alpha - \alpha H)$. When the dynamical variable α does not involve t explicitly, we may therefore write, using $\dot{\alpha}$ to denote the operator associated with the dynamical variable $\dot{\alpha}$,

$$\dot{\alpha} = \frac{i}{\hbar}(H\alpha - \alpha H). \qquad \langle 27 \rangle$$

Equation $\langle 27 \rangle$ is called the *equation of motion* of α; in quantum mechanics, *the equation of motion of a dynamical variable is the equation telling what operator is to be associated with the time derivative of this dynamical variable.*

To illustrate the use of ⟨27⟩, let us identify once more the dynamical variable $\dot{x}$. The operator associated with $\dot{x}$ is, according to ⟨27⟩,

$$\dot{x} = \frac{i}{\hbar}(Hx - xH), \tag{28}$$

that is,

$$\dot{x} = \frac{i}{\hbar}\left[\left(-\frac{\hbar^2}{2m}\frac{\partial^2}{\partial x^2}\right)x + V(x)x - x\left(-\frac{\hbar^2}{2m}\frac{\partial^2}{\partial x^2}\right) - xV(x)\right]$$

$$= -\frac{i\hbar}{2m}\left(\frac{\partial^2}{\partial x^2}x - x\frac{\partial^2}{\partial x^2}\right) = -\frac{i\hbar}{2m}\cdot 2\frac{\partial}{\partial x}, \tag{29}$$

or

$$\dot{x} = p/m, \tag{30}$$

where p is the operator associated with the momentum. Passing from operators to the corresponding dynamical variables, we get (5), that is, the result obtained before by a study of d av$_\psi$ x/dt.

In conclusion, we shall indicate the reason for the detailed resemblance between the classical and the quantum-mechanical equations connecting dynamical variables and time derivatives of dynamical variables. In the classical theory, whenever α does not depend explicitly on t, $\dot{\alpha}$ is the negative of the Poisson bracket of H and α:

$$(16^9) \qquad\qquad \dot{\alpha} = -[H, \alpha]. \tag{31}$$

Now, the quantum condition 1^{13} requires that the operator to be associated with the Poisson bracket of two variables be $-i/\hbar$ times the commutator of the operators associated with the variables themselves, so that, if α and H are the operators associated with the variables α and H, then the operator associated with the dynamical variable $-[H, \alpha] = \dot{\alpha}$ should be

$$\frac{i}{\hbar}(H\alpha - \alpha H), \tag{32}$$

that is, just the operator ⟨27⟩.

Exercises

1. Show that the operator x is Hermitian but that $\partial/\partial x$ is not. Under what condition is an operator of type c Hermitian?

2. Show that, if α and β are Hermitian, then $\alpha + \beta$ and $\alpha\beta + \beta\alpha$ are also Hermitian.

3. Show that, if α and β are Hermitian, but do not commute, then their commutator is not Hermitian, but $i(\alpha\beta - \beta\alpha)$ is Hermitian.

4. Show that the condition that the operator α be Hermitian is sufficient in order that $\text{av}_\psi \ \alpha$ be real for any (normalizable) state ψ.

5. Use the equation of motion $\langle 27 \rangle$ to identify the dynamical variable dx^2/dt; in comparing the result with the corresponding classical result, remember 14^{14}.

6. Let $g(x)$ be an operator, a function of the operator x only and admitting of a power series expansion in the operator x. Generalize the result of Exercise 6^2, and show that $(d/dx)g(x) - g(x)(d/dx) = g'(x)$, where $g'(x)$ is the operator, a function of the operator x only, obtained by a formal differentiation of $g(x)$ with respect to x.

7. Use $\langle 27 \rangle$ and the result of Exercise 6 to derive the quantum-mechanical analogue of the classical equation $\dot{p} = -\partial V(x)/\partial x$.

8. Use $\langle 27 \rangle$ to show that $d(\alpha + \beta)/dt = \dot{\alpha} + \dot{\beta}$ and $d\alpha\beta/dt = \dot{\alpha}\beta + \alpha\dot{\beta}$, and explain what these equations mean.

9. Review Exercise 2^{43} in the light of the results of the present section.

10. Show that the quantum condition 1^{13} is consistent with the requirement that the operators associated with the dynamical variables α, β, and $[\alpha, \beta]$ have only real eigenvalues.

11. Using the explicit form of the one-dimensional Schroedinger operator H, verify $\langle 23 \rangle$ for the case of normalizable ψ's by integrating by parts. Equation $\langle 25 \rangle$ can thus be derived without direct reference to the general result $\langle 19 \rangle$.

45. Constants of Motion

If the time derivative of the dynamical variable α pertaining to a given dynamical system is zero (that is, quantum mechanically, if $d \ \text{av} \ \alpha/dt$ is zero for *every* state of the system), then α is called a *constant of motion* of the system.

The reader will verify that the right side of 25^{44} vanishes for every possible ψ if and only if the operators α and H commute, and that consequently the simple criterion by which we may recognize a quantum-mechanical constant of motion is the following: if the dynamical variable α does not depend explicitly on t and if

$$\alpha H = H\alpha \qquad \langle 1 \rangle$$

(that is, if the operator α commutes with the Hamiltonian operator of the given system), then the dynamical variable α is a constant of motion of this system. This result, which can be inferred directly from the equation of motion

$$\langle 27^{44} \rangle \qquad\qquad \dot{\alpha} = \frac{i}{\hbar}(H\alpha - \alpha H), \qquad\qquad \langle 2 \rangle$$

is usually abbreviated thus: *if α commutes with the Hamiltonian of the system and does not depend explicitly on t, then α is a constant of motion of this system.*

Now, if $α$ commutes with H, then $α^k$ also commutes with H, and therefore, if $α$ is a constant of motion for the given system, then $α^k$ is also a constant of motion for this system. Hence, if $α$ is a constant of motion, then the time derivative of the average of each of its powers is zero for every state of the system; and, recalling that the distribution-in-$α$ is determined by the values of the averages of the powers of $α$, we get the result: *if α is a constant of motion, then the distribution-in-α for every state of the system is stationary.*[4]

If c is a numerical constant, then

$$\dot{c} = \frac{i}{\hbar}(Hc - cH) = 0, \qquad\qquad \langle 3 \rangle$$

so that any numerical constant such as 1, 2, m, $π$, and so on, is a (trivial) constant of motion of every dynamical system. When enumerating the constants of motion of a system, we always omit the mention of numerical constants.

If the given system is conservative, then H is independent of t and we have

$$\dot{H} = \frac{i}{\hbar}(HH - HH) = 0, \qquad\qquad \langle 4 \rangle$$

so that the energy of a conservative system is a constant of motion of this system, and, in particular, the distribution-in-E for any state of a conservative system is stationary.   Similarly, when the system is conservative, then any function of H not involving t is a constant of motion.

In the case of a free particle, we have $H = -κ^{-1}∂^2/∂x^2$, so that the momentum operator $p = -i\hbar∂/∂x$ commutes with H.   Hence the momentum is a constant of motion of the free particle, and for any state of a free particle the distribution-in-p is stationary.

It follows from the concluding remarks of §44 that every

---

[4] We emphasize the word *every*, because in the exceptional case of an energy state (when in the expectation formula 2¹⁷ the time factor of $\bar{ψ}$ cancels that of $ψ$) the distribution-in-$α$ is stationary even if $α$ is not a constant of motion, provided $α$ does not involve t explicitly.

constant of motion of a classical dynamical system is also a constant of motion of a corresponding quantum-mechanical system. For example, the momentum of a free particle, being a constant of motion in the classical case, is also a constant of motion quantum mechanically. [A more elaborate example is provided by the dynamical variables L, L_x, L_y, and L_z (the magnitude and the three components of the orbital angular momentum of the particle) when the particle moves in a three-dimensional radial field: L, L_x, L_y, and L_z, being constants of motion of a classical particle in a radial force field, are, as we shall presently see, also constants of motion of a quantum-mechanical particle in a radial force field.]

If the state of a *classical* system is specified by a maximal set of conditions (that is, by an equivalent of the precise initial conditions of motion), then each constant of motion has a definite numerical value that is independent of t. The situation is different in quantum mechanics, where maximal sets of conditions are, so to speak, less stringent; thus the value of a constant of motion may be uncertain even though the state is specified by as many conditions as it is possible to impose without contradictions; and in some cases the precise knowledge of the value of one constant of motion may even imply that the value of another constant of motion is certainly uncertain. [To illustrate: when a particle moves in a radial force field so that L_x, L_y, and L_z (the components of orbital angular momentum) are constants of motion, then it turns out that for every state for which L_x has a definite numerical value other than zero the values of both L_y and L_z are bound to be uncertain; but the distribution-in-L_x, the distribution-in-L_y, and the distribution-in-L_z are all stationary for every state; similarly, for a state for which L_y has a definite value other than zero, the values of L_z and L_x are bound to be uncertain; and so forth.] The fact that a precise knowledge of the value of a constant of motion α may be incompatible with the precise knowledge of the value of another constant of motion β shows up mathematically through the noncommutability of the operators α and β.

Exercise

1. Correlate 19^{28} and the results of Exercises 5^{20}, 1^{28}, and 8^{28} with the results of this section.

46. Dirac's Expansion Theorem

If the state of a system is described by a ψ-function that is an eigenfunction of an operator α, we call this state an *eigenstate* of α; for example, as we already mentioned in §18, an energy state of a system, being described by an eigenfunction of the operator H pertaining to this system, is called an eigenstate of H. Accordingly, the assertion that a state is an eigenstate of α means that the value of the dynamical variable α for this state is a certainty. If the ψ-function describing a state is a simultaneous eigenfunction of the operators α, β, and so on, we call this state a *simultaneous eigenstate* of α, β, and so on.

If the respective operators associated with certain dynamical variables commute with each other, then we say, for brevity, that these dynamical variables commute with each other; in particular, if the respective operators associated with certain constants of motion of a given system commute with each other, we say that these constants of motion form a set of *commuting constants of motion* of this system.

Our interest in commuting constants of motion is due principally to a theorem that we shall indicate somewhat unprecisely as follows: *if*

$$H, \alpha_2, \alpha_3, \cdots, \alpha_k, \qquad \langle 1 \rangle$$

is a set of commuting constants of motion of a dynamical system, then every state of this system is either a simultaneous eigenstate of the k quantities $\langle 1 \rangle$, *or a superposition of such simultaneous eigenstates.*[5] In other words, *every state of a system can be expanded in terms of the particular states that are simultaneous eigenstates of all the constants of motion.* This theorem can be derived from the following fundamental expansion theorem enunciated by Dirac: an arbitrary ψ can be expressed linearly in terms of the eigenfunctions of a Hermitian operator. No entirely adequate general proof of the latter theorem has as yet been constructed, however. In the sequel we shall use the term *expansion theorem* to denote the

---

[5] Strictly speaking, every particular simultaneous eigenstate of the quantities $\langle 1 \rangle$ is itself a superposition of the various simultaneous eigenstates of these quantities, a superposition in which all states except this particular one enter with zero weight; our statement, which we adopt because of its suggestiveness, is therefore tautologic.

theorem stated above in italics. This theorem was found to hold in the case of every particular system that has been investigated, and the reliance on its correctness has been a most valuable guide in the development of quantum mechanics, for example, in the theory of atomic and molecular spectra. The theorem is perhaps approached best through the branch of mathematics called *group theory*; but we shall adopt it without further question.

To illustrate: In the case of a one-dimensional free particle, a set of commuting constants of motion is

$$H = -\frac{1}{\kappa}\frac{\partial^2}{\partial x^2}, \qquad p = -i\hbar\frac{\partial}{\partial x}, \qquad \langle 2 \rangle$$

so that the expansion theorem claims that every state of a one-dimensional free particle is either a simultaneous eigenstate of H and p, or a superposition of such simultaneous eigenstates. A reference to §28 proves this claim to be correct: the simultaneous eigenstates of H and p are 6^{28} and 7^{28}; the general stationary state, 5^{28}, is a superposition of 6^{28} and 7^{28}; and the most general state, 14^{28}, is again a superposition of the simultaneous eigenstates of H and p.

The computational utility of the expansion theorem in the study of a particular dynamical system lies in the facts that constants of motion, other than H and functions of H, are usually easier to handle than H itself, and that the theorem permits us essentially to restrict our attention to the simultaneous eigenfunctions of the operators $\langle 1 \rangle$ and to arrange the work as follows: we compute first the eigenfunctions of the simplest constant of motion; then, using the arbitrary features of the ψ's so obtained, we adjust these ψ's to be also eigenfunctions of the next-simplest constant of motion; and we proceed in this manner from the simpler to the more complicated constants of motion until we identify the simultaneous eigenfunctions of them all; and when this is done we presumably know that every state of the system is either one of the states already computed or a superposition of these states.

The expansion theorem is, so to speak, the more useful the more complicated the system (provided, of course, that the system has a constant of motion simpler than H), and we are not prepared at the moment to illustrate its use in a way that does full justice to its power; the following simple example may nevertheless be of interest.

Let it be desired to compute the energy levels of a free particle; the equation $H\psi = E\psi$ is then

$$-\frac{1}{\kappa}\frac{\partial^2}{\partial x^2}\psi = E\psi, \qquad (3)$$

so that the computation consists essentially in finding the well-behaved solutions of a *second-order* differential equation. But the expansion theorem permits us to avoid actually solving (3) for ψ, as follows: Our system has the commuting constants of motion $\langle 2 \rangle$, of which p is the simpler; in fact, the eigenvalue equation $p\psi = p'\psi$ is

$$-i\hbar \frac{\partial}{\partial x} \psi = p'\psi, \tag{4}$$

that is, a *first-order* differential equation whose general solution

(4²⁷)
$$\psi = Ae^{i p' x/\hbar} \tag{5}$$

is well-behaved if p' is real. The eigenfunctions of p being available, we proceed to find next the simultaneous eigenfunctions of p and H by adjusting the number p' in (5) so that (5) would satisfy (3). Substitution of (5) into (3) yields the result $p' = \pm\sqrt{2mE}$, and hence the simultaneous eigenfunctions of H and p are

$$\psi = Ae^{\pm i\sqrt{2mE}\, x/\hbar}, \tag{6}$$

that is, apart from the time factors, just the functions 6²⁸ and 7²⁸. The expansion theorem now claims that any state of a free particle is a superposition of these simultaneous eigenfunctions (which must, of course, be multiplied by the appropriate time factors), so that our work is completed.

To summarize: in the case of the free particle, the expansion theorem enables us to solve the first-order equation (4) and then to adjust the solution to satisfy (3), rather than to solve outright the second-order equation (3). Both (3) and (4) are of course so simple that the use of the theorem in this particular problem is hardly of assistance.

47. Dynamical Variables Having no Classical Analogues

Each specific operator that we have used so far was introduced because it had been identified as the operator associated in the Schroedinger scheme with a dynamical variable that we desired to study; and each was, of course, a linear operator capable of operating on functions of x. Now, are there linear operators that are capable of operating on functions of x but that are not associated in the Schroedinger scheme with classical dynamical variables? If such operators exist, are they useful in quantum-mechanical computations? The answers to both questions are in the affirmative; and in this section we shall give two examples of operators of this kind, their use to be illustrated in the next.

Let us consider first the mathematical operation of substituting $-x$ for x in $u(x)$ and introduce the operator, to be denoted by Ω, which, when operating on $u(x)$, converts it into $u(-x)$, so that

$$\Omega u(x) = u(-x) \tag{1}$$

for every $u(x)$; for example, $\Omega e^x = e^{-x}$, $\Omega \sin x = \sin(-x) =$ $- \sin x$, $\Omega \cos x = \cos(-x) = \cos x$, $\Omega(x^2 + 3x) = x^2 - 3x$, and so forth. Equation (1) enables us to compute the result of operating with Ω on any given operand and hence defines Ω completely, even though we may not be able to express Ω in terms of operators that are more familiar to us. Ω is a linear operator, since for any $u(x)$ and $v(x)$ we have $\Omega(u + v) = \Omega u + \Omega v$ and $\Omega cu = c\,\Omega u$.

Let us next compute the eigenvalues of Ω, that is, the numbers λ for which the equation

$$(15^3) \qquad\qquad \Omega u(x) = \lambda u(x), \qquad\qquad (2)$$

that is,
$$u(-x) = \lambda u(x), \qquad\qquad (3)$$

has well-behaved solutions. Operating with Ω on both sides of (3), we get $\Omega u(-x) = \Omega \lambda u(x)$, that is,

$$u(x) = \lambda u(-x), \qquad\qquad (4)$$

and elimination of u between (3) and (4) yields $\lambda^2 = 1$, that is,

$$\lambda = \pm 1, \qquad\qquad (5)$$

so that Ω can have no eigenvalues other than 1 and -1. Setting $\lambda = 1$ in (2), we get $\Omega u(x) = u(x)$, that is, $u(-x) = u(x)$; this equation is satisfied by every even function of x and, in particular, by every well-behaved even function of x; consequently, Ω has the eigenvalue $+1$, and every well-behaved *even* function of x is an eigenfunction of Ω belonging to the eigenvalue $+1$. Setting $\lambda = -1$ in (2), we find in a similar way that Ω has the eigenvalue -1, and that every well-behaved *odd* function of x is an eigenfunction of Ω belonging to the eigenvalue -1. Each of the two eigenvalues of Ω is degenerate to an infinite degree.

If an operator is explicitly expressible in a reasonably simple way in terms of $-i\hbar\partial/\partial x$, x, and c, we have as a rule no difficulty in identifying the classical dynamical variable with which this operator is associated; but our operator Ω turns out not to bear any simple relation to the elementary Schroedinger operators, and we find it impossible to interpret it in any clear-cut way as being associated with a classical dynamical variable. As we shall see, the operator Ω can, nevertheless, be employed to advantage in certain mathematical quantum-mechanical calculations, in which it is treated on the same footing as the operators that are associated with classical dynamical variables. To make the terminology as uniform as possible, we then speak of the 'dynamical variable Ω', with the understanding that this dynamical variable has no classical analogue; thus if ψ is a normalized Schroedinger function, and if the integral

$$\int \bar{\psi}\Omega\psi \; dx, \tag{6}$$

that is, $\int \bar{\psi}(x)\psi(-x)dx$, should come into play in a mathematical calculation, we would refer to (6) as the average of the dynamical variable Ω—or simply the average of Ω—for the state ψ, and would denote (6) by $\mathrm{av}_\psi \; \Omega$, even though the 'dynamical variable Ω' has no classical analogue. Similarly, if a state is an eigenstate of Ω belonging to the eigenvalue 1 of Ω, that is, if it is specified by a ψ-function which is even in x, then we find it convenient to say that the value of Ω for this state is certainly 1, even though we are unable to describe an apparatus which is capable of measuring the 'dynamical variable Ω.'

In general, if a *linear operator* α finds application in the mathematical machinery of quantum mechanics, we speak of the *dynamical variable* α associated with it; and if, by using backwards the procedure for associating operators with dynamical variables, we find it impossible to identify a classical dynamical variable corresponding to the operator α, we say that the dynamical variable α has *no classical analogue*. This manner of speaking is, of course, merely a matter of terminology.

We consider next the linear operator, to be denoted by Γ_l or simply by Γ, which, when operating on $u(x)$, converts it into $u(x + l)$, where l is a prescribed real constant, so that

$$\Gamma u(x) = u(x + l) \tag{7}$$

for every $u(x)$; for example, $\Gamma e^x = e^{x+l} = e^l e^x$, $\Gamma \sin x = \sin(x + l)$, $\Gamma(x^2 + 3x) = (x + l)^2 + 3(x + l)$, and so forth. The operator Γ is of interest in connection with certain dynamical systems (§49), and hence it is sometimes convenient to speak of it as associated with a dynamical variable Γ, a variable to which no classical analogue can usually be ascribed.

To determine the eigenfunctions and eigenvalues of Γ, we seek the well-behaved solutions of the equation

(15^3) $$\Gamma u = \lambda u, \tag{8}$$

that is, $$u(x + l) = \lambda u, \tag{9}$$

where λ is a constant. To begin with, we suppress for a moment the conditions of good behavior and note that, if v is a periodic function of x with period l, that is, if

$$v(x + l) = v(x), \qquad (10)$$

then operating with Γ on v is equivalent to multiplying v by unity; that, if a is a constant, then operating with Γ on the function e^{ax} is equivalent to multiplying e^{ax} by the constant e^{al}; and that the function

$$u = A e^{ax} v, \qquad [v(x + l) = v(x)] \quad (11)$$

(where A and a are constants and v, as indicated, is periodic in x with period l) is the most general function which, when operated on by Γ, becomes multiplied by a constant. Returning to the boundary conditions, we now note that since v is periodic the function (11) is certain to be ill-behaved in the infinite region unless a is a pure imaginary, and that consequently we must restrict ourselves to functions of the form

$$u = e^{ikx} v, \qquad [v(x + l) = v(x)], \quad (12)$$

where k is a real constant and where A has been incorporated in v. The factor e^{ikx} and all its derivatives being continuous, the function (12) will satisfy our continuity conditions if v does so, and hence the eigenfunctions of the operator Γ are functions of the form (12), where v is any well-behaved function periodic in x with period l.

Operating with Γ on (12), we get

$$\Gamma e^{ikx} v(x) = e^{ik(x+l)} v(x + l) = e^{ikl} e^{ikx} v(x). \qquad (13)$$

The eigenvalue of Γ belonging to the eigenfunction (12) is consequently e^{ikl}; this eigenvalue is in general complex, and hence the dynamical variable Γ is to be regarded as complex rather than real.

Exercises

1. Show that $(1 + \Omega)^2 = 2(1 + \Omega)$, $(1 - \Omega)^2 = 2(1 - \Omega)$, $(1 + \Omega)(1 - \Omega) = 0$, $\Gamma \Omega \Gamma = \Omega$ and $\Gamma \Omega \Gamma^2 \Omega \Gamma = 1$.

2. Show that the operator Ω is Hermitian and that the operator Γ is not Hermitian.

3. Show that for the state 19^{21} of an oscillator av $\Omega = \exp(-x_0^2/a^2)$. Remember 23^{28}.

4. Show that for the state 19^{21} of an oscillator av Ω^n equals $\exp\ (-x_0^2/a^2)$ if n is odd and 1 if n is even; then show that the 'distribution-in-Ω' for this state is:

Possible values of Ω	1	-1
Their probabilities	$\frac{1}{2}[1 + \exp\ (-x_0^2/a^2)]$	$\frac{1}{2}[1 - \exp\ (-x_0^2/a^2)]$

Note that this distribution is stationary, even though the state is not an energy state.

48. Constants of Motion Having no Classical Analogues

A dynamical variable having no classical analogue may commute with the Hamiltonian operator, and consequently a quantum-mechanical system may have constants of motion in excess of those suggested by classical analogy. These extra constants of motion are just as useful in the study of the system as are those that do have classical analogues; in particular, the expansion theorem of §46 draws no distinction between constants of motion that do have classical analogues and those that do not.

To illustrate: we consider a particle moving in one dimension in a potential field which is even in x, so that

$$V(-x) = V(x); \tag{1}$$

unless $V(x)$ is a constant and the particle is free, classical theory then suggests that only H and functions of H are constants of motion. In fact, however, the dynamical variable Ω defined by 1^{47} is also a constant of motion in this case; indeed, for an arbitrary $u(x)$ on which the indicated operations can be performed, we have

$$\Omega H u(x) = \Omega\left[-\frac{1}{\kappa}\frac{\partial^2}{\partial x^2}u(x) + V(x)u(x)\right] \tag{2}$$

[see (1)]

$$= -\frac{1}{\kappa}\frac{\partial^2}{\partial(-x)^2}u(-x) + V(-x)u(-x)$$

$$= -\frac{1}{\kappa}\frac{\partial^2}{\partial x^2}u(-x) + V(x)u(-x)$$

$$= Hu(-x) = H\Omega u(x);$$

hence

$$\Omega H = H\Omega, \tag{3}$$

and Ω satisfies the criterion 1^{45}. Thus a system whose potential is even in x has at least the two following constants of motion:

$$H, \quad \Omega. \qquad \langle 4 \rangle$$

Let us now see to what extent the constant of motion Ω is helpful in computing the eigenfunctions of H when V is even in x. When applied to the set $\langle 4 \rangle$, the expansion theorem asserts that every eigenfunction of H is either a simultaneous eigenfunction of H and Ω, or a superposition of such simultaneous eigenfunctions. Hence, when V is even in x, the essential part of the search for the eigenfunctions of H is the identification of the simultaneous eigenfunctions of Ω and H. Now, as shown in §47, the eigenfunctions of Ω are the well-behaved even functions of x and the well-behaved odd functions of x. Consequently the expansion theorem asserts that in seeking the eigenfunctions of H when V is even in x we may from the outset restrict ourselves to operands that are even in x and to operands that are odd in x, and need not consider operands that are neither even nor odd in x (with the assurance that, if H has eigenfunctions that are neither even nor odd in x, then these eigenfunctions are superpositions of eigenfunctions of H that are even in x and eigenfunctions of H that are odd in x, and may be obtained later from the simultaneous eigenfunctions of H and Ω by taking linear combinations of the latter). Note that the claim "every eigenfunction of H that is neither even nor odd in x is a superposition of an *eigenfunction of H* that is even in x and an *eigenfunction of H* that is odd in x" is not to be confused with the almost trivial[6] claim that "every function that is neither even nor odd in x is a superposition of a *function* that is even in x and a *function* that is odd in x."

The result obtained above with the help of the expansion theorem and of the dynamical variable Ω has been to a certain extent anticipated in our previous discussion. For example, we showed in theorem 29 of §32 that, if V is even in x and the motion is bound, then every eigenfunction of H is either even or odd in x; the possibility that both even and odd eigenfunctions of H could belong to the same eigenvalue of H did not arise there, since in the bound one-dimensional case the eigenvalues of H are nonde-

---

[6] Let $u(x)$ be arbitrary; then $f(x) = \frac{1}{2}[u(x) + u(-x)]$ is even in x, $g(x) = \frac{1}{2}[u(x) - u(-x)]$ is odd in x, and $u(x)$ can be written as $u(x) = f(x) + g(x)$, that is, as a superposition of an even and an odd function.

generate. Again, in §39, we were able to devote our attention separately to the even solutions and to the odd solutions of the Schroedinger equation for the even potential of Fig. 66.

Potential lattices. The usefulness of the constants of motion not having classical analogues is illustrated perhaps more forcibly when the potential is periodic in x with period l, say, so that

$$V(x) = V(x + l); \tag{5}$$

unless $V(x)$ is a constant and the particle is free, classical theory then suggests that only H and functions of H are constants of motion. However, using the operator Γ defined by 7^{47}, we get for an arbitrary u on which the indicated operations can be performed

$$\Gamma H u(x) = \Gamma \left[-\frac{1}{\kappa} \frac{\partial^2}{\partial x^2} u(x) + V(x)u(x) \right] \tag{6}$$

[see (5)]

$$= -\frac{1}{\kappa} \frac{\partial^2}{\partial (x + l)^2} u(x + l) + V(x + l)u(x + l)$$

$$= -\frac{1}{\kappa} \frac{\partial^2}{\partial x^2} u(x + l) + V(x)u(x + l)$$

$$= H u(x + l) = H \Gamma u(x);$$

hence

$$\Gamma H = H \Gamma, \tag{7}$$

and Γ is a constant of motion. Thus a particle moving in a periodic potential or, as we shall often say, a particle moving in a *potential lattice*, has at least the two following constants of motion:

$$H, \Gamma. \tag{8}$$

The expansion theorem now asserts that, when the particle moves in a potential lattice, then every eigenfunction of H is either a simultaneous eigenfunction of H and Γ, or a superposition of such simultaneous eigenfunctions. Hence, when V is periodic in x, the essential part of the search for the eigenfunctions of H is the identification of the simultaneous eigenfunctions of Γ and H. Now, the eigenfunctions of Γ are

$$(12^{47}) \qquad\qquad u = e^{ikx}v, \qquad [v(x + l) = v(x)], \tag{9}$$

where k is a real constant and v is a well-behaved periodic function of x of period l; consequently the expansion theorem asserts that in seeking the eigenfunctions of H for a potential lattice we may from the outset restrict ourselves to operands of the form (9), with the assurance that the eigenfunctions of H which are not of the form (9) are superpositions of eigenfunctions of this form and can be obtained later by taking linear combinations of the latter. This assertion constitutes the one-dimensional form of *Bloch's theorem.*[7]

An example of a potential lattice will be taken up in the next section.

Exercises

1. Explain why the stationary character of the distribution-in-Ω computed in Exercise 4[47] is not unexpected.

2. If $\alpha\beta = -\beta\alpha \neq 0$, then the operators α and β are said to *anticommute.* Show that the operators Ω and d/dx anticommute and that the operators Γ and d/dx commute.

3. Verify that every momentum state is an eigenstate of Γ. This result is related to that of Exercise 4[7].

4. Consider a free particle, note that H and Ω comprise a set of commuting constants of motion, and verify the expansion theorem insofar as this set is concerned.

5. Consider a free particle, note that H, p, Γ (Γ with an arbitrary l) comprise a set of commuting constants of motion, and verify the expansion theorem insofar as this set is concerned.

49. Potential Lattices and Energy Bands

An electron in a crystal is subject to the fields of the regularly spaced atoms or ions comprising the crystal, and thus moves in a three-dimensional potential lattice; the quantum theory of the motion of a particle in a three-dimensional lattice is consequently of considerable interest. It turns out that some of the characteristics of such a motion show up even in the hypothetical case of a one-dimensional lattice, to which we shall restrict our attention here.

Let us then consider a one-dimensional potential lattice of period l, so that

$$V(x + l) = V(x), \tag{1}$$

and look for the energy levels of the system, that is, the values of the number E for which the Schroedinger equation $H\psi = E\psi$ or, more explicitly, the equation

$$\psi'' + \kappa[E - V(x)]\psi = 0, \tag{2}$$

---

[7] F. Bloch, *Zeits. f. Physik*, **52, 555** (1928). See also Floquet's theory of differential equations with periodic coefficients; for example, in Ince.

has well-behaved solutions. Now, having assumed the correctness of the expansion theorem, we may restrict our attention to ψ's of the form

(9^{48}) $$\psi = e^{ikx}v, \quad [v(x + l) = v(x)], \quad (3)$$

where k is a real constant and v is a well-behaved periodic function of x of period l. Substituting (3) into (2), we find that, in order that (3) be a solution of (2), v must satisfy the differential equation

$$v'' + 2ikv' + \kappa\left[E - V(x) - \frac{k^2}{\kappa}\right]v = 0. \quad (4)$$

Thus the expansion theorem permits us to look for *periodic well-behaved* solutions of (4), rather than for (periodic or not) *well-behaved* solutions of (2). To be sure, Equation (4) is somewhat more complicated than Equation (2); but the permissibility of considering only the periodic solutions of (4) usually more than offsets this.

A rectangular lattice. For a periodic $V(x)$ of actual physical interest, the treatment of (4) is complicated at best, and we shall turn at once to the idealized lattice of Fig. 74, consisting of an

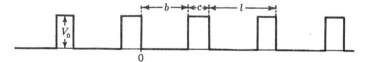

Fig. 74. A rectangular potential lattice.

infinite sequence of rectangular potential wells of width b separated by potential hills of width c and height V_0 ; the period of this lattice is

$$l = b + c. \quad (5)$$

The well whose left edge lies at $x = nl$ (where $n = \cdots, -2, -1, 0, 1, 2, \cdots,$) will be called the nth well; the hill whose left edge lies at $x = nl - c$ will be called the nth hill.

Energies smaller than V_0. We begin with the case

$$0 < E < V_0, \quad (6)$$

and, adopting the abbreviations

(6^{29}) $$\alpha = \sqrt{\kappa E}, \quad \beta = \sqrt{\kappa(V_0 - E)}, \quad (7)$$

write (4) separately for a well and a hill, getting the equations

$$\begin{cases} v'' + 2ikv' + (\alpha^2 - k^2)v = 0 & \text{(a well)} \quad (8) \\ v'' + 2ikv' - (\beta^2 + k^2)v = 0 & \text{(a hill),} \quad (9) \end{cases}$$

and then find the respective general solutions of (8) and (9), getting

$$v = \begin{cases} A_n e^{i(\alpha-k)x} + B_n e^{-i(\alpha+k)x} & \text{(the nth well)} \\ C_n e^{(\beta-ik)x} + D_n e^{-(\beta+ik)x} & \text{(the nth hill),} \end{cases} \quad (10)$$

where the A's, B's, C's, and D's, are arbitrary constants.

We now proceed to adjust v so as to make it periodic with period l. Let x be a point within the 0th well and $x + nl$ the corresponding point in the nth well. The periodicity of v is then assured insofar as the wells are concerned if

$$A_0 e^{i(\alpha-k)x} + B_0 e^{-i(\alpha+k)x} = A_n e^{i(\alpha-k)(x+nl)} + B_n e^{-i(\alpha+k)(x+nl)} \quad (11)$$

for all values of x between 0 and b, that is, if

$$A_n = A_0 e^{-i(\alpha-k)nl}, \qquad B_n = B_0 e^{i(\alpha+k)nl}. \quad (12)$$

A similar consideration of the hills yields the equations

$$C_n = C_0 e^{-(\beta-ik)nl}, \qquad D_n = D_0 e^{(\beta+ik)nl}. \quad (13)$$

The requirement of periodicity, resulting in (12) and (13), thus reduces the number of arbitrary constants in (10) from infinity to just four, say A_0, B_0, C_0, and D_0.

Our next task is to adjust A_0, B_0, C_0, and D_0 so that v is well-behaved. Since v is finite for any finite value of x and is periodic, it automatically remains finite when $|x| \to \infty$. The conditions for continuity of v and v' at $x = 0$ are, according to (10),

$$A_0 \quad + \quad B_0 = \quad C_0 \quad + \quad D_0 \quad (14)$$

$$i(\alpha - k)A_0 - i(\alpha + k)B_0 = (\beta - ik)C_0 - (\beta + ik)D_0. \quad (15)$$

The conditions for continuity of v and v' at $x = b$ are, according to (10) and (13),

$$e^{i(\alpha-k)b}A_0 \quad + \quad e^{-i(\alpha+k)b}B_0$$
$$= e^{-(\beta-ik)c}C_0 \quad + \quad e^{(\beta+ik)c}D_0 \quad (16)$$

$$i(\alpha - k)e^{i(\alpha-k)b}A_0 - i(\alpha + k)e^{-i(\alpha+k)b}B_0$$
$$= (\beta - ik)e^{-(\beta-ik)c}C_0 - (\beta - ik)e^{(\beta+ik)c}D_0. \quad (17)$$

The existence of well-behaved periodic v's thus hinges on the consistency of the four equations (14) to (17). The condition for consistency can be found, for example, by expressing A_0 and B_0 in terms of C_0 and D_0 by means of (14) and (15), then eliminating A_0 and B_0 from (16) and (17), and finally requiring that the dependence of C_0 on D_0 given by (16) be the same as that given by (17). The procedure is tedious in any case, but the result is relatively simple: Equations (14) to (17) have simultaneous solutions A_0, B_0, C_0, and D_0 (other than the trivial $A_0 = B_0 = C_0 = D_0 = 0$) if and only if

$$\cosh \beta c \cos \alpha b + \frac{\beta^2 - \alpha^2}{2\alpha\beta} \sinh \beta c \sin \alpha b = \cos lk. \qquad (18)$$

We now recall that k in (3) is a *real* constant, so that the right side of (18) is a real number lying at or between -1 and 1; Equation (18) is consequently compatible with the requisite reality of k if and only if

$$-1 \leq \cosh \beta c \cdot \cos \alpha b + \frac{\beta^2 - \alpha^2}{2\alpha\beta} \sinh \beta c \cdot \sin \alpha b \leq 1. \qquad (19)$$

The new condition (19) involves the undetermined parameter E (besides the prescribed constants m, h, b, c, and V_0) and is in fact the condition that an E lying below V_0 must satisfy in order to be a possible energy value of our system.

Numerical example. To illustrate the type of limitation that (19) imposes on E, we turn to a numerical example, set

$$V_0 b^2 \kappa = 144, \qquad c = \tfrac{1}{24} b, \qquad (20)$$

and let
$$E/V_0 = r, \qquad (21)$$

so that (19) becomes

$$-1 \leq \left[\cosh \tfrac{1}{2}\sqrt{1-r} \cdot \cos 12\sqrt{r} \right.$$

$$\left. + \frac{1-2r}{2\sqrt{r(1-r)}} \sinh \tfrac{1}{2}\sqrt{1-r} \cdot \sin 12\sqrt{r} \right] \leq 1. \qquad (22)$$

The choice $V_0 b^2 \kappa = 144$ is the same as that which we made in Exercise 3[29] while studying numerically a *single* rectangular potential well.

The bracketed term in (22) turns out to be the oscillating function of r shown graphically in Fig. 75. We note that for

$r < .03$ (that is, for $E < .03\,V_0$) the curve lies above 1; values of E lying below .03 V_0 thus fail to satisfy (22) and hence are not possible energy values of our system.   It is also seen from the graph, however, that (22) does hold for all r's lying in the interval from about .03 to about .06, indicated in Fig. 75 by a thick horizontal line; hence all E's lying in the

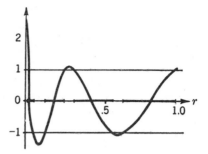

Fig. 75. Graph of the bracketed function in (22).

interval from about .03 V_0 to about .06 V_0 are possible energy values of the system.   For r's just greater than .06, the curve drops below -1, so that (22) does not hold, and consequently energies just greater than .06 V_0 are not possible; but r's lying in the interval from about .13 to about .25 satisfy (22) once again, so that all E's lying in the interval from about .13 V_0 to about .25 V_0 are possible energy values.   Fig. 75 implies, in fact, that the possible energies of our system lying below V_0 form four *bands*, spaced approximately as follows:

$$\begin{cases} \text{first band:} & .03\ V_0 \le E \le .06\ V_0 \\ \text{second band:} & .13\ V_0 \le E \le .25\ V_0 \\ \text{third band:} & .33\ V_0 \le E \le .57\ V_0 \\ \text{fourth band:} & .64\ V_0 \le E \le .99\ V_0 \,. \end{cases} \qquad (23)$$

Any E lying within one of these four bands is a possible energy value, so that within a band the energy spectrum is continuous; but the consecutive 'allowed' bands are separated by 'forbidden' bands, that is, by continuous stretches of impossible energies.

The result (23) is shown graphically on the right-hand side of Fig. 76, where the allowed energy bands are shaded; the horizontal lines on the left-hand side of this figure are the discrete energy levels of a single well for which $V_0 b^2 \kappa = 144$, taken from Fig. 31[29]. Note that the substitution of an infinite periodic sequence of rectangular wells for a single well of a similar shape causes each of the discrete levels of the single well to spread out into a continuous band.

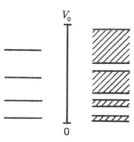

Fig. 76. The discrete levels for a rectangular well and the corresponding energy bands for a rectangular lattice.

Energies greater than V_0. Next we take up the case

$$E > V_0 \qquad (24)$$

when β in (7) is the pure imaginary quantity $\beta = i\gamma$, where

$$\gamma = \sqrt{\kappa(E - V_0)}. \qquad (25)$$

The structure of equations (8) to (19) is now the same as before, and the correction for the fact that β is imaginary can be made directly in (19). Substituting $i\gamma$ for β in (19) and recalling that $\cosh i\xi = \cos \xi$ and $\sinh i\xi = i \sin \xi$, we get the new condition

$$-1 \le \cos \gamma c \cdot \cos \alpha b - \frac{\alpha^2 + \gamma^2}{2\alpha\gamma} \sin \gamma c \cdot \sin \alpha b \le 1. \qquad (26)$$

For the particular numerical values (20) the condition (26) becomes

$$-1 \le \left[\cos 12\sqrt{r} \cdot \cos \tfrac{1}{2}\sqrt{r-1} \right.$$

$$\left. + \frac{1-2r}{2\sqrt{r(r-1)}} \sin 12\sqrt{r} \cdot \sin \tfrac{1}{2}\sqrt{r-1} \right] \le 1. \qquad (27)$$

The bracketed term in (27) is plotted at the right of $r = 1$ in Fig. 77, the left part of which is a reproduction of Fig. 75. We note

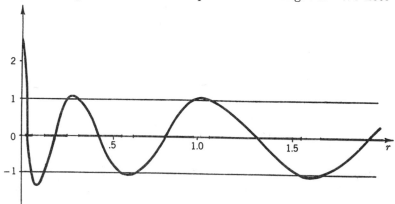

Fig. 77. Graph of the bracketed functions in (22) and (27).

that the energy spectrum of our system lying above V_0 consists
(just as in the case $E < V_0$) of continuous allowed bands separated
by continuous forbidden bands.   The lower part of the complete
energy spectrum of our system is shown on the right-hand side of
Fig. 78, where the allowed bands are shaded; the left-hand side of
this figure, a reproduction of Fig. 31^{29},
shows the lower part of the complete
energy spectrum of a single well for
which $V_0 b^2 \kappa = 144$.   Note, in particular, that the substitution of an infinite periodic sequence of rectangular
wells for a single well of a similar
shape causes the continuous energy
spectrum of the single well to break
up into bands.

Concluding remarks. We have shown
above with the help of the expansion
theorem that the possible energies of
a particle moving in the potential lattice of Fig. 74 are E's lying below V_0
and satisfying (19) and E's lying above
V_0 and satisfying (26), and that in

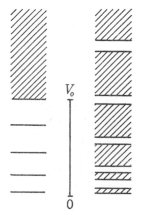

Fig. 78. Energy spectra
for a rectangular well and
for a rectangular lattice.

the special numerical case (20) the energy spectrum consists of
the bands illustrated in Fig. 78.   A more thorough treatment
of the rectangular lattice would include a study of the dependence
of the energy bands on the relative widths of the wells and the
hills, a computation of the ψ-functions for the energy states, a
study of the rôle of the parameter k and of the relation between
k and E, and so on.[8]

Energy spectra composed of alternating allowed and forbidden
bands are characteristic of potential lattices;[9] the case $V(x) =$
constant is of course an exception.   The bands for a sinusoidal
potential lattice are illustrated[10] (for a particular choice of m and
of the amplitude and period of V) in Fig. 79(b), where V is shown
by a thick line and the allowed bands are shaded; Fig. 79(a) shows
the discrete and the continuous spectra for a single sinusoidal well.

[8] R. de L. Kronig and W. G. Penney, *Proc. Roy. Soc.*, **130A**, 499 (1931),
considered an idealization of the lattice of Fig. 74 and derived a number of
results in a closed form.

[9] H. A. Kramers, *Physica*, **2**, 483 (1935).

[10] P. M. Morse, *Phys. Rev.*, **35**, 1310 (1930).

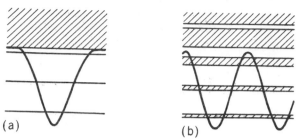

(a)   (b)

Fig. 79. A sinusoidal well and a sinusoidal lattice.

We must emphasize that our discussion deals with lattices that are strictly periodic and thus extend from $x = -\infty$ to $x = \infty$. In physical problems concerning not only the interior but also the surface of a crystal it is necessary to take into account the finite extent of the actual lattice; similarly, the computations must be modified whenever it is desired to take into account the imperfections of the crystal. These matters are discussed in writings on the theory of the solid state.[11]

Exercises

1. Show that, if $c \to 0$ while b and V_0 are held fixed, then (19) and (26) go over into 3[28]; if $b \to 0$ while c and V_0 are held fixed, then (19) and (26) go over into $E \geq V_0$; if $V_0 \to \infty$ while b and c are held fixed, then (19) goes over into 5[30] with $l = b$; if $c \to \infty$ while V_0 and b are held fixed, then (19) goes over into 19[29] with $a = \frac{1}{2}b$. Explain why these limiting forms of (19) and (26) are not unexpected.

2. Consider large values of E and use (26) to show that as E increases the allowed bands become wider and the forbidden bands narrower.

3. Just as the substitution of a periodic sequence of wells for a single well results in a spreading of each discrete level of a single well into a band, so the substitution of a finite sequence of wells for a single well results in a splitting of each discrete level of a single well into a multiplet of levels. To illustrate: consider a double well consisting of two rectangular wells each of width b and depth V_0, whose adjacent edges are separated from each other by a distance c; and show without detailed analysis that, if c is sufficiently large to make exp $\left[-\frac{1}{2}\sqrt{\kappa(V_0 - E)}\,c\right]$ much smaller that exp $\left[\frac{1}{2}\sqrt{\kappa(V_0 - E)}\,c\right]$, then the discrete energy spectrum consists of a series of doublets (pairs of levels), the separation of the members of a doublet being small compared to the separations of the doublets, and the positions of the doublets being approximately those of the singlet levels of a single rectangular well of width b and depth V_0.

---

[11] For an introductory survey and many references see F. Seitz and R. P. Johnson, *Jour. Applied Phys.*, **8**, 84–97. 186–199, and 246–260 (1937).

Chapter VIII

REMARKS ON THE MOMENTUM METHOD

50. The Framework of the Momentum Method

The present short chapter marks an important turning point in our study, for, having discussed the Schroedinger method in some detail, we now begin to consider methods other than Schroedinger's. It should perhaps be emphasized that the work of this chapter might have, in principle, preceded our study of the Schroedinger method. The reader will recall that the operator assumption I and the quantum condition II of §13, as well as the operand rule IV of §17, are quite noncommittal concerning the specific form of the operators and operands to be employed; in the light of these general assumptions, the Schroedinger methods rests, in fact, on a rather special possible choice of operators and operands, a choice, however, of the greatest all-round usefulness.

A characteristic of the one-dimensional Schroedinger method is the prominence that it gives to the coordinate x (this method may, in fact, be called the x-*method*); the Schroedinger operands, for example, are functions of x (and of t) intepreted as amplitudes of distributions-in-x. The so-called *momentum method* or p-*method*, which we shall now outline briefly for the case of one dimension, gives the corresponding prominence to the momentum p, and the operands used in this method are functions of p (and of t) interpreted as amplitudes of distributions-in-p.

The operators of interest to us now are those that can operate on functions of p, the fundamental ones being p (multiplication of an operand by p), $\partial/\partial p$ (differentiation of an operand partially with respect to p), and c (multiplication of an operand by the numerical constant c). The algebra of these operators is of course essentially the same as that of the operators x, $\partial/\partial x$, and c. For example, since for an arbitrary differentiable $u(p)$ we have

$$\frac{\partial}{\partial p} \, pu(p) = p \, \frac{\partial}{\partial p} \, u(p) + u(p) = \left[p \, \frac{\partial}{\partial p} + 1 \right] u(p), \qquad (1)$$

we find, recalling the definition of equality of operators, that $(\partial/\partial p)p = p(\partial/\partial p) + 1$, that is, that

$$\frac{\partial}{\partial p}\, p - p\, \frac{\partial}{\partial p} = 1. \qquad (2)$$

Equation (2) is analogous to 30^2. The reader will perhaps readily see that were the symbol p substituted for the symbol x *throughout* Chapter I, the mathematical content of that chapter would not be altered.

We shall be concerned with eigenvalues and eigenfunctions of operators constructed from p, $\partial/\partial p$, and c, and consequently a definition of a well-behaved function of p is required. The definition is analogous to that in the case of functions of x: $u(p)$ is well-behaved if it is not identically zero, if it remains finite when $|\,p\,| \to \infty$ (that is, when $p \to -\infty$ and also when $p \to \infty$) and if it is continuous and has an adequate number of continuous derivatives; we shall not consider the continuity-conditions in detail—insofar as the work of this chapter is concerned it is sufficient to require $u(p)$ and $\partial u(p)/\partial p$ to be continuous, that is, to impose on the operands the standard continuity conditions of §3. The definitions of the terms 'eigenvalue' and 'eigenfunction' need not be reworded, it being understood, of course, that if the operator α involves the operators p, $\partial/\partial p$, or both, then u in the equation

(15^3) $\qquad\qquad\qquad\qquad \alpha u = \lambda u \qquad\qquad\qquad\qquad (3)$

is usually a function of p.

Our next task is to identify the operators, which we denote as usual by x and p, to be associated in the p-scheme with the dynamical variables x (the coordinate) and p (the momentum), respectively. The operators x and p must, in any scheme of association, satisfy the relation

$\langle 5^{13}\rangle$ $\qquad\qquad\qquad\qquad xp - px = i\hbar, \qquad\qquad\qquad \langle 4\rangle$

and we note, consulting (2), that the associations

$$\begin{cases} \text{dynamical variable } x \rightleftarrows \text{operator } i\hbar\, \dfrac{\partial}{\partial p} \\[2ex] \text{dynamical variable } p \rightleftarrows \text{operator } p \end{cases} \qquad \langle 5\rangle$$

are consistent with $\langle 4\rangle$; further, the eigenvalues of p and $i\hbar\partial/\partial p$ are all real (Exercises 1 and 2), and consequently the associations

⟨5⟩ are suitable in every respect. These associations are the fundamental ones of the p-scheme, and are to be contrasted with the fundamental associations 3^{14} of the Schroedinger method.

For a dynamical variable that is the sum of a function of x (the coordinate) only and a function of p (the momentum) only, we then adopt the association

$$\text{dynamical variable } \alpha(x) + \beta(p) \rightleftarrows \text{operator } \alpha\left(i\hbar\frac{\partial}{\partial p}\right) + \beta(p), \quad ⟨6⟩$$

which is to be contrasted with 11^{14}. In particular, the one-dimensional Hamiltonian

$$(6^9) \qquad\qquad H = \frac{1}{2m}\,p^2 + V(x) \qquad\qquad (7)$$

is associated in the p-method with the operator

$$H = \frac{1}{2m}\,p^2 + V\left(i\hbar\frac{\partial}{\partial p}\right), \qquad\qquad ⟨8⟩$$

where $V(i\hbar\partial/\partial p)$ is the same function of $i\hbar\partial/\partial p$ as $V(x)$ is of x. The operator ⟨8⟩ is to be contrasted with our familiar Schroedinger operator 18^{14}; note that the Hamiltonian operator is usually more complicated in the p-scheme than in the Schroedinger scheme.

According to the operand rule of §17, the operands of the p-method are to be associated with states of dynamical systems. In computations carried out entirely by means of the p-method, it is convenient to denote the operands by ψ (with the understanding that ψ is a function of p and t, rather than of x and t) and to call them ψ-functions, as we shall do in this chapter; but whenever the Schroedinger method and the p-method are used concurrently it is advantageous to adopt the notation described at the end of §27 and to denote the Schroedinger ψ-functions by $(x\mid)$, and the ψ-functions of the p-scheme by $(p\mid)$; a justification for this use of the symbol $(p\mid)$ will be given in Exercise 5.

To complete the list of assumptions required for simple one-dimensional applications of the p-method we add the two following:

III_1^P. *Every operand ψ of the p-method pertaining to a one-*

dimensional system whose Hamiltonian is H depends on the time t in such a way that

$$H\psi = i\hbar \frac{\partial}{\partial t} \psi \qquad \langle 9 \rangle$$

where H is the operator $\langle 8 \rangle$.

V_1^P. *When a one-dimensional system is in the state specified in the p-method by the operand* ψ, *then the expected average,* $av_\psi \alpha$, *of any dynamical variable* α *is given by the formula*

$$av_\psi \alpha = \frac{\displaystyle\int_{-\infty}^{\infty} \bar{\psi}\alpha\psi \, dp}{\displaystyle\int_{-\infty}^{\infty} \bar{\psi}\psi \, dp}, \qquad \langle 10 \rangle$$

where α *in the integrand is the operator associated in the p-method with the dynamical variable* α.

Equation $\langle 9 \rangle$ has the same form as does the second Schroedinger equation 1^{16}, while $\langle 10 \rangle$, the expectation formula of the p-method in one dimension, resembles the one-dimensional Schroedinger expectation formula 2^{17}.

Exercises

1. Use the operator associated in the p-scheme with the coordinate x to show that all real (and no other) numbers are possible values of x, and that the eigenfunction belonging to the eigenvalue x' of x is $\psi = \psi(p) = Ae^{-ix'p/\hbar}$.

2. Use the operator associated in the p-scheme with the momentum p to show that all real (and no other) numbers are possible values of p, and that the eigenfunction belonging to the eigenvalue p' of p is[1] $\psi = \psi(p) = A\delta(p - p')$.

3. How can the distribution function of a dynamical variable for a specific state of a one-dimensional system be computed (at least in principle) within the framework of the p-method?

4. Show that in the p-scheme the operands ψ and $c\psi$, where c is a numerical constant, specify the same state.

5. Take α in $\langle 10 \rangle$ to be a function of p only and show that, in the p-scheme, $\bar{\psi}\psi$ is the distribution-in-p for the state specified by ψ, so that ψ itself is an amplitude of this distribution.

6. Working in the p-scheme, show that, if ψ is an eigenfunction of an operator α belonging to the eigenvalue a of α, then the result of a precise measurement of the dynamical variable α when the system is in the state ψ is certain to be a.

---

[1] As before, we regard δ-functions as well-behaved.

7. Let $(x \mid)$ denote an amplitude of the distribution-in-x for a state specified in the p-scheme by the ψ-function $(p \mid)$, and derive the result of Exercise 11[27] without reference to the Schroedinger method.

51. Energy Levels of an Oscillator

To illustrate the p-method, we shall now use it to compute the energy levels of a linear harmonic oscillator. The Hamiltonian being

$$(15^{10}) \qquad H = \frac{1}{2m} p^2 + \tfrac{1}{2}kx^2, \tag{1}$$

we find, using 8^{50}, that in the p-scheme the operator H for the oscillator is

$$H = \frac{1}{2m} p^2 - \tfrac{1}{2}k\hbar^2 \frac{\partial^2}{\partial p^2}, \tag{2}$$

so that our problem is to compute the eigenvalues of the operator $\langle 2 \rangle$, that is, to find the values of the number E for which the equation $H\psi = E\psi$, or

$$\left(\frac{1}{2m} p^2 - \tfrac{1}{2}k\hbar^2 \frac{\partial^2}{\partial p^2} \right)\psi = E\psi, \tag{3}$$

has well-behaved solutions; our operands are now functions of p.

The substitutions

$$s = p/b, \qquad E = \tfrac{1}{2}h\nu_c\lambda, \tag{4a, b}$$

where

$$b = \sqrt[4]{km\hbar^2}, \qquad 2\pi\nu_c = \sqrt{k/m}, \tag{5}$$

carry the differential equation (3) into

$$\left(-\frac{\partial^2}{\partial s^2} + s^2 \right)\psi = \lambda\psi, \tag{6}$$

that is, into 3^4; note that the abbreviations (5) are the same as 25^{18} and 14^{15}. The eigenvalues of (6) are

$$(28^4) \qquad \lambda_n = 2n + 1, \qquad n = 0, 1, 2, 3, \cdots, \tag{7}$$

so that, in view of (4b), the possible energies of the oscillator are

$$E_n = (n + \tfrac{1}{2})h\nu_c, \qquad n = 0, 1, 2, 3, \cdots \tag{8}$$

The result (8) is identical with our old result 15^{15}.

We have thus found the energy levels of the oscillator by a method other than Schroedinger's. In the case of the oscillator, the steps of the p-method are quite similar to those of the Schroedinger method, because the Hamiltonian is quite symmetric in x and p.

Exercises

1. Compute the eigenfunctions of (3) and show that in the p-scheme the normalized ψ-function specifying the nth quantum state of an oscillator is 41^{27}, γ_n being an arbitrary real constant.

2. Consider the normal state of the oscillator and, working entirely within the p-scheme, derive 26^{18}, 27^{18}, 18^{18}, and 19^{18}.

3. Working entirely within the p-scheme, prove the Heisenberg inequality 13^{23}.

4. Use the p-method to compute the energy spectrum of a free particle.

52. Concluding Remarks

The p-method may be built up into a theory as comprehensive as that of Schroedinger; in particular, the equation of motion 27^{44} is found to hold in the p-scheme as well as in Schroedinger's, and the expansion theorem of §46 goes over into the p-scheme without a change of wording. But the p-scheme is on the whole not as convenient as Schroedinger's for handling the more usual types of problems. The main reasons for our mentioning it are that, at least in its more elementary aspects, it affords perhaps the simplest example of a method other than Schroedinger's, and that it enables us to emphasize the generality of the operator assumption I, the quantum condition II, and the operand rule IV without invoking operators other than differential operators.

The questions now arise as to whether the p-scheme is certain to yield results in agreement with Schroedinger's, and whether it can be deduced directly from the Schroedinger method (that is, whether it can be constructed without replacing the assumptions III^S and V^S by other assumptions). The answers are in the affirmative, but the proofs, which involve a theorem on differential equations due to Laplace,[2] are beyond the scope of this book.

The process of working with the p-method is often called working in *momentum space*; a ψ-function of the p-method is often called a *momentum eigenfunction*, a term not to be confused with the term *eigenfunction of momentum*, that is, a ψ-function specifying a state

---

[2] Ince, page 187.

for which the momentum is a certainty.   The term 'p-representation' is sometimes used for 'p-method.'

It should perhaps be added that when the p-scheme is used in handling potential lattices the equation $H\psi = E\psi$ assumes a rather interesting form. For example, let $V(x) = V_0 \cos ax$, that is, let

$$V(x) = \tfrac{1}{2}V_0 e^{-iax} + \tfrac{1}{2}V_0 e^{iax}, \tag{1}$$

where V_0 and a are prescribed constants; according to 8^{50}, the operator associated with H in the p-scheme is then

$$H = \frac{1}{2m}\,p^2 + \tfrac{1}{2}V_0 e^{ah\frac{\partial}{\partial p}} + \tfrac{1}{2}V_0 e^{-ah\frac{\partial}{\partial p}}. \tag{$\langle 2\rangle$}$$

To find what happens to a function of p when the operator $\exp\,(ah\,\partial/\partial p)$ acts on it we expand $\exp\,(ah\,\partial/\partial p)$ formally into a power series and get

$$e^{ah\frac{\partial}{\partial p}} = 1 + ah\frac{\partial}{\partial p} + \frac{1}{2!}\,a^2\hbar^2\frac{\partial^2}{\partial p^2} + \frac{1}{3!}\,a^2\hbar^3\frac{\partial^3}{\partial p^3} + \cdots, \tag{$\langle 3\rangle$}$$

an equation which implies that

$$e^{ah\frac{\partial}{\partial p}}\psi(p) = \left[1 + ah\frac{\partial}{\partial p} + \frac{1}{2!}\,a^2\hbar^2\frac{\partial^2}{\partial p^2} + \cdots\right]\psi(p)$$

$$= \psi(p) + ah\psi'(p) + \frac{1}{2!}\,a^2\hbar^2\psi''(p) + \cdots, \tag{$\langle 4\rangle$}$$

where the primes denote differentiation with respect to p; now, by Taylor's theorem,

$$\psi(p) + ah\psi'(p) + \frac{1}{2!}\,a^2\hbar^2\psi''(p) + \cdots = \psi(p + ah), \tag{5}$$

and, waiving mathematical caution, we conclude that

$$e^{ah\frac{\partial}{\partial p}}\psi(p) = \psi(p + ah), \tag{6}$$

that is, that operating on $\psi(p)$ with the operator $\exp\,(ah\,\partial/\partial p)$ results in replacing p in $\psi(p)$ by $p + ah$.   In a similar way

$$e^{-ah\frac{\partial}{\partial p}}\psi(p) = \psi(p - ah). \tag{7}$$

Thus when H is $\langle 2\rangle$ the equation $H\psi = E\psi$ is

$$\frac{1}{2m}\,p^2\psi(p) + \tfrac{1}{2}V_0\psi(p + ah) + \tfrac{1}{2}V_0\psi(p - ah) = E\psi(p). \tag{8}$$

Note that (8), an equation to be solved for ψ and E under the condition that ψ be well-behaved, is not a differential equation; equations of type (8) are called *difference equations*.

Exercises

1. Starting with the result found in the paragraph following 4^{48}, show that, if $V(x)$ is even in x, then every eigenfunction of H in the p-scheme is either even or odd in p, or is a superposition of an even-in-p and an odd-in-p eigenfunction of H.

2. Let Ω_p denote the operation of replacing p by $-p$, so that $\Omega_p f(p) = f(-p)$ for every $f(p)$. Use the operator Ω_p and the expansion theorem to derive the result of Exercise 1 without reference to the Schroedinger method.

CHAPTER IX

LINEAR OPERATORS AND MATRICES

We have by now considered two distinct methods of associating specific operators with dynamical variables: the Schroedinger method and the p-method. The next method on our program is that of Heisenberg, which employs operators quite different from those that we used before, and associates dynamical variables with *matrices*. The present chapter is devoted to a preliminary mathematical discussion, which is intended for a reader whose knowledge of matrices is at best vague and which consequently begins in a rather elementary way. The more essential parts of this chapter are listed in §61.

If the reader finds any difficulties in connection with the elements of the theory of simultaneous linear algebraic equations encountered in this chapter, he should consult a book on algebra.

53. Mappings of a Plane

Vectors and rays. Let the various points of a plane, say the plane of Fig. 80, be denoted by O, u, v, w, and so on. With every point of the plane we associate a vector with a terminus at the point in question and with an origin at O; the point and the corresponding vector will be denoted by the same symbol, and the terms *point* and *vector* will be used interchangeably.

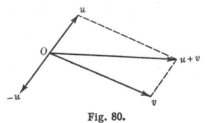

Fig. 80.

The symbol cu, where c is a real number, denotes the vector whose length is $|c|$ times that of u, and whose direction is the same as that of u if c is positive and opposite if c is negative. The vector whose origin and terminus are both at O is called the vector *zero* and is denoted by 0. The locus of the termini of all vectors of the form cu, where u is fixed but c differs from vector to vector, forms a *ray*; a ray can be specified by a single nonvanishing vector lying on it, and may be pictured as an infinite straight line through O. If a ray contains a nonvanishing vector that is perpendicular to a nonvanishing vector lying on another ray, the two rays are said to be (mutually) orthogonal. The symbol $u + v$ denotes the vector sum of u and v, that is, the vector forming, in the usual sense, the diagonal of the parallelogram with vector sides u and v. The methods of this section will be entirely geometric, so that, for example, to specify a point or a line in our plane, we must mark it, and to add two given vectors we must use ruler and compasses.

By definition, n vectors, u_I, u_{II}, $\cdots$, $u_{(n)}$, are said to be *linearly independent* if it is impossible to choose n constants, c_1, c_2, $\cdots$, c_n, not all of which are zeros, in such a way as to satisfy the equation

$$c_1 u_I + c_2 u_{II} + \cdots + c_n u_{(n)} = 0; \qquad (1)$$

otherwise, the n vectors are said to be linearly dependent. The reader will convince himself that any *three* vectors lying in a plane are linearly dependent, and that *two* vectors lying in a plane are linearly dependent if and only if they lie on the same ray.

Mappings. A process of rearranging the points comprising a plane is called a *transformation* or a *mapping* of the plane. The following mapping, which we shall call the mapping τ, is a simple

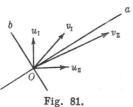

Fig. 81.

example: we draw in our plane the mutually perpendicular lines a and b shown in Fig. 81, and then move each point in the plane so that it does not cross either a or b, so that its distance from a is halved, and so that its distance from b is trebled; the point u_I in Fig. 81 is thus sent into the place v_I, the point u_{II} into the place v_{II}, and so on. To illustrate the effect of this mapping perhaps more clearly, we draw in Fig. 82 a circle with center at O and also the ellipse into which the mapping τ sends the points of this circle; the reader will verify that the specifically marked points of the circle are

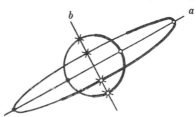

Fig. 82. A circle and the ellipse into which the mapping τ sends this circle.

sent, respectively, into the similarly marked points of the ellipse.

Mappings will usually be denoted by Greek letters. The symbolic equation

$$\alpha u = v, \tag{2}$$

read 'α times u equals v,' will mean that the mapping α sends the vector u into the position occupied, prior to the mapping, by the vector v; thus in the case of our special mapping τ we write $\tau u_\mathrm{I} = v_\mathrm{I}$, $\tau u_\mathrm{II} = v_\mathrm{II}$, and so on, where u_I, u_II, v_I, and v_II are the particular vectors so marked in Fig. 81.

If a mapping α sends each vector into a definite place, we say that α is *unambiguous*. If all distinct vectors are sent by α into distinct places (that is, if the inequality $u \neq v$ implies the inequality $\alpha u \neq \alpha v$) we say that α is *nonsingular*; otherwise (that is, if there are some u and v such that $u \neq v$ but $\alpha u = \alpha v$) we call α *singular*. If both equations

$$\alpha(cu) = c(\alpha u) \quad \text{and} \quad \alpha(u + v) = \alpha u + \alpha v, \quad c, u, v \text{ arbitrary}, \tag{3}$$

hold, we say that α is *linear*. The reader will verify that our special mapping τ is unambiguous, linear, and nonsingular. We shall use the term *mapping* for *unambiguous linear mapping*, since only such mappings will be of interest to us; further, we shall regard *mappings* as *operators* whose *operands* are *vectors*, and shall use the terms *mapping* and *operator* interchangeably.

When our τ acts on a vector, it in general moves the vector from one ray to another; for example, the vector u_I of Fig. 81 and the vector $\tau u_\mathrm{I} = v_\mathrm{I}$, into which τ sends u_I, lie on different rays. But the vectors lying on the rays a and b behave in an exceptional way; in fact, as is perhaps best seen from Fig. 82,

$$\tau u = 3u, \qquad \text{if } u \text{ lies on } a \tag{4}$$

$$\tau u = \tfrac{1}{2}u, \qquad \text{if } u \text{ lies on } b, \tag{5}$$

so that a vector lying on the ray a remains on this ray after the mapping τ is carried out, and a vector lying on b remains on b. If a nonvanishing vector u is sent by an operator α into a numerical multiple of itself, that is, if

$$\alpha u = \lambda u, \tag{6}$$

where λ is a number, we call u an *eigenvector* of α, call λ an *eigenvalue* of α, and say that the eigenvector u and the eigenvalue λ of α belong to each other; this terminology, except for the omission of references to boundary and continuity conditions, is parallel to that of §3, and (6) has precisely the same form as 15^3. Equation (4) signifies, in these terms, that any nonvanishing vector lying on a is an eigenvector of our mapping τ, belonging to the eigenvalue 3 of τ; similarly, Equation (5) signifies that any nonvanishing vector lying on b is an eigenvector of our τ, belonging to the eigenvalue $\frac{1}{2}$ of τ. A ray containing an eigenvector of an operator is called an *eigenray* or a *principal axis* of the operator; thus the ray a is the eigenray of our τ belonging to the eigenvalue 3, and b is the eigenray of our τ belonging to the eigenvalue $\frac{1}{2}$; any nonvanishing vector lying on an eigenray of a linear operator is of course an eigenvector of the operator. It is perhaps obvious on geometric grounds that the rays a and b are the only eigenrays of τ, and that consequently the only eigenvalues of our τ are the two, 3 and $\frac{1}{2}$, found above. Any two eigenvectors of τ belonging to the eigenvalue 3 are linearly dependent, and hence this eigenvalue is said to be *nondegenerate*; similarly, the eigenvalue $\frac{1}{2}$ of τ is nondegenerate. This use of the term 'nondegenerate eigenvalue' is parallel to that of §7.

Further examples of mappings. Another simple mapping, to be called γ, is the following: We draw in our plane the line A shown in Fig. 83 and then *reflect* in A every point of the plane, so

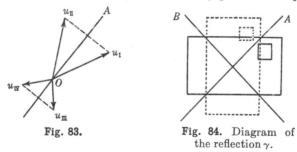

Fig. 83.

Fig. 84. Diagram of the reflection γ.

that the point u_I is sent to the place u_{II}, the point u_{II} to the place u_I, the point u_{III} to the place u_{IV}, and so forth. To illustrate the effect of γ more elaborately, we show in Fig. 84 the plane, prior to the reflection, with an outline of a postcard (full line) with center at O drawn on it; the position of the outline of the postcard after the reflection is shown by the dotted line.[1] The latter position is shown once again in Fig. 85.

---

[1] It should perhaps be emphasized that Fig. 84 is meant to illustrate the reflection of the plane in the line A and *not* the rotation of the plane

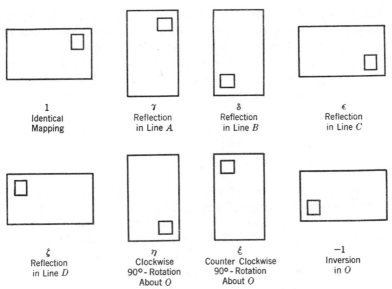

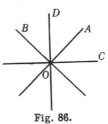

Fig. 85. Diagrams of eight mappings of a plane.   The lines A, B, C, and D are those of Fig. 86.

In general, γ shifts a vector from one ray to another, except that (Fig. 84)

$$\gamma u = u, \qquad \text{if } u \text{ lies on } A \qquad (7)$$

$$\gamma u = -u, \qquad \text{if } u \text{ lies on } B. \qquad (8)$$

The eigenvalues of our γ are consequently 1 and -1, the eigenray belonging to the eigenvalue 1 being A, and the eigenray belonging to the eigenvalue -1 being B.

The effect of a reflection of the plane in the ray A, B, C, or D of Fig. 86 is indicated in diagrams γ, δ, ϵ, and ζ of Fig. 85 by the respective position into which it sends the outline of a postcard whose initial position is shown by the full line in Fig. 84.

The mapping consisting in multiplying every vector of the plane by a constant c is

Fig. 86.

through 180° about the line A as an axis; the rotation (which would display the back of the postcard) would involve getting out into the third dimension, while the transformations that we consider now are all carried out within the plane.   Similar remarks apply to the other reflections of the plane mentioned below.

denoted by the symbol c.   Each nonvanishing vector is an eigen-vector of this mapping and belongs to the single eigenvalue c of the mapping.   Every three, but not every two, eigenvectors of the operator c are linearly dependent; for this reason the single eigenvalue c of the operator c is said to be doubly degenerate, this use of the term being parallel to that of §7.   Special cases of mappings of type c are the mapping 1 (the *identical mapping*), which leaves every vector in its original position, and the mapping -1 (the *inversion in O*), which reverses the direction of every vector without changing its length; these mappings are illustrated in Fig. 85.

A rotation of every vector in the plane about O through the same angle is another example of a mapping of the plane.   The respective effects of a clockwise 90°-rotation and of a counterclockwise 90°-rotation about O are illustrated in diagrams η and ξ of Fig. 85. Since the mapping η (as well as the mapping ξ) rotates every vector through 90° and thus removes every nonvanishing vector from its original ray, this mapping has no eigenvectors and eigen-values when regarded from the standpoint of ordinary geometry; but we shall presently generalize our viewpoint, and then both η and ξ will turn out to have imaginary eigenvalues.

The eight mappings of Fig. 85 are of course rather special examples of mappings of a plane; but they are particularly simple, and we shall often use them for illustrations.

Algebraic relations between mappings.   In dealing with map-pings, we speak of their *sums, products,* and so on, the definitions of equality, sum, and product of mappings being just those given in §2 for operators in general.   Operator-algebraic relations between mappings can be illustrated by reference to Fig. 85. We note, for example, that if an arbitrary vector is reflected in the line C (operation ϵ) and the resulting vector is turned clockwise through 90° (operation η), then the final vector is just that obtained by reflecting the original vector in the line B (operation δ); symbolically,

$$\eta\epsilon u = \delta u, \qquad u \text{ arbitrary,} \tag{9}$$

and hence $$\eta\epsilon = \delta. \tag{10}$$

Again, if an arbitrary vector is turned clockwise through 90° (operation η) and the resulting vector is reflected in the line C

(operation ϵ), then the final vector is just that obtained by reflecting the original vector in the line A (operation γ); symbolically,

$$\epsilon\eta u = \gamma u, \qquad u \text{ arbitrary}, \tag{11}$$

and hence $\qquad\qquad \epsilon\eta = \gamma. \tag{12}$

Since γ and δ are different operations, we conclude from (10) and (12) that

$$\eta\epsilon \neq \epsilon\eta, \tag{13}$$

that is, that the mappings ϵ and η do not commute.

If an arbitrary vector is turned clockwise through 90° (operation η) and the resulting vector is turned counterclockwise through 90° (operation ξ), then the final vector is just the original vector, so that ξ, so to speak, undoes what η does; symbolically, $\xi\eta u = u$ for an arbitrary u, and hence

$$\xi\eta = 1. \tag{14}$$

In a similar way we find that

$$\eta\xi = 1, \tag{15}$$

and comparison with (14) shows that η and ξ commute. Incidentally, Equations (14) and (15) suggest writing

$$\eta = \xi^{-1} \quad \text{and} \quad \xi = \eta^{-1}, \tag{16}$$

and calling η and ξ the *reciprocals* of each other. An operator may be its own reciprocal: the operators 1, γ, δ, ϵ, ζ, and -1 of Fig. 85 are examples. It will be shown in Exercise 5 that some operators have no reciprocals.

The geometric notion of mappings, discussed above with special reference to a plane, is readily extended to the case of a three-dimensional space or, as we shall say for short, a 3-space. Just as a nonsingular linear mapping of a plane in general sends a circle into an ellipse, so a nonsingular mapping of a 3-space in general sends a sphere into an ellipsoid.

Exercises

1. Identify the respective eigenrays and eigenvalues of the mappings δ, ϵ, and ζ of Fig. 85.

TABLE 11

	1	γ	δ	ϵ	ζ	η	ξ	-1
1	1	γ	δ	ϵ	ζ	η	ξ	-1
γ	γ	1	-1	ξ	η	ζ	ϵ	δ
δ	δ	-1	1	η	ξ	ϵ	ζ	γ
ϵ	ϵ	η	ξ	1	-1	γ	δ	ζ
ζ	ζ	ξ	η	-1	1	δ	γ	ϵ
η	η	ϵ	ζ	δ	γ	-1	1	ξ
ξ	ξ	ζ	ϵ	γ	δ	1	-1	η
-1	-1	δ	γ	ζ	ϵ	ξ	η	1

2. Verify Table 11, which comprises the *multiplication table* of the operators of Fig. 85; the product $\alpha\beta$ is recorded at the intersection of the column labeled β and the row labeled α.

3. Use Table 11 to show that $(1 + \gamma)(1 - \gamma) = 0$, $(1 + \gamma)^2 = 2(1 + \gamma)$, $\epsilon\eta - \eta\epsilon = 2\gamma$, and $\epsilon\eta + \eta\epsilon = 0$, and verify these relations by geometric construction. Show that, if $(\gamma\eta)^{-1}$ denotes the reciprocal of $\gamma\eta$, then $(\gamma\eta)^{-1} = \eta^{-1}\gamma^{-1}$.

4. Show geometrically that, if two eigenrays of a mapping of a plane coincide with two eigenrays of another mapping of the plane, then the two mappings commute.

5. Show geometrically that a singular mapping has no reciprocal; remember that we restrict ourselves to unambiguous mappings.

6. Show geometrically that a mapping having the eigenvalue 0 is singular, and that every singular mapping has the eigenvalue 0.

7. Let α_1, α_2, α_3, $\cdots$, be operators, and let $(\alpha_i\alpha_j)$ and $(\alpha_j\alpha_k)$ denote for the moment the operators $\alpha_i\alpha_j$ and $\alpha_j\alpha_k$, respectively; the α's are then said to obey the *associative law for multiplication* if $(\alpha_i\alpha_j)\alpha_k = \alpha_i(\alpha_j\alpha_k)$ for every i, j, and k. Verify that the operators of Fig. 85 obey this law.

8. Incidentally, a set of operators is said to form a *group* if all of the following rather stringent conditions are satisfied: (a) the members of the set obey the associative law for multiplication; (b) the set contains the operator 1; (c) every member of the set has a reciprocal, and this reciprocal is a member of the set; and (d) if α and β are any two members of the set, then $\alpha\beta$, $\beta\alpha$, α^2, and β^2 are also members of the set. Verify that the eight operators of Fig. 85 form a group, and that the four operators 1, η, ξ, and -1 also form a group when taken by themselves.

9. Show geometrically that any set of four or more vectors in 3-space is linearly dependent.

10. A certain mapping of 3-space consists in reflecting every point in a plane passing through O; show geometrically that the eigenvalues of this mapping are -1 and 1, the first being nondegenerate and the second being doubly degenerate.

11. Let σ be a reflection of 3-space in a plane S passing through O, and τ be a reflection of the 3-space in a plane T passing through O. Show geometrically that $\sigma\tau$ is a rotation about the line of intersection of the planes S and T, and that $\sigma\tau = (\tau\sigma)^{-1}$.

54. Representation of Mappings by Means of Matrices

The purely geometric methods of the preceding section become unwieldy in the case of more complicated mappings, and we shall now turn to the methods of analytic geometry. To do this, we draw in our plane a rectangular coordinate frame with origin at O, say the frame P with axes P_1 and P_2, shown in Fig. 87, which are supposed to lie along the lines C and D of Fig. 86; the basic unit vectors of this frame will be denoted by e_1^P and e_2^P. Any vector u in the plane can be resolved in terms of e_1^P and e_2^P, that is, expressed in the form

$$u = u_1^P e_1^P + u_2^P e_2^P, \tag{1}$$

where u_1^P and u_2^P are two *numbers*, called the *components of the vector u in the frame P*. The superscripts P in our symbols would be unnecessary were it not for the fact that we shall presently consider other coordinate frames and compare the results; to make the notation unambiguous, we shall agree not to use the superscripts P, Q, and R as exponents, that is, to indicate powers. Given the coordinate frame, the components of u specify u completely. If $u = cv$, where c is a constant, we have $u_1^P = cv_1^P$ and

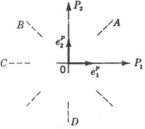

Fig. 87. The frame P.

$u_2^P = cv_2^P$, so that, in particular, if $u = v$, then $u_1^P = v_1^P$ and $u_2^P = v_2^P$. If $w = u + v$, then $w_1^P = u_1^P + v_1^P$ and $w_2^P = u_2^P + v_2^P$. If the vectors u and v are orthogonal (mutually perpendicular), then, as the reader will verify, we have

$$u_1^P v_1^P + u_2^P v_2^P = 0. \tag{2}$$

The square of the length of a vector u is

$$(u_1^P)^2 + (u_2^P)^2. \tag{3}$$

Vectors of unit length are called *unitary*; pairs of unitary and mutually orthogonal vectors are called *orthonormal*.

Let us now consider the operator γ of the last section, namely, the reflection of the plane in the line A, and find the relations between the components u_1^P and u_2^P of an arbitrary vector u and the components v_1^P and v_2^P of the vector $v = \gamma u$, that is, the vector into which γ sends the vector u. As seen from Fig. 88, $v_1^P = u_2^P$ and $v_2^P = u_1^P$, that is,

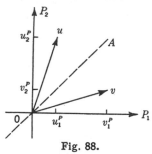

Fig. 88.

$$\begin{cases} v_1^P = 0 \cdot u_1^P + 1 \cdot u_2^P \\ v_2^P = 1 \cdot u_1^P + 0 \cdot u_2^P. \end{cases} \tag{4}$$

Equations (4) completely specify the effect of the operator γ and enable us, in particular, to compute by algebraic means the eigenvalues and the eigenrays of γ. If u is an eigenvector of γ, so that $\gamma u = v = \lambda u$, then $v_1^P = \lambda u_1^P$ and $v_2^P = \lambda u_2^P$, and hence, *if u is an eigenvector of γ*, Equations (4) go over into

$$\begin{cases} \lambda u_1^P = 0 \cdot u_1^P + 1 \cdot u_2^P \\ \lambda u_2^P = 1 \cdot u_1^P + 0 \cdot u_2^P, \end{cases} \tag{5}$$

that is, into

$$\begin{cases} -\lambda u_1^P + u_2^P = 0 \\ u_1^P - \lambda u_2^P = 0. \end{cases} \tag{6}$$

Equations (6)—which contain three unknowns, λ, u_1^P, and u_2^P—enable us to evaluate just the quantities we want, namely, λ and u_2^P/u_1^P, that is, the eigenvalues of γ and the slopes of the eigenrays of γ relative to the frame P. Indeed, in order that these simultaneous linear homogeneous equations have solutions other than the trivial $u_1^P = u_2^P = 0$, it is necessary and sufficient that the determinant of the coefficients be zero, that is, that

$$\begin{vmatrix} -\lambda & 1 \\ 1 & -\lambda \end{vmatrix} = 0, \tag{7}$$

or $\lambda^2 - 1 = 0$, and

$$\lambda = \pm 1. \tag{8}$$

The eigenvalues of our γ are thus 1 and -1, a result obtained by purely geometrical considerations in the preceding section.

To calculate the eigenvectors, or rather the eigenrays, of our γ we substitute the permissible values of λ, one by one, into (6), and find that

$$\text{for } \lambda = \quad 1, \qquad u_2^P / u_1^P = \quad 1 \qquad (9)$$

$$\text{for } \lambda = -1, \qquad u_2^P / u_1^P = -1. \qquad (10)$$

Equation (9) states that, relative to the frame P, the slope of the eigenray of γ belonging to the eigenvalue 1 is 1; Equation (10) states that, relative to the frame P, the slope of the eigenray of γ belonging to the eigenvalue -1 is -1. These results check with those of the preceding section, where we found the eigenrays of γ belonging to the eigenvalues 1 and -1 to be the rays A and B, respectively.

In Equations (4), which specify analytically the effect of our mapping γ, the components u_1^P and u_2^P are variables, and hence the structure of (4) can be adequately described by listing in some readily decipherable manner the fixed numerical coefficients on the right of (4); the standard method of doing this is to arrange the coefficients in exactly the same positions as they occur in (4), and to let the array, or *matrix*,

$$\begin{pmatrix} 0 & 1 \\ 1 & 0 \end{pmatrix}, \qquad (11)$$

summarize the essential content of Equations (4). This matrix enables us—by means of Equations (4)—to calculate the position into which γ sends any given vector; we call it 'the matrix representing the operator γ in the frame P,' denote it by γ^P, and write

$$\gamma^P = \begin{pmatrix} 0 & 1 \\ 1 & 0 \end{pmatrix}. \qquad (12)$$

We shall always mark matrices having a finite number of rows and columns by large parentheses, as in (12), and determinants by vertical lines, as in (7).

In the case of the other operators of the preceding section, the passage from geometric to analytic methods can be carried out in an entirely analogous way. For example, if u is an arbitrary vector and v is the vector ξu, that is, the vector into which u is sent by a counterclockwise 90° rotation about O, we find, as seen from Fig. 89, that

$$\begin{cases} v_1^P = 0 \cdot u_1^P - 1 \cdot u_2^P \\ v_2^P = 1 \cdot u_1^P + 0 \cdot u_2^P \end{cases} \qquad (13)$$

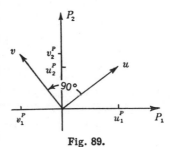

Fig. 89.

and that consequently the matrix representing the operator ξ in the frame P is

$$\xi^P = \begin{pmatrix} 0 & -1 \\ 1 & 0 \end{pmatrix}. \tag{14}$$

Similar calculations show that the eight operators of Fig. 85 are represented in the frame P by the following matrices:

$$1^P = \begin{pmatrix} 1 & 0 \\ 0 & 1 \end{pmatrix}, \; \gamma^P = \begin{pmatrix} 0 & 1 \\ 1 & 0 \end{pmatrix}, \; \delta^P = \begin{pmatrix} 0 & -1 \\ -1 & 0 \end{pmatrix}, \; \epsilon^P = \begin{pmatrix} 1 & 0 \\ 0 & -1 \end{pmatrix}$$
$$\zeta^P = \begin{pmatrix} -1 & 0 \\ 0 & 1 \end{pmatrix}, \; \eta^P = \begin{pmatrix} 0 & 1 \\ -1 & 0 \end{pmatrix}, \; \xi^P = \begin{pmatrix} 0 & -1 \\ 1 & 0 \end{pmatrix}, \; -1^P = \begin{pmatrix} -1 & 0 \\ 0 & -1 \end{pmatrix}. \tag{15}$$

In general, if the components, relative to a frame P, of every vector u and of the vector $v = \alpha u$, into which a mapping α sends u, are related by the equations

$$v_1^P = a u_1^P + b u_2^P$$
$$v_2^P = c u_1^P + d u_2^P, \tag{16}$$

where a, b, c, and d are numerical constants, we say that the matrix

$$\alpha^P = \begin{pmatrix} a & b \\ c & d \end{pmatrix} \tag{17}$$

represents the mapping α in the frame P; conversely, the statement that a mapping α is represented in the frame P by the matrix (17) means that the components of an arbitrary vector u and of the vector $v = \alpha u$, into which α sends u, are related through Equations (16). It is, of course, impossible to summarize the significance of a matrix by quoting any *single* number. When the numerical values of the constants a, b, c, and d in (16) and (17), having to do with a mapping α and the frame P, are not given explicitly, we usually denote them by α_{11}^P, α_{12}^P, α_{21}^P, and α_{22}^P; (16) and (17) then have the forms

$$\begin{cases} v_1^P = \alpha_{11}^P u_1^P + \alpha_{12}^P u_2^P \\ v_2^P = \alpha_{21}^P u_1^P + \alpha_{22}^P u_2^P \end{cases} \text{and} \quad \alpha^P = \begin{pmatrix} \alpha_{11}^P & \alpha_{12}^P \\ \alpha_{21}^P & \alpha_{22}^P \end{pmatrix}. \tag{18a, b}$$

Whenever it will be agreed to keep the coordinate frame in mind, the superscripts in (18) will be omitted; a mapping and the matrix representing it will then be denoted by the same symbol.

Vectors with complex components. The application of algebraic methods to geometric problems suggests a generalization of terminology. For example, from the purely geometric viewpoint, the straight line $y = 2x$ and the parabola $y = x^2 + 2$ of Fig. 90 do not intersect. To investigate the question of the intersection of these curves from the standpoint of analytic geometry, we look for the simultaneous solutions of the equations

Fig. 90.

$$y = 2x, \qquad y = x^2 + 2. \qquad (19)$$

The solutions

$$x_1 = 1 + i, \qquad y_1 = 2 + 2i \qquad (20a)$$

and

$$x_2 = 1 - i, \qquad y_2 = 2 - 2i \qquad (20b)$$

are complex, as is to be expected from the fact that the curves do not intersect from the geometric viewpoint. Now, the solutions (20) enable us to say, if we wish, that the straight line and the parabola of Fig. 90 *do* intersect, provided we include points whose coordinates are complex numbers.

The notion of points with complex coordinates or, what is the same thing, of vectors with complex components is a useful one because it enables us to retain geometric terminology in certain purely algebraic calculations. Although matters of terminology may at first sight seem trivial, the retention of geometric terms in our algebraic work turns out to be profitable, if only because it helps us to remember (and in some cases perhaps also to visualize) certain algebraic relations and processes. Accordingly, we shall henceforth speak freely of vectors having complex components and shall treat them on the same footing as vectors having real components. The totality of all vectors of the form (1), that is,

$$u = u_1^P e_1^P + u_2^P e_2^P, \qquad (21)$$

where now u_1^P and u_2^P are arbitrary real, imaginary, or complex numbers, will be called the *complex plane*, or simply the *plane*. The points in the physical plane of the paper in Fig. 87 comprise only a portion of our complex plane; the complete complex plane can be visualized no more readily than can the two points of intersection of the parabola and the straight line in Fig. 90. If u

is a vector in the complex plane, then the locus of the termini of all vectors of the form cu (where c is now not necessarily real) comprises a *ray*; the picture of a ray in the complex plane as a straight line through O is of course an imperfect one.

The reader should not confuse our complex plane with the plane, called the Argand diagram, used for graphical representation of complex numbers in the theory of functions of a complex variable, in the treatment of alternating currents by means of complex numbers, and so forth. In an Argand diagram the number $a + bi$ is associated with a point whose coordinate along the 'axis of the reals' is the *real* number a and whose coordinate along the 'axis of the imaginaries' is the *real* number b. Our complex plane, on the other hand, contains points whose *coordinates* are *complex*.

The uniformizing effect of working in the complex rather than in the real plane can be illustrated further as follows: In discussing the eight mappings of Fig. 85 from the geometric viewpoint, we had no difficulty in identifying their eigenvalues and eigenvectors, save in the case of the rotations η and ξ; eigenvectors and eigenvalues had in fact to be denied to η and ξ, so that these mappings appeared to be exceptional. The situation is different from the analytic standpoint. For example, the analytic significance of the rotation ξ is given by (13), so that the circumstances under which $\xi u = \lambda u$ may be determined through Equations (13). Writing $v = \lambda u$ in (13) we get

$$\begin{cases} \lambda u_1^P = 0 \cdot u_1^P - 1 \cdot u_2^P \\ \lambda u_2^P = 1 \cdot u_1^P + 0 \cdot u_2^P \end{cases} \text{ that is } \begin{cases} -\lambda u_1^P - u_2^P = 0 \\ u_1^P - \lambda u_2^P = 0. \end{cases} \quad \text{(22a, b)}$$

These equations have solutions other than $u_1^P = u_2^P = 0$ if the determinant of the coefficients vanishes, that is, if $\lambda^2 + 1 = 0$, or

$$\lambda = \pm i. \quad \text{(23)}$$

The eigenvalues of our ξ are consequently i and $-i$; this result was foreshadowed in Table 11, according to which $\xi^2 = -1$.

To compute the eigenrays of ξ we substitute the eigenvalues (23), one by one, into (22) and find that

$$\text{for } \lambda = \quad i, \qquad u_2^P / u_1^P = -i \qquad \textbf{(24)}$$

$$\text{for } \lambda = -i, \qquad u_2^P / u_1^P = i. \qquad \textbf{(25)}$$

The vectors having these imaginary 'slopes' relative to the frame P are thus not removed from their original rays when the plane undergoes a counterclockwise $90°$ rotation; instead, they are multiplied, respectively, by the constants i and $-i$. In terms of the complex plane, our ξ has two distinct eigenvalues and, just as every other nondegenerate mapping in Fig. 85, two eigenrays.

When the plane under consideration is complex, the expression (3) for the square of the length of a vector needs modification, since (3) may be negative or complex when u_1^P and u_2^P are complex; we then adopt the expression

$$(u_1^P)^*u_1^P + (u_2^P)^*u_2^P \tag{26}$$

for the square of the length of u, $(u_1^P)^*$ and $(u_2^P)^*$ being the complex conjugates of the numbers u_1^P and u_2^P. Similarly, we take the condition

$$(u_1^P)^*v_1^P + (u_2^P)^*v_2^P = 0, \tag{27}$$

or the equivalent condition $(v_1^P)^*u_1^P + (v_2^P)^*u_2^P = 0$, as the condition for orthogonality of u and v. When the components of u and v are real, (26) and (27) go over into (3) and (2), respectively.

Consecutive operations. Let the matrices representing two mappings α and β in some frame be

$$\alpha = \begin{pmatrix} \alpha_{11} & \alpha_{12} \\ \alpha_{21} & \alpha_{22} \end{pmatrix} \quad \text{and} \quad \beta = \begin{pmatrix} \beta_{11} & \beta_{12} \\ \beta_{21} & \beta_{22} \end{pmatrix}. \tag{28}$$

What is the matrix representing in the same frame the mapping $\alpha\beta$? Now, if β sends u into v, and α sends v into w, then, by definition, the mapping $\alpha\beta$ will send u directly into w; our task is consequently that of expressing the components of w in terms of the components of u, it being given that

$$\begin{cases} v_1 = \beta_{11}u_1 + \beta_{12}u_2 \\ v_2 = \beta_{21}u_1 + \beta_{22}u_2 \end{cases} \text{and} \begin{cases} w_1 = \alpha_{11}v_1 + \alpha_{12}v_2 \\ w_2 = \alpha_{21}v_1 + \alpha_{22}v_2. \end{cases} \tag{29a, b}$$

Eliminating v_1 and v_2 from (29b) by means of (29a), we get

$$\begin{cases} w_1 = (\alpha_{11}\beta_{11} + \alpha_{12}\beta_{21})u_1 + (\alpha_{11}\beta_{12} + \alpha_{12}\beta_{22})u_2 \\ w_2 = (\alpha_{21}\beta_{11} + \alpha_{22}\beta_{21})u_1 + (\alpha_{21}\beta_{12} + \alpha_{22}\beta_{22})u_2 \end{cases} \tag{30}$$

for an arbitrary u, and it follows that the desired matrix, which is denoted by $\alpha\beta$, is

$$\alpha\beta = \begin{pmatrix} \alpha_{11}\beta_{11} + \alpha_{12}\beta_{21} & \alpha_{11}\beta_{12} + \alpha_{12}\beta_{22} \\ \alpha_{21}\beta_{11} + \alpha_{22}\beta_{21} & \alpha_{21}\beta_{12} + \alpha_{22}\beta_{22} \end{pmatrix}. \tag{31}$$

The reader may recognize the matrix (31) as what is called in algebra *the product $\alpha\beta$ of the matrices α and β* given by (28); our result can thus be stated in the following readily remembered way: the matrix representing the product $\alpha\beta$ of the operators α and β is the product $\alpha\beta$ of the matrices representing, respectively, the operators α and β.

In algebra, the matrix product $\begin{pmatrix} a_{11} & a_{12} \\ a_{21} & a_{22} \end{pmatrix}\begin{pmatrix} b_{11} & b_{12} \\ b_{21} & b_{22} \end{pmatrix}$ of the matrices $\begin{pmatrix} a_{11} & a_{12} \\ a_{21} & a_{22} \end{pmatrix}$ and $\begin{pmatrix} b_{11} & b_{12} \\ b_{21} & b_{22} \end{pmatrix}$ is *defined* to be the matrix written on the right side of the following matrix equation:

$$\begin{pmatrix} a_{11} & a_{12} \\ a_{21} & a_{22} \end{pmatrix}\begin{pmatrix} b_{11} & b_{12} \\ b_{21} & b_{22} \end{pmatrix} = \begin{pmatrix} a_{11}b_{11} + a_{12}b_{21} & a_{11}b_{12} + a_{12}b_{22} \\ a_{21}b_{11} + a_{22}b_{21} & a_{21}b_{12} + a_{22}b_{22} \end{pmatrix}. \quad (32)$$

The reader should carefully memorize the arrangement of the entries in (32), noting, in particular, that the entry in the nth row and mth column of the product is constructed from the entries in the nth row of the left factor and the mth column of the right factor; the following diagram illustrates the computation of the entry in the *first row* and the *second column* of the product:

$$\begin{pmatrix} a_{11} & a_{12} \\ \cdots & \cdots \end{pmatrix}\begin{pmatrix} \cdots & b_{12} \\ \cdots & b_{22} \end{pmatrix} = \begin{pmatrix} \cdots & a_{11}b_{12} + a_{12}b_{22} \\ \cdots & \cdots \end{pmatrix}. \quad (33)$$

The multiplication of matrices having more than two rows and two columns will be discussed presently.

To illustrate the implications of our result (31) let us take from (15) the matrices $\eta^P = \begin{pmatrix} 0 & 1 \\ -1 & 0 \end{pmatrix}$ and $\epsilon^P = \begin{pmatrix} 1 & 0 \\ 0 & -1 \end{pmatrix}$ and use matrix multiplication to compute the matrix representing in the frame P the mapping $\eta\epsilon$. We have

$$\begin{pmatrix} 0 & 1 \\ -1 & 0 \end{pmatrix}\begin{pmatrix} 1 & 0 \\ 0 & -1 \end{pmatrix} = \begin{pmatrix} 0\cdot 1 + 1\cdot 0 & 0\cdot 0 + 1\cdot(-1) \\ (-1)\cdot 1 + 0\cdot 0 & (-1)\cdot 0 + 0\cdot(-1) \end{pmatrix}$$

$$= \begin{pmatrix} 0 & -1 \\ -1 & 0 \end{pmatrix}, \quad (34)$$

that is, in the light of (15),

$$\eta^P \epsilon^P = \delta^P. \quad (35)$$

Equation (35) is of course to be expected in view of 10^{53}

To compute the matrix representing the mapping $\beta\alpha$ when the matrices representing the mappings α and β are given to be (28), we consider the vectors $\alpha u = v$ and $\beta v = w$, where u is arbitrary, and express the components of w in terms of those of u. The desired matrix, denoted by $\beta\alpha$, turns out to be

$$\beta\alpha = \begin{pmatrix} \beta_{11}\alpha_{11} + \beta_{12}\alpha_{21} & \beta_{11}\alpha_{12} + \beta_{12}\alpha_{22} \\ \beta_{21}\alpha_{11} + \beta_{22}\alpha_{21} & \beta_{21}\alpha_{12} + \beta_{22}\alpha_{22} \end{pmatrix}; \tag{36}$$

this result could have been obtained directly from (31) by interchanging the symbols α and β, but leaving all the subscripts as they stand. According to the definition (32), the matrix (36) is just the matrix product $\beta\alpha$ of the matrices (28). Comparison of (36) with (31) shows that the matrices $\alpha\beta$ and $\beta\alpha$ are usually different from each other, so that matrix multiplication is in general noncommutative.

To illustrate: let us take from (15) the matrices η^P and ϵ^P, and compute the matrix representing in the frame P the mapping $\epsilon\eta$. We have

$$\begin{pmatrix} 1 & 0 \\ 0 & -1 \end{pmatrix}\begin{pmatrix} 0 & 1 \\ -1 & 0 \end{pmatrix} = \begin{pmatrix} 1\cdot 0 + 0\cdot(-1) & 1\cdot 1 + 0\cdot 0 \\ 0\cdot 0 + (-1)\cdot(-1) & 0\cdot 1 + (-1)\cdot 0 \end{pmatrix}$$

$$= \begin{pmatrix} 0 & 1 \\ 1 & 0 \end{pmatrix}, \tag{37}$$

and comparison with (34) shows that the matrices η^P and ϵ^P do not commute. Incidentally, according to (15), Equation (37) means that

$$\epsilon^P \eta^P = \gamma^P, \tag{38}$$

as is to be expected from 12^{53}.

Sums of operators. If the matrices representing two mappings α and β in some frame are (28), what matrix represents in the same frame the mapping $\alpha + \beta$? Now, according to 12^2, $\alpha + \beta$ is that mapping which sends any vector u into the sum of the vectors αu and βu, so that, if $(\alpha + \beta)u = v$, then $v = \alpha u + \beta u$; consequently

$$\begin{cases} v_1 = \alpha_{11}u_1 + \alpha_{12}u_2 + \beta_{11}u_1 + \beta_{12}u_2 \\ \qquad = (\alpha_{11} + \beta_{11})u_1 + (\alpha_{12} + \beta_{12})u_2 \\ v_2 = \alpha_{21}u_1 + \alpha_{22}u_2 + \beta_{21}u_1 + \beta_{22}u_2 \\ \qquad = (\alpha_{21} + \beta_{21})u_1 + (\alpha_{22} + \beta_{22})u_2 \end{cases} \tag{39}$$

and hence the desired matrix, which we shall denote by $\alpha + \beta$, is

$$\alpha + \beta = \begin{pmatrix} \alpha_{11} + \beta_{11} & \alpha_{12} + \beta_{12} \\ \alpha_{21} + \beta_{21} & \alpha_{22} + \beta_{22} \end{pmatrix}. \tag{40}$$

In algebra the *sum* of the matrices $\begin{pmatrix} a_{11} & a_{12} \\ a_{21} & a_{22} \end{pmatrix}$ and $\begin{pmatrix} b_{11} & b_{12} \\ b_{21} & b_{22} \end{pmatrix}$ is *defined* as the matrix written on the right side of the following matrix equation:

$$\begin{pmatrix} a_{11} & a_{12} \\ a_{21} & a_{22} \end{pmatrix} + \begin{pmatrix} b_{11} & b_{12} \\ b_{21} & b_{22} \end{pmatrix} = \begin{pmatrix} a_{11} + b_{11} & a_{12} + b_{12} \\ a_{21} + b_{21} & a_{22} + b_{22} \end{pmatrix}; \qquad (41)$$

the reader should carefully memorize the rule for matrix addition expressed by (41). Our result (40) can now be stated thus: the matrix representing the sum of the operators α and β is the sum of the matrices representing, respectively, the operators α and β. For example, according to (15), the matrix representing in the frame P the sum of our mappings γ and ξ is $\begin{pmatrix} 0 & 0 \\ 2 & 0 \end{pmatrix}$.

Representation of vectors by columns of numbers. In treating mappings by analytic methods, we found it convenient to represent them by square arrays of numbers, that is, by square matrices. A certain regularity is introduced into our formalism if we also agree, when listing the components of a vector, to arrange the components into a column. Thus, when working in some coordinate frame that is to be kept in mind, we shall write

$$u = \begin{pmatrix} u_1 \\ u_2 \end{pmatrix} \qquad (42)$$

instead of saying that the components of a vector u are u_1 and u_2 For example, we shall write

$$v = \begin{pmatrix} 1 \\ 3 \end{pmatrix} \qquad (43)$$

instead of saying that the components of the particular vector v with respect to the given frame are $v_1 = 1$ and $v_2 = 3$. Column symbols such as (42) and (43) are called *representatives* of our vectors; but for brevity we shall usually refer to column symbols simply as *vectors*.

We shall next set up rules for the manipulation of the column symbols. First of all, whenever $u = v$, we agree to write

$$\begin{pmatrix} u_1 \\ u_2 \end{pmatrix} = \begin{pmatrix} v_1 \\ v_2 \end{pmatrix}, \qquad (44)$$

so that (44) will imply the two equations

$$u_1 = v_1 , \qquad\qquad u_2 = v_2 , \qquad\qquad (45)$$

and conversely. Substituting the column symbols for u, v, and w into the equation $w = u + v$, we get

$$\begin{pmatrix} w_1 \\ w_2 \end{pmatrix} = \begin{pmatrix} u_1 \\ u_2 \end{pmatrix} + \begin{pmatrix} v_1 \\ v_2 \end{pmatrix}; \qquad\qquad (46)$$

now, if $w = u + v$, then $w_1 = u_1 + v_1$ and $w_2 = u_2 + v_2$; consequently, in order that (46) may imply the equation $w = u + v$, we must adopt the following rule for addition of our column symbols:

$$\begin{pmatrix} u_1 \\ u_2 \end{pmatrix} + \begin{pmatrix} v_1 \\ v_2 \end{pmatrix} = \begin{pmatrix} u_1 + v_1 \\ u_2 + v_2 \end{pmatrix}. \qquad\qquad (47)$$

Similarly, if $v = cu$, where c is a constant, a direct substitution of our new symbols yields

$$\begin{pmatrix} v_1 \\ v_2 \end{pmatrix} = c \begin{pmatrix} u_1 \\ u_2 \end{pmatrix}; \qquad\qquad (48)$$

now, if $v = cu$, then $v_1 = cu_1$ and $v_2 = cu_2$; consequently, in order that (48) may imply the equation $v = cu$, we must adopt the following rule for multiplying a column symbol by a constant:

$$c \begin{pmatrix} u_1 \\ u_2 \end{pmatrix} = \begin{pmatrix} cu_1 \\ cu_2 \end{pmatrix}. \qquad\qquad (49)$$

Finally, if $\alpha u = v$, the direct substitution of our symbols gives

$$\begin{pmatrix} \alpha_{11} & \alpha_{12} \\ \alpha_{21} & \alpha_{22} \end{pmatrix} \begin{pmatrix} u_1 \\ u_2 \end{pmatrix} = \begin{pmatrix} v_1 \\ v_2 \end{pmatrix}. \qquad\qquad (50)$$

But the equation $\alpha u = v$ means that v_1 and v_2 are related to u_1 and u_2 through Equations (18); hence, in order that (50) may be equivalent to $\alpha u = v$, we must adopt the rule

$$\begin{pmatrix} \alpha_{11} & \alpha_{12} \\ \alpha_{21} & \alpha_{22} \end{pmatrix} \begin{pmatrix} u_1 \\ u_2 \end{pmatrix} = \begin{pmatrix} \alpha_{11} u_1 + \alpha_{12} u_2 \\ \alpha_{21} u_1 + \alpha_{22} u_2 \end{pmatrix}. \qquad\qquad (51)$$

The rule (51) for the multiplication of a vector by a matrix resembles the rule (32) for the multiplication of a matrix by a matrix; the following diagram illustrates the computation of the entry in the second row of the right side of (51):

$$\begin{pmatrix} \cdots & \cdots \\ \alpha_{21} & \alpha_{22} \end{pmatrix}\begin{pmatrix} u_1 \\ u_2 \end{pmatrix} = \begin{pmatrix} \cdots \\ \alpha_{21}u_1 + \alpha_{22}u_2 \end{pmatrix}. \tag{52}$$

According to (9), any eigenvector u of our mapping γ, belonging to the eigenvalue 1 of γ, satisfies the equation $u_2^P/u_1^P = 1$, so that the vector

$$u = \begin{pmatrix} 1 \\ 1 \end{pmatrix}, \tag{53}$$

in the frame P, may be taken as a sample eigenvector of γ belonging to the eigenvalue 1. Multiplying (53) by γ^P from (15), we get

$$\begin{pmatrix} 0 & 1 \\ 1 & 0 \end{pmatrix}\begin{pmatrix} 1 \\ 1 \end{pmatrix} = \begin{pmatrix} 0 \cdot 1 + 1 \cdot 1 \\ 1 \cdot 1 + 0 \cdot 1 \end{pmatrix} = \begin{pmatrix} 1 \\ 1 \end{pmatrix}, \tag{54}$$

that is,

$$\begin{pmatrix} 0 & 1 \\ 1 & 0 \end{pmatrix}\begin{pmatrix} 1 \\ 1 \end{pmatrix} = 1\begin{pmatrix} 1 \\ 1 \end{pmatrix}; \tag{55}$$

Equation (55) means that operating on the vector (53) with the matrix γ^P is equivalent to multiplying (53) by the constant 1; Equation (55) thus restates that the vector (53), when the column symbol is interpreted in terms of the frame P, is an eigenvector of γ belonging to the eigenvalue 1. Similarly, according to (10), a sample eigenvector of γ belonging to the eigenvalue -1, when referred to the frame P, is $u = \begin{pmatrix} 1 \\ -1 \end{pmatrix}$; multiplying this vector by γ^P, we indeed get $\begin{pmatrix} 0 & 1 \\ 1 & 0 \end{pmatrix}\begin{pmatrix} 1 \\ -1 \end{pmatrix} = \begin{pmatrix} 0 \cdot 1 + 1 \cdot (-1) \\ 1 \cdot 1 + 0 \cdot (-1) \end{pmatrix} = \begin{pmatrix} -1 \\ 1 \end{pmatrix}$, that is, $\begin{pmatrix} 0 & 1 \\ 1 & 0 \end{pmatrix}\begin{pmatrix} 1 \\ -1 \end{pmatrix} = -1\begin{pmatrix} 1 \\ -1 \end{pmatrix}$.

The rules for the analytic treatment of mappings of a plane presented above will be presently extended to mapping of spaces of higher dimensionality.

Exercises

1. Show that a mapping consisting in multiplying every vector of a plane by a constant c is represented by the matrix $\begin{pmatrix} c & 0 \\ 0 & c \end{pmatrix}$, and justify

the following rule for the multiplication of a matrix by a constant:

$$c\begin{pmatrix} \alpha_{11} & \alpha_{12} \\ \alpha_{21} & \alpha_{22} \end{pmatrix} = \begin{pmatrix} c\alpha_{11} & c\alpha_{12} \\ c\alpha_{21} & c\alpha_{22} \end{pmatrix}.$$

2. Show that $\begin{pmatrix} 1 & 2 \\ -3 & -4 \end{pmatrix} + \begin{pmatrix} 7 & 5 \\ 8 & 6 \end{pmatrix} = \begin{pmatrix} 8 & 7 \\ 5 & 2 \end{pmatrix}$, $\begin{pmatrix} 1 & 2 \\ -3 & -4 \end{pmatrix}\begin{pmatrix} 7 & 5 \\ 8 & 6 \end{pmatrix} =$

$\begin{pmatrix} 23 & 17 \\ -53 & -39 \end{pmatrix}$, $\begin{pmatrix} 7 & 5 \\ 8 & 6 \end{pmatrix}\begin{pmatrix} 1 & 2 \\ -3 & -4 \end{pmatrix} = -2\begin{pmatrix} 4 & 3 \\ 5 & 4 \end{pmatrix}$, $\begin{pmatrix} 1 & 2 \\ -3 & -4 \end{pmatrix}\begin{pmatrix} 5 \\ 6 \end{pmatrix} =$

$\begin{pmatrix} 17 \\ -39 \end{pmatrix}$, and $\begin{pmatrix} 7 & 5 \\ 8 & 6 \end{pmatrix}\begin{pmatrix} 5 \\ 6 \end{pmatrix} = \begin{pmatrix} 65 \\ 76 \end{pmatrix}$.

3. Verify that the multiplication table of the matrices (15) is Table 11[53]

4. Use the matrices (15) and matrix algebra to verify the relations $(1 + \gamma)(1 - \gamma) = 0$, $(1 + \gamma)^2 = 2(1 + \gamma)$, $\epsilon\eta - \eta\epsilon = 2\gamma$, and $\epsilon\eta + \eta\epsilon = 0$ derived geometrically in Exercise 3^{53}.

5. Working in the frame P and using the matrices (15), show that, if

$$v = \begin{pmatrix} 1 \\ 4 \end{pmatrix}, \text{ then } \gamma v = \begin{pmatrix} 4 \\ 1 \end{pmatrix}, \ \delta v = \begin{pmatrix} -4 \\ -1 \end{pmatrix}, \ \epsilon v = \begin{pmatrix} 1 \\ -4 \end{pmatrix}, \ \zeta v = \begin{pmatrix} -1 \\ 4 \end{pmatrix},$$

$\eta v = \begin{pmatrix} 4 \\ -1 \end{pmatrix}$, and $\xi v = \begin{pmatrix} -4 \\ 1 \end{pmatrix}$, where the mappings are those of Fig. 85.

6. Use the matrices (15) to investigate analytically the eigenvalues and eigenvectors of the mappings of Fig. 85, and verify Table 12.

7. Show that the two eigenrays of every one of the mappings of Table 12 are orthogonal. Show that the length of each of the particular eigenvectors of γ, δ, η, and ξ listed in this table is $\sqrt{2}$.

8. A certain mapping σ of the plane is represented in the frame P by the matrix $\begin{pmatrix} 1.04 & .72 \\ .72 & 1.46 \end{pmatrix}$. Show analytically that the eigenvalues of σ are .5 and 2.0, and that sample eigenvectors of σ, belonging, respectively, to these eigenvalues, can be represented in the frame P by $\begin{pmatrix} .8 \\ -.6 \end{pmatrix}$ and $\begin{pmatrix} .6 \\ .8 \end{pmatrix}$. Note the orthogonality of the eigenrays of σ.

Draw graphs of a unit circle and of the ellipse into which σ sends this circle; note that the axes of the ellipse lie on the eigenrays of σ.

TABLE 12

Mapping	Eigenvalue	Sample eigenvector (frame P)	Eigenvalue	Sample eigenvector (frame P)
γ	1	$\begin{pmatrix} 1 \\ 1 \end{pmatrix}$	-1	$\begin{pmatrix} 1 \\ -1 \end{pmatrix}$
δ	1	$\begin{pmatrix} 1 \\ -1 \end{pmatrix}$	-1	$\begin{pmatrix} 1 \\ 1 \end{pmatrix}$
ϵ	1	$\begin{pmatrix} 1 \\ 0 \end{pmatrix}$	-1	$\begin{pmatrix} 0 \\ 1 \end{pmatrix}$
ζ	1	$\begin{pmatrix} 0 \\ 1 \end{pmatrix}$	-1	$\begin{pmatrix} 1 \\ 0 \end{pmatrix}$
η	i	$\begin{pmatrix} 1 \\ i \end{pmatrix}$	$-i$	$\begin{pmatrix} 1 \\ -i \end{pmatrix}$
ξ	i	$\begin{pmatrix} 1 \\ -i \end{pmatrix}$	$-i$	$\begin{pmatrix} 1 \\ i \end{pmatrix}$

9. A certain mapping ρ of the plane is represented in the frame P by the matrix $\begin{pmatrix} 2.5 & 1.0 \\ 2.0 & 1.5 \end{pmatrix}$. Show analytically that the eigenvalues of ρ are .5 and 3.5, and that the corresponding eigenrays of ρ are not orthogonal.

Draw graphs of a unit circle and of the ellipse into which ρ sends this circle; note that the axes of the ellipse do not lie on the eigenrays of ρ.

55. Different Coordinate Frames May Yield Different Representatives for a Given Operator

The matrices representing the eight mappings of Fig. 85 were computed in §54 with reference to the particular frame P of Fig. 87; to illustrate that the representatives of mappings, as well as of vectors, may be different in different coordinate frames, we shall now make some computations using the frame Q, shown in Fig. 91, whose axes Q_1 and Q_2 are supposed to lie along the

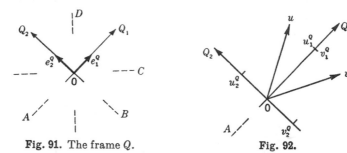

Fig. 91. The frame Q.   Fig. 92.

lines A and B of Fig. 86; the basic unit vectors of this frame will be denoted by e_1^Q and e_2^Q. Any vector u in the plane can be resolved in terms of e_1^Q and e_2^Q, the numbers u_1^Q and u_2^Q in

$$u = u_1^Q e_1^Q + u_2^Q e_2^Q \tag{1}$$

being the components of u with respect to the frame Q.

Let us consider first the relations between the components u_1^Q and u_2^Q of an arbitrary vector u, and the components v_1^Q and v_2^Q of the vector $v = \gamma u$, that is, the vector into which our mapping γ sends the vector u, γ being the reflection of the plane in the line A. As seen from Fig. 92, $v_1^Q = u_1^Q$ and $v_2^Q = -u_2^Q$, that is,

$$\begin{cases} v_1^Q = 1 \cdot u_1^Q + 0 \cdot u_2^Q \\ v_2^Q = 0 \cdot u_1^Q - 1 \cdot u_2^Q. \end{cases} \tag{2}$$

Consequently the matrix that represents γ in the frame Q and that we denote by γ^Q is

$$\gamma^Q = \begin{pmatrix} 1 & 0 \\ 0 & -1 \end{pmatrix}. \tag{3}$$

This matrix is different from the matrix γ^P representing γ in the frame P; it is, as we might expect, the same as ϵ^P.

Next, let us calculate the eigenvalues of γ, using the frame Q. If u is an eigenvector of γ, so that $v = \gamma u = \lambda u$, then $v_1^Q = \lambda u_1^Q$ and $v_2^Q = \lambda u_2^Q$, and (2) becomes

$$\begin{cases} (1 - \lambda)u_1^Q + 0 \cdot u_2^Q = 0 \\ 0 \cdot u_1^Q + (-1 - \lambda)u_2^Q = 0. \end{cases} \tag{4}$$

Equations (4) have solutions other than $u_1^Q = u_2^Q = 0$ if and only if the determinant of their coefficients vanishes, that is, if and only if

$$\begin{vmatrix} (1 - \lambda) & 0 \\ 0 & (-1 - \lambda) \end{vmatrix} = 0. \tag{5}$$

The solutions of (5) are $\lambda = \pm 1$, and hence the eigenvalues of our γ are 1 and -1, in agreement with 8^{54} and with the geometric conclusions of §53.

The reader will have made a long step toward understanding the discussion which is to follow if he remembers that the eigenvalues of a mapping are intrinsic attributes of the mapping itself, and that, consequently, whatever procedure may be adopted in an analytic computation (for example, whatever coordinate frame may be used in representing the mapping by a matrix), the results of the computation of the eigenvalues of a given mapping should be quite the same.

Finally, let us compute the eigenrays of γ, using the frame Q. Setting $\lambda = 1$ in (4), we find that the slope u_2^Q/u_1^Q, relative to the frame Q, of the eigenray of γ belonging to the eigenvalue 1 is 0; this eigenray consequently coincides with the Q_1-axis and is the ray A, first identified in §53. Treating the case $\lambda = -1$ in a similar way, we find that the following column symbols represent, in the frame Q, sample eigenvectors of γ:

$$\lambda = 1, \quad u = \begin{pmatrix} 1 \\ 0 \end{pmatrix}; \qquad \lambda = -1, \quad u = \begin{pmatrix} 0 \\ 1 \end{pmatrix}. \tag{6}$$

The column symbols referring to the frame Q and representing the particular sample eigenvectors of γ that are listed in Table 12 are obtained by multiplying the column symbols given in (6) by $\sqrt{2}$; the resulting symbols are, as we might expect, different from the corresponding symbols listed in Table 12 and referring to the frame P.

The eigenvectors of a mapping are intrinsic attributes of the mapping itself, and hence, whatever analytic method may be adopted in computing the eigenvectors of a given mapping, the results should be the same; but the column symbol representing an eigenvector is usually different for different coordinate frames.

Exercises

1. Show that the following matrices represent the mappings of Fig. 85 in the frame Q, and compare them with 15[54]:

$$1^Q = \begin{pmatrix} 1 & 0 \\ 0 & 1 \end{pmatrix}, \quad \gamma^Q = \begin{pmatrix} 1 & 0 \\ 0 & -1 \end{pmatrix}, \quad \delta^Q = \begin{pmatrix} -1 & 0 \\ 0 & 1 \end{pmatrix}, \quad \epsilon^Q = \begin{pmatrix} 0 & -1 \\ -1 & 0 \end{pmatrix}$$

$$\zeta^Q = \begin{pmatrix} 0 & 1 \\ 1 & 0 \end{pmatrix}, \quad \eta^Q = \begin{pmatrix} 0 & 1 \\ -1 & 0 \end{pmatrix}, \quad \xi^Q = \begin{pmatrix} 0 & -1 \\ 1 & 0 \end{pmatrix}, \quad -1^Q = \begin{pmatrix} -1 & 0 \\ 0 & -1 \end{pmatrix}. \tag{7}$$

2. Verify that the multiplication table of the matrices (7) is Table 11.

3. Work out Exercise 4[54], using (7) rather than 15[54].

4. Use the matrices (7) to investigate analytically the eigenvalues and eigenvectors of the mappings of Fig. 85; verify Table 13 and compare it with Table 12.

5. Show that a counterclockwise rotation of a real plane through the angle ϕ about O is represented in every (real) coordinate frame by the matrix

$$\begin{pmatrix} \cos\phi & -\sin\phi \\ \sin\phi & \cos\phi \end{pmatrix}.$$

TABLE 13

Mapping	Eigenvalue	Sample eigen-vector (frame Q)	Eigenvalue	Sample eigen-vector (frame Q)
γ	1	$\begin{pmatrix} 1 \\ 0 \end{pmatrix}$	-1	$\begin{pmatrix} 0 \\ 1 \end{pmatrix}$
δ	1	$\begin{pmatrix} 0 \\ 1 \end{pmatrix}$	-1	$\begin{pmatrix} 1 \\ 0 \end{pmatrix}$
ϵ	1	$\begin{pmatrix} 1 \\ -1 \end{pmatrix}$	-1	$\begin{pmatrix} 1 \\ 1 \end{pmatrix}$
ζ	1	$\begin{pmatrix} 1 \\ 1 \end{pmatrix}$	-1	$\begin{pmatrix} 1 \\ -1 \end{pmatrix}$
η	i	$\begin{pmatrix} 1 \\ i \end{pmatrix}$	$-i$	$\begin{pmatrix} 1 \\ -i \end{pmatrix}$
ξ	i	$\begin{pmatrix} 1 \\ -i \end{pmatrix}$	$-i$	$\begin{pmatrix} 1 \\ i \end{pmatrix}$

56. Matrices and Vectors

In §54, while systematizing the algebraic procedure for the study of mappings of a plane, we introduced matrices such as $\begin{pmatrix} \alpha_{11} & \alpha_{12} \\ \alpha_{21} & \alpha_{22} \end{pmatrix}$, $\begin{pmatrix} \beta_{11} & \beta_{12} \\ \beta_{21} & \beta_{22} \end{pmatrix}$, and so on, and column symbols, or vectors, such as $\begin{pmatrix} u_1 \\ u_2 \end{pmatrix}$, $\begin{pmatrix} v_1 \\ v_2 \end{pmatrix}$, and so on, and evolved certain rules for combining such arrays with one another. We shall now state the rudiments of the algebra of arrays of a more general kind. Our definitions and rules will be direct generalizations of those of §54, and the numbers at the left of some of the formulas below will refer to the corresponding formulas of §54. In the next section we shall show how a helpful quasi-geometric significance can be read into the algebraic steps of this section.

Arrays of numbers such as

$$\alpha = \begin{pmatrix} \alpha_{11} & \alpha_{12} & \cdots & \alpha_{1N} \\ \alpha_{21} & \alpha_{22} & \cdots & \alpha_{2N} \\ & & \cdots & \\ \alpha_{N1} & \alpha_{N2} & \cdots & \alpha_{NN} \end{pmatrix}, \quad \beta = \begin{pmatrix} \beta_{11} & \beta_{12} & \cdots & \beta_{1N} \\ \beta_{21} & \beta_{22} & \cdots & \beta_{2N} \\ & & \cdots & \\ \beta_{N1} & \beta_{N2} & \cdots & \beta_{NN} \end{pmatrix}, \quad (1)$$

and so forth, are called *square matrices* of N rows and N columns, *N-by-N matrices*, or simply *matrices*, and are usually denoted by single letters, as in (1). The N^2 individual numerical entries comprising a matrix α are called *elements* or *components* of α; the element α_{nm} of α, that is, the element in the nth row and mth column of α, is called the nmth element of α; the range of each of the subscripts occurring in this section will be 1, 2, $\cdots$, N, and all matrices considered below will have the same N.

If (and only if) all of the corresponding elements of two matrices α and β are equal, that is, if

$$\alpha_{nm} = \beta_{nm} \qquad (2)$$

for all values of n and m, we write

$$\alpha = \beta \qquad (3)$$

and say that the matrices α and β are equal to each other. The symbolic equation (3) is essentially an abbreviation for the N^2 equations (2).

The rule for adding two matrices is:

$$\begin{pmatrix} \alpha_{11} & \alpha_{12} & \cdots & \alpha_{1N} \\ \alpha_{21} & \alpha_{22} & \cdots & \alpha_{2N} \\ & & \cdots & \\ \alpha_{N1} & \alpha_{N2} & \cdots & \alpha_{NN} \end{pmatrix} + \begin{pmatrix} \beta_{11} & \beta_{12} & \cdots & \beta_{1N} \\ \beta_{21} & \beta_{22} & \cdots & \beta_{2N} \\ & & \cdots & \\ \beta_{N1} & \beta_{N2} & \cdots & \beta_{NN} \end{pmatrix}$$

$$= \begin{pmatrix} \alpha_{11} + \beta_{11} & \alpha_{12} + \beta_{12} & \cdots & \alpha_{1N} + \beta_{1N} \\ \alpha_{21} + \beta_{21} & \alpha_{22} + \beta_{22} & \cdots & \alpha_{2N} + \beta_{2N} \\ & & \cdots & \\ \alpha_{N1} + \beta_{N1} & \alpha_{N2} + \beta_{N2} & \cdots & \alpha_{NN} + \beta_{NN} \end{pmatrix}. \quad (4)$$

The matrix on the right side of (4) is called the *sum* of the matrices α and β, and is denoted by $\alpha + \beta$; thus we have the N^2 relations

$$(\alpha + \beta)_{nm} = \alpha_{nm} + \beta_{nm}, \quad (5)$$

where $(\alpha + \beta)_{nm}$ is the nmth element of the matrix $\alpha + \beta$.

The rule for multiplying a matrix α by a constant c is:

$$c \begin{pmatrix} \alpha_{11} & \alpha_{12} & \cdots & \alpha_{1N} \\ \alpha_{21} & \alpha_{22} & \cdots & \alpha_{2N} \\ & & \cdots & \\ \alpha_{N1} & \alpha_{N2} & \cdots & \alpha_{NN} \end{pmatrix} = \begin{pmatrix} c\alpha_{11} & c\alpha_{12} & \cdots & c\alpha_{1N} \\ c\alpha_{21} & c\alpha_{22} & \cdots & c\alpha_{2N} \\ & & \cdots & \\ c\alpha_{N1} & c\alpha_{N2} & \cdots & c\alpha_{NN} \end{pmatrix}. \quad (6)$$

The matrix on the right side of (6) is called the *product* of the matrix α and the constant c, and is denoted by $c\alpha$; thus we have the N^2 relations

$$(c\alpha)_{nm} = c\alpha_{nm}, \quad (7)$$

where $(c\alpha)_{nm}$ is the nmth element of the matrix $c\alpha$.

The rule for multiplying a matrix β from the left by a matrix α is:

$$\begin{pmatrix} \alpha_{11} & \alpha_{12} & \cdots & \alpha_{1N} \\ \alpha_{21} & \alpha_{22} & \cdots & \alpha_{2N} \\ & & \cdots & \\ \alpha_{N1} & \alpha_{N2} & \cdots & \alpha_{NN} \end{pmatrix} \cdot \begin{pmatrix} \beta_{11} & \beta_{12} & \cdots & \beta_{1N} \\ \beta_{21} & \beta_{22} & \cdots & \beta_{2N} \\ & & \cdots & \\ \beta_{N1} & \beta_{N2} & \cdots & \beta_{NN} \end{pmatrix}$$

$$= \begin{pmatrix} \sum \alpha_{1i}\beta_{i1} & \sum \alpha_{1i}\beta_{i2} & \cdots & \sum \alpha_{1i}\beta_{iN} \\ \sum \alpha_{2i}\beta_{i1} & \sum \alpha_{2i}\beta_{i2} & \cdots & \sum \alpha_{2i}\beta_{iN} \\ & & \cdots & \\ \sum \alpha_{Ni}\beta_{i1} & \sum \alpha_{Ni}\beta_{i2} & \cdots & \sum \alpha_{Ni}\beta_{iN} \end{pmatrix}, \quad (8)$$

where the summation index i runs through the values $1, 2, \cdots, N$. The matrix on the right side of (8) is called the *product* $\alpha\beta$ of the matrices α and β, and is denoted by $\alpha\beta$; thus we have the N^2 relations

$$(\alpha\beta)_{nm} = \sum_i \alpha_{ni}\beta_{im}, \quad i = 1, 2, \cdots, N, \quad (9)$$

where $(\alpha\beta)_{nm}$ is the nmth element of the matrix $\alpha\beta$.

Interchanging α and β in (8), we get

$$\begin{pmatrix} \beta_{11} & \beta_{12} & \cdots & \beta_{1N} \\ \beta_{21} & \beta_{22} & \cdots & \beta_{2N} \\ & \cdots & \\ \beta_{N1} & \beta_{N2} & \cdots & \beta_{NN} \end{pmatrix} \begin{pmatrix} \alpha_{11} & \alpha_{12} & \cdots & \alpha_{1N} \\ \alpha_{21} & \alpha_{22} & \cdots & \alpha_{2N} \\ & \cdots & \\ \alpha_{N1} & \alpha_{N2} & \cdots & \alpha_{NN} \end{pmatrix}$$

$$= \begin{pmatrix} \sum \beta_{1i}\alpha_{i1} & \sum \beta_{1i}\alpha_{i2} & \cdots & \sum \beta_{1i}\alpha_{iN} \\ \sum \beta_{2i}\alpha_{i1} & \sum \beta_{2i}\alpha_{i2} & \cdots & \sum \beta_{2i}\alpha_{iN} \\ & \cdots & \\ \sum \beta_{Ni}\alpha_{i1} & \sum \beta_{Ni}\alpha_{i2} & \cdots & \sum \beta_{Ni}\alpha_{iN} \end{pmatrix} \quad (10)$$

The matrix on the right side of (10) is called the *product $\beta\alpha$* of the matrices α and β, and is denoted by $\beta\alpha$; thus we have

$$(\beta\alpha)_{nm} = \sum_i \beta_{ni}\alpha_{im}, \qquad i = 1, 2, \cdots, N. \quad (11)$$

Comparison of (8) and (10) shows that the matrices $\alpha\beta$ and $\beta\alpha$ are in general not equal to each other, so that matrix multiplication is usually noncommutative.

Single-file arrays of numbers such as

$$u = \begin{pmatrix} u_1 \\ u_2 \\ \cdots \\ u_N \end{pmatrix}, \qquad v = \begin{pmatrix} v_1 \\ v_2 \\ \cdots \\ v_N \end{pmatrix}, \quad (12)$$

and so on, are called *column symbols, N-vectors*, or simply *vectors* (strictly, they are matrices of N rows and one column), and are usually denoted by single letters, as in (12). The N individual numerical entries comprising a vector u are called *components* of u; the component u_k, that is, the entry in the kth row of u, is called the kth component of u; all vectors considered below will have the same N, this N being equal to that of the matrices discussed above. The N-vector whose N components are all zeros is called the vector *zero* and is denoted by 0. The number

(26[54]) $$\sum_i u_i^* u_i, \qquad i = 1, 2, \cdots, N, \quad (13)$$

where u_i^* is the complex conjugate of u_i, is called the *square of the length* of the vector u. If

$$(27^{54}) \qquad \sum_i u_i^* v_i = 0, \qquad i = 1, 2, \cdots, N, \quad (14)$$

the vectors u and v are said to be *orthogonal*.

If (and only if) all of the corresponding components of two vectors u and v are equal, that is, if

$$u_k = v_k \tag{15}$$

for all values of k, we write

$$u = v \tag{16}$$

and say that the vectors u and v are equal to each other. The symbolic equation (16) is essentially an abbreviation for the N equations (15).

The rule for adding two vectors is:

$$(47^{54}) \qquad \begin{pmatrix} u_1 \\ u_2 \\ \cdots \\ u_N \end{pmatrix} + \begin{pmatrix} v_1 \\ v_2 \\ \cdots \\ v_N \end{pmatrix} = \begin{pmatrix} u_1 + v_1 \\ u_2 + v_2 \\ \cdots \\ u_N + v_N \end{pmatrix}. \tag{17}$$

The vector on the right side of (17) is called the *sum* of the vectors u and v, and is denoted by $u + v$; thus we have the N relations

$$(u + v)_k = u_k + v_k, \tag{18}$$

where $(u + v)_k$ is the kth component of the vector $u + v$.

The rule for multiplying a vector u by a constant c is:

$$(49^{54}) \qquad c \begin{pmatrix} u_1 \\ u_2 \\ \cdots \\ u_N \end{pmatrix} = \begin{pmatrix} cu_1 \\ cu_2 \\ \cdots \\ cu_N \end{pmatrix}. \tag{19}$$

The vector on the right side of (19) is called the *product* of the vector u and the constant c, and is denoted by cu; thus we have the N relations

$$(cu)_k = cu_k, \tag{20}$$

where $(cu)_k$ is the kth component of the vector cu. The totality of vectors of the form cu, where u is a fixed nonvanishing vector and the constant c (which is allowed to be complex) varies from vector to vector, is said to form a *ray*.

Finally, the rule for multiplying a vector u by a matrix α is:

$$(51^{54}) \quad \begin{pmatrix} \alpha_{11} & \alpha_{12} & \cdots & \alpha_{1N} \\ \alpha_{21} & \alpha_{22} & \cdots & \alpha_{2N} \\ & & \cdots & \\ \alpha_{N1} & \alpha_{N2} & \cdots & \alpha_{NN} \end{pmatrix} \cdot \begin{pmatrix} u_1 \\ u_2 \\ \cdots \\ u_N \end{pmatrix} = \begin{pmatrix} \sum \alpha_{1i} u_i \\ \sum \alpha_{2i} u_i \\ \cdots \\ \sum \alpha_{Ni} u_i \end{pmatrix}, \qquad (21)$$

where the summation index i runs through the values $1, 2, \cdots, N$. The vector on the right side of (21) is denoted by αu; thus we have the N relations

$$(\alpha u)_k = \sum_i \alpha_{ki} u_i, \qquad\qquad i = 1, 2, \cdots, N, \quad (22)$$

where $(\alpha u)_k$ is the kth component of the vector αu.

In the first column of the accompanying table we list the fundamental symbolic equations that may hold between N-by-N matrices α, β, and so on, and N-vectors u, v, and so on; the second column gives the sets of numerical equations that the respective symbolic equations imply according to the definitions given above; the number of numerical equations in a set is given in the third column. The summation indices i run through the values $1, 2, \cdots, N$; it is of course immaterial what letter, not employed otherwise, is used for a summation index. The rules (23) to (31) apply also when N is infinite, that is, when the matrices have an infinite number of rows and columns and the vectors have an infinite number of rows.

$\alpha = \beta$	$\alpha_{nm} = \beta_{nm}$	N^2	(23)
$\gamma = \alpha + \beta$	$\gamma_{nm} = \alpha_{nm} + \beta_{nm}$	N^2	(24)
$\beta = c\alpha$	$\beta_{nm} = c\alpha_{nm}$	N^2	(25)
$\gamma = \alpha\beta$	$\gamma_{nm} = \sum_i \alpha_{ni}\beta_{im}$	N^2	(26)
$\delta = \beta\alpha$	$\delta_{nm} = \sum_i \beta_{ni}\alpha_{im}$	N^2	(27)
$u = v$	$u_k = v_k$	N	(28)
$w = u + v$	$w_k = u_k + v_k$	N	(29)
$v = cu$	$v_k = cu_k$	N	(30)
$v = \alpha u$	$v_k = \sum_i \alpha_{ki} u_i$	N	(31)

Repeated applications of these rules lead to the identification of more complicated combinations of matrices and vectors. For example, in the case of the matrix

$$(\alpha\beta)\gamma \tag{32}$$

(that is, the product, in the given order, of the matrices $\alpha\beta$ and γ), we have according to (9)

$$[(\alpha\beta)\gamma]_{nm} = \sum_i (\alpha\beta)_{ni}\gamma_{im} , \tag{33}$$

where $[(\alpha\beta)\gamma]_{nm}$ is the nmth component of $(\alpha\beta)\gamma$; now, again according to (9), $(\alpha\beta)_{ni} = \sum_j \alpha_{nj}\beta_{ji}$, so that we finally get

$$[(\alpha\beta)\gamma]_{nm} = \sum_j \sum_i \alpha_{nj}\beta_{ji}\gamma_{im} . \tag{34}$$

Similarly, in the case of the matrix

$$\alpha(\beta\gamma) \tag{35}$$

(that is, the product, in the given order, of the matrices α and $\beta\gamma$) we have

$$[\alpha(\beta\gamma)]_{nm} = \sum_j \alpha_{nj}(\beta\gamma)_{jm} , \tag{36}$$

or, since $(\beta\gamma)_{jm} = \sum_i \beta_{ji}\gamma_{im}$,

$$[\alpha(\beta\gamma)]_{nm} = \sum_j \sum_i \alpha_{nj}\beta_{ji}\gamma_{im} . \tag{37}$$

Comparison of (34) and (37) shows that

$$(\alpha\beta)\gamma = \alpha(\beta\gamma), \tag{38}$$

and hence matrix multiplication is said to be associative (Exercise 7[53]). This result enables us, in particular, to use without ambiguity the symbol $\alpha\beta\gamma$ for the product, in the given order, of three matrices α, β, and γ, and to write

$$\alpha\beta\gamma = (\alpha\beta)\gamma = \alpha(\beta\gamma), \tag{39}$$

it being immaterial which of the two interpretations is given to the symbol $\alpha\beta\gamma$. Similarly, the vectors $\alpha(\beta u)$ and $(\alpha\beta)u$ are equal to each other, so that the symbol $\alpha\beta u$ can be used without ambiguity:

$$\alpha\beta u = \alpha(\beta u) = (\alpha\beta)u. \tag{40}$$

The k N-vectors u_I , u_{II} , $\cdots$, $u_{(k)}$ are said to be *linearly independent* if it is impossible to choose k constants c_1 , c_2 , $\cdots$, c_k , not all of which are zeros, in such a way as to satisfy the equation $c_1 u_I + c_2 u_{II} + \cdots + c_k u_{(k)} = 0$, where 0 denotes the N-vector zero; otherwise the k vectors are said to be *linearly dependent*.

The matrices on the one hand and the vectors on the other are treated in our algebra as entities of essentially different kinds; thus, the addition of a vector to a matrix is not provided for; also, although we have a rule for multiplying a vector from the left by a matrix (that is, a rule for interpreting the symbol αu), we have no rule for multiplying a matrix from the left by a vector, so that a symbol such as $u\alpha$ is meaningless. In fact, the distinction that our algebra makes between matrices and vectors is just the distinction between operators and operands. Accordingly, in the study of the interplay between matrices and vectors it is convenient to regard *matrices* as *operators* and *vectors* as their *operands*, and to interpret the equation

$$(31) \qquad\qquad \alpha u = v \qquad\qquad (41)$$

as meaning that the matrix α, when operating on the vector u, sends it into the vector v. We shall leave it as an exercise for the reader to prove that the rules (23) to (31) are entirely consistent with an operator-operand interpretation of matrices and vectors, that is, that these rules define equality, sums, and products in a manner consistent with the definitions of equality, sums, and products which we adopted in §2 while discussing operators and operands.

Eigenvalues and eigenvectors of matrices. If a matrix α and a nonvanishing vector u are so related that

$$\alpha u = \lambda u, \qquad\qquad (42)$$

where λ is a number (that is, if u, when operated on by α, is sent into a numerical multiple of itself), then u is said to be an *eigenvector* of the matrix α, λ is said to be an *eigenvalue* of the matrix α, and the eigenvector u and the eigenvalue λ of α are said to belong to each other. If u is an eigenvector of α belonging to the eigenvalue λ, then the ray cu is called an *eigenray* of α belonging to the eigenvalue λ.

For example, if we multiply the vector $u = \begin{pmatrix} 1 \\ 2 \\ 2 \end{pmatrix}$ by the matrix

$$\rho = \begin{pmatrix} 11 & -6 & 2 \\ -6 & 10 & -4 \\ 2 & -4 & 6 \end{pmatrix} \qquad\qquad (43)$$

we get according to (21)

$$\rho u = \begin{pmatrix} 11 & -6 & 2 \\ -6 & 10 & -4 \\ 2 & -4 & 6 \end{pmatrix} \begin{pmatrix} 1 \\ 2 \\ 2 \end{pmatrix} = \begin{pmatrix} 11 \cdot 1 - 6 \cdot 2 + 2 \cdot 2 \\ -6 \cdot 1 + 10 \cdot 2 - 4 \cdot 2 \\ 2 \cdot 1 - 4 \cdot 2 + 6 \cdot 2 \end{pmatrix} = \begin{pmatrix} 3 \\ 6 \\ 6 \end{pmatrix} = 3 \begin{pmatrix} 1 \\ 2 \\ 2 \end{pmatrix} \quad (44)$$

and hence

$$\rho u = 3u. \quad (45)$$

The vector $\begin{pmatrix} 1 \\ 2 \\ 2 \end{pmatrix}$ is consequently an eigenvector of the matrix ρ, the corre-

sponding eigenvalue of ρ being 3; and the ray $c \begin{pmatrix} 1 \\ 2 \\ 2 \end{pmatrix}$ is the eigenray of ρ

belonging to the eigenvalue 3.

The procedure for computing the eigenvalues of a given matrix is as follows: According to (28) the symbolic equation (42) is an abbreviation for the N numerical equations $(\alpha v)_k = (\lambda u)_k$, that is, [see (31) and (30)] for the N equations $\sum \alpha_{ki} u_i = \lambda u_k$ or $\sum \alpha_{ki} u_i - \lambda u_k = 0$, which, when written out in detail, are

$$\begin{cases} (\alpha_{11} - \lambda)u_1 + \alpha_{12}u_2 + \cdots + \alpha_{1N}u_N = 0 \\ \alpha_{21}u_1 + (\alpha_{22} - \lambda)u_2 + \cdots + \alpha_{2N}u_N = 0 \\ \cdots\cdots\cdots\cdots\cdots\cdots\cdots\cdots\cdots\cdots\cdots\cdots\cdots \\ \alpha_{N1}u_1 + \alpha_{N2}u_2 + \cdots + (\alpha_{NN} - \lambda)u_N = 0. \end{cases} \quad (46)$$

In order that the system (46) have solutions other than the trivial $u_1 = u_2 = \cdots = u_N = 0$, it is necessary and sufficient that the determinant of the coefficients vanish, that is, that

$$\begin{vmatrix} (\alpha_{11} - \lambda) & \alpha_{12} & \cdots & \alpha_{1N} \\ \alpha_{21} & (\alpha_{22} - \lambda) & \cdots & \alpha_{2N} \\ & \cdots & & \\ \alpha_{N1} & \alpha_{N2} & \cdots & (\alpha_{NN} - \lambda) \end{vmatrix} = 0. \quad (47)$$

Now, besides the preassigned quantities α_{nm}, Equation (47) involves only the parameter λ, so that (42) has nontrivial solutions if and only if λ satisfies (47). Equation (47)—an equation of the Nth degree in the parameter λ—is called the *secular equation* of the matrix α, and we have the result: the eigenvalues of a matrix are the roots of the secular equation of the matrix. Note that the computation of the eigenvalues of a given matrix can be carried out directly through the secular equation (47), and without reference to the defining equation (42).

For example, the eigenvalues of the matrix (43) are defined to be those values of λ for which the equation $\rho u = \lambda u$, that is,

$$\begin{pmatrix} 11 & -6 & 2 \\ -6 & 10 & -4 \\ 2 & -4 & 6 \end{pmatrix} \begin{pmatrix} u_1 \\ u_2 \\ u_3 \end{pmatrix} = \lambda \begin{pmatrix} u_1 \\ u_2 \\ u_3 \end{pmatrix}, \tag{48}$$

holds (u_1, u_2, and u_3, at least one of which is required to be different from zero, are then the components of an eigenvector of ρ belonging to the eigenvalue λ of ρ); however, to compute the eigenvalues of ρ we need not write down Equation (48), but may turn directly to the secular equation (47), which in the case of the matrix ρ is

$$\begin{vmatrix} (11 - \lambda) & -6 & 2 \\ -6 & (10 - \lambda) & -4 \\ 2 & -4 & (6 - \lambda) \end{vmatrix} = 0, \tag{49}$$

that is, $(11 - \lambda) \cdot (10 - \lambda) \cdot (6 - \lambda) + (-6) \cdot (-4) \cdot 2 + (-6) \cdot (-4) \cdot 2 - 2 \cdot (10 - \lambda) \cdot 2 - (-6) \cdot (-6) \cdot (6 - \lambda) - (11 - \lambda) \cdot (-4) \cdot (-4) = 0$, or simply

$$-\lambda^3 + 27\lambda^2 - 180\lambda + 324 = 0. \tag{50}$$

The roots of (50) are $\lambda_1 = 3$, $\lambda_2 = 6$, and $\lambda_3 = 18$, so that the matrix ρ has just three eigenvalues: 3, 6, and 18. For no other values of λ is it possible to find three numbers u_1, u_2, and u_3 which satisfy (48) and which are not all zero.

The following example will illustrate the procedure for computing the eigenrays of a matrix.

Let it be required to find the eigenray of our matrix ρ belonging to the eigenvalue 3 of ρ. Equation (48), when written in the detailed form (46), yields

$$(11 - \lambda)u_1 - 6u_2 + 2u_3 = 0$$
$$-6u_1 + (10 - \lambda)u_2 - 4u_3 = 0 \tag{51}$$
$$2u_1 - 4u_2 + (6 - \lambda)u_3 = 0$$

so that for $\lambda = 3$ we get

$$8u_1 - 6u_2 + 2u_3 = 0$$
$$-6u_1 + 7u_2 - 4u_3 = 0 \tag{52}$$
$$2u_1 - 4u_2 + 3u_3 = 0.$$

The determinant of the coefficients of this set of three simultaneous linear homogeneous equations in three unknowns is known to be zero because of the special choice of λ, and hence the set has nontrivial solutions. If u_1, u_2, and u_3 satisfy (52), then au_1, au_2, and au_3 also satisfy it, whatever the value of the constant a may be; consequently we may ascribe an arbitrary value to one of the u's, for example, let $u_1 = c$. Equations (52) then become

$$-6u_2 + 2u_3 = -8c$$
$$7u_2 - 4u_3 = 6c \tag{53}$$
$$-4u_2 + 3u_3 = -2c,$$

that is, a set of three linear inhomogeneous equations in two unknowns The consistency of these equations is assured, and we may restrict ourselves to just two of them, say the first and the second:

$$-6u_2 + 2u_3 = -8c$$
$$7u_2 - 4u_3 = 6c. \tag{54}$$

We now have a set of two inhomogeneous equations in two unknowns' Since the determinant of the coefficients of (54) is not zero, the set has one and only one solution, which is readily found to be $u_2 = 2c$ and $u_3 = 2c$; as a check, we verify that $u_2 = 2c$ and $u_3 = 2c$ satisfy the third equation in (53). The components of an eigenvector of ρ belonging to the eigenvalue 3 are consequently $u_1 = c$, $u_2 = 2c$, and $u_3 = 2c$, and the eigenray of ρ belonging to the eigenvalue 3 is

$$c \begin{pmatrix} 1 \\ 2 \\ 2 \end{pmatrix}, \tag{55}$$

that is, the ray first mentioned just below (45).

Any two eigenvectors of our matrix ρ belonging to the eigenvalue 3 differ from each other at most through a multiplicative constant and are consequently linearly dependent; for this reason the eigenvalue 3 of ρ is said to be *nondegenerate*. If every $n + 1$ but not every n eigenvectors of a matrix α belonging to the eigenvalue λ of α are linearly dependent, the eigenvalue λ is said to be *n-fold degenerate*, or to be of *multiplicity n*; an example of degeneracy will be given in Exercise 6. According to the theory of simultaneous linear equations, the maximum number of linearly independent eigenvectors that may belong to a given eigenvalue of an N-by-N matrix is equal to the number of times this eigenvalue occurs among the N roots of the secular equation

of the matrix. A matrix having one or more degenerate eigenvalues is called *degenerate*. The totality of the eigenvalues of a
matrix is called its *eigenvalue spectrum*.

Exercises

1. Illustrate by diagrams similar to 33^{54} and 52^{54} the processes of multiplying a matrix by a matrix and a vector by a matrix when $N > 2$.

2. Show that if $\alpha = \begin{pmatrix} 1 & -2 & 3 & -4 \\ 4 & 3 & 2 & 1 \\ 4 & -3 & 2 & -1 \\ 1 & 2 & -3 & 4 \end{pmatrix}$ and $\beta = \begin{pmatrix} 1 & 4 & -1 & -4 \\ 2 & -3 & 2 & 3 \\ 3 & 2 & -3 & -2 \\ 4 & -1 & 4 & 1 \end{pmatrix}$,

then $\alpha + \beta = \begin{pmatrix} 2 & 2 & 2 & -8 \\ 6 & 0 & 4 & 4 \\ 7 & -1 & -1 & -3 \\ 5 & 1 & 1 & 5 \end{pmatrix}$, $\alpha\beta = \begin{pmatrix} -10 & 20 & -30 & -20 \\ 20 & 10 & 0 & -10 \\ 0 & 30 & -20 & -30 \\ 12 & -12 & 28 & 12 \end{pmatrix}$,

$\beta\alpha = \begin{pmatrix} 9 & 5 & 21 & -15 \\ 1 & -13 & -5 & -1 \\ -3 & 5 & 13 & -15 \\ 17 & -21 & 15 & -17 \end{pmatrix}$, $\alpha^2 = \begin{pmatrix} 1 & -25 & 17 & -25 \\ 25 & -3 & 19 & -11 \\ -1 & -25 & 13 & -25 \\ 1 & 21 & -11 & 17 \end{pmatrix}$,

$\beta^2 = \begin{pmatrix} -10 & -6 & -6 & 6 \\ 14 & 18 & -2 & -18 \\ -10 & 2 & 2 & -2 \\ 18 & 26 & -14 & -26 \end{pmatrix}$, and $(\alpha + \beta)^2 = \begin{pmatrix} -10 & -6 & 2 & -54 \\ 60 & 12 & 12 & -40 \\ -14 & 12 & 8 & -72 \\ 48 & 14 & 18 & -14 \end{pmatrix}$;

verify that $(\alpha + \beta)^2 = \alpha^2 + \alpha\beta + \beta\alpha + \beta^2$.

3. Let $u = \begin{pmatrix} 5 \\ 1 \\ 2 \\ 6 \end{pmatrix}$ and let α and β be the matrices so labeled in Exercise 2;

show that $\alpha u = \begin{pmatrix} -15 \\ 33 \\ 15 \\ 25 \end{pmatrix}$ and $\beta u = \begin{pmatrix} -17 \\ 29 \\ -1 \\ 33 \end{pmatrix}$.

4. Show that the eigenrays of the matrix (43) belonging to its respective

eigenvalues 3, 6, and 18 are $c_1 \begin{pmatrix} 1 \\ 2 \\ 2 \end{pmatrix}$, $c_2 \begin{pmatrix} 2 \\ 1 \\ -2 \end{pmatrix}$, and $c_3 \begin{pmatrix} 2 \\ -2 \\ 1 \end{pmatrix}$, where c_1,

c_2, and c_3 are arbitrary nonvanishing constants. Using the explicit expressions for the eigenvectors, show that any two eigenvectors of (43) belonging to different eigenvalues are orthogonal.

5. Show that the eigenvalues of the matrix $\begin{pmatrix} 1 & 0 & 6 \\ 0 & -2 & 0 \\ 6 & 0 & 6 \end{pmatrix}$ are -3, -2, and 10. Compute the eigenrays of this matrix, and, using the explicit expressions for the eigenrays, show that any two of its eigenvectors belonging to different eigenvalues are orthogonal.

6. Show that the eigenvalues of the matrix $\begin{pmatrix} 9 & 0 & -2 \\ 0 & 10 & 0 \\ -2 & 0 & 6 \end{pmatrix}$ are 5 and 10, the first of which is nondegenerate and the second is doubly degenerate. Show that the eigenvectors belonging to the eigenvalue 5 of this matrix have the form $c_1 \begin{pmatrix} 1 \\ 0 \\ 2 \end{pmatrix}$, and the eigenvectors belonging to the eigenvalue 10 the form $c_2 \begin{pmatrix} 0 \\ 1 \\ 0 \end{pmatrix} + c_3 \begin{pmatrix} 2 \\ 0 \\ -1 \end{pmatrix}$, where c_1, c_2, and c_3 are arbitrary constants. Verify that every three but not every two eigenvectors belonging to the eigenvalues 10 are linearly dependent. Using the explicit expressions for the eigenvectors, show that any two eigenvectors of this matrix belonging to different eigenvalues are orthogonal.

7. Show that the eigenvalues of each of the three matrices 12^{86} are 1 and -1; and that sample eigenvectors of σ_x are $\begin{pmatrix} 1 \\ 1 \end{pmatrix}$ and $\begin{pmatrix} 1 \\ -1 \end{pmatrix}$, those of σ_y are $\begin{pmatrix} 1 \\ i \end{pmatrix}$ and $\begin{pmatrix} 1 \\ -i \end{pmatrix}$, and those of σ_z are $\begin{pmatrix} 1 \\ 0 \end{pmatrix}$ and $\begin{pmatrix} 0 \\ 1 \end{pmatrix}$.

8. Let α and β be two matrices such that $\alpha u = \beta u$ for every vector u; show that then $\alpha = \beta$ in the sense of the definition of matrix equality adopted in this section. Recall the definition of equality of operators given in §2, and discuss the bearing of the present result on the operator-operand interpretation of matrices and vectors. Consider, in the light of the definitions of operator sum and operator product given in §2, the definitions of matrix sum and matrix product adopted in this section.

9. Show that, if the terminology is appropriately adjusted, then the theorems of Exercises 2^6 and 3^6 hold for matrices.

57. N-Dimensional Spaces

N-by-N matrices and N-component column symbols arise, often in disguise, in all kinds of problems in mathematics, classical physics, and quantum mechanics; but an intuitive insight into those of their properties which will be of special interest to us is gained particularly readily if in discussing them we speak of them as though they have to do with mappings of an N-dimensional space; it is for this reason that we have already introduced some geometric terms in the purely algebraic discussion of the last section. Accordingly, now and then in our algebraic study of matrices and column symbols, we shall

(a) speak of an N-dimensional space (N-space) within which there is fixed a coordinate frame whose origin is at a point O, whose N axes are mutually perpendicular, and whose scale unit is the same for all axes;

(b) interpret an N-component column symbol as representing a vector in this N-space, that is, as being a properly ordered list of the components (relative to our coordinate frame) of an N-dimensional vector; and

(c) interpret an N-by-N matrix as the representative (relative to our frame) of a mapping of the N-space.

If $N = 2$ or $N = 3$ and if all the components of the matrices and column symbols concerned are real, then the steps enumerated above can be actually pictured in terms of a plane or the ordinary three-dimensional space, so that our interpretation is then truly geometric rather than quasi-geometric; if $N > 3$ and all components are real, then the N-space invoked is a fictitious one and is similar to the phase spaces used in statistical mechanics; in general, our N-space will be complex and hence still more abstract. Incidentally, the orientation and the scale unit of the coordinate frame referred to in (a) will be quite immaterial for our purposes.

The algebraic meaning of the symbolic equation $\alpha u = v$ is that the components of the column symbols u and v and of the matrix α are related through the equations 31^{56}; the quasi-geometric interpretation of this equation is that a mapping α (represented by the matrix α) of an N-space sends the vector u (represented by the column symbol u) into the vector v (represented by the column symbol v). In particular, the quasi-geometric interpretation of the symbolic equation $\alpha u = \lambda u$ is that the vector u of an N-space is an eigenvector of the mapping α belonging to the eigenvalue λ of the mapping, that is, that the mapping α does not remove the vector u from its original ray but merely multiplies it by the constant λ. Thus *the eigenvalues of a matrix* (that is, the roots of the secular equation of the matrix) *are the eigenvalues of a mapping that the matrix may be interpreted to represent.*

The introduction of quasi-geometrical notions is of course essentially a matter of terminology. Thus an N-vector was defined in §56 as an ordered single-file array of N numbers; and it will remain just that, whether or not we try to picture it as a point in a fictitious N-dimensional space.

Exercises

1. Interpret the matrix 43^{56} as representing a mapping of a 3-space, and investigate the figure into which this mapping sends a unit sphere with center at O.

2. Consider along the lines of the preceding exercise the matrix of Exercise 6^{56}. What, in particular, is the geometric implication of the degeneracy of this matrix?

58. Further Remarks on Matrices

The elements α_{11}, α_{22}, $\cdots$, and α_{NN}, lying on the principal diagonal of a matrix α, are the *diagonal* elements of α; the remaining elements are the *off-diagonal* elements of α. A matrix all of whose off-diagonal elements are zeros, that is, a matrix of the form

$$\begin{pmatrix} \alpha_{11} & 0 & \cdots & 0 \\ 0 & \alpha_{22} & \cdots & 0 \\ & & \cdots & \\ 0 & 0 & \cdots & \alpha_{NN} \end{pmatrix}, \tag{1}$$

is a *diagonal matrix*. The special matrices

$$\begin{pmatrix} c & 0 & \cdots & 0 \\ 0 & c & \cdots & 0 \\ & \cdots & \\ 0 & 0 & \cdots & c \end{pmatrix}, \quad \begin{pmatrix} 1 & 0 & \cdots & 0 \\ 0 & 1 & \cdots & 0 \\ & \cdots & \\ 0 & 0 & \cdots & 1 \end{pmatrix}, \quad \begin{pmatrix} 0 & 0 & \cdots & 0 \\ 0 & 0 & \cdots & 0 \\ & \cdots & \\ 0 & 0 & \cdots & 0 \end{pmatrix}, \tag{2}$$

are denoted by c, 1, and 0, and are called the matrix c, the *unit matrix*, and the *matrix zero*, respectively; since $1\alpha = \alpha 1 = \alpha$, whatever α may be, the symbol 1 is usually omitted when the unit matrix is involved as a factor in a matrix product. The sum of the diagonal elements of a matrix α is denoted by the symbol $\operatorname{tr} \alpha$ and is called the *trace*[2] of the matrix α:

$$\operatorname{tr} \alpha = \alpha_{11} + \alpha_{22} + \cdots + \alpha_{NN} \; ; \tag{3}$$

[2] The German term is *Spur*, meaning *trace* or *spoor*.

for example, if ρ is the matrix 43^{56}, we have tr $\rho = 11 + 10 + 6 = 27$. The following determinant, denoted by det α, is called the *determinant of the matrix* α:

$$\det \alpha = \begin{vmatrix} \alpha_{11} & \alpha_{12} & \cdots & \alpha_{1N} \\ \alpha_{21} & \alpha_{22} & \cdots & \alpha_{2N} \\ & & \cdots & \\ \alpha_{N1} & \alpha_{N2} & \cdots & \alpha_{NN} \end{vmatrix} ; \tag{4}$$

for example, if ρ is the matrix 43^{56}, we have

$$\det \rho = \begin{vmatrix} 11 & -6 & 2 \\ -6 & 10 & -4 \\ 2 & -4 & 6 \end{vmatrix} = 324.$$

If det $\alpha = 0$, the matrix α is said to be *singular*.

The determinant

$$\begin{vmatrix} (\alpha_{11} - \lambda) & \alpha_{12} & \cdots & \alpha_{1N} \\ \alpha_{21} & (\alpha_{22} - \lambda) & \cdots & \alpha_{2N} \\ & & \cdots & \\ \alpha_{N1} & \alpha_{N2} & \cdots & (\alpha_{NN} - \lambda) \end{vmatrix} , \tag{5}$$

that is, the left side of the secular equation 47^{56}, is called the *secular determinant* of the matrix α; the secular determinant of α is a polynomial of the Nth degree in the parameter λ, and its numerical value depends of course on that of λ. If $\lambda = 0$ the secular determinant becomes det α, and hence, when the secular determinant is expanded in powers of λ, the term independent of λ is just det α; further, the terms involving λ^N and λ^{N-1} all come from the product of the diagonal elements of the secular determinant; and, since $(\alpha_{11} - \lambda) \cdot (\alpha_{22} - \lambda) \cdots (\alpha_{NN} - \lambda) = (-\lambda)^N + (-\lambda)^{N-1} \operatorname{tr} \alpha + \cdots$, we conclude that the secular determinant has the form

$$(-\lambda)^N + (-\lambda)^{N-1} \operatorname{tr} \alpha + \cdots + \det \alpha. \tag{6}$$

The coefficients of λ^{N-2}, λ^{N-3}, and so on, in (6) are also definite combinations of the elements of α, but we need not consider them in detail here.

The secular equation of α thus has the form

$$(-\lambda)^N + (-\lambda)^{N-1} \operatorname{tr} \alpha + \cdots + \det \alpha = 0. \tag{7}$$

Now, if λ_1, λ_2, $\cdots$, and λ_N denote the N roots of (7), then (7) can be written in the factored form

$$(\lambda_1 - \lambda) \cdot (\lambda_2 - \lambda) \cdots (\lambda_N - \lambda) = 0; \tag{8}$$

expanding the left side of (8), we get

$$(-\lambda)^N + (-\lambda)^{N-1} (\lambda_1 + \lambda_2 + \cdots + \lambda_N) + \cdots$$

$$+ \lambda_1 \cdot \lambda_2 \cdots \lambda_N = 0, \quad (9)$$

and comparison with (7) shows that

$$\lambda_1 + \lambda_2 + \cdots + \lambda_N = \operatorname{tr} \alpha, \tag{10}$$

and

$$\lambda_1 \cdot \lambda_2 \cdots \lambda_N = \det \alpha. \tag{11}$$

Thus the sum and the product of the eigenvalues of a matrix are equal, respectively, to the trace and to the determinant of the matrix. It follows from (11) that a matrix having the eigenvalue 0 is singular, and conversely.

The *reciprocal* of matrix α is the matrix, denoted by α^{-1}, which, when multiplied into α from either side, yields the unit matrix as the product:

$$\alpha\alpha^{-1} = \alpha^{-1}\alpha = 1. \tag{12}$$

The nmth element of α^{-1} turns out to be

$$(\alpha^{-1})_{nm} = \frac{1}{\det \alpha} \frac{\partial \det \alpha}{\partial \alpha_{mn}}; \tag{13}$$

the quantity $\partial \det \alpha/\partial \alpha_{mn}$ is called the *cofactor* of the element α_{mn}. For example, if

$$\alpha = \begin{pmatrix} \alpha_{11} & \alpha_{12} \\ \alpha_{21} & \alpha_{22} \end{pmatrix}, \tag{14}$$

then $\det \alpha = \alpha_{11}\alpha_{22} - \alpha_{12}\alpha_{21}$, so that $\partial \det \alpha/\partial \alpha_{11} = \alpha_{22}$, $\partial \det \alpha/\partial \alpha_{12} = -\alpha_{21}$, $\partial \det \alpha/\partial \alpha_{21} = -\alpha_{12}$, and $\partial \det \alpha/\partial \alpha_{22} = \alpha_{11}$; hence, writing the common factor $(\det \alpha)^{-1}$ outside, we have

$$\alpha^{-1} = \frac{1}{\alpha_{11}\alpha_{22} - \alpha_{12}\alpha_{21}} \begin{pmatrix} \alpha_{22} & -\alpha_{12} \\ -\alpha_{21} & \alpha_{11} \end{pmatrix}. \tag{15}$$

The factor $(\det \alpha)^{-1}$ in (13) shows that a singular matrix has no reciprocal; it then follows from (11) that a matrix has no reciprocal if it has the eigenvalue 0.

The matrix

$$\tilde{\alpha} = \begin{pmatrix} \alpha_{11} & \alpha_{21} & \cdots & \alpha_{N1} \\ \alpha_{12} & \alpha_{22} & \cdots & \alpha_{N2} \\ & & \cdots & \\ \alpha_{1N} & \alpha_{2N} & \cdots & \alpha_{NN} \end{pmatrix}, \tag{16}$$

where α_{nm} is the nmth element of the matrix α, is the *transpose* of the matrix α; for example,

$$\text{if } \alpha = \begin{pmatrix} 1 & 2+i & 3-2i \\ 4 & 5-i & 6+3i \\ 7 & 2 & 9 \end{pmatrix}, \quad \text{then } \tilde{\alpha} = \begin{pmatrix} 1 & 4 & 7 \\ 2+i & 5-i & 2 \\ 3-2i & 6+3i & 9 \end{pmatrix}. \tag{17}$$

Denoting the nmth element of $\tilde{\alpha}$ by $\tilde{\alpha}_{nm}$, we have the N^2 relations

$$\tilde{\alpha}_{nm} = \alpha_{mn}. \tag{18}$$

The matrix

$$\bar{\alpha} = \begin{pmatrix} \alpha_{11}^* & \alpha_{21}^* & \cdots & \alpha_{N1}^* \\ \alpha_{12}^* & \alpha_{22}^* & \cdots & \alpha_{N2}^* \\ & & \cdots & \\ \alpha_{1N}^* & \alpha_{2N}^* & \cdots & \alpha_{NN}^* \end{pmatrix}, \tag{19}$$

where α_{nm}^* is the complex conjugate of the nmth element of the matrix α, is the *complex conjugate* of the matrix α; for example,

$$\text{if } \alpha = \begin{pmatrix} 1 & 2+i & 3-2i \\ 4 & 5-i & 6+3i \\ 7 & 2 & 9 \end{pmatrix}, \quad \text{then } \bar{\alpha} = \begin{pmatrix} 1 & 4 & 7 \\ 2-i & 5+i & 2 \\ 3+2i & 6-3i & 9 \end{pmatrix}. \tag{20}$$

Denoting the nmth element of $\bar{\alpha}$ by $\bar{\alpha}_{nm}$, we have the N^2 relations

$$\bar{\alpha}_{nm} = \alpha_{mn}^*. \tag{21}$$

Note that the computation of $\bar{\alpha}$ involves a transposition of rows and columns of α, so that, usually, $\bar{\alpha}$ is *not* the matrix whose elements are the complex conjugates of the corresponding elements of α.

If

$$\alpha = \bar{\alpha}, \tag{22}$$

that is, if

$$\alpha_{nm} = \alpha_{mn}^*, \tag{23}$$

the matrix α is said to be *Hermitian*; the matrix 43^{56}, the matrices 12^{86}, and the matrix $\begin{pmatrix} 5 & 3+2i \\ 3-2i & 7 \end{pmatrix}$ are examples of Hermitian matrices.   According to (23) the diagonal elements of a Hermitian matrix are all real.   We shall show in §69 that *every eigenvalue of a Hermitian matrix is real*, and that *any two eigenvectors of a Hermitian matrix belonging to different eigenvalues of the matrix are orthogonal*; for the present the correctness of these assertions will be taken for granted.

If a vector u is simultaneously an eigenvector of two matrices α and β, that is, if $\alpha u = \lambda u$ and $\beta u = \mu u$, where λ and μ are constants, then u is a *simultaneous eigenvector* of α and β.   If $\alpha\beta = \beta\alpha$, the matrices α and β *commute*; if $\alpha\beta = -\beta\alpha$, the matrices α and β *anticommute*; the matrix $\alpha\beta - \beta\alpha$ is the *commutator* of α and β.

Exercises

1. One of the eigenvalues of a 3-by-3 matrix α is 5, tr α is 12, and det α is 60; find the remaining eigenvalues of α.

2. Show that det $(\alpha\beta)$ = det $(\beta\alpha)$ = (det α)·(det β), and that det $(c\alpha)$ = c^N det α.

3. Show that the eigenvalues of a diagonal matrix are its diagonal elements.

4. Use (13) to compute α^{-1} when α is a 3-by-3 matrix with unspecified elements α_{11}, α_{12}, and so on; check the result by matrix multiplication.

5. Show that

$$(\alpha\beta)^{-1} = \beta^{-1}\alpha^{-1}, \qquad \widetilde{\alpha\beta} = \tilde{\beta}\tilde{\alpha}, \qquad \overline{\alpha\beta} = \bar{\beta}\bar{\alpha}; \qquad \text{(24a, b, c)}$$

here $(\alpha\beta)^{-1}$, $\widetilde{\alpha\beta}$, and $\overline{\alpha\beta}$ are the reciprocal, the transpose, and the complex conjugate, respectively, of the matrix $\alpha\beta$.   Generalize these results to products of more than two matrices.   Reconcile the equation given in Exercise 11^{53} with (24a).

6. Show that, if N is finite, then tr $(\alpha\beta - \beta\alpha) = 0$; note that this result cannot be extended to the case when N is infinite, since the infinite series that are then involved may fail to converge absolutely.

7. Let a mapping ξ of a plane be represented in some coordinate frame by the matrix ξ, so that the components $(\xi u)_1$ and $(\xi u)_2$ of a vector ξu are related to those of u through the equations

(18a^{54})
$$(\xi u)_1 = \xi_{11}u_1 + \xi_{12}u_2$$
$$(\xi u)_2 = \xi_{21}u_1 + \xi_{22}u_2$$
(25)

and let U_1 and U_2 be two *vectors* in the plane which, before the mapping is carried out, coincide with the basic unit vectors e_1 and e_2 of the coordinate frame.   When the mapping ξ is carried out, U_1 and U_2 are sent into ξU_1

and ξU_2; the latter vectors in general no longer coincide with e_1 and e_2, which, being fixed with respect to the coordinate frame, are not affected by the mapping. Show that the vectors ξU_1, ξU_2, U_1, and U_2 satisfy the equations

$$\xi U_1 = \xi_{11} U_1 + \xi_{12} U_2$$
$$\xi U_2 = \xi_{21} U_1 + \xi_{22} U_2 . \tag{26}$$

8. Show, adjusting the terminology whenever necessary, that the theorems of Exercises 6[6] and 3[7], and the last theorem of §6 hold for matrices and vectors in general; and that those of Exercises 2[44] and 3[44] hold for Hermitian matrices.

9. Use the quasi-geometric interpretation of matrices as mappings to convince yourself that (a) a matrix having the eigenvalue 0 can have no reciprocal, (b) the eigenvalues of a diagonal matrix are its diagonal elements, and (c) the eigenvectors of a diagonal matrix belonging to distinct eigenvalues of the matrix are mutually orthogonal.

10. Let $\alpha\beta = \beta\alpha$, where α is a nondegenerate diagonal matrix; show that then β is also diagonal.

11. Write down a singular 2-by-2 matrix with simple nonvanishing numerical elements; interpret it as representing a mapping of a plane and construct the figure into which the mapping sends the unit circle.

12. Explain why the following argument is fallacious: "According to a result of Exercise 4[54], the matrix γ^P listed in 15[54] satisfies the equation $(1 + \gamma^P)(1 + \gamma^P) = 2(1 + \gamma^P)$; multiplying both sides of this equation on the right by the reciprocal of the matrix $1 + \gamma^P$, we get $(1 + \gamma^P)(1 + \gamma^P)(1 + \gamma^P)^{-1} = 2(1 + \gamma^P)(1 + \gamma^P)^{-1}$, that is, $1 + \gamma^P = 2$; hence $\gamma^P = 1$."

13. Show that every two of the three matrices 12[86] anticommute with each other; that every two of the four matrices 10[91] anticommute with each other.

59. Function Space

We have already seen that *mapping operators* can be represented by matrices; our next task is to show that *differential operators* can also be represented by matrices. As a preliminary step we shall show that differential operators can be interpreted as mappings of a certain space, called *function space*.[3]

To introduce the notion of a function space we begin with a simple case.[4] Let $f_1 = f_1(x)$ and $f_2 = f_2(x)$, to which we shall

---

[3] Our use of the term *function space* will be somewhat unprecise. See *function space* and *Hilbert space* in Kemble.

[4] D. Jackson, *Am. Math. Monthly*, **31**, 461 (1924).

refer as the *basic f's*, be two real functions of x which are orthonormal in an interval (a, b), so that

$$\int_a^b f_1^2 \, dx = 1, \qquad \int_a^b f_2^2 \, dx = 1, \qquad \int_a^b f_1 f_2 \, dx = 0; \qquad (1)$$

and let us restrict ourselves to real functions $u = u(x)$ which are linear combinations of f_1 and f_2, and thus have the form

$$u = c_1 f_1 + c_2 f_2, \qquad (2)$$

where c_1 and c_2 are arbitrary real constants. To specify any particular u, it is necessary and sufficient to quote two specific real numbers c_1 and c_2; that is, a particular u is specified in the same manner as is a particular point in a real plane. This suggests that we may associate each of our u's with a vector in a plane by drawing, as in Fig. 93, a rectangular coordinate frame, associating the basic f's with the basic unit vectors of this frame, and associating a function u with the vector whose components are c_1 and c_2. Note that if $w = u + v$, where u and v are both real linear combinations of f_1 and f_2, then the vector associated with w is the sum, in the usual sense, of the vectors associated, respectively, with the functions u and v.

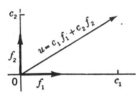

Fig. 93. A function plane.

We call the plane shown in Fig. 93 the *function plane* of the functions (2), because each vector in this plane can be associated with a particular function of type (2), and conversely.

For example, if the basic f's are

$$f_1 = N \sin x, \qquad\qquad f_2 = N \sin 2x, \qquad (3)$$

where $N = \pi^{-\frac{1}{2}}$, then every function u of the form

$$u = c_1 f_1 + c_2 f_2 = c_1 N \sin x + c_2 N \sin 2x, \qquad (4)$$

where the c's are real, can be associated with a vector in the plane of Fig. 94; the plane of Fig. 94 is then the function plane of functions of the form (4). An interval over which the f's are orthonormal in this case is $(-\pi, \pi)$.

The various geometric quantities pertaining to a function plane stand in a one-to-one corre-

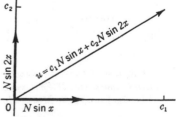

Fig. 94. The plane of the functions (4).

spondence with certain analytic expressions pertaining to the functions u. For example, according to Fig. 93, the square of the length of the vector u is $c_1^2 + c_2^2$; now, $\int u^2 dx = \int (c_1 f_1 + c_2 f_2)^2 dx = c_1^2 \int f_1^2 dx + 2 c_1 c_2 \int f_1 f_2 dx + c_2^2 \int f_2^2 dx$, so that in view of (1) we have $\int_a^b u^2 dx = c_1^2 + c_2^2$, and hence

$$\int_a^b u^2 dx = \text{square of the length of the vector } u. \qquad (5)$$

We speak of the length of the vector associated with a function u simply as the *length of the function u*.

Angles in our function plane also have a direct analytical meaning. Indeed, according to Fig. 95, in which both u and v have the form (2),

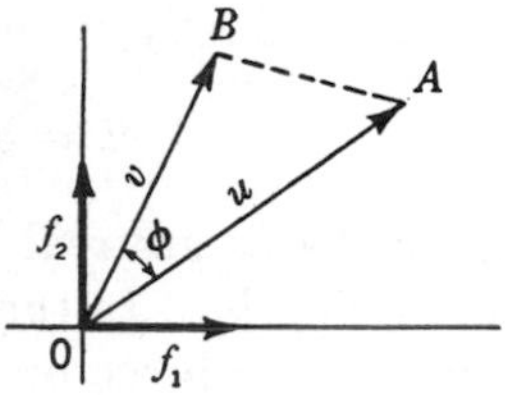

Fig. 95.

$$OA^2 + OB^2 - 2 \cdot OA \cdot OB \cdot \cos \phi = AB^2; \qquad (6)$$

now, in view of (5), $OA^2 = \int_a^b u^2 dx$, $OB^2 = \int_a^b v^2 dx$, and $AB^2 = \int_a^b (u - v)^2 dx = \int_a^b u^2 dx + \int_a^b v^2 dx - 2 \int_a^b uv dx$; substituting these integrals into (6) and solving for $\cos \phi$, we get

$$\cos \phi = \frac{\int_a^b uv dx}{\sqrt{\int_a^b u^2 dx \int_a^b v^2 dx}}. \qquad (7)$$

We speak of the angle between the respective vectors associated with two functions u and v simply as the *angle between the functions u and v*. If

$$\int_a^b uv dx = 0, \qquad (8)$$

then, according to (7), the vectors associated with u and v are mutually perpendicular; perhaps the term *orthogonal*, which we used all along for real functions satisfying (8), will now appear particularly appropriate.

If f_1, f_2, and f_3 are three real functions of x that are orthonormal in an interval (a, b), then the functions

$$u = c_1 f_1 + c_2 f_2 + c_3 f_3 , \qquad (9)$$

where the c's are arbitrary real constants, can be associated with vectors in a real three-dimensional space, the three basic f's being now associated with the three unit vectors of a rectangular coordinate frame. The formulas (5) and (7) carry over directly to this case.

More generally, we may be concerned with functions of the form

$$u = c_1 f_1 + c_2 f_2 + \cdots + c_N f_N , \qquad (10)$$

where the f's are real functions of x that are orthonormal in an interval (a, b). In this case we can still speak of the u's as being associated with vectors in a certain space; but the space now has N dimensions, and our interpretation is quasi-geometric. The formulas (5) and (7) are taken over for this case without change.

A further generalization lies in allowing N in (10) to be infinite, so that the u's are infinite series:[5]

$$u = c_1 f_1 + c_2 f_2 + \cdots + c_k f_k + \cdots . \qquad (11)$$

This case is of particular interest, since it arises in connection with expansions of real functions in terms of infinite orthonormal sets of real functions, such as the trigonometric functions (Fourier series), the Hermite functions (Gram-Charlier series), and so on. The function space now has an infinite (though countable) number of dimensions.

The final generalization to be considered at present is that when the basic f's and the c's in (11) are allowed to be complex, so that the u's under consideration are, in general, complex functions of x. The *function space* now invoked is a complex space of infinitely many dimensions, and is therefore very much of an abstraction. The formula (5) is now no longer suitable, and we adopt the following instead:

$$\int_a^b \bar{u} u \, dx = \text{square of the length of the vector } u. \qquad (12)$$

---

[5] For our present purposes, the notation of (11) is somewhat more convenient than that of 8^8.

The formula (7) for the cosine of the angle between two functions now also needs modification, which, however, we need not consider here; suffice it to state that the condition for the orthogonality of the vectors associated with two functions u and v is

$$(3^8) \qquad\qquad \int_a^b \bar{u}v\,dx = 0 \qquad\qquad (13)$$

rather than (8).

To summarize: When two real functions of x, orthonormal in an interval (a, b), are given, then each function u that is a real linear combination of these two functions can be associated with a vector in a plane called a function plane of the u's; the association is readily visualizable, and to the geometrical elements of the plane, such as lengths and angles, there correspond simple analytical expressions. The situation is no more complicated when all functions u under consideration are real linear combinations of three real orthonormal functions; the 'function space' then has three dimensions, but is still directly visualizable. Quasi-geometric abstraction begins when we consider functions that are real linear ·combinations of more than three (in particular, infinitely many) orthonormal functions, or when we deal with complex functions; a direct intuitive grasp of the entire function space is then no longer possible; the notion of a function space, nevertheless is still useful because it enables us to employ geometric terminology and geometric analogy in a rather suggestive way.

Mappings of function space. The concept of function space enables us under certain circumstances to interpret differential operators as mappings. We begin once again with an example.

Suppose that we are investigating the effect of the particular operator $-d^2/dx^2$ (which we shall denote by ξ) on the particular functions (4). We have

$$\xi u = -\frac{d^2}{dx^2} u = -\frac{d^2}{dx^2} (c_1 N \sin x + c_2 N \sin 2x)$$

$$= c_1 N \sin x + 4c_2 N \sin 2x. \qquad\qquad (14)$$

Thus ξu is again a real linear combinaton of the functions (3), and hence the functions ξu, as well as the functions u, can be associated with vectors in the plane of Fig. 94. The respective vectors associated with u and with ξu are indicated in Fig. 96, where the f's stand for the particular functions (3), u stands for a function of the particular form (4), and ξ stands for

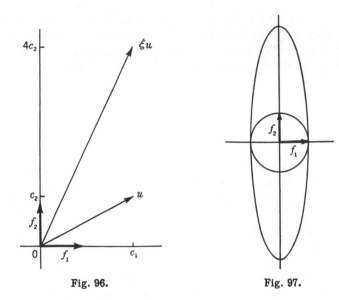

Fig. 96.   Fig. 97.

the particular operator $-d^2/dx^2$. We can therefore interpret the process
of operating with $-d^2/dx^2$ on our u's as a *mapping of a function plane*;
the ellipse into which this mapping sends the unit circle is shown in Fig. 97,
together with the unit circle.

In general, let the functions u under consideration have the
form

(11) $$u = c_1 f_1 + c_2 f_2 + \cdots + c_k f_k + \cdots ,$$ (15)

where the c's are constants and where the f's are orthonormal in
some interval; and let an operator ξ be such that for an arbitrary u
of the form (15) we have

$$\xi u = d_1 f_1 + d_2 f_2 + \cdots + d_k f_k + \cdots ,$$ (16)

where the d's are constants, and the f's are the same as in (15).
The function space that 'accommodates' the u's will then also
accommodate the functions ξu; and hence the effect of the operator
ξ on the functions u may be pictured as *a mapping of a function
space*.

When a function space is used, it is sometimes convenient to
represent a function by a column symbol whose elements are the

'components' of the function relative to the coordinate frame of the function space. The functions (2), for example, can be written in the form

$$u = \begin{pmatrix} c_1 \\ c_2 \end{pmatrix}, \qquad (17)$$

the basic functions f_1 and f_2 being kept in mind. Had we used the symbols u_1 and u_2 for the numbers c_1 and c_2 in (2), the notation of (17) would have been precisely like that of 42^{54}.

Exercises

1. Use a function plane to show geometrically that, if the functions u_1 and u_2 are orthonormal in an interval (a, b), then the functions $v_1 = (u_1 + u_2)/\sqrt{2}$ and $v_2 = (u_1 - u_2)/\sqrt{2}$ are also orthonormal in (a, b). Verify this result analytically, allowing u_1 and u_2 to be complex.

2. Prove (5) and (7) when u and v have the form (9).

3. Let u_1, u_2, and u_3 be real functions, orthonormal in $(-\infty, \infty)$. Verify the equation $\int(u_1 + \frac{1}{2}u_2 + \frac{1}{2}u_3)^2\, dx = \frac{3}{2}$ and correlate it with the fact that the distance between a vertex of a unit cube and the center of a nonadjacent face is $\sqrt{\frac{3}{2}}$. Verify the equation

$$[\int(u_1 + u_2)(u_1 + u_3)\, dx] \cdot [\int(u_1 + u_2)^2\, dx]^{-\frac{1}{2}}[\int(u_1 + u_3)^2\, dx]^{-\frac{1}{2}} = \frac{1}{2}$$

and correlate it with the fact that the face diagonals of a cube, passing through a common vertex, make an angle of 60° with each other.

4. Discuss the significance of the fact that the basic f's do not appear in (5), (7), (12), and (13).

5. Let $u = \Sigma_i c_i f_i$ be the expansion of a real function u in terms of an orthonormal set of real functions; express c_k as an integral and show, in the light of (7) and (5), that c_k may be properly called the kth *component* of u.

6. Discuss the relation between the eigenvectors of the mapping of Fig. 97 and the eigenfunctions [having the form (4)] of the operator $-d^2/dx^2$; do the same for the eigenvalues.

7. Convince yourself on quasi-geometric grounds that, if an operator ξ satisfying (16) is interpreted as a mapping of a function space, then the eigenfunctions of ξ having the form (15) are associated with the eigenvectors of the mapping; consider the eigenvalues of the operator and of the mapping in a similar light.

8. Show that the operator d/dx cannot be interpreted as a mapping of the plane of Fig. 94. Use two functions from the set 25^8 to construct a function plane in terms of which the operator d/dx can be interpreted as a mapping; what conclusion regarding the eigenvalues of d/dx can be drawn from the geometry of this mapping?

60. Representation of Differential Operators by Means of Matrices

As we have just seen, a differential operator can under certain circumstances be interpreted as a mapping. This mapping can in turn be represented by a matrix; and the matrix so obtained is said *to represent the differential operator.*

For example, insofar as the effect of the operator $\xi = -d^2/dx^2$ on functions of type 4^{59} is concerned, this operator can be interpreted as a mapping of a plane—in fact, as the mapping pictured in Fig. 97. Now, inspection of Fig. 96 shows that, in terms of the coordinate frame given in the figure, the mapping in question is represented by the matrix

$$\xi = \begin{pmatrix} 1 & 0 \\ 0 & 4 \end{pmatrix}. \tag{1}$$

This matrix is said to *represent* the operator $-d^2/dx^2$ insofar as the effect of the latter on functions of type 4^{59} is concerned.

The matrix (1) can be found also by the following systematic method: If ξ is a mapping of a plane, and U_1 and U_2 are the vectors which, before the mapping is carried out, coincide with the unit vectors of the coordinate frame, then

(26^{58})

$$\xi U_1 = \xi_{11} U_1 + \xi_{12} U_2$$
$$\xi U_2 = \xi_{21} U_1 + \xi_{22} U_2 , \tag{2}$$

where $\bar{\xi}_{nm}$ are the elements of the transpose of the matrix representing the mapping. Now, the vectors coinciding with the unit vectors of the coordinate frame of our function plane are f_1 and f_2 , so that we may rewrite (2) as

$$\xi f_1 = \xi_{11} f_1 + \xi_{12} f_2$$
$$\xi f_2 = \xi_{21} f_1 + \xi_{22} f_2 , \tag{3}$$

where ξ is the differential operator whose matrix representative we are seeking, and where f_1 and f_2 are the basic f's. The elements of the matrix ξ are thus the coefficients in the expansions of the functions ξf_1 and ξf_2 in terms of f_1 and f_2 . Since f_1 and f_2 are orthonormal in some interval (a, b), the expansion coefficients can be evaluated by means of 21^8; in fact,

$$\xi_{11} = \int_a^b \bar{f}_1 \xi f_1 \, dx, \, \xi_{12} = \int_a^b \bar{f}_2 \xi f_1 \, dx, \, \xi_{21} = \int_a^b \bar{f}_1 \xi f_2 \, dx, \text{ and } \xi_{22} = \int_a^b \bar{f}_2 \xi f_2 \, dx.$$

These four relations can be summarized by writing $\xi_{nm} = \int_a^b \bar{f}_m \xi f_n \, dx$, and consequently

$$\xi_{nm} = \int_a^b \bar{f}_n \xi f_m \, dx. \tag{4}$$

In our special case, ξ is $-d^2/dx^2$, the f's are given by 3^{59}, and the interval (a, b) can be taken as $(-\pi, \pi)$. Substituting into (4), we then get, for example, $\xi_{11} = \int_{-\pi}^{\pi} f_1 \xi f_1 \, dx = \int_{-\pi}^{\pi} N \sin x (-d^2/dx^2) N \sin x \, dx = 1$, in agreement with (1). The reader should verify that the three remaining elements of (1) are also given correctly by the formula (4).

In dealing with the problem of representing differential operators by means of matrices, we shall be concerned with the case when the functions u under consideration have the form

$$(15^{59}) \qquad u = c_1 f_1 + c_2 f_2 + \cdots + c_k f_k + \cdots , \qquad (5)$$

where the c's are constants and the f's are orthonormal in an interval (a, b), and when an operator ξ is such that for an arbitrary u of the form (5) we have

$$(16^{59}) \qquad \xi u = d_1 f_1 + d_2 f_2 + \cdots + d_k f_k + \cdots , \qquad (6)$$

where the f's are the same as in (5) and the d's are constants. As pointed out in §59, the effect of ξ on the u's can in this case be interpreted as a mapping of a function space, and our problem is to compute the matrix representing this mapping when the unit vectors of the coordinate frame of the function space are the vectors associated with the basic f's. The reader will perhaps readily convince himself that quasi-geometric reasoning, patterned after the geometric reasoning of the preceding example, leads to the conclusion that the nmth element of the matrix ξ (representing the operator ξ) is again given by (4). The matrix now has an infinite number of rows and columns. In the sequel we shall usually deal with operators ξ, functions u, and sets of basic f's satisfying the four following conditions: the f's are orthonormal in the infinite interval, so that (4) becomes

$$\xi_{nm} = \int_{-\infty}^{\infty} f_n \xi f_m dx; \qquad (7)$$

the f's form a set that is complete with respect to normalizable functions; the u's are normalizable; and the functions ξu are also normalizable.

In an exposition not employing quasi-geometric inferences, Equation (4) would be written down as the *definition* of the matrix ξ representing the differential operator ξ; and Equation (7) would be regarded as the special case of this definition, referring to basic f's that are orthonormal in the infinite interval.

Quasi-geometric reasoning suggests that if, using a specific set of basic f's, we compute the matrices representing, respectively, the three differential operators α, β, and $\gamma = \alpha + \beta$, then the matrix representing γ should be the sum of the matrices representing α and β. This surmise is readily verified analytically: denoting the three matrices by α, β, and γ, and recalling 29^8, we have according to (7)

$$\gamma_{nm} = \int \bar{f}_n \gamma f_m dx = \int \bar{f}_n (\alpha + \beta) f_m dx = \int \bar{f}_n \alpha f_m dx + \int \bar{f}_n \beta f_m dx, \quad (8)$$

and it follows that $\gamma_{nm} = \alpha_{nm} + \beta_{nm}$, that is, that the matrices satisfy the equation $\gamma = \alpha + \beta$.

Similarly (as quasi-geometric reasoning again suggests) the matrix representing the differential operator $\gamma = \alpha\beta$ is the product $\alpha\beta$ of the matrices α and β representing the operators α and β. Indeed, according to (7), the nmth element of the matrix representing γ is

$$\gamma_{nm} = \int \bar{f}_n \alpha\beta f_m dx; \quad (9)$$

expanding βf_m in terms of the f's, we get

$$\beta f_m = \sum_i b_i f_i, \quad (10)$$

where, according to 21^8, $b_i = \int \bar{f}_i \beta f_m dx$; comparison with (7) now shows that $b_i = \beta_{im}$, where β is the matrix representing the operator β; hence (10) can be written as

$$\beta f_m = \sum_i \beta_{im} f_i, \quad (11)$$

and (9) as

$$\gamma_{nm} = \sum_i \beta_{im} \int \bar{f}_n \alpha f_i dx; \quad (12)$$

according to (7) the integral in (12) is just the nith element of the matrix representing the operator α, and hence $\gamma_{nm} = \sum_i \beta_{im} \alpha_{ni}$; now, α_{ni} and β_{im} being ordinary numbers, the last equation can be written as $\gamma_{nm} = \sum_i \alpha_{ni} \beta_{im}$, and hence the matrix equation $\gamma = \alpha\beta$ has been proved. In consequence of this theorem, and the one preceding, *every operator-algebraic relation that holds between two or more differential operators holds also between the matrices representing these operators, provided all the matrices are computed with reference to the same set of basic f's.*

One of the main reasons for our interest in the subject of representation of differential operators by means of matrices is that, whenever every eigenfunction of a differential operator ξ can be expanded in terms of the basic f's, *every eigenvalue of the differential operator ξ is also an eigenvalue of the matrix representing ξ*; hence a search for the eigenvalues of a differential operator may be replaced by a search for the eigenvalues of a matrix representing this operator. The proof runs as follows: Let u be an eigenfunction of ξ belonging to the eigenvalue λ, so that

$$\xi u = \lambda u; \tag{13}$$

let $\boldsymbol{\xi}$ denote for the moment the matrix representing ξ, so that

$$\xi_{ki} = \int \bar{f}_k \xi f_i dx; \tag{14}$$

and let $\boldsymbol{u}$ denote for the moment the vector (column symbol) with components

$$u_i = \int \bar{f}_i u dx, \tag{15}$$

which are infinitely many in number.[6] Expanding u in terms of the basic f's, we have $u = \sum_i c_i f_i$, where $c_i = \int \bar{f}_i u dx$, that is, $c_i = u_i$, so that (13) can be written as

$$\sum_i u_i \xi f_i = \lambda \sum_i u_i f_i . \tag{16}$$

Multiplying (16) through by $\bar{f}_k$ and integrating, we get $\sum_i u_i \int \bar{f}_k \xi f_i dx = \lambda \sum_i u_i \int \bar{f}_k f_i dx$, that is, $\sum_i u_i \xi_{ki} = \lambda \sum_i u_i \int \bar{f}_k f_i dx$; on account of the orthonormality of the f's, this becomes $\sum_i u_i \xi_{ki} = \lambda u_k$, so that

$$\sum_i \xi_{ki} u_i = \lambda u_k . \tag{17}$$

Now, the right side of (17) is the kth component of the vector $\lambda \boldsymbol{u}$, while according to 31[56] the left side of (17) is the kth component of the vector $\boldsymbol{\xi} \boldsymbol{u}$; and since (17) holds for every value of k we conclude that

$$\boldsymbol{\xi} \boldsymbol{u} = \lambda \boldsymbol{u}, \tag{18}$$ •

---

[6] The vector $\boldsymbol{u}$ is associated in function space with the function u, that is, with the eigenfunction of ξ belonging to the eigenvalue λ; recall Exercise 7[59].

that is, that the vector u is an eigenvector of the matrix ξ belonging to the eigenvalue λ of ξ. Consequently an eigenvalue of the operator ξ is also an eigenvalue of the matrix representing ξ.

Note that according to (7) the elements of a matrix representing a given operator depend in general on the choice of the basic f's, so that the term '*the* matrix representing the operator ξ' should be used only when a definite set of f's is referred to. From the quasi-geometric standpoint, a choice of the f's has to do with a choice of a coordinate frame in function space; and, as indicated by the simple examples of §55, the structure of a matrix representing a mapping may depend on the coordinate frame employed in constructing the matrix.

Exercises

1. Using 41[8] and 43[8], show that, if the Hermite functions u_k listed in 33[8] are chosen as the basic f's in such a way that $f_k = u_k$, then the matrices (denoted by x and x^2) representing respectively the operators x and x^2 have the forms given below. These matrices have infinitely many rows and columns, and only their upper left-hand corners are shown. Note that in view of the labeling of the present f's the rows and the columns of the matrices should be labeled $0, 1, 2, \cdots$, rather than $1, 2, 3, \cdots$

$$x = \frac{1}{\sqrt{2}} \begin{vmatrix} 0 & \sqrt{1}' & 0 & 0 & 0 & \cdots \\ \sqrt{1}' & 0 & \sqrt{2}' & 0 & 0 & \cdots \\ 0 & \sqrt{2}' & 0 & \sqrt{3}' & 0 & \cdots \\ 0 & 0 & \sqrt{3}' & 0 & \sqrt{4}' & \cdots \\ \cdots & \cdots & \cdots & \cdots & \cdots & \cdots \end{vmatrix} \tag{19}$$

$$x^2 = \tfrac{1}{2} \begin{vmatrix} 1 & 0 & \sqrt{2}' & 0 & 0 & \cdots \\ 0 & 3 & 0 & \sqrt{6}' & 0 & \cdots \\ \sqrt{2}' & 0 & 5 & 0 & \sqrt{12}' & \cdots \\ 0 & \sqrt{6}' & 0 & 7 & 0 & \cdots \\ \cdots & \cdots & \cdots & \cdots & \cdots & \cdots \end{vmatrix} \tag{20}$$

The apostrophe is used in (19) and (20) in the same way as in Exercise 7[8], so that the entry $\sqrt{1}'$ in the top row of (19) stands for $\sqrt{1}e^{i(\gamma_1 - \gamma_0)}$, the entry $\sqrt{1}'$ in the next row of (19) stands for $\sqrt{1}e^{i(\gamma_0 - \gamma_1)}$, and so on.

2. Verify by matrix multiplication that the matrix (20) is the square of the matrix (19); in this calculation it is of course necessary to write out in full the phase factor of each element.

3. Show that in terms of the basic f's of Exercise 1 the matrices representing the operators d/dx and d^2/dx^2 are

$$\frac{d}{dx} = \frac{1}{\sqrt{2}} \begin{vmatrix} 0 & \sqrt{1}' & 0 & 0 & 0 & \cdots \\ -\sqrt{1}' & 0 & \sqrt{2}' & 0 & 0 & \cdots \\ 0 & -\sqrt{2}' & 0 & \sqrt{3}' & 0 & \cdots \\ 0 & 0 & -\sqrt{3}' & 0 & \sqrt{4}' & \cdots \\ \cdots & \cdots & \cdots & \cdots & \cdots & \cdots \end{vmatrix} \quad (21)$$

$$\frac{d^2}{dx^2} = \frac{1}{2} \begin{vmatrix} -1 & 0 & \sqrt{2}' & 0 & 0 & \cdots \\ 0 & -3 & 0 & \sqrt{6}' & 0 & \cdots \\ \sqrt{2}' & 0 & -5 & 0 & \sqrt{12}' & \cdots \\ 0 & \sqrt{6}' & 0 & -7 & 0 & \cdots \\ \cdots & \cdots & \cdots & \cdots & \cdots & \cdots \end{vmatrix} \quad (22)$$

4. Show that, if the basic f's are chosen to be the functions

$$f_n = \begin{cases} 0 & x \leqq 0 \\ \sqrt{\dfrac{2}{\pi}} \sin nx & 0 \leqq x \leqq \pi \quad (23) \\ 0 & \pi \leqq x, \end{cases}$$

where $n = 1, 2, 3, \cdots$, then the matrix representing the operator x is

$$x = \frac{1}{450\pi} \begin{vmatrix} 225\pi^2 & -800 & 0 & \cdots \\ -800 & 225\pi^2 & -864 & \cdots \\ 0 & -864 & 225\pi^2 & \cdots \\ \cdots & \cdots & \cdots & \cdots \end{vmatrix} \quad (24)$$

The requisite integrals can be evaluated by reference to 13^{31}. Note that this matrix x is quite different from (19).

5. The operators x and d/dx satisfy the equation $(d/dx)x - x(d/dx) = 1$; verify that the matrices (19) and (21) also satisfy it. Why cannot the matrices (24) and (21) be expected to satisfy it?

6. Show that, if the basic f's are taken to be the normalized eigenfunctions of a Hermitian differential operator ξ having a nondegenerate spectrum, then ξ itself is represented by a diagonal matrix. Why cannot a similar statement be made if ξ is a degenerate Hermitian operator?

7. What matrix represents the operator $-d^2/dx^2 + x^2$ when the basic f's are the Hermite functions of Exercise 1?

8. Restrict yourself to the case when the basic f's are orthonormal in the infinite region, and show that a matrix representing a Hermitian operator is a Hermitian matrix.

9. Verify that the matrices (19) and (20) are Hermitian; remember that i appears in the phase factors. Find the matrix representing the operator $-id/dx$ when the basic f's are the Hermite functions, and verify that this matrix is Hermitian.

61. Concluding Remarks

The principal aims of this chapter were: first, to outline in §§56 and 58 the fundamentals of matrix algebra; and second, to show in §60 how and in what sense differential operators can be represented by matrices. The main results of §60 are the formulas 4^{60} and 7^{60}, and the three theorems following 7^{60}. Note that, apart from the use of some geometric terms, the contents of §§56 and 58 are entirely algebraic and that, as already mentioned, insofar as the contents of §60 are concerned, we might *define* the matrix representing a differential operator ξ by means of 4^{60} and thus eliminate the quasi-geometric aspects of the discussion.

The reason for our having discussed mappings and introduced geometric and quasi-geometric notions in spite of the fact that these are not absolutely essential for the problems that are to follow is twofold: first, a study of mappings and of their representation provides a beginner with suitable drill in the manipulation of matrices; and second, such a study helps to acquire an intuitive grasp of the content of some of the purely algebraic results of this and of the following chapters. The extent to which the quasi-geometric standpoint is helpful varies of course from person to person.

CHAPTER X

ELEMENTS OF THE HEISENBERG METHOD

62. Heisenberg Matrices

The Heisenberg theory was the first form of quantum mechanics to be invented;[1] the formulation of the Schroedinger theory followed within a few months;[2] and the fact that the two outwardly dissimilar theories, suggested to their respective authors by independent and entirely different considerations, are nevertheless fundamentally identical from the mathematical standpoint was proved a few months later.[3] In approaching the Heisenberg theory, we might begin with Heisenberg's original assumptions, quite independently of all the discussion of quantum mechanics which we presented so far; or we might do as we did in the case of the p-method, namely, begin with our general postulates I, II, and IV, and then, without regard for our work with the Schroedinger method, add further assumptions, stated now in a form appropriate to the Heisenberg method; it is, however, most expedient for us to introduce certain features of the Heisenberg method in the light of our knowledge of the Schroedinger method. This approach has the disadvantage of not making it at once clear how the Heisenberg method could have been invented before Schroedinger's; but this disadvantage is quite offset by the simplification of the presentation which this approach permits. Besides, it is often advantageous in practice to use the Schroedinger method in some parts and the Heisenberg method in other parts of the same computation; and consequently it is perhaps more important for us to emphasize the interrelation between the two methods, rather than to stress the fact that either of them can be formulated without reference to the other.

Our discussion will be confined to bound one-dimensional

---

[1] W. Heisenberg, *Zeits. f. Physik*, **33**, 879 (1925).

[2] E. Schroedinger, *Ann. der Physik*, **79**, 361, 489, 734; **80**, 437; **81**, 109 (January to June, 1926).

[3] E. Schroedinger, *Ann. der Physik*, **79**, 734 (1926); C. Eckart, *Phys. Rev.*, **28**, 711 (1926).

motion of a particle in a conservative field (in which case the Schroedinger eigenfunctions of the Hamiltonian are normalizable and the energy levels are discrete and nondegenerate) and to dynamical variables that do not involve t explicitly; but many of our results hold more generally.

The operators associated with dynamical variables in the Heisenberg method are matrices, and the procedure for computing the Heisenberg matrix α which is associated with the dynamical variable α pertaining to a dynamical system whose Hamiltonian is H consists of the following steps:

(a) We identify the Schroedinger operator H associated with the Hamiltonian of the dynamical system under consideration, and compute the *normalized* time-dependent Schroedinger eigenfunctions of H, say

$$\psi_1 , \psi_2 , \psi_3 , \cdots \tag{1}$$

belonging to the energy levels $E_1 , E_2 , E_3 , \cdots$;

(b) we identify the Schroedinger operator α associated with the dynamical variable α under consideration; and

(c) using 7^{60} and taking the basic f's to be the ψ's in (1), we compute the matrix α representing the Schroedinger operator α; this matrix, that is, the matrix with elements

$$\alpha_{nm} = \int_{-\infty}^{\infty} \bar{\psi}_n \alpha \psi_m \, dx, \tag{2}$$

is the desired Heisenberg operator.

The procedure outlined above can be summarized in the following statement, which we adopt as the definition of Heisenberg matrices: *the Heisenberg matrix α, associated with the dynamical variable α pertaining to a dynamical system with a Hamiltonian H, is the matrix representing the Schroedinger operator α when the basic f's are the normalized time-dependent Schroedinger eigenfunctions of H.*

It follows from this definition and from the theorem stated in italics just below 12^{60} that *every operator-algebraic relation that holds between two or more Schroedinger operators holds also between the corresponding Heisenberg matrices.* In particular, the Schroedinger operators satisfy the commutation rules required by the quantum condition 1^{13}, and hence the Heisenberg operators also conform to this condition.

It also follows from this definition and from the result of Exercise 8^{60} that *Heisenberg matrices are Hermitian, and consequently their eigenvalues are real.*[4] Hence the use of Heisenberg matrices as operators to be associated with dynamical variables is compatible with the operator assumption I of §13.

Examples. To illustrate Heisenberg matrices, we shall now construct some matrices pertaining to a linear harmonic oscillator. In this case the Schroedinger operator associated with the Hamiltonian is

$$H = -\frac{1}{\kappa} \frac{\partial^2}{\partial x^2} + \tfrac{1}{2}kx^2, \tag{3}$$

where $\kappa = 2m/\hbar^2$, and the normalized time-dependent Schroedinger eigenfunctions of the Hamiltonian are (see 7^{16})

$$\psi_n = e^{i\gamma_n} N_n H_n\left(\frac{x}{a}\right) e^{-\frac{1}{2}\left(\frac{x}{a}\right)^2} e^{-iE_n t/\hbar}, \qquad n = 0, 1, 2, \cdots, \tag{4}$$

where

$$E_n = (n + \tfrac{1}{2})h\nu_c, \qquad a = \sqrt[4]{\frac{\hbar^2}{km}}, \qquad \nu_c = \frac{1}{2\pi}\sqrt{\frac{k}{m}}, \tag{5}$$

and $N_n = 1/\sqrt{a 2^n n! \pi^{\frac{1}{2}}}$, where H_n is the Hermite polynomial 37^4, and where the γ's are arbitrary real constants, independent of both x and t; we shall also use the abbreviation

$$(25^{18}) \qquad\qquad b = \hbar/a = a\sqrt{km} = \sqrt[4]{km\hbar^2}. \tag{6}$$

According to the definition $\langle 2 \rangle$, the Heisenberg matrix associated with the coordinate x, when the system under consideration is the linear harmonic oscillator, has the elements

$$x_{nm} = \int \bar{\psi}_n x \psi_m \, dx, \tag{7}$$

where the ψ's are given by (4), and x in the integrand is the Schroedinger operator associated with the coordinate x; the subscript m in $\langle 7 \rangle$, which takes on the values $0, 1, 2, \cdots$, is of

---

[4] The reality of the eigenvalues of a Hermitian matrix, taken for granted in §58, will be proved in §69.

course not to be confused with the mass of the particle. The integral in $\langle 7 \rangle$ is essentially of the form 41^8, and we get

$$
x_{nm} = \begin{cases} a\sqrt{\tfrac{1}{2}n}\, e^{-i(\gamma_n - \gamma_m)}\, e^{i(E_n - E_m)t/\hbar} & \text{if } m = n - 1 \\ a\sqrt{\tfrac{1}{2}(n+1)}\, e^{-i(\gamma_n - \gamma_m)}\, e^{i(E_n - E_m)t/\hbar} & \text{if } m = n + 1 \\ 0 & \text{otherwise.} \end{cases} \quad (8)
$$

Using the apostrophe, as before, for the phase factor $\exp[-i(\gamma_n - \gamma_m)]$ and the prime for the time factor $\exp[i(E_n - E_m)t/\hbar]$, we can abbreviate (8) to

$$
x_{nm} = \begin{cases} a\sqrt{\tfrac{1}{2}n}'' & \text{if } m = n - 1 \\ a\sqrt{\tfrac{1}{2}(n+1)}'' & \text{if } m = n + 1 \\ 0 & \text{otherwise.} \end{cases} \quad (9)
$$

The matrix x thus has the form

$$
x = \frac{a}{\sqrt{2}} \begin{bmatrix} 0 & \sqrt{1}'' & 0 & 0 & 0 & \cdots \\ \sqrt{1}'' & 0 & \sqrt{2}'' & 0 & 0 & \cdots \\ 0 & \sqrt{2}'' & 0 & \sqrt{3}'' & 0 & \cdots \\ 0 & 0 & \sqrt{3}'' & 0 & \sqrt{4}'' & \cdots \\ \cdots & \cdots & \cdots & \cdots & \cdots & \cdots \end{bmatrix} \quad (10)
$$

Note that the rows and columns in (10) are to be labeled $0, 1, 2, \cdots$, rather than $1, 2, 3, \cdots$.

Similarly, the Heisenberg matrix p associated with the momentum of the linear harmonic oscillator has the elements

$$
p_{nm} = \int \bar{\psi}_n p \psi_m \, dx, \quad \langle 11 \rangle
$$

where the ψ's are given by (4) and p in the integrand is the Schroedinger operator $p = -i\hbar \partial/\partial x$ associated with the momentum, so that, more explicitly,

$$
p_{nm} = \int \bar{\psi}_n \left(-i\hbar \frac{\partial}{\partial x} \right) \psi_m \, dx. \quad (12)
$$

Comparison of (12) with 42^8 shows that

$$
p_{nm} = \begin{cases} ib\sqrt{\tfrac{1}{2}n}\, e^{-i(\gamma_n - \gamma_m)}\, e^{i(E_n - E_m)t/\hbar} & \text{if } m = n - 1 \\ -ib\sqrt{\tfrac{1}{2}(n+1)}\, e^{-i(\gamma_n - \gamma_m)}\, e^{i(E_n - E_m)t/\hbar} & \text{if } m = n + 1 \\ 0 & \text{otherwise,} \end{cases} \quad (13)
$$

that is, that

$$p_{nm} = \begin{cases} ib\sqrt{\tfrac{1}{2}n}'' & \text{if } m = n - 1 \\ -ib\sqrt{\tfrac{1}{2}(n+1)}'' & \text{if } m = n + 1 \\ 0 & \text{otherwise.} \end{cases} \tag{14}$$

The matrix p thus has the form

$$p = \frac{ib}{\sqrt{2}} \begin{vmatrix} 0 & -\sqrt{1}'' & 0 & 0 & 0 & \cdots \\ \sqrt{1}'' & 0 & -\sqrt{2}'' & 0 & 0 & \cdots \\ 0 & \sqrt{2}'' & 0 & -\sqrt{3}'' & 0 & \cdots \\ 0 & 0 & \sqrt{3}'' & 0 & -\sqrt{4}'' & \cdots \\ \cdots & \cdots & \cdots & \cdots & \cdots & \cdots \end{vmatrix} \tag{15}$$

where the labeling of rows and columns, as in the case of all Heisenberg matrices pertaining to the oscillator, is the same as in (10).

Again, the Heisenberg matrix H associated with the energy of the linear harmonic oscillator has the elements

$$H_{nm} = \int \bar{\psi}_n H \psi_m \, dx, \tag{16}$$

where the ψ's are given by (4), and H in the integrand is the Schroedinger operator $\langle 3 \rangle$ associated with the Hamiltonian of the oscillator. Since ψ_m in $\langle 16 \rangle$ is the eigenfunction of H belonging to the eigenvalue E_m, we have $H_{nm} = E_m \int \bar{\psi}_n \psi_m \, dx$, so that in view of the orthonormality of the ψ's

$$H_{nm} = \begin{cases} E_n & \text{if } m = n \\ 0 & \text{if } m \neq n. \end{cases} \tag{17}$$

Now, $E_n = (n + \tfrac{1}{2})h\nu_c$, and hence

$$H = \begin{vmatrix} \tfrac{1}{2}h\nu_c & 0 & 0 & 0 & \cdots \\ 0 & \tfrac{3}{2}h\nu_c & 0 & 0 & \cdots \\ 0 & 0 & \tfrac{5}{2}h\nu_c & 0 & \cdots \\ 0 & 0 & 0 & \tfrac{7}{2}h\nu_c & \cdots \\ \cdots & \cdots & \cdots & \cdots & \cdots \end{vmatrix} \tag{18}$$

Thus H is a diagonal matrix whose diagonal elements are the energy levels of the oscillator.

If the Heisenberg matrix associated with a dynamical variable α is available, then the matrix pertaining to the same dynamical system and associated with a dynamical variable that is a function of α can be computed by matrix algebra without invoking the defining equation $\langle 2 \rangle$. For example, if the matrix x for the oscillator, that is, the formula (9), is available, then the matrix x^2 for the oscillator can be computed by squaring the matrix x. In fact, we have

$$(26^{56}) \qquad x^2_{nm} = \sum_i x_{ni} x_{im}, \qquad (19)$$

where, in our case, $i = 0, 1, 2, \cdots$; according to (9), x_{ni} vanishes unless $i = n - 1$ or $i = n + 1$, so that, for a fixed n, two terms, at most, on the right of (19) are different from zero, and (19) reduces to

$$x^2_{nm} = x_{n,n-1} x_{n-1,m} + x_{n,n+1} x_{n+1,m} ; \qquad (20)$$

now, again according to (9), $x_{n-1,m}$ vanishes unless $m = n - 2$ or $m = n$, while $x_{n+1,m}$ vanishes unless $m = n$ or $m = n + 2$; hence the only elements of x^2 which do not necessarily vanish are

$$\begin{cases} x^2_{n,n-2} = x_{n,n-1} x_{n-1,n-2} \\ x^2_{nn} = x_{n,n-1} x_{n-1,n} + x_{n,n+1} x_{n+1,n} \\ x^2_{n,n+2} = x_{n,n+1} x_{n+1,n+2} . \end{cases} \qquad (21)$$

Substituting the appropriate elements of x from (9) into Equations (21) with due attention to the phase and time factors, we finally get

$$x^2_{nm} = \begin{cases} \frac{1}{2}a^2 \sqrt{n(n-1)}'' & \text{if } m = n - 2 \\ a^2(n + \frac{1}{2}) & \text{if } m = n \\ \frac{1}{2}a^2 \sqrt{(n+1)(n+2)}'' & \text{if } m = n + 2 \\ 0 & \text{otherwise.} \end{cases} \qquad (22)$$

Incidentally, in the notation due to Dirac, the matrix element denoted above by α_{nm} is denoted instead by $(n \mid \alpha \mid m)$; thus the nmth element of the matrix x is denoted by $(n \mid x \mid m)$, the nmth element of the matrix p^2 by $(n \mid p^2 \mid m)$, and so forth. The symbol $(n \mid \alpha \mid m)$ fits in with the symbols $(x \mid n)$ and $(m \mid x)$ for ψ_n and $\bar{\psi}_m$ discussed at the end of §27. In this notation the definition $\langle 2 \rangle$ of a Heisenberg matrix element becomes

$$(n \mid \alpha \mid m) = \int (n \mid x)\alpha(x \mid m) \, dx, \qquad \langle 23 \rangle$$

where α in the integrand is the Schroedinger operator associated with the dynamical variable α, and where $(x \mid m)$ and $(n \mid x)$ are normalized.

Exercises

1. Verify (22) by means of $\langle 2 \rangle$.
2. Compute the matrix (17) by matrix algebra from the matrices (9) and (14), using the equation $H = p^2/2m + \frac{1}{2}kx^2$.
3. Verify by matrix algebra that the matrices (9) and (14) satisfy the equation $xp - px = i\hbar$.
4. Compute the matrix (14) by matrix algebra from the matrices (9) and (17), using the relation $p = m\dot{x}$ and the equation of motion 27[44].
5. Set γ_n in (4) equal to $\gamma_0 - n(\gamma + \frac{3}{2}\pi)$, where $\dot{\gamma}_0$ and γ are arbitrary real constants, and show that *for large values of* n the matrix elements (8) then become

$$
x_{n,n-r} =
\begin{cases}
-i \sqrt{\dfrac{E_n}{2k}}\, e^{i\gamma} e^{i(E_n - E_{n-1})t/\hbar} & \text{if } r = 1 \\[2ex]
i \sqrt{\dfrac{E_n}{2k}}\, e^{-i\gamma} e^{i(E_n - E_{n+1})t/\hbar} & \text{if } r = -1 \\[2ex]
0 & \text{otherwise.}
\end{cases}
\tag{24}
$$

Show also that with the same choice of phases the elements of the matrix p^2 pertaining to the oscillator become, *for large values of* n,

$$
p^2_{n,n-r} =
\begin{cases}
\frac{1}{2}mE_n e^{2i\gamma} e^{i(E_n - E_{n-2})t/\hbar} & \text{if } r = 2 \\
mE_n & \text{if } r = 0 \\
\frac{1}{2}mE_n e^{-2i\gamma} e^{i(E_n - E_{n+2})t/\hbar} & \text{if } r = -2 \\
0 & \text{otherwise.}
\end{cases}
\tag{25}
$$

6. Compute a few elements in the upper left-hand corner of the Heisenberg matrix associated with the coordinate x of a particle moving in a one-dimensional box extending from $x = 0$ to $x = l$, and note that this matrix resembles 24[60] and is quite different from (10).

63. Heisenberg Matrices (Continued)

We shall now enumerate certain further properties of the Heisenberg matrices. In deriving these properties we shall use the definition 2[62]; but note that these properties themselves, as well as some of those that were pointed out in the preceding section, can be described without reference to the Schroedinger method. As before, we restrict ourselves to bound one-dimensional motion.

A. As we have seen in §14, the structure of the Schroedinger operator associated with a specific dynamical variable $\alpha(x, p)$ is quite independent of the dynamical system in connection with which the operator is to be used; for example, the respective Schroedinger operators associated with the coordinate x and the momentum p of a particle are always x and $-i\hbar\partial/\partial x$, whatever the dynamical system under consideration may be. On the other hand, *the structure of the Heisenberg matrix associated with a dynamical variable* $\alpha(x, p)$ *depends on the dynamical system under consideration*. This property of the Heisenberg matrices, illustrated in Exercise 6^{62}, follows from the fact that the ψ's in 2^{62} differ from system to system.

B. Taking the phase and time factors of the ψ's in 2^{62} outside the integral sign, we find that the nmth element of a Heisenberg matrix α has the form

$$\alpha_{nm} = a_{nm} e^{-i(\gamma_n - \gamma_m)} e^{i(E_n - E_m)t/h}, \qquad (1)$$

where a_{nm} is a numerical constant,[5] the γ's are the arbitrary phases of the ψ's, and E_n and E_m are the respective energies of the nth and the mth energy states of the system under consideration. Thus *the nmth element of every Heisenberg matrix pertaining to a given dynamical system has the same phase factor* $e^{-i(\gamma_n - \gamma_m)}$; the phase factors of the off-diagonal elements are interrelated, but are not fixed unless the arbitrary phases of the Schroedinger eigenfunctions of H are fixed by 'a suitable convention (we speak of this arbitrariness of the phase factors as their *standard arbitrariness*); the phase factors of the diagonal elements are equal to 1, so that these elements are free from any arbitrariness. Further, *the nmth element of every[5] Heisenberg matrix pertaining to a given dynamical system depends on t through the same time factor* $e^{i(E_n - E_m)t/h}$; this factor is periodic in t with frequency $(E_n - E_m)/h$, which we denote by ν_{nm} :

$$\nu_{nm} = (E_n - E_m)/h; \qquad (2)$$

comparison with 4^{31} now shows that the frequency of a (non-vanishing) off-diagonal element α_{nm} equals the frequency of the light that would be emitted in the transition of the system from the nth to the mth energy state; in particular, the *diagonal* elements of a Heisenberg matrix are independent of t.

It is the standard form of the phase and time factor of α_{nm} that permits us to abbreviate them without confusion by an apostrophe and a prime, respectively, and to write (1) as α_{nm}

---

[5] Remember that the dynamical variables under consideration do not involve t explicitly.

$= a_{nm}{}''$; in quantum-mechanical literature it is customary not to indicate these factors at all, but to have the reader keep them in mind.

C. *The Heisenberg matrix* H *associated with the Hamiltonian of the system under consideration is a diagonal matrix whose diagonal elements are the energy levels of the system*:

$$H_{nm} = \begin{cases} E_n & \text{if } m = n \\ 0 & \text{if } m \neq n. \end{cases} \tag{3}$$

The proof is the same as that leading to 17^{62} in the special case of the oscillator.

D. Comparing the definition 2^{62} with the Schroedinger expectation formula 2^{17} and remembering that the ψ's in 2^{62} are normalized, we find that

$$\alpha_{nn} = \mathrm{av}_n \alpha, \tag{4}$$

that is, that *the nth diagonal element of the Heisenberg matrix* α *is the expected average of the dynamical variable* α *for the nth quantum state of the system under consideration.*

E. Using 2^{62}, we can write 6^{31} as

$$A_{n \to m} = \frac{64 \pi^4 \epsilon^2 (\nu_{n \to m})^3}{3 h c^3} \cdot |x_{nm}|^2, \tag{5}$$

so that *the off-diagonal elements of the Heisenberg matrix associated with* x *are intimately related to the transition probabilities of the system under consideration.* The off-diagonal elements of Heisenberg matrices associated with dynamical variables other than coordinates do not have as direct a physical interpretation. The elements of all Heisenberg matrices are, however, asymptotically connected to certain classical quantities; this connection will be illustrated later in this section.

F. A Heisenberg matrix α depends in general on t; denoting it for the moment by $\alpha(t)$ and adapting to the case of matrices the standard definition of a time derivative, we *define* the time derivative of α as the matrix

$$\dot{\alpha} = \lim_{\Delta t \to 0} \frac{\alpha(t + \Delta t) - \alpha(t)}{\Delta t}. \tag{6}$$

It follows that

$$\dot{\alpha}_{nm} = \lim_{\Delta t \to 0} \frac{\alpha_{nm}(t + \Delta t) - \alpha_{nm}(t)}{\Delta t} = \frac{d}{dt} \alpha_{nm}, \tag{7}$$

where $\dot{\alpha}_{nm}$ is the nmth element of the matrix $\dot{\alpha}$ and $d\,\alpha_{nm}/dt$ is the time derivative of α_{nm}; accordingly, *the time derivative of a Heisenberg matrix α is the matrix whose elements are the time derivatives of the corresponding elements of α.* In view of (1) and (2), Equation (7) becomes, in the case of Heisenberg matrices,

$$\dot{\alpha}_{nm} = \frac{i(E_n - E_m)}{\hbar}\,\alpha_{nm} = 2\pi i \nu_{nm}\alpha_{nm}\,. \qquad (8)$$

G. Next we show that the time derivative, $\dot{\alpha}$, of a Heisenberg matrix α is $i\hbar^{-1}$ times the commutator of the Heisenberg matrices H and α, where H is the Heisenberg matrix associated with the Hamiltonian of the system under consideration. Indeed, taking the nmth elements of both sides of the matrix equation

$$\dot{\alpha} = \frac{i}{\hbar}(H\alpha - \alpha H), \qquad \langle 9 \rangle$$

we get

$$\dot{\alpha}_{nm} = \frac{i}{\hbar}\left(\sum_j H_{nj}\alpha_{jm} - \sum_j \alpha_{nj}H_{jm}\right); \qquad (10)$$

in view of (3) this reduces to

$$\dot{\alpha}_{nm} = \frac{i}{\hbar}(H_{nn}\alpha_{nm} - \alpha_{nm}H_{mm}) = \frac{i(E_n - E_m)}{\hbar}\,\alpha_{nm}, \qquad (11)$$

and a comparison with (8) completes the verification of $\langle 9 \rangle$. Now, according to the equation of motion 27^{44}, the right side of $\langle 9 \rangle$ is the operator to be associated with the time derivative of the dynamical variable α, and hence *the Heisenberg matrix associated with the time derivative of a dynamical variable α is the time derivative of the Heisenberg matrix associated with the dynamical variable α.*

H. We shall now illustrate an asymptotic connection between the elements of Heisenberg matrices and the coefficients of the classical Fourier expansions of the corresponding dynamical variables. When the classical motion of a one-dimensional system is periodic with a period T, then every dynamical variable α pertaining to the system can be expressed classically as a Fourier series

$$\alpha = \sum_r \alpha_r e^{ir\omega t}, \qquad r = \cdots, -2, -1, 0, 1, 2, \cdots, \qquad (12)$$

where $\omega = 2\pi/T$ is 2π times the fundamental frequency of the motion, and where α_r is the (complex) amplitude of the rth harmonic of α; note that when complex exponentials rather than trigonometric functions are used in the Fourier series the harmonics are numbered $\cdots, -2, -1, 0, 1, 2, \cdots$. For example, the classical Fourier series for the coordinate of an oscillator is

$$(19^{10}) \qquad x = \left(i\sqrt{\frac{E}{2k}}\, e^{-i\gamma}\right) e^{-i\omega t} + \left(-i\sqrt{\frac{E}{2k}}\, e^{i\gamma}\right) e^{i\omega t}; \qquad (13)$$

in this case the amplitude of the harmonic numbered -1 is $i\sqrt{E/2k}\, e^{-i\gamma}$, that of the harmonic numbered 1 is $-i\sqrt{E/2k}\, e^{i\gamma}$, and the amplitudes of all other harmonics vanish, so that the various amplitudes can be listed as follows:

TABLE 14

r	$\cdots$	-3	-2	-1	0	1	2	3	$\cdots$
Amplitude of the classical rth harmonic of x	$\cdots$	0	0	$i\sqrt{\dfrac{E}{2k}}\, e^{-i\gamma}$	0	$-i\sqrt{\dfrac{E}{2k}}\, e^{i\gamma}$	0	0	$\cdots$

Let us turn next to the Heisenberg matrix representing the coordinate of the oscillator and consider those of its elements x_{nm} for which both n and m are large. These elements are listed in 24^{62}, so that, disregarding the standard time factors, we get:

TABLE 15

r	$\cdots$	-3	-2	-1	0	1	2	3	$\cdots$
$x_{n,n-r}$ for large n and apart from time factor	$\cdots$	0	0	$i\sqrt{\dfrac{E_n}{2k}}\, e^{-i\gamma}$	0	$-i\sqrt{\dfrac{E_n}{2k}}\, e^{i\gamma}$	0	0	$\cdots$

Comparison of the two tables now shows that, when n is large, the matrix element $x_{n,n-r}$ is, apart from its time factor, precisely the classical amplitude of the rth harmonic of x, except that the E of Table 14 is replaced in Table 15 by E_n.

Similarly, for the square of the momentum of the oscillator, we get from 22^{10} and from 25^{62}:

TABLE 16

r	$\cdots$	-3	-2	-1	0	1	2	3	$\cdots$
Amplitude of the classical rth harmonic of p^2	$\cdots$	0	$\frac{1}{2}mEe^{-2i\gamma}$	0	mE	0	$\frac{1}{2}mEe^{2i\gamma}$	0	$\cdots$
$p^2_{n,n-r}$ for large n and apart from time factor	$\cdots$	0	$\frac{1}{2}mE_ne^{-2i\gamma}$	0	mE_n	0	$\frac{1}{2}mE_ne^{2i\gamma}$	0	$\cdots$

The asymptotic agreement between matrix elements and classical Fourier amplitudes is again apparent.

The two examples given above illustrate the theorem that we shall call the *correspondence rule* for the Heisenberg matrices, a theorem stating essentially that *for large values of n and small values of r the matrix element $\alpha_{n,n-r}$ of the Heisenberg matrix associated with a dynamical variable α is simply related to the rth classical harmonic of α.* The proof of this theorem will be omitted, since it employs advanced classical mechanics; nor shall we attempt to state the theorem more explicitly than we did above. Note that the *precise* agreement of, say, Tables 14 and 15 is due in part to the special choice of the γ_n's adopted in Exercise 5[62].

The correspondence rule is in accord with the *Bohr correspondence principle* formulated before the advent of quantum mechanics, which postulates asymptotic connections between atomic mechanics and classical mechanics in the region of the higher energies. Bohr's principle played a fundamental rôle in the considerations that led Heisenberg to the formulation of matrix mechanics.

Exercises

1. In view of 30[44] and the result of Exercise 7[44], the Heisenberg matrices pertaining to a specific dynamical system must satisfy the equations $p = m\dot{x}$ and $m\ddot{x} = -V'$. Verify that the matrices 9[62] and 14[62] satisfy these relations.

2. Use (3) and 5[30] to fill in the explicit values of the elements in the upper left-hand corner of the Heisenberg matrix associated with the Hamiltonian of a particle in a box. Note that this matrix is different from 18[62].

3. Verify the correspondence rule for the dynamical variables p, x^2, and xp for an oscillator.

4. Show that in the case of the linear harmonic oscillator the time factor of a Heisenberg matrix element $\alpha_{n,n-r}$ is the same as that of the *r*th harmonic of the classical dynamical variable α; to what special feature of the energy spectrum of the oscillator is this coincidence due?

5. Show that, if the motion of a system is bound, then the diagonal elements of the Heisenberg matrix p pertaining to this system are all zeros.

6. Recall the criterion 1[45] and show that, if the energy spectrum of a system is nondegenerate, the Heisenberg matrix associated with a constant of motion of the system is diagonal; see Exercise 7 for an example. Then use the rule for time differentiation of Heisenberg matrices to verify that the matrix associated with the time derivative of a constant of motion is the matrix zero.

7. Compute the Heisenberg matrix representing the dynamical variable Ω of §47 when the dynamical system under consideration is a linear harmonic oscillator. For what class of one-dimensional dynamical systems is the Heisenberg matrix Ω the same as it is for a linear harmonic oscillator?

8. Show that the constants of motion of a bound one-dimensional system all commute with one another.

9. Show that, if a system has noncommuting constants of motion, then its energy spectrum is degenerate. (On account of the result of Exercise 8, this theorem is of no interest in connection with bound one-dimensional systems.)

10. Assume the matrix H to be degenerate (a case that does not arise in bound one-dimensional motion), recall the criterion 1[45], and show that, although the matrix associated with a constant of motion need not then be diagonal, its time derivative, defined by (8), is nevertheless the matrix zero.

11. Show that the definition 23[62] of the Heisenberg matrix element $(n \mid \alpha \mid m)$, that is, α_{nm}, is equivalent to the following definition:

$$(n \mid \alpha \mid m) = \int_{-\infty}^{\infty} (n \mid p)\alpha(p \mid m)\, dp, \qquad (14)$$

where α in the integrand is the operator associated in the p-scheme with the dynamical variable α, $(p \mid k)$ is the normalized ψ-function of the p-scheme describing the kth energy state of the system, and $(k \mid p)$ is, as usual, the complex conjugate of $(p \mid k)$. *Hint*: first show that the equivalence holds when α is the coordinate x.

64. The Heisenberg Method

Having defined Heisenberg matrices through 2[62], we derived in the two preceding sections certain properties of these matrices, properties that can be described without reference to the Schroedinger theory. Now, it turns out that, if we should require a set of matrices to have these properties, then the conditions imposed on the matrices are so stringent that the matrices become uniquely determined, apart from just the standard arbitrariness of the phase factors of their elements. In other words, *Heisenberg matrices can be computed without reference to the Schroedinger theory*, and, in particular, to 2^{62}. This fact enables us to treat quantum-mechanical problems by the Heisenberg method, which we shall now describe (insofar as it concerns the computation of the possible values of real dynamical variables not involving t explicitly and pertaining to a conservative system) by stating the rules for associating specific operators with dynamical variables and the rule for inferring the possible values of a dynamical variable from the operator associated with it.

A. *The Heisenberg operators to be associated with dynamical variables are Hermitian matrices that fulfill the quantum conditions* 1^{13} *and satisfy the time-derivative, sum, and product relations satisfied by the corresponding dynamical variables themselves*; further, *the matrix associated with the Hamiltonian of the system is to be diagonal*; and lastly, *the nmth element of every matrix, associated with a dynamical variable not involving t explicitly, is to depend on t through the time factor* $e^{i(E_n - E_m)t/\hbar}$; the rule for time differentiation of the matrices is therefore

(8^{63})
$$\dot{\alpha}_{nm} = \frac{i(E_n - E_m)}{\hbar}\alpha_{nm},$$
(1)

where the E's are the energy levels of the system, whose theoretical values are of course usually unknown at the beginning of a calculation.

B. Once the matrices satisfying the conditions A have been found, *the possible values of a dynamical variable are the eigenvalues of the matrix associated with it*. This is the fundamental physical assumption of the Heisenberg method when this method is viewed apart from our postulate I of §13.

The major computational problem in the application of the Heisenberg method to a specific dynamical system is usually the identification of the matrices to be associated with dynamical variables, that is, matrices satisfying the conditions A. In practice we usually first choose the matrix H to be a diagonal matrix with undetermined diagonal elements, then associate with every remaining dynamical variable a matrix whose elements are undetermined except for the form of their time factors, and finally force these matrices to satisfy the quantum conditions and the relations holding between the corresponding dynamical variables until their elements become fully determined, that is, until only the standard arbitrariness in the phase factors remains. This procedure must be carried out separately for each dynamical system. Incidentally, since the matrix H is required to be diagonal, it follows from B that *the diagonal elements of the matrix H are the energy levels of the system.*

In the light of our previous work the conditions A are not unexpected; but the considerations that led Heisenberg in his pioneer work to formulate an essentially equivalent set of conditions were of course quite different from those discussed above.

65. Energy Levels of an Oscillator

To illustrate the Heisenberg procedure we shall now use it to compute the energy levels of a linear harmonic oscillator. According to the conditions A of §64, the Heisenberg matrices x, p, and H must in this case satisfy the special relations

$$m\ddot{x} = -kx \tag{1}$$

and

$$H = \frac{1}{2m} p^2 + \tfrac{1}{2}kx^2, \tag{2}$$

and also the standard relations

$$p = m\dot{x} \tag{3}$$

and

$$xp - px = i\hbar; \tag{4}$$

further, the matrices must be Hermitian, the matrix H must be diagonal, and the time factors of the various matrix elements must be of the standard form, so that, in particular, $\dot{x}_{nl} = i(E_n - E_l)\hbar^{-1}x_{nl}$,

$$\ddot{x}_{nl} = -(E_n - E_l)^2 \hbar^{-2} x_{nl}, \tag{5}$$

and

$$p_{nl} = mi(E_n - E_l)\hbar^{-1} x_{nl}. \tag{6}$$

As noted in the preceding section, it is a claim of the Heisenberg theory that, if the matrices x, p, and H satisfy these conditions, then the diagonal elements of H are the energy levels of the oscillator.

To simplify our problem, we shall assume outright that the

energy spectrum of the oscillator is discrete and nondegenerate, and possesses a lowest level E_0 , so that the matrix H has the form

$$H = \begin{vmatrix} E_0 & 0 & 0 & 0 & \cdots \\ 0 & E_1 & 0 & 0 & \cdots \\ 0 & 0 & E_2 & 0 & \cdots \\ 0 & 0 & 0 & E_3 & \cdots \\ \cdots & \cdots & \cdots & \cdots & \cdots \end{vmatrix} \qquad (7)$$

where the E's are as yet undetermined. The rows and columns of all matrices of this section will be labeled 0, 1, 2, $\cdots$.

To simplify the problem still further, we shall also assume that the correspondence rule holds to the extent that if the classical rth harmonic of x is zero then the corresponding elements of the matrix x (that is, the elements $x_{n,n-r}$) are also zero, and if the classical rth harmonic of x is not zero then the corresponding elements of the matrix x are also not zero. It then follows from 19^{10} that

$$\begin{cases} x_{nl} = 0 & \text{if } l \neq n \pm 1 \\ x_{nl} \neq 0 & \text{if } l = n \pm 1, \end{cases} \qquad (8)$$

where the nonvanishing elements are as yet undetermined except for the form of their time factors. In other words, the correspondence rule suggests that the matrix x has the form

$$x = \begin{vmatrix} 0 & x_{01} & 0 & 0 & \cdots \\ x_{10} & 0 & x_{12} & 0 & \cdots \\ 0 & x_{21} & 0 & x_{23} & \cdots \\ 0 & 0 & x_{32} & 0 & \cdots \\ \cdots & \cdots & \cdots & \cdots & \cdots \end{vmatrix} \qquad (9)$$

where the elements not shown as zeros are not zeros. In view of (6) and the assumed nondegeneracy of the energy spectrum, the matrix p has a similar form.

Our problem is now to identify the various matrices, in particular the matrix H, by adjusting their as yet undetermined elements in such a way that the matrices satisfy the conditions summarized above. The procedure is quite straightforward. According to $\langle 1 \rangle$

$$m\ddot{x}_{n,n-1} = -kx_{n,n-1} , \tag{10}$$

which, on account of (5), becomes $[k - m(E_n - E_{n-1})^2 \hbar^{-2}]x_{n,n-1} = 0$; therefore, in view of (8), $k - m(E_n - E_{n-1})^2 \hbar^{-2} = 0$, and

$$(E_n - E_{n-1})^2 = \hbar^2 \nu_c^2 , \tag{11}$$

where ν_c is our usual abbreviation for the classical frequency of the oscillator. Taking square roots and remembering that, according to our labeling convention, E_n is greater than E_{n-1}, we get

$$E_n - E_{n-1} = h\nu_c , \tag{12}$$

so that

$$E_n = nh\nu_c + E_0 . \tag{13}$$

Thus a great deal of information about the energy levels (their spacing relative to each other) has been obtained almost at once.

To complete the computation of the energy levels, it remains to evaluate E_0, that is, the matrix element H_{00}. Now, according to $\langle 2 \rangle$,

$$H_{00} = \frac{1}{2m} p_{00}^2 + \tfrac{1}{2}kx_{00}^2 \tag{14}$$

where p_{00}^2 and x_{00}^2 are the 00th elements of the matrices p^2 and x^2; hence

$$H_{00} = \frac{1}{2m} \sum_j p_{0j}p_{j0} + \tfrac{1}{2}k \sum_j x_{0j}x_{j0}, \qquad j = 0, 1, 2, \cdots . \tag{15}$$

In view of (8) and (6), the only nonvanishing terms in the sums go with $j = 1$, so that (15) reduces to

$$H_{00} = \frac{1}{2m} p_{01}p_{10} + \tfrac{1}{2}kx_{01}x_{10} . \tag{16}$$

On account of (6), this becomes

$$H_{00} = \frac{1}{2m} [im(E_0 - E_1)\hbar^{-1}x_{01}][im(E_1 - E_0)\hbar^{-1}x_{10}] + \tfrac{1}{2}kx_{01}x_{10}, \tag{17}$$

and, using (13), we get

$$H_{00} = \frac{4\pi^2 m^2 \nu_c^2}{2m} x_{01}x_{10} + \tfrac{1}{2}kx_{01}x_{10} = kx_{01}x_{10} . \tag{18}$$

To evaluate $x_{01}x_{10}$ we turn to $\langle 4 \rangle$, which has not yet been used. We have $(xp - px)_{00} = i\hbar$, that is,

$$\sum_j x_{0j}p_{j0} - \sum_j p_{0j}x_{j0} = i\hbar, \qquad j = 0, 1, 2, \cdots. \qquad (19)$$

The only value of j yielding nonvanishing terms is again 1, so that

$$x_{01}p_{10} - p_{01}x_{10} = i\hbar. \qquad (20)$$

Using (6) and (13), we convert this into $x_{01}(2\pi i m \nu_c x_{10})$ $- (-2\pi i m \nu_c x_{01})x_{10} = i\hbar$, and therefore

$$x_{01}x_{10} = \frac{\hbar}{4\pi m \nu_c} = \frac{h}{4\pi\sqrt{km}}. \qquad (21)$$

Equation (18) now yields $H_{00} = \frac{1}{2}h\nu_c$, and it follows from (13) that

$$E_n = (n + \tfrac{1}{2})h\nu_c, \qquad n = 0, 1, 2, \cdots, \qquad (22)$$

in agreement with the result obtained in §15 by the Schroedinger method and in §51 by the p-method.

The reader will have noted (a) that our acquaintance with the classical theory of the oscillator, which was of no assistance in computing the energy levels of the oscillator by the Schroedinger method, has been of great help in the work of this section, since it enabled us through the correspondence rule to determine from the outset the general form of the Heisenberg matrices; and (b) that the mathematical methods of this section, being on the whole purely algebraic, are somewhat simpler than in the Schroedinger case. For reasons such as these a person intimately acquainted with the classical theory of a dynamical system and skilled in judicious application of the correspondence rule will sometimes prefer to make calculations regarding the corresponding quantum-mechanical system directly by the Heisenberg method and without reference to the Schroedinger theory.

·Heisenberg matrices, other than H, pertaining to the oscillator are also readily computed without the aid of Schroedinger functions by extending the calculations given above. For example, since x must be a Hermitian matrix, we have $x_{10} = x_{01}^*$, so that $x_{01}x_{10} = |x_{01}|^2$, and (21) becomes

$$|x_{01}|^2 = \tfrac{1}{2}a^2, \qquad (23)$$

where a is given in 5^{62}. Hence the modulus of x_{01} is $2^{-\frac{1}{2}}a$, and x_{01} differs from $2^{-\frac{1}{2}}a$ by a factor of the form $e^{i\delta}$, where δ is real; this factor must include the standard time factor of x_{01} and must therefore be of the form $e^{i\gamma}e^{i(E_0-E_1)t/\hbar}$, where γ remains arbitrary. We may, if we wish, set $\gamma = \gamma_1 - \gamma_0$, where γ_0 and γ_1 are arbitrary real constants, and write

$$x_{01} = \frac{1}{\sqrt{2}}\, ae^{-i(\gamma_0-\gamma_1)}e^{i(E_0-E_1)t/\hbar} = \frac{1}{\sqrt{2}}\, a''. \qquad (24)$$

This result is in agreement with the middle line in 8^{62} for $n = 0$. The calculation of the matrix x will be completed in Exercises 2 and 3.

The computation of the Heisenberg matrices for the oscillator by the Heisenberg method becomes of course more involved when carried out without the aid of the correspondence rule. On the assumption that the energy spectrum is nondegenerate, it is not difficult to show that every row or column of the matrix x contains, at most, two nonvanishing elements, but the identification of the positions of these is somewhat tedious.[6]

Exercises

1. Derive (13) by equating the $(n, n + 1)$th elements [rather than the $(n, n - 1)$th elements] of the two sides of $\langle 1 \rangle$.

2. Equate the nth diagonal elements of the two sides of $\langle 4 \rangle$ and show, using (8), that $|\, x_{n,n+1}\,|^2 - |\, x_{n,n-1}\,|^2 = \frac{1}{2}a^2$; then show that $|\, x_{n,n+1}\,|^2 = \frac{1}{2}(n + 1)a^2$.

3. Deduce 8^{62} from the final result of Exercise 2.

4. Equate the nlth elements of the two sides of $\langle 1 \rangle$ and show, assuming nondegeneracy of the energy spectrum, but not using the correspondence rule, that every row as well as every column of the matrix x for the oscillator contains at most two nonvanishing elements.

5. Recall Exercise 6^{58} and show that, since $\langle 4 \rangle$ holds for any dynamical system, all Heisenberg matrices have an infinite number of rows and columns.

6. Equate the nnth elements of the two sides of $\langle 4 \rangle$ and show that every row as well as every column of the Heisenberg matrix x for any dynamical system contains at least one nonvanishing element.

---

[6] See for example, G. Birtwistle, *The New Quantum Mechanics*, Chapter X; Cambridge: The University Press, 1928. Or M. Born and P. Jordan, *Elementare Quantenmechanik*, §23; Berlin: Springer, 1930. Born and Jordan consider the problem with a minimum of assumptions and show that the Heisenberg method leads to unique matrices for the oscillator.

66. Diagonalization of Matrices

In this and in the following section we shall take up certain mathematical preliminaries to the Heisenberg perturbation theory.

Frame changes. If we begin with an analytical description of vectors and mappings of a space in terms of some coordinate frame P and then go over to their description in terms of another frame Q, we say that we have carried out a *transformation of coordinates* or a *frame change*. Our immediate problem is to set up a convenient analytical method for describing frame changes.

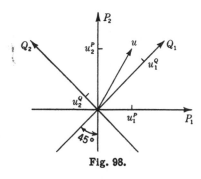

Fig. 98.

We start with a two-dimensional example and indicate in Fig. 98 a plane, an arbitrary vector u in this plane, and the two coordinate frames P and Q of Fig. 87[54] and Fig. 91[55]; the process of substituting the frame Q for the frame P will be called for brevity the frame change S.

A frame change (unlike a mapping) does not affect the *vectors* of our plane; for example, the vector u in Fig. 98 remains the same whatever frame may be used in describing the plane analytically. But a frame change does in general affect the *components* of a vector; thus the components u_1^P and u_2^P of the vector u in Fig. 98 are different from the components u_1^Q and u_2^Q of the same vector, the relations between the two sets of components being

$$
\begin{cases}
u_1^Q = \dfrac{1}{\sqrt{2}}\, u_1^P + \dfrac{1}{\sqrt{2}}\, u_2^P \\[2mm]
u_2^Q = -\dfrac{1}{\sqrt{2}}\, u_1^P + \dfrac{1}{\sqrt{2}}\, u_2^P.
\end{cases}
\tag{1}
$$

Now, the knowledge of the matrix of the coefficients on the right side of Equations (1) is sufficient for the computation of u_1^Q and u_2^Q whenever u_1^P and u_2^P are known; in fact, we adopt the matrix

$$
S = \begin{pmatrix} \dfrac{1}{\sqrt{2}} & \dfrac{1}{\sqrt{2}} \\[2mm] -\dfrac{1}{\sqrt{2}} & \dfrac{1}{\sqrt{2}} \end{pmatrix}
\tag{2}
$$

as a standard description of our frame change S. Using u^P to denote a column symbol with components u_1^P and u_2^P, and u^Q to denote a column symbol with components u_1^Q and u_2^Q, we may now symbolize Equations (1) by writing $u^Q = Su^P$.

If u is an arbitrary vector in an N-space, and if its components u_i^Q in a frame Q are related to its components u_i^P in a frame P through the equations

$$u_1^Q = s_{11} u_1^P + s_{12} u_2^P + \cdots + s_{1N} u_N^P$$

$$u_2^Q = s_{21} u_1^P + s_{22} u_2^P + \cdots + s_{2N} u_N^P \qquad (3)$$

$$\cdots\cdots\cdots\cdots\cdots\cdots\cdots\cdots\cdots\cdots$$

$$u_N^Q = s_{N1} u_1^P + s_{N2} u_2^P + \cdots + s_{NN} u_N^P,$$

then we adopt the matrix

$$S = \begin{pmatrix} s_{11} & s_{12} & \cdots & s_{1N} \\ s_{21} & s_{22} & \cdots & s_{2N} \\ & & \cdots & \\ s_{N1} & s_{N2} & \cdots & s_{NN} \end{pmatrix} \qquad (4)$$

as the analytical description of the transformation from the frame P to the frame Q and, denoting the column symbol with components u_i^Q by u^Q and the column symbol with components u_i^P by u^P, we symbolize Equations (3) by writing

$$u^Q = S u^P. \qquad (5)$$

The effect of frame changes on representatives of mappings. Let a mapping α of a space send an arbitrary vector u into the vector v, so that

$$\alpha u = v, \qquad (6)$$

and let this mapping and the vectors u and v be represented in a frame P by the matrix α^P and column symbols u^P and v^P, respectively, so that

$$\alpha^P u^P = v^P; \qquad (7)$$

further, let this mapping and the vectors u and v be represented in another frame Q by the matrix α^Q and column symbols u^Q and v^Q, respectively, so that

$$\alpha^Q u^Q = v^Q. \qquad (8)$$

Our problem is to find the relation between α^Q and α^P when the transformation from the frame P to the frame Q is described by a matrix S, so that

$$u^Q = S u^P \qquad (9)$$

$$v^Q = S v^P. \qquad (10)$$

Eliminating u^Q and v^Q from (8) by means of (9) and (10), we get

$$\alpha^Q S u^P = S v^P, \tag{11}$$

that is,

$$\alpha^Q S u^P = S \alpha^P u^P. \tag{12}$$

Since the vector u is arbitrary, the column symbol u^P in (12) has arbitrary components; recalling Exercise 8[56], we then conclude that

$$\alpha^Q S = S \alpha^P. \tag{13}$$

If S^{-1} exists, we get from (13) the equation

$$\alpha^Q = S \alpha^P S^{-1}, \tag{14}$$

which enables us to compute α^Q in terms of α^P and S.

To illustrate, we return for a moment to the reflection γ discussed in §54; this reflection is represented in the frame P of Fig. 98 by the matrix

(15[54])
$$\gamma^P = \begin{pmatrix} 0 & 1 \\ 1 & 0 \end{pmatrix}. \tag{15}$$

We shall use (14) to find the matrix γ^Q representing the same mapping but constructed relatively to the frame Q. The frame change from P to Q is in this case described by the matrix (2), so that according to 15[58]

$$S^{-1} = \begin{pmatrix} \dfrac{1}{\sqrt{2}} & -\dfrac{1}{\sqrt{2}} \\ \dfrac{1}{\sqrt{2}} & \dfrac{1}{\sqrt{2}} \end{pmatrix}. \tag{16}$$

Equation (14) now yields

$$\gamma^Q = S\gamma^P S^{-1} = \begin{pmatrix} \dfrac{1}{\sqrt{2}} & \dfrac{1}{\sqrt{2}} \\ -\dfrac{1}{\sqrt{2}} & \dfrac{1}{\sqrt{2}} \end{pmatrix} \begin{pmatrix} 0 & 1 \\ 1 & 0 \end{pmatrix} \begin{pmatrix} \dfrac{1}{\sqrt{2}} & -\dfrac{1}{\sqrt{2}} \\ \dfrac{1}{\sqrt{2}} & \dfrac{1}{\sqrt{2}} \end{pmatrix} = \begin{pmatrix} 1 & 0 \\ 0 & -1 \end{pmatrix} \tag{17}$$

in agreement with 7[55].

From the quasi-geometric standpoint that we have employed in this section, it is of course obvious that the matrices α^Q and α^P have the same eigenvalues, namely, the eigenvalues of the one mapping that both matrices represent. To prove (algebraically, and without ascribing to the matrices any geometrical significance) that, if the matrices α^Q, α^P, and S satisfy (14), then every eigenvalue of α^P is also an eigenvalue of α^Q, we may proceed as follows: Let α^P, the constant λ, and the column symbol u^P satisfy the equation

$$\alpha^P u^P = \lambda u^P, \tag{18}$$

so that λ is an eigenvalue of α^P. Construct the column symbol Su^P, denote it, say, by u^Q, and operate on it with the matrix α^Q. The result is

$$\alpha^Q u^Q = \alpha^Q S u^P = S\alpha^P S^{-1} S u^P = S\alpha^P u^P, \tag{19}$$

so that, in view of (18), $\alpha^Q u^Q = S\lambda u^P = \lambda S u^P$, that is

$$\alpha^Q u^Q = \lambda u^Q, \tag{20}$$

and hence λ is an eigenvalue of α^Q.

If three matrices, α', α, and β, are related through the equation

$$\alpha' = \beta\alpha\beta^{-1}, \tag{21}$$

that is, through an equation of the form (14), then α' is called the *transform* of α by β, β is called the *transformation matrix*, and the process of constructing α' from α and β is called a *similarity transformation*; similarly, the matrix $\alpha'' = \gamma\alpha\gamma^{-1}$ is called the transform of α by γ, and so on. We have shown above, quite apart from any quasi-geometric significance that may be attached to matrices, that *the eigenvalues of a transform of a matrix are the same as those of the matrix itself.* This result provides the clue for our interest in the topics now under discussion, because it shows that the computation of the eigenvalues of a matrix can, by a similarity transformation of the given matrix, be reduced to the computation of the eigenvalues of another matrix, which might perhaps be easier to handle than the given matrix.

Unitary frame changes. Let $u, v, \cdots, z$ be N orthonormal vectors in an N-space, represented in a frame P by the column symbols

$$\begin{pmatrix} u_1 \\ u_2 \\ \cdots \\ u_N \end{pmatrix}, \begin{pmatrix} v_1 \\ v_2 \\ \cdots \\ v_N \end{pmatrix}, \ldots, \begin{pmatrix} z_1 \\ z_2 \\ \cdots \\ z_N \end{pmatrix}, \tag{22}$$

so that we have the N equations (recall 13^{53} and 14^{56})

$$\sum_i u_i^* u_i = \sum_i v_i^* v_i = \cdots = \sum_i z_i^* z_i = 1 \tag{23}$$

and the $\frac{1}{2}N(N-1)$ equations

$$\sum_i u_i^* v_i = \sum_i u_i^* w_i = \cdots = \sum_i u_i^* z_i = 0$$
$$\sum_i v_i^* w_i = \cdots = \sum_i v_i^* z_i = 0 \qquad (24)$$
$$\cdots\cdots\cdots\cdots\cdots\cdots$$
$$\sum_i y_i^* z_i = 0,$$

and let S be the special frame change described by the matrix

$$S = \begin{pmatrix} u_1^* & u_2^* & \cdots & u_N^* \\ v_1^* & v_2^* & \cdots & v_N^* \\ & & \cdots & \\ z_1^* & z_2^* & \cdots & z_N^* \end{pmatrix}. \qquad (25)$$

Our present problem is to identify the frame Q that the special frame change S substitutes for the frame P.

Operating with the matrix S in turn on each of the symbols (22), we get the column symbols

$$\begin{pmatrix} 1 \\ 0 \\ \cdots \\ 0 \end{pmatrix}, \begin{pmatrix} 0 \\ 1 \\ \cdots \\ 0 \end{pmatrix}, \cdots, \begin{pmatrix} 0 \\ 0 \\ \cdots \\ 1 \end{pmatrix}. \qquad (26)$$

Now according to (5), the symbols (26) are the representatives in the frame Q of our vectors u, v, $\cdots$, z; and inspection of (26) shows that Q is that frame whose basic unit vectors lying along the respective axes Q_1, Q_2, $\cdots$, Q_N are just our unit vectors u, v, $\cdots$, z. This result enables us to construct the matrix describing a transformation from a given orthogonal frame to another having the same origin, the same scale unit, and a prescribed orientation relative to the first.

A transformation from one orthogonal frame to another orthogonal frame without change of scale unit and origin, and a matrix describing such a transformation are called, respectively, a *unitary frame change* and a *unitary matrix*. The matrix (25), whose elements satisfy Equations (23) and (24), is thus a unitary matrix. The complex conjugate of (25) is

$$\bar{S} = \begin{pmatrix} u_1 & v_1 & \cdots & z_1 \\ u_2 & v_2 & \cdots & z_2 \\ & & \cdots & \\ u_N & v_N & \cdots & z_N \end{pmatrix}, \qquad (27)$$

and we find, using (23) and (24), that

$$S\bar{S} = 1, \tag{28}$$

that is, that

$$S^{-1} = \bar{S}. \tag{29}$$

Equation (29), which can be shown to imply the $\frac{1}{2}N(N+1)$ equations (23) and (24), provides a succinct algebraic definition of a unitary matrix: *a matrix is unitary if its complex conjugate equals its reciprocal.*

Diagonalization of Hermitian matrices. Let a mapping α be represented in a frame P by a *Hermitian* matrix

$$\alpha^P = \begin{pmatrix} \alpha_{11} & \cdots & \alpha_{1N} \\ \cdots & \cdots & \cdots \\ \alpha_{N1} & \cdots & \alpha_{NN} \end{pmatrix} \tag{30}$$

and let Q be an orthogonal frame whose axes lie along the eigenvectors of α. We shall show that the matrix α^Q representing the mapping α in the frame Q is diagonal.

Let the unitary eigenvectors[7] of α belonging to its eigenvalues $\lambda_1, \lambda_2, \cdots, \lambda_N$, be represented in the frame P by the column symbols (22), so that

$$\begin{pmatrix} \alpha_{11} & \cdots & \alpha_{1N} \\ \cdots & \cdots & \cdots \\ \alpha_{N1} & \cdots & \alpha_{NN} \end{pmatrix} \begin{pmatrix} u_1 \\ \cdots \\ u_N \end{pmatrix} = \lambda_1 \begin{pmatrix} u_1 \\ \cdots \\ u_N \end{pmatrix}, \tag{31a}$$

$$\begin{pmatrix} \alpha_{11} & \cdots & \alpha_{1N} \\ \cdots & \cdots & \cdots \\ \alpha_{N1} & \cdots & \alpha_{NN} \end{pmatrix} \begin{pmatrix} v_1 \\ \cdots \\ v_N \end{pmatrix} = \lambda_2 \begin{pmatrix} v_1 \\ \cdots \\ v_N \end{pmatrix}, \tag{31b}$$

and so forth, or, more explicitly,

$$\sum_i \alpha_{ki} u_i = \lambda_1 u_k, \qquad \sum_i \alpha_{ki} v_i = \lambda_2 v_k, \cdots, \tag{32}$$

---

[7] As noted in §58, any two eigenvectors of a Hermitian matrix belonging to different eigenvalues of the matrix are orthogonal. If α^P is nondegenerate, the mapping α has just N eigenrays, and each of its normalized eigenvectors is undetermined only to the extent of a numerical factor of modulus unity, which we absorb in the elements of (22). If α^P is degenerate, the mapping α has an infinite number of eigenrays; we then restrict ourselves to eigenvectors lying along N mutually orthogonal eigenrays; it is immaterial for our purpose how these N rays are chosen.

where $k = 1, 2, \cdots, N$. Our task is to find, with the help of (32), the matrix representing α in the frame whose basic unit vectors are represented in the frame P by the column symbols (22), so that the transformation matrix and its reciprocal are just (25) and (27); Equations (24) are of course consistent with the fact that α^P is Hermitian. Using (14), we get

$$\alpha^Q = S\alpha^P S^{-1}$$

$$= \begin{pmatrix} u_1^* & \cdots & u_N^* \\ \cdots & \cdots & \cdots \\ z_1^* & \cdots & z_N^* \end{pmatrix} \begin{pmatrix} \alpha_{11} & \cdots & \alpha_{1N} \\ \cdots & \cdots & \cdots \\ \alpha_{N1} & \cdots & \alpha_{NN} \end{pmatrix} \begin{pmatrix} u_1 & \cdots & z_1 \\ \cdots & \cdots & \cdots \\ u_N & \cdots & z_N \end{pmatrix}. \quad (33)$$

Now,

$$\begin{pmatrix} \alpha_{11} & \cdots & \alpha_{1N} \\ \cdots & \cdots & \cdots \\ \alpha_{N1} & \cdots & \alpha_{NN} \end{pmatrix} \begin{pmatrix} u_1 & \cdots & z_1 \\ \cdots & \cdots & \cdots \\ u_N & \cdots & z_N \end{pmatrix}$$

$$= \begin{pmatrix} \sum \alpha_{1i} u_i & \cdots & \sum \alpha_{1i} z_i \\ \cdots & \cdots & \cdots \\ \sum \alpha_{Ni} u_i & \cdots & \sum \alpha_{Ni} z_i \end{pmatrix} = \begin{pmatrix} \lambda_1 u_1 & \cdots & \lambda_N z_1 \\ \cdots & \cdots & \cdots \\ \lambda_1 u_N & \cdots & \lambda_N z_N \end{pmatrix}, \quad (34)$$

and hence

$$\alpha^Q = \begin{pmatrix} u_1^* & \cdots & u_N^* \\ \cdots & \cdots & \cdots \\ z_1^* & \cdots & z_N^* \end{pmatrix} \begin{pmatrix} \lambda_1 u_1 & \cdots & \lambda_N z_1 \\ \cdots & \cdots & \cdots \\ \lambda_1 u_N & \cdots & \lambda_N z_N \end{pmatrix}$$

$$= \begin{pmatrix} \lambda_1 \sum u_i^* u_i & \cdots & \lambda_N \sum u_i^* z_i \\ \cdots & \cdots & \cdots \\ \lambda_1 \sum z_i^* u_i & \cdots & \lambda_N \sum z_i^* z_i \end{pmatrix}, \quad (35)$$

that is,

$$\alpha^Q = \begin{pmatrix} \lambda_1 & 0 & \cdots & 0 \\ 0 & \lambda_2 & \cdots & 0 \\ & & \cdots & \\ 0 & 0 & \cdots & \lambda_N \end{pmatrix}. \quad (36)$$

The process of subjecting a matrix to a similarity transformation such that the transform of the matrix is diagonal is called *diagonalization* of the matrix or, even in purely algebraic discussions, *transformation of the matrix to its principal axes*. A similarity transformation employing a unitary transformation matrix is called a *unitary transformation*. We have shown above that a Hermitian matrix can be diagonalized by means of a unitary transformation, and that the appropriate transformation matrix can be constructed as soon as the eigenvectors of the given matrix have been computed.

To illustrate, we shall diagonalize the matrix γ^P given by (15). According to Table 12[54], the normalized eigenvectors of γ^P belonging to its respective eigenvalues 1 and -1 are $\dfrac{e^{i\delta_1}}{\sqrt{2}}\begin{pmatrix} 1 \\ 1 \end{pmatrix}$ and $\dfrac{e^{i\delta_2}}{\sqrt{2}}\begin{pmatrix} 1 \\ -1 \end{pmatrix}$, where the δ's are arbitrary real constants whose values are immaterial for our purpose; to save writing, we let $\delta_1 = 0$ and $\delta_2 = \pi$, getting the particular unitary eigenvectors

$$\begin{pmatrix} \dfrac{1}{\sqrt{2}} \\ \dfrac{1}{\sqrt{2}} \end{pmatrix} \quad \text{and} \quad \begin{pmatrix} -\dfrac{1}{\sqrt{2}} \\ \dfrac{1}{\sqrt{2}} \end{pmatrix}. \tag{37}$$

Using (37) to construct the transformation matrix S after the manner in which (25) is constructed from (22), we find that S is just the matrix (2). That the transform of γ^P by this S is diagonal is seen from (17).

Summary of algebraic results. So far as strict matrix algebra is concerned, we defined in this section the terms transform of a matrix, transformation matrix, similarity transformation, unitary matrix, unitary transformation, and diagonalization of a matrix; and, restricting ourselves to matrices with a finite number of rows and columns, we proved algebraically that the eigenvalues of a transform of a matrix are the same as those of the matrix itself, and that a Hermitian matrix can be diagonalized by means of a unitary transformation.

The process of diagonalization throws a matrix into a form in which its eigenvalues are displayed in full view (Exercise 3[58]); nevertheless, in most cases, this process is not useful for the *computation* of eigenvalues, because to set up the appropriate transformation matrix we must know the eigenvectors of the given matrix, while to compute the eigenvectors it is necessary first to find the eigenvalues. But the process of diagonalization is of computational value in certain approximate calculations to be considered in the next section.

Exercises

1. Show that a counterclockwise rotation of a rectangular coordinate frame of a real plane through an angle ϕ about O is described by the matrix $\begin{pmatrix} \cos \phi & \sin \phi \\ -\sin \phi & \cos \phi \end{pmatrix}$. Contrast this matrix with that of Exercise 5[55].

2. Use (14) to compute each of the matrices 7^{55} from the corresponding matrix in 15^{54}.

3. Diagonalize the matrix of Exercise 8^{54}.

4. Show that every algebraic relation that holds between two or more matrices holds also between the respective transforms of these matrices, provided each matrix is subjected to *the same* similarity transformation.

5. Show that, if two matrices do not commute, then they cannot be diagonalized simultaneously, that is, by means of the same similarity transformation.

6. The transformation from a frame P to a frame Q is described by a matrix S; the transformation from the frame Q to a frame R is described by a matrix T; compute the matrix describing the transformation from the frame P directly to the frame R.

7. Show that a product of two unitary matrices is unitary.

8. Show that the transform of a Hermitian matrix by a unitary matrix is Hermitian.

9. Show that the elements of (25) satisfy the equations

$$u_k^* u_l + v_k^* v_l + \cdots + z_k^* z_l = \begin{cases} 1 & \text{if } k = l \\ 0 & \text{if } k \neq l. \end{cases} \tag{38}$$

Note the appropriateness of saying that the rows of a unitary matrix are orthonormal, and that so are its columns.

10. Show that, if a unitary matrix S commutes with a nondegenerate diagonal matrix, then S is diagonal and each of its diagonal elements is of modulus unity.

11. Diagonalize the matrix ξ^P in 15^{54}; the procedure developed in the text is applicable in this case, since a Hermitian matrix can be formed by multiplying ξ^P by i. Reconcile the result of the diagonalization with that of Exercise 5^{55}.

12. Show that the condition (29), when imposed on the matrix (27), implies the $\frac{1}{2}N(N + 1)$ equations (23) and (24).

67. Approximate Diagonalization of Matrices

If a matrix α has the form

$$\alpha = \alpha^0 + \epsilon \alpha^{\mathrm{I}} + \epsilon^2 \alpha^{\mathrm{II}} + \cdots , \tag{1}$$

where α^0 is *diagonal*, so that

$$\alpha_{nm}^0 = 0 \quad \text{if } n \neq m, \tag{2}$$

where α^0, α^{I}, and so on, are matrices not involving ϵ, and where ϵ is a sufficiently small numerical parameter, then we call α a *perturbed* matrix, call α^0 the *unperturbed* matrix, and call $\epsilon \alpha^{\mathrm{I}}$

$+ \epsilon^2 \alpha^{II} + \cdots$ the *perturbing matrix* or the *perturbation.* Thus, if ϵ is small, then the matrix

$$\alpha = \begin{pmatrix} 1 + 3\epsilon & 2\epsilon \\ 2\epsilon & 4 + \epsilon^2 \end{pmatrix} \tag{3}$$

is an example of a perturbed 2-by-2 matrix, the unperturbed matrix being $\alpha^0 = \begin{pmatrix} 1 & 0 \\ 0 & 4 \end{pmatrix}$, and the perturbation being $\epsilon \alpha^I + \epsilon^2 \alpha^{II} = \epsilon \begin{pmatrix} 3 & 2 \\ 2 & 0 \end{pmatrix} + \epsilon^2 \begin{pmatrix} 0 & 0 \\ 0 & 1 \end{pmatrix}$. The purpose of this section is to show how matrix diagonalization can be used for approximate calculation of the eigenvalues of a Hermitian perturbed matrix without explicit use of the secular equation.

We begin with a few remarks concerning the eigenvalues of the particular matrix (3). If ϵ is entirely negligible, then (3) reduces to the unperturbed matrix

$$\begin{pmatrix} 1 & 0 \\ 0 & 4 \end{pmatrix} \tag{4}$$

whose eigenvalues are 1 and 4; thus to the zeroth approximation the eigenvalues of (3) are 1 and 4. If ϵ is small enough to permit neglecting the terms in ϵ^2, but not small enough to permit neglecting the terms in ϵ^1, then (3) goes over into

$$\begin{pmatrix} 1 + 3\epsilon & 2\epsilon \\ 2\epsilon & 4 \end{pmatrix}; \tag{5}$$

this matrix is not diagonal, and we are not prepared to determine its eigenvalues by inspection.

Let us now compute, correctly to terms[8] in ϵ^2, the transform α' of (3) by the special matrix

$$S = 1 + \epsilon S^I, \quad \text{where } S^I = \begin{pmatrix} 0 & -\frac{2}{3} \\ \frac{2}{3} & 0 \end{pmatrix}; \tag{6}$$

the reason for choosing this particular S will appear presently. Since ϵ is small, the reciprocal of (6) can be found by the formula $(1 + \delta)^{-1} = 1 - \delta + \delta^2 - \cdots$, so that, correctly to terms in ϵ^2, we have $S^{-1} = 1 - \epsilon S^I + \epsilon^2 (S^I)^2$, that is,

$$S^{-1} = 1 - \epsilon \begin{pmatrix} 0 & -\frac{2}{3} \\ \frac{2}{3} & 0 \end{pmatrix} + \epsilon^2 \begin{pmatrix} -\frac{4}{9} & 0 \\ 0 & -\frac{4}{9} \end{pmatrix}. \tag{7}$$

---

[8] 'Correctly to terms in ϵ^n' means that the terms in $\epsilon, \epsilon^2, \cdots, \epsilon^n$ are correct, while the terms in $\epsilon^{n+1}, \epsilon^{n+2}$, and so on, are not necessarily correct.

Thus

$$\alpha' = S\alpha S^{-1} = \begin{pmatrix} 1 & -\frac{2}{3}\epsilon \\ \frac{2}{3}\epsilon & 1 \end{pmatrix} \begin{pmatrix} 1 + 3\epsilon & 2\epsilon \\ 2\epsilon & 4 + \epsilon^2 \end{pmatrix} \begin{pmatrix} 1 - \frac{4}{9}\epsilon^2 & \frac{2}{3}\epsilon \\ -\frac{2}{3}\epsilon & 1 - \frac{4}{9}\epsilon^2 \end{pmatrix}. \quad (8)$$

When we carry out the matrix multiplication and neglect powers higher than ϵ^2 in the result, (8) reduces to

$$\alpha' = \begin{pmatrix} 1 + 3\epsilon - \frac{4}{3}\epsilon^2 & 2\epsilon^2 \\ 2\epsilon^2 & 4 + \frac{7}{3}\epsilon^2 \end{pmatrix} \quad (9)$$

Comparison of (9) with (3) shows that the effect of our transformation has been to cause linear terms in ϵ to appear only in the diagonal elements or, as we say for short, to diagonalize (3) to terms in ϵ^1. If ϵ^2 can be neglected, (9) becomes the diagonal matrix

$$\begin{pmatrix} 1 + 3\epsilon & 0 \\ 0 & 4 \end{pmatrix} \quad (10)$$

whose eigenvalues are $1 + 3\epsilon$ and 4. Recalling that the eigenvalues of a transform of a matrix are the same as those of the matrix itself, we conclude that, correctly to terms in ϵ^1, the eigenvalues of (3) are also $1 + 3\epsilon$ and 4.

Since terms in ϵ^2 appear off the diagonal in (9), we are not prepared to determine by inspection the eigenvalues of α correctly to terms in ϵ^2. A similarity transformation can, however, be found which diagonalizes (3) to terms in ϵ^2, and then the eigenvalues can be obtained by inspection correctly to terms in ϵ^2. The remainder of this section will deal with a systematic procedure for such approximate computations.

Let S be an as yet undetermined unitary matrix of the form

$$S = S^0 + \epsilon S^{\mathrm{I}} + \epsilon^2 S^{\mathrm{II}} + \cdots, \quad (11)$$

where the superscripted S's are matrices independent of ϵ; let α be our perturbed Hermitian matrix (1); and let us try to adjust S in such a way that the matrix

$$A = S\alpha S^{-1} \quad (12)$$

is diagonal, that is, that

$$A_{nm} = 0 \text{ if } n \neq m. \quad (13)$$

Since A is a diagonal transform of α, the diagonal elements of A are the eigenvalues of α, so that if these eigenvalues are appropriately numbered, we have

$$A_{nn} = \lambda_n ; \quad (14)$$

we assume that each eigenvalue is a power series in ϵ, so that A has the form

$$A = A^0 + \epsilon A^{\mathrm{I}} + \epsilon^2 A^{\mathrm{II}} + \cdots, \tag{15}$$

where the superscripted A's are diagonal matrices independent of ϵ.

To find how S is to be chosen, we multiply (12) by S from the right, getting

$$AS = S\alpha, \tag{16}$$

that is,

$$\begin{aligned}(A^0 + \epsilon A^{\mathrm{I}} + \epsilon^2 A^{\mathrm{II}} + \cdots)(S^0 + \epsilon S^{\mathrm{I}} + \epsilon^2 S^{\mathrm{II}} + \cdots)\\ = (S^0 + \epsilon S^{\mathrm{I}} + \epsilon^2 S^2 + \cdots)(\alpha^0 + \epsilon \alpha^{\mathrm{I}} + \epsilon^2 \alpha^{\mathrm{II}} + \cdots),\end{aligned} \tag{17}$$

and combine like powers of ϵ:

$$\left.\begin{array}{c} A^0 S^0 \\ \epsilon(A^0 S^{\mathrm{I}} + A^{\mathrm{I}} S^0) \\ \epsilon^2(A^0 S^{\mathrm{II}} + A^{\mathrm{I}} S^{\mathrm{I}} + A^{\mathrm{II}} S^0) \\ \cdots \end{array}\right\} = \left\{\begin{array}{c} S^0 \alpha^0 \\ \epsilon(S^0 \alpha^{\mathrm{I}} + S^{\mathrm{I}} \alpha^0) \\ \epsilon^2(S^0 \alpha^{\mathrm{II}} + S^{\mathrm{I}} \alpha^{\mathrm{I}} + S^{\mathrm{II}} \alpha^0) \\ \cdots \end{array}\right. \tag{18}$$

Thus, if (16) is to hold identically in ϵ, the following sequence of matrix equations must be satisfied:

$$A^0 S^0 = S^0 \alpha^0 \tag{19}$$

$$A^0 S^{\mathrm{I}} + A^{\mathrm{I}} S^0 = S^0 \alpha^{\mathrm{I}} + S^{\mathrm{I}} \alpha^0 \tag{20}$$

$$A^0 S^{\mathrm{II}} + A^{\mathrm{I}} S^{\mathrm{I}} + A^{\mathrm{II}} S^0 = S^0 \alpha^{\mathrm{II}} + S^{\mathrm{I}} \alpha^{\mathrm{I}} + S^{\mathrm{II}} \alpha^0 \tag{21}$$

$$\cdots = \cdots$$

The only quantities in these equations which are known from the outset are the α's. The equations, however, enable us to set up one after another the matrices A^0, S^0, A^{I}, S^{I}, and so on, and, through the A's, to determine the eigenvalues of α correctly to any desired power of ϵ.

We first turn to (19). If $\epsilon \to 0$, then $\alpha \to \alpha^0$ and $A \to A^0$, so that, since the eigenvalues of A are the same as those of α, the eigenvalues of A^0 must be the same as those of α^0; and, since both A^0 and α^0 are diagonal, these matrices can differ only in the order of their diagonal elements. We can without loss of generality require that the diagonal elements of A^0 be arranged in the same order as those of α^0, in which case

$$A^0 = \alpha^0, \tag{22}$$

and (19) becomes

$$\alpha^0 S^0 = S^0 \alpha^0. \tag{23}$$

Now, if $\epsilon \to 0$, then $S \to S^0$, so that, since S is to be unitary for any value of ϵ, S^0 must itself be unitary. It now follows from (23) and the result of Exercise 10[66] that, *if the unperturbed matrix α^0 is nondegenerate*, then S^0 is a diagonal matrix each of whose diagonal elements is of modulus unity. We adopt the simplest possibility, namely

$$S^0 = 1. \tag{24}$$

We shall see presently that when α^0 is degenerate this choice of the unit matrix for S^0 is not satisfactory.

Having determined A^0 and S^0, we turn to (20), which now has the form $\alpha^0 S^I + A^I = \alpha^I + S^I \alpha^0$, that is,

$$\alpha^0 S^I - S^I \alpha^0 = \alpha^I - A^I. \tag{25}$$

Equating the nnth elements of the two sides of (25), we get

$$\sum_i \alpha^0_{ni} S^I_{in} - \sum_j S^I_{nj} \alpha^0_{jn} = \alpha^I_{nn} - A^I_{nn}. \tag{26}$$

Since α^0 is diagonal, the left side of (26) is $\alpha^0_{nn} S^I_{nn} - S^I_{nn} \alpha^0_{nn} = 0$, and hence

$$A^I_{nn} = \alpha^I_{nn}. \tag{27}$$

If powers of ϵ higher than the first are neglected, (15) reduces to $A = A^0 + \epsilon A^I$, so that (14) becomes $\lambda_n = A^0_{nn} + \epsilon A^I_{nn}$, or, according to (22) and (27),

$$\lambda_n = \alpha^0_{nn} + \epsilon \alpha^I_{nn}. \tag{28}$$

Thus, *if the unperturbed matrix is nondegenerate, then the diagonal elements of the perturbed matrix give the eigenvalues of the perturbed matrix correctly to terms in the first power of ϵ.* For example, we can now tell by inspection that the eigenvalues of (3), correct to terms in ϵ^I, are $1 + 3\epsilon$ and 4.

A calculation of S^I from (20), followed by a calculation of A^{II} from (21), yields the next approximation for the eigenvalues:

$$\lambda_n = \alpha^0_{nn} + \epsilon \alpha^I_{nn} + \epsilon^2 \left[\alpha^{II}_{nn} + \sum_i{}' \frac{\alpha^I_{ni} \alpha^I_{in}}{\alpha^0_{nn} - \alpha^0_{ii}} \right], \tag{29}$$

where i runs through the values $1, 2, \cdots, n-1, n+1, \cdots, N$; the prime after the $\sum$ is a reminder that i skips the value n.

When the unperturbed matrix α^0 is degenerate, the formula (29) acquires vanishing denominators, indicating that our procedure then needs modification. A closer study, which we shall not undertake here, shows that, in the degenerate case, S^0 can and must be chosen to be nondiagonal, and that new formulas take the place of (28) and (29). In particular, *if the unperturbed matrix is degenerate it is no longer possible to find the eigenvalues of the perturbed matrix correctly to terms in ϵ^1 by merely inspecting its diagonal elements.*

Formulas for the eigenvalues correct to any power of ϵ whenever the process is convergent are given, for example, by Condon and Shortley, page 34.

In their detailed presentation of the matrix perturbation theory, Condon and Shortley consider as an illustration the particular matrix

$$\begin{pmatrix} 10 + 5\epsilon & 0 & 10\epsilon \\ 0 & 10 & 30\epsilon \\ 10\epsilon & 30\epsilon & 0 \end{pmatrix} \quad (30)$$

and plot its precise eigenvalues as functions of ϵ in a graph reproduced[9] in part in Fig. 99. The unperturbed matrix in (30) is degenerate, its eigenvalues being 10, 10,

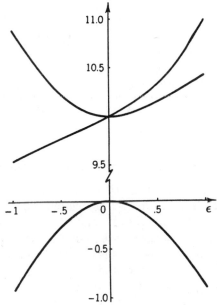

Fig. 99. The eigenvalues of (30), plotted against ϵ.

and 0; but for $\epsilon \neq 0$ the matrix has three distinct eigenvalues, and we say that *the perturbation has removed the degeneracy.*

Exercises

1. Use (29) to show that the eigenvalues of (3), correct to terms in ϵ^2, are $1 + 3\epsilon - \frac{4}{3}\epsilon^2$, and $4 + \frac{7}{3}\epsilon^2$.

---

[9] By permission of The Cambridge University Press and The Macmillan Company, publishers.

2. Compute the exact eigenvalues of (3), using the secular equation; then allow ϵ to be small, substitute a power series for the radical in the precise expression for the eigenvalues, and verify the result of Exercise 1.

3. Use (29) to compute correctly to terms in ϵ^2 the eigenvalues of the matrix $\begin{pmatrix} 1 & \epsilon & 4\epsilon \\ \epsilon & 2 & \epsilon \\ 4\epsilon & \epsilon & 3 \end{pmatrix}$. Use 10^{58} and 11^{58} as partial checks.

4. Show, using the secular equation, that the eigenvalues of the matrix $\begin{pmatrix} 1 & \epsilon \\ \epsilon & 1 \end{pmatrix}$ are $1 + \epsilon$ and $1 - \epsilon$. Why is (29) not applicable to this case, even when ϵ is small?

5. Show that in view of (25) and (27) the matrix S^{I} can be taken to be

$$S^{\mathrm{I}}_{nm} = \begin{cases} 0 & \text{if } m = n \\ \dfrac{\alpha^{\mathrm{I}}_{nm}}{\alpha^0_{nn} - \alpha^0_{mm}} & \text{if } m \neq n. \end{cases} \tag{31}$$

6. Verify that (31), when used with (3), yields the S^{I} of (6).

7. Show that, when α^0 is nondegenerate, the similarity transformation of (1) by the matrix $1 + \epsilon S^{\mathrm{I}}$, where S^{I} is given by (31), diagonalizes (1) to terms in ϵ^1.

8. Derive (29).

68. The Matrix Perturbation Method for Nondegenerate States

As we return to physics, we recall that the structure of the Heisenberg matrix associated with a dynamical variable $\alpha(x, p)$ depends on the dynamical system under consideration; for example, as noted in Exercise 6[62], the matrix associated with the coordinate x is one matrix when the dynamical system in question is the oscillator, and quite another matrix when the system is a particle in a box. We also recall that the Heisenberg matrix H associated with the Hamiltonian of a system is diagonal and has the elements

$$(3^{63}) \qquad H_{nm} = \begin{cases} E_n & \text{if } m = n \\ 0 & \text{if } m \neq n, \end{cases} \tag{1}$$

where the E_n's are the energy levels of the system; thus the respective Heisenberg energy matrices pertaining to two different systems are both diagonal and differ from each other only through the numerical values of their diagonal elements—recall Exercise 2^{63}.

Let the Hamiltonian function of some specific dynamical system be

$$H^0 = \frac{1}{2m} p^2 + V^0(x) \qquad (2)$$

and let the Heisenberg matrices (which we denote by x^0, p^0, H^0, and so on) associated, respectively, with the coordinate, the momentum, the Hamiltonian, and so on, of this system be known. The availability of these matrices is then usually of no assistance in the computation of the matrices x, p, and H, associated, respectively, with the coordinate, the momentum, and the Hamiltonian of another specific dynamical system whose Hamiltonian function is

$$H = \frac{1}{2m} p^2 + V(x); \qquad (3)$$

for example, the availability of the various Heisenberg matrices pertaining to the linear harmonic oscillator is of no assistance in computing the various matrices pertaining to a particle in a box. An exceptional case arises, however, if

(1^{36})
$$V(x) = V^0(x) + V^P(x), \qquad (4)$$

where the term $V^P(x)$ is small, that is, if the second system differs from the first only through a small perturbing potential; in this case the knowledge of the matrices pertaining to the first (the *unperturbed*) system is very useful in the treatment—at least the approximate treatment—of the second (the *perturbed*) system.

We now proceed to show how the Heisenberg matrices pertaining to the unperturbed system can be used for an approximate computation of the energy levels of the perturbed system. Our first steps are to note that the Hamiltonian functions (2) and (3) satisfy the relation

$$H = H^0 + V^P(x) \qquad (5)$$

and to set up the auxiliary matrix

$$\mathbf{H} = H^0 + V^P(x^0), \qquad \langle 6 \rangle$$

where H^0 is the energy matrix of the unperturbed system, x^0 is the coordinate matrix of the unperturbed system, and the matrix $V^P(x^0)$ is the same function of the matrix x^0 as the perturbing potential $V^P(x)$ is of the coordinate x.

To illustrate: Let the unperturbed system be a linear harmonic oscillator and let the various Heisenberg matrices which pertain to it and which we distinguish by the superscript zero be available; in particular, the matrices 10^{62} and 18^{62}, that is,

$$
x^0 = \frac{a}{\sqrt{2}}
\begin{vmatrix}
0 & \sqrt{1}'' & 0 & \cdots \\
\sqrt{1}'' & 0 & \sqrt{2}'' & \cdots \\
0 & \sqrt{2}'' & 0 & \cdots \\
\cdots & \cdots & \cdots & \cdots
\end{vmatrix}
\qquad
H^0 =
\begin{vmatrix}
\frac{1}{2}h\nu_c & 0 & 0 & \cdots \\
0 & \frac{3}{2}h\nu_c & 0 & \cdots \\
0 & 0 & \frac{5}{2}h\nu_c & \cdots \\
\cdots & \cdots & \cdots & \cdots
\end{vmatrix}
\qquad (7a, b)
$$

are then available. Further, let the perturbing potential have the special form $V^P(x) = \epsilon kx$. Then

$$
V^P(x^0) = \epsilon kx^0 = \frac{\epsilon ka}{\sqrt{2}}
\begin{vmatrix}
0 & \sqrt{1}'' & 0 & \cdots \\
\sqrt{1}'' & 0 & \sqrt{2}'' & \cdots \\
0 & \sqrt{2}'' & 0 & \cdots \\
\cdots & \cdots & \cdots & \cdots
\end{vmatrix}
\qquad \langle 8 \rangle
$$

so that the auxiliary matrix H is

$$
\mathrm{H} = H^0 + V^P(x^0) =
\begin{vmatrix}
\frac{1}{2}h\nu_c & \epsilon\sqrt{\frac{1}{2}}ka'' & 0 & \cdots \\
\epsilon\sqrt{\frac{1}{2}}ka'' & \frac{3}{2}h\nu_c & \epsilon\sqrt{\frac{2}{2}}ka'' & \cdots \\
0 & \epsilon\sqrt{\frac{2}{2}}ka'' & \frac{5}{2}h\nu_c & \cdots \\
\cdots & \cdots & \cdots & \cdots
\end{vmatrix}
\qquad \langle 9 \rangle
$$

The energy matrix H of the perturbed system is not available, although we know that it is diagonal. Our purpose is to show how H can be approximated with the help of the matrix H.

To establish the property of H which is responsible for our interest in this matrix, we proceed as follows: According to the fundamental formula 2^{62}, the elements of the matrix H (the energy matrix of the perturbed system) are

$$
H_{nm} = \int \bar{\psi}_n H \psi_m \, dx, \qquad \langle 10 \rangle
$$

where H in the integrand is the Schroedinger operator associated with the Hamiltonian of the perturbed system and the ψ's are normalized eigenfunctions[10] of this operator; in view of (5), Equation $\langle 10 \rangle$ can be written as

$$H_{nm} = \int \bar{\psi}_n [H^0 + V^P(x)] \psi_m \, dx, \qquad \langle 11 \rangle$$

where H^0 is the Schroedinger operator associated with the Hamiltonian of the unperturbed system. Similarly, the elements of the matrix H^0 (the energy matrix of the unperturbed system) are

$$H^0_{nm} = \int \bar{\psi}^0_n H^0 \psi^0_m \, dx, \qquad \langle 12 \rangle$$

where H^0 in the integrand is the Schroedinger operator associated with the Hamiltonian of the unperturbed system, and the ψ^0's are normalized eigenfunctions[10] of this operator. Again, the nmth element of the matrix x^0 (the coordinate matrix of the unperturbed system) is $\int \bar{\psi}^0_n x \psi^0_m dx$, and the nmth element of the matrix $V^P(x^0)$ is [11]

$$\int \bar{\psi}^0_n V^P(x) \psi^0_m \, dx. \qquad (13)$$

In view of $\langle 6 \rangle$, $\langle 12 \rangle$, and (13), we thus have the result

$$\mathrm{H}_{nm} = \int \bar{\psi}^0_n [H^0 + V^P(x)] \psi^0_m \, dx. \qquad \langle 14 \rangle$$

Now, according to $\langle 11 \rangle$, the matrix H is the representative of the Schroedinger operator $H^0 + V^P(x)$ when the basic f's are the Schroedinger eigenfunctions of the perturbed Hamiltonian. Similarly, according to $\langle 14 \rangle$, the matrix H is the representative of the same Schroedinger operator when the basic f's are the Schroedinger eigenfunctions of the unperturbed Hamiltonian. Thus the matrices H and H represent the same differential operator, though with respect to different sets of basic f's; and, since the eigenvalues of any matrix representing a differential operator are the same as those of the differential operator itself, we conclude that *the eigenvalues of the matrix H are the same as those of the matrix* H. In other words, the energy levels of the perturbed system are the eigenvalues of the auxiliary matrix H. Since we have not yet

---

[10] Insofar as our argument is concerned, it is quite immaterial whether the explicit forms of these eigenfunctions are available or not.

[11] In practice we would perhaps prefer to compute the matrix $V^P(x^0)$ by matrix algebra in terms of the matrix x^0, rather than by an extra integration; but for our present purposes it is important to note that the nmth element of $V^P(x^0)$ *can* be expressed in the form (13).

used the assumption that $V^P(x)$ is small, this conclusion is quite general.

Perturbation formulas. We now turn to the case when the energy spectrum E_0^0, E_1^0, E_2^0, $\cdots$, of the unperturbed system is nondegenerate and when the perturbing potential can be expanded into a power series in a small parameter ϵ, so that

$$(12^{36}) \qquad H = H^0 + \epsilon v^{\mathrm{I}}(x) + \epsilon^2 v^{\mathrm{II}}(x) + \cdots, \qquad (15)$$

where the v's are functions of x independent of ϵ. The auxiliary matrix H can then be written as

$$\mathrm{H} = H^0 + \epsilon v^{\mathrm{I}}(x^0) + \epsilon^2 v^{\mathrm{II}}(x^0) + \cdots . \qquad \langle 16 \rangle$$

The matrix H thus has the form 1^{67}, so that its eigenvalues (which, as we have seen, are the same as those of H) can be approximated by means of 29^{67}. The correlation of the symbols of the present section with those of §67 is as follows: $\alpha = \mathrm{H}$, $\alpha^0 = H^0$, $\alpha^{\mathrm{I}} = v^{\mathrm{I}}(x^0)$, $\alpha^{\mathrm{II}} = v^{\mathrm{II}}(x^0)$, and so on; λ_n in §67 denotes the nth eigenvalue of α (that is, of H), and since the eigenvalues of H are the energy levels of the perturbed system we write $\lambda_n = E_n$; further, since the diagonal elements of H^0 are the energy levels of the unperturbed system, we write $\alpha_{nn}^0 = E_n^0$. When we substitute the new symbols into 29^{67} and, to simplify appearances, suppress the argument x^0 of the v's, we get the formula

$$E_n = E_n^0 + \epsilon v_{nn}^{\mathrm{I}} + \epsilon^2 \left[v_{nn}^{\mathrm{II}} + \sum_i{}' \frac{v_{ni}^{\mathrm{I}} v_{in}^{\mathrm{I}}}{E_n^0 - E_i^0} \right], \quad [v = v(x^0)]. \quad (17)$$

The supplementary equation $v = v(x^0)$ in (17) is a reminder that v_{nn}^{I} stands for the nnth element of the matrix $v^{\mathrm{I}}(x^0)$, v_{ni}^{I} stands for the nith element of the matrix $v^{\mathrm{I}}(x^0)$, and so on. As before, the prime after the $\sum$ means that the term $i = n$ is to be omitted in the summation.

Equation (17) is the perturbation formula of matrix mechanics giving the energy levels of the perturbed system correctly to terms in ϵ^2, provided the unperturbed system is nondegenerate.

To illustrate the use of (17) we return to the oscillator perturbed by the potential $V^P(x) = \epsilon kx$. In this case, $v^{\mathrm{I}}(x) = kx$ and $v^{\mathrm{II}}(x) = v^{\mathrm{III}}(x) = \cdots = 0$; the matrices involved in (17) therefore are [remember that we write v for $v(x^0)$] $v^{\mathrm{I}} = kx^0$ and $v^{\mathrm{II}} = 0$. The matrix x^0, shown in (7), has the elements 9^{62}, so that

$$
v^{\mathrm{I}}_{nm} = \begin{cases} ka\sqrt{\tfrac{1}{2}n}\,'' & \text{if } m = n - 1 \\ ka\sqrt{\tfrac{1}{2}(n + 1)}\,'' & \text{if } m = n + 1 \\ 0 & \text{otherwise,} \end{cases} \tag{18}
$$

while $v^{\mathrm{II}}_{nm} = 0$ for all values of n and m. In particular, it follows from (18) that

$$
v^{\mathrm{I}}_{ni} v^{\mathrm{I}}_{in} = \begin{cases} \tfrac{1}{2} n k^2 a^2 & \text{if } i = n - 1 \\ \tfrac{1}{2} (n + 1) k^2 a^2 & \text{if } i = n + 1 \\ 0 & \text{otherwise.} \end{cases} \tag{19}
$$

Substituting these results into (17) we get

$$
E_n = E^0_n + \epsilon^2 \left[\frac{\tfrac{1}{2} n k^2 a^2}{E^0_n - E^0_{n-1}} + \frac{\tfrac{1}{2}(n + 1) k^2 a^2}{E^0_n - E^0_{n+1}} \right], \tag{20}
$$

which, in view of the relations 5^{62}, reduces to

$$
E_n = E^0_n - \tfrac{1}{2} \epsilon^2 k. \tag{21}
$$

On the basis of the present computation we may expect that the precise expressions for E_n might involve terms in ϵ^3, ϵ^4, and so on; but in fact the result (21) is exact, as shown in Exercise 2^{36}.

By extending the developments of §67 and applying the results to our physical perturbation problem, we may evaluate one by one the terms of E_n involving ϵ^3, ϵ^4, and so on; but in practice it is seldom of interest to go beyond the second-order correction included in (17). Note that the first-order correction given by (17) is $\epsilon v^{\mathrm{I}}_{nn}$, so that this correction vanishes whenever the diagonal elements of $V^P(x^0)$ are free from first powers of ϵ; but remember that (17) was derived for the case when H^0 is nondegenerate. We shall leave it to the reader (Exercise 1) to show that *the perturbation formula* (17) *is precisely equivalent to the Schroedinger perturbation formulas derived in* §36.

Exercises

1. Identify the integrals in 22^{36} and 31^{36} with Heisenberg matrix elements, and show that these formulas, when taken together, are equivalent to (17).

2. Assume the matrices (7) to be available, and approximate by means of (17) the energy levels of an oscillator perturbed by the potential $\tfrac{1}{2}\epsilon k x^2$. Use 10^{36} to check the result for the normal state of the perturbed system.

3. Assume the matrices (7) to the available, and approximate by means of (17) the energy levels of an oscillator perturbed by the potential ϵx^3; check the result by a reference to Exercise 4[36].

4. The matrix each of whose elements is the time average of the corresponding element of a given matrix is said to be the time average of the given matrix. Show that, if the unperturbed system is nondegenerate, then the time average of the auxiliary matrix H [that is, the matrix ⟨6⟩] is a diagonal matrix whose diagonal elements are the energy levels of the perturbed system correct to terms in ϵ^1.

69. More Matrix Algebra

The first and the second subscripts in the symbol α_{kl} for a matrix element denote, respectively, the row and the column of the matrix α in which this element belongs. The formulas to be discussed in this section take on a somewhat more readily remembered form if we adopt a similar two-subscript notation for the elements of column symbols, and denote the kth component of the column symbol u by u_k. rather than by u_k as we did before; the first subscript (the subscript k) then tells us the row of the column symbol u in which the element u_k. belongs, while the second (the subscript $\cdot$) reminds us that the symbol u has only one column. The new notation is illustrated in Equations (7), (10), and (13); we note, in particular, the similarity between (7) and (6), between (10) and (9), and between (13) and (12).

Now, if we replace each element of a matrix α by its complex conjugate and transpose the matrix so obtained, then the resulting matrix, introduced in 19[58], is called the complex conjugate of the matrix α and is denoted by $\bar{\alpha}$. If we treat a column symbol u in a similar manner the result is a *row symbol*; this symbol is called *the complex conjugate of the column symbol* u and is denoted by $\bar{u}$. Thus the complex conjugate of the column symbol $u = \begin{pmatrix} 1 \\ i \end{pmatrix}$ is the row symbol $\bar{u} = (1, -i)$, the complex conjugate of $v = \begin{pmatrix} 1 \\ -i \\ 2+i \end{pmatrix}$ is $\bar{v} = (1, i, 2 - i)$, and so forth. The elements of a row symbol $\bar{u}$ will be numbered from left to right and the kth element will be denoted by $\bar{u}_{\cdot k}$, so that, by definition,

$$\bar{u}_{\cdot k} = (u_k.)^*, \tag{1}$$

where $(u_k.)^*$ is the complex conjugate of the number $u_k.$. Note that the two-subscript notation for the elements of $\bar{u}$ fits in with that for the elements of a matrix and of a column symbol: the first subscript (the subscript $\cdot$) in $\bar{u}._k$ reminds us that the symbol in question has only one row, while the second (the subscript k) tells the column of $\bar{u}$ in which this element belongs.[12] Whenever we speak of a column symbol u as the *vector u*, we speak of the row symbol $\bar{u}$ as the *complex conjugate of the vector u*. The matrices of this section will each have N rows and N columns, while the column symbols and row symbols will each have N elements.

If the corresponding elements of two row symbols $\bar{v}$ and $\bar{u}$ are equal to each other, that is, if

$$\bar{u}._k = \bar{v}._k , \qquad k = 1, 2, \cdots , N, \tag{2}$$

we write

$$\bar{u} = \bar{v} \tag{3}$$

and say that the row symbols $\bar{v}$ and $\bar{u}$ are equal to each other. The symbolic equation (3) and its interpretation (2) are recorded in (8); note the similarity between (8), (7), and (6).

The rules for multiplying a row symbol by a constant and for adding two or more row symbols are patterned after the corresponding rules for matrices and column symbols. Thus, if two row symbols $\bar{u}$ and $\bar{v}$ are so related that

$$\bar{v}._k = c\bar{u}._k , \qquad k = 1, 2, \cdots , N, \tag{4}$$

where c is a constant, then we write

$$\bar{v} = c\bar{u} \tag{5}$$

and say that $\bar{v}$ equals c times $\bar{u}$. The symbolic equation (5) and its interpretation (4) are recorded in (14); note the similarity between (14), (13), and (12). Again, if three row symbols $\bar{u}$, $\bar{v}$, and $\bar{w}$ are so related that $\bar{w}._k = \bar{u}._k + \bar{v}._k$ for every value of k, then we write $\bar{w} = \bar{u} + \bar{v}$ and say that $\bar{w}$ is the sum of $\bar{u}$ and $\bar{v}$; this definition is recorded in (11).

Our rules for adding two symbols require the addition of the similarly placed elements of the addends, and are thus unsuited for the case when the numbers of rows and columns of one symbol

---

[12] Note that the kth element of $\bar{u}$ can be denoted without ambiguity by $u._k$ rather than by $\bar{u}._k$.

do not match those of the other; accordingly, our algebra does not provide for the addition of a matrix and a vector, a matrix and the complex conjugate of a vector, or a vector and the complex conjugate of a vector.

(23⁵⁶)	$\alpha = \beta$	$\alpha_{kl} = \beta_{kl}$	N^2	(6)
(28⁵⁶)	$u = v$	$u_{k\cdot} = v_{k\cdot}$	N	(7)
	$\bar{u} = \bar{v}$	$\bar{u}_{\cdot k} = \bar{v}_{\cdot k}$	N	(8)
(24⁵⁶)	$\gamma = \alpha + \beta$	$\gamma_{kl} = \alpha_{kl} + \beta_{kl}$	N^2	(9)
(29⁵⁶)	$w = u + v$	$w_{k\cdot} = u_{k\cdot} + v_{k\cdot}$	N	(10)
	$\bar{w} = \bar{u} + \bar{v}$	$\bar{w}_{\cdot l} = \bar{u}_{\cdot l} + \bar{v}_{\cdot l}$	N	(11)
(25⁵⁶)	$\beta = c\alpha$	$\beta_{kl} = c\alpha_{kl}$	N^2	(12)
(30⁵⁶)	$v = cu$	$v_{k\cdot} = cu_{k\cdot}$	N	(13)
	$\bar{v} = c\bar{u}$	$\bar{v}_{\cdot l} = c\bar{u}_{\cdot l}$	N	(14)
(26⁵⁶)	$\gamma = \alpha\beta$	$\gamma_{kl} = \Sigma\alpha_{ki}\beta_{il}$	N^2	(15)
(27⁵⁶)	$\delta = \beta\alpha$	$\delta_{kl} = \Sigma\beta_{ki}\alpha_{il}$	N^2	(16)
(31⁵⁶)	$v = \alpha u$	$v_{k\cdot} = \Sigma\alpha_{ki}u_{i\cdot}$	N	(17)
	$\bar{v} = \bar{u}\alpha$	$\bar{v}_{\cdot l} = \Sigma\bar{u}_{\cdot i}\alpha_{il}$	N	(18)
	$c = \bar{u}v$	$c_{\cdot\cdot} = \Sigma\bar{u}_{\cdot i}v_{i\cdot}$	1	(19)

Our old rules for multiplying two symbols, neither of which is simply a number, imply that the left factor has as many columns as the right factor has rows, and hence allow for the multiplication of two matrices and for the multiplication of a vector from the left by a matrix; but they do not allow for the multiplication of a matrix from the left by a vector, so that the symbol $u\alpha$ is to be regarded as meaningless. When these rules are extended to include row symbols, we find that the symbol $\alpha\bar{u}$ has no meaning, but that the symbol $\bar{u}\alpha$ can be defined as the row symbol whose kth element $(\bar{u}\alpha)_{\cdot k}$ equals $\sum_i \bar{u}_{\cdot i}\alpha_{ik}$; this definition is recorded in (18). Again, the symbol $v\bar{u}$ (as well as the symbol $u\bar{v}$) has no meaning, while, as recorded in (19), the symbol $\bar{u}v$ can be defined as the number $\sum_i \bar{u}_{.i} v_{i.}$; the two dot subscripts of $c_{..}$ in (19), though they are not altogether necessary, remind us that the quantity $\bar{u}v$ is a numerical constant (having only one row and only one column), and make (19) quite similar in appearance to the four equations preceding it. Examples of products involving row symbols are given in Exercise 1.

Since the product $\bar{u}\alpha$ is a row symbol, the product $(\bar{u}\alpha)v$ is a number; this number turns out to be the same as $\bar{u}(\alpha v)$, that is, the product of $\bar{u}$ and the column symbol αv; therefore we can use without ambiguity the symbol $\bar{u}\alpha v$:

$$\bar{u}\alpha v = (\bar{u}\alpha)v = \bar{u}(\alpha v). \tag{20}$$

We shall leave it to the reader to show that

$$\bar{u}\alpha v = \sum_i \sum_j \bar{u}_{.i}\alpha_{ij}v_{j.}, \qquad i, j = 1, 2, \cdots, N. \tag{21}$$

According to (19), $\bar{u}u = \sum_i \bar{u}_{.i}u_{i.}$, so that, recalling the interpretation of 13^{56}, we get

$$\bar{u}u = \text{square of length of } u. \tag{22}$$

Similarly, the condition 14^{56} for the orthogonality of two vectors u and v can be written as

$$\bar{u}v = 0 \tag{23}$$

or as $\bar{v}u = 0$.

We shall leave it to the reader to show that *the complex conjugate of a product of our symbols is the product of the complex conjugates of the factors taken in the reverse order*, except that the position of a numerical factor is of course immaterial. For example,

$$\overline{cu} = \bar{c}\bar{u}, \qquad \overline{\alpha u} = \bar{u}\bar{\alpha}, \qquad \overline{\bar{u}\alpha} = \bar{\alpha}u, \qquad \overline{\bar{u}v} = \bar{v}u \tag{24}$$

and

$$\overline{\bar{u}\alpha v} = \bar{v}\bar{\alpha}u. \tag{25}$$

These results are an extension of $24c^{58}$.

Hermitian matrices. The following proofs of the two theorems taken for granted in §58 illustrate the convenience of our symbolism.

Every eigenvalue of a Hermitian matrix is real. Let α be a Hermitian matrix, so that

$$(22^{58}) \qquad\qquad \bar{\alpha} = \alpha, \tag{26}$$

and let λ be the eigenvalue of α belonging to the eigenvector u of α, so that

$$\alpha u = \lambda u. \tag{27}$$

Multiplying (27) from the left by $\bar{u}$, we get

$$\bar{u}\alpha u = \lambda \bar{u}u. \tag{28}$$

Taking the complex conjugates of the two sides of (28), we get $\overline{\bar{u}\alpha u} = \overline{\lambda \bar{u}u}$, that is, $\bar{u}\bar{\alpha}u = \bar{\lambda}\bar{u}u$; and since α satisfies (26) this becomes

$$\bar{u}\alpha u = \bar{\lambda}\bar{u}u. \tag{29}$$

It now follows from (28) and (29) that $\bar{\lambda} = \lambda$, and the theorem is proved.

The eigenvectors of a Hermitian matrix belonging to distinct eigenvalues are orthogonal. Let α be Hermitian and let u and v be eigenvectors of α belonging, respectively, to the eigenvalues λ and μ, so that

$$\alpha u = \lambda u, \qquad \alpha v = \mu v, \tag{30a, b}$$

where, according to the theorem just proved, both λ and μ are real. Multiplying (30a) from the left by $\bar{v}$ and (30b) from the left by $\bar{u}$, we get

$$\bar{v}\alpha u = \lambda \bar{v}u, \qquad \bar{u}\alpha v = \mu \bar{u}v. \tag{31a, b}$$

Taking the complex conjugates of both sides of (31b), we get $\overline{\bar{u}\alpha v} = \overline{\mu \bar{u}v}$, that is, $\bar{v}\bar{\alpha}u = \bar{\mu}\bar{v}u$, which reduces to

$$\bar{v}\alpha u = \mu \bar{v}u. \tag{32}$$

Subtracting (32) from (31a), we finally get

$$(\lambda - \mu)\bar{v}u = 0, \tag{33}$$

so that $\bar{v}u = 0$ whenever $\lambda \neq \mu$, and the theorem is proved.

Quasi-geometric interpretation. Just as N-component column symbols u, v, w, and so on, may be interpreted as representing points in an N-space (u representing the point whose coordinates are the numbers $u_1.$, $u_2.$, $\cdots$, $u_N.$; and so on), so N-component row symbols $\bar{u}$, $\bar{v}$, $\bar{w}$, and so on may be interpreted as representing points in *another* N-space ($\bar{u}$ representing the point whose coordinates are the numbers $\bar{u}_{.1}$, $\bar{u}_{.2}$, $\cdots$, $\bar{u}_{.N}$; and so on); the second N-space is then called the *dual* of the first, and vice versa.

It should perhaps be emphasized that it is improper to interpret column symbols and row symbols as representing points within *the same N*-space, since such an interpretation would lead to inconsistencies;[13] for example, this interpretation would suggest that a column symbol and a row symbol can be added together, while the rules of our algebra do not provide for such an addition. When a mapping α is carried out in the space containing u, v, w, and so on, a corresponding mapping takes place in the dual space, since the row symbols $\bar{u}$, $\bar{v}$, $\bar{w}$, and so on, are sent, respectively, into $\bar{u}\alpha$, $\bar{v}\alpha$, $\bar{w}\alpha$, and so on; but we need not discuss these mappings here.

Exercises

1. Show that if $u = \begin{pmatrix} 1 \\ 2 \\ i \end{pmatrix}$, $v = \begin{pmatrix} 0 \\ 2 \\ i \end{pmatrix}$, $w = \begin{pmatrix} 1 + i \\ i \\ 2 \end{pmatrix}$, and $\alpha = \begin{pmatrix} 1 & 2 & 3 \\ i & 4 & 5 \\ 6 & 7 & i \end{pmatrix}$ then
$\bar{u}\alpha = (1 - 4i, 10 - 7i, 14)$, $\bar{u}\alpha - \bar{v}\alpha = (1, 2, 3)$, $\bar{u}v = 5$, $\bar{v}u = 5$, $\bar{u}u = 6$, $\bar{v}v = 5$, $\bar{u}\alpha v = 20$, $\bar{v}\bar{\alpha}u = 20$, $\bar{v}\alpha u = 16 - 7i$, $\overline{\bar{u}\alpha}v = 16 + 7i$, $\bar{u}w = 1 + i$, $\bar{w}u = 1 - i$, $\bar{v}w = 0$, and $\bar{w}v = 0$.

2. Show that when u, v, α, and β are arbitrary we have $\bar{u}\alpha + \bar{v}\alpha = (\bar{u} + \bar{v})\alpha$, $\alpha u + \alpha v = \alpha(u + v)$, $\bar{u}\alpha + \bar{u}\beta = \bar{u}(\alpha + \beta)$, $\alpha u + \beta u = (\alpha + \beta)u$, and $\bar{u}\alpha v + \bar{u}\beta v = \bar{u}(\alpha + \beta)v$.

3. Prove (20) and (21).

4. Prove (24) and (25).

5. If u and v are vectors and α and β are matrices, what is $\bar{u}\alpha\beta v$? Write down the complex conjugate of $\bar{u}\alpha\beta v$ in terms of u, $\bar{\alpha}$, β, and $\bar{v}$, and verify your result by a simple nontrivial numerical example.

6. Show that in order for the matrix α to be Hermitian it is necessary and sufficient that the equation $\bar{u}\alpha v = \bar{v}\bar{\alpha}u$ hold when u and v are arbitrary. Writing this as $\bar{u}\alpha v = \overline{u}\bar{\alpha}v$ and then as $\bar{u}\alpha v = \overline{\bar{\alpha}u}\cdot v$, we get the matrix equivalent of 19[44].

7. Construct straightforward algebraic proofs (not involving symbolic manipulation) of the two theorems concerning the reality of the eigenvalues and the orthogonality of the eigenvectors of Hermitian matrices, proved in the text by symbolic methods.

---

[13] N-component column symbols and row symbols can, however, be interpreted without inconsistencies in terms of a single N-space by associating the column symbols with points and the row symbols with $(N - 1)$-dimensional elements of the space. Thus when 2-component column symbols are interpreted as representing *points* in a plane, then 2-component row symbols can be interpreted as representing straight *lines* in the same plane; when 3-component column symbols are interpreted as representing *points* in a 3-space, then 3-component row symbols can be interpreted as representing *planes* in the same 3-space; and so forth.

70. The Heisenberg Representation of States

The Heisenberg method is particularly well adapted to the search for the possible values of dynamical variables, since it allows this search to be conducted without explicit reference to the representatives of the states of the system, that is, to the operands of the Heisenberg matrices; thus in computing the energy levels of the oscillator in §65 we dealt only with the Heisenberg operators (matrices) associated with dynamical variables, and had no need to consider the operands of these operators. In the Schroedinger method, on the other hand, the study of the behavior of the operands is essential for the identification of the eigenvalues of the operator associated with a dynamical variable. The Heisenberg operands, however, come into play in studies, carried out by the Heisenberg method, of detailed properties of states; for example, in problems concerning the distribution-in-x for a given state. But, as we shall see, the Heisenberg method is not particularly well adapted to problems of this kind.

According to the operand rule IV of §17, states of dynamical systems are to be associated with the operands of the quantum-mechanical operators. The Heisenberg operators are matrices; accordingly, their operands, which we shall denote by ψ, are vectors, that is, column symbols. Now, according to the definition 2^{62}, the Heisenberg matrix α associated with the dynamical variable α pertaining to a dynamical system with a Hamiltonian H, is the matrix representing the Schroedinger operator α when the basic f's are the normalized time-dependent Schroedinger eigenfunctions of H; similarly, we adopt the definition: *the Heisenberg vector ψ associated with a state ψ of a dynamical system whose Hamiltonian is H is the vector representing the Schroedinger function ψ when the basic f's are the normalized time-dependent Schroedinger eigenfunctions of H.*

To identify with the help of the Schroedinger theory a Heisenberg vector ψ associated with the state ψ, we then take a Schroedinger function ψ associated with the state ψ, expand it in terms of the normalized Schroedinger eigenfunctions ψ_1, ψ_2, ψ_3, $\cdots$ of H, getting

$$\psi = c_1\psi_1 + c_2\psi_2 + c_3\psi_3 + \cdots , \tag{1}$$

and construct the vector

$$\psi = \begin{pmatrix} c_1 \\ c_2 \\ c_3 \\ \cdots \end{pmatrix}. \tag{2}$$

This is a Heisenberg vector representing the state ψ; it has, in general, infinitely many nonvanishing components. In particular, the Heisenberg vectors associated with the energy states of the (nondegenerate) system are, apart from an arbitrary multiplicative constant going with each vector,

$$\psi_1 = \begin{pmatrix} 1 \\ 0 \\ 0 \\ \cdots \end{pmatrix}, \qquad \psi_2 = \begin{pmatrix} 0 \\ 1 \\ 0 \\ \cdots \end{pmatrix}, \qquad \psi_3 = \begin{pmatrix} 0 \\ 0 \\ 1 \\ \cdots \end{pmatrix}, \cdots. \tag{3}$$

According to §16, the c's in (1) are numerical constants, and consequently *the Heisenberg ψ's are independent of t*; in the Heisenberg method, the time variation of the properties of a system in a given state is taken care of by the time dependence of the operators associated with dynamical variables, this situation being just the reverse of that in the Schroedinger method.

The rôle of the Schroedinger $\bar{\psi}$'s is taken over in the Heisenberg method by the row symbols, which are conjugate to the Heisenberg vectors and which, for a reason to be given later, we denote by ϕ's rather than by $\bar{\psi}$'s. Thus the ϕ corresponding to the ψ given by (2) is

$$\phi = (\bar{c}_1, \bar{c}_2, \bar{c}_3, \cdots) \tag{4}$$

and the ϕ's corresponding to the stationary states (3) are

$$\phi_1 = (1, 0, 0, 0, \cdots)$$
$$\phi_2 = (0, 1, 0, 0, \cdots) \tag{5}$$
$$\phi_3 = (0, 0, 1, 0, \cdots)$$

and so forth.

Note that, in view of the rules of the preceding section, *a Heisenberg ψ and a Heisenberg ϕ cannot be added to one another*. Since a

Schroedinger ψ can obviously be added to a Schroedinger $\bar{\psi}$, this result may at first sight seem strange. But as our previous work with the Schroedinger theory illustrates, the necessity of adding a ψ and a $\bar{\psi}$ never arises in the formalism of the Schroedinger method. Similarly, the necessity of adding a ψ to a ϕ never arises in the Heisenberg theory, and consequently the impossibility of carrying out such an addition causes no difficulty.

We shall now identify the Heisenberg equivalent of the Schroedinger expectation formula

$$\langle 2^{18} \rangle \qquad\qquad \mathrm{av}_\psi \alpha = \int \bar{\psi} \alpha \psi \, dx, \qquad\qquad \langle 6 \rangle$$

where α in the integrand is the Schroedinger operator associated with the dynamical variable α, and ψ is a normalized Schroedinger function describing the state ψ. Expanding ψ in the form (1), we get

$$\mathrm{av}_\psi \alpha = \int \left(\sum_i \bar{c}_i \bar{\psi}_i \right) \alpha \left(\sum_j c_j \psi_j \right) dx$$
$$= \sum_i \sum_j \bar{c}_i \left[\int \bar{\psi}_i \alpha \psi_j \, dx \right] c_j ; \qquad\qquad \langle 7 \rangle$$

the bracketed integral is the Heisenberg matrix element α_{ij}, so that $\langle 7 \rangle$ becomes

$$\mathrm{av}_\psi \alpha = \sum_i \sum_j \bar{c}_i \alpha_{ij} c_j . \qquad\qquad \langle 8 \rangle$$

The right side of $\langle 8 \rangle$ has precisely the same form as that of 21^{69}; recalling that c_j is the jth element of the Heisenberg vector ψ and that $\bar{c}_i$ is the ith element of the corresponding Heisenberg ϕ, we finally replace $\langle 8 \rangle$ by

$$\mathrm{av}_\psi \alpha = \phi \alpha \psi, \qquad\qquad \langle 9 \rangle$$

which is thus the Heisenberg equivalent of $\langle 6 \rangle$. If the Schroedinger ψ-function is not normalized, then $\mathrm{av}_\psi \alpha$ is given by 2^{17} rather than by $\langle 6 \rangle$, and $\langle 9 \rangle$ becomes replaced by

$$\mathrm{av}_\psi \alpha = \frac{\phi \alpha \psi}{\phi \psi}, \qquad\qquad \langle 10 \rangle$$

where α in the numerator is the Heisenberg matrix associated with the dynamical variable α, ψ is the Heisenberg vector representing the state ψ, and ϕ, a row symbol, is the complex conjugate of the vector ψ. Equation $\langle 10 \rangle$, the *Heisenberg expectation formula*, reduces to $\langle 9 \rangle$ whenever $\phi\psi = 1$, that is, whenever the Heisenberg vector ψ is normalized.

Note that, as a comparison of $\langle 6 \rangle$ and $\langle 9 \rangle$ shows, the Heisenberg expression $\phi\alpha\psi$ is equivalent in the one-dimensional case to the Schroedinger expression $\int \bar{\psi}\alpha\psi \, dx$ and *not* to the Schroedinger expression $\bar{\psi}\alpha\psi$; in particular, both $\phi\alpha\psi$ and $\int \bar{\psi}\alpha\psi \, dx$ are numbers, while $\bar{\psi}\alpha\psi$ is a function of x. It is to lessen the possibility of confusion in this connection that we denote the conjugates of the Heisenberg ψ's by symbols other than $\bar{\psi}$'s.

Now, how can the Heisenberg ψ's (identified above with the help of the Schroedinger theory) be constructed without reference to the Schroedinger ψ's? To do this we interpret $\langle 10 \rangle$ as a *fundamental assumption* of the Heisenberg method; this assumption might be labeled V^H, since it plays the same rôle in the Heisenberg method that the assumption V^S of §17 does in the Schroedinger theory. The procedure for constructing the Heisenberg ψ that specifies a given state of a given system then consists in identifying the column symbol which, when used in $\langle 10 \rangle$ in conjunction with the Heisenberg matrices pertaining to this system, yields average values of the various dynamical variables in agreement with the data that specify the state verbally. Unless the state in question is an energy state, this procedure is usually complicated.

When the Heisenberg matrices pertaining to a dynamical system are available and the Heisenberg ψ specifying a state of this system is given, then $\langle 10 \rangle$ enables us to compute the average of any dynamical variable for this state. In particular, we may then compute the averages of all integral powers of a given dynamical variable and hence infer, at least in principle, the distribution function of this variable for this state; but unless the dynamical variable in question is a constant of motion, this procedure is usually tedious, if not altogether impracticable, when the explicit form of the distribution function is desired.

Exercises

1. Infer from 16^{21} the Heisenberg ψ specifying the state of an oscillator which in the Schroedinger theory is specified by the ψ-function 19^{21}; then use $\langle 9 \rangle$ to show, with the help of 9^{62}, that for this state of the oscillator av $x = x_0 \cos \omega t$, where $\omega = 2\pi\nu_c$. (In §21 we deduced this result from 20^{21}.)

2. Suppose that the Heisenberg ψ of Exercise 1 is available and explain how the distribution-in-x for the corresponding state can then be found, at least in principle, without reference to Schroedinger functions.

3. Recall 9^{20} and explain how the distribution-in-E for a state can be obtained by inspecting the Heisenberg ψ specifying this state.

4. Recall that the Heisenberg energy matrices are diagonal and use $\langle 10 \rangle$ to show, without reference to the Schroedinger ψ's, that the Heisenberg ψ's specifying the energy states of a nondegenerate system have the form (3). Remember that the nth energy state is one for which av $E = E_n$ and $\Delta E = 0$.

5. Deduce 4^{63} from $\langle 10 \rangle$.

CHAPTER XI

REMARKS ON THE SYMBOLIC METHOD

We have by now illustrated three quantum-mechanical methods of associating *specific* operators with dynamical variables: the Schroedinger method, the p-method, and the Heisenberg method. The quantum condition $\alpha\beta - \beta\alpha = i\hbar[\alpha, \beta]$ of §13, however, fixes the commutation rules that the quantum-mechanical operators must satisfy, but does not specify in detail the individual operators themselves; and, as pointed out in §13, this implies that detailed specification of the individual operators is not necessary for the computation of the theoretical data to be compared with experiment, and that quantum-mechanical calculations may be carried out by the purely symbolic methods of operator algebra. In this chapter we make a few remarks concerning the symbolic method introduced by Dirac and emphasized in his book, *The Principles of Quantum Mechanics*.

71. Symbolic Operators and Operands

The symbolic method can be formulated without reference to the Schroedinger method, the Heisenberg method, and so forth; but to a beginner its rules, which are of necessity abstract, are then likely to appear rather strange, and we shall therefore first list a few of the more abstract properties of our familiar operators and operands.

We begin with the operands, which we have uniformly denoted by ψ's and which are functions of x in the Schroedinger method, functions of p in the p-method, and column symbols in the Heisenberg method. The ψ's used in any *one* of these three methods have the following properties:

(a) it has a meaning to say that two ψ's are equal to one another;[1]

---

[1] Given two Schroedinger functions, ψ_1 and ψ_2, we can, of course, determine whether $\psi_1 = \psi_2$ or $\psi_1 \neq \psi_2$; again, given two Heisenberg column symbols, ψ_1 and ψ_2, we can determine whether $\psi_1 = \psi_2$ or $\psi_1 \neq \psi_2$. At present, however, we are concerned merely with the fact that an equation of the form $\psi_1 = \psi_2$ has a meaning (one meaning in Schroedinger's case,

(b) any two ψ's can be added together, the result being a ψ;

(c) there exists a ψ, called zero, which, when added to any other ψ, leaves the latter unaltered.

The Heisenberg ψ's, being column symbols, cannot be multiplied together; the Schroedinger ψ's can be multiplied together from the *mathematical* standpoint, and so can the ψ's of the p-scheme, but the need for such a multiplication never arises in the *quantum-mechanical* calculations; thus, quantum mechanically,

(d) the multiplication of two ψ's together is meaningless.

Turning next to the operators, to be denoted for the moment by α's, we find that the α's used in any *one* of the three methods have the following properties:

(e) it has a meaning to say that two α's are equal to one another;

(f) any two α's can be added together, the result being an α;

(g) any two α's can be multiplied together in two ways, depending on the order of the factors; and the two products, both of which are α's, are usually different, so that the multiplication of the α's is usually noncommutative;

(h) some α's, called constants or numbers, commute with every α; and

(i) the multiplication of the α's is associative.

Insofar as the interplay of operators and operands is concerned, we note that within any *one* of the three methods

(j) the addition of an α and a ψ is meaningless;

(k) any ψ can be multiplied from the left by any α, and the product $\alpha\psi$ is a ψ;

(l) the multiplication of an α from the left by a ψ is meaningless; and

(m) the α's are linear operators.

Now, in the symbolic approach, the mathematical form of the operators associated with dynamical variables is left unspecified; that is, the α's are not required to be differential operators, or matrices, or operators of any other particular type. The mathematical form of the operands associated with states is also left unspecified; that is, the ψ's are not required to be functions of x, or functions of p, or column symbols, or operands of any other

---

another in Heisenberg's, and still another in the case of the p-method), and not with the tests necessary to verify such an equation. Similar remarks apply to the assertion (e) of this section and the assertion (n) of §73.

definite type. The symbolic α's and ψ's are, however, required to have the thirteen properties (a) to (m) listed above, and consequently they embody the essential more abstract characteristics of the various specific quantum-mechanical operators and operands.

If a symbolic operator α, a symbolic operand ψ other than 0, and a number λ satisfy the symbolic equation

$$\alpha\psi = \lambda\psi, \qquad \langle 1 \rangle$$

we say that λ is an eigenvalue of α, ψ is an eigen-ψ of α, and that the eigenvalue λ of α and the eigen-ψ ψ of α belong to one another. The noncommittal term 'eigen-ψ' now takes the place of the more explicit terms 'eigenfunction' and 'eigenvector.'

72. Energy Levels of an Oscillator

Before further abstract discussion, we shall illustrate the symbolic scheme by computing the energy levels of a linear harmonic oscillator by a method due to Dirac. Apart from the fact that we shall use symbolic operands, our procedure should not seem unfamiliar, because we have already handled symbolic operators—for example, in Exercise 7^2. But the procedure will be somewhat indirect, the main reason for this being that our computations are symbolic equivalents of integrations; and even elementary integrations often use indirect approaches.

The classical Hamiltonian of the oscillator is $H = p^2/2m + \frac{1}{2}kx^2$, so that, if the symbolic operators associated respectively with the coordinate x and the momentum p are denoted by x and p, the symbolic Hamiltonian is

$$H = \frac{1}{2m} p^2 + \frac{1}{2} kx^2. \qquad \langle 1 \rangle$$

According to the operator assumption I of §13, our mathematical problem is to find the eigenvalues of the operator $\langle 1 \rangle$, that is, the values of the number E for which the symbolic equation

$$H\psi = E\psi \qquad \langle 2 \rangle$$

has symbolic solutions ψ, other than $\psi = 0$. We know further that, according to the quantum condition 1^{13}, the symbolic operators x and p satisfy the commutation rule

$$\langle 5^{13} \rangle \qquad\qquad xp - px = i\hbar. \qquad \langle 3 \rangle$$

Let us first suppose for the moment that the oscillator has an energy state for which E is negative. For this state, as for any other state, the average value of the energy would equal the sum of the respective averages of $p^2/2m$ and $\tfrac{1}{2}kx^2$. Since the state in question is an energy state, the average of the energy would be just E; and since E has been assumed to be negative it follows that for this state the average of $p^2/2m$, or the average of $\tfrac{1}{2}kx^2$, or both, would have to be negative. But all experimentally possible values of $p^2/2m$ and $\tfrac{1}{2}kx^2$ are obviously positive. We therefore conclude that the assumption that E is negative is not tenable, and that

$$E \geq 0. \tag{4}$$

We next introduce the symbolic operators

$$X = \sqrt{k}x, \qquad P = p/\sqrt{m}, \tag{5}$$

and find, using $\langle 3 \rangle$, that

$$XP - PX = ih\nu_c\,, \tag{6}$$

where ν_c is the classical frequency of the oscillator, and that

$$H = \tfrac{1}{2}P^2 + \tfrac{1}{2}X^2. \tag{7}$$

Now,

$$(P + iX)(P - iX) = P^2 + X^2 + i(XP - PX)$$
$$= 2H - h\nu_c \tag{8}$$

and

$$(P - iX)(P + iX) = P^2 + X^2 - i(XP - PX)$$
$$= 2H + h\nu_c\,, \tag{9}$$

so that, on the one hand,

$$(P - iX)(P + iX)(P - iX)$$
$$= (P - iX)[(P + iX)(P - iX)] = (P - iX)(2H - h\nu_c), \tag{10}$$

while on the other

$$(P - iX)(P + iX)(P - iX)$$
$$= [(P - iX)(P + iX)](P - iX) = (2H + h\nu_c)(P - iX). \tag{11}$$

Thus

$$(P - iX)(2H - h\nu_c) = (2H + h\nu_c)(P - iX), \qquad \langle 12 \rangle$$

or, since $h\nu_c$ is a number and therefore commutes with $P - iX$,

$$(P - iX)(H - h\nu_c) = H(P - iX). \qquad \langle 13 \rangle$$

Let us now suppose that H has an as yet undetermined eigenvalue E_n, so that there exists a nonvanishing symbolic operand, say ψ_n, satisfying the equation

$$H\psi_n = E_n\psi_n. \qquad \langle 14 \rangle$$

Subtracting $h\nu_c\psi_n$ from both sides of $\langle 14 \rangle$, we get

$$(H - h\nu_c)\psi_n = (E_n - h\nu_c)\psi_n, \qquad \langle 15 \rangle$$

and multiplying both sides of $\langle 15 \rangle$ from the left by the operator $P - iX$, we get

$$(P - iX)(H - h\nu_c)\psi_n = (P - iX)(E_n - h\nu_c)\psi_n. \qquad \langle 16 \rangle$$

In view of $\langle 13 \rangle$ and the fact that $E_n - h\nu_c$ is a number, this reduces to

$$H(P - iX)\psi_n = (E_n - h\nu_c)(P - iX)\psi_n, \qquad \langle 17 \rangle$$

or, if we use the notation

$$(P - iX)\psi_n = \psi_{n-1}, \qquad \langle 18 \rangle$$

to

$$H\psi_{n-1} = (E_n - h\nu_c)\psi_{n-1}. \qquad \langle 19 \rangle$$

Equation $\langle 19 \rangle$ has the form $\langle 2 \rangle$ and means that [unless $\psi_{n-1} = (P - iX)\psi_n = 0$, a possibility which for the moment we disregard] ψ_{n-1} is an eigen-ψ of H, the corresponding eigenvalue of H being $E_n - h\nu_c$. We have thus shown, barring the possibility that $\psi_{n-1} = 0$, that, if E_n is an eigenvalue of H, then $E_n - h\nu_c$ is also an eigenvalue of H. Repetition of the argument shows that, if $E_n - h\nu_c$ is an eigenvalue of H, then [barring the possibility that $\psi_{n-2} = (P - iX)\psi_{n-1} = 0$] $E_n - 2h\nu_c$ is also an eigenvalue of H, and so on, so that, if E_n is an eigenvalue of H, then the energies

$$E_n, E_n - h\nu_c, E_n - 2h\nu_c, E_n - 3h\nu_c, \cdots, \qquad (20)$$

are each an eigenvalue of H.

Now, unless the series (20) terminates, it will include negative terms that according to (4) are impossible. Consequently the series must terminate, and we must investigate the circumstances that lead to termination. If we denote the last term in (20) by E_0 and the corresponding symbolic eigen-ψ of H by ψ_0, our mathematical problem is to find the condition under which the equation

$$H\psi_0 = E_0\psi_0, \qquad\qquad [\psi_0 \neq 0] \quad \langle 21 \rangle$$

when treated in the same way as we treated $\langle 14 \rangle$, will *not* lead to the conclusion that $E_0 - h\nu_c$ is also an eigenvalue of H.

If we replace ψ_n by ψ_0 in $\langle 14 \rangle$, Equation $\langle 17 \rangle$ becomes

$$H(P - iX)\psi_0 = (E_0 - h\nu_c)(P - iX)\psi_0 \qquad\qquad \langle 22 \rangle$$

and implies that $E_0 - h\nu_c$ is an eigenvalue of H unless

$$(P - iX)\psi_0 = 0. \qquad\qquad \langle 23 \rangle$$

But if $\langle 23 \rangle$ holds, then

$$(P + iX)(P - iX)\psi_0 = 0, \qquad\qquad \langle 24 \rangle$$

so that according to $\langle 8 \rangle$

$$(2H - h\nu_c)\psi_0 = 0, \qquad\qquad \langle 25 \rangle$$

that is,

$$H\psi_0 = \tfrac{1}{2}h\nu_c\psi_0, \qquad\qquad \langle 26 \rangle$$

and, according to $\langle 21 \rangle$,

$$E_0\psi_0 = \tfrac{1}{2}h\nu_c\psi_0 ; \qquad\qquad \langle 27 \rangle$$

the angular brackets in the number of the last equation remind us that the operand ψ_0 is symbolic. Since $\psi_0 \neq 0$, Equation $\langle 23 \rangle$ is thus equivalent to the equation

$$E_0 = \tfrac{1}{2}h\nu_c, \qquad\qquad (28)$$

and we conclude: the series (20) fails to terminate unless it contains the term $\tfrac{1}{2}h\nu_c$, and if it contains this term it terminates with it. Since (20) must terminate, it follows that (20) has the form

$$E_n, E_n - h\nu_c, E_n - 2h\nu_c, \cdots, \tfrac{1}{2}h\nu_c, \qquad\qquad (29)$$

that is,

$$[n + \tfrac{1}{2}]h\nu_c, [(n - 1) + \tfrac{1}{2}]h\nu_c, \cdots, \tfrac{1}{2}h\nu_c, \qquad (30)$$

where n is some positive integer. This result is our familiar

$$E_n = (n + \tfrac{1}{2})h\nu_c, \qquad n = 0, 1, 2, \cdots, \quad (31)$$

except that we have not yet shown that the series (30) should extend without limit to the left (Exercise 1).

These computations show how the formula (31), which we have now obtained for the fourth time, can be derived symbolically, that is, without ascribing explicit mathematical forms to the quantum-mechanical operators and operands. Another example of symbolic calculations will be given in §85.

Exercises

1. Show symbolically that, if E is an eigenvalue of $\langle 7 \rangle$, then $E + h\nu_c$ is certainly also an eigenvalue of $\langle 7 \rangle$.

2. Correlate the symbolic result that $\langle 19 \rangle$ follows from $\langle 14 \rangle$ with the nonsymbolic formula 55^4, and find a nonsymbolic equivalent of the fact that (28) follows symbolically from $\langle 23 \rangle$.

73. The Symbolic ϕ's

We now turn back to the Heisenberg method and note that the Heisenberg α's, which are matrices, the Heisenberg ψ's, which are column symbols, and the Heisenberg ϕ's, which are row symbols conjugate to the ψ's, have the following properties in addition to those listed in §71:

(n) it has a meaning to say that two ϕ's are equal to one another;

(o) any two ϕ's can be added together, the result being a ϕ;

(p) there exists a ϕ that when added to any other ϕ leaves the latter unaltered;

(q) the addition of a ϕ and a ψ is meaningless;

(r) any ψ can be multiplied from the left by any ϕ, and the product $\phi\psi$ is a number;

(s) the multiplication of a ψ from the right by a ϕ is meaningless;

(t) any α can be multiplied from the left by any ϕ, and the product $\phi\alpha$ is a ϕ;

(u) the multiplication of an α from the right by a ϕ is meaningless unless α is a number;

(v) if c is a number, then $c\phi = \phi c$; and

(w) the numbers $\phi(\alpha\psi)$ and $(\phi\alpha)\psi$ are equal to one another, so that either can be denoted simply by $\phi\alpha\psi$.

Now, the symbolic method employs, besides the symbolic ψ's and the symbolic α's, also symbolic ϕ's that are postulated to have the properties (n) to (w) listed above. These ϕ's are called by Dirac *conjugate imaginaries* of the symbolic ψ's. No specific mathematical form is ascribed to these ϕ's; in particular, they are not required to be row symbols.

One of the physical assumptions of the symbolic method is

V. If a system is in the state specified by the symbol ψ, then the expected average of any dynamical variable α is

$$\mathrm{av}_\psi \alpha = \frac{\phi\alpha\psi}{\phi\psi}, \qquad\qquad \langle 1 \rangle$$

where α in the numerator is the symbolic operator associated with the dynamical variable α, and ϕ is the conjugate imaginary of ψ.

Equation $\langle 1 \rangle$, the *symbolic expectation formula,* is the symbolic generalization of the Schroedinger expectation formula 1^{17}, of the complete expectation formula of the p-method (of which 10^{50} is a special case), and of the Heisenberg expectation formula 10^{70} (which has exactly the same appearance as $\langle 1 \rangle$, but in which ψ and ϕ are a column symbol and a row symbol, rather than purely abstract symbols). If ψ is such that

$$\phi\psi = 1, \qquad\qquad \langle 2 \rangle$$

in which case the symbol ψ is said to be *normalized,* then $\langle 1 \rangle$ reduces to

$$\mathrm{av}_\psi \alpha = \phi\alpha\psi. \qquad\qquad \langle 3 \rangle$$

To give an example of a symbolic computation involving ϕ's, we shall now show that, if ψ is an eigen-ψ of α belonging to the eigenvalue a of α, that is, if

$$\alpha\psi = a\psi, \qquad\qquad \langle 4 \rangle$$

then the value of the dynamical variable α for the state ψ is certainly a. Indeed, multiplying $\langle 4 \rangle$ from the left by the conjugate imaginary of ψ, we get $\phi\alpha\psi = \phi a\psi$, that is, $\phi\alpha\psi = a\phi\psi$, and $\phi\alpha\psi/\phi\psi = a$, so that, according to $\langle 1 \rangle$,

$$\mathrm{av}_\psi \alpha = a; \qquad\qquad (5)$$

multiplying $\langle 4 \rangle$ from the left by α, we get $\alpha^2\psi = \alpha a\psi = a\alpha\psi$, so that

$$\alpha^2\psi = a^2\psi, \qquad\qquad \langle 6 \rangle$$

from which it follows that $\phi\alpha^2\psi = a^2\phi\psi$, that is,

$$\text{av}_\psi\,\alpha^2 = a^2; \qquad\qquad \langle 7 \rangle$$

thus $\text{av}_\psi\,\alpha^2 = (\text{av}_\psi\,\alpha)^2$, and the fact that the value of α for the state ψ is certainly a follows from (5) and 20[11].

The Schroedinger equivalent of the multiplication of a symbolic equation by ϕ (which multiplication must be done from the left) is the *multiplication of the corresponding equation of the Schroedinger scheme from the left by $\bar{\psi}$, followed by integration*, rather than merely multiplication by $\bar{\psi}$; for example, in the one-dimensional case, the Schroedinger equivalent of the symbolic step from the equation $\alpha\psi = a\psi$ to the equation $\phi\alpha\psi = \phi a\psi$ is the step from the equation $\alpha\psi = a\psi$ to the equation $\int\bar{\psi}\alpha\psi\,dx = \int\bar{\psi}a\psi\,dx$. Hence the Schroedinger equivalents of the symbolic ϕ's, which we shall not discuss, are not recognized as readily as are their Heisenberg equivalents.

We may, if we wish, picture the symbolic ψ's as vectors in a certain space, the ψ-space, and picture the symbolic α's as mappings of this space; the symbolic ϕ's are then to be pictured as vectors in another place, the ϕ-space. That such a quasi-geometric interpretation will not lead to contradictions follows from the complete parallelism between the rules for handling the symbolic ψ's, α's, and ϕ's, and those for handling the Heisenberg ψ's, α's, and ϕ's.

With these few remarks, we end our discussion of the symbolic method. To build up systematically the rules for manipulating the symbolic ψ's, α's, and ϕ's, and to introduce such notions as the orthogonality of two ψ's, the complex conjugate of an α, and so on, would merely mean rewording appropriately our familiar vector-matrix rules and definitions; but to go further than that, to show, for example, how Schroedinger functions can be expressed in terms of the symbolic ψ's, would require rather advanced discussion.

Exercises

1. Correlate the symbolic steps that we used in deducing the physical implications of $\langle 4 \rangle$ with the explicit steps used in §17 in deducing the physical implications of 7^{17}.

2. If the symbolic operator α satisfies the equation $\overline{\phi_r \alpha \psi_s} = \phi_s \alpha \psi_r$ for every pair of symbolic operands ψ_r and ψ_s, then α is said to be *Hermitian*. Correlate this definition with 19[44], and show symbolically that every eigenvalue of a Hermitian operator is real.

3. Show that in view of the assumption V the second sentence in the operator assumption I of §13 can be deleted.

CHAPTER XII

PROBLEMS IN THREE-DIMENSIONAL MOTION; THE SCHROEDINGER METHOD

We shall now consider a few problems concerning phenomena taking place in our physical three-dimensional space. The Schroedinger method for handling these problems is a direct extension of that of Chapters III to VII, referring to fictitious one-dimensional motion; several of the more general results of these chapters will, in fact, reappear almost word for word in the present chapter. Some of the numbers at the left of our new equations are those of the corresponding one-dimensional equations.

74. Mathematical Preliminaries

We use the Cartesian frame of Fig. 100 and denote the point whose coordinates are x, y, and z by the symbol xyz; wherever the symbol xyz is used for the product of the Cartesian coordinates of a point rather than for the point itself, this fact will be stated explicitly. The vector with origin at O and terminus at xyz is called the *position vector* and is denoted by $\mathbf{r}$; its length is denoted by r. We denote functions of x, y, and z by $u(x, y, z)$, $v(x, y, z)$, $f(x, y, z)$, and so on, or simply by u, v, f, and so on; their complex conjugates by $\bar{u}(x, y, z)$, $\bar{v}(x, y, z)$, $\bar{f}(x, y, z)$, and so on, or by $\bar{u}$, $\bar{v}$, $\bar{f}$, and so forth; and their moduli by $|u(x, y, z)|$, $|v(x, y, z)|$, $|f(x, y, z)|$, and so forth, or by $|u|$, $|v|$, $|f|$, and so forth.

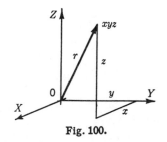

Fig. 100.

If u is everywhere a continuous function of x, of y, and of z, and if each of the three partial derivatives $\partial u/\partial x$, $\partial u/\partial y$, and $\partial u/\partial z$ is everywhere a continuous function of x, of y, and of z, except perhaps at isolated points, then we say that u satisfies our *standard continuity conditions*. If u has a single value at each point in space, we call it *single-valued*. If u satisfies our standard continuity conditions, is single-valued, and is not identically

401

zero, and if $|u|$ is everywhere finite,[1] then we say that u is *well-behaved.*

We also use the spherical polar frame of Fig. 101 and denote the point whose coordinates are r, θ, and ϕ by the symbol $r\theta\phi$. The relations between the Cartesian and the polar coordinates of a given point are

$$\begin{cases} x = r \sin\theta\cos\phi & r = \sqrt{x^2 + y^2 + z^2} \\[2ex] y = r \sin\theta\sin\phi & \theta = \cos^{-1}\dfrac{z}{\sqrt{x^2 + y^2 + z^2}} \\[2ex] z = r\cos\theta & \phi = \tan^{-1}\dfrac{y}{x} \end{cases} \quad (1)$$

Note that, while in the Cartesian frame every point has an unambiguous single set of three coordinates, this is not so in the polar frame; for example, the set $r = 1$, $\theta = \frac{1}{2}\pi$, and $\phi = \frac{1}{2}\pi$ specifies the same point in space as does the set $r = 1$, $\theta = \frac{1}{2}\pi$, and $\phi = \frac{5}{2}\pi$; this property of the polar frame is in part responsible for the stress that we now put on single-valuedness. If x, y, and z are eliminated from the function $u = u(x, y, z)$ by means

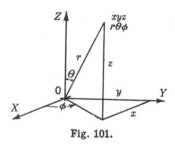

Fig. 101.

of r, θ, and ϕ, then we denote the resulting function of r, θ, and ϕ by $u(r, \theta, \phi)$ or simply by u [strictly, the u in $u(r, \theta, \phi)$ should then be replaced by another symbol]; for example, if $u = u(x, y, z) = e^{x^2+y^2+z^2}$, then we write $u = u(r, \theta, \phi) = e^{r^2}$, although in this particular case we may write $u = u(r) = e^{r^2}$.

---

[1] By "$|u|$ is everywhere finite" we mean not only that $|u|$ is finite (that is, not infinite) at every particular point, but also that $|u|$ does not increase without limit when $r \to \infty$, that is, when the point xyz recedes (in any manner whatever) from the origin O; thus the function $e^{x^2-y^2-z^2}$ is not well-behaved because, for example, it grows without limit if the point xyz recedes from O along the x-axis. Incidentally, the complete conditions for good behavior of u, which we need not consider in our elementary work, allow u to become infinite at isolated points, provided its infinities are so mild that certain integrals involving u are finite; see Kemble, §23d.

In accordance with the convention stated above Equation 29[8], we use the abbreviations

$$\int f dx = \int_{-\infty}^{\infty} f dx, \quad \int f dy = \int_{-\infty}^{\infty} f dy, \quad \int f dz = \int_{-\infty}^{\infty} f dz, \quad (2)$$

and

$$\int f dr = \int_{0}^{\infty} f dr, \quad \int f d\theta = \int_{0}^{\pi} f d\theta, \quad \int f d\phi = \int_{0}^{2\pi} f d\phi. \quad (3)$$

Further, we denote the differential volume element by $d\tau$ and use the symbol

$$\int f \, d\tau \quad (4)$$

for the definite integral of f taken over the entire space. For example, if Cartesian coordinates are used, so that $d\tau = dx \, dy \, dz$, we let

$$\int f d\tau = \int_{-\infty}^{\infty} \int_{-\infty}^{\infty} \int_{-\infty}^{\infty} f(x, y, z) dx \, dy \, dz; \quad (5)$$

again, if spherical polar coordinates are used, so that $d\tau = r^2 \, dr \sin \theta \, d\theta \, d\phi$, we let

$$\int f d\tau = \int_{0}^{2\pi} \int_{0}^{\pi} \int_{0}^{\infty} f(r, \theta, \phi) r^2 dr \sin \theta \, d\theta \, d\phi, \quad (6)$$

the integration with respect to ϕ extending from 0 to 2π, that with respect to θ extending from 0 to π, and that with respect to r extending from 0 to ∞.

If the integral $\int \bar{u}u \, d\tau$ is finite, then u is said to be of *integrable square* or *quadratically integrable* (in the infinite region). If

$$(19^8) \qquad\qquad \int \bar{u}u \, d\tau = 1, \qquad\qquad (7)$$

then u is said to be *normal, unitary, normalized to unity*, or simply *normalized* (in the infinite region). If f is quadratically integrable (in the infinite region) and N is a number such that

$$(22^8) \qquad\qquad \bar{N}N = (\int \bar{f}f \, d\tau)^{-1}, \qquad\qquad (8)$$

then the function Nf is normalized (in the infinite region); the number N (the *normalizing factor* of f) is indeterminate to the extent of a phase factor $e^{i\gamma}$, where γ is an arbitrary real constant.

If the functions u and v satisfy the condition

(3^8) $$\int \bar{u}v \, d\tau = 0 \qquad (9)$$

or the equivalent condition $\int \bar{v}u \, d\tau = 0$, then they are said to be mutually *orthogonal* (in the infinite region). If every two functions in the set

$$u_1, u_2, u_3, \cdots \qquad (10)$$

are mutually orthogonal in the infinite region, then the *set* is said to be *orthogonal* (in this region); if, in addition, each u_k is normalized, then the set is said to be *orthonormal* (in the infinite region).

If a function f admits of an expansion in terms of the orthogonal set (10), that is, if f can be expressed throughout the infinite region in the form

(8^8) $$f = \sum_k c_k u_k, \quad k = 1, 2, 3, \cdots, \quad (11)$$

then the expansion coefficients are given by the formula

(12^8) $$c_k = \frac{\int \bar{u}_k f d\tau}{\int \bar{u}_k u_k d\tau}, \qquad (12)$$

which reduces to

(21^8) $$c_k = \int \bar{u}_k f d\tau \qquad (13)$$

whenever the set (10) is orthonormal. The proof of (12) runs quite parallel to that of 12^8.

Differential operators. The operators with which we shall now deal and which for lack of a better short name we call *differential operators* are combinations of the operators x, y, and z (which stand, respectively, for the multiplication of operands by the variable x, the variable y, and the variable z), the operators $\partial/\partial x$, $\partial/\partial y$, and $\partial/\partial z$ (which stand, respectively, for partial differentiation of operands with respect to x, with respect to y, and with respect to z), and the operators of type c (which stand for the multiplication of operands by numerical constants). Equality, addition, multiplication, and so forth, of these operators are defined as in §2, and so are such terms as commutator, and so forth. We shall leave it to the reader to show, in particular, that any two of the three operators x, y, and z commute with each other, that any two of the three operators $\partial/\partial x$, $\partial/\partial y$, and $\partial/\partial z$ commute with each other, and that

$$\frac{\partial}{\partial x} x - x \frac{\partial}{\partial x} = 1 \qquad \frac{\partial}{\partial y} y - y \frac{\partial}{\partial y} = 1 \qquad \frac{\partial}{\partial z} z - z \frac{\partial}{\partial z} = 1 \qquad (14)$$

$$\frac{\partial}{\partial x} y - y \frac{\partial}{\partial x} = 0 \qquad \frac{\partial}{\partial y} z - z \frac{\partial}{\partial y} = 0 \qquad \frac{\partial}{\partial z} x - x \frac{\partial}{\partial z} = 0 \qquad (15)$$

$$\frac{\partial}{\partial x} z - z \frac{\partial}{\partial x} = 0 \qquad \frac{\partial}{\partial y} x - x \frac{\partial}{\partial y} = 0 \qquad \frac{\partial}{\partial z} y - y \frac{\partial}{\partial z} = 0. \qquad (16)$$

The differential operator $\partial^2/\partial x^2 + \partial^2/\partial y^2 + \partial^2/\partial z^2$ is called the *Laplace operator*, or the *Laplacian*; we abbreviate it by the symbol ∇^2, usually read *del squared*:

$$\nabla^2 = \frac{\partial^2}{\partial x^2} + \frac{\partial^2}{\partial y^2} + \frac{\partial^2}{\partial z^2}. \qquad (17)$$

Other differential operators of interest to us are combinations of the operators r, θ, ϕ, $\partial/\partial r$, $\partial/\partial\theta$, $\partial/\partial\phi$, and c; these (polar) operators can be expressed in terms of the (Cartesian) operators introduced above, and vice versa. To illustrate, we consider the operator $\partial/\partial z$. According to the rules for partial differentiation,

$$\frac{\partial}{\partial z} u = \frac{\partial r}{\partial z} \frac{\partial}{\partial r} u + \frac{\partial \theta}{\partial z} \frac{\partial}{\partial \theta} u + \frac{\partial \phi}{\partial z} \frac{\partial}{\partial \phi} u; \qquad (18)$$

in view of (1),

$$\frac{\partial r}{\partial z} = \frac{\partial}{\partial z} \sqrt{x^2 + y^2 + z^2} = \frac{z}{\sqrt{x^2 + y^2 + z^2}} = \frac{z}{r} = \cos\theta, \qquad (19)$$

$$\frac{\partial \theta}{\partial z} = \frac{\partial}{\partial z} \cos^{-1}\frac{z}{r} = -\frac{1}{\sqrt{1 - z^2/r^2}} \frac{\partial}{\partial z} \frac{z}{r}$$

$$= -\frac{1}{\sqrt{1 - z^2/r^2}} \frac{1}{r} \sin^2\theta = -\frac{1}{r}\sin\theta, \qquad (20)$$

and

$$\frac{\partial \phi}{\partial z} = 0, \qquad (21)$$

so that (18) becomes

$$\frac{\partial}{\partial z} u = \cos\theta \frac{\partial}{\partial r} u - \frac{1}{r}\sin\theta \frac{\partial}{\partial \theta} u; \qquad (22)$$

and since (22) holds for an arbitrary operand u on which the indicated operations can be performed, we conclude that

$$\frac{\partial}{\partial z} = \cos\theta \, \frac{\partial}{\partial r} - \frac{1}{r}\sin\theta \, \frac{\partial}{\partial\theta}. \tag{23}$$

Eigenvalues and eigenfunctions. If a differential operator α, a *well-behaved* operand u, and a numerical constant λ satisfy the equation

$$(15^3) \qquad\qquad \alpha u = \lambda u, \tag{24}$$

then we say, as before, that λ is an eigenvalue of α, that u is an eigenfunction of α, and that the eigenvalue λ and the eigenfunction u of the operator α belong to each other. The computation of the eigenvalues of operators in the three-dimensional case is of course usually more involved than in the one-dimensional case, but is much the same in principle except for the new emphasis on single-valuedness.

To illustrate the effect of requiring that u in (24) be single-valued, we shall compute the eigenvalues of the operator $-i\,\partial/\partial\phi$ for which (24) becomes the differential equation

$$-i\,\frac{\partial}{\partial\phi}\,u = \lambda u. \tag{25}$$

The general solution of (25) is

$$u = A(r,\,\theta)e^{i\lambda\phi}, \tag{26}$$

where $A(r,\,\theta)$ is an arbitrary function of r and θ, and it remains to determine the circumstances under which (26) is well-behaved. Now, the behavior of (26) depends of course on that of both $A(r,\,\theta)$ and $e^{i\lambda\phi}$; of $A(r,\,\theta)$ we can say only that it should not spoil the behavior of u [the choice $A(r,\,\theta) =$ constant, for example, is satisfactory]; but the second factor, whose explicit form is available, enables us to derive a limitation to be put on λ. Indeed, since the two sets of coordinates $(r,\,\theta,\,\phi)$ and $(r,\,\theta,\,\phi + 2\pi)$ specify the same point in space, the value of the function u, *if u is to be single-valued*, must remain unaltered when we replace ϕ by $\phi + 2\pi$; in other words, the condition of single-valuedness requires that (26) satisfy the equation

$$A(r,\,\theta)e^{i\lambda\phi} = A(r,\,\theta)e^{i\lambda(\phi+2\pi)}, \tag{27}$$

that is,

$$1 = e^{2\pi i\lambda}. \tag{28}$$

Equation (28) holds if and only if

$$\lambda = \cdots, -2, -1, 0, 1, 2, \cdots, \tag{29}$$

so that *the eigenvalues of* $-i\dfrac{\partial}{\partial\phi}$ *are the positive and the negative integers, zero included.*   Note that, because of the cyclic character of the coordinate ϕ, the eigenvalue spectrum of $-i\,\partial/\partial\phi$ is discrete, and is quite different from that of, say, $-i\,\partial/\partial x$.   In dealing with the operator $-i\,\partial/\partial\phi$, the symbol λ is usually replaced by the symbol m, and the eigenfunctions of $-i\,\partial/\partial\phi$ are then written as

$$u_m = A_m(r, \theta)e^{im\phi}, \qquad m = 0, \pm 1, \pm 2, \cdots, \tag{30}$$

where the subscript m of A reminds us that the arbitrary well-behaved factor $A(r, \theta)$ may be different for different values of m The ϕ-factors in (30) have the form 28[8], and hence the quantity $\int \bar{u}_m u_{m'}\,d\phi$ vanishes whenever $m \neq m'$; for this reason the set (30) is said to be 'orthogonal in ϕ.'

The Legendrian.[2]   An operator of special interest to us is

$$-\frac{1}{\sin\theta}\frac{\partial}{\partial\theta}\sin\theta\frac{\partial}{\partial\theta} - \frac{1}{\sin^2\theta}\frac{\partial^2}{\partial\phi^2}, \tag{31}$$

which we call the *Legendre operator,* or simply the *Legendrian*; its Cartesian form, with a reversed algebraic sign, is shown on the left side of (74).   To compute the eigenvalues of the Legendrian, we look for the values of λ for which the equation

$$\left(-\frac{1}{\sin\theta}\frac{\partial}{\partial\theta}\sin\theta\frac{\partial}{\partial\theta} - \frac{1}{\sin^2\theta}\frac{\partial^2}{\partial\phi^2}\right)u = \lambda u \tag{32}$$

---

[2] The Legendre operator plays a fundamental rôle in the quantum theory of angular momentum; our discussion of it is, however, not extensive, and one of the important tasks that the reader should eventually take up is a more elaborate study of the eigenfunctions of this operator, called surface spherical harmonics and discussed in mathematical works on spherical harmonics, in classical treatments of potential theory, and in some books on quantum mechanics.   A clear elementary presentation (but written from a standpoint somewhat different from that adopted here) is given in Chapter VIII of Jeans; our presentation follows in part that of §2A of Sommerfeld.

has well-behaved solutions. The Legendrian does not involve r or $\partial/\partial r$, and consequently we may temporarily take u to be a function of θ and ϕ only, and later permit the arbitrary constants in the solutions of (32) to be functions of r.

Separation of variables. The partial differential equation (32), called the *Legendre equation*, can be separated into two ordinary differential equations in much the same way that the partial differential equation 7^{42} was separated into the two ordinary differential equations 11^{42} and 12^{42}. Indeed, turning to u's of the special form $u = \Theta(\theta)\Phi(\phi)$, or, for short,

$$u = \Theta\Phi \tag{33}$$

(where Θ is a function of θ only, and Φ is a function of ϕ only), substituting (33) into (32), and dividing the resulting equation by $-\Theta\Phi/\sin^2\theta$, we get

$$\frac{\sin\theta}{\Theta}\frac{\partial}{\partial\theta}\left(\sin\theta\frac{\partial\Theta}{\partial\theta}\right) + \lambda\sin^2\theta = -\frac{1}{\Phi}\frac{\partial^2\Phi}{\partial\phi^2}. \tag{34}$$

Note that in (34) the parentheses are not strictly necessary, and ∂'s can be replaced by d's. Now, the left side of (34) depends only on θ, while its right side depends only on ϕ, so that (34) has the form $f(\theta) = g(\phi)$; and, since θ and ϕ are *independent* variables, it follows that the left side of (34) cannot in fact depend even on θ, while its right side cannot in fact depend even on ϕ. In other words, each side of (34) is a numerical constant, say c:

$$\frac{\sin\theta}{\Theta}\frac{\partial}{\partial\theta}\left(\sin\theta\frac{\partial\Theta}{\partial\theta}\right) + \lambda\sin^2\theta = c \tag{35}$$

and

$$-\frac{\partial^2}{\partial\phi^2}\Phi = c\Phi. \tag{36}$$

We shall call (35) and (36) the 'θ-equation' and the 'ϕ-equation,' respectively.

The ϕ-equation. The operator $-\partial^2/\partial\phi^2$ is the square of the operator $-i\,\partial/\partial\phi$, so that its eigenvalues are the squares of the eigenvalues of $-i\,\partial/\partial\phi$, that is, the squares of the integers (29). Therefore Equation (36), which is just the eigenvalue equation for the operator $-\partial^2/\partial\phi^2$, has well-behaved solutions if and only if

$$c = m^2, \qquad\qquad m = 0, \pm 1, \pm 2, \cdots. \tag{37}$$

Replacing c in (36) by m^2, we find that

$$\Phi = Ae^{im\phi} + Be^{-im\phi}, \tag{38}$$

where A and B are arbitrary constants—constants in the sense that they are independent of both ϕ and θ.

The θ-equation. Replacing c in (35) by m^2 and changing from ∂'s to d's, we get

$$\frac{1}{\sin\theta}\frac{d}{d\theta}\left(\sin\theta\,\frac{d\Theta}{d\theta}\right) + \left(\lambda - \frac{m^2}{\sin^2\theta}\right)\Theta = 0. \tag{39}$$

When we introduce the new independent variable

$$\mu = \cos\theta \tag{40}$$

whose range is

$$-1 \le \mu \le 1, \tag{41}$$

and note that $\dfrac{d}{d\theta} = \dfrac{d\mu}{d\theta}\dfrac{d}{d\mu} = -\sin\theta\,\dfrac{d}{d\mu}$, Equation (39) becomes

$$(1-\mu^2)\frac{d^2\Theta}{d\mu^2} - 2\mu\frac{d\Theta}{d\mu} + \left(\lambda - \frac{m^2}{1-\mu^2}\right)\Theta = 0. \tag{42}$$

Our purpose is now to find the value of λ for which (42) has well-behaved solutions.

In treating (42) it is convenient to write

$$\Theta = (1-\mu^2)^{\frac{1}{2}|m|}v(\mu), \tag{43}$$

where v is an as yet undetermined function of μ; substituting (43) into (42), we then find that

$$(1-\mu^2)v'' - 2(|m|+1)\mu v' + (\lambda - |m| - m^2)v = 0, \tag{44}$$

where $v' = dv/d\mu$, and so on.

We now proceed to solve (44) by power series; the method is similar to that used in the case of 17^4, and we shall outline it but briefly. We let

$$v = \sum_i a_i\mu^i, \qquad i = \tau,\ \tau+1,\ \tau+2,\ \cdots, \tag{45}$$

where τ and the a's are as yet undetermined constants and $a_\tau \ne 0$, and, substituting (45) into (44), get

$$\sum_i \{a_i i(i-1)\mu^{i-2} + a_i[\lambda - (i+|m|)(i+|m|+1)]\mu^i\} = 0. \tag{46}$$

The coefficient of μ^k in (46) is

$$(k + 2)(k + 1)a_{k+2} + [\lambda - (k + |m|)(k + |m| + 1)]a_k. \quad (47)$$

In order that (46) may hold, the coefficient (47) must vanish for every value of k, so that

$$\frac{a_{k+2}}{a_k} = \frac{(k + |m|)(k + |m| + 1) - \lambda}{(k + 1)(k + 2)}. \quad (48)$$

To determine τ, we note that the coefficient of the lowest power of μ, that is, of $\mu^{\tau-2}$, in (46) is $a_\tau \tau(\tau - 1)$, so that the equation $\tau(\tau - 1) = 0$ must hold, and we have the two possibilities $\tau = 0$ and $\tau = 1$. The series, which we denote by V_0, obtained from (45) by letting $\tau = 0$, letting $a_0 = 1$, and omitting the odd powers of μ, that is,

$$V_0(\mu) = 1 + a_2 \mu^2 + a_4 \mu^4 + \cdots, \quad (49)$$

is a particular solution of (44), provided of course that the a's satisfy (48); the case $\tau = 1$ yields another particular solution,

$$V_1(\mu) = \mu + a_3 \mu^3 + a_5 \mu^5 + \cdots, \quad (50)$$

and the general solution of (44) is

$$v = A V_0(\mu) + B V_1(\mu). \quad (51)$$

If the series (49) terminates, that is, if V_0 is a polynomial, then V_0 is finite throughout the region $-1 \leq \mu \leq 1$ and, when substituted into (43), yields a well-behaved Θ. On the other hand, if (49) is an infinite series, then V_0, when substituted into (43), yields an ill-behaved Θ. Indeed, for $\mu = 1$ we have

$$V_0(1) = 1 + a_2 + a_4 + \cdots; \quad (52)$$

this series diverges, and a more complete study shows that the factor $(1 - \mu^2)^{\frac{1}{2}|m|}$ in (43) fails to keep Θ finite when v is infinite. The series V_1 behaves in a similar way. Thus the permissible values of λ are those which lead to a terminating v, that is, the values

$$\lambda = (k + |m|)(k + |m| + 1), \quad (53)$$

which, according to (48), cause the vanishing of a_{k+2}, a_{k+4}, a_{k+6}, and so on.

Therefore, the only way to obtain a well-behaved solution of the θ-equation (42) is

(a) to let $\lambda = (k + |m|)(k + |m| + 1)$, where k is a positive integer or zero (thus causing V_0 to terminate if k is even, or V_1 if k is odd), and

(b) to set the arbitrary multiplier of the nonterminating series in (51) equal to zero.

Since $|m|$ in (53) takes on the values 0, 1, 2, $\cdots$, and since k (the exponent of the highest power of μ in the polynomial v) also takes on these values, we may set

$$k + |m| = l, \quad l = 0, 1, 2, \cdots \quad (54)$$

and rewrite (53) as

$$\lambda = l(l + 1), \quad l = 0, 1, 2, \cdots ; \quad (55)$$

the eigenvalues of the Legendrian are thus the special integers 0, 2, 6, 12, 20, $\cdots$.

The well-behaved solutions of the θ-equation. Since our interest is restricted to well-behaved solutions, we may now rewrite (42) as

$$(1 - \mu^2) \frac{d^2\Theta}{d\mu^2} - 2\mu \frac{d\Theta}{d\mu} + \left[l(l + 1) - \frac{m^2}{1 - \mu^2} \right]\Theta = 0, \quad (56)$$

and (44) as

$$(1 - \mu^2)v'' - 2(|m| + 1)\mu v' + [l(l + 1) - |m| - m^2]v = 0. \quad (57)$$

It follows from (54) that, for a preassigned l, only the following $2l + 1$ values of m yield polynomial solutions of (57):

$$m = -l, -(l - 1), \cdots, -1, 0, 1, \cdots, (l - 1), l. \quad (58)$$

It can be shown[3] that the polynomial solutions of (57) can be written, apart from a multiplicative constant, as

$$v = \frac{d^{l+|m|}}{d\mu^{l+|m|}} (\mu^2 - 1)^l. \quad (59)$$

According to (43), a well-behaved solution of (56) can be obtained by multiplying (59) by $(1 - \mu^2)^{\frac{1}{2}|m|}$; the result, when divided by a conventional factor $2^l l!$, is denoted by $P_l^{|m|}$ and is called an *associated Legendre function of the first kind*, except that when $m = 0$ the symbol P_l is used instead of P_l^0 and the resulting

---

[3] Jeans, §240.

function is called a *Legendre polynomial*. Thus, apart from an arbitrary multiplicative constant, the well-behaved solutions of (56) are

$$P_l^{|m|}(\mu) = \frac{1}{2^l l!} (1 - \mu^2)^{\frac{1}{2}|m|} \frac{d^{l+|m|}}{d\mu^{l+|m|}} (\mu^2 - 1)^l. \tag{60}$$

For many quantum-mechanical purposes, however, it is particularly convenient to introduce the following function,[4] to be denoted either by $\Theta(l m)$ or by Θ_l^m:

$$\Theta(lm) = \Theta_l^m = (-1)^{\frac{1}{2}(m+|m|)} \sqrt{\frac{(2l + 1)(l - |m|)!}{2(l + |m|)!}} P_l^{|m|}(\mu), \tag{61}$$

and to write the well-behaved solutions of (56) either as $\Theta = A\Theta(l m)$ or as $\Theta = A\Theta_l^m$, where A is an arbitrary nonvanishing constant. We shall ordinarily denote the function (61) by Θ_l^m, and shall reserve the symbol $\Theta(l m)$ for cases that would otherwise involve complicated typesetting.

A few Θ_l^m's, grouped according to the values of l, are:

$$\Theta_0^0 = \sqrt{\frac{1}{2}}$$

$$\begin{cases} \Theta_1^0 = \sqrt{\frac{3}{2}} \mu = \sqrt{\frac{3}{2}} \cos \theta \\ \\ \Theta_1^1 = -\sqrt{\frac{3}{4}} (1 - \mu^2)^{\frac{1}{2}} = -\sqrt{\frac{3}{4}} \sin \theta \qquad = -\Theta_1^{-1} \end{cases}$$

$$\begin{cases} \Theta_2^0 = \sqrt{\frac{5}{8}} (3\mu^2 - 1) = \sqrt{\frac{5}{8}} (3 \cos^2 \theta - 1) \\ \\ \Theta_2^1 = -\sqrt{\frac{15}{4}} (1 - \mu^2)^{\frac{1}{2}}\mu = -\sqrt{\frac{15}{4}} \sin \theta \cos \theta \qquad = -\Theta_2^{-1} \\ \\ \Theta_2^2 = \sqrt{\frac{15}{16}} (1 - \mu^2) = \sqrt{\frac{15}{16}} \sin^2 \theta \qquad = \Theta_2^{-2} \end{cases}$$

---

[4] Condon and Shortley, page 52.

$$\begin{cases} \Theta_3^0 = \sqrt{\dfrac{7}{8}}\,(5\mu^3 - 3\mu) = \sqrt{\dfrac{7}{8}}\,(5\cos^3\theta - 3\cos\theta) \\[2em] \Theta_3^1 = -\sqrt{\dfrac{21}{32}}\,(1-\mu^2)^{\frac{1}{2}}(5\mu^2-1) \\[2em] \qquad\quad = -\sqrt{\dfrac{21}{32}}\,(5\sin\theta\cos^2\theta - \sin\theta) \quad = -\Theta_3^{-1} \\[2em] \Theta_3^2 = \sqrt{\dfrac{105}{16}}\,(1-\mu^2)\mu = \sqrt{\dfrac{105}{16}}\,\sin^2\theta\cos\theta \qquad = \Theta_3^{-2} \\[2em] \Theta_3^3 = -\sqrt{\dfrac{35}{32}}\,(1-\mu^2)^{\frac{3}{2}} = -\sqrt{\dfrac{35}{32}}\,\sin^3\theta \qquad = -\Theta_3^{-3}. \end{cases}$$

The Θ_l^m's satisfy the equations

$$\int_{-1}^{1} \Theta_l^m(\mu)\Theta_{l'}^m(\mu)\,d\mu$$

$$= \int_0^{\pi} \Theta_l^m(\cos\theta)\Theta_{l'}^m(\cos\theta)\,\sin\theta\,d\theta = \begin{cases} 1 & \text{if } l = l' \\ 0 & \text{if } l \neq l' \end{cases} \quad (62)$$

and are therefore said to be 'orthonormal in θ.'

The eigenfunctions of the Legendrian. We now recall (33), multiply (61) by (38), and, for the moment, set $B = 0$. The result, that is, the function

$$A\,\Theta_l^m e^{im\phi}, \tag{63}$$

is an eigenfunction of the Legendrian belonging to the eigenvalue $l(l + 1)$.

Now, the value of l having been fixed, the parameter m in the θ-equation can be given any one of the $2l + 1$ values (58). The products of the corresponding Θ-factors (61) with the first term in the Φ-factor (38) are, if we omit the arbitrary multipliers,

$$\Theta_l^{-l} e^{-il\phi},\, \Theta_l^{-(l-1)} e^{-i(l-1)\phi},\, \cdots,\, \Theta_l^{-1} e^{-i\phi},\, \Theta_l^0,\, \Theta_l^1 e^{i\phi},\, \cdots,$$
$$\Theta_l^{l-1} e^{i(l-1)\phi},\, \Theta_l^l e^{il\phi}. \tag{64}$$

Since $\Theta_l^{-m} = (-1)^m \Theta_l^m$ and since the arbitrary constants are omitted, the Θ's with negative superscripts may be replaced by the Θ's with the corresponding positive superscripts—this is not unexpected, because the θ-equation is unchanged when m is replaced by $-m$; but we shall adopt the notation of (64) on account of its symmetry.

When we turn to the second term in the Φ-factor (38) and proceed as before, we find that, since this term differs from the first only through the sign of m, it contributes nothing new to our list (64). Hence the eigenfunctions of the Legendrian belonging to the eigenvalue $l(l + 1)$ are just the $2l + 1$ functions (64), their multiples, and their linear combinations. The members of (64) are linearly independent, and hence the eigenvalue $l(l + 1)$ of the Legendrian is degenerate to the degree $2l + 1$.

It is convenient to define the symbols $\Upsilon(l\,m)$ and Υ_l^m by writing

$$\Upsilon(l\,m) = \Upsilon_l^m = \Theta(l\,m)\,\frac{e^{im\phi}}{\sqrt{2\pi}} = \Theta_l^m\,\frac{e^{im\phi}}{\sqrt{2\pi}} \tag{65}$$

and to rewrite the list (64) as

$$\Upsilon_l^{-l},\; \Upsilon_l^{-l+1},\; \cdots,\; \Upsilon_l^{-1},\; \Upsilon_l^0,\; \Upsilon_l^1,\; \cdots,\; \Upsilon_l^{l-1},\; \Upsilon_l^l, \tag{66}$$

the compensating factors $\sqrt{2\pi}$ being absorbed in the unwritten arbitrary multipliers. The Υ's and their numerical multiples are called *surface spherical harmonics.* Any well-behaved function of θ and ϕ can be expressed as a linear combination of surface spherical harmonics,[3] and consequently our having restricted ourselves to solutions of the Legendre equation of the rather special form $u = \Theta\Phi$ has not impaired the generality of our results.

A few Υ's, grouped according to the values of l, are:

$$\Upsilon_0^0 = \sqrt{\frac{1}{4\pi}}$$

$$\Upsilon_2^{-2} = \sqrt{\frac{15}{32\pi}}\,\sin^2\theta\,e^{-2i\phi}$$

$$\Upsilon_2^{-1} = \sqrt{\frac{15}{8\pi}}\,\sin\theta\cos\theta\,e^{-i\phi}$$

$$\Upsilon_1^{-1} = \sqrt{\frac{3}{8\pi}}\,\sin\theta\,e^{-i\phi}$$

$$\Upsilon_2^0 = \sqrt{\frac{5}{16\pi}}\,(3\cos^2\theta - 1)$$

$$\Upsilon_1^0 = \sqrt{\frac{3}{4\pi}}\,\cos\theta$$

$$\Upsilon_2^1 = -\sqrt{\frac{15}{8\pi}}\,\sin\theta\cos\theta\,e^{i\phi}$$

$$\Upsilon_1^1 = -\sqrt{\frac{3}{8\pi}}\,\sin\theta\,e^{i\phi}$$

$$\Upsilon_2^2 = \sqrt{\frac{15}{32\pi}}\,\sin^2\theta\,e^{2i\phi}.$$

We finally note that, if R is any well-behaved function of r, then the function

$$u_{lm} = R\Upsilon_l^m, \qquad \text{where} \begin{cases} l = 0, 1, 2, \cdots \\ m = 0, \pm 1, \pm 2, \cdots, \pm l, \end{cases} \qquad (67)$$

is a simultaneous eigenfunction of the Legendrian and of the operator $-i\,\partial/\partial\phi$, belonging to the eigenvalue $l(l + 1)$ of the Legendrian and the eigenvalue m of $-i\,\partial/\partial\phi$; conversely, every simultaneous eigenfunction of the Legendrian and of $-i\,\partial/\partial\phi$ has the form (67).

Exercises

1. Show that

$$\frac{\partial}{\partial x} = \sin\theta\cos\phi\frac{\partial}{\partial r} + \frac{1}{r}\cos\theta\cos\phi\frac{\partial}{\partial\theta} - \frac{1}{r}\frac{\sin\phi}{\sin\theta}\frac{\partial}{\partial\phi} \qquad (68)$$

$$\frac{\partial}{\partial y} = \sin\theta\sin\phi\frac{\partial}{\partial r} + \frac{1}{r}\cos\theta\sin\phi\frac{\partial}{\partial\theta} + \frac{1}{r}\frac{\cos\phi}{\sin\theta}\frac{\partial}{\partial\phi} \qquad (69)$$

$$\frac{\partial}{\partial z} = \cos\theta\frac{\partial}{\partial r} - \frac{1}{r}\sin\theta\frac{\partial}{\partial\theta} \qquad (70)$$

$$y\frac{\partial}{\partial z} - z\frac{\partial}{\partial y} = -\sin\phi\frac{\partial}{\partial\theta} - \cot\theta\cos\phi\frac{\partial}{\partial\phi} \qquad (71)$$

$$z\frac{\partial}{\partial x} - x\frac{\partial}{\partial z} = \cos\phi\frac{\partial}{\partial\theta} - \cot\theta\sin\phi\frac{\partial}{\partial\phi} \qquad (72)$$

$$x\frac{\partial}{\partial y} - y\frac{\partial}{\partial x} = \frac{\partial}{\partial\phi} \qquad (73)$$

$$\left(y\frac{\partial}{\partial z} - z\frac{\partial}{\partial y}\right)^2 + \left(z\frac{\partial}{\partial x} - x\frac{\partial}{\partial z}\right)^2 + \left(x\frac{\partial}{\partial y} - y\frac{\partial}{\partial x}\right)^2 \qquad (74)$$

$$= \frac{1}{\sin\theta}\frac{\partial}{\partial\theta}\sin\theta\frac{\partial}{\partial\theta} + \frac{1}{\sin^2\theta}\frac{\partial^2}{\partial\phi^2}.$$

2. Show by comparing the Cartesian forms[5] of the operators (71) and (73) that the eigenvalues of $i\sin\phi\frac{\partial}{\partial\theta} + i\cot\theta\cos\phi\frac{\partial}{\partial\phi}$ are the integers (29).

---

[5] That is, the forms given on the left sides of (71) and (73).

3. Let $\{\alpha, \beta\}$ denote the commutator $\alpha\beta - \beta\alpha$, and show that

$$\left\{ y\frac{\partial}{\partial z} - z\frac{\partial}{\partial y}, z\frac{\partial}{\partial x} - x\frac{\partial}{\partial z} \right\} = -\left(x\frac{\partial}{\partial y} - y\frac{\partial}{\partial x} \right) \tag{75}$$

$$\left\{ z\frac{\partial}{\partial x} - x\frac{\partial}{\partial z}, x\frac{\partial}{\partial y} - y\frac{\partial}{\partial x} \right\} = -\left(y\frac{\partial}{\partial z} - z\frac{\partial}{\partial y} \right) \tag{76}$$

$$\left\{ x\frac{\partial}{\partial y} - y\frac{\partial}{\partial x}, y\frac{\partial}{\partial z} - z\frac{\partial}{\partial y} \right\} = -\left(z\frac{\partial}{\partial x} - x\frac{\partial}{\partial z} \right). \tag{77}$$

4. Recall Exercise 7^6 and show that, if u is a simultaneous eigenfunction of any two of the operators (71), (72), and (73), then it is also an eigenfunction of the third, and the eigenvalues of (71), (72), and (73) belonging to this u are all zero.

5. Using first their Cartesian and then their polar forms, show in detail that each of the three operators (71), (72), and (73) commutes with (74). Note that this result is a special case of that of Exercise 8^6.

6. Using the Cartesian forms of the operators (71) to (74), show in detail that each of these operators commutes with the operator $r = \sqrt{x^2 + y^2 + z^2}$ and with every operator involving the operator r only; verify by inspecting the polar forms.

7. Use (61) and (60) to show that

$$\Theta_l^l = (-1)^l \frac{1}{2^l l!} \sqrt{\frac{(2l+1)!}{2}} \sin^l\theta \tag{78}$$

and that Θ_l^m is identically zero if $|m| > l$.

8. Extend the table of Θ's on pages 412 and 413 through $l = 4$.

9. Verify Equations 2^A to 6^A for sundry special cases using Θ's from the table on pages 412 and 413.

10. Use Equations 3^A to 5^A to show that

$$\sin\theta \frac{d}{d\theta} \Theta_l^m = l A_l^m \Theta_{l+1}^m - (l+1) B_l^m \Theta_{l-1}^m.$$

11. Show that if $m \neq 0$ then 2^A follows from 3^A, 4^A, and 6^A.

12. Extend the table of Υ's on page 414 through $l = 3$.

13. Taking (62) for granted, show that the functions (65) form a set that is *orthonormal in the angles*, that is,

$$\int_0^{2\pi}\int_0^{\pi} \bar{\Upsilon}_l^m \Upsilon_{l'}^{m'} \sin\theta \, d\theta \, d\phi = \begin{cases} 1 & \text{if } l = l' \text{ and } m = m' \\ 0 & \text{otherwise.} \end{cases} \tag{79}$$

75. Remarks on Classical Mechanics

The time derivatives $\dot{x}$, $\dot{y}$, and $\dot{z}$ of the Cartesian coordinates of a particle are the Cartesian components v_x, v_y, and v_z of its *velocity*; the velocity itself is a vector, denoted by v. The quantities

$$p_x = m\dot{x}, \qquad p_y = m\dot{y}, \qquad p_z = m\dot{z} \qquad (1)$$

(where m is the mass of the particle), are the components of the *linear momentum* of the particle; the linear momentum itself is a vector, denoted by p. In vector notation, the three equations (1) are summarized by writing

$$p = m\dot{r}, \qquad (2)$$

where $\dot{r}$ is the time derivative of the position vector r.

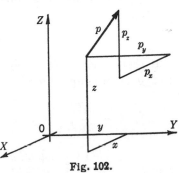

Fig. 102.

If we consider Fig. 102 and compute the 'moment' of the vector p about the x-axis (in the manner used in statics to compute the moment of a force about an axis), we find the result to be $yp_z - zp_y$; similarly, the respective moments of p about the y-axis and about the z-axis are $zp_x - xp_z$ and $xp_y - yp_x$. We write

$$L_x = yp_z - zp_y, \quad L_y = zp_x - xp_z, \quad L_z = xp_y - yp_x, \qquad (3)$$

and call L_x , L_y , and L_z the components of the *orbital angular momentum* of the particle about the point O. The orbital angular momentum itself is a vector, denoted by L; its magnitude is denoted by L, so that

$$L^2 = L_x^2 + L_y^2 + L_z^2 . \qquad (4)$$

Orbital angular momentum is often called by the more descriptive name *moment of momentum*. In vector notation, the three equations (3) are summarized by means of the equation

$$L = r \times p, \qquad (5)$$

which is read "L equals r cross p."

Let the force (a vector) acting on the particle when the particle is at[6] xyz be denoted by $f(x, y, z)$, or simply by f, and let its

---

[6] We exclude from consideration the case when the force depends on the velocity of the particle, as it does, for example, when an electrically charged particle moves in a magnetic field.

Cartesian components be denoted by $f_x(x, y, z)$, $f_y(x, y, z)$, and $f_z(x, y, z)$, or simply by f_x, f_y, and f_z. The classical equations of motion of the particle then are

$$m\ddot{x} = f_x, \qquad m\ddot{y} = f_y, \qquad m\ddot{z} = f_z. \qquad (6)$$

In vector notation, the three equations (6) are summarized by writing

$$m\ddot{r} = f.$$

If there exists a function of x, y, and z, which we denote by $V(x, y, z)$, or simply by V, such that

$$f_x = -\frac{\partial V}{\partial x}, \qquad f_y = -\frac{\partial V}{\partial y}, \qquad f_z = -\frac{\partial V}{\partial z}, \qquad (7)$$

then V is called the *potential function* of the system, or simply the *potential*, and the force field is said to be *conservative*. In vector notation, the three equations (7) are summarized by means of the equation

$$f = -\operatorname{grad} V, \qquad (8)$$

which is read "f equals minus the gradient of V."

Whenever Equations (7) hold, the quantity

$$\tfrac{1}{2}m(\dot{x}^2 + \dot{y}^2 + \dot{z}^2) + V(x, y, z) \qquad (9)$$

remains constant as the particle proceeds with its motion. This quantity is called the *energy* of the particle and is denoted by E; the first term in (9) is the *kinetic energy* of the particle, while $V(x, y, z)$ is its *potential energy*. If (9) is expressed in terms of x, y, z, p_x, p_y, and p_z (rather than the terms of $x, y, z, \dot{x}, \dot{y}$, and $\dot{z}$) the result is called the *Hamiltonian function* of the system, or simply the *Hamiltonian* of the system, and is denoted by H:

$$H = \frac{1}{2m}(p_x^2 + p_y^2 + p_z^2) + V(x, y, z). \qquad (10)$$

To indicate that the energy of the system preserves its numerical value E, we write

$$H = E. \qquad (11)$$

The set (6) of three simultaneous second-order differential equations is equivalent to the following set of six first-order differential equations, called *Hamilton's canonical equations*:

$$\dot{x} = \frac{\partial H}{\partial p_x} \qquad \dot{y} = \frac{\partial H}{\partial p_y} \qquad \dot{z} = \frac{\partial H}{\partial p_z}$$

$$\dot{p}_x = -\frac{\partial H}{\partial x} \qquad \dot{p}_y = -\frac{\partial H}{\partial y} \qquad \dot{p}_z = -\frac{\partial H}{\partial z}. \tag{12}$$

If the six variables q_1, q_2, q_3, p_1, p_2, and p_3 are such that H can be expressed entirely in terms of them and that when this is done the six equations

$$\dot{q}_i = \frac{\partial H}{\partial p_i} \qquad \dot{p}_i = -\frac{\partial H}{\partial q_i} \qquad i = 1, 2, 3 \tag{13}$$

hold, then q_i and p_i are said to be *canonically conjugate*. Comparison of (13) with (12) shows that, in particular, the coordinate x and the x-component p_x of the linear momentum are canonically conjugate, that so are y and p_y, and that so are z and p_z.

The dynamical variable denoted by $[\xi, \eta]$ and constructed from two dynamical variables ξ and η according to the formula

$$[\xi, \eta] = \left(\frac{\partial \xi}{\partial x}\frac{\partial \eta}{\partial p_x} - \frac{\partial \xi}{\partial p_x}\frac{\partial \eta}{\partial x}\right) + \left(\frac{\partial \xi}{\partial y}\frac{\partial \eta}{\partial p_y} - \frac{\partial \xi}{\partial p_y}\frac{\partial \eta}{\partial y}\right)$$
$$+ \left(\frac{\partial \xi}{\partial z}\frac{\partial \eta}{\partial p_z} - \frac{\partial \xi}{\partial p_z}\frac{\partial \eta}{\partial z}\right) \tag{14}$$

is called the *Poisson bracket* of ξ and η. The Poisson brackets of some of the simpler dynamical variables are listed in Table 17. We note, in particular, that

$$[L_x, L_y] = L_z \qquad [L_y, L_z] = L_x \qquad [L_z, L_x] = L_y. \tag{15}$$

Distribution functions. If the information available about a particle moving in three dimensions falls short of being equivalent to the specification of the precise initial conditions of the motion (of which there are six), then a study of the motion usually involves probability considerations. The following remarks are restricted to probabilities concerning the *position* of a particle; for definiteness, we write down our definitions in terms of a Cartesian frame.

TABLE 17

Examples of Poisson brackets. $[\xi, \eta]$ is shown at the intersection of row labeled ξ and column labeled η.

	x	y	z	p_x	p_y	p_z	L_x	L_y	L_z
x	0	0	0	1	0	0	0	z	$-y$
y	0	0	0	0	1	0	$-z$	0	x
z	0	0	0	0	0	1	y	$-x$	0
p_x	-1	0	0	0	0	0	0	p_z	$-p_y$
p_y	0	-1	0	0	0	0	$-p_z$	0	p_x
p_z	0	0	-1	0	0	0	p_y	$-p_x$	0
L_x	0	z	$-y$	0	p_z	$-p_y$	0	L_z	$-L_y$
L_y	$-z$	0	x	$-p_z$	0	p_x	$-L_z$	0	L_x
L_z	y	$-x$	0	p_y	$-p_x$	0	L_y	$-L_x$	0

If the x-, the y-, and the z-coordinate of the particle have values lying, respectively, somewhere between x and $x + dx$, somewhere between y and $y + dy$, and somewhere between z and $z + dz$, then we say for short that the particle is 'in $dxdydz$ at xyz.' If the probability that the particle is in $dxdydz$ at xyz is expressed in the form

$$P(x, y, z)dxdydz, \tag{16}$$

we call $P(x, y, z)$ the (absolute)[7] *distribution function for position, the distribution-in-position*, the *distribution-in-xyz*, or the *probability density*. The probability that the particle is inside a volume V can be computed by integrating $P(x, y, z)$ over this volume; since the particle is certain to be somewhere in the infinite region, we have, in particular,

$$\iiint P(x, y, z)\, dx\, dy\, dz = 1. \tag{17}$$

When the (absolute) distribution-in-xyz is $P(x, y, z)$, then the (expected) *average*, $\operatorname{av} f(x, y, z)$, and the (expected) *inexactitude*, $\Delta f(x, y, z)$, of a function $f(x, y, z)$ are defined as follows:

$$\operatorname{av} f(x, y, z) = \iiint f(x, y, z)P(x, y, z)\, dx\, dy\, dz, \tag{18}$$

$$\Delta f(x, y, z) = \sqrt{\iiint [f(x,y,z) - \operatorname{av} f(x,y,z)]^2 P(x,y,z)\, dx\, dy\, dz}. \tag{19}$$

---

[7] *Relative* probabilities can be introduced in the manner of §11.

We note that

$$(20^{11}) \qquad \Delta^2 f(x, y, z) = \text{av} \left[f(x, y, z) \right]^2 - \text{av}^2 f(x, y, z). \qquad (20)$$

The formulas (18) to (20) apply of course also in the cases when the function denoted by $f(x, y, z)$ depends in fact only on x, or only on y, or only on x and y, and so on.

If the distribution-in-xyz depends on the time t, and thus has the form $P(x, y, z, t)$, it is called *nonstationary*; otherwise it is called *stationary*.

If the distribution-in-xyz vanishes or nearly vanishes everywhere except in a limited region, it is sometimes called a *probability packet*; the point with coordinates av x, av y, and av z is then called the *center* of the packet. The distribution function

$$P(x, y, z) = \frac{1}{\sigma_x \, \sigma_y \, \sigma_z (2\pi)^{\frac{3}{2}}} e^{ -\frac{(x-x_0)^2}{2\sigma_x^2} - \frac{(y-y_0)^2}{2\sigma_y^2} - \frac{(z-z_0)^2}{2\sigma_z^2} }, \qquad (21)$$

where x_0, y_0, z_0, and the σ's are constants, is an example of a stationary probability packet. The center of this packet is at the point $x_0 y_0 z_0$; should one or more of the quantities x_0, y_0, and z_0 depend on t, the packet would be a moving one.

Certain distribution functions are conveniently expressed in terms of the polar frame. For example, if the parameters in (21) satisfy the relations $x_0 = y_0 = z_0 = 0$ and $\sigma_x = \sigma_y = \sigma_z = \sigma$, then (21) becomes $P(x, y, z) = [\sigma^3 (2\pi)^{\frac{3}{2}}]^{-1} \exp \left(-r^2/2\sigma^2 \right)$, so that the probability density at the point $r\theta\phi$ is

$$P(r, \theta, \phi) = \frac{1}{\sigma^3 (2\pi)^{\frac{3}{2}}} e^{ -\frac{r^2}{2\sigma^2} }; \qquad (22)$$

the probability of finding the particle in the polar volume element $r^2 \, dr \sin \theta \, d\theta \, d\phi$ at the point $r\theta\phi$ is consequently

$$P(r, \theta, \phi) r^2 dr \sin \theta \, d\theta \, d\phi = \frac{1}{\sigma^3 (2\pi)^{\frac{3}{2}}} e^{ -\frac{r^2}{2\sigma^2} } r^2 dr \sin \theta \, d\theta \, d\phi. \qquad (23)$$

The distribution (22) is seen to be spherically symmetric, that is, independent of the angles θ and ϕ; we denote it nevertheless by $P(r, \theta, \phi)$, rather than simply by $P(r)$, in order to emphasize the fact that it *does* contain information about the angles as well as about r.

The probability that the distance of the particle from the origin has a value lying between r and $r + dr$ (that is, the probability of finding the particle between two spheres with radii r and $r + dr$ and with centers at O) is often of interest; if this probability is expressed in the form $P_r\, dr$, then P_r, a function of r, is the *distribution-in-r*. We have, by definition,

$$P_r\, dr = \int_0^{2\pi} \int_0^{\pi} \int_r^{r+dr} P(r,\, \theta,\, \phi) r^2\, dr\, \sin\theta\, d\theta\, d\phi \qquad (24)$$

or simply (see 10^{12}),

$$P_r\, dr = \left[r^2 \int_0^{2\pi} \int_0^{\pi} P(r,\, \theta,\, \phi) \sin\theta\, d\theta\, d\phi \right] dr. \qquad (25)$$

For example, in the special case (22), which is particularly simple because of the spherical symmetry, we have

$$P_r = \frac{4\pi}{\sigma^3(2\pi)^{\frac{3}{2}}} r^2 e^{-\frac{r^2}{2\sigma^2}}. \qquad (26)$$

The reason for our denoting the distribution-in-r by P_r rather than by $P(r)$ is to diminish the possibility of confusing the symbol for this distribution with $P(r, \theta, \phi)$, that is, with our symbol for the polar form of the probability density.

Probability currents. If the distribution-in-xyz is nonstationary and thus has the form $P(x, y, z, t)$, we may speak of it as flowing from place to place and may introduce the notion of probability currents, or, more precisely, *probability-current densities*, as follows: Let dA be a small area located at the point xyz and parallel to the yz-plane; the time rate at which the probability flows in the positive x-direction across this area at the instant t is then proportional to dA and is in general dependent on x, y, z, and t, so that we may express it in the form $s_x(x, y, z, t)\, dA$; the function $s_x(x, y, z, t)$, or simply s_x, is then called the x-component of the probability-current density at xyz at the instant t; it is negative whenever the flow is in the negative x-direction. The y- and the z-component of this current density are defined in a similar manner and are denoted by $s_y(x, y, z, t)$ and $s_z(x, y, z, t)$, or simply by s_y and s_z. The current density itself is now defined to be the vector whose components are s_x, s_y, and s_z, and is denoted by $\mathbf{s}(x, y, z, t)$ or simply by $\mathbf{s}$. The direction of $\mathbf{s}$ at any point is that of the total current at this point, and the magnitude of **s** at any point is that of the total current density at this point.

Since probability is, so to speak, neither created nor destroyed, the time rate at which the probability of finding the particle in a given volume increases should equal the time rate at which the probability enters this volume across its surface (if the probability of finding the particle within the volume actually decreases, then the rate at which it increases is negative, and probability leaves rather than enters across the surface). To express this conservation property in mathematical terms, we consider the volume element $dxdydz$ about the point xyz, shown in Fig. 103. The probability of finding the particle in this volume is $P(x, y, z, t) \times dxdydz$ or simply $Pdxdydz$, and the time rate at which this probability varies is $\dfrac{\partial P}{\partial t} dxdydz$.

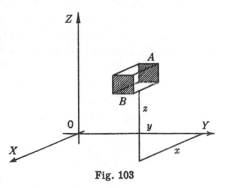

Fig. 103

The rate at which probability flows *into* the volume through the shaded face marked A is $s_x(x, y, z, t) \times dydz$ or simply $s_x dydz$; the rate at which probability *leaves* the volume through the shaded face B is $s_x(x + dx, y, z, t)\, dydz$ or [when terms in dx^2, dx^3, and so on, are omitted] $s_x(x, y, z, t)\, dydz$ $+ \dfrac{\partial s_x(x, y, z, t)}{\partial x}\, dxdydz$, that is, $s_x dydz + \dfrac{\partial s_x}{\partial x} dxdydz$; the rate of net *influx* through the two shaded faces is consequently $-\dfrac{\partial s_x}{\partial x} dxdydz$. The two remaining pairs of faces contribute to the net influx the terms $-\dfrac{\partial s_y}{\partial y} dxdydz$ and $-\dfrac{\partial s_z}{\partial z} dxdydz$. Equating the total influx to $\dfrac{\partial P}{\partial t} dxdydz$ and canceling the factor $dxdydz$, we now get the so-called *continuity equation*

$$\frac{\partial s_x}{\partial x} + \frac{\partial s_y}{\partial y} + \frac{\partial s_z}{\partial z} = -\frac{\partial P}{\partial t}, \tag{27}$$

which summarizes the conservation of probability in mathematical terms. In vector notation, Equation (27) is written as

$$\text{div } s = -\frac{\partial P}{\partial t} \tag{28}$$

and is read "the divergence of s equals $-\frac{\partial P}{\partial t}$."

Plane complex waves. If k_x, k_y, k_z, and c are real constants, then the equation

$$k_x x + k_y y + k_z z = c \tag{29}$$

is the equation of a plane. We shall leave it to the reader to verify that the x-, the y-, and the z-intercept of the plane (29) are c/k_x, c/k_y, and c/k_z; that the x-, the y-, and the z-coordinate of the point in this plane lying nearest to O are $k_x c/(k_x^2 + k_y^2 + k_z^2)$, $k_y c/(k_x^2 + k_y^2 + k_z^2)$, and $k_z c/(k_x^2 + k_y^2 + k_z^2)$; that the distance of this plane from O is $| c |/(k_x^2 + k_y^2 + k_z^2)^{\frac{1}{2}}$; that the cosines of the angles α_x, α_y, and α_z which a normal to this plane makes with the x-, the y-, and the z-axis are

$$\cos \alpha_x = \frac{k_x}{\sqrt{k_x^2 + k_y^2 + k_z^2}}, \qquad \cos \alpha_y = \frac{k_y}{\sqrt{k_x^2 + k_y^2 + k_z^2}},$$

$$\cos \alpha_z = \frac{k_z}{\sqrt{k_x^2 + k_y^2 + k_z^2}}; \tag{30}$$

and that the plane

$$k_x x + k_y y + k_z z = c' \tag{31}$$

is parallel to the plane (29) and lies a distance $| c - c' |/(k_x^2 + k_y^2 + k_z^2)^{\frac{1}{2}}$ from it.

Let k denote the vector with components k_x, k_y, and k_z; the cosines of the angles that this vector makes with the three axes are just (30), and consequently the plane (29) is perpendicular to the vector k. In vector notation, (29) is written as

$$k \cdot r = c \tag{32}$$

and is read "k dot r equals c." The magnitude of k will be denoted by k, so that $k = \sqrt{k_x^2 + k_y^2 + k_z^2}$.

If t is the time, A is a constant (real, imaginary, or complex),

ν is a positive constant, and k_x, k_y, and k_z are real constants, then the expression

$$u = A e^{2\pi i (k_x x + k_y y + k_z z - \nu t)} \tag{33}$$

or, in vector notation,

$$u = A e^{2\pi i (\mathbf{k} \cdot \mathbf{r} - \nu t)} \tag{34}$$

is called a *plane monochromatic complex wave*. This wave is said to be plane because, at any fixed instant, u has a constant value over any one plane perpendicular to the vector $\mathbf{k}$. A is the (complex) *amplitude* of u; ν is the *frequency* of u [note that at any fixed point in space u has the form constant $\times e^{-2\pi i \nu t}$]; the quantity

$$\lambda = \frac{1}{\sqrt{k_x^2 + k_y^2 + k_z^2}} = \frac{1}{k} \tag{35}$$

is the *wave length* of u [note that if the distance between two planes, both of which are perpendicular to $\mathbf{k}$, is an integral multiple of (35), then the value of u at any instant is the same over both planes], and k is the *wave number* of u. As time goes on, the values of u drift, so to speak, in the direction of the vector $\mathbf{k}$ [which for this reason is called the *propagation vector*] with the velocity

$$v_\phi = \lambda \nu, \tag{36}$$

called the *phase velocity* of u.

The plane monochromatic waves encountered in the classical theory of the vibrations of continuous media are real waves, expressible in the form[8]

$$u = \mathrm{Re}\, A e^{2\pi i (\mathbf{k} \cdot \mathbf{r} - \nu t)}, \tag{37}$$

where the symbol Re is that of 2^8.

Exercises

1. Verify Table 17.
2. Show that Equation 16^9, that is, $\dot{\xi} = [\xi, H]$, holds in three-dimensional motion whenever ξ does not involve t explicitly. If $\dot{\xi} = 0$ for all time, then ξ is called a *constant of motion* of the system.

---

[8] If A in (37) is to be the true amplitude of the real wave, then it must be required to be real, and a further real constant, the initial phase ϕ, must be added within the parentheses of the exponent of (37). See 16^{40}.

3. Show that Equations 14⁹ hold in the three-dimensional case.

4. Show that, if $f(r)$ is an arbitrary function of r and $f(p)$ is an arbitrary function of p, where $p = \sqrt{p_x^2 + p_y^2 + p_z^2}$, then

$$[L_x, f(r)] = [L_y, f(r)] = [L_z, f(r)] = [L^2, f(r)] = 0 \qquad (38)$$

$$[L_x, f(p)] = [L_y, f(p)] = [L_z, f(p)] = [L^2, f(p)] = 0. \qquad (39)$$

5. The quantity $m\dot{r}$, denoted by p_r, is called *radial momentum*. Show that, when the force field is conservative, the energy of a particle can be expressed in the form

$$\frac{1}{2m} p_r^2 + \frac{1}{2mr^2} L^2 + V(r, \theta, \phi), \qquad (40)$$

where $V(r, \theta, \phi)$ is the potential energy expressed in terms of polar coordinates.

6. If the force acting on the particle is everywhere directed either toward or away from the origin O, then the force field is called *central* or *radial*. Show that, if the potential energy of the particle depends only on the distance from O, that is, if the potential function has the special form $V = V(r)$, then the force field is central. Show also that, if the force field is central and conservative, then the potential function has the form $V = V(r)$.

7. Show that, if the force field is central and conservative, then L_x, L_y, L_z, and L^2 are constants of motion.

8. Show that some of the constants of motion of a free particle moving in three dimensions are H, p_x, p_y, p_z, L_x, L_y, L_z, and L^2.

9. A particle attracted toward O with a force proportional to its distance r from O is called an *isotropic spatial harmonic oscillator*, or simply an *isotropic oscillator*; its potential function is $V(x, y, z) = \frac{1}{2}k(x^2 + y^2 + z^2)$, or simply $V(r) = \frac{1}{2}kr^2$, where k is the *restoring constant*. Show that the quantities H, L_x, L_y, L_z, and L^2, and also the quantities $H^A = p_x^2/2m + \frac{1}{2}kx^2$, $H^B = p_y^2/2m + \frac{1}{2}ky^2$, and $H^C = p_z^2/2m + \frac{1}{2}kz^2$ are each a constant of motion of the isotropic oscillator.

10. Verify that for the distribution (21) av $x = x_0$, av $y = y_0$, av $z = z_0$, $\Delta x = \sigma_x$, $\Delta y = \sigma_y$, and $\Delta z = \sigma_z$.

11. Suppose that a particle confined inside a sphere of radius R with center at O is equally likely to be anywhere within this sphere, and show that then av $r = \frac{3}{4}R$, $\Delta r = \sqrt{\dfrac{3}{80}} R$, av $\dot{x} = 0$, and $\Delta x = \sqrt{\dfrac{1}{5}} R$.

12. Show that the function (33)—a plane wave—is a simultaneous eigenfunction of the operators $-i\,\partial/\partial x$, $-i\,\partial/\partial y$, $-i\,\partial/\partial z$, and $-\nabla^2$, belonging to the respective eigenvalues $2\pi k_x$, $2\pi k_y$, $2\pi k_z$, and $4\pi^2(k_x^2 + k_y^2 + k_z^2)$ of these operators.

76. Elements of the Schroedinger Method

According to the operator assumption I of §13, the properties of dynamical variables pertaining to three-dimensional motion are investigated in quantum mechanics through a mathematical study of the properties of operators to be associated with these variables. These operators are required to satisfy the quantum condition

$$\langle 1^{13} \rangle \qquad\qquad \alpha\beta - \beta\alpha = i\hbar[\alpha, \beta], \qquad\qquad \langle 1 \rangle$$

the formula for the Poisson bracket now being 14^{75}. It follows from $\langle 1 \rangle$ and Table 17 that the operators x, y, z, p_x, p_y, and p_z (whatever their specific forms may be), associated in *any* quantum-mechanical scheme with the coordinates and the components of momentum of a particle, must satisfy the following commutation rules: the operators x, y, z must commute with one another; the operators p_x, p_y, and p_z must commute with one another; and we must have

$$xp_x - p_x x = i\hbar \quad yp_y - p_y y = i\hbar \quad zp_z - p_z z = i\hbar \qquad \langle 2 \rangle$$

$$yp_x - p_x y = 0 \quad zp_y - p_y z = 0 \quad xp_z - p_z x = 0 \qquad \langle 3 \rangle$$

$$zp_x - p_x z = 0 \quad xp_y - p_y x = 0 \quad yp_z - p_z y = 0. \qquad \langle 4 \rangle$$

Schroedinger operators. The Schroedinger method employs the following *particular* scheme of associating specific operators with the fundamental dynamical variables:

$$\left\{ \begin{array}{l} \text{dynamical variables } x, y, z \rightleftarrows \text{operators } x, y, z, \text{respectively} \\[2mm] \text{dynamical variables } p_x, p_y, p_z, \rightleftarrows \text{operators } -i\hbar \dfrac{\partial}{\partial x}, -i\hbar \dfrac{\partial}{\partial y}, \quad \langle 5 \rangle \\[4mm] \qquad\qquad\qquad\qquad\qquad -i\hbar \dfrac{\partial}{\partial z}, \text{respectively.} \end{array} \right.$$

This scheme is a direct extension of the one-dimensional scheme 3^{14}. The operators $\langle 5 \rangle$ satisfy the requisite commutation rules, and their eigenvalues are all real.

A further Schroedinger association, of which the associations $\langle 5 \rangle$ are special cases, is

dynamical variable $\alpha(x, y, z) + \beta(p_x, p_y, p_z)$

$$\rightleftarrows \text{operator } \alpha(x, y, z) + \beta\left(-i\hbar \frac{\partial}{\partial x}, -i\hbar \frac{\partial}{\partial y}, -i\hbar \frac{\partial}{\partial z} \right). \qquad \langle 6 \rangle$$

The respective operators to be associated with dynamical variables of the most general form $\alpha(x, y, z, p_x, p_y, p_z)$, involving products of the coordinates and the p's, must usually be each identified separately because of the noncommutability of x and p_x, and so forth.

According to $\langle 6 \rangle$, the Schroedinger operator associated with a Hamiltonian

$$(10^{75}) \qquad H = \frac{1}{2m}\,(p_x^2 + p_y^2 + p_z^2) + V(x, y, z) \qquad (7)$$

is
$$H = -\frac{1}{\kappa}\left(\frac{\partial^2}{\partial x^2} + \frac{\partial^2}{\partial y^2} + \frac{\partial^2}{\partial z^2}\right) + V(x, y, z), \qquad \langle 8 \rangle$$

that is,
$$H = -\frac{1}{\kappa}\,\nabla^2 + V(x, y, z), \qquad \langle 9 \rangle$$

where the operator $V(x, y, z)$ is the same function of the operators x, y, and z that the potential function $V(x, y, z)$ is of the coordinates x, y, and z, and where, as before,

$$(17^{14}) \qquad\qquad \kappa = \frac{8\pi^2 m}{h^2} = \frac{2m}{\hbar^2}. \qquad (10)$$

The Schroedinger operators are differential operators; accordingly, the Schroedinger operands are functions of x, y, and z, or of whatever other coordinates may be employed. These operands, denoted by $\psi(x, y, z, t)$, by $\psi(r, \theta, \phi, t)$, or simply by ψ, are required to depend on the time t so as to satisfy the second Schroedinger equation 1^{16}; but for the present we shall disregard their time dependence and shall thus restrict ourselves to instantaneous ψ's.

When the Schroedinger operator associated with a dynamical variable α has been identified, then the computation of the possible values of this dynamical variable reduces, according to the operator assumption I of §13, to the computation of the eigenvalues of the operator α, that is, to the computation of the values of the number λ for which the eigenvalue equation

$$\alpha\psi(x, y, z, t) = \lambda\psi(x, y, z, t) \qquad \langle 11 \rangle$$

or simply
$$\alpha\psi = \lambda\psi \qquad \langle 12 \rangle$$

has well-behaved solutions. In particular, the computation of the energy levels of a system whose Hamiltonian is H reduces to the calculation of the values of the number E for which the following equation has well-behaved solutions:

$$H\psi = E\psi, \qquad\qquad \langle 13 \rangle$$

that is,
$$\left[-\frac{1}{\kappa} \nabla^2 + V(x, y, z) \right] \psi = E\psi, \qquad\qquad (14)$$

that is,
$$\frac{\partial^2 \psi}{\partial x^2} + \frac{\partial^2 \psi}{\partial y^2} + \frac{\partial^2 \psi}{\partial z^2} + \kappa [E - V(x, y, z)]\psi = 0. \qquad (15)$$

Equation $\langle 13 \rangle$, in its forms (14) or (15), is called the (three-dimensional) *first Schroedinger equation*, the *Schroedinger amplitude equation*, the *Schroedinger wave equation*, or simply the *Schroedinger equation*. Note that (14) and (15) must be modified whenever a magnetic field is involved.

We shall take it for granted that the *equation of motion*

$$\langle 27^{44} \rangle \qquad\qquad \dot{\alpha} = \frac{i}{\hbar} (H\alpha - \alpha H) \qquad\qquad \langle 16 \rangle$$

holds in the three-dimensional case; this equation tells us how to construct the operator associated with the dynamical variable $\dot{\alpha}$ from the operators associated with α itself and with H. If α commutes with H, then the operator $\dot{\alpha}$ is zero, and α is called a *constant of motion* of the system. Just as in the one-dimensional case, if α is a constant of motion, then the time derivatives of the expected averages of α and of all of its powers are zero for every state of the system, and consequently the distribution-in-α is stationary for every state of the system. Again, just as in the one-dimensional case, a dynamical variable that is a constant of motion of a classical system is also a constant of motion of a corresponding quantum-mechanical system.[9]

We shall also take it for granted that the expansion theorem of §46 holds in the three-dimensional case.

The remainder of this section will be devoted to illustrations of the use of the eigenvalue equation in the Schroedinger method.

Linear momentum. In the case of the x-component of the linear momentum, the eigenvalue equation $\langle 12 \rangle$ can be written as

$$p_x \psi = p_x' \psi, \qquad\qquad \langle 17 \rangle$$

---

[9] Exceptions to this assertion arise, however, in the relativistic theory discussed in Chapter XIV.

where p_x is the operator associated with the dynamical variable p_x and where the symbol p_x' replaces the symbol λ; in the Schroedinger scheme we have, explicitly,

$$-i\hbar \frac{\partial}{\partial x} \psi = p_x'\psi. \tag{18}*$$

The solution of (18),

$$\psi_{p_x'} = A(y, z)e^{ip_x'x/\hbar} \tag{19}$$

(where $A(y, z)$ is an arbitrary well-behaved function of y and z), is well-behaved for every real value of p_x', and hence the eigenvalue spectrum of the operator p_x extends continuously from $-\infty$ to ∞. Accordingly, just as in classical mechanics, any real value of p_x is a possible one, so that p_x is not quantized.

In the case of the dynamical variables p_y and p_z, the computations and the results are of course similar to those given above: p_y and p_z are not quantized. The eigenfunction of the operator p_y belonging to its eigenvalue p_y' turns out to be

$$\psi_{p_y'} = B(z, x)e^{ip_y'y/\hbar}, \tag{20}$$

where $B(z, x)$ is an arbitrary well-behaved function of z and x; the eigenfunction of the operator p_z belonging to its eigenvalue p_z' is

$$\psi_{p_z'} = C(x, y)e^{ip_z'z/\hbar}, \tag{21}$$

where $C(x, y)$ is an arbitrary well-behaved function of x and y.

The free particle; Cartesian quantization.[10] Taking the potential of a free particle to be $V(x, y, z) = 0$, we find that the Schroedinger Hamiltonian operator $\langle 8 \rangle$ is

$$H = -\frac{1}{\kappa}\left(\frac{\partial^2}{\partial x^2} + \frac{\partial^2}{\partial y^2} + \frac{\partial^2}{\partial z^2}\right). \tag{22}$$

Our problem is to find the eigenvalues of this H, that is, the values of the number E for which the Schroedinger equation $H\psi = E\psi$ or, explicitly,

$$-\frac{1}{\kappa}\left(\frac{\partial^2}{\partial x^2} + \frac{\partial^2}{\partial y^2} + \frac{\partial^2}{\partial z^2}\right)\psi = E\psi, \tag{23}$$

has well-behaved solutions.

---

[10] The term *Cartesian quantization* means that the computations are carried out in Cartesian coordinates; incidentally, we shall find that the energy of a free particle is in fact not quantized.

Our procedure will rely on the expansion theorem.   As shown in Exercise 8[75], the dynamical variables

$$H, \; p_x, \; p_y, \; p_z \tag{24}$$

are constants of motion of a free particle in the classical theory. Each of the operators

$$p_x = -i\hbar \frac{\partial}{\partial x}, \qquad p_y = -i\hbar \frac{\partial}{\partial y}, \qquad p_z = -i\hbar \frac{\partial}{\partial z} \tag{25}$$

commutes with our operator H, so that, in quantum mechanics also, the set (24) is a set of constants of motion of a free particle. Further, the operators $\langle 25 \rangle$ commute with one another, and hence (24) is a set of *commuting* constants of motion.   Consequently, in looking for the eigenvalues of our H, we may, according to the expansion theorem, restrict our attention to eigenfunctions of H that are simultaneously eigenfunctions of the three p's.

The respective eigenfunctions of p_x, p_y, and p_z are (19), (20), and (21), so that a simultaneous eigenfunction of the three p's has the form $\psi = Ae^{ip'_x x/\hbar}e^{ip'_y y/\hbar}e^{ip'_z z/\hbar}$, that is,

$$\psi = Ae^{i(p'_x x + p'_y y + p'_z z)/\hbar}, \tag{26}$$

where A is an arbitrary constant (independent of either x, y, or z) and where p'_x, p'_y, and p'_z are arbitrary *real* constants.   It thus remains to adjust the constants in (26) so as to make it an eigenfunction of our H belonging to the eigenvalue E.   We have

$$HAe^{i(p'_x x + p'_y y + p'_z z)/\hbar} = -\frac{1}{\kappa}\left(\frac{\partial^2}{\partial x^2} + \frac{\partial^2}{\partial y^2} + \frac{\partial^2}{\partial z^2}\right) Ae^{i(p'_x x + p'_y y + p'_z z)/\hbar}$$

$$= \frac{1}{2m}(p'^2_x + p'^2_y + p'^2_z)Ae^{i(p'_x x + p'_y y + p'_z z)/\hbar}, \tag{27}$$

and consequently the proper adjustment is to choose the p''s in such a way that

$$\frac{1}{2m}(p'^2_x + p'^2_y + p'^2_z) = E. \tag{28}$$

Equation (28) is to be expected by classical analogy.

Now, the p''s being real, Equation (28) cannot be satisfied if E is negative; but, if $E \geq 0$, then a suitable choice of the p''s can always be made.   It follows that any positive E, zero included, is an eigenvalue of our H, that is, that *any positive energy value, zero included, is a possible energy value of a free particle* (when the potential $V(x, y, z)$ is taken to be zero).

We note that, if $E = 0$, then (28) can be satisfied in only one way, namely, by letting $p_x' = p_y' = p_z' = 0$, in which case (26) reduces to a numerical constant; but, if $E > 0$, then the p''s can be chosen in an infinite variety of ways, different choices of the p''s yielding linearly independent ψ's. Consequently, the eigenvalue 0 of our H is nondegenerate, while every other eigenvalue of H is degenerate to an infinite degree.

According to the expansion theorem, any eigenfunction of H belonging to the eigenvalue E is a superposition of the solutions (26) whose p''s satisfy (28); and, since (except when $E = 0$) the p''s can vary continuously within certain limits, the superposition may be either discrete or continuous.

Separation of variables. The solutions of (23), found above with the help of the expansion theorem, can be found also by separating the variables in (23). Restricting our attention to ψ's of the form

$$\psi = XYZ \tag{29}$$

[that is, $\psi = X(x)Y(y)Z(z)$], substituting (29) into (23), dividing through by $-XYZ/\kappa$, and using primes in the conventional way (compare 10[42]), we get

$$\frac{X''}{X} + \frac{Y''}{Y} + \frac{Z''}{Z} = -\kappa E. \tag{30}$$

Equation (30) has the form $f(x) + g(y) + h(z) = $ constant, and, since x, y, and z are *independent* variables, it follows that the terms X''/X, Y''/Y, and Z''/Z are each a constant. Thus we may write

$$X''/X = -a^2, \qquad Y''/Y = -b^2, \qquad Z''/Z = -c^2, \tag{31}$$

where, in accordance with (30), the constants a, b, and c must satisfy the equation

$$a^2 + b^2 + c^2 = \kappa E. \tag{32}$$

The respective general solutions of the ordinary differential equations (31) are

$$X = A_1 e^{iax} + A_2 e^{-iax}, \ \ Y = B_1 e^{iby} + B_2 e^{-iby}, \ \ Z = C_1 e^{icz} + C_2 e^{-icz}. \tag{33}$$

Substituting these solutions into (29), we get a sum of eight terms; and, since (32) allows a, b, and c to have either algebraic sign, each term has the form

$$\psi = A e^{i(ax+by+cz)}. \tag{34}$$

To obtain good behavior, we must now restrict a, b, and c to be real. Writing $a = p'_x/\hbar$, $b = p'_y/\hbar$, and $c = p'_z/\hbar$, we may convert (34) into (26) and (32) into (28).

It should perhaps be emphasized that the present procedure is no more rigorous from the mathematical standpoint than that which uses the expansion theorem: to complete the argument in either case, it is necessary to show that every well-behaved solution of (23) can be expanded as a linear combination of the special solutions (26). Our assumption that the expansion theorem is correct amounts in the present case just to the assumption that such an expansion is possible.

The isotropic oscillator; Cartesian quantization. In the case of this oscillator, defined in Exercise 9^{75}, the potential is $\frac{1}{2}k(x^2 + y^2 + z^2)$, so that the Schroedinger Hamiltonian operator is

$$H = -\frac{1}{\kappa}\left[\frac{\partial^2}{\partial x^2} + \frac{\partial^2}{\partial y^2} + \frac{\partial^2}{\partial z^2}\right] + \frac{1}{2}k(x^2 + y^2 + z^2), \quad (35)$$

and the Schroedinger equation, $H\psi = E\psi$, is

$$-\frac{1}{\kappa}\left[\frac{\partial^2}{\partial x^2} + \frac{\partial^2}{\partial y^2} + \frac{\partial^2}{\partial z^2}\right]\psi + \frac{1}{2}k(x^2 + y^2 + z^2)\,\psi = E\psi. \quad (36)$$

We shall again rely on the expansion theorem. The quantities

$$H^A = \frac{1}{2m}p_x^2 + \frac{1}{2}kx^2, \qquad H^B = \frac{1}{2m}p_y^2 + \frac{1}{2}ky^2,$$

$$H^C = \frac{1}{2m}p_z^2 + \frac{1}{2}kz^2 \quad (37)$$

are, as shown in Exercise 9^{75}, constants of motion in the classical case, so that they are also constants of motion in the quantum theory of the oscillator. Further, the corresponding operators

$$H^A = -\frac{1}{\kappa}\frac{\partial^2}{\partial x^2} + \frac{1}{2}kx^2, \qquad H^B = -\frac{1}{\kappa}\frac{\partial^2}{\partial y^2} + \frac{1}{2}ky^2,$$

$$H^C = -\frac{1}{\kappa}\frac{\partial^2}{\partial z^2} + \frac{1}{2}kz^2 \quad (38)$$

commute with one another, and consequently the set

$$H, H^A, H^B, H^C \quad (39)$$

is a set of commuting constants of motion. In looking for the eigenvalues of H, we may, therefore, according to the expansion theorem, restrict our attention to simultaneous eigenfunctions of all four quantities (39).

The operators H^A, H^B and H^C are all of the same form and are all simpler than the operator H, which is their sum. We begin with H^A. The operator

$$H^A = -\frac{1}{\kappa}\frac{\partial^2}{\partial x^2} + \frac{1}{2}kx^2 \qquad (40)$$

is identical with 2^{15}, that is, with the Hamiltonian operator of a *linear* harmonic oscillator, and consequently its eigenvalues and eigenfunctions can be identified by referring to 15^{15} and to Exercise 2^{15}. Replacing the symbol n by α, denoting the eigenvalues of H^A by E_α^A and the corresponding eigenfunctions by ψ_α^A, and disregarding normalization, we then get

$$E_\alpha^A = (\alpha + \tfrac{1}{2})h\nu_c \qquad \alpha = 0, 1, 2, \cdots \qquad (41)$$

and

$$\psi_\alpha^A = A(y, z)H_\alpha\left(\frac{x}{a}\right)e^{-\frac{1}{2}\left(\frac{x}{a}\right)^2}, \qquad (42)$$

where $2\pi\nu_c = \sqrt{k/m}$, $a = \sqrt[4]{\hbar^2/km}$, and H_α is the αth Hermite polynomial. As the symbol $A(y, z)$ implies, the arbitrary factor in (42), though independent of x, is allowed to be a (well-behaved) function of y and z.

The operator H^B differs from H^A only through the replacement of x by y; consequently its eigenvalues and eigenfunctions are

$$E_\beta^B = (\beta + \tfrac{1}{2})h\nu_c \qquad \beta = 0, 1, 2, \cdots \qquad (43)$$

and

$$\psi_\beta^B = B(z, x)H_\beta\left(\frac{y}{a}\right)e^{-\frac{1}{2}\left(\frac{y}{a}\right)^2}. \qquad (44)$$

Similarly the eigenvalues and eigenfunctions of H^C are

$$E_\gamma^C = (\gamma + \tfrac{1}{2})h\nu_c, \qquad \gamma = 0, 1, 2, \cdots \qquad (45)$$

and

$$\psi_\gamma^C = C(x, y)H_\gamma\left(\frac{z}{a}\right)e^{-\frac{1}{2}\left(\frac{z}{a}\right)^2}. \qquad (46)$$

It follows from (42), (44), and (46) that the simultaneous eigenfunctions of H^A, H^B, and H^C, which we denote by $\psi_{\alpha\beta\gamma}$, are

$$\psi_{\alpha\beta\gamma} = AH_\alpha\left(\frac{x}{a}\right)e^{-\frac{1}{2}\left(\frac{x}{a}\right)^2}H_\beta\left(\frac{y}{a}\right)e^{-\frac{1}{2}\left(\frac{y}{a}\right)^2}H_\gamma\left(\frac{z}{a}\right)e^{-\frac{1}{2}\left(\frac{z}{a}\right)^2}, \qquad (47)$$

that is,

$$\psi_{\alpha\beta\gamma} = A H_\alpha\left(\frac{x}{a}\right) H_\beta\left(\frac{y}{a}\right) H_\gamma\left(\frac{z}{a}\right) e^{-\frac{1}{2}\left(\frac{r}{a}\right)} , \tag{48}$$

where A is independent of x, y, and z.

Now,

$$\begin{aligned}
H\psi_{\alpha\beta\gamma} &= (H^A + H^B + H^C)\psi_{\alpha\beta\gamma} = H^A\psi_{\alpha\beta\gamma} + H^B\psi_{\alpha\beta\gamma} + H^C\psi_{\alpha\beta\gamma} \\
&= E^A_\alpha\psi_{\alpha\beta\gamma} + E^B_\beta\psi_{\alpha\beta\gamma} + E^C_\gamma\psi_{\alpha\beta\gamma} = (E^A_\alpha + E^B_\beta + E^C_\gamma)\psi_{\alpha\beta\gamma} ,
\end{aligned} \tag{49}$$

so that $\psi_{\alpha\beta\gamma}$ is an eigenfunction of H belonging to the eigenvalue

$$E_{\alpha\beta\gamma} = E^A_\alpha + E^B_\beta + E^C_\gamma = (\alpha + \beta + \gamma + \tfrac{3}{2})h\nu_c \tag{50}$$

of H. Recalling the expansion theorem and the fact that the quantum numbers α, β, and γ may each have any value from the list $0, 1, 2, \cdots$, we conclude that *the energy levels of the isotropic spatial harmonic oscillator are*

$$\tfrac{3}{2}h\nu_c , \tfrac{5}{2}h\nu_c , \tfrac{7}{2}h\nu_c , \cdots . \tag{51}$$

Equation (50) involves α, β, and γ only in the combination $\alpha + \beta + \gamma$, so that we may write it as

$$E_n = (n + \tfrac{1}{2})h\nu_c , \qquad\qquad n = 1, 2, 3, \cdots , \tag{52}$$

where

$$n = \alpha + \beta + \gamma + 1. \tag{53}$$

The integer n (whose range is to be contrasted with that of the n in 15[15]) is called the *principal* quantum number of the oscillator. Except in the case $n = 1$ (when the oscillator is in its normal state, that is, its state of lowest energy), several distinct choices of α, β, and γ will yield the same value of n; the ψ-functions (47) corresponding to these distinct choices belong to the same eigenvalue of H but are linearly independent, and consequently all excited energy states of the isotropic oscillator are degenerate.

Components of orbital angular momentum. The dynamical variables

$$(3^{75}) \quad L_x = yp_z - zp_y , \quad L_y = zp_x - xp_z , \quad L_z = xp_y - yp_x \tag{54}$$

do not involve products of variables associated with noncommuting operators, and consequently the corresponding Schroedinger operators can be identified at once by a reference to $\langle 5 \rangle$. In fact, we have

$$L_x = i\hbar \left(z \frac{\partial}{\partial y} - y \frac{\partial}{\partial z} \right) = i\hbar \left(\sin \phi \frac{\partial}{\partial \theta} + \cot \theta \cos \phi \frac{\partial}{\partial \phi} \right) \qquad \langle 55 \rangle$$

$$L_y = i\hbar \left(x \frac{\partial}{\partial z} - z \frac{\partial}{\partial x} \right) = i\hbar \left(- \cos \phi \frac{\partial}{\partial \theta} + \cot \theta \sin \phi \frac{\partial}{\partial \phi} \right) \qquad \langle 56 \rangle$$

$$L_z = i\hbar \left(y \frac{\partial}{\partial x} - x \frac{\partial}{\partial y} \right) = - i\hbar \frac{\partial}{\partial \phi} , \qquad \langle 57 \rangle$$

where the polar forms are taken from Exercise 1^{74}.

Of the operators $\langle 55 \rangle$ to $\langle 57 \rangle$, the polar form of L_z , that is,

$$L_z = -i\hbar \frac{\partial}{\partial \phi} , \qquad \langle 58 \rangle$$

is the simplest, and hence we shall restrict our attention to it; it is perhaps obvious that investigating L_z is equivalent to investigating the component of orbital angular momentum in *any* prescribed direction, because the coordinate frame can always be so chosen that its polar axis points in this direction.

To find the possible values of L_z , we must compute the eigenvalues of the operator $\langle 58 \rangle$, that is, the values of the number λ for which the equation

$$L_z \psi = \lambda \psi, \qquad \langle 59 \rangle$$

or, explicitly,

$$-i\hbar \frac{\partial}{\partial \phi} \psi = \lambda \psi , \qquad (60)$$

has well-behaved solutions. Now, the operator L_z is $\hbar$ times the operator $-i \, \partial/\partial \phi$ whose eigenvalues are the integers 29^{74}, and consequently the eigenvalues of L_z are $\hbar$ times these integers. Hence, *the possible values of L_z (or, for that matter, of the component of L in any direction) are*

$$\cdots , \ -2\hbar, \ -\hbar, \ 0, \ \hbar, \ 2\hbar, \ \cdots . \qquad (61)$$

Abbreviating the words "the possible values of the dynamical variable α are" by the symbol "$\alpha \overset{\circ}{=},$" we write this result in the form

$$L_z \overset{\circ}{=} m_l \hbar, \qquad m_l = 0, \ \pm 1, \ \pm 2, \ \cdots . \qquad (62)$$

The integer m_l in (62) is called the *axial, magnetic, or equatorial quantum number*. The subscript l in m_l serves to remind us that we are dealing with a component of the *orbital* angular momentum L, to be distinguished from the *spin* angular momentum that we shall take up later. The quantity $\hbar$-is called the *Bohr unit* of angular momentum. The formula (62) is common to both the quantum theory and the Bohr theory.

It follows from 30[74] that the eigenfunctions of L_z belonging to the eigenvalue $m_l\hbar$ of L_z [we denote them by $\psi(m_l)$] have the form

$$\psi(m_l) = A(r, \theta)e^{im_l \phi}, \tag{63}$$

where $A(r, \theta)$ is an arbitrary well-behaved function of r and θ. The eigenfunctions of L_z form a set that is orthogonal in ϕ.

Magnitude of orbital angular momentum. According to 4[75] and ⟨55⟩ to ⟨57⟩ the Schroedinger operator L^2 associated with the square of the magnitude of the orbital angular momentum is

$$L^2 = -\hbar^2\left[\left(z\frac{\partial}{\partial y} - y\frac{\partial}{\partial z}\right)^2 + \left(x\frac{\partial}{\partial z} - z\frac{\partial}{\partial x}\right)^2 + \left(y\frac{\partial}{\partial x} - x\frac{\partial}{\partial y}\right)^2\right], \quad ⟨64⟩$$

that is, according to 74[74],

$$L^2 = -\hbar^2\left(\frac{1}{\sin\theta}\frac{\partial}{\partial\theta}\sin\theta\frac{\partial}{\partial\theta} + \frac{1}{\sin^2\theta}\frac{\partial^2}{\partial\phi^2}\right). \tag{⟨65⟩}$$

The operator L^2 is thus $\hbar^2$ times the Legendre operator 31[74].

The possible values of L^2 are the eigenvalues of ⟨65⟩, that is, $\hbar^2$ times the eigenvalues of the Legendrian, which are listed in 55[74]; hence, *the possible values of L^2, the square of the magnitude of the orbital angular momentum, are*

$$0, 2\hbar^2, 6\hbar^2, 12\hbar^2, 20\hbar^2, \cdots . \tag{66}$$

Using the notation introduced just above (62) we summarize this result by writing

$$L^2 \overset{\circ}{=} l(l+1)\hbar^2, \qquad l = 0, 1, 2, \cdots . \tag{67}$$

The eigenfunctions of L^2 belonging to the eigenvalue $l(l+1)\hbar^2$ are the $2l + 1$ functions

$$(67^{74}) \qquad \psi(l\,m_l) = R\Upsilon(l\,m_l) \qquad m_l = 0, \pm 1, \cdots, \pm l \tag{68}$$

and their linear combinations; the arbitrary well-behaved functions R of r in the set (68) are of course independent of one another.

As recorded in 14^A and 15^A, each of the functions in the set (68) is a simultaneous eigenfunction of L^2 and L_z, belonging to the eigenvalue $l(l + 1)\hbar^2$ of L^2 and the eigenvalue $m_l\hbar$ of L_z; hence the notation $\psi(l\,m_l)$.

The possible values of L, the magnitude of the orbital angular momentum, are the positive square roots of the possible values of L^2:

$$L \overset{\circ}{=} \sqrt{l(l + 1)}\hbar, \qquad\qquad l = 0, 1, 2, \cdots. \quad (69)$$

Comparison of (69) with (62) reveals a curious feature of our results: while the possible values of L_z are *integral* multiples of $\hbar$, the possible values of L are (except for the value 0) *irrational* multiples of $\hbar$.

The integer l in Equations (67) to (69), whose values are $0, 1, 2, \cdots$, is called the *azimuthal quantum number*; it should not be confused with the azimuthal quantum number k of the Bohr theory.

Exercises

1. Compute the possible energies of a free particle, taking the potential to be $V(x, y, z) = V_0 = \text{constant} \neq 0$.

2. Derive (48) and (52) by separating the variables in (36).

3. Show that, for a preassigned n, the integers α, β, and γ in (53) can be chosen in $\frac{1}{2}n(n + 1)$ distinct ways,[11] and that hence the multiplicity (degree of degeneracy) of the nth level of the isotropic oscillator is $\frac{1}{2}n(n + 1)$.

4. Show that to normalize (48) we must set $A = e^{i\delta}(a^3 2^{\alpha+\beta+\gamma}\alpha!\beta!\gamma!\pi^{\frac{3}{2}})^{-\frac{1}{2}}$, where δ is real and independent of x, y, and z, but otherwise arbitrary.

5. A particle moving in the potential field

$$V(x, y, z) = \tfrac{1}{2}k^A x^2 + \tfrac{1}{2}k^B y^2 + \tfrac{1}{2}k^C z^2,$$

where the k's are constants not all equal to one another, is called an *aniso-tropic spatial harmonic oscillator*. Identify a set of commuting constants of motion of this system, a set similar to (39); find the eigenfunctions of H, both by the expansion theorem and by separating variables; show that the energy levels are $E_{\alpha\beta\gamma} = (\alpha + \tfrac{1}{2})h\nu_c^A + (\beta + \tfrac{1}{2})h\nu_c^B + (\gamma + \tfrac{1}{2})h\nu_c^C$, where $\alpha, \beta, \gamma = 0, 1, 2, \cdots$, and $2\pi\nu_c^A = \sqrt{k^A/m}$, and so on; point out the circumstances under which this energy spectrum is degenerate.

---

[11] Note that this problem is identical with that of computing the number of ways in which $n - 1$ indistinguishable balls can be distributed among 3 distinguishable boxes.

6. Show that the quantum condition $\langle 1 \rangle$ requires the operators L_x, L_y, L_z, and L^2 to satisfy the following commutation rules:

$$L_xL_y - L_yL_x = i\hbar L_z, \quad L_yL_z - L_zL_y = i\hbar L_x, \quad L_zL_x - L_xL_z = i\hbar L_y, \quad \langle 70 \rangle$$

and

$$L_xL^2 - L^2L_x = L_yL^2 - L^2L_y = L_zL^2 - L^2L_z = 0 \qquad \langle 71 \rangle$$

and verify that the Schroedinger operators L_x, L_y, L_z, and L^2 satisfy these rules.

7. Recall Exercise 4[74] and show that (63) is not an eigenfunction of L_z unless $m_l = 0$, and $A(r, \theta)$ depends on r only.

8. Verify in detail that, if the force field is central and conservative, then the Schroedinger operators L_x, L_y, L_z, and L^2 each commute with the operator $\langle 8 \rangle$, and that consequently the classical result of Exercise 7[75] holds in the Schroedinger theory.

9. Show that in the Schroedinger scheme

$$p_x \pm ip_y = -i\hbar e^{\pm i\phi}\left(\sin\theta\,\frac{\partial}{\partial r} + \frac{\cos\theta}{r}\frac{\partial}{\partial\theta} \pm \frac{i}{r\sin\theta}\frac{\partial}{\partial\phi}\right) \qquad \langle 72 \rangle$$

$$p_z = -i\hbar\left(\cos\theta\,\frac{\partial}{\partial r} - \frac{\sin\theta}{r}\frac{\partial}{\partial\theta}\right) \qquad \langle 73 \rangle$$

$$L_x \pm iL_y = \hbar e^{\pm i\phi}\left(\pm\frac{\partial}{\partial\theta} + i\cot\theta\,\frac{\partial}{\partial\phi}\right) \qquad \langle 74 \rangle$$

$$L_z = -i\hbar\frac{\partial}{\partial\phi}. \qquad \langle 75 \rangle$$

10. If the potential $V(x, y, z)$ is periodic in x, in y, and in z, with respective periods a, b, and c, that is, if for every choice of x, y, and z

$$V(x, y, z) = V(x + a, y + b, z + c), \qquad (76)$$

then we call it a (spatial) *potential lattice.*

Consider a particle moving in a potential lattice, recall the procedure of §48, construct three constants of motion similar to the Γ of §48, and show that in computing the energy spectrum of this system we may restrict ourselves to eigenfunctions of H having the special form

$$\psi = e^{i(k_xx + k_yy + k_zz)}v(x, y, z), \qquad (77)$$

where k_x, k_y, and k_z are real numerical constants, and where the factor $v(x, y, z)$ has the periodicity of the lattice, that is,

$$v(x, y, z) = v(x + a, y + b, z + c). \qquad (78)$$

This result is the three-dimensional form of the Bloch's theorem referred to in §48.

11. Show by an example[12] that the sum of the possible values of two (or more) dynamical variables is in general not a possible value of the sum of these variables; then consider the set (39) and explain why the eigenvalues of H (which equals $H^A + H^B + H^C$) can nevertheless be computed by merely adding the respective eigenvalues of H^A, H^B, and H^C.

77. Elements of the Schroedinger Method (Continued)

Quantum numbers. The general solution of a Schroedinger eigenvalue equation $\alpha\psi = \lambda\psi$ involves the parameter λ; the requirement that ψ be well-behaved is imposed by ruling out the values of λ for which ψ is ill-behaved; and the remaining values of λ are the eigenvalues of α. The general expression for the eigenfunctions of α thus contains a parameter, called a *quantum number*, whose values are usually restricted. For example, the eigenfunctions 19^{76} of the operator p_x contain the quantum number p_x', restricted to be real; the eigenfunctions 42^{76} of the operator H^A contain the quantum number α, restricted to the values 0, 1, 2, $\cdots$; the eigenfunctions 63^{76} of the operator L_z contain the quantum number m_l, restricted to the values 0, ± 1, ± 2, $\cdots$; and so on. Accordingly, the general expression for the simultaneous eigenfunctions of several operators, which are not simply functions of one another, contains several quantum numbers; for example, the simultaneous eigenfunctions 68^{76} of L_z and L contain the two quantum numbers m_l and l. In the three-dimensional case, the general expression for the simultaneous eigenfunction of a sufficiently large set of commuting constants of motion usually contains three quantum numbers; for example, 26^{76} contains p_x', p_y', and p_z', while 48^{76} contains α, β, and γ.

The eigenfunctions of a Schroedinger operator having a discrete eigenvalue spectrum form an orthogonal set, just as in the one-dimensional case; for example, the eigenfunctions 63^{76} of L_z form a set orthogonal in ϕ, the eigenfunctions 68^{76} form a set orthogonal in the angles, the eigenfunctions 42^{76} of H^A form a set orthogonal in x and so on. In particular, the simultaneous eigenfunctions of a sufficiently large set of commuting constants of motion, including H, form a set orthogonal in the infinite region whenever the spectrum of each of these constants of motion is discrete—the set 47^{76} of the simultaneous eigenfunctions of H, H^A, H^B, and H^C

---

[12] For instance, consider the kinetic energy, the potential energy, and the total energy of a linear harmonic oscillator.

is an example; denoting the three quantum numbers appearing in such eigenfunctions by λ, μ, and ν, we may then write

$$\int \bar{\psi}_{\lambda\mu\nu}\psi_{\lambda'\mu'\nu'}\, d\tau = 0 \quad \text{unless } \lambda = \lambda', \quad \mu = \mu', \quad \nu = \nu'. \quad (1)$$

For the present, we can illustrate (1) only by a reference to 47^{76}, in which case $\lambda = \alpha$, $\mu = \beta$, and $\nu = \gamma$.

With the help of suitable conventions, the triply subscripted symbols $\psi_{\lambda\mu\nu}$ can be replaced by singly subscripted ψ's (thus in 47^{76} we might denote ψ_{000} by ψ_0, ψ_{100} by ψ_1, ψ_{010} by ψ_2, ψ_{001} by ψ_3, ψ_{200} by ψ_4, ψ_{110} by ψ_5, and so on); but the three-subscript notation is usually more convenient because it is quite explicit. When this notation is used, some of our familiar formulas have to be somewhat modified in appearance; for example, if a function ψ admits of an expansion in terms of the triply subscripted ψ's, we write

(11^{74})
$$\psi = \sum_\lambda \sum_\mu \sum_\nu c_{\lambda\mu\nu}\psi_{\lambda\mu\nu}, \quad (2)$$

where λ, μ, and ν run through their respective mutually consistent values, and find, using (1), that

(12^{74})
$$c_{\lambda\mu\nu} = \frac{\int \bar{\psi}_{\lambda\mu\nu}\psi\, d\tau}{\int \bar{\psi}_{\lambda\mu\nu}\psi_{\lambda\mu\nu}\, d\tau}. \quad (3)$$

Whenever one or more of the subscripts in $\psi_{\lambda\mu\nu}$ has a continuous range of values (that is, whenever the spectrum of one or more of the constants of motion under consideration is continuous), the corresponding summation or summations in (2) must be replaced by integration, and the formula (3) must be adjusted accordingly.

The time dependence of the Schroedinger operands that pertain to a given dynamical system is governed, as in the one-dimensional case, by the second Schroedinger equation

$\langle 1^{16} \rangle$
$$H\psi = i\hbar\frac{\partial}{\partial t}\psi, \quad \langle 4 \rangle$$

where H is the Schroedinger operator associated with the Hamiltonian of this system. In conservative three-dimensional motion of a single particle in the absence of magnetic fields, this operator is 8^{76}, that is, $-\kappa^{-1}\nabla^2 + V(x, y, z)$.

Arguments similar to those of §16 yield the following results for the three-dimensional case:

(a) Every Schroedinger eigenfunction of H belonging to the eigenvalue E has the form

$$(4^{16}) \qquad\qquad \psi_E = \psi_E^0 e^{-iEt/\hbar}, \qquad\qquad (5)$$

where ψ_E^0 is an instantaneous eigenfunction of H belonging to the eigenvalue E. Note our standard time factor $e^{-iEt/\hbar}$.

(b) If an instantaneous Schroedinger function ψ^0 referring to the instant $t = 0$ is not an eigenfunction of H, then the corresponding time-dependent Schroedinger function is

$$(14^{16}) \qquad\qquad \psi = \sum_\lambda \sum_\mu \sum_\nu c_{\lambda\mu\nu} \psi_{\lambda\mu\nu}, \qquad\qquad (6)$$

where the $\psi_{\lambda\mu\nu}$'s are time-dependent eigenfunctions of H and the c's are the same as those in the expansion

$$(13^{16}) \qquad\qquad \psi^0 = \sum_\lambda \sum_\mu \sum_\nu c_{\lambda\mu\nu} \psi_{\lambda\mu\nu}^0, \qquad\qquad (7)$$

in which the $\psi_{\lambda\mu\nu}^0$'s are the $\psi_{\lambda\mu\nu}$'s of Equation (6) with t set equal to zero. Hence, to compute ψ when we are given ψ^0, we set up the expansion (7) and then multiply each $\psi_{\lambda\mu\nu}^0$ in (7) by the appropriate standard time factor. If all but one c in (7) vanish, the result is of course just (5).

Whenever continuous spectra are involved, the appropriate summations in (6) and (7) are to be replaced by the integrations.

Specification of states. In the case of a three-dimensional motion of a single particle, the 'configuration space' is the ordinary three-dimensional space, so that the assumption V^8 of §17 takes the following form:

V_3^8. *When a system consisting of a single particle in three dimensions is in the state specified by the Schroedinger function ψ, then the expected average, $\mathrm{av}_\psi\,\alpha$, of any dynamical variable α is given by the formula*

$$\langle 2^{17} \rangle \qquad\qquad \mathrm{av}_\psi\, \alpha = \frac{\int \bar\psi \alpha \psi\, d\tau}{\int \bar\psi \psi\, d\tau}, \qquad\qquad \langle 8 \rangle$$

where α in the integrand is the Schroedinger operator associated with the dynamical variable α, and where, as indicated, the integrals extend over the entire three-dimensional space.

The operator α in $\langle 8 \rangle$ operates only on ψ and *not* on the functions of the coordinates that may be contained in $d\tau$; a more explicit notation for the numerator of $\langle 8 \rangle$ is $\int \bar\psi(\alpha\psi)\, d\tau$. If ψ is normalized, then $\langle 8 \rangle$, the (three-dimensional) *Schroedinger expectation formula*, reduces to

$$\langle 2^{18} \rangle \qquad \qquad \operatorname{av}_\psi \alpha = \int \bar{\psi} \alpha \psi \, d\tau. \qquad \qquad \langle 9 \rangle$$

Given the Schroedinger ψ-function specifying a state of a system, the expectation formula $\langle 8 \rangle$ enables us, at least in principle, to compute (by studying the averages of the powers of ξ) the distribution function for this state of any dynamical variable ξ pertaining to this system, and thus to find the possible values of ξ for this state and their respective probabilities; in other words, given the Schroedinger ψ, the formula $\langle 8 \rangle$ enables us to compute everything we might want to know about the corresponding state of the system. Conversely, given a verbal specification of a state, the formula $\langle 8 \rangle$ enables us, at least in principle, to identify the Schroedinger ψ that specifies this state mathematically: the procedure is to construct a ψ-function which, when used in $\langle 8 \rangle$, yields the results contained in the verbal description of the state.

Arguments similar to those of §17 yield the following results for the three-dimensional case:

(c) If c is a numerical constant, then the Schroedinger functions ψ and $c\psi$ specify the same state.

(d) The distribution-in-xyz (or the distribution-in-$r\theta\phi$, and so on, if non-Cartesian coordinates are used) for a state specified by a Schroedinger function ψ is $\bar{\psi}\psi$. For this reason, Schroedinger ψ's are called *amplitudes of probability density*, or simply *probability amplitudes*.

(e) If ψ is an eigenfunction of the operator α belonging to the eigenvalue a of α, then the result of a precise measurement of the dynamical variable α when the system is in the state ψ is certainly a.

If ψ is not an eigenfunction of the operator α, then the result of a precise measurement of the dynamical variable α for the state ψ is not a certainty; the probability that this result will be a particular eigenvalue of α can be computed either by calculating the distribution-in-α for the state ψ, or by inspecting the expansion of ψ in terms of the eigenfunctions of α. For example, let $P(E_n)$ denote the probability that a precise energy measurement will yield the result E_n when the state is specified by a *normalized*

Schroedinger function ψ and E_n is a nondegenerate level; then [compare 9^{20}] $P(E_n)$ equals the square of the modulus of the coefficient of ψ_n in the expansion of ψ in terms of the normalized eigenfunctions of H. In case of degeneracy, this result is generalized as follows: *To determine $P(E_n)$, expand the given (normalized) ψ in terms of the normalized eigenfunctions of H, pick out in the expansion the coefficients of the eigenfunctions of H belonging to the eigenvalue E_n, and add the squares of their moduli—the resulting sum is $P(E_n)$.* Our wording of this rule implies that the energy spectrum is discrete; in the case of a wholly or partly continuous spectrum, the rule must be modified in detail.

To illustrate: Let the state of an isotropic oscillator be represented at some instant by the Schroedinger function

$$\psi = \left(1 + 4\frac{x}{a} - 6\frac{y}{a}\right) e^{-\frac{1}{2}\left(\frac{r}{a}\right)^2}; \tag{10}$$

what is the probability that the energy of the oscillator in this state is $\frac{5}{2}h\nu_c$?

The expansion of (10) in terms of the eigenfunctions of H can be obtained without recourse to integration, for, writing (10) as

$$\psi = \left[e^{-\frac{1}{2}\left(\frac{r}{a}\right)^2}\right] + 2\left[2\frac{x}{a}e^{-\frac{1}{2}\left(\frac{r}{a}\right)^2}\right] - 3\left[2\frac{y}{a}e^{-\frac{1}{2}\left(\frac{r}{a}\right)^2}\right], \tag{11}$$

we recognize the bracketed functions as just the functions[13] $\psi_{[000]}$, $\psi_{[100]}$, and $\psi_{[010]}$ of 48^{76} with $A = 1$. But the expansion (11) is not quite what we want; in the first place, the eigenfunctions of H appearing in brackets in (11) are not normalized, and, secondly, our ψ is itself not normalized. So, using the normalizing factors of Exercise 4^{76} and denoting the *normalized* functions 48^{76} by triply subscripted ψ's, we rewrite (11) as

$$\psi = \sqrt{a^3\pi^{3/2}}\psi_{[000]} + 2\sqrt{2a^3\pi^{3/2}}\psi_{[100]} - 3\sqrt{2a^3\pi^{3/2}}\psi_{[010]}, \tag{12}$$

and it remains to normalize ψ itself. Multiplying the right side of (12) by its complex conjugate, integrating the result over all space, and remembering the orthonormality of the triply subscripted ψ's, we find that $\int \bar{\psi}\psi \, d\tau = a^3\pi^{3/2} + 4\cdot 2a^3\pi^{3/2} + 9\cdot 2a^3\pi^{3/2} = 27a^3\pi^{3/2}$. Dividing (12) through by $(27a^3\pi^{3/2})^{1/2}$, we finally get the equation

$$\frac{1}{\sqrt{27a^3\pi^{3/2}}}\psi = \sqrt{\frac{1}{27}}\psi_{[000]} + \sqrt{\frac{8}{27}}\psi_{[100]} - \sqrt{\frac{18}{27}}\psi_{[010]}. \tag{13}$$

The left side of (13) is a normalized Schroedinger function specifying the state in question; the right side is the expansion of this function in terms of the normalized eigenfunctions of H.

---

[13] The bracketed subscripts of the ψ's are the numerical values of the quantum numbers α, β, and γ, in this order.

Now, we are interested in the probability that the energy of the oscillator is $\frac{5}{2}h\nu_c$, and consequently we pick out in (13) the eigenfunctions of H belonging to the eigenvalue $\frac{5}{2}h\nu_c$. These eigenfunctions are $\psi_{[100]}$ and $\psi_{[010]}$, and their coefficients in (13) are $\sqrt{8/27}$ and $-\sqrt{18/27}$. The sum of the squares of the moduli of these coefficients is $\frac{26}{27}$, and hence the probability that a precise measurement of the energy of our oscillator will yield the result $\frac{5}{2}h\nu_c$ is $\frac{26}{27}$.

The rule given above in italics holds for real dynamical variables other than the energy. Thus, if $P(\alpha_n)$ denotes the probability that a precise measurement of the dynamical variable α will yield the numerical result α_n when the state is specified by a normalized Schroedinger function ψ, then, *to determine $P(\alpha_n)$, expand the given (normalized) ψ in terms of the normalized eigenfunctions of the operator α, pick out in the expansion the coefficients of the eigenfunctions of α belonging to the eigenvalue α_n, and add the squares of their moduli—the resulting sum is $P(\alpha_n)$.* Our wording of this rule implies that the eigenvalue spectrum of α is discrete; in the case of a wholly or partly continuous spectrum, the rule must be modified in detail.

Probability-current density. The distribution-in-xyz and the components of probability-current density satisfy the continuity equation

$$(27^{75}) \qquad \frac{\partial s_x}{\partial x} + \frac{\partial s_y}{\partial y} + \frac{\partial s_z}{\partial z} = -\frac{\partial P}{\partial t}. \qquad (14)$$

Now, the Schroedinger expression for the distribution-in-xyz for a state ψ is $\bar{\psi}\psi$, and consequently the Schroedinger expressions for s_x, s_y, and s_z for the state ψ must satisfy the equation

$$\frac{\partial s_x}{\partial x} + \frac{\partial s_y}{\partial y} + \frac{\partial s_z}{\partial z} = -\frac{\partial}{\partial t} \bar{\psi}\psi. \qquad (15)$$

The one-dimensional formula 6^{37} (which refers of course to probability current rather than to probability-current density) suggests the expressions

$$\begin{cases} s_x = \dfrac{\hbar}{2im} \left(\bar{\psi}\, \dfrac{\partial \psi}{\partial x} - \dfrac{\partial \bar{\psi}}{\partial x}\, \psi \right) \\[3mm] s_y = \dfrac{\hbar}{2im} \left(\bar{\psi}\, \dfrac{\partial \psi}{\partial y} - \dfrac{\partial \bar{\psi}}{\partial y}\, \psi \right) \\[3mm] s_z = \dfrac{\hbar}{2im} \left(\bar{\psi}\, \dfrac{\partial \psi}{\partial z} - \dfrac{\partial \bar{\psi}}{\partial z}\, \psi \right). \end{cases} \qquad (16)$$

The quantities (16) do indeed satisfy (15) whenever H has the form 8[76], and we adopt them[14] as the components of probability-current density for the state ψ for the case when H is given by 8[76].

In vector notation, Equations (16) are summarized by writing

$$s = \frac{\hbar}{2im} [\bar{\psi}(\text{grad } \psi) - (\text{grad } \bar{\psi})\psi]. \tag{17}$$

Exercises

1. The state of a free particle is specified at $t = 0$ by the ψ-function 26[76]. Use $\langle 4 \rangle$ to verify in detail that then the time-dependent ψ-function is

$$\psi = A e^{i(p_x' x + p_y' y + p_z' z - Et)/\hbar}, \tag{18}$$

where $E = (p_x'^2 + p_y'^2 + p_z'^2)/2m$.

2. Show that the x-, y-, and z-component of the linear momentum of a free particle in the state (18) have certainly the respective numerical values p_x', p_y', and p_z'. For this reason we may say that (18) describes a particle moving in the direction having direction cosines p_x'/p', p_y'/p', and p_z'/p' relative to the coordinate axes; here $p' = \sqrt{p_x'^2 + p_y'^2 + p_z'^2}$.

3. Set $p_x' = p_y' = 0$ in (18) and show that, as expected by classical analogy, the z-component of the angular momentum of a free particle moving in the z-direction is certainly zero.

4. Show that the component of L in the direction of the motion of the particle in the state (18) is certainly zero.

5. The state of a free particle is specified at $t = 0$ by the ψ-function.

$$\psi^0 = e^{i(ax+by)} + e^{i(cx-by)}, \tag{19}$$

where a, b, and c are real constants, and $a^2 \neq c^2$. Construct the time-dependent ψ. Compute the possible values of E, p_x, p_y, and p_z for this state, and the respective probabilities of these values.

6. Write down the time-dependent and normalized form of 48[76]; include the arbitrary phase, which is now independent of x, y, z, and t.

7. Show that, if an isotropic oscillator is in its normal state, then each of the dynamical variables 37[76] has certainly the value $\frac{1}{2}h\nu_c$, and each of the dynamical variables L_x, L_y, L_z, and L has certainly the value 0.

8. The state of an isotropic oscillator is specified at $t = 0$ by the instantaneous ψ-function (10). Construct the time-dependent ψ and find the distribution-in-E for the instant t.

9. According to 48[76], the following instantaneous ψ-functions belong to the (triply degenerate) first excited state of an isotropic oscillator:

$$\psi_{[100]} = xe^{-\frac{1}{2}\left(\frac{r}{a}\right)^2}, \quad \psi_{[010]} = ye^{-\frac{1}{2}\left(\frac{r}{a}\right)^2}, \quad \psi_{[001]} = ze^{-\frac{1}{2}\left(\frac{r}{a}\right)^2}. \tag{20}$$

(a) Show that $L_x\psi_{[100]} = 0$, $L_y\psi_{[100]} = -i\hbar\psi_{[001]}$, $L_z\psi_{[100]} = i\hbar\psi_{[010]}$;

---

[14] Both 8[76] and (16) are to be modified when the particle is electrically charged and moves in a magnetic field.

$L_x\psi_{[010]} = i\hbar\psi_{[001]}$, $L_y\psi_{[010]} = 0$, $L_z\psi_{[010]} = -i\hbar\psi_{[100]}$; $L_x\psi_{[001]} = -i\hbar\psi_{[010]}$, $L_y\psi_{[001]} = i\hbar\psi_{[100]}$, $L_z\psi_{[001]} = 0$.

(b) Show that, for the state $\psi_{[001]}$, the energy of the oscillator is certainly $\frac{5}{2}h\nu_c$, H^A is certainly $\frac{1}{2}h\nu_c$, H^B is also certainly $\frac{1}{2}h\nu_c$, H^C is certainly $\frac{3}{2}h\nu_c$, L_z is certainly 0, L is certainly $\sqrt{2}\,\hbar$, L_x is uncertain and equally likely to be[15] $\hbar$ or $-\hbar$, and L_y is also uncertain and equally likely to be $\hbar$ or $-\hbar$. Make similar computations for the states $\psi_{[100]}$ and $\psi_{[010]}$.

(c) Show that, for the state of the isotropic oscillator described by the Schroedinger function $\psi_{[100]} + i\psi_{[010]}$, the energy is certainly $\frac{5}{2}h\nu_c$; H^C is certainly $\frac{1}{2}h\nu_c$; L_z is certainly $\hbar$; L is certainly $\sqrt{2}\,\hbar$; L_x (and also L_y) is uncertain, its possible values being $\hbar$, 0, and $-\hbar$, and the respective probabilities of these values being $\frac{1}{4}$, $\frac{1}{2}$, and $\frac{1}{4}$; H^A (and also H^B) is uncertain and equally likely to be $\frac{1}{2}h\nu_c$ or $\frac{3}{2}h\nu_c$.

(d) Construct a linear combination of the ψ-functions (20) describing a state for which L_z is certainly $-\hbar$, and consider this state along the lines of part (c).

(e) Construct a linear combination of the ψ-functions (20) describing a state for which L_y is certainly $\hbar$, and consider this state along the lines of part (c).

(f) We are told that the energy of an isotropic oscillator is certainly $\frac{5}{2}h\nu_c$ and that no other information is available; write down the Schroedinger function that summarizes this information, and discuss the significance of its arbitrary features.

(g) Show that, if the energy of an isotropic oscillator is certainly $\frac{5}{2}h\nu_c$, then the magnitude of its orbital angular momentum is certainly $\sqrt{2}\,\hbar$.

10. Show that the functions (20) can be written as

$$\psi_{[100]} = -RT_1^1 + RT_1^{-1} \tag{21}$$

$$\psi_{[010]} = iRT_1^1 + iRT_1^{-1} \tag{22}$$

$$\psi_{[001]} = \sqrt{2}\,RT_1^0, \tag{23}$$

where $R = \sqrt{\frac{2}{3}\pi}\,r \exp(-r^2/2a^2)$.

11. Use Equations (21) to (23) to verify by inspection the results of parts (b), (c), (d), and (g) of Exercise 9 concerned with L_z and L.

12. Describe by diagrams the distribution-in-xyz of an isotropic oscillator in the normal state; in the state $\alpha = 1$, $\beta = 0$, $\gamma = 0$.

13. Show that for an isotropic oscillator[16] $\mathrm{av}_{[0:0]}\,x^2 = \frac{1}{2}a^2$, $\mathrm{av}_{[000]}\,r^2 = \frac{3}{2}a^2$, $\mathrm{av}_{[000]}\,p_x^2 = \frac{1}{2}kma^2$, $\mathrm{av}_{[100]}\,x^2 = \frac{3}{2}a^2$, $\mathrm{av}_{[100]}\,y^2 = \frac{1}{2}a^2$, $\mathrm{av}_{[100]}\,r^2 = \frac{5}{2}a^2$.

14. Recall Exercise 5[76] and show that, if the total energy of an anisotropic oscillator having a nondegenerate energy spectrum is certainly $E_{\alpha\beta\gamma}$, then the respective averages of the potential and the kinetic energies are $\frac{1}{2}E_{\alpha\beta\gamma}$ each.

15. Show that, if the total energy of an isotropic oscillator is certainly

---

[15] To verify this distribution-in-L_x, compute $\mathrm{av}\,L_x^k$ for $k = 0$, 1, 2, and so forth, and then use the uniqueness theorem of §11.

[16] The subscripts of the symbol av are the values of the quantum numbers α, β, and γ for the energy state in question.

E_n , then the respective averages of the potential and the kinetic energies are $\frac{1}{2}E_n$ each; remember the degeneracy of the energy spectrum.

16. Show that the quantities (16) satisfy (15) whenever H is given by 8[76].

17. Compute the distribution-in-xyz and the probability current for a free particle in the state (18), and note that the direction of the current is that of the motion of the particle.

18. The ψ-function (18) is called a *plane monochromatic de Broglie wave*. Show that the direction of propagation of this wave is that of the motion of the particle, and that the correlations 4[41], 5[41], and 9[41] hold in the three-dimensional case.

19. Derive the theorem concerning the distribution-in-E stated in italics on page 444.

20. Derive the Heisenberg inequalities 14[23].

21. Use the Hamiltonian 8[76] and the equation of motion 16[76] to show that the Schroedinger operator associated with the radial momentum[17] p_r (that is, with $m\dot{r}$) is

$$p_r = -i\hbar\left(\frac{\partial}{\partial r} + \frac{1}{r}\right), \tag{24}$$

and verify that $p_r^2 = -\hbar^2 \dfrac{1}{r^2}\dfrac{\partial}{\partial r} r^2 \dfrac{\partial}{\partial r}$.

78. Central Fields[18]

We shall now consider a particle moving in a (conservative) central field, in which case the potential function has the special form $V = V(r)$, and consequently the Schroedinger Hamiltonian operator is

$$H = -\frac{1}{\kappa}\left(\frac{\partial^2}{\partial x^2} + \frac{\partial^2}{\partial y^2} + \frac{\partial^2}{\partial z^2}\right) + V(r) \tag{1}$$

or, when the Cartesian derivatives are replaced by their polar equivalents,[19]

$$H = -\frac{1}{\kappa}\left(\frac{1}{r^2}\frac{\partial}{\partial r} r^2 \frac{\partial}{\partial r} + \frac{1}{r^2\sin\theta}\frac{\partial}{\partial \theta}\sin\theta\frac{\partial}{\partial \theta} + \frac{1}{r^2\sin^2\theta}\frac{\partial^2}{\partial \phi^2}\right) + V(r). \tag{2}$$

---

[17] Radial momentum is an example of a quantity having a classical analogue but not admitting of a precise quantum-mechanical measurement; see Kemble, footnote on page 335. Lest our Equation ⟨24⟩ appear to contradict some of the statements on page 297 of Kemble, we must mention that Professor Kemble transforms operators and ψ-functions from one coordinate frame to another by a method that is different from our elementary method.

[18] For brevity, we say 'central field' for 'conservative central field,' and 'central motion' for 'motion in a conservative central field.'

[19] An elementary though tedious procedure for identifying the polar form of ∇^2 is to square and add the right sides of 68[74], 69[74], and 70[74].

Using the operators L^2 and p_r given by 65^{76} and 24^{77}, we can rewrite (2) in the condensed form

$$H = \frac{1}{2m} p_r^2 + \frac{1}{2mr^2} L^2 + V(r), \tag{3}$$

which is precisely the form taken in the case of a central field by the classical Hamiltonian 40^{75}.

Constants of motion. A most important characteristic of classical motion in a central field is that, quite independently of the explicit form of $V(r)$, the orbital momentum is conserved, that is, L_x, L_y, L_z, and L are constants of motion. We have verified in Exercise 8^{76} that this characteristic persists in the Schroedinger theory of central motion, and it follows that according to (nonrelativistic) quantum mechanics *the distribution-in-L_x, the distribution-in-L_y, the distribution-in-L_z, and the distribution-in-L are all stationary for every state of a particle moving in a central field.*

The operators L_x, L_y, and L_z do not commute with one another (recall 70^{76}), and consequently ψ-functions that are simultaneous eigenfunctions of these operators are rather an exception; in fact, it follows from Exercise 7^{76} that only spherically symmetric ψ's, that is, ψ's depending on r only, are simultaneous eigenfunctions of L_x, L_y, and L_z. Hence, although the respective distributions in L_x, in L_y, and in L_z are all stationary in central motion, the fact that the value of one of these variables is a certainty for some state usually implies that the values of the other two are not certainties for this state. In the exceptional case of states specified by spherically symmetric ψ's and called *s-states*, the values of L_x, L_y, L_z, and L are all certainly zero.

Eigenfunctions of H. When the field is central, the set

$$H, L, L_z \tag{4}$$

is a set of commuting constants of motion.[20] The simultaneous eigenfunctions of H, L, and L_z will be called for brevity the *basic* ψ's or, more precisely, the *basic polar* ψ's, where the word *polar* means that we use the spherical polar coordinate frame. According to the expansion theorem, every ψ-function pertaining to a

---

[20] The set H, L, and L_x and the set H, L, and L_y are also sets of commuting constants of motion; but they are not as convenient as (4) because the polar forms of the operators L_x and L_y are not as simple as the polar form of the operator L_z.

given system with a spherically symmetric potential is either a basic (polar) ψ of the system or a superposition of the basic (polar) ψ's.

Now, the simultaneous eigenfunctions of L and L_z are

$$(68^{76}) \qquad\qquad \psi(l\ m_l) = R\Upsilon(l\ m_l), \qquad\qquad (5)$$

where R is an arbitrary well-behaved function of r. To compute the basic ψ's, it thus remains to adjust R so as to make (5) an eigenfunction of H belonging to an eigenvalue E of H, that is, to adjust R so as to satisfy the equation

$$H\psi(l\ m_l) = E\psi(l\ m_l). \qquad\qquad \langle 6\rangle$$

Using the form $\langle 3\rangle$ of H and remembering that $\psi(l\ m_l)$ is an eigenfunction of L^2 belonging to the eigenvalue $l(l+1)\hbar^2$, we find that

$$H\psi(l\ m_l) = \frac{1}{2m}\ p_r^2\psi(l\ m_l) + \frac{1}{2mr^2}L^2\psi(l\ m_l) + V\psi(l\ m_l)$$

$$= \frac{1}{2m}\ p_r^2\psi(l\ m_l) + \frac{1}{2mr^2}l(l+1)\hbar^2\psi(l\ m_l) + V\psi(l\ m_l) \qquad \langle 7\rangle$$

$$= \left[\frac{1}{2m}\ p_r^2\ R + \frac{l(l+1)}{\kappa r^2}\ R + VR\right]\Upsilon(l\ m_l).$$

Equating this to the right side of $\langle 6\rangle$ and canceling the common angle factor, we finally get the equation

$$\frac{1}{2m}\ p_r^2 R + \frac{l(l+1)}{\kappa r^2}\ R + V(r)R = ER, \qquad\qquad \langle 8\rangle$$

that is,

$$-\frac{1}{\kappa}\frac{1}{r^2}\frac{d}{dr}\ r^2\frac{dR}{dr} + \frac{l(l+1)}{\kappa r^2}\ R + V(r)R = ER, \qquad (9)$$

called the *radial equation*.

We now introduce the function

$$\chi(r) = rR \qquad\qquad (10)$$

and find with the help of (9) that it satisfies the equation

$$\left[-\frac{1}{\kappa}\frac{d^2}{dr^2} + \frac{l(l+1)}{\kappa r^2} + V(r)\right]\chi = E\chi. \qquad (11)$$

This equation has the general form of a one-dimensional Schroedinger equation describing the radial motion of a particle in a potential field[21] $l(l + 1)/\kappa r^2 + V(r)$, and we may expect by analogy with the true[22] one-dimensional case that solutions of the χ-equation (11) which yield well-behaved R's exist only for restricted values of E, and that in the process of solving (11) an extra quantum number, say n, would usually come into play. The well-behaved R's would therefore usually involve n, called the *principal quantum number*, in addition to the azimuthal quantum number l appearing in (9), and we may denote them by $R(n\,l)$; the basic polar ψ's then take the form

$$\psi(n\,l\,m_l) = R(n\,l)\Upsilon(l\,m_l). \tag{12}$$

The value of E in (9) belonging to $R(n\,l)$ and denoted by E_{nl} is independent of the axial quantum number m_l, since m_l does not appear in the radial equation. It follows that *the energy spectrum of a particle in central motion is degenerate with respect to the axial quantum number*; in fact, a level having a specific value of l consists of $2l + 1$ *coincident levels*. Indeed, to construct a basic ψ when a specific $R(n\,l)$ is given, we must let l in $\Upsilon(l\,m_l)$ be the same as in $R(n\,l)$; but, this done, we may choose m_l in $\Upsilon(l\,m_l)$ in any one of the $2l + 1$ ways consistent with the given l, each choice yielding a distinct $\psi(n\,l\,m_l)$ belonging to the same eigenvalue of H.

The conclusion that the energy spectrum for central motion must be degenerate can, of course, be drawn directly from the result of Exercise 9[63] and the fact that L_x, L_y, and L_z, which are constants of motion for central fields, do not commute with each other.

A state for which the value of L is certainly 0 is called an *s-state*; one for which L is certainly $\sqrt{2}\,\hbar$ is a *p-state*, one for which L is certainly $\sqrt{6}\,\hbar$ is a *d-state*, and one for which L is certainly $\sqrt{12}\,\hbar$ is an *f-state*; the symbols s, p, and d have their

---

[21] The term $l(l + 1)/\kappa r^2$ in (11), associated with the term $L^2/2mr^2$ in $\langle 3 \rangle$, represents a centrifugal effect; note that classically $L^2/2mr^2$ is that part of the kinetic energy which arises because of the tangential motion of the particle, that is, the motion at right angles to r.

[22] Note that the independent variable r in (11) has the range $(0, \infty)$, rather than $(-\infty, \infty)$ as in the true one-dimensional case, and that, according to (10), good behavior, of R usually implies that χ vanishes at $r = 0$.

origin in the experimental classification of spectral series into *sharp*, *principal*, and *diffuse*. For states described by the basic functions (12) we then have the following names:

TABLE 18

Value of l	Name of state
0	s-state
1	p-state
2	d-state
3	f-state

For states with larger l's the names are assigned alphabetically, starting with g.

The radial equation, which involves $V(r)$, must be studied separately for each specific central field, so that we cannot go further in classifying energy levels without turning to special cases.

Exercises

1. Show that, if (12) is normalizable and R in (12) is real, except perhaps for a complex multiplicative constant, then the average of p_r for the state (12) is zero. Explain why this result is to be expected on intuitive physical grounds.

2. Using the abbreviation $B(r, \theta) = (\hbar/mr \sin \theta) \, | \, R(n \, l) \, |^2 \, [\Theta(l \, m_l)]^2$, show that, if R in (12) is real, except perhaps for a complex multiplicative constant, then the components of the relative probability current for the state $\psi(n \, l \, m_l)$ are $s_x = -m_l B(r, \theta) \sin \phi$, $s_y = m_l B(r, \theta) \cos \phi$, and $s_z = 0$. Show that hence the lines of flow of the probability current are circles centered on the z-axis and parallel to the xy-plane,[23] and that the direction of the flow is consistent with the fact that $\psi(n \, l \, m_l)$ specifies a state for which L_z is certainly $m_l \hbar$.

3. Write down the Schroedinger equation $H\psi = E\psi$, where H is given by (2), assume that ψ has the form $R(r)\Theta(\theta)\Phi(\phi)$, and derive the radial equation (9) by separating variables.

79. The Free Particle; Polar Quantization

Perhaps the simplest example of a central motion is offered by a free particle, in which case

$$V = V(r) = 0, \qquad (1)$$

---

[23] The symmetry of the current about the z-axis may on first thought seem surprising; this point will be taken up in §80.

and the χ-equation 11^{78} becomes

$$\left[-\frac{1}{\kappa}\frac{d^2}{dr^2} + \frac{l(l+1)}{\kappa r^2}\right]\chi = E\chi. \tag{2}$$

When we introduce the new independent variable

$$s = \sqrt{\kappa E}\,r \tag{3}$$

and use the subscript l with χ to help in classifying the solutions, (2) becomes

$$\left[\frac{d^2}{ds^2} + 1 - \frac{l(l+1)}{s^2}\right]\chi_l(s) = 0. \tag{4}$$

A particular solution of this equation is

$$\chi_l(s) = s^{\frac{1}{2}}J_{l+\frac{1}{2}}(s), \tag{5}$$

where $J_{l+\frac{1}{2}}$, the *Bessel function* of order $l + \frac{1}{2}$, is[24]

$$\begin{aligned}
J_{l+\frac{1}{2}}(s) = \frac{1}{\sqrt{2\pi s}}\Bigg[&e^{is}\sum_{k=0}^{l}\frac{i^{k-l-1}(l+k)!}{k!(l-k)!(2s)^k} \\
&+ e^{-is}\sum_{k=0}^{l}\frac{(-i)^{k-l-1}(l+k)!}{k!(l-k)!(2s)^k}\Bigg]
\end{aligned} \tag{6}$$

so that, for example,

$$J_{\frac{1}{2}}(s) = \sqrt{\frac{2}{\pi s}}\,\sin s \tag{7}$$

$$J_{\frac{3}{2}}(s) = \sqrt{\frac{2}{\pi s}}\left(\frac{\sin s}{s} - \cos s\right) \tag{8}$$

$$J_{\frac{5}{2}}(s) = \sqrt{\frac{2}{\pi s}}\left[\left(\frac{3}{s^2} - 1\right)\sin s - 3\frac{\cos s}{s}\right]. \tag{9}$$

Each $J_{l+\frac{1}{2}}$ vanishes at $s = 0$ and, as s increases, oscillates about the s-axis with gently decreasing amplitude; the nodes of the J's are unequally spaced except in the case of $J_{\frac{1}{2}}$.

Equation (4), being of the second order, has solutions that are linearly independent of the particular solution (5); but these solutions yield ill-behaved R's and hence are of no interest to us.

---

[24] It should perhaps be emphasized that (6) is correct only when l is zero or a positive integer, which is so in our case.

Dividing (5) by r, multiplying the quotient for the sake of appearances by $(\kappa E)^{-\frac{1}{2}}$, and denoting the result by[25] $R(E, l)$, we get

$$R(E, l) = s^{-\frac{1}{2}} J_{l+\frac{1}{2}}(s), \qquad\qquad s = \sqrt{\kappa E}\, r. \qquad (10)$$

According to 10^{78} the functions (10) are, apart from arbitrary multiplicative constants, the radial factors of the basic polar ψ's for a free particle. In particular, apart from arbitrary multiplicative constants,[26]

$$R(E, 0) = \frac{\sin s}{s} \qquad\qquad (11)$$

$$R(E, 1) = \frac{\sin s}{s^2} - \frac{\cos s}{s} \qquad\qquad (12)$$

$$R(E, 2) = \left(\frac{3}{s^3} - \frac{1}{s}\right) \sin s - 3\, \frac{\cos s}{s^2}. \qquad (13)$$

Graphs of these functions are shown in Fig. 104.

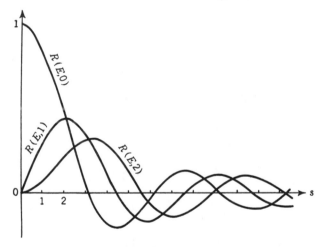

Fig. 104. The functions (11), (12), and (13).

The functions (10) involve the parameter E through s. The function $R(E, 0)$ is well-behaved if $E \geq 0$ and is ill-behaved other-

[25] We write $R(E, l)$ rather than $R(n\, l)$ because the energy of a free particle is not quantized.

[26] Note that in going from (10) to (11), (12), and (13), we omitted the factors $\sqrt{2/\pi}$ that appear in the J's.

wise; the remaining R's are well-behaved if $E > 0$ and are ill-behaved otherwise (they vanish identically for $E = 0$). Thus every positive value of E in (2), zero included, yields well-behaved R's, so that, as we have already shown in §76, *every positive energy value, zero included, is a possible energy value of a free particle* (when the potential is taken to be zero).

According to (10) and 12[78], the basic polar ψ's for a free particle of energy E are,[27] when we include the time factors but omit the arbitrary multiplicative constants,

$$\psi(E, l, m_l) = s^{-\frac{1}{2}} J_{l+\frac{1}{2}}(s) \Upsilon(l\ m_l) e^{-iEt/\hbar}, \tag{14}$$

so that we can write, omitting further numerical coefficients,

$$\psi(E, 0, 0) = \frac{\sin s}{s} e^{-iEt/\hbar} \tag{15}$$

$$\left\{ \begin{array}{l} \psi(E, 1, -1) = \left(\dfrac{\sin s}{s^2} - \dfrac{\cos s}{s} \right) \sin \theta\, e^{-i\phi}\, e^{-iEt/\hbar} \qquad (16) \\[2em] \psi(E, 1, 0) = \left(\dfrac{\sin s}{s^2} - \dfrac{\cos s}{s} \right) \cos \theta\, e^{-iEt/\hbar} \qquad (17) \\[2em] \psi(E, 1, 1) = \left(\dfrac{\sin s}{s^2} - \dfrac{\cos s}{s} \right) \sin \theta\, e^{i\phi}\, e^{-iEt/\hbar} \qquad (18) \end{array} \right.$$

and so forth.

If E in (14) is greater than zero, then every one of the functions (14), and hence also every linear combination of these functions, is an eigenfunction of the Hamiltonian (of the free particle) belonging to the eigenvalue E, so that every energy level of a free particle, except the level $E = 0$, is degenerate to an infinite degree; this result was obtained once before in §76. The degeneracy of the energy spectrum of a free particle is thus much greater than the minimum degeneracy pointed out in italics on page 451.

Relations between the polar and the Cartesian ψ-functions for a free particle. Let us call for the moment the functions (14) the (basic) *polar* ψ's of the free particle, and the functions

$$(18^{77}) \qquad \psi_{p'_x p'_y p'_z} = e^{i(p'_x x + p'_y y + p'_z z)/\hbar} e^{-iEt/\hbar} \tag{19}$$

the (basic) *Cartesian* ψ's of the free particle.

---

[27] Only (15) belongs to $E = 0$.

The Cartesian ψ's were computed by the use of the commuting constants of motion H, p_x, p_y, and p_z ; and each of them represents a state for which not only the energy but also p_x, p_y, and p_z are certainties.

The polar ψ's were computed by the use of the commuting constants of motion H, L, and L_z ; and each of them represents a state for which not only the energy but also L and L_z are certainties.

H, L, and L_z being a set of commuting constants of motion of a free particle, the expansion theorem claims that every ψ-function of a free particle is a superposition[28] of the polar ψ's of a free particle. Thus the expansion theorem claims, in particular, that each of the functions (19) is a superposition of the functions (14). This is indeed so. To illustrate, we consider the Cartesian ψ

$$e^{ip_z'z/\hbar}, \tag{20}$$

which represents instantaneously a free particle of definite energy moving in the z-direction, and which can be written as[29]

$$e^{is \cos \theta}, \tag{21}$$

where $s = \sqrt{\kappa E}\, r$. The function (21) satisfies the relation[30]

$$e^{is \cos \theta} = \sum_{l=0}^{\infty} [i^l \pi \sqrt{2(2l+1)}] s^{-\frac{1}{2}} J_{l+\frac{1}{2}}(s) \Upsilon_l^0, \tag{22}$$

and we recognize the right side of (22) as a linear combination of our instantaneous polar ψ's (14). The possibility of expanding the Cartesian ψ's in terms of the polar ψ's has thus been verified for the special case of a particle moving in the z-direction.

Similarly, the set H, p_x, p_y, and p_z being a set of commuting constants of motion of a free particle, the expansion theorem claims that every ψ-function of a free particle is a superposition of the Cartesian ψ's of a free particle. Thus the expansion theorem claims, in particular, that each of the functions (14) is a superposition of the functions (19). This claim can also be verified rigorously.

---

[28] A superposition may of course involve only one term.

[29] Note that $z = r \cos \theta$ and that, when $p_x' = p_y' = 0$, then, according to 28^{76}, $p_z' = \sqrt{2mE}$ and $p_z'/\hbar = \sqrt{\kappa E}$.

[30] See *Bauer's formula* in a book on Bessel functions.

Exercises

1. The state of a free particle is specified at $t = 0$ by the ψ-function $r^{-1} \sin \alpha r \cos \beta r$, where α and β are nonvanishing real constants having the physical dimensions cm^{-1}. Show that the energy of the particle is not a certainty, and that its possible values are $(\alpha + \beta)^2/\kappa$ and $(\alpha - \beta)^2/\kappa$; and construct the time-dependent ψ.

2. Verify the result of Exercise 3[77] by inspecting (22).

3. Use polar quantization to compute the possible energies of a free particle when $V(r) = V_0 = $ constant $\neq 0$.

80. The Bohr Formula for the Hydrogen Atom; Fixed Nucleus

We consider next an electron (mass m and charge[31] $-e$) which, when at a distance r from the origin O, is urged toward O with the *inverse-square* or *Coulomb* force of magnitude e^2/r^2, as though a nucleus of charge e were permanently located at O. This system we call, rather loosely, a *hydrogen atom*. For the present we neglect relativity effects and effects due to the so-called electron spin.

Our potential function is now[32]

$$V(r) = -\frac{e^2}{r} ; \tag{1}$$

our basic polar ψ's, as always in central fields, are of the form

$$(12^{78}) \qquad \psi(n \, l \, m_l) = R(n \, l)\Upsilon(l \, m_l); \tag{2}$$

and the equation 11^{78} satisfied by the function

$$(10^{78}) \qquad \chi = rR \tag{3}$$

is now

$$\left[-\frac{1}{\kappa}\frac{d^2}{dr^2} + \frac{l(l+1)}{\kappa r^2} - \frac{e^2}{r} \right] \chi = E\chi. \tag{4}$$

The χ-equation (4) has the form of a Schroedinger equation for the linear motion of a particle in the potential field

---

[31] This e, having the value of approximately 4.8×10^{-10} electrostatic units, is not to be confused with the base of natural logarithms.

[32] Note that our V denotes the potential energy of the electron in the field of the nucleus, and not the electrostatic potential due to the nucleus.

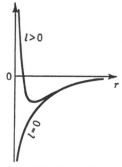

Fig. 105. Functions of the form $l(l+1)/\kappa r^2 - e^2/r$.

$l(l + 1)/\kappa r^2 - e^2/r$, indicated without regard for scale in Fig. 105; and, by analogy with the one-dimensional case of conditional binding[33] shown in Fig. 48(a), we may expect that the energy spectrum of our system consists of a continuous part extending upward from $E = 0$ and a discrete part lying below $E = 0$. In proving this to be the case, we shall consider separately the positive and the negative values of E in (4). Incidentally, Fig. 105 suggests that when $l > 0$ the particle is strongly repelled from the origin in the vicinity of the origin; consequently we may expect that for states other than s-states the ψ-functions should vanish at O.

The case $E > 0$. If E is positive, the substitutions

$$\mu = \tfrac{1}{2}e^2\sqrt{\kappa/E}, \qquad\qquad \xi = 2\sqrt{\kappa E}\, r, \qquad (5)$$

reduce (4) to

$$\frac{d^2\chi(\xi)}{d\xi^2} + \left[\frac{1}{4} + \frac{\mu}{\xi} - \frac{l(l + 1)}{\xi^2}\right]\chi(\xi) = 0, \qquad (6)$$

where μ is a positive parameter. To determine the possible positive values of E we must find the positive values of μ for which (6) has solutions that are well-behaved when divided by r, that is, solutions that yield well-behaved R's.

The solutions of (6) can be expected to be free from ill behavior except perhaps at the origin and at infinity, and hence we can restrict our attention to these extremes. To determine the behavior of χ at $\xi = 0$ we assume that

$$\chi(\xi) = a_\tau\xi^\tau + a_{\tau+1}\xi^{\tau+1} + a_{\tau+2}\xi^{\tau+2} + \cdots, \qquad (7)$$

where $a_\tau \neq 0$, substitute (7) into the left side of (6), and find that the term containing the lowest power of ξ in the result is $a_\tau[\tau(\tau - 1) - l(l + 1)]\xi^{\tau-2}$. In order that this term ·vanish we must have $\tau(\tau - 1) = l(l + 1)$, that is, $\tau = l + 1$ or $\tau = -l$.

---

[33] Such analogy is not always reliable; see, for example, the discussion of the inverse-cube field by G. H. Shortley, *Phys. Rev.*, **38**, 120 (1931).

The power-series solutions of (6) near the origin thus have the form

$$\chi(\xi) = a\xi^{l+1} + \text{higher powers of } \xi, \tag{8}$$

or the form

$$\chi(\xi) = b\xi^{-l} + \text{higher powers of } \xi, \tag{9}$$

where a and b are arbitrary nonvanishing constants. Now, the series (8), when divided by r, vanishes for $r = 0$ when $l = 1, 2, \cdots$, and has a finite nonvanishing value for $r = 0$ when $l = 0$; this series thus always yields an R that is well-behaved at the origin. Hence for every positive value of E the radial equation has particular solutions which are well-behaved at the origin and differ from one another by constant factors. The series (9), on the other hand, is of no interest to us since, when divided by r, it is ill-behaved at 0 even when $l = 0$.

For large values of ξ, Equation (6) reduces to the approximate equation $\chi'' + \frac{1}{4}\chi \cong 0$, so that its general solution has, for large values of ξ, the form

$$\chi \cong Ae^{\frac{1}{2}i\xi} + Be^{-\frac{1}{2}i\xi}. \tag{10}$$

Dividing this result by r, we find that for every positive value of E the general solution of the radial equation is well-behaved at infinity.

Now, whatever the form of a solution of (6) may be near $\xi = 0$, this solution will have the form (10) when $\xi \to \infty$. In particular, the solutions that have the form (8) for small ξ's will have the form (10) for large ξ's. Since (8) is well-behaved for small and (10) for large ξ's and since solutions of the form (8) exist for every positive E, we conclude that the radial equation has well-behaved solutions for every positive value of E. And it finally follows that *an electron moving in the Coulomb potential* $-e^2/r$ *may have any positive energy whatever.*

The case $E < 0$. If E is negative, the substitutions

$$\lambda = \tfrac{1}{2}e^2\sqrt{-\kappa/E}, \qquad \rho = 2\sqrt{-\kappa E}\, r \tag{11a, b}$$

reduce (4) to

$$\frac{d^2\chi(\rho)}{d\rho^2} + \left[-\frac{1}{4} + \frac{\lambda}{\rho} - \frac{l(l+1)}{\rho^2} \right] \chi(\rho) = 0. \tag{12}$$

For small values of ρ, Equation (12) reduces to the same form as does (6) for small values of ξ, so that for every negative value of E the radial equation has particular solutions that are well-behaved at the origin and differ from one another by constant factors.

For large values of ρ, Equation (12) reduces to the approximate equation $\chi'' - \frac{1}{4}\chi \cong 0$. This equation has the solution $e^{\frac{1}{2}\rho}$, which misbehaves when $\rho \to \infty$, and the solution $e^{-\frac{1}{2}\rho}$, which vanishes when $\rho \to \infty$; for large values of ρ, it also has the approximate solutions $\rho e^{-\frac{1}{2}\rho}$, $\rho^2 e^{-\frac{1}{2}\rho}$, and so forth, which vanish when $\rho \to \infty$. Hence, for every negative value of E the radial equation has particular solutions that are well-behaved at infinity and particular solutions that are ill-behaved there.

It follows that, for a specific negative value of E, the particular solutions of the radial equation which are well-behaved at $r = 0$ are either all well-behaved at infinity or all ill-behaved at infinity, and consequently we may expect quantization.

To determine the precise values of the discrete energy levels, we take up (12) anew and, taking the hint from the forms of its solutions that are well-behaved at $\rho = 0$ and of its solutions that are well-behaved when $\rho \to \infty$, write χ in the form

$$\chi = \rho^{l+1} e^{-\rho/2} v(\rho), \tag{13}$$

where $v(\rho)$ is as yet undetermined. From this point the procedure is quite similar to that which we used in the case of 3^4, and we shall omit the details.[34] When we express v as the power series

$$v(\rho) = a_\tau \rho^\tau + a_{\tau+1} \rho^{\tau+1} + a_{\tau+2} \rho^{\tau+2} + \cdots, \tag{14}$$

with $a_\tau \neq 0$, it turns out that $\tau = 0$ or $\tau = -2l - 1$, that the successive coefficients in (14) are related through the equations

$$\frac{a_{\nu+1}}{a_\nu} = \frac{\lambda - \nu - l - 1}{(\nu + 1)(\nu + 2l + 2)}, \tag{15}$$

---

[34] Our discussion of the motion in a Coulomb field is quite brief; but the problem is an important one, and the reader should at the first opportunity study it in detail. See, for example, Pauling and Wilson, Chapter V; and Slater and Frank, Chapter XXXIII. For a very detailed treatment, see H. Bethe, "Quantenmechanik der Ein- und Zwei-Elektronenprobleme" [hereafter cited as Bethe], *Handbuch der Physik*, second Edition, Volume XXIV-1; Berlin: Springer, 1933.

and that the solutions (14) are well-behaved if $\tau = 0$ and if v is a terminating polynomial, and are ill-behaved otherwise. According to (15), v terminates if and only if

$$\lambda = \nu + l + 1, \quad \nu = 0, 1, 2, \cdots, \quad (16)$$

that is, if and only if λ is an integer greater than zero, say

$$\lambda = n, \quad n = 1, 2, 3, \cdots. \quad (17)$$

Using (11a), we now find that *the discrete energy spectrum of an electron moving in the Coulomb potential* $-e^2/r$ consists of the following levels:

$$E_n = -\frac{2\pi^2 m e^4}{h^2 n^2}, \quad n = 1, 2, 3, \cdots. \quad (18)$$

This celebrated result was first obtained by Bohr in 1913 and marked the first triumph of his atomic theory.

The polynomial $v(\rho)$, starting with a term in ρ^0 and terminating with a term in ρ^ν, that is, in ρ^{n-l-1}, turns out to be, apart from a constant factor, the polynomial

$$\frac{d^{2l+1}}{d\rho^{2l+1}} \left[e^\rho \frac{d^{n+l}}{d\rho^{n+l}} (\rho^{n+l} e^{-\rho}) \right]. \quad (19)$$

The polynomial $e^x \dfrac{d^k}{dx^k} (x^k e^{-x})$ is denoted by $L_k(x)$ and is called the *Laguerre polynomial* of the kth degree; the mth derivative of $L_k(x)$ with respect to x is denoted by $L_k^m(x)$, so that the polynomial (19) is denoted by $L_{n+l}^{2l+1}(\rho)$. Thus the χ's yielding well-behaved R's, if we omit the arbitrary constants, are

$$\chi(n\,l) = \rho^{l+1} e^{-\rho/2} L_{n+l}^{2l+1}(\rho). \quad (20)$$

Introducing the constant

$$a_o = \frac{\hbar^2}{me^2}, \quad (21)$$

called *the radius of the first Bohr orbit in hydrogen,* and recalling (11b) and (18), we find that the independent variable in (20) is

$$\rho = \frac{2}{na_0} r. \quad (22)$$

Dividing (20) by r, we get $R(n\,l)$; the result, when normalized in such a way that $\displaystyle\int_0^\infty \bar{R}(n\,l)R(n\,l)r^2\,dr = 1$, is

$$R(n\,l) = e^{i\gamma} N(n\,l)\rho^l e^{-\rho/2} L_{n+l}^{2l+1}(\rho), \quad (23)$$

where γ [strictly, γ_{nl}] is an arbitrary real constant, and where

$$N(nl) = \sqrt{\frac{4(n-l-1)!}{a_0^3 n^4 [(n+l)!]^3}}. \tag{24}$$

The normalized basic ψ's specifying instantaneously the discrete energy states are consequently

$$\psi(n\ l\ m_l) = e^{i\gamma}N(n\ l)\rho^l e^{-\rho/2}L_{n+l}^{2l+1}(\rho)\Upsilon(l\ m_l), \tag{25}$$

where the γ's [strictly, the $\gamma(n\ l\ m_l)$'s] are arbitrary real constants. In particular, the instantaneous normalized ψ-function for the normal state (that is, the state with $n = 1$, $l = 0$, and $m_l = 0$) is

$$\psi(1\ 0\ 0) = e^{i\gamma}\sqrt{\frac{1}{\pi a_0^3}}\,e^{-r/a_0}. \tag{26}$$

Degeneracy of the discrete spectrum. Since (12) has satisfactory solutions only for particular values of λ, and since it involves from the outset the azimuthal quantum number l, we may expect that its satisfactory solutions and also the possible values of E would involve at least two quantum numbers, one of which is l. As shown by (25), this is true insofar as the ψ-functions are concerned; but, as shown by (18), this is not true for the energy levels: the energy levels depend only on the principal quantum number n, and are degenerate with respect to the azimuthal quantum number l. This 'accidental' degeneracy means that the degeneracy of the discrete energy spectrum of a hydrogen atom is greater than the minimum degeneracy pointed out in italics on page 451.

According to (16) and (17),

$$n \geq l + 1, \tag{27}$$

so that the following n values of l are compatible with a prescribed value n of the principal quantum number:

$$l = 0, 1, 2, \cdots, (n-1). \tag{28}$$

Now, there are $2l + 1$ values of m_l which are compatible with a prescribed value l of the azimuthal quantum number, and therefore there are

$$[2\cdot 0 + 1] + [2\cdot 1 + 1] + [2\cdot 2 + 1]$$
$$+ \cdots + [2\cdot(n-1) + 1] = n^2 \tag{29}$$

distinct pairs of values of l and m_l which are compatible with a prescribed value n of the principal quantum number. And, since the energy formula (18) involves only n, it follows that *in the Coulomb case the degeneracy of the nth quantum state is n^2-fold*.

The continuous energy spectrum of the hydrogen atom (that is, the spectrum consisting of all positive values of E) is also degenerate. But a discussion of this degeneracy lies outside the scope of this book.

Concluding remarks. A particle moving classically in a central field remains in a plane that is perpendicular to the orbital angular momentum L; consequently, should we expect the motion to exhibit any symmetry at all, this symmetry would be with respect to an axis having the direction of L and thus inclined to the z-axis at an angle whose cosine is L_z/L. To determine the direction of L it is of course necessary to know all the three quantities L_x, L_y, and L_z. Now, quantum mechanically, the knowledge of L_x and L_y is incompatible with that of L_z (except for s-states), and consequently, quantum mechanically, the *direction* of L is never known. For states for which both L_z and L are known and $L \neq 0$, we may, however, picture L as lying somewhere on a cone that makes with the z-axis the angle whose cosine is L_z/L. It then follows that states with known L_z and L, if they should exhibit any symmetry at all, should exhibit it with respect to the z-axis. This is indeed the case: note, recalling 12^{78}, that our basic $\overline{\psi}\psi$'s are independent of ϕ and, recalling Exercise 2^{78}, that the probability currents associated with the basic ψ's are also independent of ϕ.

A particle moving classically in a central field may remain in the equatorial plane (the xy-plane); this case arises when L is directed along the z-axis, so that L_z has the largest value consistent with the value of L, that is, the value $L_z = L$. According to quantum mechanics, the largest value of L_z consistent with the value $\sqrt{l(l+1)}\,\hbar$ of L is $l\hbar$, and consequently the smallest angle that L can make with the z-axis has the cosine $l/\sqrt{l(l+1)}$. This cosine approaches 1 for large values of l, and we may therefore expect by classical analogy that, for a state having a large l and having as large an m_l as is consistent with this l, namely, $m_l = l$, the particle should be very likely to be near the equatorial plane. It will be shown in Exercise 5 that this is so.

If $L = 0$, the classical motion of a particle in a central field takes place along a straight line, passing through O, whose direction can be ascertained as soon as the initial conditions of the motion are known; but if *all* we know is the energy of the system and the fact that $L = 0$, then the direction of this line is entirely indeterminate, and hence the distribution-in-position of the particle is spherically symmetric about O. Since states for which $L = 0$, that is, *s*-states, are described by spherically symmetric ψ's, the situation is quite analogous in quantum mechanics.

For the basic polar states, the possible orientations of L with respect to the *z*-axis (not the orientations of L *in space*, which are never known) can be pictured by vector diagrams. Thus the first diagram of Fig. 106, which refers to the case $l = 1$, shows the vector L of length $L = \sqrt{1 \cdot 2}\,\hbar$ in the three positions corresponding to the respective possible values $-\hbar$, 0, and $\hbar$ of its *z*-component L_z; the second diagram refers in a similar way to *d*-states.

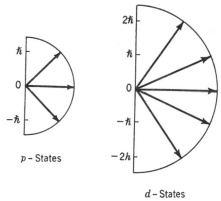

p - States

d - States

Fig. 106. Vector diagrams for L.

Exercises

1. Consider the normal state (26) of a hydrogen atom and show that: (a) the most probable value of r for this state is a_0; (b) $\mathrm{av}_{100}\, r^{-1} = a_0^{-1}$; (c) $\mathrm{av}_{100}\, r^{-2} = 2a_0^{-2}$; (d) if $k = 1, 2, 3 \cdots$, then $\mathrm{av}_{100}\, r^k = (k+2)!\, a_0^k/2^{k+1}$; (e) $\mathrm{av}_{100}\, p_x^2 = \hbar^2/3a_0^2$; (f) $\mathrm{av}_{100}\, V(r) = -e^2/a_0$; (g) the average potential energy equals twice the total energy; (h) the average kinetic energy equals minus the total energy.

2. The state of a hydrogen atom is specified at $t = 0$ by the ψ-function $(8 - \rho \sin \theta\, e^{i\phi})e^{-\rho/2}$; compute the distribution-in-E, the distribution-in-L, and the distribution-in-L_z; and set up the time-dependent ψ.

3. An electron moves in the fixed Coulomb field Ze^2/r^2 as though a nucleus of charge Ze were permanently located at O. Show by inspection that the energy levels of this system[35] and the various ψ's pertaining to it

---

[35] This system is of interest in connection with the so-called *hydrogenic* or *hydrogen-like* atoms which, like the deuterium atom, the singly ionized helium atom, and so forth, consist of a nucleus and a single electron.

can be obtained from the corresponding results of this section by merely replacing e^2 by Ze^2; this means, in particular, that, in results expressed entirely in terms of a_0, a_0 is to be replaced by a_0/Z.

4. An electron moving in the fixed Coulomb field of Exercise 3 is in the normal state. Show that then the average electrostatic potential in space due to both the fixed field and the field of the electron itself is $e(Z - 1)/r + (eZ/a_0 + e/r)e^{-\frac{2Zr}{a_0}}$.

5. Recall 78[74] and show that for a basic polar state with l large and with $m_l = l$ the particle is very likely to be near the equatorial plane.

6. Note that the motion of a spatial isotropic harmonic oscillator is central, and compute the energy levels 52[76] using the constants of motion H, L, and L_z, that is, using polar quantization.

7. Show that the functions RT_1^{-1}, RT_1^0, and RT_1^1 of Exercise 10[77] are the basic polar ψ's of the isotropic oscillator belonging to the first excited state.

8. Show on physical grounds that, if a basic Cartesian ψ of an isotropic oscillator (that is, a ψ of the form 48[76]) belonging to the nth energy level is expanded in terms of the basic polar ψ's of the oscillator (that is, ψ's of the form 12[78]), then only the polar ψ's belonging to the nth level will appear in the expansion. The expansions of Exercise 10[77] illustrate this result, the converse of which is of course also true.

81. The Bohr Formula for the Hydrogen Atom; Free Nucleus

We now proceed to remove the physically unsatisfactory condition that the nucleus of our hydrogen atom be held fixed, and turn to the problem of an electron (mass m, charge $-e$) and a proton (mass M, charge e) moving nonrelativistically in each other's field and free from external influences.

As we have seen in a number of instances, the quantum-mechanical study of a dynamical system is made quite systematic as soon as the constants of motion of the system are identified. And since the constants of motion of a classical system, which are usually identified rather easily, are certain to be constants of motion of a corresponding nonrelativistic quantum-mechanical system, we begin with a few remarks on the classical theory of our present system.

The coordinates and the components of the linear momentum of the electron will carry the subscript 1, those of the proton the subscript 2. The distance between the two particles is then $[(x_1 - x_2)^2 + (y_1 - y_2)^2 + (z_1 - z_2)^2]^{\frac{1}{2}}$, their mutual electric potential energy when they are at this distance apart is

$-e^2/[(x_1 - x_2)^2 + (y_1 - y_2)^2 + (z_1 - z_2)^2]^{\frac{1}{2}}$, and the Hamiltonian of the system is

$$H = \frac{1}{2m}(p_{x_1}^2 + p_{y_1}^2 + p_{z_1}^2) + \frac{1}{2M}(p_{x_2}^2 + p_{y_2}^2 + p_{z_2}^2)$$

$$- \frac{e^2}{\sqrt{(x_1 - x_2)^2 + (y_1 - y_2)^2 + (z_1 - z_2)^2}}. \qquad (1)$$

Since the forces exerted by the proton on the electron, and conversely, are directed along the straight line joining the proton and the electron, and since there are no external forces, it is perhaps obvious that the center of gravity of the two particles, whose coordinates are

$$X = \frac{mx_1 + Mx_2}{m + M}, \qquad Y = \frac{my_1 + My_2}{m + M}, \qquad Z = \frac{mz_1 + Mz_2}{m + M}, \qquad (2)$$

will move uniformly in a straight line, while the electron and the proton revolve about their center of gravity as though this center were at rest.   Hence we may expect a simplification if we replace the six coordinates of the electron and proton by the three coordinates (2) and by three additional *internal* coordinates describing the internal configuration of the system; for the latter we choose the three coordinates

$$x = x_1 - x_2, \qquad y = y_1 - y_2, \qquad z = z_1 - z_2 \qquad (3)$$

of the electron with respect to the proton.

Rewriting (1) in terms of the new variables (2) and (3) and the quantities

$$P_x = (m + M)\dot{X}, \quad P_y = (m + M)\dot{Y}, \quad P_z = (m + M)\dot{Z} \qquad (4)$$

and

$$p_x = \mu\dot{x}, \qquad\qquad p_y = \mu\dot{y}, \qquad\qquad p_z = \mu\dot{z}, \qquad (5)$$

where μ, defined as

$$\mu = \frac{mM}{m + M}, \qquad (6)$$

is called the *reduced mass* of the system, we get

$$H = H^o + H^i, \qquad (7)$$

where

$$H^c = \frac{1}{2(m+M)} (P_x^2 + P_y^2 + P_z^2) \qquad (8)$$

and

$$H^i = \frac{1}{2\mu} (p_x^2 + p_y^2 + p_z^2) - \frac{e^2}{r}, \qquad (9)$$

r being the distance between the electron and the proton.

The term H^c in (7) refers to the motion of the center of gravity and is the Hamiltonian of a free particle of mass $m + M$; the term H^i refers to the internal motion and is the Hamiltonian of a particle of mass μ moving in a fixed Coulomb field with $V = -e^2/r$; H^c and H^i have no variables in common, so that the motion of the center of gravity and the internal motion are independent of one another. The total energy E of the system has the form

$$E = E^c + E^i; \qquad (10)$$

here E^c is the translational kinetic energy $(P_x^2 + P_y^2 + P_z^2)/2(m + M)$, computed as though the total mass $m + M$ were concentrated at the center of gravity; and E^i is the internal energy, that is, the energy of the electron and the proton moving under each other's influence about their center of gravity as though this center were at rest, or, if we use the particular internal coordinates (3), the energy of a particle of reduced mass μ and charge $-e$ moving about a fixed nucleus of charge e.

Insofar as the motion of the center of gravity is concerned, the quantities P_x, P_y, and P_z are constants, and since this motion is independent of the internal motion the P's are constants of motion of the complete system; similarly, the constants of the internal motion are also constants of motion of the complete system.

Schroedinger theory. In the present problem we encounter for the first time the task of identifying the Schroedinger operators to be associated with the coordinates and the components of linear momentum of *two interacting* particles. The procedure (which can be justified by a study of Poisson brackets relating to a system containing two particles) is a direct extension of that for the case of a single particle: with the variables x_1, y_1, z_1, p_{x_1}, p_{y_1}, and p_{z_1} pertaining to the electron we associated the respective operators x_1, y_1, z_1, $-i\hbar \, \partial/\partial x_1$, $-i\hbar \, \partial/\partial y_1$, and $-i\hbar \, \partial/\partial z_1$; and with the variables x_2, y_2, z_2, p_{x_2}, p_{y_2}, and p_{z_2} pertaining to the proton we associate the respective operators x_2, y_2, z_2, $-i\hbar\,\partial/\partial x_2$, $-i\hbar\,\partial/\partial y_2$, and $-i\hbar\,\partial/\partial z_2$. The operands of these operators are well-behaved functions of the six variables x_1, y_1, z_1, x_2, y_2, and z_2; good behavior[36] is now defined by a direct generalization of the definition of §74.

The Schroedinger operator associated with the Hamiltonian (1) is

$$H = -\frac{\hbar^2}{2m}\left(\frac{\partial^2}{\partial x_1^2} + \frac{\partial^2}{\partial y_1^2} + \frac{\partial^2}{\partial z_1^2}\right)$$

$$-\frac{\hbar^2}{2M}\left(\frac{\partial^2}{\partial x_2^2} + \frac{\partial^2}{\partial y_2^2} + \frac{\partial^2}{\partial z_2^2}\right) - \frac{e^2}{r}. \qquad \langle 11 \rangle$$

The classical procedure suggests that we introduce the new coordinates defined by (2) and (3), and the new momentum operators

$$P_x = -i\hbar\,\frac{\partial}{\partial X}, \qquad P_y = -i\hbar\,\frac{\partial}{\partial Y}, \qquad P_z = -i\hbar\,\frac{\partial}{\partial Z} \qquad \langle 12 \rangle$$

and

$$p_x = -i\hbar\,\frac{\partial}{\partial x}, \qquad p_y = -i\hbar\,\frac{\partial}{\partial y}, \qquad p_z = -i\hbar\,\frac{\partial}{\partial z}. \qquad \langle 13 \rangle$$

In terms of these, the operator $\langle 11 \rangle$ becomes

$$H = H^c + H^i, \qquad \langle 14 \rangle$$

where

$$H^c = -\frac{\hbar^2}{2(m + M)}\left(\frac{\partial^2}{\partial X^2} + \frac{\partial^2}{\partial Y^2} + \frac{\partial^2}{\partial Z^2}\right) \qquad \langle 15 \rangle$$

---

[36] It should perhaps be emphasized that the two particles under consideration here—electron and proton—are *distinguishable*. In the case of *identical* particles, the ψ-functions must not only be well-behaved but must also satisfy certain symmetry conditions (to put it roughly, the additional conditions take care of the experimental impossibility of detecting an interchange of two indistinguishable particles); this extremely important point lies outside the scope of this book.

Incidentally, in the case of two particles, the configuration space referred to in the general Schroedinger expectation formula 1^{17} is a fictitious 6-dimensional space; its axes refer to the six coordinates x_1, y_1, z_1, x_2, y_2, and z_2, so that every configuration of the *two particles* in 3-space is represented by a *single point* in the configuration space.

and

$$H^i = -\frac{\hbar^2}{2\mu}\left(\frac{\partial^2}{\partial x^2} + \frac{\partial^2}{\partial y^2} + \frac{\partial^2}{\partial z^2}\right) - \frac{e^2}{r}. \qquad \langle 16\rangle$$

The commuting dynamical variables

$$H, P_x, P_y, P_z \qquad \langle 17\rangle$$

are among the constants of motion of our system, and we begin by determining the form of their simultaneous eigenfunctions. The simultaneous eigenfunctions of the P's are

$$\psi = u(x, y, z)e^{i(P'_x x + P'_y y + P'_z z)/\hbar}, \qquad (18)$$

where the P''s are arbitrary real constants and $u(x, y, z)$ is an arbitrary well-behaved function of the internal coordinates. Now, if we operate on (18) with H and write

$$\frac{1}{2(m + M)}[P'^2_x + P'^2_y + P'^2_z] = E^c, \qquad (19)$$

we get

$$H\psi = H^c\psi + H^i\psi = E^c\psi + H^i\psi, \qquad \langle 20\rangle$$

so that if (18) is to satisfy the Schroedinger equation $H\psi = E\psi$ we must have

$$E^c\psi + H^i\psi = E\psi. \qquad \langle 21\rangle$$

When (18) is explicitly substituted into $\langle 21\rangle$ the exponential factor cancels out, and we are left with

$$E^c u(x, y, z) + H^i u(x, y, z) = Eu(x, y, z). \qquad \langle 22\rangle$$

If we finally write

$$E - E^c = E^i, \qquad (23)$$

Equation $\langle 22\rangle$ becomes

$$H^i u(x, y, z) = E^i u(x, y, z). \qquad \langle 24\rangle$$

We therefore conclude that the simultaneous eigenfunctions of the variables $\langle 17\rangle$ have the form (18) where $u(x, y, z)$ is a well-behaved function satisfying $\langle 24\rangle$, and (since the values of the P''s remain unrestricted) that the quantity E^c, which we may call the translational energy of our system, is not quantized.

Now, in view of $\langle 16 \rangle$, Equation $\langle 24 \rangle$ is just the Schroedinger equation for a single particle of mass μ moving in the fixed Coulomb potential $-e^2/r$, and consequently the possible values of the parameter E^i in $\langle 24 \rangle$, that is, of the internal energy of our system, can be obtained from the results of the preceding section by writing μ for m. The conclusion is that all positive values of the internal energy are possible, while its possible negative values are

$$E_n^i = -\frac{2\pi^2 \mu e^4}{h^2 n^2}, \quad n = 1, 2, 3, \cdots. \quad (25)$$

Exercise

1. Compare the energy levels of the internal motion of the hydrogen atom, the deuterium atom, and a singly ionized helium atom of mass 4.

82. The Fine Structure of the Hydrogen Levels

When the spectrum of atomic hydrogen is studied with apparatus of moderate resolving power, the discrete energy levels are found to be just those given by the Bohr formula

$$(18^{80}) \qquad\qquad E_n = -2\pi^2 me^4/n^2 h^2, \qquad\qquad (1)$$

provided this formula is corrected for nuclear motion,[37] as we have done in §81. But when high resolution is employed it is found that the levels which the Bohr formula requires to be singlets are, in fact, with the exception of the lowest level, very narrow multiplets.

The fine structure of the lower portion of the hydrogen energy spectrum is shown schematically in[38] Fig. 107. The long thin lines mark the positions of the singlet levels required by the Bohr formula; these levels are shown as equally spaced, although their separations, in fact, decrease with increasing n. The short thick lines show the actual levels. The displacement of each member of the nth multiplet below the nth Bohr level, measured in terms of the unit

$$me^8/2c^2 \hbar^4 n^4, \qquad\qquad (2)$$

---

[37] In the remainder of our work with the hydrogen atom we shall disregard the corrections for nuclear motion.

[38] By permission of The Cambridge University Press and The Macmillan Company, publishers, our energy-level diagrams for hydrogen are patterned after Fig. 2^5 of Condon and Shortley.

is indicated by the number at the right of the corresponding short line. Since the unit (2) decreases with n, the diagram exaggerates the widths of the higher multiplets; it also exaggerates the separations of the members of a multiplet compared to the separations of the Bohr levels.

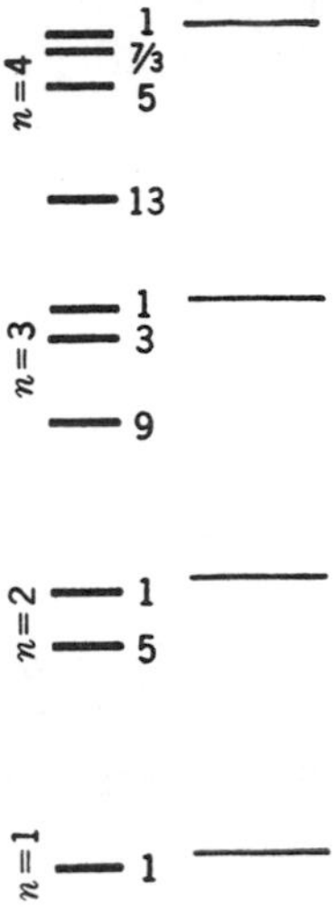

The formula that gives the levels correctly was obtained in 1915 by Sommerfeld,[39] who extended Bohr's quantization rules to an electron moving in a Coulomb field according to the laws of Einstein's theory of relativity, rather than the laws of Newtonian mechanics. Sommerfeld's *fine-structure formula* is

$$E_{nk} = mc^2 \left[1 + \left(\frac{\alpha}{n - k + \sqrt{k^2 - \alpha^2}} \right)^2 \right]^{-\frac{1}{2}} \quad (3)$$

where the principal quantum number n takes on the values

$$n = 1, 2, 3, \cdots, \quad (4)$$

and the auxiliary quantum number k takes on, for a prescribed value of n, the n values

$$k = 1, 2, \cdots, n. \quad (5)$$

The symbol c denotes the speed of light, while α, defined as

$$\alpha = \frac{e^2}{c\hbar} \quad (6)$$

and called the *Sommerfeld fine-structure constant*, is a pure number whose value is approximately $\frac{1}{137}$.

Since α^2 is very small compared to k^2, the term $-k$ in (3) is almost canceled by the radical following this term, and therefore the levels having the same n but different k's lie very close together compared with levels having different n's; the formula (3) thus describes a series of narrow multiplets. To reveal their structure more clearly we expand the right side of (3) into a power series

Fig. 107. Fine structure of hydrogen levels.

---

[39] A. Sommerfeld, *Annalen der Physik*, **51**, 1 (1916).

in α and then drop the terms containing $1/c^4$, $1/c^6$, and so on. The resulting highly accurate approximation is

$$E_{nk} = E_n - \frac{|E_n|\,\alpha^2}{4n^2}\left(\frac{4n}{k} - 3\right) + mc^2, \qquad (7)$$

where E_n is given by (1) and the factor $|E_n|\,\alpha^2/n^2$ is just the quantity (2). The term mc^2 in (7) is called the *relativistic rest energy* of the electron.

The levels computed by means of (7), with the rest energy left out, and their Sommerfeld classification in terms of the quantum numbers n and k are shown on the right side of Fig. 108; the left part of this figure is a reproduction of Fig. 107 (Fig. 107 has, in fact, been computed from Equation (7) rather than from experimental data).

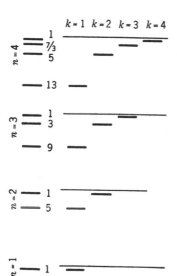

Fig. 108. Fine-structure levels of hydrogen, and their Sommerfeld classification.

So far, our quantum-mechanical computations concerning the hydrogen atom have led to the Bohr formula; but since Sommerfeld's, rather than Bohr's, formula agrees with experiment, we should expect the theory to yield Sommerfeld's formula or one much like it. Our study is thus as yet incomplete; and, guided by the fact that Sommerfeld's computations invoked the theory of relativity, we proceed to investigate the relativity corrections to our quantum-mechanical result.

Exercises

1. Deduce (7) from (3).
2. Extend Fig. 108 through $n = 5$.

83. Relativity Corrections for Hydrogen

In relativity theory, the Newtonian relation $E - V = (p_x^2 + p_y^2 + p_z^2)/2m$ between the kinetic energy $E - V$ and the

Cartesian components p_x, p_y, and p_z of the linear momentum of a particle is replaced by the relation

$$\frac{1}{c^2}(E - V)^2 = p_x^2 + p_y^2 + p_z^2 + m^2c^2,\tag{1}$$

where c is the speed of light and m is the so-called *rest mass* of the particle, that is, mass as determined by an observer with respect to whom the particle is at rest. In the case of a free particle at rest, or, more precisely, in the case $V = 0$ and $p_x = p_y = p_z = 0$, Equation (1) reduces to $E^2 = m^2c^4$ and yields for the energy of the particle the positive value

$$E_0 = mc^2\tag{2}$$

and the negative value $-mc^2$. The second alternative is of no interest in classical relativity, while (2) is interpreted to mean that, even when at rest, the particle possesses a *mass energy* or *rest energy* of the amount mc^2. According to relativity theory, a Cartesian component of the linear momentum of a particle may have any value between $-\infty$ and ∞, while the speed of the particle cannot exceed the speed of light c; hence the relativistic relation ($p_x = m\dot{x}/\sqrt{1 - v^2/c^2}$, and so on) between linear momentum and velocity, which we need not discuss here, is more complicated than the corresponding Newtonian relation.

The fundamental problem of the relativistic quantum mechanics of a single particle, namely, the construction of the operator H that should replace the Schroedinger Hamiltonian operator when the Newtonian energy equation is replaced by the relativistic equation (1), will be taken up in §91. For the present we shall employ a somewhat indirect procedure that avoids the use of the explicit form of the operator H; critical comments on this procedure will be made in §91.

We consider a state ψ for which the total energy of the system is certainly E, rewrite (1) as

$$\frac{1}{c^2}(E - V)^2 - p_x^2 - p_y^2 - p_z^2 = m^2c^2,\tag{3}$$

and find that the Schroedinger operator associated with the quantity on the left side of (3) is

$$\frac{1}{c^2}(E - V)^2 + \hbar^2\left(\frac{\partial^2}{\partial x^2} + \frac{\partial^2}{\partial y^2} + \frac{\partial^2}{\partial z^2}\right),\tag{4}$$

where E is the numerical value of the total energy and V is the Schroedinger operator associated with the potential energy. Now, according to (3), the quantity on the left side of (3) is simply the number m^2c^2; we interpret this fact to mean quantum mechanically that the Schroedinger function ψ describing an energy state of energy E is an eigenfunction of the operator (4) belonging to the eigenvalue m^2c^2 of (4), and write

$$\left[\frac{1}{c^2}(E - V)^2 + \hbar^2\left(\frac{\partial^2}{\partial x^2} + \frac{\partial^2}{\partial y^2} + \frac{\partial^2}{\partial z^2}\right)\right]\psi = m^2c^2\psi. \qquad (5)$$

The energy levels of the system can now be found by computing the numerical values of E for which (5) has well-behaved solutions.

Recalling the steps from 1^{78} to 3^{78}, we may rewrite (5) as

$$\left[-p_r^2 - \frac{L^2}{r^2} + \frac{(E - V)^2}{c^2}\right]\psi = m^2c^2\psi, \qquad \langle 6 \rangle$$

where L^2 and p_r are the operators 65^{76} and 24^{77}.

Let us now consider central fields, when V in $\langle 6 \rangle$ has the form $V(r)$. The straightforward mathematical procedure for studying $\langle 6 \rangle$ in this case is to try separating the variables by assuming that ψ has the form $R(r)\Theta(\theta)\Phi(\phi)$. We can, however, skip a step or two because nonrelativistic analogy suggests that L_z and L^2 are constants of motion in our case, and that hence, according to the expansion theorem, we may restrict ourselves at once to ψ's of the more specific form

(68^{76}) $\qquad\qquad\qquad \psi = R\Upsilon(l\,m_l). \qquad\qquad (7)$

Substituting (7) into $\langle 6 \rangle$, where now $V = V(r)$, and using 15^A, we find that the angle factors cancel out and that we are left with the radial equation

$$\left[-p_r^2 - \frac{l(l + 1)\hbar^2}{r^2} + \frac{1}{c^2}\{E - V(r)\}^2\right]R = m^2c^2R. \qquad \langle 8 \rangle$$

The cancellation of the angle factors provides a mathematical justification for the form (7).

When we finally restrict ourselves to the Coulomb case

(1^{80}) $\qquad\qquad\qquad V = -e^2/r \qquad\qquad\qquad (9)$

and make our standard substitution

$$(10^{78}) \qquad\qquad \chi = rR, \qquad\qquad (10)$$

Equation ⟨8⟩ reduces to

$$\left\{ -\frac{1}{\kappa}\frac{d^2}{dr^2} + \left[\frac{l(l+1)}{\kappa} - \frac{e^4}{2mc^2}\right]\frac{1}{r^2} - \frac{E}{mc^2}\frac{e^2}{r} \right\} \chi$$
$$= \left[\frac{E^2}{2mc^2} - \frac{1}{2}mc^2\right]\chi. \qquad (11)$$

Apart from the differences in the numerical coefficients, our new χ-equation (11) is of the same form as the nonrelativistic χ-equation

$$(4^{80}) \qquad\qquad \left\{ -\frac{1}{\kappa}\frac{d^2}{dr^2} + \frac{l(l+1)}{\kappa}\frac{1}{r^2} - \frac{e^2}{r} \right\} \chi = E\chi. \qquad (12)$$

Hence the precise values of E for which (11) has satisfactory solutions can be found in essentially the same way as in the case of (12), and we may omit details.[40] It turns out that the positive[41] values of E for which (11) has solutions yielding well-behaved R's are the continuum of all values lying above mc^2 and also the discrete values

$$E_{nl} = mc^2\left[1 + \left(\frac{\alpha}{n - (l + \frac{1}{2}) + \sqrt{(l + \frac{1}{2})^2 - \alpha^2}}\right)^2 \right]^{-\frac{1}{2}}, \qquad (13)$$

where α is the fine-structure constant $e^2/c\hbar$, where the principal quantum number n takes on the values

$$n = 1, 2, 3, \cdots, \qquad\qquad (14)$$

and where, for a prescribed n, the azimuthal quantum number l runs through the n values

$$l = 0, 1, 2, \cdots, (n - 1). \qquad\qquad (15)$$

If the right side of (13) is expanded in powers of α, and the terms containing $1/c^4$, $1/c^6$, and so on, are dropped, (13) reduces to the approximate formula

$$E_{nl} = E_n - \frac{|E_n|\alpha^2}{4n^2}\left(\frac{4n}{l + \frac{1}{2}} - 3\right) + mc^2, \qquad (16)$$

---

[40] Sommerfeld, page 112.

[41] Equation (11) contains E^2 as well as E, and yields both positive and negative energy levels; the latter are of no interest in the work of this section.

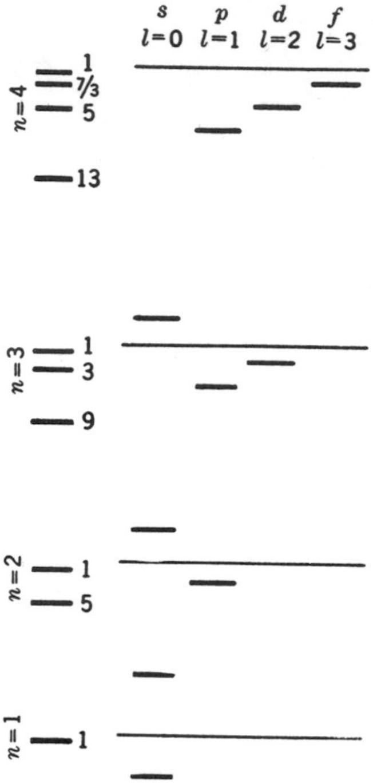

$$\begin{array}{cccc}
s & p & d & f \\
l=0 & l=1 & l=2 & l=3
\end{array}$$

Fig. 109. Relativity corrections for hydrogen. The Sommerfeld levels are shown at the left.

where E_n is the Bohr energy 18[80]. The second of the three terms on the right side of (16) is called the *relativity correction* for hydrogen.

Equation (13) is of substantially the same form as the Sommerfeld fine-structure formula 3[82]; but, since Sommerfeld's k is an integer, while our $l + \frac{1}{2}$ is not, the two formulas differ in an important detail. The levels given by (16) are contrasted with the correct levels in Fig. 109. We conclude that, in quantum mechanics, in contradistinction to the Bohr theory, the relativity correction alone is not sufficient to bring agreement with experiment.

We shall find in §89 that the approximate Sommerfeld formula 7[82] can be obtained by combining the relativity correction with a correction for the so-called electron spin; and in §96 we shall see how the fine structure of the hydrogen levels can be found precisely with the help of the correct relativistic Hamiltonian operator.

Exercises

1. Extend Fig. 109 through $n = 5$.

2. Show that, if $c \to \infty$, then (11) reduces to (12); remember that the relativistic E of (11) includes the rest energy, while the nonrelativistic E of (12) does not.

CHAPTER XIII

ELEMENTS OF PAULI'S THEORY OF ELECTRON SPIN

84. The Electron-Spin Hypothesis

Our failure to get quantum mechanically a correct formula for the hydrogen levels may be ascribed to the fact that we have so far disregarded the phenomenon of *electron spin*. This phenomenon has no classical analogue, and in approaching its theory we shall begin by recounting an empirical clue.

Bohr's theory does not lend itself to an accurate computation of the energy levels of atoms having several electrons; but it does enable one to infer quite a few important features of the levels, and during the decade following its inception a large amount of work was done in trying to apply it to the interpretation of spectral data. It was found, however, that a fairly coherent picture could be obtained only with the help of certain extraneous assumptions.

In 1925, Uhlenbeck and Goudsmit[1] proposed that each electron spins while revolving about a nucleus and has a quantized *spin angular momentum* and, being an electrically charged body,[2] a *spin magnetic moment*. This proposal was remarkably successful in correlating spectral data for both unperturbed and perturbed complex atoms, and in interpreting the results of the Stern-Gerlach experiment concerned with the deflection of atoms projected into an inhomogeneous magnetic field; but the reason why Sommerfeld succeeded in getting a correct formula for hydrogen *without* introducing electron spin became obscure.

The essence of the Uhlenbeck-Goudsmit hypothesis is that[3]

(a) each electron has a spin angular momentum s whose com-

---

[1] G. E. Uhlenbeck and S. Goudsmit, *Naturwissenschaften*, **13**, 953 (1925); *Nature*, **117**, 264 (1926).

[2] S. J. Barnett, "Gyromagnetic and Electron-Inertia Effects," *Rev. Mod. Physics*, **7**, 129 (1935).

[3] Our present s's are not to be confused with probability-current densities.

ponent in any direction can have only the value $\frac{1}{2}\hbar$ or the value $-\frac{1}{2}\hbar$, so that, in particular,

$$s_z \overset{\circ}{=} \pm\tfrac{1}{2}\hbar, \tag{1}$$

and that

(b) each electron has a spin magnetic moment $\mathbf{\mu}$ such that, in electromagnetic units,

$$\mathbf{\mu} = -\frac{e}{mc}\,\mathbf{s}. \tag{2}$$

Here $-e$ is the charge, m the mass, and $\mathbf{s}$ the spin angular momentum of the electron, while c is the ratio of electrostatic and electromagnetic units, that is, the speed of light.

From the standpoint of the Bohr theory, and also from the standpoint of that part of quantum mechanics which we have discussed so far, the assumption (a) seems strange for two main reasons: the possible values of s_z are taken to be *halves* rather than *integral multiples* of the Bohr unit of angular momentum $\hbar$, and only *two* values of s_z are assumed possible. The assumption (b) is also somewhat strange because the factor e/mc in (2) is larger than we might expect, that is, the magnetic moment of the electron is assumed to be anomalously large when compared with the assumed spin angular momentum of the electron. Incidentally, according to classical theory,[2] the magnetic moment of an atom arising because of the *orbital* motion of an electron is

$$-\frac{e}{2mc}\,\mathbf{L}, \tag{3}$$

where $\mathbf{L}$ is the orbital angular momentum of the electron; the expression (3) is supported by spectroscopic evidence.

We shall see in the next chapter that the phenomenon of electron spin finds a direct quantum-mechanical interpretation as soon as we satisfy the requirements of the theory of relativity in a thoroughgoing manner. But first, with the help of a method due to Pauli,[4] we shall show how the hypothesis of electron spin can be grafted onto nonrelativistic quantum mechanics.

Both values of s_z assumed in (1) vanish when $h \to 0$, so that electron spin disappears in the limit $h \to 0$ and thus has no classical analogue (the situation is of course different in the case of orbital angular momentum because, since $m_l = 0, \pm1, \pm2, \cdots$,

---

[4] W. Pauli, *Zeits. f. Physik*, **43**, 601 (1927). We shall not discuss the relativistic form of Pauli's method.

a decrease of the factor h in $m_l h$ does not delimit the value of $m_l h$). Hence there is no obvious way (in fact, there is not any way) in which the operators that might be associated with s_z can be constructed from the operators associated with our familiar classical dynamical variables.

In the applications of the electron-spin idea to the Bohr theory, the spin angular momentum is treated on quite the same footing as orbital angular momentum; and the success of these applications would therefore suggest that at least the more fundamental properties of spin angular momentum must be similar to those of orbital angular momentum. Now, perhaps the most fundamental property of classical orbital angular momentum is the set of Poisson bracket relations 15[75], so that perhaps the most fundamental property of the quantum-mechanical operators associated with the components of orbital angular momentum is the set of relations[5]

$$\langle 70^{76} \rangle \qquad \begin{array}{c} L_x L_y - L_y L_x = i\hbar L_z , \qquad L_y L_z - L_z L_y = i\hbar L_x , \\[2mm] L_z L_x - L_x L_z = i\hbar L_y . \end{array} \qquad (4)$$

Taking the hint from (4), we now *assume* that the operators s_x, s_y, and s_z to be associated with the components of spin angular momentum satisfy the commutation rules

$$s_x s_y - s_y s_x = i\hbar s_z , \qquad s_y s_z - s_z s_y = i\hbar s_x , \qquad s_z s_x - s_x s_z = i\hbar s_y . \quad (5)$$

We shall show in the next section that the eigenvalues required by (1) are compatible with these commutation rules.

Exercise

1. Recall Exercises 9[76] and 10[74], and derive Equations 12[A], 13[A], and 18[A] from Equations 2[A] to 6[A]. In a similar way verify the terms containing dR/dr in 16[A] and 17[A].

85. Possible Values of Components of Angular Momenta[6]

We shall now compute symbolically the eigenvalues of three Hermitian operators, J_x, J_y, and J_z, defined through the commutation rules

$$J_x J_y - J_y J_x = i\hbar J_z , \qquad J_y J_z - J_z J_y = i\hbar J_x ,$$
$$J_z J_x - J_x J_z = i\hbar J_y , \qquad (1)$$

---

[5] We no longer use angular brackets in equation numbers.

[6] Condon and Shortley, page 46. The reader who omitted Chapter XI may also omit §85.

that is, rules of the form 4^{84} and 5^{84}; we use the symbols J to emphasize that in this section we are not restricting ourselves to orbital angular momenta denoted by L's or to spin angular momenta denoted by s's, but are instead treating angular momenta in general. We note that the operator

$$J^2 = J_x^2 + J_y^2 + J_z^2 \qquad (2)$$

commutes with J_x, J_y, and J_z, and that

$$(J_x + iJ_y)J_z = (J_z - \hbar)(J_x + iJ_y). \qquad (3)$$

Since J_x, J_y, and J_z enter symmetrically in (1), the eigenvalues of one of these operators are the same as those of another, and we shall focus our attention on J_z. Further, we shall restrict ourselves to ψ's that are simultaneous eigen-ψ's of J_z and J^2; the permissibility of this follows from the general expansion theorem quoted a few lines below 1[46]. Each of our four J's is Hermitian, and consequently the eigenvalues of each are all real.

Let ψ be a simultaneous eigen-ψ of J_z and J^2, belonging to the eigenvalue a of J_z and the eigenvalue b^2 of J^2, so that

$$J_z\psi = a\psi, \qquad J^2\psi = b^2\psi, \qquad \psi \neq 0. \qquad \text{(4a, b, c)}$$

From (4a) we get

$$(J_x + iJ_y)J_z\psi = a(J_x + iJ_y)\psi, \qquad (5)$$

or, according to (3), $(J_z - \hbar)(J_x + iJ_y)\psi = a(J_x + iJ_y)\psi$, that is,

$$J_z[(J_x + iJ_y)\psi] = (a + \hbar)[(J_x + iJ_y)\psi]. \qquad (6)$$

Hence, if a is an eigenvalue of J_z, then $a + \hbar$ is also an eigenvalue of J_z, provided the operand $(J_x + iJ_y)\psi$ does not vanish. Since

$$J^2[(J_x + iJ_y)\psi] = (J_x + iJ_y)J^2\psi = (J_x + iJ_y)b^2\psi$$
$$= b^2[(J_x + iJ_y)\psi], \qquad (7)$$

the operand $(J_x + iJ_y)\psi$, unless it vanishes, is an eigen-ψ of J^2 belonging to the eigenvalue b^2 of J^2, the same eigenvalue that belongs to ψ. Iterating this argument, we get the series

$$a, a + \hbar, a + 2\hbar, a + 3\hbar, \cdots \qquad (8)$$

for the eigenvalues of J_z, and find that each of the corresponding eigen-ψ's of J_z is an eigen-ψ of J^2 belonging to the eigenvalue b^2 of J^2.

Multiplying (4a) by $J_x - iJ_y$, rather than by $J_x + iJ_y$, we find by analogous arguments that, if a is an eigenvalue of J_z, then $a - \hbar$ is also an eigenvalue of J_z, so that the series (8) becomes augmented to

$$\cdots, a - 2\hbar, a - \hbar, a, a + \hbar, a + 2\hbar, \cdots. \tag{9}$$

For any state, av $J^2 =$ av $J_x^2 +$ av $J_y^2 +$ av J_z^2, and consequently for a simultaneous eigenstate of J_z and J^2 the square of the eigenvalue of J_z cannot be greater than the eigenvalue of J^2. Now, the respective eigen-ψ's of J_z belonging to its eigenvalues (9) are all eigen-ψ's of J^2 belonging to the eigenvalue b^2 of J^2, and therefore the series (9) must terminate on both sides, for otherwise it would include terms whose squares are greater than b^2.

Let A be the greatest eigenvalue of J_z consistent with the eigenvalue b^2 of J^2, and let the corresponding simultaneous eigen-ψ of J_z and J^2 be ψ_A. Substituting A for a in (6), we get $J_z[(J_x + iJ_y)\psi_A] = (A + \hbar)[(J_x + iJ_y)\psi_A]$, so that, contrary to hypothesis, J_z would have the eigenvalue $A + \hbar$ unless

$$(J_x + iJ_y)\psi_A = 0. \tag{10}$$

Multiplying (10) by $J_x - iJ_y$ and rearranging the result, we get $(J_x - iJ_y)(J_x + iJ_y)\psi_A = [J_x^2 + J_y^2 + i(J_xJ_y - J_yJ_x)]\psi_A = (J_x^2 + J_y^2 - \hbar J_z)\psi_A = (J^2 - J_z^2 - \hbar J_z)\psi_A = (b^2 - A^2 - \hbar A)\psi_A = 0$, so that, since $\psi_A \not= 0$,

$$b^2 - A^2 - \hbar A = 0. \tag{11}$$

The greater root of (11), which alone is of interest to us, is

$$A = -\tfrac{1}{2}\hbar + \tfrac{1}{2}\sqrt{\hbar^2 + 4b^2}. \tag{12}$$

A similar argument shows that the least eigenvalue of J_z consistent with the eigenvalue b^2 of J^2 is $\tfrac{1}{2}\hbar - \tfrac{1}{2}\sqrt{\hbar^2 + 4b^2}$, that is, $-A$.

The eigenvalues of J_z consistent with a preassigned eigenvalue of J^2 thus form the series

$$-A, -A + \hbar, -A + 2\hbar, \cdots, A - 2\hbar, A - \hbar, A, \tag{13}$$

and the difference between A and $-A$ must therefore be an integral multiple of $\hbar$, so that $2A = m'\hbar$, where m' is a positive integer or zero, that is,

$$A = \tfrac{1}{2}m'\hbar, \qquad m' = 0, 1, 2, \cdots. \tag{14}$$

If m' is even, say $m' = 2m$, then (13) takes the form

$$-m\hbar, \ -(m-1)\hbar, \ \cdots, \ -\hbar, \ 0, \ \hbar, \ \cdots, \ (m-1)\hbar, \ m\hbar, \quad (15)$$

where $m = 0, 1, 2, \cdots$; but if m' is odd, say $m' = 2m + 1$, we get

$$-(m+\tfrac{1}{2})\hbar, \ -(m-\tfrac{1}{2})\hbar, \ \cdots, \ -\tfrac{1}{2}\hbar, \ \tfrac{1}{2}\hbar, \ \cdots, \ (m-\tfrac{1}{2})\hbar,$$
$$(m+\tfrac{1}{2})\hbar, \quad (16)$$

where, as before, $m = 0, 1, 2, \cdots$.

The result (15), which means that the eigenvalues of a component of an angular momentum may be integral multiples of $\hbar$, is in agreement with our old result 62^{76} obtained for *orbital* angular momenta. But the result (16), which means that the eigenvalues of a component of an angular momentum may be half-odd integer multiples of $\hbar$, is new; according to it, *the assumption that the possible values of a component of spin angular momentum are $\tfrac{1}{2}\hbar$ and $-\tfrac{1}{2}\hbar$ is not inconsistent with quantum mechanics*, provided the quantum-mechanical definition of angular momenta is taken to be the commutation rules (1).

We summarize (15) and (16) by writing

$$J_z \overset{\circ}{=} m_j\hbar, \qquad m_j = 0, \ \pm\tfrac{1}{2}, \ \pm1, \ \pm\tfrac{3}{2}, \ \pm2, \ \cdots. \quad (17)$$

Exercises

1. Justify in detail the step from (8) to (9), and verify that the smallest eigenvalue of J_z consistent with the eigenvalue b^2 of J^2 is the negative of (12).

2. Show that

$$J \overset{\circ}{=} \sqrt{j(j+1)} \ \hbar, \quad j = 0, \tfrac{1}{2}, 1, \tfrac{3}{2}, 2, \cdots \quad (18)$$

and note that (18) includes 69^{76}.

3. Correlate Equations 12^A to 15^A with the various intermediate results obtained symbolically in this section.

86. The Pauli Operators and Operands

The spin operators are to satisfy the commutation rules

$$(5^{84}) \quad s_x s_y - s_y s_x = i\hbar s_z, \quad s_y s_z - s_z s_y = i\hbar s_x, \quad s_z s_x - s_x s_z = i\hbar s_y. \quad (1)$$

Further, according to the assumption (a) of §84, each of the operators s_x, s_y, and s_z must have just the two eigenvalues $\tfrac{1}{2}\hbar$ and $-\tfrac{1}{2}\hbar$; in view of 16^{85} these eigenvalues are not inconsistent with (1).

We introduce three auxiliary operators, σ_x, σ_y, and σ_z, such that

$$s_x = \tfrac{1}{2}\hbar\sigma_x, \qquad s_y = \tfrac{1}{2}\hbar\sigma_y, \qquad s_z = \tfrac{1}{2}\hbar\sigma_z. \tag{2}$$

The following properties of the σ's are of immediate interest to us. Since the eigenvalues of each s are to be just $\tfrac{1}{2}\hbar$ and $-\tfrac{1}{2}\hbar$, the eigenvalues of each σ must be just 1 and -1. Each of the operators σ_x^2, σ_y^2, and σ_z^2 must therefore have only the one eigenvalue 1; and since the only operator having the lone eigenvalue 1 is the unit operator we conclude that

$$\sigma_x^2 = \sigma_y^2 = \sigma_z^2 = 1. \tag{3}$$

According to (1) the commutation rules satisfied by the σ's must be

$$\sigma_x\sigma_y - \sigma_y\sigma_x = 2i\sigma_z, \qquad \sigma_y\sigma_z - \sigma_z\sigma_y = 2i\sigma_x,$$

$$\sigma_z\sigma_x - \sigma_x\sigma_z = 2i\sigma_y. \tag{4}$$

Now,

$$2i(\sigma_x\sigma_y + \sigma_y\sigma_x) = (2i\sigma_x)\sigma_y + \sigma_y(2i\sigma_x) \tag{5}$$

$$= (\sigma_y\sigma_z - \sigma_z\sigma_y)\sigma_y + \sigma_y(\sigma_y\sigma_z - \sigma_z\sigma_y)$$

$$= -\sigma_z\sigma_y^2 + \sigma_y^2\sigma_z = -\sigma_z + \sigma_z$$

$$= 0.$$

Hence $\sigma_x\sigma_y = -\sigma_y\sigma_x$, so that σ_x and σ_y anticommute; similar arguments show that any two of the σ's anticommute:

$$\sigma_x\sigma_y = -\sigma_y\sigma_x, \quad \sigma_y\sigma_z = -\sigma_z\sigma_y, \quad \sigma_z\sigma_x = -\sigma_x\sigma_z. \tag{6}$$

Finally, it follows from (4) and (6) that

$$\sigma_x\sigma_y = i\sigma_z, \quad \sigma_y\sigma_z = i\sigma_x, \quad \sigma_z\sigma_x = i\sigma_y. \tag{7a, b, c}$$

We now look for a set of explicit operators having the properties of the σ's. Since each σ has just two eigenvalues, 2-by-2 matrices may be expected to serve the purpose, and we begin by associating with σ_z the simplest 2-by-2 matrix having the eigenvalues 1 and -1:

$$\sigma_z = \begin{pmatrix} 1 & 0 \\ 0 & -1 \end{pmatrix} \tag{8}$$

Now,

$$\begin{pmatrix} a & b \\ c & d \end{pmatrix}\begin{pmatrix} 1 & 0 \\ 0 & -1 \end{pmatrix} = \begin{pmatrix} a & -b \\ c & -d \end{pmatrix} \tag{9}$$

and

$$\begin{pmatrix} 1 & 0 \\ 0 & -1 \end{pmatrix} \begin{pmatrix} a & b \\ c & d \end{pmatrix} = \begin{pmatrix} a & b \\ -c & -d \end{pmatrix} \qquad (10)$$

so that every matrix that anticommutes with (8), as σ_x and σ_y do according to (6), must have the form

$$\begin{pmatrix} 0 & b \\ c & 0 \end{pmatrix}. \qquad (11)$$

The eigenvalues of (11) are $\pm\sqrt{bc}$, so that if they are to be 1 and -1 we must set $bc = 1$. Perhaps the simplest possibility is to let $b = c = 1$, and to adopt for σ_x the matrix $\begin{pmatrix} 0 & 1 \\ 1 & 0 \end{pmatrix}$. It then follows from (7c) that the matrix to be associated with σ_y is $\begin{pmatrix} 0 & -i \\ i & 0 \end{pmatrix}$, and hence our complete list of σ's becomes

$$\sigma_x = \begin{pmatrix} 0 & 1 \\ 1 & 0 \end{pmatrix}, \qquad \sigma_y = \begin{pmatrix} 0 & -i \\ i & 0 \end{pmatrix}, \qquad \sigma_z = \begin{pmatrix} 1 & 0 \\ 0 & -1 \end{pmatrix}. \quad (12)$$

The matrices (12) are called the *Pauli spin matrices*.

Using (12) in (2), we get the following set of specific operators suitable for associating with the components of spin angular momentum:

$$s_x = \tfrac{1}{2}\hbar \begin{pmatrix} 0 & 1 \\ 1 & 0 \end{pmatrix}, \qquad s_y = \tfrac{1}{2}\hbar \begin{pmatrix} 0 & -i \\ i & 0 \end{pmatrix}, \qquad s_z = \tfrac{1}{2}\hbar \begin{pmatrix} 1 & 0 \\ 0 & -1 \end{pmatrix}. \quad (13)$$

Two-component ψ's. Since the Pauli theory uses the operators (13), which are 2-by-2 matrices, the Pauli operands are two-component column symbols; and, since the theory retains in essence the Schroedinger operators for dynamical variables having classical analogues, the components of these column symbols are functions of x, y, and z (or of r, θ, and ϕ; and so forth). An (instantaneous) Pauli operand ψ thus has the form[7]

$$\psi = \begin{pmatrix} \psi_1(x, y, z) \\ \psi_2(x, y, z) \end{pmatrix} \qquad (14)$$

or, as we shall write for brevity,

$$\psi = \begin{pmatrix} \psi_1 \\ \psi_2 \end{pmatrix}. \qquad (15)$$

---

[7] Two-component ψ-functions were first used, in treating spin, by C. G. Darwin: *Nature*, **119**, 282 (1927); *Proc. Roy. Soc.*, **116A**, 227 (1927). Pauli's mathematical procedure is equivalent to Darwin's in spite of a difference in the approach to the problem.

A Pauli ψ is said to be *well-behaved* if at least one of its components is different from zero and if each of its nonvanishing components is well-behaved in the sense of the Schröedinger theory. The Pauli $\bar{\psi}$ corresponding to (15) is the row symbol

(1^{69}) $$\bar{\psi} = (\bar{\psi}_1, \bar{\psi}_2),$$ (16)

so that $\bar{\psi}\psi$ is the following ordinary function of x, y, and z:

$$\bar{\psi}\psi = (\bar{\psi}_1, \bar{\psi}_2)\begin{pmatrix} \psi_1 \\ \psi_2 \end{pmatrix} = \bar{\psi}_1\psi_1 + \bar{\psi}_2\psi_2.$$ (17)

If

$$\int \bar{\psi}\psi \, d\tau = 1,$$ (18)

that is, if $\int (\bar{\psi}_1\psi_1 + \bar{\psi}_2\psi_2)d\tau = 1$, then the Pauli ψ is said to be *normalized*; as indicated by the crossed d, the integral in (18) extends over the entire three-dimensional space.

Further Pauli operators. In order that a differential[8] operator ξ may combine with the spin matrices or operate on two-component ψ's, it is first thrown into a matrix form by the following rule:

$$\xi = \xi 1 = \xi \begin{pmatrix} 1 & 0 \\ 0 & 1 \end{pmatrix} \doteq \begin{pmatrix} \xi & 0 \\ 0 & \xi \end{pmatrix}.$$ (19)

For example, the Pauli operators associated with x, p_x, and L_z are

$$x = \begin{pmatrix} x & 0 \\ 0 & x \end{pmatrix}, \qquad p_x = \begin{pmatrix} p_x & 0 \\ 0 & p_x \end{pmatrix}, \qquad L_z = \begin{pmatrix} L_z & 0 \\ 0 & L_z \end{pmatrix},$$ (20)

where the matrix elements are the appropriate Schroedinger operators. Since the Schroedinger operators associated with x, p_x, and L_z are x, $-i\hbar \, \partial/\partial x$, and $-i\hbar \, \partial/\partial \phi$, the explicit forms of the Pauli operators (20) are

$$x = \begin{pmatrix} x & 0 \\ 0 & x \end{pmatrix}, \qquad p_x = \begin{pmatrix} -i\hbar \dfrac{\partial}{\partial x} & 0 \\ 0 & -i\hbar \dfrac{\partial}{\partial x} \end{pmatrix},$$

$$L_z = \begin{pmatrix} -i\hbar \dfrac{\partial}{\partial \phi} & 0 \\ 0 & -i\hbar \dfrac{\partial}{\partial \phi} \end{pmatrix}.$$ (21)

---

[8] As before, the term *differential operator* denotes an operator constructed from one or more of the operators x, $\partial/\partial x$, y, $\partial/\partial y$, and so on.

The various Pauli operators are added together by the standard rules of matrix algebra; for example,

$$L_z + s_z = -i\hbar \frac{\partial}{\partial\phi} + \tfrac{1}{2}\hbar \begin{pmatrix} 1 & 0 \\ 0 & -1 \end{pmatrix}$$

$$= \hbar \begin{pmatrix} -i\dfrac{\partial}{\partial\phi} + \dfrac{1}{2} & 0 \\ 0 & -i\dfrac{\partial}{\partial\phi} - \dfrac{1}{2} \end{pmatrix}. \quad (22)$$

The Pauli operators are multiplied together by the standard rules of matrix algebra; for example,

$$p_x s_x = \begin{pmatrix} p_x & 0 \\ 0 & p_x \end{pmatrix} \tfrac{1}{2}\hbar \begin{pmatrix} 0 & 1 \\ 1 & 0 \end{pmatrix} = \tfrac{1}{2}\hbar \begin{pmatrix} 0 & p_x \\ p_x & 0 \end{pmatrix}$$

$$= -\tfrac{1}{2}i\hbar^2 \begin{pmatrix} 0 & \dfrac{\partial}{\partial x} \\ \dfrac{\partial}{\partial x} & 0 \end{pmatrix}. \quad (23)$$

But when multiplying together matrices with noncommuting elements we must preserve both the order of the matrix factors and the order of the element factors. For example,

$$xp_x = \begin{pmatrix} x & 0 \\ 0 & x \end{pmatrix} \begin{pmatrix} -i\hbar \dfrac{\partial}{\partial x} & 0 \\ 0 & -i\hbar \dfrac{\partial}{\partial x} \end{pmatrix} = -i\hbar \begin{pmatrix} x\dfrac{\partial}{\partial x} & 0 \\ 0 & x\dfrac{\partial}{\partial x} \end{pmatrix}, \quad (24)$$

while

$$p_x x = \begin{pmatrix} -i\hbar \dfrac{\partial}{\partial x} & 0 \\ 0 & -i\hbar \dfrac{\partial}{\partial x} \end{pmatrix} \begin{pmatrix} x & 0 \\ 0 & x \end{pmatrix} = -i\hbar \begin{pmatrix} \dfrac{\partial}{\partial x} x & 0 \\ 0 & \dfrac{\partial}{\partial x} x \end{pmatrix}. \quad (25)$$

The Pauli operators operate on the two-component ψ's according to the standard rule 51[54]. For example,

$$\sigma_x \begin{pmatrix} \psi_1 \\ \psi_2 \end{pmatrix} = \begin{pmatrix} 0 & 1 \\ 1 & 0 \end{pmatrix} \begin{pmatrix} \psi_1 \\ \psi_2 \end{pmatrix} = \begin{pmatrix} \psi_2 \\ \psi_1 \end{pmatrix} \quad (26)$$

$$\sigma_y \begin{pmatrix} \psi_1 \\ \psi_2 \end{pmatrix} = \begin{pmatrix} 0 & -i \\ i & 0 \end{pmatrix} \begin{pmatrix} \psi_1 \\ \psi_2 \end{pmatrix} = \begin{pmatrix} -i\psi_2 \\ i\psi_1 \end{pmatrix} \quad (27)$$

$$\sigma_z \begin{pmatrix} \psi_1 \\ \psi_2 \end{pmatrix} = \begin{pmatrix} 1 & 0 \\ 0 & -1 \end{pmatrix} \begin{pmatrix} \psi_1 \\ \psi_2 \end{pmatrix} = \begin{pmatrix} \psi_1 \\ -\psi_2 \end{pmatrix}. \quad (28)$$

Similarly,

$$s_x \begin{pmatrix} \psi_1 \\ \psi_2 \end{pmatrix} = \tfrac{1}{2}\hbar \begin{pmatrix} \psi_2 \\ \psi_1 \end{pmatrix}, \qquad s_y \begin{pmatrix} \psi_1 \\ \psi_2 \end{pmatrix} = \tfrac{1}{2}\hbar \begin{pmatrix} -i\psi_2 \\ i\psi_1 \end{pmatrix},$$

$$s_z \begin{pmatrix} \psi_1 \\ \psi_2 \end{pmatrix} = \tfrac{1}{2}\hbar \begin{pmatrix} \psi_1 \\ -\psi_2 \end{pmatrix}. \tag{29}$$

The rule remains formally the same when the elements of a matrix are differential operators; for example,

$$p_x \psi = \begin{pmatrix} p_x & 0 \\ 0 & p_x \end{pmatrix} \begin{pmatrix} \psi_1 \\ \psi_2 \end{pmatrix} = \begin{pmatrix} p_x\psi_1 \\ p_x\psi_2 \end{pmatrix} = \begin{pmatrix} -i\hbar\partial\psi_1/\partial x \\ -i\hbar\partial\psi_2/\partial x \end{pmatrix}. \tag{30}$$

A Pauli operator can usually be written in various forms having different degrees of explicitness. For example, in the case of the x-component of linear momentum, we have the alternative forms

$$p_x, \qquad \begin{pmatrix} p_x & 0 \\ 0 & p_x \end{pmatrix}, \qquad \begin{pmatrix} -i\hbar \dfrac{\partial}{\partial x} & 0 \\ 0 & -i\hbar \dfrac{\partial}{\partial x} \end{pmatrix}, \qquad -i\hbar \begin{pmatrix} \dfrac{\partial}{\partial x} & 0 \\ 0 & \dfrac{\partial}{\partial x} \end{pmatrix}, \tag{31}$$

and so on, any one of which can be substituted for another as occasion demands.

Eigenvalues and eigen-ψ's are defined in Pauli's theory in our standard way: if an operator α, a well-behaved operand ψ, and a number λ satisfy the equation

$$\alpha\psi = \lambda\psi, \tag{32}$$

then ψ is said to be an *eigen-ψ* of α, λ is said to be an *eigenvalue* of α, and the eigen-ψ ψ and the eigenvalue λ of α are said to belong to each other.

If α is a matrix with numerical elements, then (32) is an ordinary matrix eigenvalue equation, and the eigenvalues of α are computed by the methods of §56, that is, by means of the secular equation. The eigen-ψ's are then also found by the standard matrix methods, except that ψ_1 and ψ_2 are now allowed to be well-behaved functions of x, y, and z.

If α is a differential operator, then, according to (19), Equation (32) takes the form

$$\begin{pmatrix} \alpha\psi_1 \\ \alpha\psi_2 \end{pmatrix} = \begin{pmatrix} \lambda\psi_1 \\ \lambda\psi_2 \end{pmatrix} \tag{33}$$

and splits up into the following pair of simultaneous equations

$$\begin{cases} \alpha\psi_1 = \lambda\psi_1 \\ \alpha\psi_2 = \lambda\psi_2 \end{cases} \tag{34}$$

which does not have dependent variables in common, and each member of which is just the Schroedinger eigenvalue equation for the operator α. It follows, in particular, that the Pauli theory and the Schroedinger theory agree as to the possible values of such dynamical variables as linear momenta and orbital angular momenta.

If α involves both matrices and differential operators, then (32) again splits up into a pair of (usually differential) equations; if the matrices involved in α are not diagonal, then ψ_1 and ψ_2 become interrelated, and the problem of solving the equations for ψ_1 and ψ_2 may become complicated.

The handling of the eigenvalue equation will be illustrated in the Exercises and in §87.

Concluding remarks. Every Pauli ψ pertaining to a system whose Hamiltonian is H is required to depend on the time t in such a way as to satisfy the equation

$$H\psi = i\hbar \frac{\partial \psi}{\partial t}, \tag{35}$$

where H is the Pauli operator associated with the Hamiltonian, and

$$\frac{\partial}{\partial t} \psi = \frac{\partial}{\partial t} \begin{pmatrix} \psi_1 \\ \psi_2 \end{pmatrix} = \begin{pmatrix} \partial\psi_1/\partial t \\ \partial\psi_2/\partial t \end{pmatrix}. \tag{36}$$

Equation (35) has the form of the second Schroedinger equation.

The expected average of a dynamical variable α for a state ψ is taken in Pauli's theory to be

$$\mathrm{av}_\psi \alpha = \frac{\int \bar\psi \alpha \psi \, d\tau}{\int \bar\psi \psi \, d\tau}, \tag{37}$$

where α in the numerator is the Pauli operator associated with the dynamical variable α and where, as indicated, the integrals extend over all space. Note that the Pauli expectation formula (37) is formally identical with the Schroedinger expectation formula 8^{77}.

Exercises

1. Show that the rules given in the text for handling Pauli operators are consistent with the definitions of operator sum and operator product adopted in §2.

2. Verify that the Pauli operators x and p_x satisfy the equation $xp_x - p_xx = i\hbar$.

3. Show that, if $\psi = \begin{pmatrix} f(r, \theta)e^{i\phi} \\ f(r, \theta)e^{-i\phi} \end{pmatrix}$, then $\text{av}_\psi \, L_z = 0$, $\text{av}_\psi \, L_z^2 = \hbar^2$, $\text{av}_\psi \, L_z^3 = 0$, and so on. What is the distribution-in-L_z for this state?

4. Let $\psi(\sigma_i^+)$ denote the eigen-ψ's of the spin matrix σ_i belonging to the eigenvalue 1 of σ_i, and $\psi(\sigma_i^-)$ denote the eigen-ψ's of σ_i belonging to the eigenvalue -1 of σ_i. Show that then

$$\psi(\sigma_x^+) = \begin{pmatrix} f_1 \\ f_1 \end{pmatrix}, \qquad \psi(\sigma_y^+) = \begin{pmatrix} f_2 \\ if_2 \end{pmatrix}, \qquad \psi(\sigma_z^+) = \begin{pmatrix} f_3 \\ 0 \end{pmatrix}$$

$$\psi(\sigma_x^-) = \begin{pmatrix} g_1 \\ -g_1 \end{pmatrix}, \qquad \psi(\sigma_y^-) = \begin{pmatrix} ig_2 \\ g_2 \end{pmatrix}, \qquad \psi(\sigma_z^-) = \begin{pmatrix} 0 \\ g_3 \end{pmatrix}.$$

where each f and g is an arbitrary well-behaved function of x, y, and z. Note that $\psi(\sigma_x^+)$ is an eigen-ψ of s_x belonging to the eigenvalue $\frac{1}{2}\hbar$ of s_x, and so forth.

5. Show that, for a state for which the value of any one of the three variables s_x, s_y, and s_z is a certainty, the values of each of the other two s's are equally likely to be $\frac{1}{2}\hbar$ or $-\frac{1}{2}\hbar$.

6. Adopt $s_x \cos \alpha + s_y \cos \beta + s_z \cos \gamma$ (that is, the expression suggested by classical analogy) for the operator associated with the component of spin angular momentum s in the direction making the angles α, β, and γ with the x-, y-, and z-axis, and show that the possible values of a component of s, quite independently of the direction in which the component may be taken, are $\pm\frac{1}{2}\hbar$.

7. Let J denote the *total* angular momentum of the electron (Fig. 110), so that

$$J = L + s, \tag{38}$$

$$J_x = L_x + s_x, \qquad J_y = L_y + s_y, \qquad J_z = L_z + s_z, \tag{39}$$

and

$$J^2 = J_x^2 + J_y^2 + J_z^2 = (L_x + s_x)^2 + (L_y + s_y)^2 + (L_z + s_z)^2. \tag{40}$$

Show that the Pauli operators associated with J_z and J^2 are

(22) $$J_z = \begin{pmatrix} L_z + \frac{1}{2}\hbar & 0 \\ 0 & L_z - \frac{1}{2}\hbar \end{pmatrix} \tag{41}$$

and

$$J^2 = \begin{pmatrix} L^2 + \hbar L_z + \frac{3}{4}\hbar^2 & \hbar(L_x - iL_y) \\ \hbar(L_x + iL_y) & L^2 - \hbar L_z + \frac{3}{4}\hbar^2 \end{pmatrix} \tag{42}$$

where the L's are the appropriate Schroedinger operators.

8. Show that the operators J_x, J_y, and J_z satisfy the commutation rules 1[85].

9. Show that the Pauli operators J^2, J_z, and L^2 commute with each other. In these computations, the forms $J_z = L_z + \frac{1}{2}\hbar\sigma_z$ and $J^2 = L^2 + \hbar(L_x\sigma_x + L_y\sigma_y + L_z\sigma_z) + \frac{3}{4}\hbar^2$ are more convenient than the more explicit forms (41) and (42).

87. The Simultaneous Eigen-ψ's of J_z, L^2, and J^2

Let us now consider briefly an electron that possesses a spin angular momentum and a spin magnetic moment and that moves *classically* in a central electrostatic field. The orbital angular momentum L of the electron, its spin angular momentum s, and its total angular momentum J are shown diagramatically in Fig. 110.

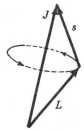

Fig. 110.
Classical vector diagram for orbital, spin, and total angular momenta.

Since the central electrostatic field exerts no torque on our electron, its total angular momentum is conserved:

(a) the total angular momentum J is a constant of motion; that is, J_x, J_y, J_z, and J are each a constant of motion.

Now, the orbital motion of the electron, which may be likened to the flow of an electric current, produces an orbital magnetic moment, whose value is given by 3[84]. This magnetic moment exerts a torque on the spin magnetic moment and thus tends to alter the direction, though not the magnitude, of the latter, that is, it causes the latter to precess; and, since the spin angular momentum and the spin magnetic moment are proportional to one another, we conclude that

(b) the spin angular momentum s undergoes a precession and is therefore not a constant of motion; but its magnitude s is a constant of motion.

Considering the torque exerted by the spin magnetic moment on the orbital magnetic moment, we find in a similar way that

(c) the angular momentum L undergoes a precession and is therefore not a constant of motion; but its magnitude L is a constant of motion.

It finally follows from (a), (b), and (c) that

(d) the vectors L and s precess about the vector J.

These precessions are indicated in Fig. 110 by the curved arrows.

We shall see in the next section that in the Pauli theory of an electron in a central electrostatic field the dynamical variables J_x, J_y, J_z, J, s, and L are constants of motion, just as the classical arguments indicated above would lead us to expect. In particular, the dynamical variables

$$J_z,\ L^2,\ J^2,\qquad\qquad (1)$$

which were shown in Exercise 9^{86} to commute with one another, are a set of *commuting constants of motion*. We prefer the set (1) to such sets as J_x, L^2, and J^2, or J_z, L, and J, because of the relative convenience of the operators involved. We omit s and s^2 from the set because these constants of motion are merely *numerical* constants and therefore are not helpful in computations; indeed, $s^2 = s_x^2 + s_y^2 + s_z^2 = (\tfrac{1}{2}\hbar)^2(\sigma_x^2 + \sigma_y^2 + \sigma_z^2) = \tfrac{3}{4}\hbar^2$, and $s = \tfrac{1}{2}\sqrt{3}\hbar$.

In computing the eigen-ψ's of a Hamiltonian H, we may, according to the expansion theorem, restrict ourselves to those eigen-ψ's of H which are simultaneously eigen-ψ's of a set of commuting constants of motion. In particular, in treating the central motion of an electron by the Pauli method we may restrict ourselves to those eigen-ψ's of H which are simultaneously eigen-ψ's of J_z, L^2, and J^2. Therefore, in preparation for the problem of central motion, we shall now compute the simultaneous eigen-ψ's of J_z, L^2, and J^2.

The eigen-ψ's of J_z. We denote the eigenvalues of J_z by $m\hbar$, where m is as yet undetermined.[9] In view of 41^{86}, the eigenvalue equation

$$J_z\psi = m\hbar\psi \tag{2}$$

takes the form

$$\begin{pmatrix} L_z + \tfrac{1}{2}\hbar & 0 \\ 0 & L_z - \tfrac{1}{2}\hbar \end{pmatrix} \begin{pmatrix} \psi_1 \\ \psi_2 \end{pmatrix} = m\hbar \begin{pmatrix} \psi_1 \\ \psi_2 \end{pmatrix} \tag{3}$$

and splits up into the two equations

$$\begin{cases} (L_z + \tfrac{1}{2}\hbar)\psi_1 = m\hbar\psi_1 \\ (L_z - \tfrac{1}{2}\hbar)\psi_2 = m\hbar\psi_2, \end{cases} \tag{4}$$

that is,

$$\begin{cases} \left(-i\dfrac{\partial}{\partial\phi} + \tfrac{1}{2}\right)\psi_1 = m\psi_1 \\ \left(-i\dfrac{\partial}{\partial\phi} - \tfrac{1}{2}\right)\psi_2 = m\psi_2. \end{cases} \tag{5}$$

The respective general solutions of the differential equations (5) are

$$\psi_1 = A_1(r, \theta)e^{i(m-\frac{1}{2})\phi}, \qquad \psi_2 = A_2(r, \theta)e^{i(m+\frac{1}{2})\phi}, \tag{6}$$

---

[9] This m must not be confused with the mass of the electron. A more explicit symbol for the eigenvalues of J_z is $m_j\hbar$.

and we note that to assure single-valuedness of ψ_1 and ψ_2 we must restrict m to the values $\pm\frac{1}{2}$, $\pm\frac{3}{2}$, $\pm\frac{5}{2}$, $\cdots$; and hence

$$J_z \stackrel{\circ}{=} m\hbar, \quad m = \pm\tfrac{1}{2}, \pm\tfrac{3}{2}, \pm\tfrac{5}{2}, \cdots. \quad (7)$$

The case of a single spinning electron thus corresponds to the possibility 16^{85} rather than 15^{85}.

The eigen-ψ's of J_z belonging to the eigenvalue $m\hbar$ of J_z, which we denote by $\psi(m)$, are, accordingly,

$$\psi(m) = \begin{pmatrix} A_1(r, \theta)e^{i(m-\frac{1}{2})\phi} \\ A_2(r, \theta)e^{i(m+\frac{1}{2})\phi} \end{pmatrix}, \quad (8)$$

where the values of m are those given in (7) and where $A_1(r, \theta)$ and $A_2(r, \theta)$ are arbitrary well-behaved functions of r and θ, except that one of them can be taken as zero.

The simultaneous eigen-ψ's of J_z and L^2. Since the eigenvalues of L^2 are known to be $l(l + 1)\hbar^2$, with $l = 0, 1, 2, \cdots$, we write the eigenvalue equation for L^2 from the outset as

$$L^2 \begin{pmatrix} \psi_1 \\ \psi_2 \end{pmatrix} = l(l + 1)\hbar^2 \begin{pmatrix} \psi_1 \\ \psi_2 \end{pmatrix}. \quad (9)$$

This equation splits up into the two Schroedinger eigenvalue equations

$$\begin{cases} L^2\psi_1 = l(l + 1)\hbar^2\psi_1 \\ L^2\psi_2 = l(l + 1)\hbar^2\psi_2, \end{cases} \quad (10)$$

and it follows from 67^{74} that

$$\psi_1 = R_1 \Upsilon(l, m'), \qquad \psi_2 = R_2 \Upsilon(l, m''), \quad (11)$$

or, more explicitly (we absorb the factor $(2\pi)^{-\frac{1}{2}}$ of the Υ's in the R's),

$$\psi_1 = R_1 \Theta_l^{m'} e^{im'\phi}, \qquad \psi_2 = R_2 \Theta_l^{m''} e^{im''\phi}, \quad (12)$$

where R_1 and R_2 are arbitrary well-behaved functions of r, and m' and m'' are integers, zero included, such that $|\,m'\,| \leq l$ and $|\,m''\,| \leq l$.

Comparison of (11) with (8) now shows that to get a ψ [we denote such a ψ by $\psi(lm)$] that is simultaneously an eigen-ψ of J_z belonging to the eigenvalue $m\hbar$ of J_z and an eigen-ψ of L^2

belonging to the eigenvalue $l(l + 1)\hbar^2$ of L^2 we must set $m' = m - \frac{1}{2}$ and $m'' = m + \frac{1}{2}$, so that

$$\psi(l\ m) = \begin{pmatrix} R_1 \Upsilon(l, m - \frac{1}{2}) \\ R_2 \Upsilon(l, m + \frac{1}{2}) \end{pmatrix}. \tag{13}$$

The well-behaved radial factors R_1 and R_2 remain undetermined and unrelated, except that at most one of them can be taken as zero.

The simultaneous eigenfunctions of J_z, L^2, and J^2. We finally proceed to adjust (13) so as to make it an eigenfunction of J^2; that is, writing the eigenvalues of J^2 in the form $j(j + 1)\hbar^2$, with j as yet undetermined, we proceed to force (13) to satisfy the eigenvalue equation

$$J^2 \begin{pmatrix} R_1 \Upsilon_l^\alpha \\ R_2 \Upsilon_l^\beta \end{pmatrix} = j(j + 1)\hbar^2 \begin{pmatrix} R_1 \Upsilon_l^\alpha \\ R_2 \Upsilon_l^\beta \end{pmatrix}, \tag{14}$$

where we have used the temporary abbreviations

$$\alpha = m - \tfrac{1}{2}, \qquad\qquad \beta = m + \tfrac{1}{2}. \tag{15}$$

Using J^2 in the form 42^{86}, we find that (14) splits up into the two equations[10]

$$\begin{cases} (L^2 + \hbar L_z + \frac{3}{4}\hbar^2)R_1 \Upsilon_l^\alpha + \hbar(L_x - iL_y)R_2 \Upsilon_l^\beta = j(j + 1)\hbar^2 R_1 \Upsilon_l^\alpha \\ \hbar(L_x + iL_y)R_1 \Upsilon_l^\alpha + (L^2 - \hbar L_z + \frac{3}{4}\hbar^2)R_2 \Upsilon_l^\beta = j(j + 1)\hbar^2 R_2 \Upsilon_l^\beta, \end{cases} \tag{16}$$

which, in view of Equations 12^A to 15^A, reduce to

$$\begin{cases} [l(l + 1) + \alpha + \frac{3}{4}]R_1 \Upsilon_l^\alpha + H_l^\beta R_2 \Upsilon_l^\alpha = j(j + 1)R_1 \Upsilon_l^\alpha \\ G_l^\alpha R_1 \Upsilon_l^\beta + [l(l + 1) - \beta + \frac{3}{4}]R_2 \Upsilon_l^\beta = j(j + 1)R_2 \Upsilon_l^\beta \end{cases} \tag{17}$$

where, according to 10^A,

$$H_l^\beta = G_l^\alpha = \sqrt{(l + \tfrac{1}{2})^2 - m^2}. \tag{18}$$

The angle factors in each of the equations (17) cancel out, and we get

$$\begin{cases} [l(l + 1) - j(j + 1) + m + \frac{1}{4}]R_1 + \sqrt{(l + \frac{1}{2})^2 - m^2}\, R_2 = 0 \\ \sqrt{(l + \frac{1}{2})^2 - m^2}\, R_1 + [l(l + 1) - j(j + 1) - m + \frac{1}{4}]R_2 = 0. \end{cases} \tag{19}$$

---

[10] We restrict ourselves to the case when both Υ's in (13) are different from zero, but write our final results in completed form; see Exercises 1 and 3.

Thus in an eigen-ψ of J^2 the radial factors R_1 and R_2 are no longer unrelated.

Equations (19) can be made consistent by a proper choice of the quantum number j, called the *inner quantum number*, which so far has been undetermined. Inspection of (19) shows that the condition for the vanishing of the determinant of the coefficients is

$$[l(l+1) - j(j+1) + \tfrac{1}{4}]^2 = (l + \tfrac{1}{2})^2, \qquad (20)$$

that is,

$$l(l+1) - j(j+1) + \tfrac{1}{4} = \pm(l + \tfrac{1}{2}). \qquad (21)$$

Taking the lower sign, we get the possibility

$$j(j+1) = l(l+1) + (l + \tfrac{1}{2}) + \tfrac{1}{4} = (l + \tfrac{1}{2})(l + \tfrac{3}{2}). \qquad (22)$$

One root of this equation is

$$j = l + \tfrac{1}{2}, \qquad l = 0, 1, 2, \cdots, \qquad (23)$$

and the second root is $-l - \tfrac{3}{2}$; but, since j appears in (19) only in the combination $j(j+1)$, the second root adds nothing new. Similarly, the upper sign in (21) yields

$$j(j+1) = l(l+1) - (l + \tfrac{1}{2}) + \tfrac{1}{4} = (l - \tfrac{1}{2})(l + \tfrac{1}{2}), \qquad (24)$$

so that

$$j = l - \tfrac{1}{2}, \qquad l = 1, 2, 3, \cdots, \qquad (25)$$

while the second root of (24) adds nothing new. The inclusion of $l = 0$ in (23) and its omission in (25) are justified by a special consideration of the case $l = 0$, to be taken up in Exercise 3.

Substituting (23) into (19), we find that $R_1/R_2 = \sqrt{l + \tfrac{1}{2} + m}/\sqrt{l + \tfrac{1}{2} - m}$, that is,

$$R_1 = \sqrt{l + \tfrac{1}{2} + m}\,R, \qquad R_2 = \sqrt{l + \tfrac{1}{2} - m}\,R, \qquad (26)$$

where R is an arbitrary (well-behaved) function of r. The result of substituting (26) into (13) will be denoted by $\psi(l, j = l + \tfrac{1}{2}, m)$:

$$\psi(l, j = l + \tfrac{1}{2}, m)$$
$$= \begin{pmatrix} \sqrt{l + \tfrac{1}{2} + m}\,R\Upsilon(l, m - \tfrac{1}{2}) \\ \sqrt{l + \tfrac{1}{2} - m}\,R\Upsilon(l, m + \tfrac{1}{2}) \end{pmatrix}, \qquad l = 0, 1, 2, \cdots. \qquad (27)$$

The expression (27) is *one* form of the simultaneous eigen-ψ's of J_z, L^2, and J^2.

To get the remaining simultaneous eigen-ψ's of J_z, L^2, and J^2, which we denote by $\psi(l, j = l - \frac{1}{2}, m)$, we substitute (25) into (19) and find that

$$R_1 = \sqrt{l + \tfrac{1}{2} - m}\, R, \qquad R_2 = -\sqrt{l + \tfrac{1}{2} + m}\, R, \qquad (28)$$

and that hence

$$\psi(l, j = l - \tfrac{1}{2}, m)$$

$$= \begin{pmatrix} \sqrt{l + \tfrac{1}{2} - m}\, R\Upsilon(l, m - \tfrac{1}{2}) \\ -\sqrt{l + \tfrac{1}{2} + m}\, R\Upsilon(l, m + \tfrac{1}{2}) \end{pmatrix}, \qquad l = 1, 2, 3, \cdots, \qquad (29)$$

where the radial factor R need not be related to that in (27).

Exercises

1. Set $m = l + \frac{1}{2}$ in (13) and show that the corresponding simultaneous eigen-ψ of J_z, L^2, and J^2 is included in (27); show that (29) does not provide for the case $m = l + \frac{1}{2}$ and explain why this is to be expected on intuitive physical grounds. Consider in a similar way the case $m = -l - \frac{1}{2}$.

2. Show that, if $m = \pm(l + \frac{1}{2})$, then the simultaneous eigen-ψ's of J_z, L^2, and J^2 are also eigen-ψ's of L_z and s_z, and explain why this is to be expected on intuitive physical grounds.

3. Use the result of Exercise 1 to justify the inclusion of $l = 0$ in (27) and its omission in (29).

4. Verify that for a state of the form (27) we have:

J_z: certainly $m\hbar$

L^2: certainly $l(l + 1)\hbar^2$

J^2: certainly $j(j + 1)\hbar^2 = (l + \frac{1}{2})(l + \frac{3}{2})\hbar^2$

L_z: av $L_z = \dfrac{2lm\hbar}{2l + 1}$; $\begin{cases} \text{possible values:} \quad (m - \frac{1}{2})\hbar \qquad (m + \frac{1}{2})\hbar \\ \text{rel. probabilities:} (l + \frac{1}{2} + m) \qquad (l + \frac{1}{2} - m) \end{cases}$

s_z: av $s_z = \dfrac{m\hbar}{2l + 1}$; $\begin{cases} \text{possible values:} \qquad \frac{1}{2}\hbar \qquad\qquad -\frac{1}{2}\hbar \\ \text{rel. probabilities:} (l + \frac{1}{2} + m) \qquad (l + \frac{1}{2} - m). \end{cases}$

5. Consider states of the form (29) along the lines of Exercises 4 and show that the differences between the new and the former results are consistent with the fact that now $J^2 < L^2$, while formerly $J^2 > L^2$.

6. Show that (27) and (29) are eigen-ψ's of the operator

$$L_x s_x + L_y s_y + L_z s_z,$$

which is usually denoted by $L \cdot s$, and that in fact

$$L \cdot s\, \psi(l, j = l + \tfrac{1}{2}, m) = \tfrac{1}{2}l\hbar^2 \psi(l, j = l + \tfrac{1}{2}, m) \qquad (30)$$

and

$$L \cdot s\, \psi(l, j = l - \tfrac{1}{2}, m) = -\tfrac{1}{2}(l + 1)\hbar^2 \psi(l, j = l - \tfrac{1}{2}, m). \qquad (31)$$

88. Spin-Orbit Interaction and the Spin Correction

We now proceed to set up the Pauli Hamiltonian for an electron in a central electrostatic field described by a potential function $V(r)$. The total energy of the electron now consists of three parts: the kinetic energy, the potential energy, and the energy due to the interaction of the spin magnetic moment $-es/mc$ with the orbital magnetic moment $-eL/2mc$; the latter energy is called the *spin-orbit* interaction energy. The kinetic and potential energies are quantities with which we are familiar; but new considerations are required for the spin-orbit interaction.

Now, the case of two bar magnets suggests that the spin-orbit interaction energy should be proportional to the respective magnitudes of the orbital magnetic moment and the spin magnetic moment, and to the cosine of the angle between the two moments; that is, because of the proportionality of the orbital magnetic moment to L and the proportionality of the spin magnetic moment to s, we may expect the spin-orbit interaction energy to contain the factor $L \cdot s$, that is, $L_x s_x + L_y s_y + L_z s_z$. Further, we would expect this energy to depend on the distance of the electron from the center of the field. The interaction energy would thus be expected to have the form

$$\xi(r) L \cdot s, \tag{1}$$

where $\xi(r)$ is a function of r whose form depends on the potential field.

The intricate problem of evaluating the spin-orbit interaction energy was considered in the light of classical analogy by Thomas[11] and by Frenkel;[11] and both concluded that this energy is given by (1) with

$$\xi(r) = \frac{1}{2m^2 c^2} \frac{1}{r} \frac{dV(r)}{dr}. \tag{2}$$

For example, in the case of the Coulomb potential $-e^2/r$, the spin-orbit interaction energy is computed to be

$$\frac{e^2}{2m^2 c^2} \frac{1}{r^3} L \cdot s. \tag{3}$$

---

[11] L. H. Thomas, *Nature*, **117**, 514 (1926). J. Frenkel, *Zeits. f. Physik*, **37**, 243 (1926). Kemble, Section 58d.

Recalling 3^{78}, we now write our complete Hamiltonian operator as

$$H = \frac{1}{2m} p_r^2 + \frac{1}{2mr^2} L^2 + V(r) + \xi(r) L \cdot s, \tag{4}$$

where

$\langle 24^{77} \rangle$
$$p_r = -i\hbar \left(\frac{\partial}{\partial r} + \frac{1}{r} \right). \tag{5}$$

Constants of motion and the two radial equations. The operators

$$J_z , L^2, J^2, \tag{6}$$

which, according to Exercise 9^{86}, commute with each other, do not involve the operators r or $\partial/\partial r$ and consequently commute with operators involving only r and $\partial/\partial r$. Further, since $J^2 = (L + s)^2 = L^2 + s^2 + 2(L_x s_x + L_y s_y + L_z s_z) = L^2 + \frac{3}{4}\hbar^2 + 2L \cdot s$, so that

$$2L \cdot s = J^2 - L^2 - \tfrac{3}{4}\hbar^2, \tag{7}$$

the operators (6) also commute with the operator $L \cdot s$. Hence J_z, L^2, and J^2 commute with every term in the Hamiltonian (4) and, as already mentioned in §87, constitute a set of commuting constants of motion in the Pauli theory of an electron in a central field. In computing the eigenvalues of (4) we therefore may, according to the expansion theorem, restrict ourselves to ψ's that are simultaneous eigen-ψ's of J_z, L^2, and J^2, that is, to ψ's of the forms 27^{87} and 29^{87}. In other words, instead of treating the eigenvalue equation $H\psi = E\psi$ in its generality, we may restrict ourselves to the simpler problem of studying separately the two equations

$$H\psi(l, j = l + \tfrac{1}{2}, m) = E\psi(l, j = l + \tfrac{1}{2}, m) \tag{8}$$

and

$$H\psi(l, i = l - \tfrac{1}{2}, m) = E\psi(l, j = l - \tfrac{1}{2}, m). \tag{9}$$

Now,

$$H\psi(l, j = l + \tfrac{1}{2}, m) = \left[\frac{1}{2m} p_r^2 + \frac{1}{2mr^2} L^2 \right.$$
$$\left. + V(r) + \xi(r) L \cdot s \right] \psi(l, j = l + \tfrac{1}{2}, m), \tag{10}$$

so that, in view of 30[87] and the fact that our ψ is an eigen-ψ of L^2 belonging to the eigenvalue $l(l + 1)\hbar^2$,

$$H\psi(l, j = l + \tfrac{1}{2}, m) = \left[\frac{1}{2m} p_r^2 + \frac{l(l + 1)\hbar^2}{2mr^2} + V(r) + \tfrac{1}{2}l\hbar^2\xi(r)\right]\psi(l, j = l + \tfrac{1}{2}, m). \quad (11)$$

The bracketed operator in (11) is free from matrices and hence does not mix the two components of ψ. Therefore, when we introduce the explicit form 27[87] for ψ, and (8) splits up into two equations, the angle factors cancel out in each equation and both equations reduce to the same radial equation, namely,

$$\left[\frac{1}{2m} p_r^2 + \frac{l(l + 1)\hbar^2}{2mr^2} + V(r) + \tfrac{1}{2}l\hbar^2\xi(r)\right]R = ER.$$

$$\begin{cases} j = l + \tfrac{1}{2} \\ l = 0, 1, 2, \cdots. \end{cases} \quad (12)$$

Treating (9) in a similar way, we get another radial equation, namely,

$$\left[\frac{1}{2m} p_r^2 + \frac{l(l + 1)\hbar^2}{2mr^2} + V(r) - \tfrac{1}{2}(l + 1)\hbar^2\xi(r)\right]R = ER$$

$$\begin{cases} j = l - \tfrac{1}{2} \\ l = 1, 2, 3, \cdots. \end{cases} \quad (13)$$

The energy levels of our system are thus the values of E which yield well-behaved solutions of (12) and also the values of E which yield well-behaved solutions of (13).

Apart from the terms in $\xi(r)$, Equations (12) and (13) are both identical with the Schroedinger radial equation

$$\langle 8^{78}\rangle \qquad \left[\frac{1}{2m} p_r^2 + \frac{l(l + 1)\hbar^2}{2mr^2} + V(r)\right]R = ER. \quad (14)$$

Since spin effects are known to be small, we may consider the terms in $\xi(r)$ as perturbing potentials and may handle (12) and (13) by perturbation methods.

The spin corrections for hydrogen. If $\psi(n\,l\,m_l)$ is the normalized Schroedinger eigenfunction 25^{80} of the Hamiltonian of hydrogen, then[12]

$$\int \bar{\psi}(n\,l\,m_l) \frac{1}{r^3} \psi(n\,l\,m_l)\,d\tau = \frac{1}{n^3 l(l+\frac{1}{2})(l+1)}\frac{1}{a_0^3}, \quad (15)$$

where a_0 is the Bohr radius 21^{80}. For hydrogen, $\xi(r) = e^2/2m^2c^2r^3$, so that for the hydrogen state $\psi(n\,l\,m_l)$ the average value of the quantity $\frac{1}{2}l\hbar^2\,\xi(r)$, that is, of the perturbing potential in (12), is

$$\frac{1}{2}l\hbar^2 \cdot \frac{e^2}{2m^2c^2} \cdot \frac{1}{n^3 l(l+\frac{1}{2})(l+1)a_0^3} = \frac{|E_n|\,\alpha^2}{4n^2}\frac{4n}{(2l+1)(l+1)}, \quad (16)$$

where E_n is the nth Bohr level 18^{80} and α is the fine-structure constant 6^{82}. Similarly, for the hydrogen state $\psi(n\,l\,m_l)$, the average value of $-\frac{1}{2}(l+1)\hbar^2\xi(r)$, that is, of the perturbing potential in (13), is

$$-\frac{|E_n|\,\alpha^2}{4n^2}\frac{4n}{l(2l+1)}. \quad (17)$$

Now, in three-dimensional perturbed motion, just as in the one-dimensional case treated in §36, the first-order energy correction for a nondegenerate perturbed level equals the average of the perturbing potential for the corresponding unperturbed state. A closer study shows that this simple result holds in our present case in spite of the degeneracy of the Bohr levels; and consequently the eigenvalue of (12) which belongs to the state $\psi(n, l, j = l + \frac{1}{2}, m)$ and which we denote by $E(n, l, j = l + \frac{1}{2})$ can be obtained in the hydrogen case to the first approximation[13] by adding the quantity (16) to the energy E_n of the Schroedinger state $\psi(n\,l\,m_l)$. Treating (13) in a similar way, we get our final results:

$$\begin{cases} E(n, l, j = l + \tfrac{1}{2}) = E_n + \dfrac{|E_n|\,\alpha^2}{4n^2}\dfrac{4n}{(2l+1)(l+1)} & (18a) \\[3mm] E(n, l, j = l - \tfrac{1}{2}) = E_n - \dfrac{|E_n|\,\alpha^2}{4n^2}\dfrac{4n}{l(2l+1)}. & (18b) \end{cases}$$

The levels (18) are shown in Fig. 111, the left portion of which is a reproduction of Fig. 107^{82}. The values of j are indicated at

---

[12] Condon and Shortley, page 117.

[13] Here 'to the first approximation' means 'correctly to terms in $1/c^2$.'

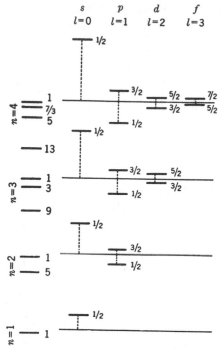

Fig. 111. Spin corrections for hydrogen. The Sommerfeld levels are shown at the left. The odd half-integers are the values of j.

the right of the levels; the vertical lines connect the sublevels with their parent Bohr levels. Note that each s-level is raised and each of the other levels is split up into a doublet; each sub-level is of course degenerate with respect to m. The arrangement of the levels is different from that required by experiment, and their number is almost twice too great. The spin corrections alone are thus insufficient to bring agreement with experiment; but we shall see in the next section that we do get the desired results when the spin corrections are combined with the relativity corrections.

The s-levels. The quantity $L \cdot s$ is zero whenever $L = 0$, so that the spin-orbit interaction energy (3) is zero whenever $L = 0$. Since $L = 0$ for s-states, the formula (3) thus implies that the spin-orbit interaction energy is zero for s-states, that is, that the spin causes no displacement in s-levels. This conclusion is borne out by (12), which becomes identical with the Schroedinger radial equation (14) whenever $l = 0$.

Yet (18a) gives a nonvanishing spin correction even when $l = 0$; and, what is more, the correction it gives when $l = 0$ is correct. Two questions therefore arise: Why does (18a) give a *nonvanishing* correction when $l = 0$? And why does (18a) give the *correct* nonvanishing correction when $l = 0$? The answer to the first question lies in the fact that the average value of r^{-3} given by (15) contains the factor l in the denominator, and that in getting the correction (16) we have canceled this l with the l

that multiplies $\xi(r)$ in (12). To the second question there is perhaps no satisfactory answer, and we may summarize the situation as follows: the Pauli method fails when applied specifically to an s-state; but, perhaps fortuitously, the correct spin correction for an s-state can nevertheless be found by extrapolating to the case $l = 0$ the Pauli results computed for $l > 0$.

Exercises

   1. Derive the radial equation (13).
   2. Extend Fig. 111 through $n = 5$.

89. The Spin-and-Relativity Correction for Hydrogen

We now turn to a Pauli electron moving relativistically in a Coulomb field. One way of treating this problem is to replace the nonrelativistic Pauli Hamiltonian 4^{88} by the appropriate relativistic Pauli Hamiltonian and to compute the eigenvalues of the latter.[14] But the simpler way, which we shall follow, is merely to combine the relativity corrections for the Schroedinger hydrogen atom, found in §83 to be

$$(16^{83}) \qquad -\frac{|E_n|\,\alpha^2}{4n^2}\left(\frac{4n}{l+\frac{1}{2}}-3\right)+mc^2, \qquad (1)$$

with the Pauli spin corrections for the Schroedinger hydrogen atom computed in §88.

In the case $j = l + \frac{1}{2}$, the spin correction is

$$(18a^{88}) \qquad \frac{|E_n|\,\alpha^2}{4n^2}\,\frac{4n}{(2l+1)(l+1)}. \qquad (2)$$

The sum of (1) and (2) is

$$-\frac{|E_n|\,\alpha^2}{4n^2}\left(\frac{4n}{l+1}-3\right)+mc^2, \qquad (3)$$

that is, since $j = l + \frac{1}{2}$,

$$-\frac{|E_n|\,\alpha^2}{4n^2}\left(\frac{4n}{j+\frac{1}{2}}-3\right)+mc^2. \qquad (4)$$

---

[14] Compare C. G. Darwin, *Proc. Roy. Soc.*, **116A**, 227 (1927).

In the case $j = l - \frac{1}{2}$, the sum of the relativity correction (1) and the spin correction given by 18b[88] is

$$- \frac{|E_n|\,\alpha^2}{4n^2}\left(\frac{4n}{l} - 3\right) + mc^2, \tag{5}$$

so that we get the expression (4) once again. Thus the spin-and-relativity corrections depend only on j and, except for the limitations that the value of l places on the values of j, are independent of l.

Adding (4) to Bohr's E_n and denoting the resulting energy levels by E_{nj}, we finally get

$$E_{nj} = E_n - \frac{|E_n|\,\alpha^2}{4n^2}\left(\frac{4n}{j + \frac{1}{2}} - 3\right) + mc^2. \tag{6}$$

Since $j = \frac{1}{2}, \frac{3}{2}, \frac{5}{2}, \cdots$, this formula is identical with the Sommerfeld formula 7[82], in which $k = 1, 2, 3, \cdots$. We conclude that, when the Schroedinger theory of the isolated hydrogen atom is corrected to terms in $1/c^2$ for both the relativity effects and the spin effects, its results are in agreement (to terms in $1/c^2$) with experiment insofar as the possible energies of the atom are concerned.

The energy levels required by (6) are shown, apart from the term mc^2, in Fig. 112, whose left portion is a reproduction of Fig. 107. Comparing this figure with Fig. 111, we note, in particular, that the relativity corrections shift adjacent spin doublets in such a way as to reduce the number of *levels* to that required by the Sommerfeld formula; but the number of basic *states* is still almost twice as great as in the Sommerfeld theory, so that

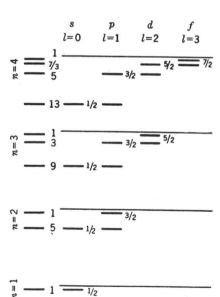

Fig. 112. Spin-and-relativity corrections for hydrogen. The Sommerfeld levels are shown at the left. The half-odd integers are the values of j.

our present hydrogen atom responds to external perturbing fields somewhat differently from the Sommerfeld hydrogen atom.

Exercises

1. Extend Fig. 112 through $n = 5$.

2. Show that the operators $L \cdot s + \frac{1}{2}\hbar^2$ (where $L \cdot s = L_x s_x + L_y s_y + L_z s_z$) and $\mathbf{\delta} \cdot \mathbf{p}$ ($= \sigma_x p_x + \sigma_y p_y + \sigma_z p_z$) anticommute with each other, and that $\hbar^2(2\hbar^{-2}L \cdot s + 1)^2 = J^2 + \frac{1}{4}\hbar^2$. Note that commutators such as $L_x p_y - p_y L_x$ can be found, except for the factor $i\hbar$, in Table 177[5].

90. Space Functions and Spin Functions

In many applications of Pauli's theory it is convenient to use a notation that is less explicit but more concise than our previous notation.

Every instantaneous Pauli ψ has the form

$$\psi = \begin{pmatrix} f(x, y, z) \\ g(x, y, z) \end{pmatrix} \tag{1}$$

and can therefore be written as

$$\psi = \begin{pmatrix} 1 \\ 0 \end{pmatrix} f + \begin{pmatrix} 0 \\ 1 \end{pmatrix} g, \tag{2}$$

where f and g are functions of the coordinates and are called *space functions*. Replacing the coefficients of f and g in (2) by the single letters α and β, we now rewrite (2) as

$$\psi = \alpha f + \beta g \tag{3}$$

and call α and β *spin functions*.

In order to be able to manipulate Pauli ψ's written in the form (3) so as to get the same results that are obtained when the more explicit form (2) is used, we must develop rules for handling the spin functions α and β. In the first place, we must have the rule

$$(\alpha f_1 + \beta g_1) + (\alpha f_2 + \beta g_2) = \alpha(f_1 + f_2) + \beta(g_1 + g_2). \tag{4}$$

Since the two column symbols in (2) are eigenvectors of σ_z belonging, respectively, to the eigenvalues 1 and -1 of σ_z, we require further that

$$\sigma_z(\alpha f + \beta g) = \alpha f - \beta g. \tag{5}$$

Similarly

$$\sigma_x(\alpha f + \beta g) = \alpha g + \beta f \tag{6}$$

and

$$\sigma_y(\alpha f + \beta g) = -i\alpha g + i\beta f. \tag{7}$$

To take care of the normalization and the orthogonality of the two column symbols in (2) we introduce the equations

$$\alpha^2 = 1, \qquad \beta^2 = 1, \qquad \alpha\beta = \beta\alpha = 0, \tag{8}$$

although the equations $\bar{\alpha}\alpha = 1$, $\bar{\beta}\beta = 1$, and $\bar{\alpha}\beta = \bar{\beta}\alpha = 0$ would perhaps be more appropriate. Since operators not involving the σ's operate only on the space functions, we have

$$L_z(\alpha f + \beta g) = \alpha L_z f + \beta L_z g, \tag{9}$$

and so on.

To illustrate the new notation, we shall recompute the eigen-ψ's of J_z. The eigenvalue equation 2^{87}, $J_z\psi = m\hbar\psi$, now reads $J_z(\alpha f + \beta g) = m\hbar(\alpha f + \beta g)$, that is,

$$(L_z + \tfrac{1}{2}\hbar\sigma_z)(\alpha f + \beta g) = m\hbar(\alpha f + \beta g). \tag{10}$$

Using the rules for handling α and β, we reduce (10) to

$$\alpha L_z f + \beta L_z g + \tfrac{1}{2}\hbar\alpha f - \tfrac{1}{2}\hbar\beta g = \alpha m\hbar f + \beta m\hbar g \tag{11}$$

and then to

$$\alpha(L_z - m\hbar + \tfrac{1}{2}\hbar)f + \beta(L_z - m\hbar - \tfrac{1}{2}\hbar)g = 0. \tag{12}$$

Multiplying (12) through separately by α and by β and recalling (8), we now get the two equations

$$(L_z - m\hbar + \tfrac{1}{2}\hbar)f = 0, \qquad (L_z - m\hbar - \tfrac{1}{2}\hbar)g = 0, \tag{13}$$

which are just the equations 4^{87}. From this point the procedure is the same as in §87, but the final result appears in the form

$$\psi(m) = \alpha A_1(r, \theta)e^{i(m-\frac{1}{2})\phi} + \beta A_2(r, \theta)e^{i(m+\frac{1}{2})\phi} \tag{14}$$

rather than in the equivalent form 8^{87}.

Exercise

1. Compute the simultaneous eigen-ψ's of J_z, L^2, and J^2, using the notation of this section.

CHAPTER XIV

ELEMENTS OF DIRAC'S THEORY OF THE ELECTRON

We finally turn to the highest refinement of quantum mechanics which is at present available, namely, the Dirac theory of the electron. In order to be able to present the elements of this theory in a particularly simple way, we shall restrict ourselves to the case of an electron moving in a purely electrostatic external field. Now, a field that is purely electrostatic from the standpoint of one observer may involve a magnetic field from the standpoint of a second observer who moves relative to the first. Consequently our restriction is a serious one; in particular, we shall have to forego the discussion of one of the most important features of the Dirac theory, namely, its invariance under the so-called Lorentz transformations of the relativity theory.

It should perhaps be emphasized that Dirac's theory is specifically a theory of the *electron*, rather than of any other particle.

The manner in which Pauli's theory forms an approximation to Dirac's is discussed in Exercise 9[97].

91. The Dirac Equation for an Electron in an Electrostatic Field

The relativistic equation that connects the total energy E, the potential energy $V = V(x, y, z)$, and the components of linear momentum p_x, p_y, and p_z of a particle of rest mass m is

$$(1^{83}) \qquad \frac{1}{c^2}(E - V)^2 = p_x^2 + p_y^2 + p_z^2 + m^2 c^2. \qquad (1)$$

Solving (1) for E, and then writing H for E, we get the Hamiltonian

$$H = V \pm c\sqrt{p_x^2 + p_y^2 + p_z^2 + m^2 c^2}. \qquad (2)$$

A reference to (1) shows that the upper sign in (2) corresponds to positive values of the kinetic energy $E - V$, while the lower sign yields negative values of the kinetic energy; in classical relativity the second alternative is of no physical interest and can be disregarded.

If we associate the appropriate Schroedinger operators with the quantities on the right side of (2), we get the operator

$$H = V \pm c\sqrt{-\hbar^2 \left(\frac{\partial^2}{\partial x^2} + \frac{\partial^2}{\partial y^2} + \frac{\partial^2}{\partial z^2} \right) + m^2 c^2}. \tag{3}$$

This operator is complicated at best: if it should be used, the equation $H\psi = E\psi$ would no longer be a differential equation of finite order.   The fundamental difficulty, however, is that adopting this operator makes it impossible to construct expressions for probability current and probability density which satisfy a relativistic equation for the conservation of probability.

Now, in §83, we avoided the operator (3) by not solving (1) explicitly for E; but this procedure is also unsatisfactory in several respects.   For example, it prevents us from determining the time dependence of ψ-functions directly through the second Schroedinger equation $H\psi = i\hbar\, \partial\psi/\partial t$.   The straightforward way out of this particular difficulty is as follows: We recall that an eigenfunction of H satisfies simultaneously the two equations $H\psi = E\psi$ and $H\psi = i\hbar\, \partial\psi/\partial t$, so that insofar as an eigenfunction of H is concerned the number E can be replaced by the operator $i\hbar\, \partial/\partial t$; we then replace E by $i\hbar\, \partial/\partial t$ in 5^{83} and get a differential equation that fixes the time dependence of ψ.   But, as inspection of 5^{83} will show, the equation so obtained is of the *second order* in $\partial/\partial t$, and hence the knowledge of the ψ-function pertaining to the instant $t = 0$ is insufficient for the computation of ψ for a later instant of time; to compute ψ for all time we would, in fact, have to know not only ψ for $t = 0$ but also $\partial\psi/\partial t$ for $t = 0$.   This feature is of course in direct contradiction to the quantum-mechanical method.

The problem of formulating a relativistic quantum mechanics thus leads us directly into an impasse: Equation (1) is unsatisfactory for quantum-mechanical purposes whether or not we solve it explicitly for E.   The way out was found by Dirac: *to get the correct Hamiltonian, we must free the Hamiltonian* (2) *from the radical that it now contains.*   This idea, which in retrospect seems simple, led to one of the most important equations of all quantum theory.

Linearization of H.   To free (2) from the radical, we must express the quantity $p_x^2 + p_y^2 + p_z^2 + m^2 c^2$ as a perfect square;

and perhaps the simplest possibility that preserves the symmetry between p_x, p_y, p_z, and mc is to write

$$p_x^2 + p_y^2 + p_z^2 + m^2 c^2 = (\alpha_x p_x + \alpha_y p_y + \alpha_z p_z + \alpha_m mc)^2, \quad (4)$$

where the coefficients α_x, α_y, α_z, and α_m are yet to be determined.

Now, we obviously cannot satisfy (4) by taking the α's to be ordinary numbers; in fact we have

$$(\alpha_x p_x + \alpha_y p_y + \alpha_z p_z + \alpha_m mc)^2$$

$$= \alpha_x^2 p_x^2 + \alpha_x \alpha_y p_x p_y + \alpha_x \alpha_z p_x p_z + \alpha_x \alpha_m p_x mc$$

$$+ \alpha_y \alpha_x p_y p_x + \alpha_y^2 p_y^2 + \alpha_y \alpha_z p_y p_z + \alpha_y \alpha_m p_y mc$$

$$+ \alpha_z \alpha_x p_z p_x + \alpha_z \alpha_y p_z p_y + \alpha_z^2 p_z^2 + \alpha_z \alpha_m p_z mc$$

$$+ \alpha_m \alpha_x mc p_x + \alpha_m \alpha_y mc p_y + \alpha_m \alpha_z mc p_z + \alpha_m^2 m^2 c^2, \quad (5)$$

so that if the α's are ordinary numbers the right side of (4) involves cross-products of the p's which do not appear on the left. But we note that if we take the α's to be *operators* which anti-commute with one another, so that

$$\begin{cases} \alpha_x \alpha_y = -\alpha_y \alpha_x & \alpha_x \alpha_z = -\alpha_z \alpha_x & \alpha_x \alpha_m = -\alpha_m \alpha_x \\ \alpha_y \alpha_z = -\alpha_z \alpha_y & \alpha_y \alpha_m = -\alpha_m \alpha_y & \alpha_z \alpha_m = -\alpha_m \alpha_z, \end{cases} \quad (6)$$

then, since the p's commute with one another, the cross-products cancel out and the right side of (4) reduces to $\alpha_x^2 p_x^2 + \alpha_y^2 p_y^2 + \alpha_z^2 p_z^2 + \alpha_m^2 m^2 c^2$; and if we require further that

$$\alpha_x^2 = \alpha_y^2 = \alpha_z^2 = \alpha_m^2 = 1, \quad (7)$$

then (4) is satisfied in every detail. We therefore conclude that, if the α's are operators satisfying (6) and (7), then the square root of $p_x^2 + p_y^2 + p_z^2 + m^2 c^2$ can be written as $\alpha_x p_x + \alpha_y p_y + \alpha_z p_z + \alpha_m mc$ and that, adopting the lower sign in (2), we can write (2) as

$$H = V - c\alpha_x p_x - c\alpha_y p_y - c\alpha_z p_z - \alpha_m mc^2. \quad (8)$$

A closer study shows that the α's should be linear operators, independent of the coordinates, of the p's, and of t; but apart from this no further restrictions are placed on the α's. Note that the replacement of the α's by $-\alpha$'s does not alter (6) and (7), so that it is immaterial whether we take the upper or the lower sign in (2); this conclusion implies that in Dirac's theory we cannot restrict ourselves from the outset to states of positive kinetic energy.

Replacing the p's in (8) by the appropriate Schroedinger operators, we get the operator

$$H = V + ic\hbar\alpha_x \frac{\partial}{\partial x} + ic\hbar\alpha_y \frac{\partial}{\partial y} + ic\hbar\alpha_z \frac{\partial}{\partial z} - \alpha_m mc^2. \qquad (9)$$

This *linear* operator is the celebrated Dirac Hamiltonian for an electron in an electrostatic field.

The matrix α's and the four-component ψ's. Although the theory does not require that we ascribe specific mathematical forms to the α's, in practice it is usually expedient to do so. We therefore proceed to identify a set of four linear operators that satisfy (6) and (7), and that do not depend on the coordinates, the p's, and t; this problem is like that of finding specific operators satisfying the Pauli conditions 3^{86} and 6^{86}, except that now we look for *four* anticommuting operators. Just as in Pauli's case, it is convenient to take our operators to be matrices; we find, however, that no four 2-by-2 matrices will anticommute with one another, and that 3-by-3 matrices also will not suit our purposes. Turning to 4-by-4 matrices, we find a variety of possibilities, of which the following is adopted by Dirac:

$$\alpha_x = \begin{pmatrix} 0 & 0 & 0 & 1 \\ 0 & 0 & 1 & 0 \\ 0 & 1 & 0 & 0 \\ 1 & 0 & 0 & 0 \end{pmatrix}, \quad \alpha_y = \begin{pmatrix} 0 & 0 & 0 & -i \\ 0 & 0 & i & 0 \\ 0 & -i & 0 & 0 \\ i & 0 & 0 & 0 \end{pmatrix},$$

$$\alpha_z = \begin{pmatrix} 0 & 0 & 1 & 0 \\ 0 & 0 & 0 & -1 \\ 1 & 0 & 0 & 0 \\ 0 & -1 & 0 & 0 \end{pmatrix}, \quad \alpha_m = \begin{pmatrix} 1 & 0 & 0 & 0 \\ 0 & 1 & 0 & 0 \\ 0 & 0 & -1 & 0 \\ 0 & 0 & 0 & -1 \end{pmatrix}. \qquad (10)$$

An advanced argument shows that any other choice of the α's will lead to the same physical conclusions, even if we use matrices of more than four rows and columns.

Now, if the Dirac operators are to involve 4-by-4 matrices, then the Dirac operands must have four components; that is, a Dirac ψ-function ψ must have the form

$$\psi = \begin{pmatrix} \psi_1 \\ \psi_2 \\ \psi_3 \\ \psi_4 \end{pmatrix}, \qquad (11)$$

where each of the four components is an ordinary function of x, y, z, and t. These ψ's, which, except for the doubling of the number of components, are like the Pauli ψ's, are manipulated in essentially the same way as the Pauli ψ's. In particular, the Dirac $\bar{\psi}$ corresponding to (11) is the row symbol

$$(16^{86}) \qquad \bar{\psi} = (\bar{\psi}_1, \bar{\psi}_2, \bar{\psi}_3, \bar{\psi}_4), \qquad (12)$$

and the corresponding Dirac $\bar{\psi}\psi$ is the following ordinary function:

$$(17^{86}) \qquad \bar{\psi}\psi = \bar{\psi}_1\psi_1 + \bar{\psi}_2\psi_2 + \bar{\psi}_3\psi_3 + \bar{\psi}_4\psi_4. \qquad (13)$$

Two Dirac ψ's, ψ^{I} and ψ^{II}, are said to be orthogonal to each other if $\int \bar{\psi}^{\mathrm{I}}\psi^{\mathrm{II}} \, d\tau = 0$, that is, if $\int (\bar{\psi}_1^{\mathrm{I}}\psi_1^{\mathrm{II}} + \bar{\psi}_2^{\mathrm{I}}\psi_2^{\mathrm{II}} + \bar{\psi}_3^{\mathrm{I}}\psi_3^{\mathrm{II}} + \bar{\psi}_4^{\mathrm{I}}\psi_4^{\mathrm{II}}) \, d\tau = 0$. The time dependence of a Dirac ψ pertaining to a system whose Hamiltonian is H is determined through the equation

$$H\psi = i\hbar \frac{\partial \psi}{\partial t}, \qquad (14)$$

where H is the Hamiltonian operator (9) and where

$$(36^{86}) \qquad \frac{\partial \psi}{\partial t} = \frac{\partial}{\partial t} \begin{pmatrix} \psi_1 \\ \psi_2 \\ \psi_3 \\ \psi_4 \end{pmatrix} = \begin{pmatrix} \partial\psi_1/\partial t \\ \partial\psi_2/\partial t \\ \partial\psi_3/\partial t \\ \partial\psi_4/\partial t \end{pmatrix}. \qquad (15)$$

Note that (14) is formally the same as the second Schroedinger equation.

When Dirac's α's have the explicit forms (10), the Dirac operators associated with 'ordinary' dynamical variables are obtained by throwing the corresponding Schroedinger operators into a matrix form after the manner of 19^{86}, except that now the 4-by-4 unit matrix is used in the transformation.

It is a fundamental assumption of the Dirac theory that the average value of a dynamical variable α for a state ψ is given by our familiar expectation formula

$$\langle 8^{77} \rangle \qquad \mathrm{av}_\psi \alpha = \frac{\int \bar{\psi}\alpha\psi \, d\tau}{\int \bar{\psi}\psi \, d\tau}, \qquad (16)$$

where α in the integrand is now the Dirac operator associated with the dynamical variable α. Note that the α in (16) is *any* dynamical variable, and not necessarily one of the subscripted α's in (10).

The equation of motion of a dynamical variable not involving t explicitly retains in the Dirac theory the form 16[76].

The Dirac equation.   The equation $H\psi = E\psi$, with H given by (8), that is, the equation

$$(V - c\alpha_x p_x - c\alpha_y p_y - c\alpha_z p_z - \alpha_m mc^2)\psi = E\psi, \qquad (17)$$

with $p_x = -i\hbar\partial/\partial x$, and so on, is called the *Dirac equation* for an electron in an electrostatic field.   The computation of the energy levels of an electron moving relativistically in an electrostatic field consists in Dirac's theory in the calculation of the numerical values of the parameter E for which (17) has well-behaved solutions.

To rewrite the Dirac equation in a more explicit form, we replace the α's by the specific matrices (10), replace ψ by a four-component column symbol, and, for uniformity, multiply V by the 4-by-4 unit matrix.   The result is

$$\begin{pmatrix} V - mc^2 & 0 & -cp_z & -c(p_x - ip_y) \\ 0 & V - mc^2 & -c(p_x + ip_y) & cp_z \\ -cp_z & -c(p_x - ip_y) & V + mc^2 & 0 \\ -c(p_x + ip_y) & cp_z & 0 & V + mc^2 \end{pmatrix} \begin{pmatrix} \psi_1 \\ \psi_2 \\ \psi_3 \\ \psi_4 \end{pmatrix} = E \begin{pmatrix} \psi_1 \\ \psi_2 \\ \psi_3 \\ \psi_4 \end{pmatrix}, \qquad (18)$$

so that (17) reduces to the four simultaneous equations

$$\begin{cases} (V - mc^2)\psi_1 - cp_z\psi_3 - c(p_x - ip_y)\psi_4 = E\psi_1 \\ (V - mc^2)\psi_2 + cp_z\psi_4 - c(p_x + ip_y)\psi_3 = E\psi_2 \\ (V + mc^2)\psi_3 - cp_z\psi_1 - c(p_x - ip_y)\psi_2 = E\psi_3 \\ (V + mc^2)\psi_4 + cp_z\psi_2 - c(p_x + ip_y)\psi_1 = E\psi_4 . \end{cases} \qquad (19)$$

Finally, we replace p_x by $-i\hbar\,\partial/\partial x$, and so on, and after a slight rearrangement get the equations

$$\begin{cases} \dfrac{i}{\hbar}\left(\dfrac{E - V}{c} + mc\right)\psi_1 + \left(\dfrac{\partial}{\partial x} - i\dfrac{\partial}{\partial y}\right)\psi_4 + \dfrac{\partial}{\partial z}\psi_3 = 0 \\[2mm] \dfrac{i}{\hbar}\left(\dfrac{E - V}{c} + mc\right)\psi_2 + \left(\dfrac{\partial}{\partial x} + i\dfrac{\partial}{\partial y}\right)\psi_3 - \dfrac{\partial}{\partial z}\psi_4 = 0 \\[2mm] \dfrac{i}{\hbar}\left(\dfrac{E - V}{c} - mc\right)\psi_3 + \left(\dfrac{\partial}{\partial x} - i\dfrac{\partial}{\partial y}\right)\psi_2 + \dfrac{\partial}{\partial z}\psi_1 = 0 \\[2mm] \dfrac{i}{\hbar}\left(\dfrac{E - V}{c} - mc\right)\psi_4 + \left(\dfrac{\partial}{\partial x} + i\dfrac{\partial}{\partial y}\right)\psi_1 - \dfrac{\partial}{\partial z}\psi_2 = 0. \end{cases} \qquad (20)$$

Thus the single symbolic Dirac equation (17) amounts to the four explicit simultaneous partial differential equations (20). And, to determine the energy levels of an electron moving relativistically in an electrostatic field in which the potential energy of the electron is $V = V(x, y, z)$, we must compute the values of the numerical values of the parameter E for which the system of equations (20) has well-behaved solutions; by 'well-behaved' we mean here that at least one of the component functions ψ_1, ψ_2, ψ_3, and ψ_4 is different from zero, and that each of the nonvanishing component functions is well-behaved in the sense of the Schroedinger theory.

Exercises

1. Show that according to (7) the only eigenvalues of α_x, α_y, α_z, and α_m are 1 and -1, and verify in detail that the particular α's given by (10) have just these eigenvalues.

2. Use (9) and 16^{76} to show that the operator associated in Dirac's theory with $\dot{p}_x$, that is, with the x-component of the force acting on an electron in an electrostatic field, is $-\partial V/\partial x$.

3. Use (9) and 16^{76} to show that the operator associated in Dirac's theory with the x-component $\dot{x}$ of the electron velocity is $-c\alpha_x$, and that consequently *the only possible results of a precise measurement of a component of the electron velocity are c and $-c$.* The fact that $m\dot{x}$ is not equal to p_x is in line with classical relativity (for example, relativistically, the absolute value of $\dot{x}$ cannot exceed c, while p_x can have any real value whatever); but the result stated in italics is new.[1]

4. Show that each of the two matrices $\pm\alpha_x\alpha_y\alpha_z\alpha_m$ anticommutes with every α in (10) and becomes 1 when squared.

5. Show that $\pm\alpha_x\alpha_y\alpha_z\alpha_m$ are the only 4-by-4 matrices that anticommute with every α in (10) and become 1 when squared.

6. To verify in a small way that the properties of the Dirac Hamiltonian (9) do not depend in any essential way on the choice of the α's, provided Equations (6) and (7) are satisfied, replace α_z in (10) by its negative and, replacing the symbol ψ in (17) by ψ', set up the equations that then take the place of (20); then show that these equations become identical with (20) if the symbols ψ_1', ψ_2', ψ_3', and ψ_4' are replaced, respectively, by $-\psi_1$, ψ_2, ψ_3, and $-\psi_4$.

7. Relate the result of Exercise 6 to the fact that when α_z in (9) is replaced by $-\alpha_z$ the resulting operator is the transform of (9) by the matrix $i\alpha_x\alpha_y\alpha_m$.

---

[1] G. Breit, *Proc. Nat. Acad. Sci.*, **14**, 553 (1928). See also E. L. Hill and R. Landshoff, *Rev. Mod. Phys.*, **10**, 116 (1938).

92. The Dirac σ's

In some computations it is convenient to rewrite the Dirac Hamiltonian 8^{91} in a slightly different form. We introduce the five matrices

$$\sigma_x = \begin{pmatrix} 0 & 1 & 0 & 0 \\ 1 & 0 & 0 & 0 \\ 0 & 0 & 0 & 1 \\ 0 & 0 & 1 & 0 \end{pmatrix}, \quad \sigma_y = \begin{pmatrix} 0 & -i & 0 & 0 \\ i & 0 & 0 & 0 \\ 0 & 0 & 0 & -i \\ 0 & 0 & i & 0 \end{pmatrix},$$

$$\sigma_z = \begin{pmatrix} 1 & 0 & 0 & 0 \\ 0 & -1 & 0 & 0 \\ 0 & 0 & 1 & 0 \\ 0 & 0 & 0 & -1 \end{pmatrix} \tag{1}$$

and

$$\rho_1 = \begin{pmatrix} 0 & 0 & 1 & 0 \\ 0 & 0 & 0 & 1 \\ 1 & 0 & 0 & 0 \\ 0 & 1 & 0 & 0 \end{pmatrix}, \quad \rho_3 = \begin{pmatrix} 1 & 0 & 0 & 0 \\ 0 & 1 & 0 & 0 \\ 0 & 0 & -1 & 0 \\ 0 & 0 & 0 & -1 \end{pmatrix} \tag{2}$$

and note that the square of each σ and each ρ is unity, that the σ's anticommute with each other, that the ρ's anticommute with each other, and that each σ commutes with each ρ. Our ρ_3 equals the α_m of 10^{91}—the relabeling of α_m is due partly to the convenience of being able to say "the ρ's commute with the σ's" rather than "ρ_1 and α_m commute with the σ's." Dirac's theory employs besides ρ_1 and ρ_3 a matrix labeled ρ_2, but we shall not need this matrix here.

Now, the σ's, the ρ's, and the α's of 10^{91} satisfy the equations

$$\alpha_x = \rho_1 \sigma_x, \qquad \alpha_y = \rho_1 \sigma_y, \qquad \alpha_z = \rho_1 \sigma_z, \qquad \alpha_m = \rho_3, \tag{3}$$

and consequently the Hamiltonian 8^{91} can be written as

$$H = V - c\rho_1(\sigma_x p_x + \sigma_y p_y + \sigma_z p_z) - \rho_3 mc^2. \tag{4}$$

The Dirac σ's (1) are just like the Pauli σ's 12^{86} except for a 'doubling'; their physical significance will be demonstrated in the next section.

93. The Existence of a 'Spin' Angular Momentum

To exhibit a remarkable feature of the Dirac equation, we turn to the case of a central electrostatic field, when the Dirac Hamiltonian 4^{92} becomes

$$H = V(r) - c\rho_1(\sigma_x p_x + \sigma_y p_y + \sigma_z p_z) - \rho_3 mc^2, \quad (1)$$

and look for constants of motion.

Classically, L_x, the x-component of the orbital angular momentum, is a constant of motion in a central field. To check whether this is so also in the Dirac theory, we recall the equation of motion 16^{76} and compute the commutator of the Dirac operator L_x and the Dirac H. Since L_x commutes with every quantity in (1) except p_y and p_z, we have

$$L_x H - H L_x = -c\rho_1[\sigma_y(L_x p_y - p_y L_x) + \sigma_z(L_x p_z - p_z L_x)]$$
$$= -c\rho_1[\sigma_y(i\hbar p_z) + \sigma_z(-i\hbar p_y)]$$
$$= -i\hbar c\rho_1(\sigma_y p_z - \sigma_z p_y) \neq 0. \quad (2)$$

Hence, in the Dirac theory, in contradistinction to classical mechanics, the x-component of the orbital angular momentum of an electron moving in a central electrostatic field is not a constant of motion.

But we note also that, since σ_x commutes with every quantity in (1) except σ_y and σ_z, we have

$$\sigma_x H - H\sigma_x = -c\rho_1[(\sigma_x\sigma_y - \sigma_y\sigma_x)p_y + (\sigma_x\sigma_z - \sigma_z\sigma_x)p_z]$$
$$= -c\rho_1[(2i\sigma_z)p_y + (-2i\sigma_y)p_z]$$
$$= 2ic\rho_1(\sigma_y p_z - \sigma_z p_y). \quad (3)$$

Thus $L_x H - H L_x = -\frac{1}{2}\hbar(\sigma_x H - H\sigma_x)$ and

$$(L_x + \tfrac{1}{2}\hbar\sigma_x)H - H(L_x + \tfrac{1}{2}\hbar\sigma_x) = 0, \quad (4)$$

so that the dynamical variable $L_x + \frac{1}{2}\hbar\sigma_x$ is a constant of motion in a central field.

The quantity $\frac{1}{2}\hbar\sigma_x$, which must be added to L_x before we get a constant of motion, has its origin in the relativistic considerations that led us to adopt the Dirac Hamiltonian 9^{91} as the correct Hamiltonian, and therefore represents a deeply rooted relativistic effect. This quantity has essentially the same form as that associated in the Pauli theory with the x-component of the spin angular momentum of the electron and, to put the matter roughly, is in a large part responsible for the fact that Dirac's theory accounts for the phenomena that have been previously attributed to a rotary motion of the electron.   For these reasons it is called the x-component of the *spin angular momentum* of the electron although, since the question of the rotation of the electron does not arise at all in Dirac's theory, this name is somewhat misleading.

We introduce the notation

$$(2^{86}) \qquad s_x = \tfrac{1}{2}\hbar\sigma_x , \qquad s_y = \tfrac{1}{2}\hbar\sigma_y , \qquad s_z = \tfrac{1}{2}\hbar\sigma_z , \qquad (5)$$

where the σ's are Dirac's, and also the notation

$$(39^{86}) \quad J_x = L_x + s_x , \quad J_y = L_y + s_y , \quad J_z = L_z + s_z . \quad (6)$$

The quantity J_x, which we call the x-component of the total angular momentum of the electron, was shown above to be a constant of motion in central fields.   Similar arguments show that J_y and J_z, and with them the quantity $J^2 = J_x^2 + J_y^2 + J_z^2$, are also constants of motion.

A more advanced argument shows that according to Dirac's equation an electron behaves in a magnetic field as though it possesses a 'spin' magnetic moment $\mathbf{u}$ related to the spin angular $\mathbf{s}$ through the equation $\mathbf{u} = -e\mathbf{s}/mc$, that is, the equation postulated by Uhlenbeck and Goudsmit.   In short, *Dirac's equation automatically endows the electron with the properties that account for the phenomena previously ascribed to a hypothetical spinning motion of the electron.*

94. Constants of Motion for a Central Field

Dirac's equation, that is, the system of the four equations 20^{91}, is not easy to handle directly even if $V = V(r)$, and in treating central motion we shall therefore once again have recourse to the expansion theorem.   Our first task is to identify a suitable set of commuting constants of motion for the case when H is given by 1^{93}.

In §93 the quantities J_x, J_y, J_z, and J^2 were found to be constants of motion for central fields; J_x, J_y, and J_z do not commute with one another, but each commutes with J^2, so that we may adopt the set

$$J_z = L_z + s_z, \qquad J^2 = (L + s)^2 = L^2 + 2L \cdot s + \tfrac{3}{4}\hbar^2. \quad (1)$$

Written out more explicitly, the operators are

$$J_z = \begin{pmatrix} L_z + \tfrac{1}{2}\hbar & 0 & 0 & 0 \\ 0 & L_z - \tfrac{1}{2}\hbar & 0 & 0 \\ 0 & 0 & L_z + \tfrac{1}{2}\hbar & 0 \\ 0 & 0 & 0 & L_z - \tfrac{1}{2}\hbar \end{pmatrix} \quad (2)$$

and

$$J^2 = \begin{pmatrix} L^2 + \hbar L_z + \tfrac{3}{4}\hbar^2 & \hbar(L_x - iL_y) & 0 & 0 \\ \hbar(L_x + iL_y) & L^2 - \hbar L_z + \tfrac{3}{4}\hbar^2 & 0 & 0 \\ 0 & 0 & L^2 + \hbar L_z + \tfrac{3}{4}\hbar^2 & \hbar(L_x - iL_y) \\ 0 & 0 & \hbar(L_x + iL_y) & L^2 - \hbar L_z + \tfrac{3}{4}\hbar^2 \end{pmatrix}. \quad (3)$$

Comparison with 41^{86} and 42^{86} shows that Dirac's J_z and J^2 are just like Pauli's except for a doubling.

On account of the way in which the p's appear in the Hamiltonian 1^{93}, the operator L^2 does not commute with H, so that the magnitude of the orbital angular momentum is not a constant of motion in Dirac's theory of central fields. This implies, incidentally, that in Dirac's theory it is not quite correct to picture the vectors L and s as simply precessing about the vector J as shown in Fig. 110^{87}.

The loss of L^2 as a constant of motion is fortunately offset by the fact that the quantity

$$K = \rho_3\!\left(\frac{2}{\hbar^2} L \cdot s + 1\right), \quad (4)$$

that is,

$$K = \frac{1}{\hbar} \begin{pmatrix} L_z + \hbar & L_x - iL_y & 0 & 0 \\ L_x + iL_y & -L_z + \hbar & 0 & 0 \\ 0 & 0 & -L_z - \hbar & -L_x + iL_y \\ 0 & 0 & -L_x - iL_y & L_z - \hbar \end{pmatrix}, \quad (5)$$

constructed by Dirac, commutes with H and also with J_z and J^2.

In central fields we thus have the commuting constants of motion

$$J_z, \ J^2, \ K, \quad (6)$$

Exercises

1. Show that K commutes with J_z, J^2, and with the Hamiltonian 1^{93}.

2. Verify Equations (12).

3. Show that

$$\hbar^2 K^2 = J^2 + \tfrac{1}{4}\hbar^2 \tag{18}$$

and that consequently every eigen-ψ of K belonging to the eigenvalue k of K is automatically an eigen-ψ of J^2 belonging to the eigenvalue $(k - \tfrac{1}{2})(k + \tfrac{1}{2})\hbar^2$ of J^2. Note that hence the set of the two commuting constants of motion J_z and K is equivalent to the set of the three constants J_z, J^2, K used in the text.

4. Use (10) and (18) to show that (13) includes *all* eigenvalues of K.

5. Compute the ψ's (16) and (17), without using the Pauli ψ's, as follows: (a) Require a ψ with components ψ_1, ψ_2, ψ_3, and ψ_4 to be an eigen-ψ of J_z belonging to the eigenvalue $m\hbar$ of J_z, with m as yet undetermined, and thus find the dependence of ψ_1, ψ_2, ψ_3, and ψ_4 on the angle ϕ. (b) Require the eigen-ψ of J_z to be an eigen-ψ of $J^2 - \hbar^2 K$ belonging to the eigenvalue λ' of $J^2 - \hbar^2 K$ and, restricting yourself to the components ψ_1 and ψ_2, determine their dependence on the angle θ. (c) Require the eigen-ψ of J_z to be an eigen-ψ of $J^2 + \hbar^2 K$ belonging to the eigenvalue λ'' of $J^2 + \hbar^2 K$ and, restricting yourself to the components ψ_3 and ψ_4, determine their dependence on θ. (d) Write down the simultaneous eigen-ψ's of J_z, $J^2 - \hbar^2 K$, and $J^2 + \hbar^2 K$, and require them to be eigen-ψ's of K belonging to the eigenvalue k of K.

6. Show that j can be eliminated from (16) and (17) with the help of the quantities k, $|k|$, and $k^\dagger = k/|k|$ in such a way that (16) and (17) become identical in form.

95. The Radial Equations

Having computed the simultaneous eigen-ψ's of J_z, J^2, and K, we proceed to consider the simultaneous eigen-ψ's of J_z, J^2, K, and H for a central field. Our problem is to find the conditions that the Dirac equation, taken in the form 19^{91}, with the understanding that $V = V(r)$, imposes on the four components of ψ after these components have already been partly determined by the requirement that ψ be an eigen-ψ of J_z, J^2, and K, that is, that ψ have the form 16^{94} or the form 17^{94}.

We begin with $\psi(j, k = j + \tfrac{1}{2}, m)$, substitute ψ_1, ψ_2, ψ_3, and ψ_4 from 16^{94} into the *first* of the four equations 19^{91}, and get the equation

$$(V - mc^2)\sqrt{j + m}\, R^{\mathrm{I}}\Upsilon(j - \tfrac{1}{2}, m - \tfrac{1}{2})$$
$$- cp_z\sqrt{j + 1 - m}\, R^{\mathrm{II}}\Upsilon(j + \tfrac{1}{2}, m - \tfrac{1}{2})$$
$$+ c(p_x - ip_y)\sqrt{j + 1 + m}\, R^{\mathrm{II}}\Upsilon(j + \tfrac{1}{2}, m + \tfrac{1}{2})$$
$$= E\sqrt{j + m}\, R^{\mathrm{I}}\Upsilon(j - \tfrac{1}{2}, m - \tfrac{1}{2}), \tag{1}$$

which in view of 17^A and 18^A reduces to

$$(E - V + mc^2)R^I - ic\hbar \sqrt{\frac{j+1}{j}} \left[\frac{dR^{II}}{dr} + (j + \tfrac{3}{2}) \frac{R^{II}}{r} \right] = 0, \quad (2)$$

or, since in the present case $k = j + \tfrac{1}{2}$, to

$$(E - V + mc^2)R^I - ic\hbar \sqrt{\frac{k+\tfrac{1}{2}}{k-\tfrac{1}{2}}} \left[\frac{dR^{II}}{dr} + (k + 1) \frac{R^{II}}{r} \right] = 0. \quad (3)$$

The *second* of the four equations 19^{91} leads once again to (3), while the *third* and *fourth* each yield the same new equation

$$i \sqrt{\frac{k+\tfrac{1}{2}}{k-\tfrac{1}{2}}} (E - V - mc^2)R^{II} + c\hbar \left[\frac{dR^I}{dr} - (k - 1) \frac{R^I}{r} \right] = 0. \quad (4)$$

Turning to the $\psi(j, k = -j - \tfrac{1}{2}, m)$ given by 17^{94}, we find that the first of the four equations 19^{91} yields an equation slightly different from (2); but when we eliminate j from this equation by means of k, which now equals $-j - \tfrac{1}{2}$, we get (3) once again. Similarly, the second of the equations 19^{91} also yields (3), while the third and fourth each yield (4). The fact that $\psi(j, k = j + \tfrac{1}{2}, m)$ and $\psi(j, k = -j - \tfrac{1}{2}, m)$ give identical results when these results are expressed in terms of k rather than j is not unexpected in view of the conclusion of Exercise 6^{94}.

The substitution

$$R_a = R^I, \qquad R_b = i \sqrt{\frac{k + \tfrac{1}{2}}{k - \tfrac{1}{2}}} R^{II} \qquad (5)$$

reduces (3) and (4) to the equations

$$\begin{cases} \dfrac{1}{c\hbar} [E - V(r) + mc^2] R_a - \dfrac{dR_b}{dr} - (k + 1) \dfrac{R_b}{r} = 0 \\[2mm] \dfrac{1}{c\hbar} [E - V(r) - mc^2] R_b + \dfrac{dR_a}{dr} - (k - 1) \dfrac{R_a}{r} = 0. \end{cases} \qquad (6)$$

Since these equations incorporate both of the special cases $\psi(j, k = j + \tfrac{1}{2}, m)$ and $\psi(j, k = -j - \tfrac{1}{2}, m)$, the quantum number k in (6) runs through its complete range:

$$(13^{94}) \qquad\qquad k = \pm 1, \pm 2, \pm 3, \cdots \qquad (7)$$

We now conclude that the problem of computing the energy levels of an electron moving in a central electrostatic field reduces in the Dirac theory to the problem of computing the numerical values of the parameter E for which the system of the two simultaneous first-order ordinary differential equations (6) has well-behaved solutions R_a and R_b. These equations, called the *radial equations*, must be studied separately for each particular form of $V(r)$; an example is given in the next section.

The substitutions

$$(3^{80}) \qquad\qquad \chi_a = rR_a, \qquad \chi_b = rR_b \qquad\qquad (8)$$

reduce (6) to the more convenient form

$$\begin{cases} \dfrac{1}{c\hbar}[E - V(r) + mc^2]\chi_a - \dfrac{d\chi_b}{dr} - \dfrac{k}{r}\chi_b = 0 \\[3mm] \dfrac{1}{c\hbar}[E - V(r) - mc^2]\chi_b + \dfrac{d\chi_a}{dr} - \dfrac{k}{r}\chi_a = 0. \end{cases} \qquad (9)$$

A method for deriving the radial equations without the use of constants of motion was given by Darwin;[2] a symbolic method for deriving the χ-equations (9) was given by Dirac.[3]

Exercises

1. Eliminate R_a between the two equations (6) and show that R_b, which we shall denote simply by R, satisfies the equation

$$\frac{1}{c\hbar}(E - V - mc^2)R + c\hbar\left(\frac{d}{dr} - \frac{k-1}{r}\right)(E - V + mc^2)^{-1}\left(\frac{d}{dr} + \frac{k+1}{r}\right)R = 0,$$

$$\qquad\qquad (10)$$

where $V = V(r)$.

2. Show that, with the help of 24^{77} and 2^{88}, Equation (10) can be written as

$$2mc^2(E - V + mc^2)^{-1}\left[\frac{1}{2m}p_r^2 + \frac{k(k+1)}{\kappa r^2}\right]R + VR$$

$$-2m^2c^4\hbar^2(E - V + mc^2)^{-2}\left[(k+1)\xi(r)R + r\xi(r)\frac{dR}{dr}\right]$$

$$= (E - mc^2)R. \quad (11)$$

---

[2] C. G. Darwin. *Proc. Roy. Soc.*, **118a**, 654 (1928).
[3] Dirac, §73

96. The Energy Levels of the Hydrogen Atom.[4]

We now consider along the lines of the Dirac theory an electron moving in the fixed Coulomb potential e/r; the potential energy of the electron then is

$$(1^{80}) \qquad\qquad V(r) = -\frac{e^2}{r}, \qquad\qquad (1)$$

and Dirac's χ-equations 9^{95} become

$$\begin{cases} \dfrac{1}{c\hbar}\left(E + \dfrac{e^2}{r} + mc^2\right)\chi_a - \dfrac{d\chi_b}{dr} - \dfrac{k}{r}\chi_b = 0 \\[2mm] \dfrac{1}{c\hbar}\left(E + \dfrac{e^2}{r} - mc^2\right)\chi_b + \dfrac{d\chi_a}{dr} - \dfrac{k}{r}\chi_a = 0. \end{cases} \qquad (2)$$

This problem is one of the few that can be solved precisely.

Using primes to denote differentiation with respect to r and introducing the abbreviations

$$A = (mc^2 + E)/c\hbar, \qquad B = (mc^2 - E)/c\hbar, \qquad (3)$$

and the fine-structure constant

$$(6^{82}) \qquad\qquad \alpha = e^2/\hbar c, \qquad\qquad (4)$$

we rewrite (2) as

$$\begin{cases} A\chi_a + \alpha\chi_a/r - \chi_b' - k\chi_b/r = 0 \\[1mm] B\chi_b - \alpha\chi_b/r - \chi_a' + k\chi_a/r = 0. \end{cases} \qquad (5)$$

Next we write the functions χ_a and χ_b in the forms

$$\chi_a = e^{-Cr}\sum_s a_s r^s, \qquad s = \tau, \tau+1, \tau+2, \cdots, \qquad (6)$$

$$\chi_b = e^{-Cr}\sum_s b_s r^s, \qquad s = \tau, \tau+1, \tau+2, \cdots. \qquad (7)$$

The constant C is as yet undetermined; the a's and b's are also undetermined, but to avoid trivialities we require that at least

---

[4] Dirac, §74. Just as in our previous computations involving relativity or spin, we make no correction for nuclear motion.

one of the two coefficients a_r and b_r be different from zero. Substituting (6) and (7) into (5), we get

$$\begin{cases} \sum_s \{[Aa_s + Cb_s]r^s + [\alpha a_s - (s+k)b_s]r^{s-1}\} = 0 \\ \sum_s \{[Bb_s + Ca_s]r^s - [\alpha b_s + (s-k)a_s]r^{s-1}\} = 0. \end{cases} \tag{8}$$

To determine τ, that is, the exponent of r with which the series in (6) and (7) begin, we equate to zero the coefficients of the lowest [the $(\tau - 1)$th] power of r in (8); the resulting equations

$$\alpha a_r - (\tau + k)b_r = 0$$
$$\alpha b_r + (\tau - k)a_r = 0 \tag{9}$$

have nonvanishing solutions a_r and b_r if

$$\tau = \sqrt{k^2 - \alpha^2} \tag{10}$$

and also if τ is the negative of (10); the second possibility is of no interest to us, since it yields χ's that are ill-behaved at the origin.

We now proceed to correlate the a's and the b's in (6) and (7). Collecting the $(s - 1)$th powers of r in (8) and equating the sums of their coefficients to zero, we get

$$Aa_{s-1} + Cb_{s-1} + \alpha a_s - (s+k)b_s = 0 \tag{11a}$$

$$Ca_{s-1} + Bb_{s-1} - (s-k)a_s - \alpha b_s = 0. \tag{11b}$$

Two of the four unknowns, namely, a_{s-1} and b_{s-1}, can both be eliminated from Equations (11) provided we choose the as yet undetermined constant C so as to make the determinant of the coefficients of a_{s-1} and b_{s-1} vanish; so we set

$$C = \sqrt{AB} = \sqrt{m^2c^4 - E^2}/\hbar c. \tag{12}$$

If we now multiply (11a) by C and (11b) by A, and subtract, we find that the a's and the b's are related as follows:

$$[C\alpha + (s-k)A]a_s + [A\alpha - (s+k)C]b_s = 0. \tag{13}$$

Next we consider the behavior of the a's and b's for large values of s, when (13) reduces to the approximate equation

$$Aa_s \cong Cb_s. \tag{14}$$

Eliminating the b's from (11b) with the help of (14) and the equation $Aa_{s-1} \cong Cb_{s-1}$ which follows from (14), we get

$$[C + AB/C]a_{s-1} - [(s - k) + A\alpha/C]a_s \cong 0, \qquad (15)$$

or, since s is large, $[C + AB/C]a_{s-1} - sa_s \cong 0$, that is

$$a_s/a_{s-1} \cong 2C/s. \qquad (16)$$

Eliminating the a's from (16) with the help of (14), we find that, for large values of s, $b_s/b_{s-1} \cong 2C/s$.

Since the right side of (16) is just the ratio of the coefficients of the successive powers of r in the power series for e^{2Cr}, we conclude that for large values of r the series in (6) and (7) behave like e^{2Cr} unless they terminate, so that the χ's themselves behave like e^{Cr}. Now, according to (12), C is positive if $E^2 < m^2c^4$ and imaginary if $E^2 > m^2c^4$. Hence our χ's are well-behaved when $r \to \infty$ if $E^2 > m^2c^4$ and, unless the series in (6) and (7) terminate, are ill-behaved if $E^2 < m^2c^4$. We conclude: *the electron in a Coulomb field may have any energy greater than mc^2 or smaller than $-mc^2$*; but not all energies lying between $-mc^2$ and mc^2 are possible.

Finally we turn to the case when the series in (6) terminates, say with a term in r^s, so that $a_s \neq 0$ and $a_{s+1} = a_{s+2} = \cdots = 0$; according to (13), the series in (7) then also terminates with a term in r^s. Since, as we have seen, both series start with a term in r^τ and the exponents of r increase by steps of unity, we have

$$S - \tau = \text{positive integer or zero.} \qquad (17)$$

Introducing the integer n having the range

$$n = |k|, |k| + 1, |k| + 2, \cdots, \qquad (18)$$

we may write (17) as $S - \tau = n - |k|$, or, in view of (10), as

$$S = n - |k| + \sqrt{k^2 - \alpha^2}. \qquad (19)$$

We may now use (11) and (13) to compute the value of a_s/a_{s-1} without assuming s to be large, and then find the condition under which a_{s+1}/a_s is zero; but a simpler procedure is as follows: We write S for $s - 1$ in (11a) and set a_{s+1} and b_{s+1} equal to zero, getting

$$Aa_S + Cb_S = 0. \qquad (20)$$

Elimination of b_s from (20) by means of (13) then yields the equation $2SAC = (A^2 - C^2)\alpha$, which, in view of (3) and (12), reduces to

$$S\sqrt{m^2c^4 - E^2} = E\alpha. \tag{21}$$

Squaring both sides of (21) and recalling (19), we get the equation

$$\left(n - |k| + \sqrt{k^2 - \alpha^2}\right)^2 (m^2c^4 - E^2) = \alpha^2 E^2, \tag{22}$$

which has the positive solution

$$E = mc^2 \left[1 + \left(\frac{\alpha}{n - |k| + \sqrt{k^2 - \alpha^2}}\right)^2\right]^{-\frac{1}{2}} \tag{23}$$

and a second solution that is just the negative of (23); the negative solution, however, does not satisfy (21), and is therefore of no interest to us. The ranges of k and n in (23), given by 7[95] and (18), can be reindicated as follows:

$$n = 1, 2, 3, \cdots, \tag{24}$$

$$k = \pm 1, \pm 2, \cdots, \pm(n - 1), -n. \tag{25}$$

The reason for omitting the value $k = n$ in (25) is taken up in Exercise 3.

We note that, except for the duplicity of the levels for which $|k| < n$, the formula (23) is identical with the Sommerfeld fine-structure formula 3[82].

Besides the continuous energy spectrum extending from mc^2 to ∞ and the discrete spectrum described by Equations (23) to (25) and lying just below mc^2,[5] the Dirac electron in a Coulomb field has, as we found on the preceding page, also a continuous energy spectrum extending from $-mc^2$ to $-\infty$. It is a characteristic of the Dirac theory that, in addition to levels for which the kinetic energy of the electron is positive, it yields levels of negative kinetic energy; to put it roughly, the mathematical reason for this is that, since the algebraic signs of the α's in 9[91] are immaterial, the ambiguous sign of 2[91] is implicitly contained in Dirac's Hamiltonian.

In classical relativity the states of negative kinetic energy can be disregarded altogether. But according to the Dirac theory the probabilities for quantum jumps from states of positive to states of negative kinetic energy do not all vanish, and hence the latter states cannot be disregarded

---

[5] The value of mc^2 is approximately half a million electron volts; the lowest level of the discrete spectrum lies about 13.5 electron volts (that is, the ionization potential of the hydrogen atom in the normal state) below mc^2.

without introducing inconsistencies into the theory; further, certain mathematical expansions are impossible if the ψ's describing states of negative kinetic energy are left out.

These difficulties were reduced by Dirac through the hypothesis—which we state very roughly—that the states of negative kinetic energy are already filled with electrons, that transitions from states of positive to states of negative kinetic energy are therefore impossible, and that electrons having negative kinetic energies (and correspondingly curious properties) are distributed throughout space with such a high and uniform density that we are unaware of their existence; this hypothesis carried with it the theoretical implication that under certain circumstances there should come into being particles having the mass of the electron but the opposite charge—*anti-electrons*, as Dirac then called them. This forecast was verified a few years later when Anderson discovered experimentally the existence of such particles, now called *positrons*.

Exercises

1. Consider the consequences of reversing the algebraic sign of C in (12).

2. Construct the respective second-order differential equations approximately satisfied separately by χ_a and χ_b in (5) for large values of r, and from their solutions determine the possible values of C in (6) and (7).

3. Show that, if the series in (6) and (7) each contain only a single term, so that $S = r$, then (13) is automatically satisfied in view of (9) and is therefore useless for the computation of the levels; then assume from the outset that the series (6) and (7) each contain only a single term, write down the equations to which Equations (8) reduce in this case, and show that when $0 < E < mc^2$ they are consistent only if k is negative; finally verify that the levels lying between 0 and mc^2 and corresponding to the single-term case are accounted for by (23) to (25).

4. Illustrate the Dirac classification of the hydrogen levels by a diagram patterned after Fig. 108[82]. Mark the values of j for each level and note that, as in Fig. 112[89], the levels having the same n's and the same j's are coincident.

97. The Normal State of the Hydrogen Atom

We shall now find explicitly the Dirac ψ's for the normal state of the hydrogen atom. In this work it is convenient to use the abbreviations

$$\gamma = \sqrt{1 - \alpha^2}, \qquad a_0 = \hbar^2/me^2, \tag{1}$$

where a_0 is the Bohr radius introduced in 21[80].

The lowest energy given by the fine structure formula 23[96] is

$$E = \gamma mc^2. \tag{2}$$

This energy corresponds to the values

$$n = 1, \qquad k = -1 \tag{3}$$

of the principal quantum number n and the auxiliary quantum number k; note that, according to 25^{96}, -1 is the only value of k consistent with $n = 1$. Equations 10^{96} and 12^{96} reduce in the present case to

$$\tau = \gamma, \qquad C = 1/a_0. \tag{4}$$

Since now $|k| = n$, the series 6^{96} and 7^{96} reduce to the single terms

$$\chi_a = a_\tau r^\tau e^{-Cr}, \qquad \chi_b = b_\tau r^\tau e^{-Cr}. \tag{5}$$

Substituting (5) into 2^{96}, we find that the χ-equations are satisfied provided

$$a_\tau / b_\tau = -\alpha/(1 + \gamma). \tag{6}$$

Hence, apart from a *common* arbitrary multiplicative constant our χ's are

$$\chi_a = \alpha r^\gamma e^{-r/a_0}, \qquad \chi_b = -(1 + \gamma) r^\gamma e^{-r/a_0}, \tag{7}$$

where γ and a_0 are defined in (1). Note that, since α is approximately $\frac{1}{137}$, and hence γ is only a little less than 1, the absolute value of χ_a is much smaller than that of χ_b.

Equation 8^{95} now yields

$$R_a = \alpha r^{\gamma-1} e^{-r/a_0}, \qquad R_b = -(1 + \gamma) r^{\gamma-1} e^{-r/a_0}. \tag{8}$$

Since γ is a little less than 1, both R_a and R_b have mild infinities at $r = 0$; they are nevertheless well-behaved.[6]

According to (8), (3), and 5^{95}, we have, for the normal state,

$$R^{\mathrm{I}} = \alpha r^{\gamma-1} e^{-r/a_0}, \qquad R^{\mathrm{II}} = i\sqrt{3}(1 + \gamma) r^{\gamma-1} e^{-r/a_0}, \tag{9}$$

and we are ready to attend to the angle factors.

The simultaneous eigen-ψ's of J_z, J^2, and K have either the form $\psi(j, k = j + \frac{1}{2}, m)$ given by 16^{94} or the form $\psi(j, k = -j - \frac{1}{2}, m)$ given by 17^{94}. Since the only possible values of j are $\frac{1}{2}$, $\frac{3}{2}$, and so on, and since in the present case $k = -1$, we are here dealing with the case $j = \frac{1}{2}$, $k = -j - \frac{1}{2} = -1$, and our interest is con-

---

[6] Recall the footnote on page 402.

fined to $\psi(j, k = -j-\frac{1}{2}, m)$. Setting $j = \frac{1}{2}$ and substituting (9) into 17^{94}, we get

$$\psi(E = \gamma mc^2, j = \frac{1}{2}, k = -1, m)$$

$$= \begin{pmatrix} \alpha \sqrt{\frac{3}{2} - m} \, \Upsilon(1, m - \frac{1}{2}) \\ -\alpha \sqrt{\frac{3}{2} + m} \, \Upsilon(1, m + \frac{1}{2}) \\ i \sqrt{3} \, (1 + \gamma) \sqrt{\frac{1}{2} + m} \, \Upsilon(0, m - \frac{1}{2}) \\ i \sqrt{3} \, (1 + \gamma) \sqrt{\frac{1}{2} - m} \, \Upsilon(0, m + \frac{1}{2}) \end{pmatrix} r^{\gamma - 1} e^{-r/a_0}. \quad (10)$$

It remains to determine the suitable values of m, whose range is given by 7^{87} as $\pm\frac{1}{2}$, $\pm\frac{3}{2}$, $\pm\frac{5}{2}$, and so on. If $|m|$ is greater than $\frac{1}{2}$, then all four components of (10) vanish; hence the only possibilities are $m = -\frac{1}{2}$ and $m = \frac{1}{2}$. In the first case we get

$$\psi(E = \gamma mc^2, j = \frac{1}{2}, k = -1, m = -\frac{1}{2})$$

$$= C_1' \begin{pmatrix} \alpha \sqrt{2} \, \Upsilon_1^{-1} \\ -\alpha \Upsilon_1^0 \\ 0 \\ i \sqrt{3} \, (1 + \gamma) \Upsilon_0^0 \end{pmatrix} r^{\gamma - 1} e^{-r/a_0}, \quad (11)$$

where C_1' is the arbitrary numerical constant that we first dropped in (7). Using the table of Υ's on page 414 and absorbing the common numerical coefficients of the elements in the arbitrary multiplier, we get, more explicitly,

$$\psi(E = \gamma mc^2, j = \frac{1}{2}, k = -1, m = -\frac{1}{2})$$

$$= C_1 \begin{pmatrix} \alpha \sin\theta \, e^{-i\phi} \\ -\alpha \cos\theta \\ 0 \\ i(1 + \gamma) \end{pmatrix} r^{\gamma - 1} e^{-r/a_0}. \quad (12)$$

Similarly, when $m = \frac{1}{2}$ we have

$$\psi(E = \gamma mc^2, j = \frac{1}{2}, k = -1, m = \frac{1}{2})$$

$$= C_2' \begin{pmatrix} \alpha \Upsilon_1^0 \\ -\alpha \sqrt{2} \, \Upsilon_1^1 \\ i \sqrt{3} \, (1 + \gamma) \Upsilon_0^0 \\ 0 \end{pmatrix} r^{\gamma - 1} e^{-r/a_0}, \quad (13)$$

that is,

$$\psi(E = \gamma mc^2, j = \tfrac{1}{2}, k = -1, m = \tfrac{1}{2})$$

$$= C_2 \begin{pmatrix} \alpha \cos \theta \\ \alpha \sin \theta \, e^{i\phi} \\ i(1 + \gamma) \\ 0 \end{pmatrix} r^{\gamma - 1} e^{-r/a_0}, \quad (14)$$

where C_2 is another arbitrary constant, independent of C_1.

The normal state of the hydrogen atom is thus doubly degenerate, and any nonvanishing linear combination of the ψ's (12) and (14) describes a state for which the energy is certain to have its normal value γmc^2.

Exercises

1. Convert the instantaneous ψ's (11) and (13) into time-dependent ψ's.

2. Show that the states (11) and (13) are mutually orthogonal.

3. Show that for the state (13) av $L_z = \alpha^2 \hbar/3(1 + \gamma)$ and av $s_z = \tfrac{1}{2}\hbar - \alpha^2 \hbar/3(1 + \gamma)$, so that electron spin is almost entirely responsible for the z-component of the total angular momentum. What are the possible values of L_z for the state (13), and what are their respective probabilities? Make similar computations for the state (11).

4. Show that for the state (13) av $L^2 = \alpha^2 \hbar^2/(1 + \gamma)$. What are the possible values of L^2 for this state and their respective probabilities? Make similar computations for the state (11). Note that, apart from terms in α^2, the value of L^2 for these states is 0.

5. For states of greatest interest, the value of E is nearly equal to mc^2. Show by inspecting 2^{96} that the absolute value of χ_b is in this case much greater than that of χ_a; Equations (7) illustrate this result. Accordingly, for states of positive kinetic energy, the components ψ_1 and ψ_2 of a Dirac ψ are called 'small,' and the components ψ_3 and ψ_4 'large,' although, on account of the angle factor, a large component may sometimes turn out to be zero, as illustrated by (12) and (14).

6. Consider the classification of the components of Dirac ψ's into 'large' and 'small' for states of negative kinetic energy having a total energy nearly equal to $-mc^2$.

7. Inspect 16^{94} and 17^{94} and use the result of Exercise 5 to show that the value of L^2 for a state $\psi(j, k, m)$ can be taken approximately as $k(k + 1)\hbar^2$; the last remark of Exercise 4 illustrates this result for the case $k = -1$. We can thus say, approximately, that the rôle of the azimuthal quantum number l is taken over in Dirac's theory by k when k is positive and by $-k - 1$ when k is negative.

8. Contrast the Dirac and the Schroedinger distributions-in-position of the electron of a hydrogen atom in the normal state; but note that the two become identical if in Dirac's distribution we let $c \to \infty$.

9. Set E nearly equal to mc^2, so that, except perhaps for very small values of r, $E - V + mc^2$ can be replaced by $2mc^2$, and show that then 11^{95} reduces to

$$\left[\frac{1}{2m} p_r^2 + \frac{k(k + 1)}{\kappa r^2} + V(r) - \tfrac{1}{2}(k + 1)\hbar^2\xi(r) \right] R - \tfrac{1}{2}\hbar^2 r\xi(r) \frac{dR}{dr}$$

$$= (E - mc^2)R. \quad (15)$$

In view of the last remark of Exercise 7, Equation (15) is essentially the same as the Pauli radial equation 12^{88} if k is negative and as the Pauli radial equation 13^{88} if k is positive, except for the straightforward relativistic replacement of E by $E - mc^2$, and the extra term $r\xi(r)R'$, which has no classical analogue. A closer study[2,7] shows that in the case of a Coulomb field the extra term can be disregarded unless $k = -1$ (that is, unless $l = 0$ and we have an s-state), while for s-states it provides just the correct spin correction; in short, this extra term removes the difficulty with s-states, discussed at the end of §88, that arises in the Pauli theory.

We conclude that in the case of radial fields the Schroedinger theory and the Pauli theory can be regarded as successive approximations to the Dirac theory; the situation is similar in the case of other fields.

---

[7] Condon and Shortley, page 130.

APPENDIX

APPENDIX

A few formulas involving Legendre functions and spherical harmonics

The functions[1]

$$(61^{74}) \quad \Theta_l^m = (-1)^{\frac{1}{2}(m+|m|)} \frac{1}{2^l l!} \sqrt{\frac{(2l+1)(l-|m|)!}{2(l+|m|)!}}$$

$$(1-\mu^2)^{\frac{1}{2}|m|} \frac{d^{l+|m|}}{d\mu^{l+|m|}} (\mu^2-1)^l, \quad (1)$$

where $\mu = \cos\theta$, $l = 0, 1, 2, \cdots$, and $m = 0, \pm 1, \pm 2, \cdots, \pm l$, are orthonormal in θ (see 62^{74}) and satisfy the equations[2]

$$\cos\theta \; \Theta_l^m = A_l^m \Theta_{l+1}^m + B_l^m \Theta_{l-1}^m \tag{2}$$

$$\begin{cases} \sin\theta \; \Theta_l^m = -C_l^m \Theta_{l+1}^{m+1} + D_l^m \Theta_{l-1}^{m+1} & (3) \\ \sin\theta \; \Theta_l^m = E_l^m \Theta_{l+1}^{m-1} - F_l^m \Theta_{l-1}^{m-1} & (4) \end{cases}$$

$$\frac{d}{d\theta} \Theta_l^m = \tfrac{1}{2} G_l^m \Theta_l^{m+1} - \tfrac{1}{2} H_l^m \Theta_l^{m-1} \tag{5}$$

$$m \cot\theta \; \Theta_l^m = -\tfrac{1}{2} G_l^m \Theta_l^{m+1} - \tfrac{1}{2} H_l^m \Theta_l^{m-1}, \tag{6}$$

where the expansion coefficients are

$$A_l^m = \sqrt{\frac{(l+m+1)(l-m+1)}{(2l+1)(2l+3)}} \qquad B_l^m = \sqrt{\frac{(l+m)(l-m)}{(2l-1)(2l+1)}} \tag{7}$$

$$C_l^m = \sqrt{\frac{(l+m+1)(l+m+2)}{(2l+1)(2l+3)}} \qquad D_l^m = \sqrt{\frac{(l-m)(l-m-1)}{(2l-1)(2l+1)}} \tag{8}$$

$$E_l^m = \sqrt{\frac{(l-m+1)(l-m+2)}{(2l+1)(2l+3)}} \qquad F_l^m = \sqrt{\frac{(l+m)(l+m-1)}{(2l-1)(2l+1)}} \tag{9}$$

$$G_l^m = \sqrt{(l-m)(l+m+1)} \qquad H_l^m = \sqrt{(l+m)(l-m+1)}. \tag{10}$$

The functions[3]

$$(65^{74}) \qquad \Upsilon_l^m = \Theta_l^m \frac{e^{im\phi}}{\sqrt{2\pi}} \tag{11}$$

---

[1] These functions are the conventional normalized Legendre functions of the first kind, except for the Condon-Shortley choice of the phase factors.

[2] Condon and Shortley, page 52. Bethe, pages 551–560; note that Bethe's $\mathfrak{R}_{lm}$ equals our $(-1)^m \Theta_l^m$.

[3] These functions are the conventional normalized complex tesseral surface spherical harmonics, except for the Condon-Shortley choice of the phase factors.

are orthonormal in the angles (see 79[74]) and satisfy the equations[4]

$$(L_x + iL_y)R\Upsilon_l^m = \hbar G_l^m R\Upsilon_l^{m+1} \tag{12}$$

$$(L_x - iL_y)R\Upsilon_l^m = \hbar H_l^m R\Upsilon_l^{m-1} \tag{13}$$

$$L_z R\Upsilon_l^m = m\hbar R\Upsilon_l^m \tag{14}$$

$$L^2 R\Upsilon_l^m = l(l+1)\hbar^2 R\Upsilon_l^m \tag{15}$$

$$(p_x + ip_y)R\Upsilon_l^m = i\hbar C_l^m\left[\frac{dR}{dr} - l\frac{R}{r}\right]\Upsilon_{l+1}^{m+1}$$
$$- i\hbar D_l^m\left[\frac{dR}{dr} + (l+1)\frac{R}{r}\right]\Upsilon_{l-1}^{m+1} \tag{16}$$

$$(p_x - ip_y)R\Upsilon_l^m = -i\hbar E_l^m\left[\frac{dR}{dr} - l\frac{R}{r}\right]\Upsilon_{l+1}^{m-1}$$
$$+ i\hbar F_l^m\left[\frac{dR}{dr} + (l+1)\frac{R}{r}\right]\Upsilon_{l-1}^{m-1} \tag{17}$$

$$p_z R\Upsilon_l^m = -i\hbar A_l^m\left[\frac{dR}{dr} - l\frac{R}{r}\right]\Upsilon_{l+1}^m - i\hbar B_l^m\left[\frac{dR}{dr} + (l+1)\frac{R}{r}\right]\Upsilon_{l-1}^m, \tag{18}$$

where R is an arbitrary function of r only, where p_z, L_x, and so on, are the standard Schroedinger operators, and where A_l^m, B_l^m, and so on, are the coefficients (7) to (10).

---

[4] Bethe, *loc. cit.*

INDEX

INDEX